Lecture Notes in Artificial Intelligence 2902

Edited by J. G. Carbonell and J. Siekmann

Subseries of Lecture Notes in Computer Science

Springer-Verlag Berlin Heidelberg GmbH

Fernando Moura Pires   Salvador Abreu (Eds.)

Progress in Artificial Intelligence

11th Portuguese Conference
on Artificial Intelligence, EPIA 2003
Beja, Portugal, December 4-7, 2003
Proceedings

Series Editors

Jaime G. Carbonell, Carnegie Mellon University, Pittsburgh, PA, USA
Jörg Siekmann, University of Saarland, Saarbrücken, Germany

Volume Editors

Fernando Moura Pires
Salvador Abreu
Universidade de Évora, Departamento de Informática
Rua Romão Ramalho, 59 - 7000 Évora, Portugal
E-mail: spa@di.uevora.pt

Cataloging-in-Publication Data applied for

A catalog record for this book is available from the Library of Congress.

Bibliographic information published by Die Deutsche Bibliothek
Die Deutsche Bibliothek lists this publication in the Deutsche Nationalbibliografie; detailed bibliographic data is available in the Internet at <http://dnb.ddb.de>.

CR Subject Classification (1998): I.2, H.2, F.1, H.3, D.1.6

ISSN 0302-9743
DOI 10.1007/978-3-540-24580-3

Springer-Verlag is a part of Springer Science+Business Media

springeronline.com

Typesetting: Camera-ready by author, data conversion by PTP-Berlin, Protago-TeX-Production GmbH
Printed on acid-free paper SPIN: 10971338 06/3142 5 4 3 2 1 0
www.springer.com/mycopy

Preface

When we set about organizing EPIA 2003 in Porto during the APPIA meeting at the previous edition of the conference, EPIA 2001, it was decided that it would be organized by Fernando Moura Pires (Fajé) and myself. We chose Beja as the venue to host the conference, as it provided a good support infrastructure and Fernando had a good working relationship with several people at the Beja Polytechnic Institute.

Shortly thereafter, Fernando came to know that he was ailing from a disease that was to take his life in May 2003. As with many other projects in which he got involved, Fernando clung to the organization of this conference with dedication and perseverance, even while knowing that he might not see the results of his work. EPIA 2003 is a tribute to his work.

Taking up on the successful experience gained from EPIA 2001, we decided to structure EPIA 2003 as a set of five distinct workshops, roughly reflecting the panorama of AI research in Portugal. Special thanks are due to the organizers of each workshop, for the quality and timeliness of the work they carried out.

The conference was all the more interesting because of the eight invited presentations and tutorials, by Alexander Bockmayr, Amílcar Cardoso, Dario Floreano, Harold Boley, Pedro Domingos, Pieter Adriaans, Veronica Dahl and Vitor Santos Costa. There are short one-page abstracts included in these proceedings for some of these presentations.

This volume reflects the organization of the conference. There were a total of 119 articles submitted across the five workshops, of which 29 (24%) were selected as full-size papers and 21 (18%) as extended abstracts, one of which could not be presented for other reasons. These numbers indicate that the present model for EPIA is a sound one, particularly when compared with those for the two previous editions (1999 and 2001).

Submissions came from 21 different countries: 37 from Portugal, 11 each from Spain and South Korea, 6 each from Brazil, France and the US, and 5 or fewer from Australia, China, the Czech Republic, Germany, Denmark, Hungary, Iran, Italy, Lithuania, Mexico, The Netherlands, Poland, Singapore, Tunisia, Turkey, Taiwan, the UK and Venezuela.

The contributions were distributed among the workshops as follows:

Workshop	Submitted	Full	Short	Total
ALEA	27	6	3	9
CLPS	13	4	2	6
EKDB	39	9	6	15
MAAII	18	5	3	8
NLTR	22	5	7	12
Total	119	29	21	50

Thanks are due to the program committee members and reviewers, without whose work the conference would not have been possible.

An acknowledgement is due to FACC/FCT (Portuguese governmental funding agency) for its financial support, to the Instituto Politécnico de Beja and to the Universidade de Évora. Other sponsors are publicly acknowledged on the conference's Web site (`http://www.di.uevora.pt/epia03/`).

Besides co-chairing one of the workshops, Paulo Quaresma assisted me in various organizational aspects of EPIA 2003, for which I am thankful. Special thanks go to the local organization, in particular to Isabel Sofia Brito and Raúl Moizão of ESTIG, Instituto Politécnico de Beja, for coordinating and mobilizing the necessary resources. The knowledge and efficiency of Mrs. Filipa Reis was essential in effectively organizing and managing the conference.

So long, Fajé,

September 2003 Salvador Abreu

Organization

EPIA 2003 was jointly organized by the Department of Computer Science, Universidade de Évora and the School of Technology and Management, Polytechnic Institute of Beja, under the auspices of APPIA (Associação Portuguesa para a Inteligência Artificial).

Program Committee Co-chairs

Fernando Moura Pires	Universidade de Évora, Portugal
Salvador Abreu	Universidade de Évora, Portugal

Workshop Organizers

ALEA – Workshop on Artificial Life and Evolutionary Algorithms

Ernesto Costa	Universidade de Coimbra, Portugal
Francisco Pereira	Instituto Politécnico de Coimbra, Portugal

CLPS – Workshop on Constraint and Logic Programming Systems

Fernando Silva	Universidade do Porto, Portugal
Pedro Barahona	Universidade Nova de Lisboa, Portugal

EKDB – Workshop on Extraction of Knowledge from Data Bases

Arlindo Oliveira	Universidade Técnica de Lisboa, Portugal
Carlos Bento	Universidade de Coimbra, Portugal
João Gama	Universidade do Porto, Portugal

MAAII – Multi-Agents and AI for the Internet

Carlos Damásio	Universidade Nova de Lisboa, Portugal
José Maia Neves	Universidade do Minho, Portugal

NLTR – Natural Language and Text Retrieval

Irene Rodrigues	Universidade de Évora, Portugal
Paulo Quaresma	Universidade de Évora, Portugal

Full Program Committees

ALEA

Carlos Fonseca (Portugal)
Conor Ryan (Ireland)
Ernesto Costa (Portugal)
Luís Correia (Portugal)
Colin Reeves (UK)
Dario Floreano (Switzerland)
Francisco Pereira (Portugal)
Luís Rocha (USA)

CLPS

Enrico Pontelli (USA)
Frederic Benhamou (France)
Inês de Castro Dutra (Brazil)
Mark Wallace (UK)
Philippe Codognet (France)
Salvador Abreu (Portugal)
Fernando Silva (Portugal)
Gopal Gupta (USA)
Manuel Carro (Spain)
Pedro Barahona (Portugal)
Ricardo Rocha (Portugal)
Thom Frühwirth (Germany)

EKDB

Alípio Jorge (Portugal)
Carlos Bento (Portugal)
João Gama (Portugal)
Lee Giles (USA)
Mário Nascimento (Canada)
Rajesh Parekh (USA)
Arlindo Oliveira (Portugal)
Fernando Moura Pires (Portugal)
José Riquelme Santos (Spain)
Luís Torgo (Portugal)
Pieter Adriaans (The Netherlands)

MAAII

Ana Paiva (Portugal)
Carlos Damásio (Portugal)
Gerd Wagner (The Netherlands)
Hélder Coelho (Portugal)
João Alexandre Leite (Portugal)
José Maia Neves (Portugal)
Manuel Filipe Santos (Portugal)
Terrance Swift (USA)
Ulrike Sattler (Germany)
Vipul Kashyap (USA)
António Mário Florido (Portugal)
Carlos Ramos (Portugal)
Graça Gaspar (Portugal)
Helena Sofia Pinto (Portugal)
José Machado (Portugal)
Luís Botelho (Portugal)
Michael Schroeder (UK)
Thomas Eiter (Austria)
Victor Alves (Portugal)
Wiebe van der Hoek (UK)

NLTR

Andrew Mowbray (Australia)
João Paulo Neto (Portugal)
Lucia Helena Machado Rino (Brazil)
Nuno Mamede (Portugal)
Vera Lúcia Strube de Lima (Brazil)
Irene Rodrigues (Portugal)
José Gabriel Pereira Lopes (Portugal)
Maria das Graças Volpe Nunes (Brazil)
Paulo Quaresma (Portugal)
Veronica Dahl (Canada)

Reviewers

Alexander Dikovsky
Alicia Troncoso
Alípio Jorge
Ana Paiva
Ana Teresa Freitas
Andrew Mowbray
Arlindo Oliveira
Arlindo Silva
Bernadete Ribero
Carlos Bento
Carlos Damásio
Carlos Fonseca
Carlos Ramos
Cláudia Antunes
Colin Reeves
Conor Ryan
Dario Floreano
Eduardo Correia

Enrico Pontelli
Ernesto Costa
Fernando Silva
Francisco Ferrer-Troyano
Francisco Pereira
Frédéric Benhamou
Frédéric Saubion
Gabriel Pereira Lopes
Gerd Wagner
Gladys Castillo
Glendon R. Holst
Gopal Gupta
Graça Gaspar
Helder Coelho
Helena Galhardas
Helena Sofia Pinto
Hervé Paulino
Hugo Santos Meinedo
Iñaki Inza
Inês de Castro Dutra
Irene Rodrigues
Jacinto Mata Vázquez
Jesús S. Aguilar-Ruiz
João Alexandre Leite
João Gama
João Paulo Neto
Jorge Tavares
José Álvarez Macías
José Machado
José Maia Neves
José Riquelme Santos
Lee Giles
Lucia Machado Rino
Luísa Coheur
Luís Botelho
Luís Correia
Luís Moniz Pereira
Luís Rocha
Luis Talavera
Luís Torgo
Manuel Carro
Manuel Filipe Santos
Maria Volpe Nunes
Mário Florido
Mário Nascimento
Mark Wallace
Michael Heusch
Michael Schroeder
Miguel Filgueiras
Nelma Moreira
Nuno Mamede
Paulo Gomes
Paulo J. Azevedo
Paulo Quaresma
Pedro Barahona
Philippe Codognet
Pieter Adriaans
Rajesh Parekh
Ralf Schweimeier
Raúl Giráldez
Renata Souza Guizzardi
Ricardo Lopes
Ricardo Rocha
Roberto Ruiz
Rogério Reis
Rokia Missaoui
Rui Batoreo Amaral
Salvador Abreu
Sara C. Madeira
Terrance Swift
Thomas Eiter
Thom Frühwirth
Ulrike Sattler
Vera Lúcia Strube Lima
Veronica Dahl
Victor Alves
Vipul Kashyap
Wiebe van der Hoek

Table of Contents

Abstracts of Invited Presentations and Tutorials

Artificial Life and Evolutionary Algorithms (ALEA)

Constraint and Logic Programming Systems (CLPS)

Extraction of Knowledge from Data Bases (EKDB)

Multi-Agents and AI for the Internet (MAAII)

Natural Language and Text Retrieval (NLTR)

Constraint Programming in Computational Molecular Biology

Alexander Bockmayr

Univ. Henri Poincaré & LORIA, Nancy, France
Alexander.Bockmayr@loria.fr

Understanding living systems through computation is a challenging new area at the interface of computer science and biology. The goal of this talk is to present some recent work on applying constraint programming to problems in computational molecular biology.

After a short general introduction to constraint problems in molecular biology, we will focus on two types of applications:

- using finite domain constraint programming for determining the structure of biological macromulecules,
- using hybrid concurrent constraint programming for modeling the functioning of biological systems on the molecular and cellular level.

Fernando Moura Pires, Salvador Abreu (Eds.): EPIA 2003, LNAI 2902, p. 1, 2003.

Computational Creativity

Amílcar Cardoso and Penousal Machado

Creative Systems Group, AILab, CISUC
Universidade de Coimbra, Portugal
amilcar@dei.uc.pt
http://www.dei.uc.pt/~amilcar

Creativity is a fundamental trait of intelligence and one of the most remarkable characteristics of the human mind. Its study has been, since a long time ago, a challenge for many scientists and researchers, particularly in areas such as Philosophy, Cognitive Science, Psychology and Education. It is not a surprise, therefore, that a growing community of Artificial Intelligence researchers is deserving serious attention to the study and proposal of abstract explanation theories and adequate computational models of creativity.

This interest comes from the belief that computational creative systems are potentially efective in a wide range of artistic, technical and scientific domains where innovation is a key issue. Scientific discovery, theorem proving and technical design are just a few examples of application problems suitable for them. Also, the development of computational tools and environments that might help humans being creative is an important motivation for some of the work in the area. The multidisciplinary nature of the research is also an interesting factor of attraction. Moreover, this endeavour may contribute to the overall understanding of the mechanisms behind creativity.

This Tutorial is intended to present an overview of current research on Computational Creativity. It will include an introduction to the basic concepts and terminology of the area, as well as to formal and computational models of creativity. A discussion on the main current challenges and application domains will also be included.

Fernando Moura Pires, Salvador Abreu (Eds.): EPIA 2003, LNAI 2902, p. 2, 2003.

From Wheels to Wings with Evolutionary Spiking Circuits

Dario Floreano[1], J.-C. Zufferey[2], and J.-D.Nicoud[3]

[1] Autonomous Systems Lab, Institute of Systems Engineering
Swiss Federal Institute of Technology (EPFL), CH-1015 Lausanne, Switzerland
dario.floreano@epfl.ch
[2] ASL-EPFL
[3] DIDEL S.A., www.didel.com

I will give an overview of the EPFL indoor flying project, whose goal is to evolve neural controllers for autonomous, adaptive, indoor micro-flyers. Indoor flight is still a challenge because it requires miniaturization, energy efficiency, and control of non-linear flight dynamics. This ongoing project consists in developing a flying, vision-based micro-robot, a bio-inspired controller composed of adaptive spiking neurons directly mapped into digital micro-controllers, and a method to evolve such a neural controller without human intervention. The talk describes the motivation and methodology used to reach our goal as well as the results of a number of preliminary experiments on vision-based wheeled and flying robots.

Fernando Moura Pires, Salvador Abreu (Eds.): EPIA 2003, LNAI 2902, p. 3, 2003.

An Introduction to Object-Oriented RuleML

Harold Boley

Institute for Information Technology – e-Business
National Research Council
Fredericton, NB, Canada
(harold.boley@nrc.gc.ca)
http://www.cs.unb.ca/~boley/

Semantic Web languages such as RDF (Schema) and OWL permit object-centered, taxonomic, and description-logic modeling in the URI-based distributed information system of the Web. Rule efforts of the Semantic Web have thus spurred interest in deductive object-oriented databases and object-extended LP approaches such as F-Logic, TRIPLE, and FORUM. Object-Oriented RuleML (OO RuleML) is an extension of the proposed standard Rule Markup Language that employs object-centered, role-keyed atoms / complex terms (ROLED), allows URI-grounded, 'webized' facts and rules (GROUNDED), and permits typed variables via URI links into Web-based taxonomies (TYPED).

ROLED: RuleML's XML/RDF-integrating system syntax augments 'type tags' by 'role tags' that represent the 'slots' or 'features' of type-tagged objects. OO RuleML makes such role tags available as a user syntax in atomic formulas and complex terms: the atom and cterm elements can now contain – before/after positional argument children – non-positional argument children '_r' (for the metarole 'role') with a required CDATA attribute 'n' (for the user-defined role 'name'). This also allows for mixed positional and object-centered representations. OO RuleML has been extended by role weights specifying the relative importance of slots. A surprisingly small change to the DTDs/Schemas was needed for permitting such user-level roles.

GROUNDED: Facts and rules in OO RuleML can be 'URI-grounded' via labels containing a Web-identifier attribute, 'wid', which has a URI value that can be referred to from a complementary 'widref' attribute. The 'wid'widref' pair was inspired both by XML's 'id'/'idref' and RDF's 'about'/'resource' pairs.

TYPED: OO RuleML variables are optionally typed/sorted via URIs referring to classes of predefined RDF Schema or OWL taxonomies. XML namespace declarations can use fragments (#) to point into the RDF Schema documents containing the required class definitions. A 'var' element can then be sorted via a 'type' attribute whose value augments the namespace prefix by the local name identifying the class.

OO RuleML will be introduced using the Positional-Roled (PR) syntax, which will also be compared to Notation 3 (N3). The status of the Java-based OO jDREW implementation of OO RuleML will be reviewed. Finally, two running applications of OO RuleML will be sketched: Rule-applying collaborative filtering (RACOFI) and weighted similarity matching (Treesim).

Fernando Moura Pires, Salvador Abreu (Eds.): EPIA 2003, LNAI 2902, p. 4, 2003.

Learning from Networks of Examples

Pedro Domingos and Matt Richardson

Department of Computer Science and Engineering
University of Washington
Seattle, WA 98195-2350, USA
pedrod@cs.washington.edu
http:///www.cs.washington.edu/homes/pedrod/

Most machine learning algorithms assume that examples are independent of each other, but many (or most) domains violate this assumption. For example, in real markets customers' buying decisions are influenced by their friends and acquaintances, but data mining for marketing ignores this (as does traditional economics). In this talk I will describe how we can learn models that account for example dependences, and use them to make better decisions. For example, in the marketing domain we are able to pinpoint the most influential customers, "seed" the network by marketing to them, and unleash a wave of word of mouth. We mine these models from collaborative filtering systems and knowledge-sharing Web sites, and show that they are surprisingly robust to imperfect knowledge of the network. I will also survey other applications of learning from networks of examples we are working on, including: combining link and content information in Google-style Web search; automatically translating between ontologies on the Semantic Web; and predicting the evolution of scientific communities.

Fernando Moura Pires, Salvador Abreu (Eds.): EPIA 2003, LNAI 2902, p. 5, 2003.

Grammar Induction and Adaptive Information Disclosure

Pieter Adriaans

Institute of Logic Language and Computation
University of Amsterdam
pietera@science.uva.nl,
http://staff.science.uva.nl/~pietera/

The adaptive information disclosure (AID) project is part of a larger effort that aims at the creation of a so-called Virtual Lab environment for e-science (VL-E). In the context of AID we are building in the coming 4 years a suite of dynamic model driven information and knowledge extraction tools on top of an architecture for grid-based distributed data analysis. Keywords are: semantic models, agent technology, formal concept analysis, datamining, textmining, gridmining, grammar induction, question answering and the dynamic maintenance of ontologies. Key research challenges are:

- How to organize the content of domain specific knowledge: The creation and maintenance of semantics models of complex scientific domains on the basis of a multitude of heterogeneous sources of information.
- How to deploy the models in the knowledge extraction process: The availability of perfect models of the domain does not guarantee a performance boost of existing knowledge extraction algorithms. For each algorithm a careful analysis of the function of the model information in various stages of its execution has to be made. Theoretical assumptions about complexity issues and search bias have to be validated against empirical evidence.
- Integration with Grid technologies: The possibility of implementing this process on the basis of an architecture of co-operative agents in a grid.

Fernando Moura Pires, Salvador Abreu (Eds.): EPIA 2003, LNAI 2902, p. 6, 2003.

Understanding Implicit Language Structures

Veronica Dahl

Simon Fraser University, Canada
veronica@cs.sfu.ca
http://www.cs.sfu.ca/~veronica/

We present a logic programming parsing methodology which is especially interesting for understanding implicit human language structures. It records parsing state constituents through linear assumptions to be consumed as the corresponding constituents materialize throughout the computation. Parsing state symbols corresponding to implicit structures remain as undischarged assumptions, rather than blocking the computation as they would if they were subgoals in a query. They can then be used to glean the meaning of elided structures, with the aid of parallel structures. Word ordering inferences are made not from symbol contiguity as in DCGs, but from invisibly handling numbered edges as parameters of each symbol. We illustrate these ideas through a metagrammatical treatment of coordination, and contrast them with constraint-based approaches, both within and outside Chomskyan-like frameworks of grammar.

Keywords: Logic grammars, assumptions, elision, coordination, constraint handling rules, property grammars.

Fernando Moura Pires, Salvador Abreu (Eds.): EPIA 2003, LNAI 2902, p. 7, 2003.

Performance Issues in Prolog Applications

Vítor Santos Costa

COPPE/Universidade Federal do Rio de Janeiro
vitor@cos.ufrj.br
http://www.cos.ufrj.br/ vitor

Prolog is an expressive programming language based on a subset of First Order Logic, and has has been widely used in Artificial Intelligence Research. Examples include Machine Learning, say, for implementing Inductive Logic Programming, and Natural Language Processing, where applications range from the well-known work in Definite Clause Grammars to automata-based parsing. In this talk, we discuss how Prolog implementations matter in achieving AI application performance and scalability, and present some solutions that are currently being researched for Prolog systems. Throughout we draw from our own experience in supporting a Prolog system, and in designing ILP applications.

We observe that excellent data-base indexing is critical. Often, applications are initially developed for smallish examples, where data-base access is guaranteed to be fast. Unfortunately, when practitioners experiment with real-life like situations, performance simply breaks down. Until recently, Prolog implementations were simply not good enough in this regard. We discuss some recent work on the B-Prolog, XSB and YAP systems that tries to address the problem.

A related issue is that efficient data-base updating must be supported. For instance, many AI systems must perform search, and use the data-base to store the search space. Many AI applications thus add and remove items often, whilst still requiring fast lookup. We discuss two solutions: the use of tries as in XSB Prolog, and extending the indexing mechanism, as done recently in YAP Prolog.

Some Prolog applications require functionality beyond what is provided by the standard Prolog engine. Sometimes, we will need Prolog extensions, but sometimes even better performance can be achieved by writing a specialised interpreter or performing a simple transformation. In one example, we discuss a small program for modelling RAS pathways on a cell. Tabling allows a declarative formulation to run for non-trivial queries. But full tabling is not necessary: a poor-man's version of tabling achieves even better results. As a second example we discuss the CLP($\mathcal{BN}$) implementation: although we need coroutining to support generic queries, we have taken advantage of meta-interpreters, for instance, to do efficient learning when complete data is available.

We believe that Prolog can be effectively used for non-trivial AI programs. To do so, collaboration between users and implementors is fundamental.

Fernando Moura Pires, Salvador Abreu (Eds.): EPIA 2003, LNAI 2902, p. 8, 2003.

Optimization of Logistic Processes in Supply-Chains Using Meta-heuristics*

Carlos A. Silva[1,2], Thomas A. Runkler[1], João M. Sousa[2], and J.M. Sá da Costa[2]

[1] Siemens AG, Corporate Technology
Information and Communications, CT IC 4
81730 Munich - Germany
{carlos.silva.external, thomas.runkler}@mchp.siemens.de
[2] Technical University of Lisbon, Instituto Superior Técnico
Dep. Mechanical Engineering - Control, Automation and Robotics Group
Av. Rovisco Pais, 1049-001 Lisbon - Portugal
{csilva,jmsousa,sadacosta}@ist.utl.pt

Abstract. This paper addresses the optimization of logistic processes in supply-chains using meta-heuristics: genetic algorithms and ant colony optimization. The dynamic assignment of components to orders and choosing the solution that is able to deliver more orders at the correct date, is a scheduling problem that classical scheduling methods can not cope with. However, the implementation of meta-heuristics is done only after a positive assessment of the performance's expectation provided by the fitness-distance correlation analysis. Both meta-heuristics are then applied to a simulation example that describes a general logistic process. The performance is similar for both methods, but the ant colony optimization method provides more information at the expenses of computational costs.

1 Introduction

A supply-chain is a modern organizational framework where the goods are purchased from another companies instead of being produced in-house. It consists of a network of suppliers, warehouses and distribution centers and its most important characteristic is the ability to quickly respond to market changes [1]. Logistics can be defined as the subprocess of the supply chain that deals with planning, handling, and control of the storage of goods between the manufacturing point and the consumption point. The goods are purchased to the suppliers, transported to cross-docking centers [2] and then shipped to the costumers. The lack of storage may increase the delivery time, but it provides a more economic and flexible structure. The key issue is to still deliver the goods on time to the costumers. Therefore, the control of a logistic process is a *scheduling problem*.

Over the last decades, a wide range of methodologies has been developed to solve different scheduling problems, which are usually NP-hard problems: *dispatching rules*, bottleneck heuristics and local search methods or meta-heuristics [3]. In real-world

* This work is supported by the German Ministry of Education and Research (BMBF) under Contract no.13N7906 (project Nivelli) and by the Portuguese Foundation for Science and Technology (FCT) under Grant no. SFRH/BD/6366/2001.

Fernando Moura Pires, Salvador Abreu (Eds.): EPIA 2003, LNAI 2902, pp. 9–23, 2003.

applications, it has been proved that the classical dispatching methods are insufficient to face the new scheduling requirements dictated by the market competition. Nowadays, meta-heuristics are considered to be the most powerful scheduling techniques [4], mainly the ones using an evolutionary metaphor, like the *genetic algorithms* (GA) [5,6]. The scheduling problem in supply chain systems is a recent problem in the scheduling theory. Shen and Norrie [7] present a review on the methods used to solve this problem. The problem has been tackled mainly by the multi-agent community [1], which use in general market-based approaches to determine the schedule [8]. To the best of our knowledge, no studies about the supply-chain management in the perspective of a normal scheduling problem have been presented.

In this paper, we present a study on the scheduling of a logistic process in a supply chain framework, using meta-heuristics. Before implementing meta-heuristics, the researchers always face two questions: are the meta-heuristics expected to perform well in the problem and in that case, what meta-heuristic should be used. To answer these questions, two meta-heuristics are presented to solve this particular scheduling problem: a genetic algorithm and an ant colony optimization approach. The meta-heuristics are compared both in the performance and algorithmic levels in order to draw some conclusions that may help to answer the raised questions. The paper is organized as follows. The logistic process is described in Section 2. There, the scheduling optimization problem is also defined, and some classical scheduling strategies are presented. In Section 3, an analysis on the applicability of meta-heuristics to this problem is presented. The implementation of genetic algorithms and ant colonies in the logistic scheduling problem is also described in this section. Section 4 presents and discusses the simulation results. Section 5 concludes the paper, giving the guidelines for future work.

2 The Logistic Process in a Supply Chain

In this section, a general logistic process is described. It describes a company that sells products, but does not manufacture them. All components are bought from external suppliers, collected at docking-centers and then delivered to the clients. This supply chain framework allows the company to sell clients the newest product type on the market just by working with several different suppliers. In this way, the client has a wide range of offers, and the company can maintain or even extend its market position.

2.1 Description of the Logistic Process

Figure 1 presents a schematic representation of a general logistic process. This process can be divided into five sequential steps:

1. *Order arrival.* Let the product needed by the client be called an *order* $o_j \in O$ with $j = 1, \cdots, m$. An order is a set of one or more different items, called the *components* $c_i \in C$ with $i = 1, \cdots, n$. When a new order arrives, it receives two labels: the *arrival date* and the *desired delivery date*, which is the date when the client wishes to receive the order. The list of orders that are waiting to be delivered is called the *order list*.

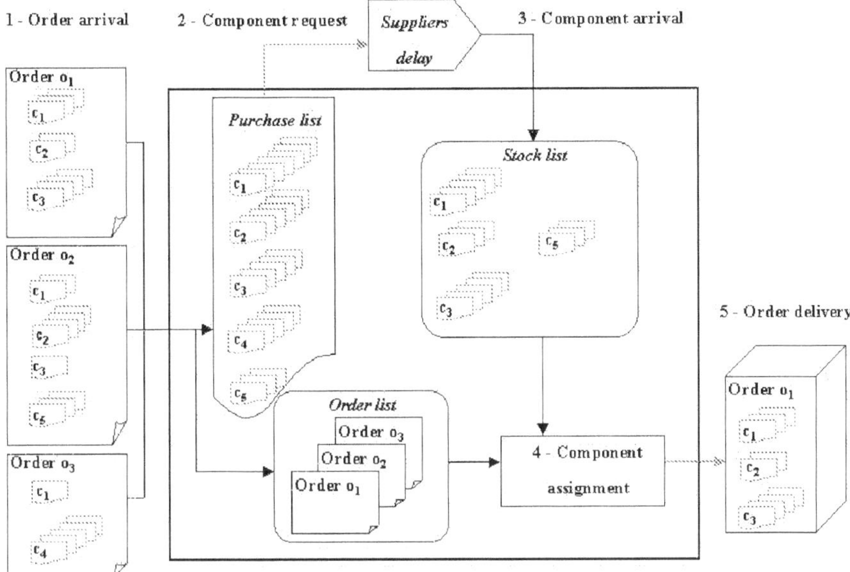

Fig. 1. General representation of a logistic process.

2. *Component request.* For every order accepted by the system, a *purchase list* with the different components and their quantities is built and these components are demanded from external suppliers. Each type of component is characterized by a certain *quantity* q_{ij} (quantity of component type c_i for order o_j) and a *suppliers delay* d_i (delay for component type c_i), which is the time that the supplier needs to deliver the component to the system.
3. *Component arrival.* The components are delivered from the suppliers to the cross-docking centers, after the supplier delay d_i. The system builds a *stock list*, which is a list with the type of components and their quantity already in the system. These components are ready to be assigned to the orders waiting in the orders list.
4. *Component assignment.* The decision process occurs at this step. The system has to observe the stock list and the orders list, and check which orders have all the components available to be delivered. It has also to check the desired delivery date, to see when it is supposed to deliver the orders. The objective is to match the delivery date with the desired date. The difference between these two dates for the order o_j is called the *tardiness* T_j. The orders should be delivered on the correct date, not before nor after, which means that the objective is to have for all orders $T_j = 0$. This decision step is done once per day, either by some dispatching rule or by some optimization procedure.
5. *Order delivery.* After the selection of the orders to be delivered has been performed by the decision process, a transporting facility picks up the components at the docking-center and the orders are delivered to the clients. After that, the stock list and the order list are updated.

This process can be described by the classical theory of queuing processes [9]. The arrival of new orders in a certain period of time can be seen as the birth process of the system and modeled by a Poisson distribution,

$$p(x, \lambda T) = \frac{(\lambda T)^x}{x!} e^{-\lambda T} \tag{1}$$

where x is the random variable *number of orders* and λT is the *birth rate*, i.e. the parameter indicating the probability of this event *occur at a certain time* T.

The delivery of orders per unit of time can be seen as the death process which is modeled by an exponential distribution

$$p(T, \mu) = \mu e^{-\mu T} \tag{2}$$

where the time T is the random variable and μ is the *death rate*, which accounts for the number of days that an order remains in the system.

The system can be influenced by two types of disturbances: disturbances in the suppliers delay d_j, when the components enter the system before or after the expected date; disturbances on the desired delivery date, when the system accepts desired delivery dates different from the expected delivery date, because a client is very important and the order cannot be lost to another competitor. These unexpected events will affect the component assignment step: if an order receives the components before expected or the desired date is very late, the order might be delivered earlier than desired ($T < 0$); if the components arrive later than expected or the desired date is to early, the orders might be delivered later than desired ($T > 0$).

It is reasonable to oblige the system to retain the orders that are going to be delivered earlier until the correct delivery date. In practice, this means that the system will never deliver orders with negative tardiness ($T \leq 0$), improving in this way the system's performance. However, this is not sufficient to control the effects of the disturbances. To do so, the system has to be able to find an efficient component scheduling, since all the other parts of the process can hardly be influenced by the company.

2.2 The Scheduling Problem

The optimization of the logistic process can be seen as a special instance of *Multiple Knapsack* problem (MKS) [10]. In the logistic system, we have n different types of items (components $c_i \in C$, where $C = \{c_1, \cdots, c_n\}$) and m different knapsacks (orders $o_j \in O$, where $O = \{o_1, \cdots, o_m\}$). Each knapsack o_j needs a set $C_j \subset C$ of different components in precise quantities q_{ij}. When a knapsack is completely full, a cost T_j is assigned to the knapsack. The objective is to find the set of knapsacks that can be filled with the available components, such that a cost function $f(T)$ is minimized. There are however two constraints. The first one is the *capacity* constraint. This means that each knapsack is either empty of full, i.e., to evaluate the cost T_j of a knapsack, it must have the complete set C_j of components. The second constraint is the *availability* constraint and it refers to the fact that to fill completely a knapsack, enough components of the same kind must be available in set C. In a mathematical framework, the problem can be described as:

$$\begin{array}{lll} \text{minimize} & f(T) & \text{(cost)} \\ \text{subject to :} & o_j = \sum_{i \in C_j} q_{ij} & \text{(capacity constrain)} \\ & \forall_{c_i \in C_j} q_{ij} \leq q_i \in C & \text{(availability constrain)} \end{array} \tag{3}$$

The objective function $f(T)$. An important question is how to measure the system's performance. It is very difficult to define an index that quantifies properly how good a solution is. One wants to have the highest number of orders delivered at the correct date, and few with positive tardiness. A classical objective function in scheduling problems is to assume the minimization of the sum of the tardiness absolute values of all orders, i.e. $\sum_{j=1}^{n} |T_j|$. However, with this function, a low global tardiness value could mask the fact that no orders are delivered at the correct date, although all of the orders are delivered with small tardiness. Therefore, we adopt a new objective function called *Null Tardiness Deviation* (NTD). Here, we impose as the most important objective the fact that the highest number of orders are delivered at the correct date, although we consider also important to have a small tardiness variance of the remaining orders. In this way the objective function to be minimized is given by

$$f(T) = \frac{1}{n_T + \frac{1}{\sum_{j=1}^{n} |T_j|}} \tag{4}$$

where $n_T = \#(T_j = 0), \forall o_j \in O$ accounts for the number of orders delivered at the correct date, and $\sum_{j=1}^{n} |T_j|$, as described previously, accounts for the tardiness of the remaining orders, which should be as small as possible.

2.3 Classical Scheduling Strategies

The companies rely very much on classical scheduling strategies because they are usually robust, simple and cheap. These properties make them very attractive and to replace them by more sophisticated methods, the companies need to be sure about the benefits of applying the new methods, comparing the costs of the change to the added value provided by this change. The problem is that the classical methods do not perform any kind of optimization of the scheduling problem and therefore, can never provide good solutions in complex environments.

Pre-assignment (PA). An easy, safe, fast (runs in $O(n)$ time) and thus common policy to schedule a logistic process within a supply chain framework, is to follow a *pre-assignment* (PA) strategy. This means that when the components of an order are purchased, they are assigned to that specific order and thus cannot be used by any other order. This strategy has proven to be insufficient to face the dynamic behavior of a logistic process. For example, the components assigned to orders that are not complete (because one component is missing) have to remain in the stock, even if they could be used to complete another order that should be delivered now. More effective strategies have to allow the exchange of components between orders.

Dispatching rule - First Desired First Served (FDFS). A dispatching rule consists of assigning a priority index to an item, based on an optimality criterion, and then schedule the activities according to the priority index. This typically gives a simple scheduling algorithm that runs in $O(n \log n)$ time. The main property is the fact that the priority of a job is determined without reference to other jobs. There are several dispatching rules that can be used in this problem. Since the objective function is to minimize the tardiness of the delivered orders as defined in (4), the most obvious dispatching rule to be used is the one where the priority index is the orders tardiness T_j. In this way, the orders with the highest tardiness will be the first to be delivered. This means that the orders with the earliest desired date are the first to be served.

2.4 Why Using Meta-heuristics

The approaches described before may be good rules for simple scheduling environments, with one single objective, but for many problems they do not yield good schedules, particularly those with precedence and release date constrains [3]. If these algorithms are not sufficient, we might consider more sophisticated scheduling approaches. These other algorithms have to take into account all the orders when making a decision about the assignment of components. Both GA and ACO approaches have the property of building solutions as a group of activities, so intrinsically when a solution is built by either of these methods, the orders are observed as part of a larger set, rather than a single individual object as it is done on the dispatching rules.

3 Meta-heuristics

Meta-heuristics are algorithms that use other heuristics to search for optimal solutions. Nowadays, genetic algorithms (or in a broader sense evolutionary algorithms) are the most used meta-heuristic used in the literature, along with simulated annealing and tabu search. However, the ant colonies have become more and more a credible option to the evolutionary algorithms, particularly in dynamic optimization problems [11]. Nevertheless, the first step before implementing a meta-heuristic is to analyze the optimization problem to find out if meta-heuristics are expected to perform well or not in the optimization problem. This is done using the fitness distance correlation analysis. Afterwards, it is presented the implementation of GA and ACO in the logistic problem.

3.1 Fitness Landscape Analysis of the Scheduling Problem

The analysis of the fitness landscape [12] became a powerful tool to use when developing optimization algorithms for NP-hard problems, after Jones and Forrest [13] proposed it as a measure for the problem difficulty in genetic algorithms applications. Since then, it has been used to evaluate the implementation of meta-heuristics in optimization problems, e.g. Stützle & Hoos [14] applied it to the Quadratic Assignment Problem (QAP).

Formally, the fitness landscape of an optimization problem is defined by:

1. The set of all possible solutions $s \in S$;
2. An objective function that assigns a fitness value $f(s)$ to every $s \in S$;
3. A neighborhood structure $N \subseteq s \times S$

The fitness landscape determines the shape of the search space as encountered by a local search algorithm. The neighborhood structure N induces a distance metric on the set of solutions. The distance $d(s, s')$ between two solutions s and s' can be defined as the minimum number of moves that has to be performed to transform s into s'. If the solutions are represented by binary vectors, $d(s, s')$ will be the number of different digits between the solutions s' and s. The correlation of this structure, can be quantified by the *fitness distance correlation coefficient* (FDC) ρ [13], which is defined as

$$\rho(f, d) = \frac{cov(f, d)}{\sigma(f)\sigma(d)} \tag{5}$$

where cov is the covariance and σ is the standard deviation. It determines how closely the fitness f and the distance d to the best known solution of several randomly generated solutions are related. If fitness increases when the distance becomes smaller then the search space is expected to be easy to search by algorithms based on the improvement of previous solutions, since there is a path to the optimum by obtaining solutions with increasing fitness.

To analyze our scheduling problem, we performed 5000 random-walks in order to estimate the fitness landscape correlation of the problem. The fitness function used was the objective function of the problem $f(T)$ defined in (4). For the distance metric d between different solutions, we considered that each solution can be seen as a binary sequence of the orders to be delivered on a specific day, with 0 value if they are not delivered and 1 if they are delivered. Then, the distance between two solutions is given by the $xor(s, s')$, i.e. the exclusive *or* between the two binary solutions, which accounts for the number of orders that had a different final value (0 or 1) from the closest optimal solution.

Figure 2 shows that there is a correlation between the distance between solutions and the fitness value, i.e. the closest a solution is from the best known solution, the closest are the fitness values. The correlation coefficient as defined in (5) has the value $\rho = 0.39$. In [13], it is proposed the reference value of $|\rho| > 0,15$ as the minimum necessary for the GA to perform well in the problem. Thus, it is expectable that any heuristic that uses some guidance based on the solution fitness is successful in achieving an optimal solution. Therefore, genetic algorithms or ant colony optimization are good candidate heuristics to solve this optimization problem.

3.2 Genetic Algorithms in the Logistic Process

Genetic Algorithms (GA) introduced by Holland in [5] and later developed by Goldberg in [15] have been widely used in the scheduling optimization field since the introductory work of Lawton [16]. To implement the algorithm on an optimization problem, there are three main aspects to take into account: the coding of the solution, the definition of the fitness function and the implementation of the basic genetic operations (selection, crossover and mutation) within the problem framework.

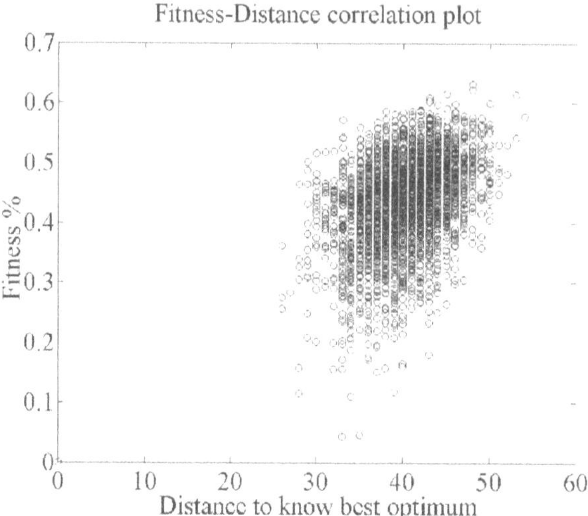

Fig. 2. Fitness distance plots for the logistic process. The x-axis gives the distance to the closest global optimum, the y-axis represents the percentage deviation from highest fitness value.

In this problem, a binary encoding is used, since the problem is intrinsically discrete. The solutions are vectors with the size of all the orders waiting to be delivered, m, with value 0 (zero) if the order is not delivered today, and value 1 if it is. Figure 3a represents an example of two solutions, A and B, in an optimization problem of $m = 5$ orders waiting to be delivered. Solution A represents that orders 1 and 3 will be delivered and solution B represents that orders 1, 4 and 5 will be delivered.

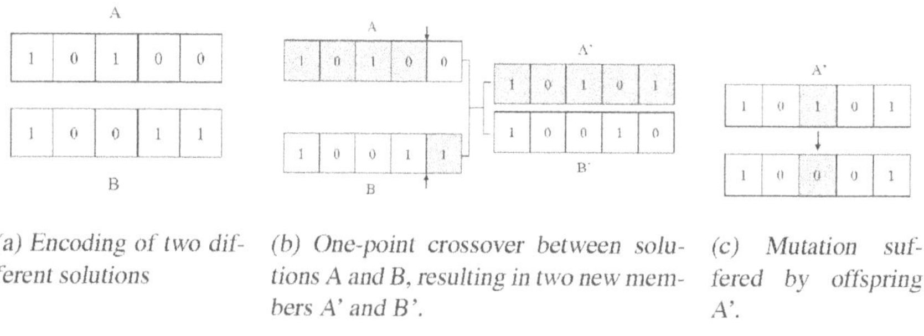

(a) Encoding of two different solutions

(b) One-point crossover between solutions A and B, resulting in two new members A' and B'.

(c) Mutation suffered by offspring A'.

Fig. 3. GA implementation to solve the logistic process.

The initial population is initialized as random binary strings. The selection consists of evaluating the fitness of each solution and then choosing the ones to create offsprings in the next generation, while the rest of the members of the population will disappear. The fitness function is the one defined in (4). The rate of individuals allowed to make offsprings is defined as the selection rate. The rest of the population is eliminated and replaced by the new offsprings. The used crossover method is the most simple and traditional way to do it, the *one-point* crossover. It consists on aligning two parents A and B, randomly chose a crossover section, and then the parents swap the segments located to the right of the crossover point, resulting in two new offsprings A' and B', as shown in Fig. 3b. The mutation is applied to a subset of the offsprings after the crossover step. It randomly changes each gene with a small probability. Figure 3c shows how the offspring A' suffered a mutation. The mutation rates are usually very low. The algorithm runs for $O(n^2)$ time.

If an infeasible solution is created after the genetic operations, this solution is transformed into a feasible solution before the algorithm proceeds. The transformation of an infeasible solution into a feasible one consists of randomly checking for each gene with value 1 if there are enough components in the stock to deliver the order associated with that gene. If yes, the gene's value remains 1 and the stock is updated. If there are not enough components in the stock, the gene's value is changed from 1 to 0.

GA parameters. The parameters tuning was done following a trial-and-error approach. Here we use a selection rate of 50% and a mutation rate of 1%. The algorithm follows an *elitist* approach, since the best individuals are maintained within the population.

3.3 Ant Colony Optimization in the Logistic Process

The meta-heuristic Ant Colony Optimization (ACO) is an optimization algorithm successfully used to solve many NP-hard optimization problems [17]. ACO algorithms are a very interesting approach to find minimum cost paths in graphs [11] specially when the connection costs in the graphics can change over time, i.e. when problems are dynamic. This algorithm has been successfully applied in the scheduling domain [18].

The algorithm is based on the fact that the ants are always able to find the shortest path between the nest and the food sources, only based on the pheromone information previously laid on the ground by other ants in the colony. The artificial ants mimic this behavior in a disjunctive-graph environment. In the scheduling problem, the orders are waiting to be delivered are the nodes of the graph, and the role of the ants is to find the minimum cost path connecting the orders that should be delivered. One important aspect of the problem is the fact that the number of visited nodes may not be the same from one ant to another (e.g., in TSP the number of nodes to visit is fixed and equal to the number of cities to visit [17]). We consider that a group of z ants is traveling on the graph. Each k ant has a bag with the available stock and is distributing it among the m orders. Each ant only visits orders whose components is able to deliver: if an order needs 2 components c_i and the ant only has one, it will not visit that order. In this way, the ACO only builds feasible solutions. When the stocks bag is empty or the remaining components are not enough to deliver any missing order, the search for this ant is finished. Since the path is not closed, the initial starting point for each ant assumes an important role. Figure 4 represents schematically the optimization graph. There, we can see that the ants have found a good schedule (orders 4,1,3 and m) and an alternative schedule (4,1,3 and m-1).

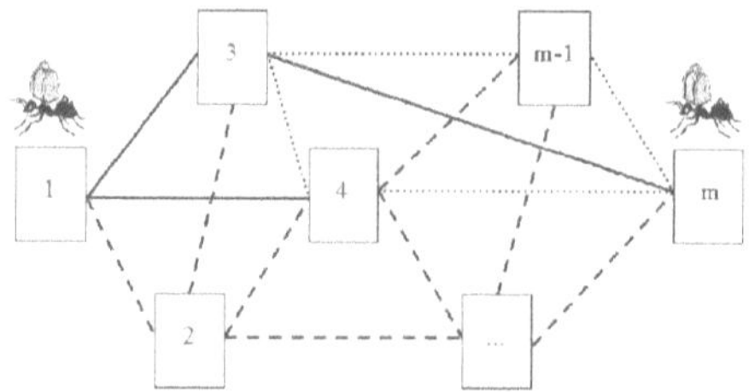

Fig. 4. Disjunctive graph representing the scheduling problem solved by the ACO. The pheromone trails have different intensities: strong (-), medium (..) and weak (- -).

The probability of an ant k in node i to choose node j as the next node to travel is given by:

$$p_{ij}^{k}(t) = \begin{cases} \frac{\tau_{ij}{}^{\alpha} \cdot \eta_{ij}{}^{\beta}}{\sum\limits_{r \notin \Gamma}^{n} \tau_{ir}{}^{\alpha} \cdot \eta_{ir}{}^{\beta}} & \text{if } j \notin \Gamma \\ 0 & \text{otherwise} \end{cases} \tag{6}$$

where τ_{ij} is the pheromone concentration in the path (i, j), η_{ij} is a *heuristic function* and Γ is a *tabu list*. The heuristic function η conduces the search with some valuable information of the problem under optimization. In the logistic process, this information is the tardiness of the order: if an order has already a positive tardiness the ant will feel a stronger attraction to visit it, because the order is already delayed. We define the heuristic function as an exponential function in the interval $[0, 1]$ where the value 0 is for the order that has the minimum tardiness T_{min} and 1 is for the most delayed order T_{max}. The objective is that the orders already delayed attract ants much more than the orders not yet delayed:

$$\eta = \frac{e^{\frac{T_j - T_{min}}{T_{max} - T_{min}}} - 1}{e - 1} \tag{7}$$

The Tabu list Γ is the list of orders already delivered by the ant and also the orders which is not possible to visit, due to lack of stocks. The parameters α and β measure the relative importance of trail pheromone and visibility, respectively.

An *iteration* t is a step from i to j done by all the z ants and a *tour* is the route made until the stock bag is empty. The update of the pheromone concentration in the trails is done at the end of each tour and is given by

$$\tau_{ij}(t + z \times m) = \tau_{ij}(t) \times (1 - \rho) + \sum_{k=1}^{z} \Delta\tau_{ij}^{k} \tag{8}$$

where $\rho \in [0, 1]$ expresses the pheromone evaporation phenomenon and $\sum_{k=1}^{z} \Delta\tau_{ij}^{k}$ are pheromones deposited in the trails (i, j) followed by all the z ants:

$$\Delta\tau_{ij}^{k} \begin{cases} \frac{1}{f_k} & \text{if arc } (i, j) \text{ was used by the } k \text{ ant} \\ 0 & \text{otherwise} \end{cases} \tag{9}$$

where f_k is the value of the evaluation function for each k ant in a minimization problem. The global update is biased by the solution found by each individual ant. Notice that the time interval taken by the z ants to do a complete tour is at the most $t + z \times m$ iterations (considering that all the m orders were visited by all the z ants. In general the number of iterations is smaller). The algorithm runs N_{max} times, where in every N^{th} tour, a new *ant colony* with z ants is released. The algorithm runs for $O(n^3)$ time.

ACO parameters. The algorithm here presented is the general ACO algorithm [11]. The implementation however, is based in the *Max-Min Ant System* (MMAS) [14]: only the best ant updates the trails in every cycle; the pheromone trail is limited to an interval $[\tau_{min}, \tau_{max}]$, in this case to the interval $[0, 1]$. However, unlike the MMAS, the pheromone update mechanism called the *pheromone trail smoothing* is not used here. The set of parameters was tuned using a trial-and-error approach. The pheromone trails are initialized with the value of 0.5 and the values $\alpha = 0.5$ and $\beta = 5$ are used. Since both τ and η are defined in the $[0, 1]$ domain, a small value of α will indicate a higher relative weight to the pheromones trail.

4 Simulation Results

Considering the description of the system presented in Section 2, it is considered a process where the number of arriving orders each day follows a Poisson distribution as in (1), with $\lambda t = 20$. Each order is a set of 1 up to 10 different types of components, and each type of component within an order can have a maximum quantity of 20. The suppliers delay follow a uniform distribution in the interval $[1, 7]$ for each type of component. The suppliers delays are constant throughout the simulation. The desired delivery date is equal to the largest supplier delay of components within the order, but it has some noise associated, which follows a normal distribution with mean 1 and standard deviation 2. This simulates both the disturbances present in the system: the fact that some of the components will miss the expected supplier delay, inducing in this way a delivery date different from the desired delivery date; it simulates also the fact that some clients ask for desired dates different from the possible delivery dates. Remember, as explained in Sec. 2, that the system retains the orders in case they are ready to be delivered before the desired date. The simulation results concern one month time (where each day is a different optimization problem). The simulations start with a stable running system, where we have already some orders to be delivered and some components in the stock. The average number of orders waiting to be delivered inside the system (queue size) is 200.

4.1 Performance-Oriented Analysis

The first analysis on the results concerns the performance of the different methods, represented by *tardiness* T. If $T = 0$ it means that the orders were delivered at the correct date, and if $T > 0$ it means that the orders were delivered after the correct date. It also shows the maximum ($\max T$) tardiness of an order as an indicator of the variance and the index $\#OD$, which is the number of orders waiting to be delivered that are

Table 1. Solutions for the problem after one month

Method	$\#T = 0$	$\#T > 0$	$\max T$	$\#OD$
PA	153	265	7	30
FDFS	282	147	4	19
GA	335	95	14	18
ACO	337	93	12	18

already delayed. Table 1 shows that both GA and ACO strategies present more orders delivered with null tardiness ($T = 0$), less delivered delayed orders ($T > 0$) and less delay orders waiting to be delivered ($\#OD$). The differences between the results of both meta-heuristics are not statistically relevant. The FDFS also outperforms clearly the PA strategy, but it is worse than the GA and the ACO methods. A more careful analysis shows that the best performance of the ACO and GA when compared to the FDFS has the counter effect of increasing the maximum tardiness of the orders ($\max T$), i.e. they are able to deliver less orders with delay, but when the orders stay in the system, they are somehow retained more than desirable.

The first conclusion is that if the system has the liberty to exchange components among the orders, it is able to face the disturbances. This explains why the all strategies except the PA are able to deal with the disturbances, since they all work with a common stock rather than a large set of small fix stocks. However, the FDFS is a dispatching rule and not a optimization method like and the ACO and GA and this explains the performance difference. FDFS attributes an index to all the orders and then sorts them, while the ACO and GA determine a set of orders, and evaluate the index of final set of orders. This originates situations where, for example, the satisfaction of one delayed single order avoids the satisfaction of three other delayed orders. With the FDFS, if the single order is one more day delayed than the others, it will be part of the solution, while with the ACO and GA, the solution for the system will state that is better to deliver three delayed orders than only one. This explains also why the ACO and GA perform worse than the FDFS strategy when it comes to the $\max T$ index.

4.2 Algorithm-Oriented Analysis

The GA and ACO are similar in terms of performance and the differences between the heuristics are not very clear. One of the questions raised in the beginning of the paper remains: which meta-heuristic should be used and why.

GA and ACO convergence. A typical run of the GA and ACO algorithms in terms of fitness improvement of the population can be seen in Figure 5. There it is presented also the one step solutions provided by the PA and the FDFS.

From this figure, we observe that the solutions of the ACO are very good right from the start; even the worst solution of the ACO is better than the first best solutions of the GA. This is explained by the fact that the ACO method is using a local heuristic to guide the search, the heuristic function η. If a similar heuristic was used in the GA, the convergence would be as fast as the ACO algorithm. This shows that even without

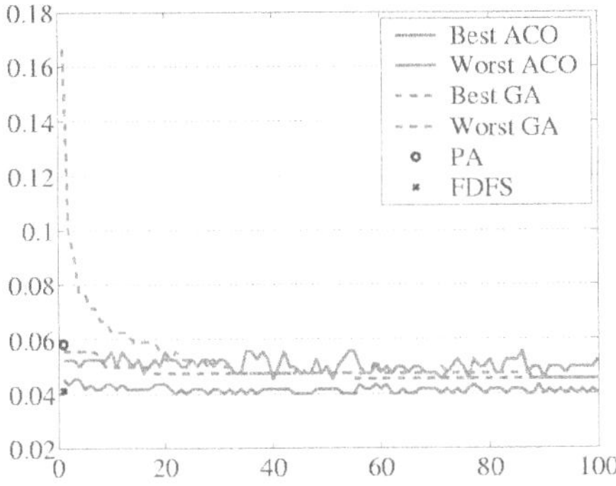

Fig. 5. Typical GA and ACO optimization after one day, in terms of best (-) and worst (- -) element of the population

the help of the local heuristic, the best solution of the GA converges to the best ACO solution after few iterations.

The fact that the ACO takes less iterations to find the optimum, does not mean that the ACO is faster. In fact, the GA algorithm is faster than the ACO algorithm, since the number of basic operations are $O(n^2)$ and $O(n^3)$ respectively. The reason that explains this difference is the fact that the GA algorithm creates a solution in one single step, while the ACO creates a solution by iterating in the graph step by step. The extra time required by the ACO algorithm is reflected in extra information at the end of the algorithm run: the pheromone matrix, which keeps a indirect record of the optimization steps towards the solutions.

It is also important to know how robust the algorithms are. A lucky run could give an extraordinary result which is not easy to repeat. On the other hand, if the method is robust, the solutions between different runs will not change considerably. Table 2 presents the average results for the same optimization problem, in terms of best result, average result and standard deviation. The results show that both the GA and ACO are quite robust methods when applied to this problem, since the average result is very near the best result and the standard deviation is rather small. The test was done for 50 different runs.

Table 2. Solutions for the problem after one day

Method	Measure	$\#T = 0$	$\#T > 0$	max T
GA	Best	24	3	5
	Average	22.6	3.2	5.7
	Deviation	0.96	0.92	1.1
ACO	Best	25	6	1
	Average	24.6	5.6	1.2
	Deviation	0.89	0.55	1.3

From this analysis we can conclude the following:

- The GA is computationally faster than the ACO. However, computational time is not a constraint in this problem.
- Both the GA and the ACO are robust algorithms in the sense that they yield always a good solution. This is proven by the fact that statistically, the solutions do not vary significantly from one run to another.

Solution's information. Let one consider that the final solution given by the GA is the one that delivers the set of orders $\{1, 3, 4, m\}$ and that the second best solution is given by $\{1, 3, 4, m-1\}$. With this information, it can be assumed that the block $\{1, 3, 4\}$ is essential to achieve a good solution, and that delivering order m or $m-1$ is not that important. Consider that the best solution given by the ACO is $(4, 1, 3, m)$ (and for this analysis we recall Fig. 4). The vectorial notation indicates a sequence mechanism. In terms of final result, it is the same solution as the GA solution $\{1, 3, 4, m\}$. However, we know that for a good solution is important to deliver first order 4, then orders 1, followed by order 3 and finally order $m-1$. If the second best solution is $(4, 1, 3, m-1)$ we still conclude the same as in the GA, that the core of a good solution is to deliver orders $(4, 1, 3)$. But this analysis in the ACO case is not purely an assumption as in the GA. The pheromone trails left by the ants in the graph really show that the stronger path connects order 3 to m, but a reasonable strong trail connects also order 3 to order $m-1$.

This information might be valuable in a fast dynamic environment, where orders can be canceled and change at any time. If we suddenly erase order 1 from our search space, the GA would have to restart the all optimization process or it would end up with a sub-optimal solution $\{3, 4, m\}$. With the ACO, a new solution is provided just by inspecting the intensity of the pheromone trails. Once again, on Fig. 4, it is possible to see that after delivering order 4, we can deliver order 3, then order m and then $m-1$. This advantage of the ACO algorithm, as a solution constructor algorithm, has already been explored in the optimization of communication networks [11], a highly dynamic problem.

5 Conclusions

This paper has two aims: the first is to present two different meta-heuristics to solve the scheduling problem of a logistic process in a supply-chain; the second is to discuss the differences between the meta-heuristics. The implemented GA and ACO strategies present very good performances in both scenarios and are easily expandable to other types of objective functions. The FDC analysis previously indicated that the meta-heuristics would perform well. Both methods have similar performances and the choice upon which should be used has to consider more variables. The GA are faster than the ACO, because the managed information during the optimization process is smaller. At the end, the GA present a black-box type of solution, while the ACO present a grey-box type of solution. It is possible to extract more information of the optimization process, which can be used if the problem becomes a dynamic problem. As future work, dynamic scenarios will be developed in order to confirm the importance of the extra information provided by the ACO algorithm.

References

1. Barbuceanu, M., Fox, M. Coordinating multiple agents in the supply chain. Proceedings of the Fifth Workshops on Enabling Technology for Collaborative Enterprises, WET ICE 96, IEEE Computer Society Press, pp. 134-141 (1996)
2. Swaminathan, J.M., Smith, S.F., Sadeh, N.M. Modeling supply chain dynamics: A multiagent approach. Decision Sciences Journal 29 (1998) 607–632
3. Pinedo, M. Scheduling: Theory, Algorithms, and Systems. Second edn. Prentice Hall (2002)
4. Jain, A., Meeran, S. A state-of-the-art review of job-shop scheduling techniques. A. S. Jain and S. Meeran. A state-of-the-art review of job-shop scheduling techniques. Technical report, Department of Applied Physics, Electronic and Mechanical Engineering, University of Dundee, Dundee, Scotland, 1998. (1998)
5. Holland, J.H. Adaptation in Natural and Artificial Systems. The University of Michigan Press (1975)
6. R, C., Gen, M., Tsujimura, Y. A total survey of job-shop scheduling problems using genetic algorithms-i. representation. Computers and Industrial Engineering 30 (1996) 983–997
7. Shen, W., Norrie, D. Agent-based systems for intelligent manufacturing: a state-of-the-art survey. Knowledge and Information Systems, an International Journal 1 (1999) 129–156
8. Dewan, P., Joshi, S. Implementation of an auction-based distributed scheduling model for a dynamic job-shop environment. International Journal of Computer Integrated Manufacturing 14 (2001) 446–456
9. Wolff, R. Stochastic Modeling and the Theory of Queues. Prentice-Hall, London (1989)
10. Martello, S., P.Toth Knapsack problems: algorithms and computer implementations. John Wiley and Sons, Ltd., New York (1990)
11. Dorigo, M., Di Caro, G. The ant colony optimization meta-heuristic. In Corne, D., Dorigo, M., Glover, F., eds.: New Ideas in Optimization. McGraw-Hill, London (1999) 11–32
12. Kauffman, S.A. Adaptation on rugged fitness landscapes. In Stein, D., ed.: Lectures in the Sciences of Complexity. Volume 1., Addsion-Weley Longman (1989) 527–618
13. Jones, T., Forrest, S. Fitness distance correlation as a measure of problem difficulty for genetic algorithms. In Kaufmann, M., ed.: Proceedings of the 6th international conference on genetic algorithms. (1995) 184–192
14. Stützle, T., Hoos, H. Max min ant system. Journal of Future Generation Computer Systems 8 (2000) 889–914
15. Goldberg, D.E. Genetic Algorithms in Search, Optimization and Machine Learning. Addison-Wesley (1989)
16. Lawton, G. Genetic algorithms for schedule optimization. AI Expert May Issue (1992) 23–27
17. Dorigo, M., Maniezzo, V., Colorni, A. The Ant System: Optimization by a colony of cooperating agents. IEEE Transactions on Systems, Man, and Cybernetics Part B: Cybernetics 26 (1996) 29–41
18. den Besten, M., Stützle, T., Dorigo, M. Ant colony optimization for the total weighted tardiness problem. In: Parallel Problem Solving from Nature – PPSN VI 6th International Conference, Paris, France, Springer Verlag (2000)

Evolutionary Neural Network Learning

Miguel Rocha[1], Paulo Cortez[2], and José Neves[1]

[1] Departamento de Informática – Universidade do Minho
Campus de Gualtar, 4710-057 Braga – PORTUGAL
{mrocha,jneves}@di.uminho.pt
[2] Departamento de Sistemas de Informação - Universidade do Minho
Campus de Azurém, 4800-058 Guimarães – PORTUGAL
pcortez@dsi.uminho.pt

Abstract. Several gradient-based methods have been developed for *Artificial Neural Network (ANN)* training. Still, in some situations, such procedures may lead to local minima, making *Evolutionary Algorithms (EAs)* a promising alternative. In this work, *EAs* using direct representations are applied to several *classification* and *regression ANN* learning tasks. Furthermore, *EAs* are also combined with local optimization, under the *Lamarckian* framework. Both strategies are compared with conventional training methods. The results reveal an enhanced performance by a macro-mutation based *Lamarckian* approach.

1 Introduction

In *MultiLayer Perceptrons (MLPs)*, one of the most popular *Artificial Neural Network (ANN)* architectures, *neurons* are grouped in *layers* and only *forward connections* exist [2]. The interest in *MLPs* was stimulated by the advent of the *Backpropagation* algorithm and since then several variants have been proposed, such as the *RPROP* [7]. Yet, these gradient-based procedures are not free from getting trapped into local minima when the error surface is rugged, being also sensitive to their parameter settings and to the network initial weights.

An alternative approach comes from the use of *Evolutionary Algorithms (EAs)*, where a number of potential solutions to a problem makes an evolving population [5,4]. *EAs* are appealing for *ANN* training since [8]: a global multi-point search is provided; no gradient information is required; and they are general purpose methods (the same *EA* may be used in different types of *ANNs*).

Following this trend, this work aims at exploring the use of *EAs* for *MLP* training, when applied to *classification* and *regression* tasks.

2 Experimental Setup

A set of ten benchmarks was considered in this work (Table 1), endorsing two main types (column **T**) of problems: *Classification (C)* and *Regression (R)* tasks. Six real-world problems were chosen from the *UCI* machine learning repository [3]. The *PRA* is based on a realistic simulation of the dynamics of a robot arm.

Fernando Moura Pires, Salvador Abreu (Eds.): EPIA 2003, LNAI 2902, pp. 24–28, 2003.

The artificial tasks include the famous *N Bit Parity* [7], the *TCC* which consists on assigning one of three colors to each block of a 3x3x3 grid cube and the *STS*, a regression task where the output is given by: $y = sin(8x) \times sin(6x)$.

Table 1. The *MLP* learning benchmarks.

Task	T	Description	C	I	H	O	W
6BP	C	Six Bit Parity	64	6	6	1	49
TCC	C	Three Color Cube	27	3	8	3	59
SMR	C	Sonar: Rocks vs Mines	104	60	6	1	373
PID	C	Pima Indians Diabetes	200	7	7	1	64
IPD	C	Iris Plant Database	150	4	3	3	27
WBC	C	Wisconsin Breast Cancer	499	9	3	1	34
STS	R	Sin Times Sin	80	1	8	1	25
PRA	R	Pumadyn Robot Arm	128	8	8	1	81
RTS	R	Rise Time Servomechanism	167	4	4	1	25
PBC	R	Prognostic Breast Cancer	198	32	4	1	137

Each problem will be modeled by a fully connected *MLP*, with one hidden layer and *bias* connections, being the topology given in Table 1, where columns **I**, **H** and **O** denote the number of input, hidden and output nodes, while column **W** shows the number of connections. Classification tasks make use of a single binary output (if two classes are present) or one boolean value per each class. In *regression* problems one real-valued output encodes the *dependent* variable. The standard logistic activation function ($\frac{1}{1+e^{-x}}$) was used in all *classification* tasks. A different strategy was adopted for the *regression* problems, since outputs may lie out of the co-domain ($[0, 1]$). Thus, the *logistic* function was adopted on the hidden nodes, while the output ones used shortcut connections and *linear* functions, to scale the range of the outputs. For all training methods, the initial weights are randomly assigned within the range $[-1; 1]$, being the accuracy of each *MLP* measured in terms of the *Root Mean Squared Error (RMSE)*.

3 Experiments with Evolutionary Algorithms

In this study, *direct* encoding is embraced (one gene per connection weight), an alternative closer to the phenotype, allowing the definition of richer genetic operators [5]. Two mutation operators were used, namely:

- *Random Mutation*, which replaces one weight by a new randomly generated value, within the range $[-1, 1]$; and
- *Gaussian Mutation*, which adds to a given gene a value taken from a gaussian distribution, with a zero mean and 0.25 standard deviation [4].

In both cases, a random number of genes is changed, between 1% to 20% of the number of *ANN* weights. The following crossover operators were also tested:

- *Two-Point*, *Uniform*, *Arithmetical* and *Sum*, standard *EA* operators [5];
- *Input* and *Output* connections, similar to a *one-point* crossover except that the set of input (output) connections to a node can not be disrupted [6]; and
- *Hidden* nodes, that combines the previous two operators; i.e., all connections to/from a hidden node can not be separated.

The *EAs* population size was set to 30, being the *selection* done by converting the fitness value (*RMSE*) into its ranking, and then applying a roulette wheel scheme, being used a substitution rate of 50% and the *elitism* value set to one. All tests were conducted using the *Java* language, running on a *Pentium III 933 MHz PC*. The termination criteria was set by CPU time (100 seconds).

The results are compiled in Table 2, which shows the quality Q_m, measured by how far (in percentage) its error ($RMSE_{m,t}$, the mean of thirty runs for the model m and task t) is from the best result (B_t), given by: $Q_m = 100 \times (\sum_{t \in T} \frac{RMSE_{m,t}}{B_t} - 1)$ where $B_t = min_{k \in M}(RMSE_{k,t})$, and T and M denote the set of learning *tasks* and *models*. In the first row, only the mutation operator is applied. For the others, each operator breeds 50% of the offspring. The best performance is achieved by *gaussian* mutation, being no gain in using a crossover operator, thus favoring *Evolutionary Programming* [4]. This may be due to the *permutation* problem; i.e., several genomes may encode the same *ANN* [8].

Table 2. The overall *EA's* results for each model m (Q_m values).

Crossover	Gaussian Mutation	Random Mutation
None	**2.1%**	148.2%
Two-Point	9.8%	143.6%
Uniform	10.3%	143.4%
Arithmetical	24.3%	146.0%
Sum	74.4%	78.3%
Input	9.3%	143.7%
Output	7.8%	143.5%
Hidden	9.5%	143.5%

4 Experiments with Lamarckian Optimization

The *EAs* performance can be improved by the use of the *Lamarckian* point of view [1]: in this work and in every generation, each individual is subject to 50 epochs of the *RPROP* algorithm [7], being the new weights encoded back into the chromosome (Figure 1). Two distinct *Lamarckian EAs (LEAs)* were tested (Table 3), with 20 individuals and one mutation operator, *gaussian* (column **GL**) or *random* (column **RL**), since the crossovers revealed poor performances. Here the comparison favors the latter *macro-mutation*, which may allow individuals to jump between local minima, while the *gaussian* mutation effect may be reversed by the *RPROP*.

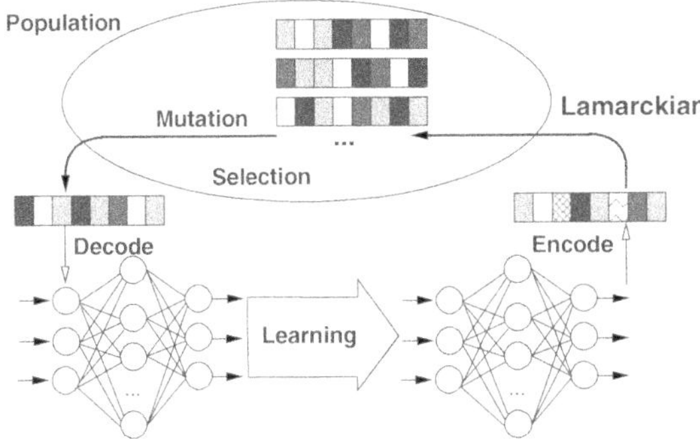

Fig. 1. An illustration of the Lamarckian strategy of inheritance.

Table 3 also compares the best *EAs* with gradient-based methods (values are presented in terms of the mean of thirty runs). The *Neural Population (NP)* model was added, where 20 *MLP's* will be trained via the *RPROP* algorithm, in order to achieve a fair comparison among *population* and *non-population* approaches. The *BackPropagation (BP)* is outperformed by the *gaussian* mutation *EA* in four benchmarks, while the *RPROP (RP)* always surpasses the *EA*. The *NP* behaves better, although the *RL* excels all methods, stressing the importance of the random mutation and selection operators.

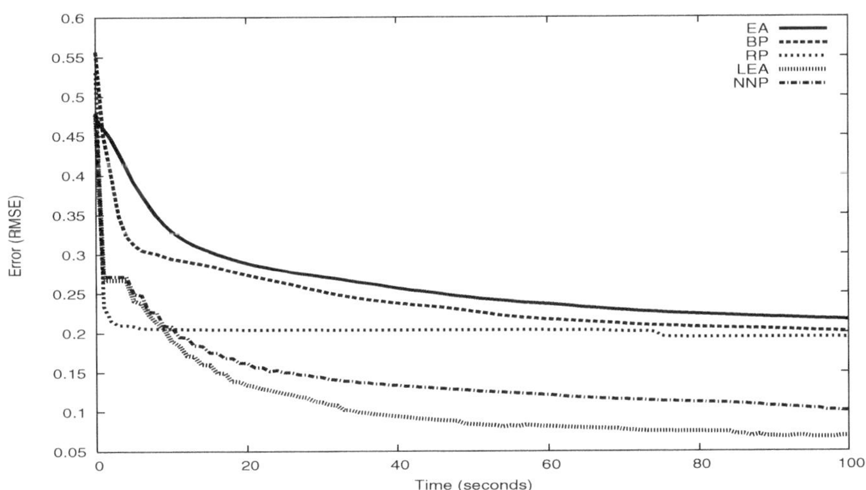

Fig. 2. The error evolution for the *TCC* task.

A temporal perspective is given in Figure 2 for the *TCC* task, reflecting each methods' traits: the *EA* and *BP* show slow learning rates; the *RP* gets the fastest convergence, but it quickly stagnates; both the random mutation *LEA* and *NP* reveal better long term performances, albeit the former method gains an advantage.

Table 3. Comparison between different training approaches (*RMSE* values).

Task	EA	GL	RL	NP	RP	BP
6BP	0.148	0.078	**0.036**	0.070	0.243	0.364
TCC	0.216	0.113	**0.069**	0.101	0.194	0.201
SMR	0.153	**0.000**	**0.000**	**0.000**	0.067	0.045
PID	0.262	0.144	**0.143**	0.151	0.175	0.164
IPD	0.081	0.045	**0.030**	0.040	0.064	0.088
WBC	0.131	**0.094**	**0.094**	0.099	0.107	0.104
STS	0.329	0.095	**0.078**	0.109	0.095	0.299
PRA	1.190	0.420	**0.390**	0.420	0.440	1.780
RTS	0.571	0.266	**0.242**	0.254	0.381	0.523
PBC	26.1	19.8	**19.0**	21.5	21.9	38.6

5 Conclusions

Results obtained by pure *EAs* stress the importance of the gaussian mutation and the difficulty in the design of crossover operators. Although other methods are more effective in supervised tasks, this approach can be quite useful for *recurrent neural networks* or *reinforcement learning*. For *classification* and *regression*, the experiments carried out have shown that the *RPROP* algorithm is the best choice when few computational resources are available. However, a better performance is achieved by the use of a *Lamarckian* approach, being shown that incorporating a macro-mutation is essential to obtain improved performances.

References

1. R. Belew, J. McInerney, and N. Schraudolph. Evolving Networks: Using the Genetic Algorithms with Connectionist Learning. CSE TR CS90-174, UCSD, 1990.
2. C. Bishop. *Neural Networks for Pattern Recognition.* Oxford Univ. Press, 1995.
3. C. Blake and C. Merz. UCI Repository of Machine Learning Databases, 1998.
4. L. J. Fogel. *Intelligence Through Simulated Evolution: Forty Years of Evolutionary Programming.* John Wiley, New York, 1999.
5. Z. Michalewicz. *Genetic Algorithms + Data Structures = Evolution Programs.* Springer-Verlag, USA, third edition, 1996.
6. D. Montana and L. Davis. Training feedforward neural networks using genetic algorithms. In *Proc. 11th IJCAI*, pages 762–767. Morgan Kaufmann, 1989.
7. M. Riedmiller. Supervised Learning in Multilayer Perceptrons – from Backpropagation to Adaptive Learning Techniques . *Comp. Stand. and Interfaces*, 16, 1994.
8. X. Yao. Evolving Artificial Neural Networks. *Proc. IEEE*, 87(9):1423–1447, 1999.

Golomb Rulers: The Advantage of Evolution

Francisco B. Pereira[1,2], Jorge Tavares[2], and Ernesto Costa[2]

[1] Instituto Superior de Engenharia de Coimbra,
Quinta da Nora, 3030 Coimbra, Portugal
[2] Centro de Informática e Sistemas da Universidade de Coimbra,
Pólo II – Pinhal de Marrocos, 3030 Coimbra, Portugal
{xico, jast, ernesto}@dei.uc.pt

Abstract. In this paper we present a new evolutionary algorithm designed to efficiently search for optimal Golomb rulers. The proposed approach uses a redundant random keys representation to codify the information contained in a chromosome and relies on a simple interpretation algorithm to obtain feasible solutions. Experimental results show that this method is successful in quickly identifying good solutions and that can be considered as a realistic alternative to massive parallel approaches that need several months or years to discover high quality Golomb rulers.

1 Introduction

A Golomb ruler is defined as a ruler that has marks unevenly spaced at integer locations in such a way that the distance between any two marks is unique. They were named after the relevant work of the mathematician Solomon Golomb [1], [2] and, unlike usual rulers, they have the ability to measure more discrete measures than the number of marks they carry. Also Golomb rulers are not redundant, since they do not measure the same distance twice.

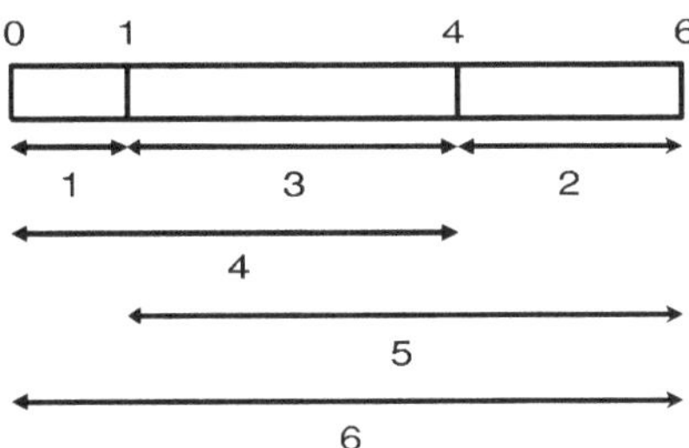

Fig. 1. A perfect Golomb ruler with 4 marks

Although the definition of a Golomb ruler does not place any restriction on the length of the ruler, researchers are usually interested in rulers with minimum length. An Optimal Golomb Ruler (OGR) is defined as the shortest length ruler

Fernando Moura Pires, Salvador Abreu (Eds.): EPIA 2003, LNAI 2902, pp. 29–42, 2003.

for a given number of marks [3]. There may exist multiple different OGRs for a specific number of marks. A perfect Golomb ruler is a particular case of an OGR: in addition to the minimum length requirement, it should measure all distances between 1 and the overall length of the ruler. In figure 1, a perfect Golomb ruler with 4 marks is presented. As you can see, all distances between 1 and 6 (the length of the ruler) can be measured. It can be proved that perfect rulers beyond 4 marks do not exist [3].

OGRs are used in a wide range of real world situations. For example, in the field of communications when setting up an interferometer for radio astronomy, placing the antennas on the marks of a Golomb ruler maximizes the recovery of information about the phases of the signal received [4], [5]. Other examples of areas where they are used include X-ray crystallography [2] or error detection and correction in the field of coding theory [3], [6].

For a small number of marks it is possible to construct OGRs by hand. As the number of marks increases, the problem becomes difficult and, for $n \geq 9$, computational approaches are required to find possible solutions. Currently, most of the techniques used to identify OGRs rely on massively parallel brute force algorithms.

In this paper we present a new Evolutionary Computation (EC) approach designed to efficiently search for good solutions. Our goal is to introduce a robust technique that has the ability to quickly identify good solutions (if possible optimum solutions) and that can be considered an alternative to brute force methods, that usually need too much time to obtain an answer and so cannot be considered as a realistic option in real world situations. The proposed algorithm uses random keys to codify possible solutions, a technique which has already showed to be effective in situations where the chromosome needs to encode a permutation [7]. We will also analyze how the addition of a simple heuristic to the EC algorithm may further improve its search performance.

Results presented here show that our evolutionary approach is successful in quickly identifying high quality rulers with several marks, confirming that they are a well-balanced technique capable of discovering good solutions within a reasonable time.

The structure of the paper is the following: in section 2 we provide a formal definition of Golomb rulers. Then, in section 3 we present an overview of some of the main techniques used to generate and verify OGRs. Section 4 comprises a description of the proposed EC model. In section 5 we present and analyze the most important experimental results achieved, while in section 6 we examine if the addition of a simple heuristic to the EC algorithm may further improve its search performance. Finally, in section 7 we draw some overall conclusions and suggest direction for future work.

2 Golomb Rulers

In this section we present a formal definition of Golomb rulers. A n-mark Golomb ruler is an ordered set of n distinct nonnegative integers $\{a_1, a_2, \ldots, a_n\}$ such that all possible differences $|a_i - a_j|$, $i, j = 1, \ldots, n$ with $i \neq j$, are distinct. Values a_i correspond to positions where marks are placed. By convention, the first mark a_1 is placed on position 0, whereas the length of the ruler is given by the position of the rightmost mark an. The ruler from figure 1 can be defined as $\{0, 1, 4, 6\}$.

The length of a segment of a ruler is defined as the distance between two consecutive marks. This way, it is also possible to represent a Golomb ruler with n marks through the specification of the length of the $n-1$ segments that compose it. According to this notation the example from figure 1 can be defined as $\{1, 3, 2\}$.

The Golomb ruler $\{a_1, a_2, \ldots, a_n\}$ is an OGR if there exists no other n-mark ruler having a smaller largest mark a_n. In such a case a_n is called the length of the n-mark OGR (OGR-n, for short).

Finding OGRs is a complex combinatorial optimization problem. Moreover, it has some specific features that differentiate it from other problems with similar characteristics, such as the Travelling Salesperson Problem (TSP). Whilst TSP can be classified as a complete ordered set (the goal is to find a permutation of the n cities that compose the problem), OGR can be considered as an incomplete ordered set [8]. Assume that we represent a ruler by a sequence composed by its segment's lengths. The OGR-n is a permutation of $n-1$ elements taken from a set of m elements, where m is defined as the maximum distance between marks (usually $n \ll m$). The construction of such a solution poses several difficulties:

- Should a maximum value for m be pre-established or should it be adjusted during the construction of a ruler?
- How to select the $n-1$ elements from a set of m values?
- How to build a valid permutation with the $n-1$ elements selected?

When we present our approach in section 4, we will describe how we addressed each one of these problems.

3 Related Work

Given its interest, both for real world applications and as a mathematical puzzle, the search for OGRs has attracted the attention of researchers over the past few decades.

One of the most important classes of algorithms proposed, aimed to construct OGRs from the scratch. Dewdney presented one of these methods in 1985 [9]. The proposed technique is composed of two phases: the ruler generation and the Golomb verification. The generation phase takes two parameters as input (the number of marks and an upper bound on the ruler length) and recursively tries to construct a Golomb ruler. The second phase of the algorithm verifies if the generated solution satisfies all requirements for a Golomb ruler. Gardner [10] and Dollas et. al. [3] presented other examples of algorithms that iteratively construct solutions. In order to improve execution time, most of these methods consider a set of search space reduction techniques.

Shearer [11] proposed a depth first backtracking algorithm. During search this method builds a Golomb ruler by selecting the position of the marks in order. At each node of the search tree the program keeps track of which differences have been used and which integers could by adjoined to the ruler without leading to an invalid solution. The algorithm backtracks when too few integers remain eligible to allow completion of the ruler.

Best solutions for OGRs with a number of marks between 20 and 23 were obtained by massive parallel distributed projects. Two projects are involved in searching for OGRs: GVANT[1] and distributed.net[2]. Both of them are collective computing projects that rely on spare CPU cycles from a large number of computers distributed over the Internet. It took several months and numerous collaborators to find optimum solutions for each one of the instances OGR-20, OGR-21, OGR-22 and OGR-23. Search for OGR-24 and OGR-25 started in July 2000.

To our knowledge there was just one attempt to apply EC techniques to search for OGRs. In 1995, Soliday et al. proposed a genetic algorithm designed to find good solutions for different Golomb ruler instances [8]. They adopted a representation where a n-mark OGR candidate is composed by a permutation of $n-1$ integers, each one of these values representing the length of a segment in the ruler. Special precautions were taken during the generation of the initial population to ensure that an individual did not contain the same segment twice. Also special genetic operators were required to guarantee that descendants were also valid permutations. Evaluation of individuals considered two fitness criteria: ruler length and number of repeated measures. Results presented in the above-mentioned paper are not very good. Best solutions evolved for rulers with 10 to 16 marks are far from the known overall bests (the lengths of the best rulers found are between 10% and 36% higher than the optimum values).

In table 1 we present the length of OGRs up to 23 marks. Also presented is the length of the best solutions found by the evolutionary approach proposed by Soliday et. al.

4 An Evolutionary Approach with Random Keys

The representation chosen for individuals plays a crucial role on the performance of EC algorithms. In the problem addressed in this paper, a candidate solution for a particular OGR-n instance must specify, either the position of the n marks, or the length of each one of the $n-1$ segments. We adopted the second approach, so a chromosome is composed by a permutation of integers representing successive segment lengths. The maximum segment length λ is specified as a parameter of the evolutionary algorithm and remains unchanged during search.

[1] GVANT project. Available at http://members.aol.com/golomb20/
[2] Distributed.net "Project OGR". Available at http://www.distributed.net/ogr/

Table 1. OGRs lengths for instances between 5 and 23 marks and best results achieved by Soliday's EC approach

Instances	Best Solutions	Soliday's EC approach
OGR-5	11	11
OGR-6	17	17
OGR-7	25	25
OGR-8	34	35
OGR-9	44	44
OGR-10	55	62
OGR-11	72	79
OGR-12	85	103
OGR-13	106	124
OGR-14	127	168
OGR-15	151	206
OGR-16	177	238
OGR-17	199	-
OGR-18	216	-
OGR-19	246	-
OGR-20	283	-
OGR-21	333	-
OGR-22	356	-
OGR-23	372	-

4.1 Chromosome Representation and Interpretation

Even though λ is known, there are two crucial decisions to make when building a solution for OGR-n: how to select $n-1$ distinct segments from the set of λ values and how to build a valid permutation with the selected elements. We adopted a representation that tries to deal efficiently with this situation:

- It provides a straightforward way to select which elements will compose the permutation;
- It finds a natural arrangement for the selected segments.

Also, the representation chosen for individuals enables a simple application of standard genetic operators guaranteeing that most of the generated descendants are legal solutions.

In our approach, the chromosome is composed by a permutation of λ distinct values. Encoding of the permutation is done with random keys (RK). RK were introduced by Bean [7] in 1994 and obtained good results in situations where the relative order of the tasks is important [7], [12]. One of their main advantages is that it is possible to apply standard genetic operators to chromosomes (e.g., one point or uniform crossover) and still obtain feasible individuals. We will just present a brief overview of RK. For a detailed description, consult [7] or [13]. RK representation uses a sequence of N random numbers to encode a permutation of length N. These numbers are typically sampled from the real interval $[0, 1]$.

Both the position and the value of the keys are important for the interpretation of the sequence. To obtain the permutation that corresponds to a given key sequence, all keys are sorted according to their values in decreasing order. Then, the original positions of the keys will be used to construct the permutation. For example, consider the following key sequence $r = \{0.5, 0.7, 0.3, 0.9, 0.4\}$. Position 4 contains the highest value of the key sequence (0.9), so 4 will be the first element of the resulting permutation. Then, the next highest value is at position 2. The ordering process continues in a similar way and at the end we get the permutation $\{4, 2, 1, 5, 3\}$. From a key sequence of length N we can always construct a permutation of N unique numbers between 1 and N (or between 0 and $N-1$ if needed).

In [13], Rothlauf et. al. proposed NetKeys, an extension of RK to problems dealing with tree network design. The situation addressed is that of the design of a minimum spanning tree over a fully connected graph with n nodes. In these circumstances, a NetKey sequence will be composed by $L = \frac{n(n-1)}{2}$ random numbers (the number of links in the graph). Positions are labelled and each one represents one possible link in the tree. The value of a particular key can be interpreted as the importance of the link it represents. The higher its value, the higher the probability that this link is used in the construction of the tree. From this sequence, a permutation of L numbers can be constructed in the same way as described for standard RK. Then the construction of the tree begins: links are added to the tree in an order that is in accordance to the value of its key. If the insertion of a link would create a cycle, then it is skipped and construction continues with the next one. The process comes to an end when $n-1$ links have been selected.

Our codification of a solution for an OGR-n follows the same principles as those expressed for NetKeys. Each one of the λ positions of the chromosome represents one possible segment. Without loss of generality, we assume that position i corresponds to a segment of length i ($i = 1, \ldots, \lambda$). Also, just like with NetKeys, the value of a given key represents the importance of the related segment. If we compare both situations, there is nevertheless one additional difficulty associated with OGRs: the interpretation algorithm must determine, not only which segments will be part of the ruler, but also its relative position. Figure 2 illustrates how decoding and interpretation (the two stages required to assign fitness to an individual) are related.

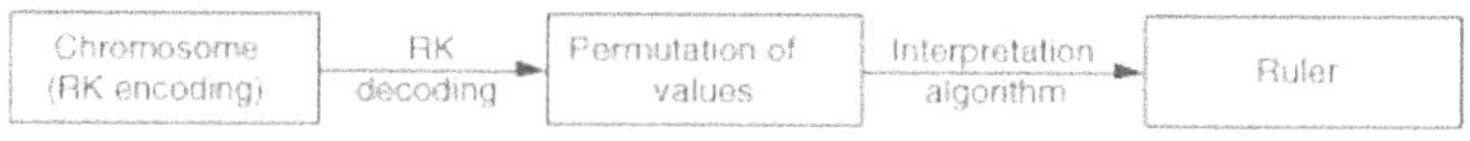

Fig. 2. Decoding and interpretation of the information contained a chromosome

A step-by-step description helps to exemplify how the decoding of the permutation and subsequent interpretation of the information contained in a chromosome is performed. Consider that we are searching for OGR-5 and that λ

is 10. Consider also that the chromosome encodes the following key sequence $\{0.87, 0.17, 0.67, 0.27, 0.86, 0.97, 0.71, 0.31, 0.38, 0.40\}$. After performing the RK decoding, the resulting permutation is $\{6, 1, 5, 7, 3, 10, 9, 8, 4, 2\}$.

During the interpretation phase, the first $n-1$ valid segments from the permutation are used to build the ruler. The iterative algorithm used to build a valid ruler tries to ensure that segments are selected in such a way that no duplicate measurements exist. It is a deterministic process and segments on the left of the permutation have higher priority. The ruler is constructed from left to right, as shown in figure 3.

1. Let R be an empty ruler and L a permutation of length λ constructed from the key sequence encoded in the chromosome. Let $curr\_seg = 1$.
2. While $curr\_seg \leq n-1$ **Repeat:**
  2.1. Starting in the beginning of L, find the first segment that can be appended to the left of the ruler R built so far without leading to duplicate measurements
  2.2. If such a segment does not exist, randomly select a value between 1 and λ and append it to the left of R.
  2.3. Increment $curr\_seg$

Fig. 3. Ruler construction algorithm

Depending on the circumstances, it might happen that in a specific position all segments lead to duplicate measurements. If this situation arises, a random value between 1 and λ is chosen and a segment with this length is appended to the ruler (see point 2.2 of the algorithm). During this operation the only restriction that applies is that there should be no duplicated segments in R.

Table 2 illustrates how these steps are applied leading to the construction of the ruler $\{6, 1, 3, 5\}$ from the permutation previously obtained.

Table 2. Iterations required to construct a Golomb ruler with 5 marks (4 segments) from the permutation {6, 1, 5, 7, 3, 10, 9, 8, 4, 2}

Iteration	Segment Selected	Ruler	Measures
1	6	$\{6, \_, \_, \_\}$	{6}
2	1	$\{6, 1, \_, \_\}$	{1,6,7}
3	3	$\{6, 1, 3, \_\}$	{1,3,4,6,7,10}
4	5	$\{6, 1, 3, 5\}$	{1,3,4,5,6,7,8,9,10,15}

Note that in the 3rd iteration segments 5 and 7 are not selected because, if inserted in the ruler, they would lead to duplicate measurements. Segment 5 is selected later because its insertion in iteration 4 does not yield any violation.

4.2 Evaluation

To evaluate an individual we follow a similar approach to the one described in [8]. We consider two criteria: ruler length and legality of the solution (i.e., whether it contains repeated measurements). The equation used to assign fitness to an individual x is the following:

$$fitness(x) = \begin{cases} \text{K - number of repeated measurements} & \text{, if } x \text{ is illegal} \\ \text{K + M - Ruler length} & \text{, if } x \text{ is legal} \end{cases} \quad (1)$$

Where K is a large constant (we used the value 1000 in our experiments) and M is an upper bound for the ruler length (for an OGR-n instance we set $M = n \times \lambda$). This formula ensures that:

- The fitness of a legal solution is always higher than the fitness of an illegal solution;
- Invalid solutions are ranked according to their illegality (number of repeated measurements);
- Legal solutions are ranked according to their length. Shorter rulers receive higher fitness.

5 Experimental Results

To evaluate our approach (which henceforth we will designate by RK-EC) we performed a set of experiments with several OGR instances. More precisely, we used the evolutionary algorithm to seek for good rulers with 10 to 19 marks.

The settings of the EC algorithm are the following: Number of generations: 20000; Population size: 200; Tournament selection with tourney size: 5; Elitist strategy; $\lambda = 30$ for instances with number of marks ≤ 13, $\lambda = 50$, for instances with 14 and 15 marks and $\lambda = 60$ for instances with number of marks ≥ 16; Two-point crossover with rate: 0.75; An evolutionary strategy like mutation operator is used. When undergoing mutation, the new value v_{new} for a given gene (i.e. a key in the chromosome) is obtained from the original value v_{old} in the following way:

$$v_{new} = v_{old} + \sigma \times N(0,1) \quad (2)$$

Where $N(0,1)$ represents a random value sampled from a standard normal distribution and σ is a parameter from the algorithm. In our experiments we used $\sigma = 0.1$. Mutation rate was set to 0.25 per gene.

For every OGR instance we performed 30 runs with the same initial conditions and with different random seeds. All initial populations were randomly generated with values for keys selected from the real interval [0, 1]. Significance of the results was tested with a t-test with level of significance 0.01.

Values for different parameters were set heuristically. Nevertheless, and even though we did not perform an extensive parametric study, we conducted some additional tests and verified that, within a moderate range, there was not an important difference in the outcomes. In table 3 we summarize, for all instances, the results achieved by the RK-EC approach. Column Best shows the length of the best solution found, whereas column Average presents the averages of the best solutions found in each one of the 30 runs. To allow an easy comparison, column Best solutions shows the length of the different OGRs.

Table 3. Results obtained by the RK-EC algorithm for all instances

Instances	Best Solutions	RK-EC	
		Best	Average
OGR-10	55	55	58.9
OGR-11	72	72	74.6
OGR-12	85	91	93.8
OGR-13	106	111	115.1
OGR-14	127	134	138.6
OGR-15	151	160	166.2
OGR-16	177	193	197.8
OGR-17	199	221	233.6
OGR-18	216	266	274
OGR-19	246	299	319

A brief perusal of the results reveals that our approach was able to consistently find good quality solutions. It found the optimal rulers for instances with 10 and 11 marks. For OGR-n instances with $12 \leq n \leq 17$ it found rulers whose length is not more than 10% larger than the optimum solutions. When applied to instances OGR-18 and OGR-19 the RK-EC approach had more difficulties and the lengths of the best rulers found are approximately 20% bigger than the OGRs. This is not an unexpected result. Golomb rulers define search spaces whose topology is very hard to sample. One reason contributing to the difficulty in finding good solutions is the number of interactions that occur between the genes that compose a chromosome. There is a high epistasis associated with this problem, since changing the position of a mark (or the length of a single segment) affects all other marks and a large number of measurements carried out by a given ruler. As the number of marks increases, it is likely that there is a growth in the difficulty of controlling the effects of changes in the ruler.

Despite these difficulties, for all instances where the comparison is possible (OGR-10 to OGR-16), the RK-EC algorithm found rulers clearly shorter than those ones discovered by the previous EC approach (consult table 1 for comparison). These results show that an EC approach can be a reliable option in situations where good quality rulers have to be quickly discovered and there is not enough time to apply massive parallel techniques that take months or even years to produce any outcome. Even in the worst cases, a 20% departure from the optimum might be considered satisfactory if the answer is found in a few minutes instead of 1 year. Also, as it can be seen from table 3, the averages of the best results found in the 30 runs are not very distant from the best solution found (this distance never exceeds 7%) showing that the RK-EC algorithm is a robust approach.

In our experiments, we selected a fairly large value for λ. It varied between 30 (for instances with no more than 13 marks) and 60 (for instances with more than 15 marks). It is known that the length of the biggest segment for OGR-10 is 13, whilst for OGR-19 is 40. As for the other instances, values are somewhere between these extremes. The gap that exists between these values and the chosen λ is likely to affect the performance of the EC algorithm. On one hand, by setting λ to a large value helps to obtain valid individuals in the interpretation phase, which might benefit the search process. On the other hand, as the chromosomes encode a large number of segments they will also contain a lot of redundant information. As an example, when seeking for OGR-19, from the 60 segments belonging to the chromosome only 18 are used to construct a ruler. This situation might slow down (or even prevent) convergence to areas of the space where good solutions are. Results presented in this paper are inconclusive in what concerns this situation and further experiments are needed to determine the real influence of λ in the performance of the evolutionary algorithm. One possible alternative that we will analyze in a near future is to let the value of λ evolve during the simulation.

6 Addition of a Simple Heuristic

In this section we will describe a final set of experiments that will enable us to analyze if the addition of a heuristic may further improve the performance of the proposed approach. In the past few years, there has been numerous attempts to combine EC algorithms with other methods, such as problem specific heuristics or generic local search techniques. In many situations, results achieved give a clear indication that this hybridization is advantageous since it enhances the ability of the evolutionary algorithm to discover good solutions [14], [15], [16].

In this paper we will just describe a straightforward test performed with a basic heuristic that favors the existence of small length segments in a ruler. Even though the occurrence of some small segments does not ensure that the fitness of a ruler is high (depending on the situation, it might be preferable to have two medium sized segments than one small and one big), it is clear that typical good solutions for OGRs will tend to contain elements with these characteristics.

In accordance to this assumption, we added to the interpretation algorithm, a heuristic that favors the insertion of small segments. This way, the modified algorithm that uses the information decoded from the chromosome to construct a ruler has the following steps presented in figure 4.

The relevant difference from the first version of the algorithm is that, with a probability ϕ, the next segment to be inserted in the ruler is selected from an ordered sequence of λ integers instead of the permutation decoded from the chromosome. Although the modification in the interpretation algorithm is minimal, when the heuristic is applied, it will introduce some variation in the construction of the ruler (the sequence order is different from the permutation which

```
1. Let R be an empty ruler, let L be a permutation of
length λ constructed from the key sequence encoded
in the chromosome and let O be an ordered sequence
of λ integers {1,2,...,λ-1,λ}. Let curr_seg = 1.
2. While curr_seg ≤ n-1 Repeat:
   2.1. R ← UniformRandomValue(0,1)
   2.2. If R ≥ φ then
        2.2.1. Selected permutation P ← L
   2.3. Else
        2.3.1. Selected permutation P ← O
    2.4. Starting in he beginning of P, find the first
   segment that can be appended to the left of the
   ruler R built so far without leading to
   duplicate measurements
   2.5. If such a segment does not exist, randomly
   select a value between 1 and λ and
   append it to the left of R.
   2.6. Increment curr_seg
```

Fig. 4. Interpretation algorithm

was decoded from the chromosome). Moreover this variation is not random, since it favors small segments. Anyway, this heuristic in no way guarantees that good solutions are obtained. When selected, it will always try to insert segments following the same order. Given this deterministic behavior, it might even induce premature convergence to local optima. That's why the application of this heuristic will be done at a moderate rate.

To examine if this modification influences the performance of the search algorithm we repeated all previous experiments. We used the same experimental settings and set $\phi = 0.25$. Results are presented in table 4.

Table 4. Results obtained by the RK-EC algorithm with heuristic for all instances

Instances	Best Solutions	RK-EC		RK-EC Heuristic	
		Best	Average	Best	Average
OGR-10	55	55	58.9	55	55.0
OGR-11	72	72	74.6	72	73.5
OGR-12	85	91	93.8	85	91.4
OGR-13	106	111	115.1	106	113.7
OGR-14	127	134	138.6	131	136.6
OGR-15	151	160	166.2	162	165.6
OGR-16	177	193	197.8	180	197.1
OGR-17	199	221	233.6	213	229.8
OGR-18	216	266	274	258	271.0
OGR-19	246	299	319	307	316.3

Even though variations in the results attained are not dramatic, there is nevertheless evidence that the addition of the described heuristic improves the search performance of the algorithm. In this new set of experiments, the optimum was found for all in-stances with $n \leq 13$. Moreover, with the exception of OGR-15 and OGR-19, best rulers found by RK-EC with heuristic are shorter than the ones discovered by RK-EC alone.

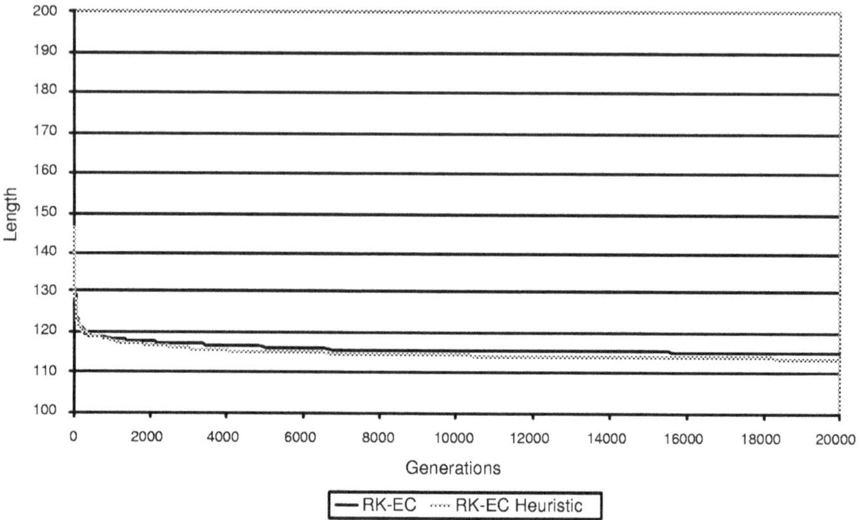

Fig. 5. Evolution of the best solution for OGR-13 in experiments with RK-EC alone and RK-EC with a heuristic. Results are averages of 30 runs

Another result that supports the advantage of the hybrid algorithm is that the average length of the best solutions found in each of the 30 runs is always smaller in experiments that used the heuristic. With the exception of OGR-15, OGR-16 and OGR-19, these differences are statistically significant.

In graphs from figures 5 and 6 we show, respectively for OGR-13 and OGR-18, the evolution of the best solutions with both versions of the algorithms (RK-EC and RK-EC with heuristic). Results are averages of the 30 runs. These graphics confirm our analysis. Even though differences are always small, the solutions found by RK-EC with the heuristic are consistently better during the whole course of the simulation.

Although it is not possible to draw definite conclusions from these results, the small advantage provided by this simple heuristic suggest that maybe a more powerful method might further improve the search performance of the EC algorithm.

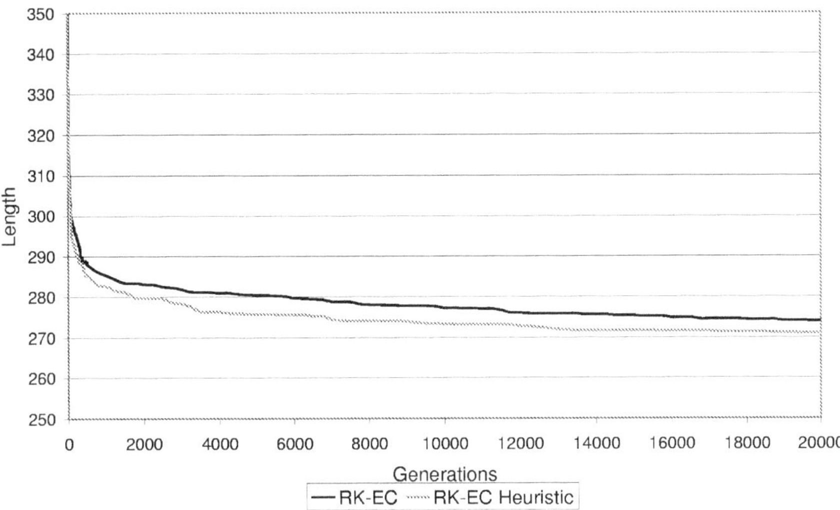

Fig. 6. Evolution of the best solution for OGR-18 in experiments with RK-EC alone and RK-EC with a heuristic. Results are averages of 30 runs

7 Conclusion

In this paper we presented a new EC algorithm used to search for good rulers for different OGR instances. Results achieved show that this evolutionary approach is effective since it was able to quickly discover good solutions. Best rulers found for all instances are clearly better than those ones achieved by the previous EC methods. Furthermore, we consider it as a realistic option to massive parallel approaches that need several months or years and a large computing power to discover high-quality Golomb rulers.

The proposed algorithm relies on RK to represent individuals from the population. One of the main advantages of this kind of representations is that they efficiently deal with permutations without requiring special precautions to build initial populations or specific genetic operators that ensure that feasible individuals are generated. Another important feature of our representation is that it encodes redundant information (there are genes, i.e., segments, that are not used to build the ruler). The proposed interpretation algorithm is an extension of a previous one proposed by Rothlauf to deal with tree network representations.

We also analyzed the effect of a simple heuristic in the performance of the EC algorithm. Even though we proposed a straightforward heuristic we verified that, in most of the OGR instances, there was a small improvement in the results achieved (both in the best solutions found and in the averages of best solutions).

Results presented in this paper can be considered as preliminary. Our approach still evidences some scalability problems. Nevertheless, after confirming that an EC algorithm based on RK representation is a viable method to search for OGRs, we intend to extend our study in order to clarify some situations that were discussed in this paper. More precisely, our future research efforts will concentrate on two topics: (1) we will deepen our investigations related to representation of possible solutions and (2) we will try to develop new heuristics that are capable to provide a more efficient assistance to EC algorithms when searching for good solutions.

References

1. Golomb, S.: How to Number a Graph. In: Graph Theory and Computing. Academic Press (1972) 23–37
2. Bloom, G., Golomb, S.: Applications of numbered undirected graphs. In: Proceedings of the IEEE. Volume 65. (1977) 562–570
3. Dollas, A., Rankin, W., McCracken, D.: New algorithms for golomb ruler derivation and proof of the 19 mark ruler. IEEE Transactions on Information Theory **44** (1998) 379–382
4. Blum, E., Biraud, F., Ribes, J.: On optimal synthetic linear arrays with applications to radioastronomy. IEEE Transactions on Antennas and Propagation **AP-22** (1974) 108–109
5. Hayes, B.: Collective wisdom. American Scientist **86** (1998) 118–122
6. Klove, T.: Bounds and construction for difference triangle sets. IEEE Transactions on Information Theory **IT-35** (1989)
7. Bean, J.: Genetic algorithms and random keys for sequencing and optimization. ORSA Journal on Computing **6** (1994) 154–160
8. Soliday, S., Homaifar, A., G., L.: Genetic algorithm approach to the search for golomb rulers. In: Proceedings of the Sixth International Conference on Genetic Algorithms (ICGA-95), Morgan Kaufmann (1995) 528–535
9. Dewdney, A.: Computer recreations. Scientific American (1985) 16–26
10. Gardner, M.: Mathematical games. Scientific American (1972) 198–112
11. Shearer, J.: Some new optimum golomb rulers. IEEE Transactions on Information Theory **IT-36** (1990) 183–184
12. Norman, B., Smith, A.: Random keys genetic algorithm with adaptive penalty function for optimization of constrained facility layout problems. In: Proceedings of the Fourth International Conference on Evolutionary Computation, IEEE (1997) 407–411
13. Rothlauf, F., Goldberg, D., Heinzl, A.D.: Network random keys - a tree representation scheme for genetic and evolutionary algorithms. Evolutionary Computation **10** (2002) 75–97
14. Magyar, G., Johnsson, G., Nevalainen, O.: An adaptive hybrid genetic algorithm fot the three-matching problem. IEEE Transactions on Evolutionary Computation **4** (2000) 135–146
15. Merz, P., Freisleben, B.: Genetic local search for the tsp: New results. In Back, T., Michalewicz, Z., Yao, X., eds.: Proceedings of the IEEE International Conference on Evolutionary Computation, IEEE Press (1997) 159–164
16. Moscato, P.: Memetic Algorithms: a Short Introduction. In: New Ideas in Optimization. McGraw-Hill (1999) 221–234

A Particle Swarm Data Miner

Tiago Sousa[1], Arlindo Silva[1,2], and Ana Neves[1,2]

[1] Escola Superior de Tecnologia, Instituto Politecnico de Castelo Branco,
Av. do Empresário, 6000 Castelo Branco – Portugal
{tsousa,arlindo, dorian}@est.ipcb.pt
http://www.est.ipcb.pt

[2] Centro de Informatica e Sistemas da Universidade de Coimbra
Polo II – Pinhal de Marrocos, 3030 Coimbra Portugal

Abstract. This paper describes the implementation of Data Mining tasks using Particle Swarm Optimisers. The object of our research has been to apply such algorithms to classification rule discovery. Results, concerning accuracy and speed performance, were empirically compared with another evolutionary algorithm, namely a Genetic Algorithm and with J48 - a Java implementation of C4.5. The data sets used for experimental testing have already been widely used and proven reliable for testing other Data Mining algorithms. The obtained results seem to indicate that Particle Swarm Optimisers are competitive with other evolutionary techniques, and could come to be successfully applied to more demanding problem domains.

1 Introduction

Data Mining (DM) and Knowledge Discovery in Databases (KDD) are the most commonly used names to describe the computational efforts meant to process database-stored information, in order to obtain valuable high level knowledge, which must conform to three main requisites: accuracy, comprehensibility and interest for the user [1].

In a nutshell, DM comprehends the actions of (semi) automatically seeking out, identifying, validating and using for prediction, structural patterns in data [2], that might be grouped into five categories: decision trees, classification rules, association rules, clusters and numeric prediction.

These patterns are ideally searched for in massive data sets, which could have origins as diverse as medicine, astronomy, fraud detection, loan granting or agriculture.

Many approaches, methods and goals have been tried out for DM. Evolutionary approaches such as Genetic Algorithms (GA) and swarm-based approaches like Ant Colonies (AC) [3] have been successfully used. In this paper we propose the use of Particle Swarm Optimisers (PSO) in classification rule discovery.

PSO are a new branch in evolutionary algorithms, which were inspired in group dynamics and its synergy and were originated from computer simulations of the coordinated motion in flocks of birds or schools of fish. As these animals

Fernando Moura Pires, Salvador Abreu (Eds.): EPIA 2003, LNAI 2902, pp. 43–53, 2003.

wander through a three-dimensional space, searching for food or evading predators, these algorithms make use of particles moving in an n-dimensional space to search for solutions for an n-variable function optimisation problem. In PSO individuals are called particles and the population is called a swarm [4].

PSO has proved to be competitive with Genetic Algorithms in several tasks, mainly in optimisation areas. Previous research, using PSO for classification tasks [5], has provided results comparing three PSO variants, namely Discrete PSO (DPSO) [6], Linear Decreasing Weight PSO (LDWPSO) [7] and Constricted PSO (CPSO) [8], laying, therefore, the foundations to our present research.

In our approach, we opted for the CPSO variant, for it proved to be more qualified when dealing with continuous attributes, which was one of our goals. Temporal complexity was another of our concerns, for without optimisation in this area, expansion to more demanding problems is seriously affected or even made impossible. Following the experimental platform, of the previously mentioned research [5], the same data sets were used, in order to assert whether this approach could offer significant improvements. These data sets were collected mainly from biology and medical science domains.

Proving the competitiveness of the PSO Data Miner in these relatively simple domains will lead to successfully applying the same algorithms to problems in the more demanding problem domains mentioned before, like molecular biology and genetics.

In section 2 the structure and algorithms used in our work are described in detail. In section 3 we describe the experimental setup and discuss the obtained results which are presented in the section 5. Conclusion and future work are in Section 4.

2 Design Structure and Algorithms

The overall structure of our work was designed to include three nested algorithms; each one fulfils a specific task and is described in details in the following sections.

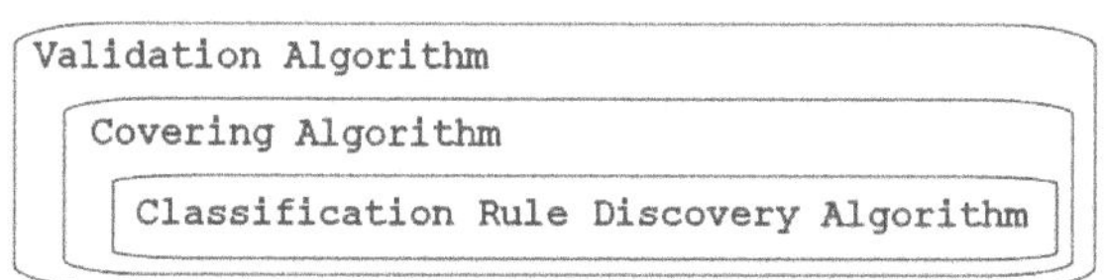

Fig. 1. Three-nested algorithm application structure

The innermost algorithm, which is the classification rule discovery algorithm, has for its task to find and return the rule, which better classifies the predominant class in a given instance, set. It is here that the PSO algorithm is used.

The covering algorithm, receives an instance set (the training set), and invokes the classification rule discovery algorithm to reduce this set by removing instances correctly classified by the rule returned by the classification rule discovery algorithm. This process is repeated until a pre-defined number of instances are left to classify in the training set. A sequential rule set is therefore created.

The aim of the validation algorithm - the out most algorithm - is not only to determine the accuracy of a rule set returned by the covering algorithm but also to gauge the liability of the whole classifying algorithm - classification rule discovery and covering algorithms altogether. This is achieved by iteratively dividing the initial data set into different test and training sets and computing average indicators, such as accuracy, time spent, rule number per set and attribute tests number per rule.

2.1 Pre-processing Routines – Data Extraction and Normalization

In a pre-processing routine, the original data set is extracted from file, parsed and analyzed. Two data structures are created: a normalized image of the data set and a structure containing metadata information.

All attribute values are normalized to the range $[0.0, t]$ with $0.0 < t < 1.0$, being t a user pre-defined value, it stands for the indifference threshold where a higher value will trigger the omission of the corresponding attribute test.

Three types of attributes were contemplated: nominal, integer and real. Instances containing missing attribute values are discarded.

Nominal attributes are normalized assigning to each different attribute value an enumerated index $\#idx$ and applying the following equation:

$$v_{norm} = \frac{idx_v \times t}{\#idx}. \quad (1)$$

idx_v is the index of the attribute value v and $\#idx$ the total number of different attribute values. Both integer and real types are normalized with equation 2.

$$v_{norm} = \frac{(v - v_{min}) \times t}{v_{max} - v_{min}}. \quad (2)$$

v_{min} and v_{max} are the lower and higher attribute values found for this attribute. A state attribute is assigned to each instance. Manipulating this state value, it is very easy and computationally efficient, to divide the data set into training and test sets and to (pseudo-) remove instances. This attribute takes the following values: TEST, TRAIN and REMOVED.

2.2 Rule Representation

Classification rules are no more than conditional clauses, involving two parts: the antecedent and the consequent. The former is a conjunction of logical tests, and the latter gives the class that applies to instances covered by this rule. These rules take the following format:

```
IF attribute_a=value_1
  AND attribute_b=value_2
  ...
  AND attribute_n=value_i
THEN class_x
```

In rule classifier systems there are two distinct approaches to individual or particle representation: the Michigan and the Pittsburgh approaches [9]. In the Michigan approach each individual encodes a single rule, whereas in the Pittsburgh approach each individual encodes a set of rules. In our work, we follow the Michigan approach and rules are encoded as a floating-point array; each attribute is represented by either one or two elements on the array, according to its type. Nominal attributes are assigned with one element on the array and attribute-matching tests are defined as follows:

$$m(v_r, v_i) = \begin{cases} true & if \ \lfloor v_r \times \#idx \rfloor = \lfloor v_i \times \#idx \rfloor \\ false & otherwise. \end{cases} \tag{3}$$

Being t the indifference threshold value, v_r the attribute value stored in the rule for testing and v_i the instance value stored in the normalized image of the data set.

Integer and real attributes are assigned with an extra element in the array in order to implement a value range instead of a single value,

$$m(v_{r1}, v_{r2}, v_i) = \begin{cases} true & if \ v_{r1} \geq t \ or \ (v_{r1} - v_{r2}) \leq v_i \ or \ (v_{r1} + v_{r2}) \geq v_i \\ false & otherwise. \end{cases} \tag{4}$$

v_{r1} can be seen as the center and v_{r1} as a neighbourhood radius, inside which matching will occur.

2.3 Classification Rule Discovery Algorithm – Particle Swarm Optimisation

As previously mentioned, the rule discovery process is achieved through a PSO algorithm. PSO are inspired in the intelligent behavior of beings as part of an experience sharing community as opposed to an isolated individual reactive response to the environment. The Adaptive Culture Model [6], which is PSO's framing theory, states that the process of cultural adaptation is rooted into three principles: evaluate, compare and imitate.

Evaluation is the capacity to qualify environmental stimuli and the *sine qua non* condition to social learning. Evaluation itself is both useless and impossible without the ability to compare; all of our metrics are but a comparison to a well-known unit and a single value becomes pointless without the values of its peers. At last, imitation is the rawest form of experience sharing from the receiver's standpoint; it involves not only observation but also the realization of purpose and timing adequacy.

In PSO algorithms, a particle decides where to move next, considering its own experience, which is the memory of its best past position, and the experience of its most successful neighbour.

There may be different concepts and values for neighbourhood; it can be seen as spatial neighbourhood where it is determined by the Euclidean distance between the positions of two particles, or as a sociometric neighbourhood (e.g.: the index position in the storing array). The latter is the most commonly used for two main motives: if space coordinates were to represent mental abilities or skills, two very similar individuals may never come to meet in their lifetime, as to elements of the same family, which may differ significantly from each other, but still, they will always be neighbours. The other motive is related with the computational effort required to process the Euclidean distance, when faced with large number of particles or dimensions - in each iteration, the distance between every two particles would have to be calculated and for each particle the nearest k neighbours would have to be sorted out.

The number of neighbours (k) usually considered is either $k = 2$ or $k = all$.

Although some actions differ from one variant of PSO to the other, the pseudo-code for PSO is as follows:

```
Initiate_Swarm()
  Loop
    For p=1 to number of particles
      Evaluate(p)
      Update_past_experience(p)
      Update_neighbourhood_best(p,k)
      For d=1 to number of Dimensions
        Move(p,d)
  Until Criterion .
```

Inevitably, with more or less iterations, the swarm converges to an optimum (possibly just a local one). In our implementation, the criterion used to trigger the ending of the loop is the realization all particles in the swarm are within a user-defined distance from the best particle in the swarm. In order to manipulate equivalent threshold distances, considering that distance ranges will differ accordingly to the dimension number, the distance formula used is the normalized Euclidean distance

$$d(p_1, p_2) = \frac{\sqrt{\sum_{i=1}^{n} (p_1^i - p_2^i)^2}}{\sqrt{d}}. \tag{5}$$

p_1 and p_2 are particles and d the dimension number, p_n^i stands for the ith coordinate value of particle p_n. As each dimension coordinate is bounded to the interval $[0.0, 1.0]$ the maximum value for $(p_1^i - p_2^i)$ is 1.0, which when squared remains 1.0, therefore to normalize a distance, all that is needed is to divide it by $\sqrt{d}$.

The output of this algorithm is the best point in the hyperspace the swarm visited - and in this case, converged to. There are several variants of PSO, typically differing in the representation: Discrete or Continuous PSO[6]; in the mechanism used to avoid spatial explosion of the swarm and guaranteeing convergence: Linear Decreasing Weight[7] or Constricted PSO[8]; or in the mechanism used to avoid premature convergence to local optima: Predator Prey[10] or Collision Avoiding Swarms[11]. The variant used in our work was the Constricted PSO (CPSO).

There is a need to maintain and update the particle's previous best position (P_{id}) and the best position in the neighbourhood (P_{gd}). There is also a velocity (V_{id}) associated with each dimension, which is an increment to be made, in each iteration, to the dimension associated (equation 6), thus making the particle change its position in the search space.

$$\begin{cases} v_{id}(t) = \chi(v_{id}(t-1) + \varphi_{1id}(P_{id} - x_{id}(t-1)) + \varphi_{2id}(P_{gd} - x_{id}(t-1))) \\ x_{id}(t) = x_{id}(t) + v_{id}(t) \end{cases} \tag{6}$$

φ_1 and φ_2 are random weights defined by an upper limit, χ is a constriction coefficient [8] set to 0.73. The general effect of equation 6 is that each particle oscillates in the search space between its previous best position and the best position of its best neighbour, hopefully finding new best points during its trajectory.

If the particle's velocity were allowed to change without bounds the swarm would never converge to an optimum, since particles oscillations would grow larger. The changes in velocity are therefore limited by χ - the constriction coefficient - forcing the swarm to converge.

The value for this parameter and for the upper limits on φ_1 and φ_2 can be chosen to guarantee convergence [8]. In our experiments χ was set o 0.73 while φ_1 and φ_2 upper limits were set to 2.05.

2.4 Rule Evaluation – Establishing Points of Reference

Rules must be evaluated during the training process in order to establish points of reference for the training algorithm: best particle positioning. The rule evaluation function must not only consider instances correctly classified but also the ones left to classify and the wrongly classified ones.

The formula used to evaluate a rule and therefore set its quality is expressed in equation 7 [9]:

$$Q(X) = \begin{cases} \frac{TP}{TP+FN} \times \frac{TN}{TN+FP} & if \quad 0.0 \leq x_i \leq 1.0, \forall i \in d \\ -1.0 & otherwise \end{cases} \tag{7}$$

Where:

- TP - True Positives = number of instances covered by the rule that are correctly classified, i.e., its class matches the training target class.
- FP - False Positives = number of instances covered by the rule that are wrongly classified, i.e., its class differs from the training target class.
- TN - True Negatives = number of instances not covered by the rule, whose class differs from the training target class.
- FN - False Negatives = number of instances not covered by the rule, whose class matches the training target class.

This formula penalizes a particle, which as moved out of legal values, assigning it with negative value (-1.0), forcing it to return to the search space.

2.5 Covering Algorithm – Rule Set Construction

The covering algorithm is basically a divide-and-conquer technique. Being given a instance training set, it runs the rule discovery algorithm in order to obtain the highest quality rule for the predominant class in the training set.

Correctly classified instances are then removed from the training set and the rule discovery algorithm is run once more. Iteratively a sequential rule set is built, and the covering algorithm runs until only a pre-defined number of instances are left to classify. This threshold criteria value is user-defined as a percentage and it is typically set to 10%.

A default rule, to capture and classify instances not classified by the previous rules is added to the rule set. Containing no attribute tests and predicting the same class as the one predominant in the remaining instances, this rule takes the form:

```
IF true
THEN class_x.
```

2.6 Validation Algorithm – Rule Set and Overall Evaluation

The purpose of the validation algorithm is to statistically evaluate the accuracy of the rule set obtained by the covering algorithm. This is done using a method known as tenfold cross validation [2].

The tenfold cross validation consists in dividing the data set into ten equal partitions and iteratively using one of this sets as a test set and the remaining nine as training sets. In the end ten different rule sets are obtained and average indicators, such as accuracy, time spent, rule number per set and attribute tests number per rule are computed.

Several other numbers for partitioning have been tried out, but theoretical research [2] has shown that ten offers the best estimate of errors.

Rule set accuracy is evaluated and presented as the percentage of instances in the test set correctly classified. An instance is considered correctly classified, when the first rule in the rule set, whose antecedent matches this instance and the consequent (predicted class) matches this instance's class.

2.7 Post-processing Routines – Rule Pruning and Rule Set Cleaning

Recall that high level knowledge extracted from databases must conform to three main requisites: accuracy, comprehensibility and interested for the user [1].

In classification rule discovery problems, the number of attribute tests per rule and the number of rules per set is a major contributor for the comprehensibility of the obtained results - fewer attribute tests and rules eases comprehensibility.

After a rule is returned from the classification rule discovery algorithm it goes through a pruning process in order to remove unnecessary attribute tests. This is done by iteratively removing each attribute test whenever the newly obtained rule has the same or higher quality value than the original rule.

Just after the covering algorithm returns a rule set, another post-processing routine is used: rule set cleaning, where rules that will never be applied are removed from the rule set.

As rules in the rule set are applied sequentially, in this routine, rules are removed from the rule set if:

- There is a previous rule in the rule set that has a subset of the rule's attribute tests.
- If it predicts the same class as the default rule and is located just before it.

So in the example below, rules number 2 and 3 will be removed and the rule set will be reduced to the first and last rules:

```
Rule #1
     If attribute_a = x_a
     Then class=c_1
Rule #2
     If attribute_a = x_a and attribute_b=x_b
     Then class=c_2
Rule #3
     If attribute_c = x_c
     Then class=c_3
Rule #4 - Default Rule
     If TRUE
     Then class=c_3.
```

3 Experimental Results

Experimental results are presented and discussed in this section. To maintain a fair experimental platform with [5] the same data sources were used: two regarding Breast-Cancer diagnosis, and the other, animal classification. These are standard benchmark problems which can easily be used to compare results with a vast number of other implemented algorithms thus allowing us to compare the effectiveness of our PSO based algorithms, not only with the other algorithms implemented by us, but also with previous results obtained from the literature.

To help benchmarking the evolutionary algorithms implemented, results were also obtained with a well-known standard tree induction algorithm, J48, a Java implementation of C4.5.

3.1 Experimental Setup

In [5] attribute testing, indifference was implemented with an extra bit (particles were coded in binary strings), as a result indifference probability occurrence will vary accordingly to the attribute assigned bit number and its range of possible values, in the interval $]1/2, 3/4]$.

In our work a user defined threshold level maintains attribute-testing indifference, therefore different values for this threshold were tested in order to evaluate its influence.

The data sources used were obtained from the Department of Computer Science, University of Waikato, Hamilton, New Zealand[13], and Information and Computer Science, University of California [14].

In section 5 we present the experimental results obtained. Accuracy values are in percentage of success, and are obtained by averaging ten-fold accuracy results.

The swarms were set to 25 particles, convergence radius to 0.1 and minimum uncovered instances to 10%.

3 data sets were used: Zoo, Wisconsin-Breast-Cancer and Breast-Cancer. Zoo is a data set that classifies animals according to their characteristics. Wisconsin-Breast-Cancer and Breast-Cancer are real data sets that classify if the tumour was malignant/benign and if recurrence of events did happen.

3.2 Discussion

Results obtained clearly state the competitiveness of CPSO with industrial tree induction algorithms like J48, a Java implementation of C4.5. Trees obtained with J48 are easily converted to rules - each path from the root to a leaf stands for a rule.

There is a clear relation between indifference threshold level value and accuracy results: best results were obtained with lower values for indifference threshold level.

Rule pruning and rule set cleaning routines indicate as expected to be strong contributors comprehensibility. Both CPSO versions did surpass J48 in the Wisconsin-Breast-Cancer relation.

Regarding accuracy, all tested algorithms seem to be equivalent. Nevertheless, temporal complexity of both CPSO versions are still much more demanding than J48, possibly due to the nature of the algorithm and processing involved.

4 Conclusions and Future Work

We proposed to improve one of the PSO variants investigated in [5] and evaluate the possible influence of the indifference threshold values. We implemented and compared this variant with the corresponding one in [5] and J48, in some benchmark data.

From the results, we can conclude that PSO can obtain competitive results against J48 in the data sets used, although there is some increase in the computational effort needed. We can also conclude, that lower values for indifference threshold offer the best accuracy results. Both post-processing routines: rule pruning and rule set cleaning, contribute greatly to comprehensibility.

Directions for future work include an empirical analysis of the influence of indifference threshold with exploration and exploitation. Applying this tool to more demanding data sources, containing continuous attributes. We hope that a more focused and better-tuned PSO based algorithm will surpass the results obtained with this approach, making PSO a real competitive technique in DM.

References

1. Fayyad, U.M., Piatetsky-Shapiro, G. and Smyth, P.: From Data Mining to Knowledge Discovery: an Overview. Advances in Knowledge Discovery and Data Mining, 1–34. AAAI/MIT, Cambridge (1996).
2. Witten, Ian H. and Frank, E.: Data Mining – Practical Machine Learning Tools and Techniques with Java Implementations. Morgan Kauffmann (1999).
3. Parpinelli, R., Lopes, H. and Freitas, A.: An Ant Colony Algorithm for Classification Rule Discovery. Idea Group (2002).
4. Kennedy, J. and Eberhart, R. C.: Particle Swarm Optimisation. Proc. IEEE, International Conference on Neural Networks. Piscataway (1995).
5. Sousa, T., Silva, A. and Neves, A.: Particle Swarm Optimisation as a New Tool for Data Mining. International Parallel and Distributed Processing Symposium (IPDPS). Nice, France, (2003).
6. J. Kennedy, Eberhart, R. C.: Swarm Intelligence Morgan Kauffman, (2001).
7. Shi, Y. and Eberhart, R. C.: Empirical Study of Particle Swarm Optimisation. Proceedings of the 1999 Congress of Evolutionary Computation. Piscatay (1999).
8. Clerc, M. and Kennedy, J.: The Particle Swarm-Explosion, Stability and Convergence in a Multidimensional Complex Space. IEEE Transactions on Evolutionary Computation, Vol. 6 No.1. (2002).
9. Lopes, H.S., Coutinho, M. S. and W. C.: An Evolutionary Approach to Simulate Cognitive Feedback Learning in Medical Domain. Genetic Algorithms and Fuzzy Logic Systems: Soft Computing Perspectives. ISBN 981-02-2423-0, World Scientific Singapore, (1997).
10. Silva, A., Neves, A. and Costa E.: Chasing the Swarm: A Predator Prey Approach to Function Optimisation. Proc. of MENDEL2002 – 8th Interna-tional Conference on Soft Computing. Brno, Czech Republic, (2002).
11. Blackwell, T. and Bentley, P. J.: Don't Push Me! Collision-Avoiding Swarms. Proc. of the Congress on Evolutionary Computation, (2002).
12. Freitas, A.: A survey of evolutionary algorithms for data mining and knowledge discovery. Ghosh, A.; Tsutsui, S. (Eds.) Advances in evolutionary computation. Springer-Verlag, (2001).
13. ftp://ftp.cs.waikato.ac.nz/pub/ml/datasets-UCI.jar
14. http://www.ics.uci.edu/ cmerz/mldb.tar.Z

5 Appendix: Results

Table 1. Relation Zoo

	J48	CPSO[5]	CPSO					
Indifference	—	0.5 - 0.7	0.1	0.5	0.7	0.1	0.5	0.7
Pruning	—	y	n	n	n	y	y	y
Rule Set Cleaning	—	y	n	n	n	y	y	y
Accuracy	92.07	76.67	89.00	86.33	80.33	89.04	77.00	46.67
Time Spent	0.09	11.75	11.00	16.00	48.00	17.36	13.01	3.35
Number of Rules	13	7	6	10	181	6	6	5
Tests per Rule	5	2	6	31	1224	5	4	4

Table 2. Relation Breast-Cancer

	J48	CPSO[5]	CPSO					
Indifference	—	0.5 - 0.7	0.1	0.5	0.7	0.1	0.5	0.7
Pruning	—	y	n	n	n	y	y	y
Rule Set Cleaning	—	y	n	n	n	y	y	y
Accuracy	72.92	76.42	75.80	74.56	74.44	76.66	75.18	73.33
Time Spent	0.03	7.04	26.45	11.54	25.73	28.13	13.19	17.81
Number of Rules	4	5	6	6	7	6	6	6
Tests per Rule	2	2	5	5	8	5	5	5

Table 3. Relation Winsconsin-Breast-Cancer

	J48	CPSO[5]	CPSO					
Indifference	—	0.5 - 0.7	0.1	0.5	0.7	0.1	0.5	0.7
Pruning	—	y	n	n	n	y	y	y
Rule Set Cleaning	—	y	n	n	n	y	y	y
Accuracy	92.82	93.92	92.89	90.63	92.00	92.84	91.81	76.61
Time Spent	0.02	17.34	117.42	87.84	114.27	85.01	67.16	18.05
Number of Rules	55	7	7	8	40	7	7	5
Tests per Rule	2	1	4	7	122	4	4	4

Yerkes-Dodson Law in Agents' Training

Šarūnas Raudys and Viktoras Justickis

Knowledge Society Management Institute, Law University of Lithuania
Ateities 20, Vilnius LT-2057, Lithuania
raudys@ktl.mii.lt, justickv@takas.lt

Abstract. Well known Yerkes-Dodson Law (YDL) claims that medium intensity stimulation encourages fastest learning. Mostly experimenters explained YDL by sequential action of two different processes. We show that YDL can be elucidated even with such simple model as nonlinear single layer perceptron and gradient descent training where differences between desired outputs values are associated with stimulation strength. Non-linear nature of curves "a number of iterations is a function of stimulation" is caused by smoothly bounded nonlinearities of the perceptron's activation function and a difference in desired outputs.

Keywords: Adaptation, Intelligent Agents, Stimulation, Y-D Law.

1 Introduction

Dependency curves between learning speed and stimulation strength remind inverted letter "U" and are described by Yerkes-Dodson Law: medium intensity stimulation encourages the fastest learning [1]. A great deal of experimental studies have confirmed YDL. Levitt [2] and Teigen [3] admit that it is "a basic relationship in nature", "a law for all seasons".

In order to elucidate "mechanics" of YDL, carefully planned large scale experiments are necessary. Up to now there was no simple convincing clarification of an origin of YDL. Most often experimenters describe YDL by sequential effect of two different processes. We consider Yerkes-Dodson law in very simple artificial learning system and explain it by effect of a single process.

Two different approaches, symbolicism [4] and connectionism [5] have been used to demonstrate YDL. French *et al.*, [5] showed that while training multilayer perceptron one can obtain "U" shaped performance curves. Shapes of these curves depend on difficulty of the task. Raudys [6-8] considered learning speed of much simpler model - single layer perceptron (SLP) trained by gradient descent minimization algorithm. It was discovered that magnitudes of starting weights and desired outputs values (targets) are "hidden" factors that determine perceptron's training speed. In present paper, we demonstrate that this model can produce Yerkes-Dodson Law if differences between desired outputs of opposite pattern classes are considered as stimulations. We show that YDL is caused by automatic change in actual cost function affected by growth of the weight vector components'. Important conclusion that follows from our research is a fact that learning speed depends dramatically on stimulation strength determined by the targets and magnitudes of initial and current weights.

Fernando Moura Pires, Salvador Abreu (Eds.): EPIA 2003, LNAI 2902, pp. 54–58, 2003.

2 The Single Layer Perceptron and Training Procedure

Nonlinear SLP consists of a number (say p) of inputs (features), $x_1, x_1, ...x_p$, one output, o, and performs operation $o = f(arg)$, where $arg = w_0 + x_1 w_1 + ... + x_p w_p$ is a weighted sum of inputs; $w_0, w_1, ..., w_p$ are weights (connection strengths), to be learned during training process [7, 9], $f(arg)$ is activation function which saturates at its left and right ends, e.g. $f(arg) = 1/(1+\exp(-arg))$, a sigmoid function. The neuron gives a significant output signal only in the case when sum arg is large and positive. We consider the SLP as a classifier. *Here the saturation of activation function is a basic ingredient in analysis of YDL.*

In order to use SLP practically, one needs to know coefficients $w_0, w_1, ..., w_p$. To learn to classify the input vectors correctly one needs to adapt weight vector $\mathbf{w} = (w_0, w_1, w_2, ..., w_p)$ to training data. In two category classification problem, training data consists of $N = N_1 + N_2$ learning vectors $\mathbf{x}_j^{(i)}$ and N indexes that denote desired outputs (targets) $t_j^{(i)} (i = 1, 2; j = 1, 2, \ldots, N_i; N = N_1 + N_2)$. Mathematically, finding of the weights (training) is formulated as optimization problem where a coast function is minimized iteratively. We are using standard sum of square errors cost function defined by differences between actual and desired outputs of the perceptron. For sigmoid activation function we can assume $t_j^{(1)} = 0, t_j^{(2)} = 1 - t_j^{(1)} = 1$. It corresponds to strong stimulation. If $t_j^{(1)} = 0.499, t_j^{(2)} = 0.501$, we have quite weak stimulation. We measure a strength of stimulation signal by $s = 1/2(t_j^{(2)} - t_j^{(1)})$. To find the weights, we utilize the *gradient descent training* iterative procedure [9]: $\mathbf{w}_{(t+1)} = \mathbf{w}_{(t)} - \eta \times (t_j^{(i)} - f(arg)) \times (\partial f(arg)/\partial arg) \times (\partial arg/\partial w)$. Here η is called learning step parameter; $t_j^{(i)} - f(arg)$ is an error signal – a bias between desired and actual outputs of the perceptron; $arg = \mathbf{w}'\mathbf{x}_j^{(i)} + w_0; \partial f(arg)/\partial arg$ is a derivative of activation function and $(p+1)$–dimensional vector $(\partial f(arg)/\partial arg) \times (\partial arg/\partial w)$ is called a gradient. Correction term and a learning speed of the perceptron depend on the gradient, $(\partial f(arg)/\partial arg) \times (\partial arg/\partial w)$, and derivative, $\partial f(arg)/\partial arg$.

3 Parameters of the Model That Affect Training Speed

Evident, relations of strength of stimulus to rapidity of habit-formation depend on the task to be learned. In adaptive agent training, a configuration of distributions of learning vectors are also affecting the gradient and training speed. Training speed we measure by a number of training epochs required to diminish generalization error until *a priori* defined threshold value, P_{goal}. Usually P_{goal} is selected close to "ideal" classification error, P_{Bayes}(Bayes error it terms of statistical decision theory). If $P_{goal} >> P_B$, we may need only very few training epochs to achieve the goal. For smaller P_{goal} one needs more epochs to achieve the goal. Thus, P_{goal} together with P_{Bayes} are two important parameters that characterize **a difficulty of the pattern recognition task**.

Parameters that affect evolution from start until a minimum of the cost are: 1) initial (starting) weight vector, 2) learning step, 3) target values, 4) regularization term added to cost function (e.g. the weight decay term, $+\lambda\mathbf{w}'\mathbf{w}$, where positive scalar λ is called a regularization constant), 5) a noise injected to inputs vectors or the weights in each training iteration, 6) desired outputs.

The target values affect a difference between the cost and classification error criterion. If targets, $t_j^{(1)}$ and $t_j^{(2)}$, are close to boundary values of $f(arg)$, 0 and 1, the weights may become large. Then the cost can come close to empirical classification error. If the targets are close to 0.5 (s is small), the sum of squares cost differs from the classification error criterion. In our research we link differences between the target values, $t_j^{(1)} - t_j^{(2)}$, with stimulation strength, s.

If **components of initial weight vector** are small, we have large derivatives of the activation function, $\partial f(arg)/\partial arg$, and fast training. At the beginning, the cost function, differs from classification error. If components of initial weight vector are large, the weighted sums, *arg*, are sizeable too. Consequently, values of the derivatives are small. Small derivatives make training slow. Large derivatives have the opposite effect. We have to note that very small and very large derivatives aggravate a possibility to climb out of a false local minimum. Thus, factors associated with initial weights and their magnitudes cannot be ignored. In [8] the weights' magnitudes were associated with agents' "age".

The learning step parameter η influences magnitudes of the weights change. Often twofold increase in η decreases the number of training epochs two times. Therefore, in our analysis η plays a role of ***dimension of a time***. At the same time η value has additional impact on training process. Small η value reduces training speed. Small η value keeps the weights to remain undersized for a long time. It means that for a longer time both the sum of squares cost and the classification error are acting as two different criteria. In addition, small η value increases a danger of being trapped into a false local minimum. Too large η value can aid the training algorithm to diverge. In such case, the algorithm never achieves the goal, the threshold value P_{goal}. Thus, both too small and too large η values also can be associated with **difficulty of the task**. In principle, learning step value can be associated with stimulation.

4 Influence of Stimulation on Training Speed

To tie gradient descent training with YDL we performed hundreds of simulation experiments with a set of s values ranging in interval [0.001 0.5], diverse Gaussian data sets and difficulties of the task (P_{goal} values). In Fig. 1*a* we present a typical result, a number of training epochs required to achieve the goal, P_{goal} = 0.03 (easy task), 0.01 (medium task) or 0.004 (difficult task). The graphs are obtained for 2D data Gaussian data with correlated components (ρ=0.7), 250+250 training vectors. Fig.1*b* differs from Fig. 1*a* only in initial weight vector: all components of $\mathbf{w}_{start}$ are 1.5 times smaller. According to [8] the agent with smaller initial weighs should be considered as a younger one. Training process becomes *easier*: we need a smaller number of iterations to achieve the goal. In both experiments for difficult cases ($P_{goal} = 0.004$) and relatively low stimulation we have curves similar to Yerkes and Dodson ones presented in [1, 3]. The minima in letter "U" relationship become less evident when the task to be learned is easier. For the easier task with smaller weight vector $\mathbf{w}_{start} = (0.08\ 1\ 2)$ and $P_{goal} > 0.01$ we have only minor minimum. In short segments of variation of parameter s, we can have increasing, decreasing or "non-sensitive" fragments. In certain segments of variation of s, however, we can obtain even inverted "U" type relationship (the very left sections of curves 2 and 3 in Fig. 1a). We pay attention to *opposing signs* for parameter s in left and right parts of Fig. 1.

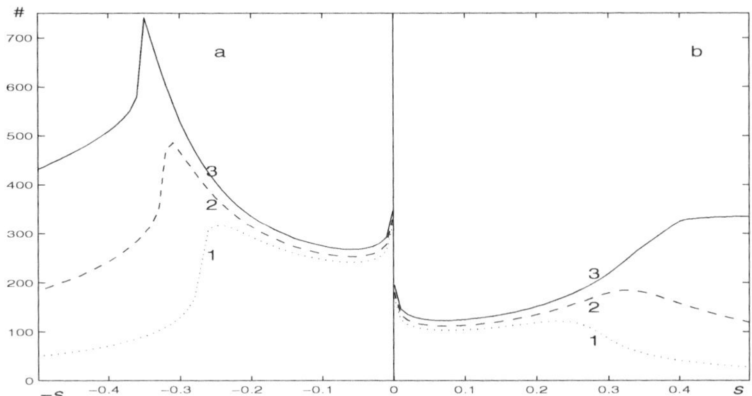

Fig. 1. Number of epochs, #, until goal P_{goal} was achieved as a function of stimulation, s: 1 – easy task ($P_{goal} = 0.03$), 2 – medium task ($P_{goal} = 0.01$), 3 – difficult task ($P_{goal} = 0.004$); a) $\mathbf{w}_{start} = (0.12\ 1.5\ 3)$; b) $\mathbf{w}_{start} = (0.08\ 1\ 2)$. P_{Bayes}=0.0023.

Non-linear nature of curves "# of iterations = *function* (s)" is caused by smoothly bounded nonlinearities of activation function and a difference in target values. Small stimulation values result in undersized weights and in small values of $arg = w_0 + x_1 w_1 + ... + x_p w_p$. In this case, we are working in linear part of function $o = f(arg)$. Then an increase in stimulation strength enlarges the gradient and speeds up training. When stimulation is high, the weights and values of arg may become large. In large weights' case, we are working in the saturated parts of activation function, $o = f(arg)$, that cause small gradient and slow training. Only for medium saturation we have fast training.

Following schema summs up effects of stimulation strength on learning speed.

Weak stimulation $\longrightarrow$ small weights $\longrightarrow$ small weighted sum, arg, $\longrightarrow$: a) cost function and classification error criteria differ essentially (speed decreases), b) high derivative of activation function ($f'(arg)$ is bounded by 1/4) (speed increases), c) small absolute values of biases $t_j^{(i)} - f(arg)$ (speed decreases).

Strong stimulation $\longrightarrow$ large weights $\longrightarrow$ large weighted sum, arg, $\longrightarrow$: a) cost function and classification error criteria are close (speed increases), b) extremely small derivative of activation function and the gradient (speed decreases), c) large values of biases $t_j^{(i)} - f(arg)$ (speed increases).

We see that in nonlinear SLP training, YDL is originated by single fact: the weight growth causes automatic saturation of the cost.

Fig. 1 indicates that for strict requirements to learning quality (P_{goal} and P_{Bayes} are close) the fastest training is obtained in interval $s \subset (0.08\ 0.2)$. It is true for the simulation conditions reported above. We already noticed notable differences between minima of the graphs presented in Fig 1*a* and Fig. 1*b*. Even individual peculiarities of randomly generated training sets' are influencing position of the minimum considered. To take into account an influence of learning step, η, on learning speed we performed experiments with *ten times smaller* parameter η, i.e. $\eta = 0.05$ instead of $\eta = 0.5$ used in previous experiments. We obtained exactly the same graphs as ones depictured in Fig 1*a* with a difference in a scale for #, the number of epochs (*ten times higher!*). It means, in present simulation experiments, parameter η played role of the time.

5 Conclusion

Yerkes-Dodson Law can be explained even with such a simple model as nonlinear single layer perceptron and gradient descent training where target values are associated with stimulation. It means that in order to achieve fast training of intelligent agents and robots, special attention to starting weights and stimulation strength should be paid. Optimal stimulation necessary to achieve fastest minimization of classification error depends on a number of factors that characterize the data, cost function and training algorithm. Fitting the parameters of the simulation model (P_{goal}, P_{Bayes}, the target values, learning step, initial weights, etc.) to applied scientist's experimental graphs could give additional explanation of phenomena under investigation, predict outcome of experiments and cut their price. It is a problem to be solved in future research.

References

1. Yerkes, R.M. and Dodson, J.D. (1908). The relation of strength of stimulus to rapidity of habit-formation. *J. Comparative Neurology and Psychology*, 18, 459–482.
2. Levitt, E. (1967). *The Psychology of Anxiety*. New York: Bobbs-Merrill.
3. Teigen, K.H. (1994) Yerkes-Dodson – a law for all seasons. *Theory and Psychology*, 4 (4): 525-547.
4. Belavkin, R. (2001) The role of emotion in problem solving. *AISB'01 Symposium on Emotion, Cognition and Affective Computing*, Heslington, York, UK, pp. 49–57.
5. French, V.A., Anderson, E., Putman, G., Alvager, T. (1999). The Yerkes-Dodson law simulated with an artificial neural network, *Complex Systems*, 5(2): 136–147.
6. Raudys, S. (1998). Evolution and generalization of a single neurone. I. SLP as seven statistical classifiers. *Neural Networks*, 11(2): 283–296.
7. Raudys, S. (2001) *Statistical and Neural Classifiers: An integrated approach to design*. Springer-Verlag. NY.
8. Raudys, S. (2002). An adaptation model for simulation of aging process. *Int. J. of Modern Physiscs, C.* 13(8): 1075–1086.
9. Haykin, S. (1999) *Neural Networks: A comprehensive foundation*. 2nd edition. Prentice-Hall, Englewood Cliffs, NJ.

SAPPO: A Simple, Adaptable, Predator Prey Optimiser

Arlindo Silva[1,3], Ana Neves[1,3], and Ernesto Costa[2,3]

[1] Escola Superior de Tecnologia, Instituto Politécnico de Castelo Branco, Av. do Empresário, 6000 Castelo Branco - Portugal
{arlindo, dorian}@est.ipcb.pt

[2] Departamento de Engenharia Informática, Universidade de Coimbra, Pólo II – Pinhal de Marrocos, 3030 Coimbra – Portugal
ernesto@dei.uc.pt

[3] Centro de Informática e Sistemas da Universidade de Coimbra, Pólo II – Pinhal de Marrocos, 3030 Coimbra – Portugal

Abstract. The balance of exploration and exploitation in particle swarm optimisation is closely related to the choice of the algorithm's parameters. Achieving the right balance is essential for the success of a given optimisation task. This choice is a difficult task, since for different functions being optimised the ideal parameter sets can also bee very different. In this paper we try to deal with this issue by introducing two new mechanisms in the basic particle swarm optimiser: a predator-prey strategy to help maintain diversity in the swarm and a symbiosis based adaptive scheme to allow the co-evolution of the algorithm parameters and the parameters of the function being optimised.

1 Introduction

The basic particle swarm algorithm was inspired on a metaphor of social interaction between individuals [1]. The result was a population based optimisation algorithm, where individuals, called particles, are represented as vectors of real numbers in a multidimensional space. A second vector is used to represent the particle's velocity. The algorithm searches for optima in the search space by changing the velocity of each particle and, as a result, its trajectory through the search space. The changes in velocity are the result of the attraction of each particle for its previous best position in the multidimensional space, as well as for the best position previously found by all its neighbours. While generally considered a form of evolutionary computation, there is no form of mutation, recombination or even explicit selection in the particle swarm algorithm. Further information on the particle swarm optimiser (PSO), its variants and the underlying cultural model can be found in [2].

As already has been mentioned by various authors [3][4], the original PSO, while successful in the optimisation of several difficult benchmark problems, presented problems in controlling the balance between exploration and exploitation,

Fernando Moura Pires, Salvador Abreu (Eds.): EPIA 2003, LNAI 2902, pp. 59–73, 2003.

namely when fine tuning around the optimum is attempted. There two main approaches in the literature to try to control this balance and thus the convergence process: the linear decreasing weight approach [4] and the constriction factor approach [5]. Both approaches rely on the careful choice and manipulation of the algorithm parameters in order to promote convergence. While successful, the different results obtained by each variant for the same problems clearly illustrate that the performance of the PSO can be heavily influenced by parameter choice.

While it is easy to establish the importance of parameter choice in the performance of this algorithm in a particular problem, the actual choice of the parameters is not as easy since it depends on information about the structure of the search space that usually is not available, at least in real world optimisation problems.

In this work we introduce two mechanisms as a first approach to the automation of the parameter definition and control of the exploration/exploitation balance. The first mechanism is based on an analogy with predator-prey interaction in nature and aims to maintain diversity in the particle swarm even in later stages of convergence. The second mechanism consists on a symbiotic scheme, where symbiotic particles encoding the algorithms parameters are attached to the original particles. Through an adequate choice of fitness function for the symbiotic particles, the algorithm parameters are co-evolved with the function parameters. This way, the parameters do not have to be predefined at the beginning of the algorithm execution. The final algorithm is named after these mechanisms: SAPPO - a Simple, Adaptive, Predator Prey Optimiser.

Experimental results are presented to illustrate the competitiveness of SAPPO with the PSO variant with best performance.

In Section 2 we describe in more detail the basic particle swarm optimiser. Section 3 introduces the new mechanisms implemented in SAPPO. Section 4 is dedicated to the presentation and discussion of the experimental results obtained. In Section 5 we draw some final conclusions to this work.

2 The Particle Swarm Optimiser

Particle swarms optimise a given n-dimensional real function by moving through the search space accordingly to the following equations:

$$\begin{aligned} V_i(t) &= \chi(wV_i(t-1) + \varphi_{1i}(P_i - X_i(t-1)) + \varphi_{2i}(P_g - X_i(t-1))) \\ X_i(t) &= X_i(t-1) + V_i(t) \end{aligned} \tag{1}$$

The position of the particle in the search space is represented by the vector X. The quality or fitness of the particle is measured by using this position as a parameter for the function being optimised. The velocity of the particle, i.e., its change in position, is represented by a vector V. The particle changes position by adding its velocity to the previous iteration position, thus obtaining the particle's position in the present iteration.

V depends on two terms: each particle i is attracted by its best previous position P_i and also its neighbours' best previous position P_p. Different neighbourhood definitions have been tried [6]. The weighted sum of these terms with a contribution from the previous velocity of the particle will result in the new velocity value for the particle. These terms model the indecision of an individual between is own convictions and the ones shared by the society it belongs to.

The weights in the velocity computation are usually called the PSO parameters. In the above formula χ is a constriction coefficient described in [5], φ_1 and φ_2 are random numbers distributed between 0 and an upper limit and different for each dimension in each particle and w is a linear decreasing weight.

From 1 we can derive the two most usual ways in which the balance between exploration and exploitation and, as a result convergence, is controlled. [4] uses $\chi = 1$ and weight w decreasing linearly from w_{max} to w_{min} during the execution of the algorithm. This approach promotes convergence by diminishing the influence of previous velocity over time. [5] theoretically guarantees convergence by choosing appropriated values for χ (called the constriction factor) and $\varphi = \varphi_1 + \varphi_2$. w is fixed and equal to 1 in this approach. We compare our results with the ones obtained with a variant of the second approach, presented in [5], since it seems to obtain the best results over a wide set of test functions.

3 A Simple, Adaptive, Predator Prey Optimiser

The initial inspiration for the Particle Swarm Optimiser, as described in [1], was the coordinated movement of groups of animals in nature, e.g. schools of fish or flocks of birds. The new mechanisms introduced in SAPPO also get their inspiration from nature. The predator prey interaction is based on the disturbance caused by predators to the groups of animals being hunted. The adaptation scheme utilized mimes the symbiotic associations between species so frequently found in nature. Both mechanisms are explained in detail in the next paragraphs.

3.1 The Predator Prey Interaction

In the PSO versions presented above both the constriction factor and the linear weigh promote the convergence of the swarm to a local optimum by damping the particles' velocity by a deliberate choice of the algorithm's parameters. An undesirable side effect of these strategies is that when the local optimum is not also the global optimum being sought particles cannot gain velocity to jump to another optimum in the search space. This phenomenon is similar to premature convergence in other evolutionary algorithms.

Our motivation for introducing the predator-prey mechanism was mainly to introduce a mechanism for creating diversity in the swarm at any moment during the run of the algorithm, by adding velocity to some particles, not depending on the level of convergence already achieved. This would allow the "escape" of particles even when convergence of the swarm around a local sub-optimum had already occurred.

There are other mechanisms used to the same effect in the literature (see [7]), but two main reasons led us to prefer the predator prey scheme. The first reason is its computational simplicity when compared to other approaches. As it will be seen when the mechanism is explained it only introduces a new particle and little computational effort in the basic algorithm. The adjective simple in SAPPO comes from this fact. A second, and less technical, motive was to maintain the swarm intelligence philosophy behind the algorithm. It seemed more appropriate to introduce a mechanism that could also be implemented as a distributed behaviour in the swarm.

The predator/prey model is based on the disturbance caused by a predator to the group of animals being hunted. Animals are driven from their favourite locations, e.g. pastures and water sources, by fear of nearby predators. Eventually, this process will result in the finding of even better locations where the arriving animals will also be chased by nearby predators.

It is this predator/prey dynamic that we try to reproduce in SAPPO. Here, a new particle is introduced into the swarm to mime the predators' behaviour. This particle, called the predator particle, is attracted by the best (fittest) particle in the swarm, according to the following equations:

$$\begin{aligned} V_p(t) &= \varphi_3(X_g(t-1) - X_p(t-1)) \\ X_p(t) &= X_p(t-1) + V_p(t) \end{aligned} \tag{2}$$

In equations 2 φ_3 is another random number distributed between 0 and an upper limit, usually 1, and X_g is the present position of the best particle in the swarm.

The predator particle can influence any particle in the swarm by changing its velocity in one or more dimensions. This influence is controlled by a "fear" probability f, which is the probability of a particle changing its velocity in one of the available dimensions due to the presence of the predator. For some particle i, if there is no change in the velocity in a dimension j, the update rules in that dimension still are:

$$\begin{aligned} v_{ij}(t) &= wv_{ij}(t-1) + \varphi_{1ij}(p_{ij} - x_{ij}(t-1)) + \varphi_{2ij}(p_{gj} - x_{ij}(t-1)) \\ x_{ij}(t) &= x_{ij}(t-1) + v_{ij}(t) \end{aligned} \tag{3}$$

The only differences from the other approaches are that w is fixed and χ is not explicitly used. But if the predator "scares" the prey (particle), i.e., if there is a change in velocity in dimension j, the rule becomes:

$$\begin{aligned} v_{ij}(t) &= wv_{ij}(t-1) + \varphi_{1ij}(p_{ij} - x_{ij}(t-1)) + \\ &\quad + \varphi_{2ij}(p_{gj} - x_{ij}(t-1)) + D(d) \\ x_{ij}(t) &= x_{ij}(t-1) + v_{ij}(t) \end{aligned} \tag{4}$$

This process is repeated for all dimensions, i.e. there can be simultaneous changes in velocity in several dimensions.

The fourth term in the first equation in 4 quantifies the repulsive influence of the predator. This term is a function of the difference between the positions of the predator and the particle. d is the Euclidean distance between predator and prey. $D(x)$ is an exponential decreasing distance function:

$$D(x) = ae^{-\frac{x}{b}} \tag{5}$$

$D(x)$ makes the influence of the predator grow exponentially with proximity. The objective of its use is to introduce more perturbation in the swarm when the particles are nearer the predator, which usually happens when convergence to a local optimum occurs. The a and b parameters define the form of the D function: a represents the maximum amplitude of the predator effect over a prey and b allows to control the distance at which the effect is still significant.

During the initial stages of the algorithm, its behaviour is similar to a traditional PSO, since the particles are scattered and the predator's influence is negligible. As convergence occurs and particles start to move to a local optimum, their distance to the best particle diminishes and the predator effect exponentially increases, accelerating some particles in new directions. When the current local optimum is not the same as the global optimum being searched, this will hopefully allow one particle to jump to another near local optima, becoming the new best particle and leading the swarm to a new exploration phase. Several repetitions of this process could lead the swarm through a chain of local optima until the global optimum is found.

3.2 The Adaptation Scheme

The analysis of previous work with the Particle Swarm Optimiser (e.g. [4][5]) has made clear that good parameter choice for the PSO, not only is important for the algorithm performance over a set of optimisation problems, but also that the performance of the algorithm for a specific problem varies significantly for different sets of parameters.

Choosing parameters to generally guarantee convergence to a local optimum can be done using the constriction factor method. But if what we are looking for is not simply convergence to a local optimum, but converge to the global optimum or at least to a "good" local optimum, finding a set of good parameters basically remains a trial and error process.

As in any other optimisation algorithm the ideal solution would be to have a built-in procedure to adapt the algorithm itself to the problem that it is trying to solve. Other evolutionary algorithms, e.g. evolutionary strategies, tried to this by encoding some of algorithm's parameters (e.g. mutation probability, variance, etc...) together with the individuals, thus trying to co-evolve solutions and algorithm's parameters.

In spite of the only relative success of past instances of this idea, we believe that PSO based algorithms in general, and specially predator-prey based ones, can greatly gain by the inclusion of co-evolution based adaptive schemes. For instance, the a parameter in the $D(x)$ function has its best influence on the algorithm when it is near the average distance between sub-optima in the search space. The algorithm could substantially gain if this parameter could be learned during execution. The same could be said for other parameters, with different roles in the algorithm.

Another important reason is the simple (one almost could say natural) way in which such a mechanism can be included in the PSO framework, as we hope to show in the next paragraphs.

Symbiotic Particles. We introduced yet a new species of particles in our algorithm as the base for the adaptation mechanism. To the original swarm - constituted by solution particles - we now add a swarm of parameter particles, encoding the algorithm's parameters. These particles interact between themselves as a normal swarm using equations 1 with a constriction factor χ of 0.729 and $\varphi = 4.1$, as recommended in [5], with only the two adjacent particles being considered as neighbours. Each particle encodes seven real valued parameters corresponding to seven adaptable parameters in SAPPO: a, b and f for the predator prey effect, N for the number of neighbours of each particle and c_1, c_2,c_3 for the velocity and position equations, which become:

$$V_i(t) = c_1 V_i(t-1) + c_2(P_i - X_i(t-1)) + c_3(P_g - X_i(t-1))) \qquad (6)$$
$$X_i(t) = X_i(t-1) + V_i(t)$$

The objective of the adaptation scheme is to find, simultaneously, a solution for an optimisation task and a set of parameters that increase the performance of the algorithm in that search. To achieve this we must link in some way the two swarms in the algorithm. We modeled this link on the symbiotic relations so common in nature, were two species live in a close relation from which both get some advantage.

In SAPPO each solution particle lives in symbiosis with a parameter particle, which encodes the parameters used when the algorithm's update equations are applied to that solution particle. The symbiotic relation is implemented trough the definition of the parameter particle fitness function.

A parameter particle has a "slower" life cycle than its companion. While a solution particle is evaluated and has its velocity and position updated every iteration, to a parameter function this only happens every i iterations (usually 10). The particle is then evaluated by comparing the actual fitness of its solution particle companion with the fitness i iterations ago. If there was an improvement, its value is stored as the parameter particle fitness, unless it is smaller than the improvement value already stored. When a new improvement value replaces an older one, the P vector is also updated with the current parameter particle's position in the search space. Velocity and position updates will then occur using equations 6. As a final element, the fitness of a parameter particle will decay slowly over every iteration of the algorithm (usually being multiplied by a decay factor $\alpha = 0.98$). This decaying ensures that a parameter particle has to keep producing improvements in the associated solution particle to maintain a high fitness.

Our approach to adaptation in SAPPO tries to maintain, as we already did with the predator-prey principle, the biological inspiration of the original PSO algorithm. We also made an effort to develop a mechanism that could be implemented following principles and ideas underlying the paradigm of swarm intelligence. Both the mechanisms introduced are based in the interaction of simple particles, with simple update rules and no centralized control. Both the solution and the behaviour of the algorithm emerge from the interactions between the individuals in this ecology of particles, and if there is intelligence in the system it is clearly not pre-programmed but emerges as a property of the system of swarms.

4 Experimental Setup and Results

4.1 Benchmark Problems

To investigate the performance of the new Simple, Adaptive, Predator Prey Optimiser (SAPPO), we compared it to a constricted version of PSO in a set of benchmark optimisation problems.

In [5] several constricted versions of the PSO, with different parameter choices, were tested in the same benchmark functions. We chose the generally best performing of those versions for comparison with SAPPO.

The benchmark problems used are a set of five non-linear functions, used as minimization problems, which present different difficulties to the optimisation algorithms. These problems are standard benchmarks not only for swarm algorithms [2][3][4][5], but also for other evolutionary algorithms (e.g. [8]). A successful and efficient optimisation of these functions is therefore an essential steppingstone for the general acceptance of swarm optimisers as reliable, general-purpose, optimisation tools.

$$\begin{aligned}
rosenbrock(x) &= \sum_{i=1}^{n-1}(100(x_{i+1}-x_i^2)^2+(x_i-1)^2) \\
rastrigin(x) &= \sum_{i-1}^{n}(x_i^2-10\cos(2\pi x_i)+10) \\
griewank(x) &= \frac{1}{4000}\sum_{i=1}^{n}(x_i-100)^2-\prod_{i=1}^{n}\cos(\frac{x_i-100}{\sqrt{i}})+1 \qquad (7) \\
ackley(x) &= -20\exp(-0.2\sqrt{\frac{1}{n}\sum_{i=1}^{n}x_i^2})-\exp(\frac{1}{n}\sum_{i=1}^{n}\cos(2\pi x_i))+20+e \\
schwefel(x) &= 418.9829n+\sum_{i=1}^{n}(-x_i\sin(\sqrt{|x_i|}))
\end{aligned}$$

In the functions above, x is a real number, n-dimensional vector and x_i is the i-th element of that vector. *rosenbrock* is the generalized Rosenbrock function, a unimodal function where the optimum is situated near the origin in a long, slightly decreasing, curved valley, where the difference between particles' fitness is very small, thus making the search difficult, since its easy for the swarm to stagnate in a non-optimal region of this valley.

rastrigin is the generalized Rastrigin function, *ackley* is the generalized Ackley function and *griewangk* the generalized Griewank function, three multimodal functions with many local minima set around the global minima in a unimodal macrostructure. In spite of this similarity in macrostructure these functions seem to pose different levels of difficulties for swarm optimisers. From swarm bibliography, it can be observed that while for *rastrigin* the PSO shows difficulties in getting near the optimum, for *griewangk* the difficulty seems to be the fine tuning stage when the particles are already near that optimum (see [4]). For the Ackley function the difficulties are the expected for this macrostructure: while the algorithm is successful in most of its runs it sometimes gets caught in a local optimum. There is a different from the other two functions in the fact that the success rate seems to be significantly higher for *ackley*.

The last function, *schwefel* - the Schwefel function, is not commonly used as a benchmark in swarm optimisation (although is common in other evolutionary approaches), since the structure of its search space makes it particularly hard for swarm optimisers. While all other functions in this benchmark set have the global optimum at the origin of the search space referential surrounded by local minima, *schwefel* has the global minimum located at the boundary of the search space and the local minima set far away from each other. The consequence of this structure is that when a swarm is caught near a local optimum it is virtually impossible for it to jump to another optimum and therefore progress towards the global minimum.

As other researchers before us, we believe that this set of benchmark functions, with each one presenting different challenges to optimisation, can be effective for the demonstration of relative weaknesses and strengths of our purposed algorithm.

4.2 Experimental Settings

Each function was optimised in 50 dimensions with its search space limited to the range presented in Table 1.

Table 1. Search space limits for each function

Function	Search Space
rosenbrock	$[-10, 10]^{50}$
rastrigin	$[-5.12, 5.12]^{50}$
griewank	$[-300, 300]^{50}$
ackley	$[-32, 32]^{50}$
schwefel	$[-500, 500]^{50}$

The PSO version used was a constricted version with $\chi = 0.729$ and $\varphi = 4.1$ and limited maximum velocity. This version was found to be generally the most efficient for the functions being optimised according to [5].

In SAPPO the most important choice was the range for the parameters encoded in the symbiotic particles. We tried to limit the range of each parameter to promising intervals. These intervals were empirically chosen after observing successful sets of parameters presented both in the literature and in our own work. The only criterion used was to keep these intervals as limited as possible, so that the total search space (for particle and parameter particles) did not increase in a way that would make the comparison with the PSO extremely unfair. The used intervals are presented in Table 2.

Table 2. Range for the parameters encoded by symbiotic particles

Parameter	Range
c_1	$[0.0, 1.0]$
c_2	$[1.7, 2.2]$
c_3	$[0.0, 0.5]$
f	$[0.0, 0.02]$
a	$[0.0, 3.0XMax]$
b	$[0.005XMax, 0.02XMax]$
N	$[1, 5]$

For both the algorithms tested, a swarm size of 30 particles was used and for each run 5000 iterations of the algorithm were performed. The results presented were obtained by averaging 100 runs of the algorithm being used.

4.3 Results and Discussion

The Particle Swarm Optimiser and the Simple, Adaptive, Predator Prey Optimiser were used to optimise the five benchmark functions using the settings presented in the previous paragraph. The average results obtained by each algorithm after 5000 iterations are presented in Table 3. The graphs presented in Fig. 1 illustrate the evolution of best fitness for both algorithms, averaged for 100 runs of each algorithm.

Table 3. Average results over 100 runs, found after 5000 iterations of each algorithm

	rosenbrock	*rastrigin*	*griewank*	*ackley*	*schwefel*
PSO	63,332424	135,332669	0,001115	0,306677	8736,404197
SAPPO	43,916634	0,039798	0,004752	0,000000	249,566755

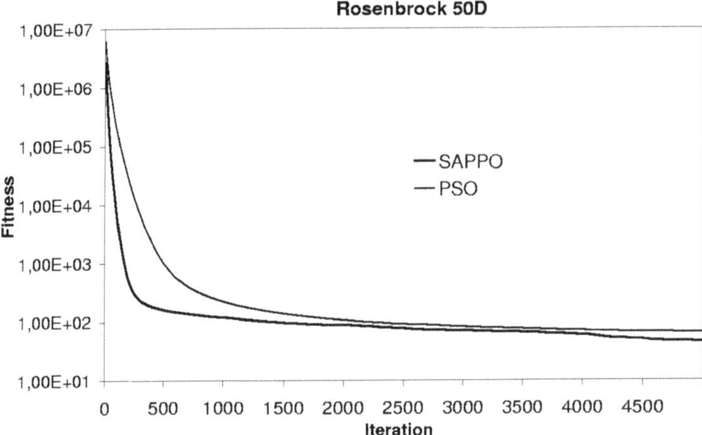

Fig. 1. Evolution of average fitness for PSO and SAPPO when optimising the Rosenbrock function. Fitness is presented in logarithmic scale.

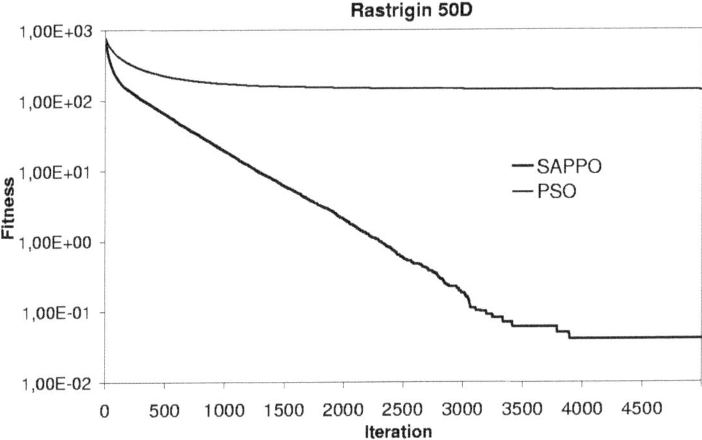

Fig. 2. Evolution of average fitness for PSO and SAPPO when optimising the Rastrigin function. Fitness is presented in logarithmic scale.

From the values in Table 3 we can conclude that the results obtained by SAPPO are clearly better for three of the five test functions (*rastrigin*, *ackley* and *schwefel*) and marginally better for one function (*rosenbrock*). SAPPO's performance was only marginally worse for the Griewangk function. These are clearly promising results for SAPPO since the introduction of the symbiotic particles introduces seven extra dimensions in the search space (one for each parameter).

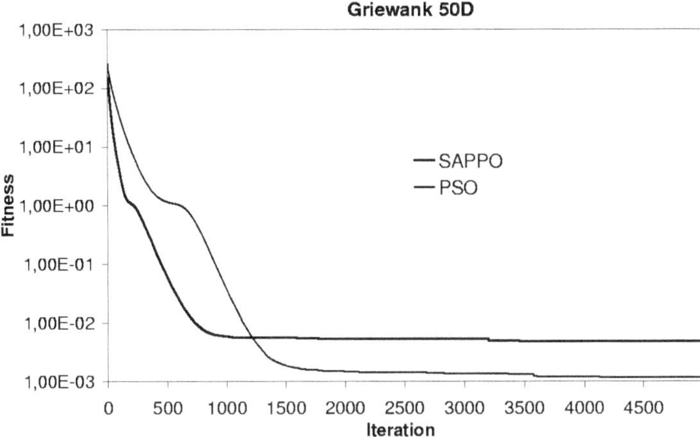

Fig. 3. Evolution of average fitness for PSO and SAPPO when optimising the Griewank function. Fitness is presented in logarithmic scale.

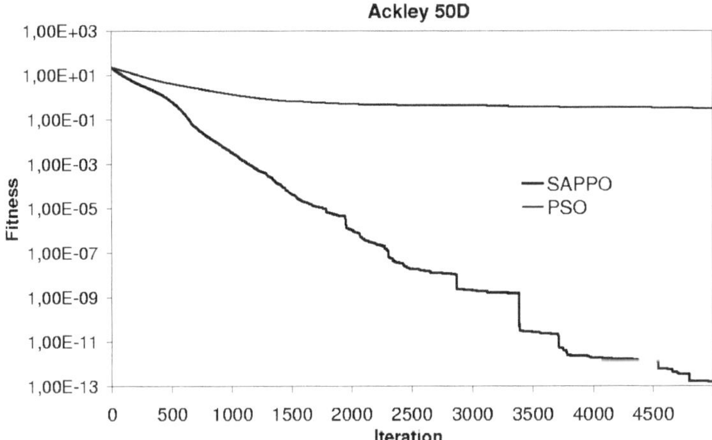

Fig. 4. Evolution of average fitness for PSO and SAPPO when optimising the Ackley function. Fitness is presented in logarithmic scale.

In a general analysis of the graphs in Figs.1–5 we can encounter some clues to this improvement in general performance. It is clear from all graphs that the adaptive scheme promotes the use of more "aggressive" search strategies, in the sense that the average fitness drops much faster for SAPPO than for PSO. This was a behaviour we expected, since the evaluation of parameter particles is clearly a greedy one: particles which produce the larger improvements are the ones that are favoured by the algorithm, so it is natural that the search strategies that result from the parameters used tend to be the ones that produce

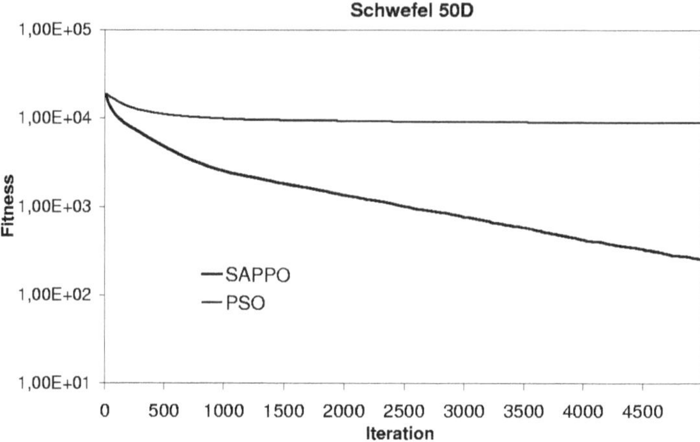

Fig. 5. Evolution of average fitness for PSO and SAPPO when optimising the Schwefel function. Fitness is presented in logarithmic scale.

large initial fitness improvements. We also expected that the fulfilment of the main objective behind any adaptive scheme - that the algorithm would adapt to the problem being solved - would result in the choice, from the "aggressive" strategies available, of one that fitted each problem, thus resulting in even faster initial convergence.

In the traditional PSO all this "aggressiveness" would lead to a short exploration phase and a quick convergence, in most cases to a local optimum. We tried to counter this effect in two ways. First, we tried to design the adaptive scheme in a way that particles that could sustain this improvement over time would emerge, mainly by allowing a decay in the parameter particles' fitness over time - if a parameter particle does not keep producing improvements in its companion fitness its own fitness will decrease and it will cease to influence its neighbours. Second, the addition of the predator-prey mechanism introduced a way of creating diversity, even under significant convergence pressure. A separate analysis of each graph can help us understand how different parts of the algorithm contributed for its performance in the optimization of each function.

For *rosenbrock* there was a very quick initial decrease in fitness for both algorithms probably when the particles where descending the walls of the function valley. When the plateau was reached both algorithms started to produce improvements very slowly as usually happens with this function. We believe the slightly better performance observed in this function for SAPPO is the result of better chosen algorithm parameters, i.e. the adaptive scheme finds a better set of parameters for this function than the ones used by the PSO. We conclude this, since, as can be seen in the next paragraphs, the effect of the predator prey mechanism seems more noticeable in search spaces with multiple optima.

The Rastrigin function is the first where SAPPO significantly outperformed the classical PSO. We have again a fast initial convergence but SAPPO keeps finding better solutions long after the stagnation of the PSO, with final bests several orders of magnitude better than the ones found by the PSO. Rastrigin is usually considered a hard function for PSO, which usually gets caught in local minima still far from the global one and is incapable of moving on. The performance of SAPPO in *rastrigin* clearly illustrates the power of the predator prey mechanism, since we believe convergence to local minima still occurs, but particles sent in new trajectories by the predator prey effect allow the swarm to jump from minimum to minimum until the global one (or at least a very good local one) is found. Griewank is the only function where SAPPO did not outperform PSO. Again we have a faster initial convergence with SAPPO but for this function neither mechanism could avoid the local minima near the optimum and a initial more "aggressive" strategy was punished with slightly worse minima than the ones found the PSO. The analysis for the Ackley function is similar to the one above for *rastrigin*, but the difference in final results is even greater, with SAPPO always finding the global minima (with six cases precision) around iteration 2000.

Finally, for the Schwefel function, which was introduced as an extreme test for both swarm based optimisers, since the structure of its search space is clearly adverse for these algorithms, the SAPPO results were again significantly better than the ones found by PSO. As expected, the standard PSO behaved very poorly for this function, as the wide positioning of the local minima in the search space makes it almost impossible for the algorithm to escape when caught around a local minimum. SAPPO behaved very differently. While for the PSO there was almost no progression after the first 500 iterations, SAPPO, even if with rather slow progress, kept improving the best fitness in the swarm until the end of each run. This was the only function for which there seemed to be yet significantly improvement possible after the 5000 iterations has elapsed, which confirms our statement that it constitutes a strong test for swarm based algorithms. Again we justify the best results of SAPPO when compared with PSO mainly by the effect of the predator prey mechanism.

Generally, we can conclude that the new mechanisms introduced combined to significantly improve the performance of our swarm optimiser on most of the benchmark functions used, with the adaptive mechanism being the main responsible for the improvement in *rosenbrock*, while the predator prey scheme clearly helped with the functions with many local minima.

5 Conclusions

We presented two biologically inspired mechanisms designed to improve specific aspects of the standard predator-prey algorithm. An adaptive scheme, based in the idea of symbiosis, was implemented using a new swarm, which encodes the algorithm main parameters. Solution particles and parameter particles are now co-evolved during the algorithm execution. The objective of the introduction of this scheme was to allow the algorithm to choose in runtime the parameters that allowed a good optimisation strategy for the problem being solved.

The second mechanism was loosely inspired in the predator prey dynamics present in animal populations, and its aim was to introduce a diversity preserving mechanism to help the algorithm escape local minima. This mechanism was implemented by introducing a new particle - a predator particle - which is attracted by the best particle in the swarm and repels all swarm particles with an intensity which is inversely proportional to the distance between prey and predator.

The new algorithm – which we call SAPPO, from Simple, Adaptive, Predator Prey Optimiser – was tested against a traditional PSO in a set of five benchmark functions, having been found that SAPPO outperformed the PSO very significantly in three of the test functions and marginally in a fourth function, while the PSO behaved marginally better in only one of the test functions.

We also tried to identify which of the new mechanisms was the main responsible for the improvement in performance in each of the test functions.

From the results and following discussion we can conclude that SAPPO can dramatically increase the performance of swarm based optimisers, at least in functions with search space structure similar to the ones used as benchmarks. Further results with other benchmark functions, problems from other and, preferably, real world problems are essential to ascertain the validity of these claims. However, we believe the principles behind the adaptive and the diversity preserving mechanisms are sane and can be useful, even if implemented in different ways, for the improvement of the traditional swarm optimisers.

A final aspect that we would like to emphasize is the swarm intelligence principle that we tried to maintain and even reinforce in the new mechanisms introduced in the algorithm. The overall behaviour of the algorithm is in no way imposed by some centralized control structure, but emerges from the interactions, governed by simple rules, of three species of particles: predator, preys and symbiots. This has the bonus effect of increasing our knowledge of how to design intelligent systems from simple, non intelligent components. As for future work, one aspect we would like to improve is the identified "greediness" of the adaptive scheme, which we think could be responsible for less satisfactory results, as the ones obtained for the Griewank function. We also believe that SAPPO, with its current characteristics, could constitute a successful approach to optimisation in dynamic environments, and wish to investigate that possibility.

Acknowledgements. This work was partially financed by the Portuguese Ministry of Science and Technology under the Program POSI.

References

1. Kennedy, J. and Eberhart, R. C.: Particle swarm optimisation. Proc. IEEE International Conference on Neural Networks. Piscataway, NJ, pp. 1942–1948, 1995.
2. Kennedy, J., Eberhart, R. C., and Shi, Y.: Swarm intelligence. Morgan Kaufmann Publishers, San Francisco. 2001
3. Angeline, P. J.: Evolutionary optimisation versus particle swarm optimisation: philosophy and performance differences. The Seventh Annual Conf. on Evolutionary Programming. 1998.
4. Shi, Y. and Eberhart, R. C.: Empirical study of particle swarm optimisation. Proceedings of the 1999 Congress on Evolutionary Computation. Piscataway, NJ, pp. 1945–1950, 1999.
5. Clerc, M. and Kennedy, J.: The particle swarm-explosion, stability, and convergence in a multidimensional complex space. IEEE Transactions on Evolutionary Computation, Vol. 6, No. 1, pp. 58–73. 2002.
6. Kennedy, J.: Small worlds and mega-minds: effects of neighborhood topology on particle swarm performance. Proc. Congress on Evolutionary Computation 1999. Piscataway, NJ, pp. 1931–1938, 1999.
7. Blackwell, T. and Bentley, P. J.: Don't Push Me! Collision-Avoiding Swarms. in Proc. of the Congress on Evolutionary Computation 2002.
8. Muhlenbein, H., and Schlierkamp-Voosen, D.: Predictive models for the breeder genetic algorithm: I. Continuous parameter optimisation. Evolutionary Computation, 1 (1), 25–49.
9. Silva, A., Neves, A. and Costa E.: Chasing the Swarm: A Predator Prey Approach to Function Optimisation. Proc. of MENDEL2002 – 8th International Conference on Soft Computing. Brno, Czech Republic, June 5–7, 2002

Evolutionary Neuroestimation of Fitness Functions*

Jesus S. Aguilar-Ruiz, Daniel Mateos, and Domingo S. Rodriguez

Department of Computer Science
University of Seville, Spain
{aguilar,mateos,dsavio}@lsi.us.es
http://www.lsi.us.es/~aguilar

Abstract. One of the most influential factors in the quality of the solutions found by an evolutionary algorithm is the appropriateness of the fitness function. Specifically in data mining, in where the extraction of useful information is a main task, when databases have a great amount of examples, fitness functions are very time consuming. In this sense, an approximation to fitness values can be beneficial for reducing its associated computational cost. In this paper, we present the Neural–Evolutionary Model (NEM), which uses a neural network as a fitness function estimator. The neural network is trained through the evolutionary process and used progressively to estimate the fitness values, what enhances the search efficiency while alleviating the computational overload of the fitness function. We demonstrate that the NEM is faster than the traditional evolutionary algorithm, under some assumptions over the total amount of estimations carried out by the neural network. The Neural–Evolutionary Model proves then useful when datasets contain vast amount of examples.

1 Introduction

Evolutionary Computation can be basically used to tackle with two sorts of problems: optimization and machine learning. In machine learning, a dataset plays the role of knowledge base, so each individual of the population is evaluated taking into account every example of that dataset, or in some cases, a representative subset of it [4]. To produce a knowledge model -in any form of knowledge representation- from a dataset is a task -among several steps of the knowledge discovery from databases (KDD) process- that consumes a lot of time when evolutionary algorithms are used, so that it is advisable to incorporate a technique able to reduce the complexity.

One of the most influential factors in the quality of the solutions found by an evolutionary algorithms (EA) is the appropiateness of the fitness function. This function assigns a value of merit (goodness) to each individual of the population

* The research was supported by the Spanish Research Agency CICYT under grant TIC2001–1143–C03–02.

Fernando Moura Pires, Salvador Abreu (Eds.): EPIA 2003, LNAI 2902, pp. 74–83, 2003.

for every generation, so that the number of calls to this function is exactly PG, where P is the size of the population and G is the number of generations. However, for machine learning problems, the fitness function needs to analyze every example from the dataset, which can have many attributes. Therefore, the overall cost of the fitness function during the evolutionary process is NMPG, where N is the number of examples of the dataset and M is the number of attributes of every example. As it is a very high cost, we then usually try to optimize the efficiency of the evolutionary algorithm, i.e. to decrease the computational cost by reducing some of these parameters.

When N is the aim of the reduction, then we are dealing with *editing or condensed algorithms* [5]. On the other hand, if we try to reduce M, the techniques are so–called *feature selection* or *attribute extraction*. As N and M are not factors of the evolutionary algorithm per se, we will call them *external factors*. In addition, P and G, which will be called *internal factors* of the evolutionary algorithm, could be also reduced. A small value of P might limit the exploration through the search space and a small value of G might reduce the explotation within the search space. These two parameters, P and G, are by far easier to modify than N or M, because they don't need a specific preprocessing algorithm but some experience.

There exist many algorithms to reduce N, most of them based on the Nearest Neighbour technique [5,6,7] or on attribute projections [2]. In the same way, other algorithms can reduce the number of attributes, such as RELIEF [8]. Editing or feature selection algorithms would not lead to a reduction in quality of results.

In this work, we deal with the reduction of the computational cost of evaluating the fitness function. None of the internal (P or G) or external (N or M) parameters are reduced, but our original approach consists in reducing directly the computational cost of the fitness function (FF) by using another "approximate" function (FF*). This function FF* will estimate the values of FF using less computational resources.

Neural networks (NN) are robust and exhibit good learning and generalization capabilities in data–rich environments and are particularly effective in modeling relationships with nonlinearities. The estimator FF* is designed as a NN, which will be trained through the evolutionary process until it can estimate by itself the fitness function, and next generations will begin to use the neural network as a FF estimator FF*, at the same time that it is trained. From a time, no more evaluations are calculated by the fitness function, but all individuals will be estimated by the neural network. NN have been chosen because they are very easy to implement, adapt well to many different search spaces, provides high quality results, and fundamentally because the training cost is very low and the test cost is virtually nil. Combinations between artificial neural networks and evolutionary algorithms have been analysed in many works, mainly for optimization tasks [9,10]. Neural networks have rarely been used as a function evaluator to facilitate EA search. In fact, little research has focused on neural networks being used for this purpose [11,12].

The main advantage of our approach resides in the significant reduction of the computational cost, since most of the evolutionary process the algorithm has not to calculate the fitness function values, as these are provided by the NN, very much faster than the fitness function. This is so because from the moment in which the NN calculates all the values, the parameters N and M disappear from the expression NMPG, having no influence on the overall cost.

The paper is organized as follows: in Section 2 the motivation of our approach is described; the NEM is presented in Section 3 and its computational cost is calculated; we demonstrate the efficiency of our approach with respect to the traditional EA in Section 4 and some properties about its use are given; finally, the most interesting conclusions and future research directions on this issue are presented in Sections 5 and 6, respectively.

2 Motivation

The computational cost of an EA can be separated into several factors: evaluation, selection, recombination, genetic operators, etc. Specifically in the supervised learning context, our ten–fold cross–validated experiments [3] carried out with datasets from the UCI repository [13] revelead that the evaluation function took approximately 85% of the total computational cost. This fact motivate us to analyze how to reduce this percentage by means of a fast evaluation of individuals from the population.

In Section 1 the internal and external factors of the EA were mentionated. Logically, internal factors as P and G have great influence on the quality of results. However, we know that a greater value for P is not necessarily going to provide better results, and an increasing of G might have the same behaviour over the EA if, for instance, the process is falling into a local minimum. We could fit these parameters, hypothetically knowing that the greater value is, better results might be found. Therefore, it is not technically appropriate to try to reduce the computational cost by decreasing the value of some of these parameters, since the quality of the results would be affected to a large extent. In addition, the range for P used to be small, for instance in machine learning problems, it is ranging from 20 to 200.

The external factors are not easily manipulated by the EA. The number of examples N and the number of attributes M should be constant values along the evolutionary process. As mentioned above, a reduction method can be tried before applying the EA, as a preprocessing technique, although the same result quality is not guaranteed. The largest value out of N, M, P and G is usually N so that dataset reduction techniques are mostly used. However, the cost of these techniques is mostly quadratic.

As calculating the fitness of an individual will have complexity NM, in some cases, a sampling method is embedded in the FF in order to reduce N to a small value N'. Nevertheless, the correct selection of the N' examples from the dataset is another difficult problem if we wish to provide exactly the same fitness value that when using the N original examples, i.e. the subset must be reliable.

Other ideas consist in conserving fitness values of individuals from older populations (previous generations) in order to save these values. We think that this technique is interesting when almost all the individuals are similar, i.e. when the population is very “old”, as the probability of two individuals are equal from consecutive populations is higher (many efficient data structures exist to store the historic information from individuals and fitness value calculations.) Nevertheless, there is relatively little work in the literature that address how to make full use of the search history to guide the future search. It is important to note that, at this point, the similarity among individuals is directly depending on the individual length and thus on the cardinality of the alphabet, what requires an appropriate enconding of the search space [1].

To deal with the problem from the point of view of M is only advisable when the dataset has hundreds or thousands of attributes. In fact, nowdays there are appearing many medical datasets with those amounts of attributes, such as the leukemia dataset used in [14] to discover the distintion between acute myeloid and acute lymphoblastic sorts of leukemia, which has 6817 attributes (genes) and only 38 examples (patients).

In short, a decreasing of N, M, P and/or G can lead to a significant reduction of the computational cost. However, this reduction can have some side effects on the quality of the results, as we have seen before.

In this work, we tackle the fitness function evaluation as an incremental learning problem, i.e. we will try to learn to calculate fitness values by using a neural network, which is progressively trained through the evolutionary process, like an embedded subprocess in the fitness function.

The aim is to achieve a neural network able to provide similar values as the fitness function, i.e. to construct a fitness function estimator. Thus, the Neuro–Evolutionary Model consists of an evolutionary algorithm and a neural network that is learning from the fitness function at the same time as estimating new values.

3 Neural–Evolutionary Model

Before presenting theoretically the Neural–Evolutionary Model (NEM), we will give some definitions. Henceforth, FF denotes the fitness function and NN is the neural network. In addition, C_{FF} is the cost of the evaluation of one individual; C_{NNT} is the cost of training the NN; and C_{NNE} is the cost of the estimation of the fitness value of an individual with the NN. A function $\varphi : \mathbb{N} \rightarrow \mathbb{N}$ indicates how many individuals will be evaluated by FF and NN at each generation. Thus, at generation i, a number φ_i of individuals will be directly evaluated by the FF and the remainder P-φ_i will be estimated by the NN.

The idea behind the NEM is very simple: at the generation i the fitness value of P-φ_i individuals will be obtained by the FF and the fitness value of φ_i individuals will be estimated by the NN, which will receive P-φ_i individuals together with P-φ_i fitness values to be trained.

```
Function NEM(E)
  var x̄: Individual
  i := 1
  P_0 :=Initialize()
  Evaluation(P_i, i)
  while i < num_generations
    i := i + 1
    for j ∈ {1, ..., |P_{i-1}|}
      x̄ :=Selection(P_{i-1}, i, j)
      P_i := P_i+Recombination(x̄, P_{i-1}, i, j)
    end for
    Evaluation(P_i, i)
  end while
  return best_of(P_i)
end NEM

Procedure Evaluation(Q, i)
  var x̄: Individual; Fitness: vector [|Q|] of real
  FFS:=φ_i individuals randomly selected from Q
  for x̄ ∈ FFS
    Fitness(x̄):=FF(x̄)
    Train NN using x̄ and Fitness(x̄)
  end for
  for x̄ ∈ Q−FFS
    Fitness(x̄):=NN(x̄)
  end for
end Evaluation
```

Fig. 1. Pseudocode of NEM.

Basically, the NEM is an EA with a more complex evaluation function, which is separated from the EA pseudocode to be better explained. In Figure 1 the EA is described, following a schema inspired by the works of Angeline and Pollack [15]. The FF is called *Evaluation*, and it is depicted at the bottom within the same Figure.

Evaluation uses a vector called Fitness, with size P, to save the fitness values of every individual. The procedure has four parts: selection of φ_i individuals; fitness calculations of φ_i individuals; training of the NN using $\bar{x}$ (an individual) and the fitness value provided by Fitness($\bar{x}$) before; and fitness value estimations by the NN. The first part involves the function φ_i, and it is depending on the number of the generation i. The selected individuals are included in a set, named FFS (Fitness Function Subset), and they will be evaluated by using the FF. Each individual $\bar{x}$ together with its fitness value Fitness($\bar{x}$) is given to the NN as a training example. After the first loop, φ_i individuals have been evaluated and the NN has been trained with them. Later, the individuals not selected before, exactly P-φ_i, are given as input to the NN to estimate the fitness values.

Table 1 shows the cost at each generation i. The cost of evaluating one individual with FF is NM; the cost of training the NN with one individual is T; the cost of estimating the fitness value of one individual with NN is E. For an EA, the cost of evaluating all the P individuals during the G generations will be C_{EA}=NMGP, as it is shown in Table 1.

Table 1. Cost of evaluating P individuals through G generations. C_{FF} is the cost of the fitness function; C_{NNT} is the cost of training the neural network; C_{NNE} is the cost of estimating the fitness values with the neural network.

Generation	C_{FF}	C_{NNT}	C_{NNE}	C_{EA}
1	φ_1 NM	φ_1 T	(P-φ_1)E	PNM
2	φ_2 NM	φ_2 T	(P-φ_2)E	PNM
⋮	⋮	⋮	⋮	⋮
i	φ_i NM	φ_i T	(P-φ_i)E	PNM
⋮	⋮	⋮	⋮	⋮
G	φ_G NM	φ_G T	(P-φ_G)E	PNM
Total	Φ NM	Φ T	(GP-Φ)E	GPNM

The total cost of the Neural–Evolutionary Model, $C_{N\diamond E}$ would be as follows:

$$C_{N\diamond E} = C_{FF} + C_{NNT} + C_{NNE}$$

$$C_{FF} = (\varphi_1 + \ldots + \varphi_G)\text{NM} = \text{NM}\sum_{i=1}^{G}\varphi_i$$

$$C_{NNT} = (\varphi_1 + \ldots + \varphi_G)\text{T} = \text{T}\sum_{i=1}^{G}\varphi_i$$

$$C_{NNE} = (\text{P} - \varphi_1 + \ldots + \text{P} - \varphi_G)\text{E} = \text{EGP-E}\sum_{i=1}^{G}\varphi_i$$

Therefore, the cost of $C_{N\diamond E}$ will be:

$$C_{N\diamond E} = (\text{NM+T-E})\Phi + \text{EGP} \tag{1}$$

where $\Phi = \sum_{i=1}^{G}\varphi_i$.

4 Efficiency

In this section, the aim is to demonstrate that $C_{N\diamond E}$ is smaller than C_{EA} under some assumptions over φ. In other words, there exist functions φ which make the NEM faster than the EA.

Theorem 1. *If $NM \geq GP$ and $\Phi <$GP-1 then the cost of the NEM, $C_{N\diamond E}$, is smaller than the cost of the EA, C_{EA}.*

Proof. Let suppose that

$$\text{NM}\Phi + \text{GP} < \text{GPNM}$$

then

$$\Phi < \frac{\text{GPNM-GP}}{\text{NM}} = \text{GP}\left(1 - \frac{1}{\text{NM}}\right)$$

if NM $\geq$ GP then

$$\Phi < \text{GP} - 1 \leq \text{GP}\left(1 - \frac{1}{\text{NM}}\right)$$

We have to note that NM has a large value in comparison to GP. The range from GP normally varies in machine learning problems from 5000 (G=100 and P=50) to 100000 (G=500 and P=200), although greater values can be used. However, since the values for N and M are previously known, we can assure that NM≥GP by searching values for G and P that satisfy the condition.

Therefore,

$$\left.\begin{array}{l} \Phi < \text{GP-1} \\ \text{NM} \geq \text{GP} \end{array}\right\} \Rightarrow \text{C}_{N\diamond E} < \text{C}_{EA}$$

In the next subsection, we are going to analyze the case of φ piece–wise linear, i.e. the number of estimations done by the NN is linear with respect to the number of generations.

4.1 Piece-Wise Linear φ.

The general case for φ is:

$$\varphi = \begin{cases} \text{P} & 0 < i < q_1 \\ -\frac{\text{P}}{q_2 - q_1}(i - q_2) & q_1 < i \leq q_2 \\ 0 & q_2 < i \leq \text{G} \end{cases} \tag{2}$$

where q_1 and q_2 are constant values within [1,G]. Figure 2 shows graphically this function.

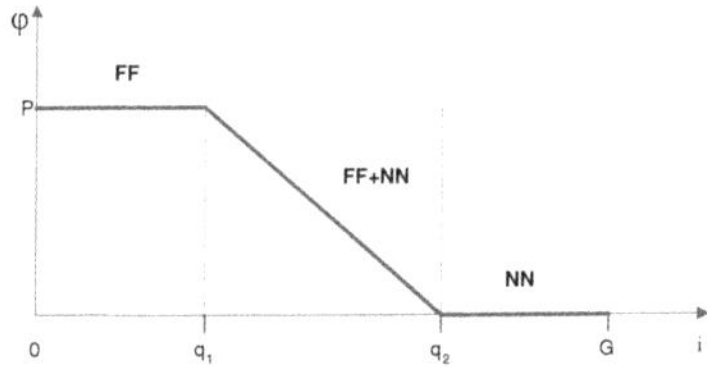

Fig. 2. Linear function φ.

During the first q_1 generations the fitness values are generated by using the FF. At generation $i = q_1 + \frac{q_2 - q_1}{\text{P}}$ the function φ_i takes the value P-1, so that the other individual is estimated by using the NN. As i increases, more individuals will be estimated with NN and lesser number of individuals will be calculated with FF. From the generation $i = q_2 + 1$, the NN estimates all of the individuals and FF is not used anymore, since NN is supposed to have learned from FF outputs. It is worth to note that q_1 determines when is NN to be used it, and q_2 when is not FF being used anymore.

The cost of Φ is as follows:

$$\Phi = \sum_{i=1}^{q_1} \varphi_i + \sum_{i=q_1+1}^{q_2} \varphi_i + \sum_{i=q_2+1}^{G} \varphi = \frac{P}{2}(q_1 + q_2 - 1) \tag{3}$$

This result is very important because the cost of the NEM is not depending on q_1 or q_2 separately, but the sum q_1+q_2. This means that the cost of NEMs will be the same if $q_1 + q_2$ are equal for both cases. Figure 3 illustrates this fact. (An open problem is to determine which NEM will have better quality, depending on the values of q_1 and q_2, for those NEMs which have the same $q_1 + q_2$ and G.)

Now, we are going to demonstrate that the cost of the function φ is actually small and satisfies the Theorem 1.

Replacing Φ from Equation 3 into Equation 1:

$$\mathrm{C}_{N \diamond E} = \mathrm{NM}\frac{\mathrm{P}}{2}(q_1 + q_2 - 1) + \mathrm{PG}$$

The cost of the NEM will be smaller than that of the EA when:

$$\mathrm{NM}\frac{\mathrm{P}}{2}(q_1 + q_2 - 1) + \mathrm{PG} < \mathrm{GPNM}$$

Simplifying,

$$\mathrm{G} > \left(\frac{q_1 + q_2 - 1}{2}\right)\left(1 + \frac{1}{\text{NM-1}}\right)$$

Assuming that NM>1 then $\frac{1}{2}\left(1 + \frac{1}{\text{NM-1}}\right) \leq 1$. Replacing, $\mathrm{G} > q_1 + q_2 - 1$ and therefore,

$$\mathrm{G} \geq q_1 + q_2 \Rightarrow \mathrm{C}_{N \diamond E} < \mathrm{C}_{EA}$$

when φ is as shown in Equation 2. By definition, $q_1 + q_2 < 2\mathrm{G}$ and $q_1 < q_2$ (as $q_1 = q_2$ means no NN is being used together with the FF), so if $q_2 = \mathrm{G} - k$, then $q_1 \leq k$, k being any value in $[0,\mathrm{G}[$.

To understand the operation of the NEM together with the linear function φ, an example of specific linear function is given, where $q_1 = 0$ and $q_2 = \mathrm{P}$. In

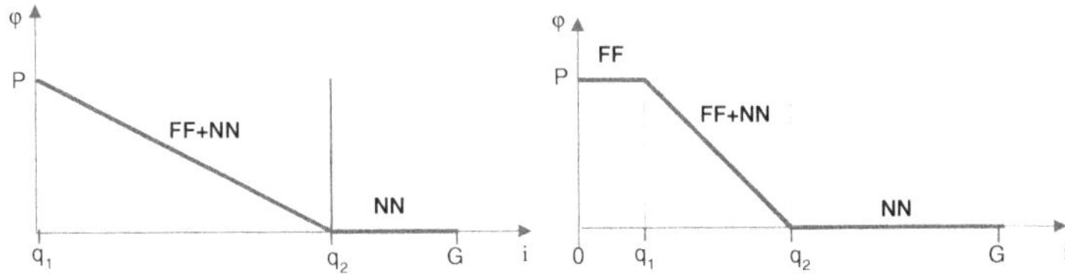

Fig. 3. Two functions φ, having the same computational cost, could provide different results with respect to the quality.

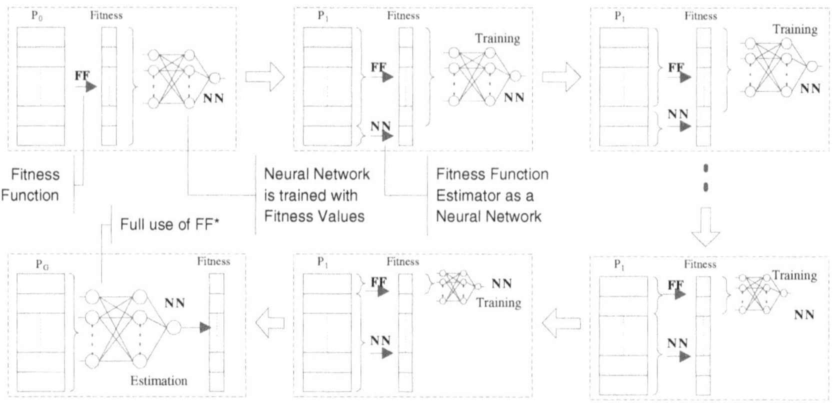

Fig. 4. The evolutionary process, within which the neural network is trained with the previously calculated fitness values.

this case, at the first generation all the individuals are evaluated with FF. At the second generation, every individual is evaluated with FF exepct for one, which is estimated with NN. With the P-1 evaluations, the NN is trained. An so on, until all of the individuals are estimated by NN, when q_2 = P+1. The process is graphically depicted in Figure 4.

5 Conclusions

Specifically, when datasets contain great amount of examples, the use of evolutionary algorithms to extract useful information in form of decision rules is a task that takes a lot of time. Fitness functions are very time consuming so that an approximation to fitness values can be beneficial for reducing its associated computational cost.

We present a Neural–Evolutionary Model (NEM), which uses a neural network as a fitness function estimator. The neural network is trained through the evolutionary process and used progressively to estimate the fitness values. We demonstrate that the NEM is faster than the traditional evolutionary algorithm, under some assumptions over the gradualness of the neural network training and its use as an estimator. In general, for greater values of N and M, better results the NEM will give with respect to efficiency.

Despite some approaches include the use of NNs together with EAs, to our knowledge, the design of the NEM is original, since the algorithm learns through two different levels: one is the evolutionary learning and the other is the neural learning, which helps to the first one.

The resulting hybrid approach find solutions with fewer computational resources devoted to the efficient evaluation of the fitness function, so the NEM is specially useful for the evolutionary extraction of interesting knowledge from datasets which have a huge size.

6 Future Works

After demonstrating the efficiency of the NEM, our research is focused on the *effectiveness* of the approached model, i.e. on experimentally proving that the quality of the results is also conserved. Another interesting future research direction consists in studying different forms for the function φ, in order to compare the quality of different approached NEMs.

References

1. Jesus S. Aguilar–Ruiz, J. C. Riquelme, and C. Del Valle, "Improving the evolutionary coding for machine learning tasks," in *Proceedings of the* 15th *European Conference on Artificial Intelligence (ECAI'02)*, Lyon, France, August 2002, pp. 173–177.
2. Jesus S. Aguilar–Ruiz, J.C. Riquelme, and M. Toro, "Data set editing by ordered projection," *Intelligent Data Analysis*, vol. 5:5, pp. 1–13, 2001.
3. Jesus S. Aguilar–Ruiz, J.C. Riquelme, and C. Del Valle, "Evolutionary learning of hierarchical decision rules," *IEEE Transactions on Systems, Man and Cybernetics, Part B*, Vol. 33, Issue 2, pp. 324–331, April 2003.
4. George H. John and Pat Langley, "Static versus dynamic sampling for data mining," in *Proceedings of the Second International Conference on Knowledge Discovery and Data Mining*, 1996.
5. B. V. Dasarathy, *Nearest Neighbor(NN) Norms: NN Pattern Classification Techniques*, IEEE Computer Society Press, 1991.
6. E. Fix and J. L. Hodges, "Discriminatory analysis, nonparametric discrimation consistency properties," Technical Report 4, US Air Force, School of Aviation Medicine, Randolph Field, TX, 1951.
7. D. R. Wilson and T. R. Martinez, "Reduction techniques for instance–based learning algorithms," *Machine Learning*, vol. 38, no. 3, pp. 257–286, 2000.
8. I. Kononenko, "Estimating attributes: analysis and extensions of relief," in *Proceedings of European Conference on Machine Learning*. 1994, Springer-Verlag.
9. Xin Yao and Young Liu, "A new evolutionary system for evolving artificial neural networks," *IEEE Transactions on Neural Networks*, vol. 8, pp. 694–7130, 1997.
10. Xin Yao, "Evolving artificial neural networks," *Proceedings of the IEEE*, vol. 87, no. 9, pp. 1423–1447, 1999.
11. A.G.Pipe, T.C. Fogarty, and A. Winfield, "Balancing exploration with exploitation - solving mazes with real numbered search spaces," in *Proceedings of the First IEEE Conference on Evolutionary Computation*, 1994, pp. 458–489.
12. D.W. Coit and A.E. Smith, "Solving the redundancy allocation problem using a combined neural network/genetic algorithm approach," *Computers & Operations Research*, 1995.
13. C. Blake and E. K. Merz, "UCI repository of machine learning databases," 1998.
14. T. R. Golub, D. K. Slonim, P. Tamayo, C. Huard, M. Gaasenbeek, J. P. Mesirov, H. Coller, M. L. Loh, J. R. Downing, M. A. Caligiuri, C. D. Bloomfield, and E. S. Lander, "Molecular classification of cancer: Class discovery and class prediction by gene expression monitoring," *Science*, , no. 285, pp. 531–537, 1999.
15. P. Angeline and J. Pollack, "Evolutionary module acquisition," in *Second Annual Conference on Evolutionary Programming*, 1993.

A Resource Sharing Model to Study Social Behaviours

Pedro Mariano and Luís Correia

Departamento de Informática
Faculdade de Ciências e Tecnologia
Universidade Nova de Lisboa
Portugal
{plm,lc}@di.fct.unl.pt

Abstract. We analyse a resource sharing game under different conditions in order to study social behaviours such as cooperation and treason. We concentrate in analysing the game under different scenarios in order to find out which one produces a more cooperative population. This is possible since the game while having multiple Pareto Optimal strategies, also has multiple pure and mixed Nash Equilibriums, which results in complex population dynamics. We introduce a simple form of agreement and compare the results with the previous cases.

Keywords: Cooperation, Agreements, Social Behaviours

1 Introduction

We have developed a game [7,6] in order to study social behaviours such as treason and exploitation. We have explicitly modelled resources while other games (Iterated Prisoner Dilemma [3,8]) do not take into account resources. Other models while having resources (fish stocks [2], rivers [4], petroleum, pollution [9]) are more difficult to analyse and to determine the important factors of social cooperation. Since our game has multiple Pareto Optimal strategies, agents need to establish some agreement regarding the playing strategy they will adopt. This in turn allows exploitative and traitor agents to appear in the population.

The contribution of this paper is twofold: the analysis of an agreement model and the effect of evolutionary operators aims at showing how cooperation can appear in a population of agents. The rest of this paper is as follows. In section 2 we introduce our model. The next section 3 discusses the results obtained with the evolutionary algorithm. We wrap in section 4 with the conclusions and final remarks.

2 Game Description and Analysis

2.1 Description

The name of the game is "Give and Take". It is played for some amount of time between two agents with one resource. During each turn of the game, the agent

Fernando Moura Pires, Salvador Abreu (Eds.): EPIA 2003, LNAI 2902, pp. 84–88, 2003.

that holds the resource, gains some wealth, while the other loses some amount of wealth. There are three general actions: *none*, *give*, *take*. An agent may do nothing, give the resource to the other agent (if it holds it), or take the resource from the other agent (if it does not hold it). This is a game whose dynamics unfolds in time. The following list shows the game parameters that are used in the game matrices:

w_g, w_l Holding the resource contributes w_g to the wealth, and lack of it incurs a penalty of w_l.

b_b, c_{pt}, c_{st} Action related parameters. The performer of the *give* action receives a bonus of b_g. Playing the *take* action costs the action performer c_{pt} and the action subject c_{st}.

From this list we obtain the two game matrices, one for each agent state:

$$A = \begin{bmatrix} w_g & -w_l - c_{st} \\ -w_l + b_g & -w_l + b_g - c_{st} \end{bmatrix} \qquad B = \begin{bmatrix} -w_l & w_g - c_{pt} \\ w_g & w_g - c_{pt} \end{bmatrix}$$

For the agent with the resource it is matrix A, where: the top row corresponds to $none_g$ action and the bottom row corresponds to *give* action. For the agent without the resource it is matrix B, where: the left column corresponds to $none_t$ action and the right column corresponds to *take* action.

2.2 Game Dynamics

In the previous section, we discussed what relations the game parameters should have in order to foster cooperation, while still maintaining the temptation to defect and explore. In this section, the focus will be on what equilibrium strategies the game has, namely the Pareto Optimal and the Nash Equilibrium. To this end, we will consider that agent strategies are described in terms of when to perform an action. We will analyse what equilibrium exists with different strategy types.

Strategies for this game can be modelled by the time agents play the *give* and *take* actions, respectively parameters t_{pg} and t_{pt}. Whenever two agents meet to play, their wealth gains will depend on the relation between their times to perform the actions. There are a total of 6 different cases (three of these have symmetric cases: $\mathcal{B}'$, $\mathcal{C}'$ and $\mathcal{E}'$). Table 1 shows examples of action sequences for all cases (with a window of 7 iterations).

From the analysis presented in [5] if follows that this game has no evolutionary stable strategy. Whenever we consider special cases such as agent's strategies being confined in cases $\mathcal{A}$ or in case $\mathcal{F}$, then agents should, respectively, give the resource as late as possible, and take the resource as late as possible. When we do not impose such restrictions, changes in agent's strategies will lead them to different cases. The possible transitions are as follows: from case $\mathcal{A}$ to either one of cases $\mathcal{B}$, $\mathcal{B}'$, or $\mathcal{D}$; from case $\mathcal{B}$ to $\mathcal{D}$; from case $\mathcal{C}$ to $\mathcal{E}$; from case $\mathcal{D}$ to case $\mathcal{B}'$; from case $\mathcal{E}$ to $\mathcal{D}$; from case $\mathcal{F}$ to either one of cases $\mathcal{D}$, $\mathcal{E}$, or $\mathcal{E}'$. These are not all the possible transitions, but rather the ones that we were able to

Table 1. Description of each case in terms of the action sequence interval. Time goes from left to right. Top agent starts with the resource.

case	action sequence	case	action sequence	case	action sequence
$\mathcal{A}$	--G---- ------G	$\mathcal{B}'$	--G---- --T---G	$\mathcal{C}'$	------- --T---G
$\mathcal{B}$	--G---T ------G	$\mathcal{D}$	--G---T --T---G	$\mathcal{E}'$	------T --T---G
$\mathcal{C}$	--G---T -------	$\mathcal{E}$	--G---T --T----	$\mathcal{F}$	------T --T----

conclude from the previous analysis. They also show that this game is similar to the rock-scissor-paper game.

The main result of these analyses is the set of relationships involving the game parameters. If we vary the game parameters, we alter the relationships and cause all strategies, except one, to be dominated (in the context of the relationships). This calls for a study of the game dynamics under several game parameters combinations. Analyses of the game matrix (in terms of when to play an action) yields several mixed Nash Equilibriums.

3 Game Implementation and Results

In order to cope with the multiple Pareto Optimal strategies, we have developed an agreement model slightly different from the one used in [6]. This model has 3 parameters related to the agreement model. They are: the time to exchange the resource, t_e^A; the probability to enter an agreement, p^A; and the probability to break an agreement, p_b^A. As before, this agent model yielded better results than the strategy without agreement.

The results were obtained from evolutionary runs. A population of 100 agents was evolved for 1000 generations. Two different population structures were used: a toroidal square grid (lattice), and a population with no neighbourhood properties (bag). This structure influenced game interactions and applicability of evolutionary operators. In the first they were constrained to the 4-Moore neighbourhood, while in the second they could occur between any pair of agents. The agent chromosome was composed of the time to perform the actions and the agreement parameters (only numeric values). Crossover picked values from two parents to create a new offspring. A crossover variant was only applied to similar parents. A similarity value was calculated based on the difference between the numeric values (of the chromosome) and the expected time they would perform their actions.

Different scenarios were considered. Scenarios differed on the evolutionary operators used and the inclusion of the agreement model (see table 2). For each scenario, different game parameters were tested. For each parameter combination 10 simulation runs were recorded. Table 3 shows the different parameter values. Crossover probability was set at 100%. The mutation operator added gaussian

Table 2. Conditions used in the different scenarios.

selection operator	tournament of 2, roulette whell
crossover operator	crossover on similars, normal crossover, not used
agreement model	used, not used

noise to the numeric values. Mutation probability was set at 5%. The selection operators used were roulette wheel and tournament of 2 agents. Agent's fitness was the average wealth gained in the games it participated. An agent played 3 games with a randomly selected group of 4 agents. On average, each agent played $3 \cdot 4 \cdot 2 = 12$ games.

Table 3. Parameters values used through the simulations.

parameter	value
w_g	5, 10, 15
w_l	0
b_g	0, 2, 4
c_{pt}	0, 5, 10, 15
c_{st}	5, 10, 15, 20
world	bag, lattice

We used as a result for each simulation run the average wealth of the entire population through all 1000 generations. The result of each parameter combination was the average of the simulation run result. This final result value was used to compare parameter combinations from different scenarios. Best results were obtained with the agreement model. Use of the crossover operators did not overall improve results. Tournament selection operator always yielded better results than roulette wheel with a few exceptions most notably $w_g = 5$, $c_{st} = 20$ and $b_g = 4$. Regarding game parameters, best results occurred when $w_g = 15$, $b_g = 4$, $c_{pt} = 0$, and $c_{st} = 5$. Generally, results varied proportionally to b_g and w_g. There was no clear trend regarding parameters c_{pt} and c_{st}.

4 Conclusions

We have presented a game whose dynamics resembles a rock-scissors-paper game, and contains multiple Pareto Optimal strategies. While its definition is simple, the dynamics that it shows are complex, due to the many pure and mixed Nash Equilibriums that can invade a population.

We have used the same framework and analysed the evolutionary dynamics under different conditions, namely how agents play the game (with or without agreements) and the effect of genetic operators. This is in contrast to others [10] that have used different games to study the same behaviours as we did. In [1] the authors have also studied cooperation but as an extension to the Iterated Prisoner Dilemma game.

We were able to obtain different results when we varied the game (possibility of agreements) and evolutionary conditions (different evolutionary operators). The way an agent is constrained to play a game affects its outcome. When agents are constrained to use the agreement protocol they are able to increase their wealth outcome. We have already observed the appearance of treason and exploitation. We will now carry on to study strategies to preclude or deal with it.

Acknowledgments. Pedro Mariano is financed by grant no. SFRH/BD/1219/2000 supported by FCT/MCT of Portugal.

References

1. Robert Axelrod. Promoting norms. In Robert Axelrod, editor, *The Complexity of Cooperation: Agent-Based Models of Competition and Collaboration*, Princeton Studies in Complexity, chapter 3. Princeton University Press, 1997.
2. Harald Bergland, Derek J. Clark, and Pål Andreas Pedersen. Rent-seeking and quota regulation of a renewable resource. *Resource and Energy Economics*, 24(3):263–279, 2002.
3. Björn Brembs. Chaos, cheating and cooperation: potential solutions to the prisoner's dilemma. *Oikos*, 76(1):14–24, 1996.
4. D. Marc Kilgour and Ariel Dinar. Are stable agreements for sharing international river waters now possible? Policy Research Working Paper WPS1474, The World Bank, 1995.
5. Pedro Mariano. Theoretical analysis of Give-Take game. PdD internal report, 2003.
6. Pedro Mariano and Luís Correia. The effect of agreements in a game with multiple strategies for cooperation. In Russell K. Standish, Mark A. Bedau, and Hussein A. Abbass, editors, *Artificial Life VIII*, pages 375–378. MIT Press, 2002.
7. Pedro Mariano and Luís Correia. A game to study coordination and cooperation. In Rino Falcone and Larry Korba, editors, *5th Workshop on Deception, Fraud and Trust in Agent Societies*, pages 101–112, 2002.
8. Martin A Nowak, S Bonhoeffer, and R M May. Spatial games and the maintenance of cooperation. *Proceedings of the National Academy of Sciences*, 91:4877–4881, 1994.
9. Santiago J. Rubio and Begoña Casino. A note on cooperative versus non-cooperative strategies in international pollution control. *Resource and Energy Economics*, 24(3):251–261, 2002.
10. Karl Sigmund, Christoph Hauert, and Martin A. Nowak. Reward and punishment in minigames. *Proceedings of the National Academy of Sciences*, 98(19):10757–10762, 2001.

Improving Self-Confidence: An Advise-Based Evolutionary Model

Ivette C. Martínez, Miguel A. Castro, and Carlos D. Castillo

Grupo de Inteligencia Artificial
Universidad Simón Bolívar
Caracas 1080-1, Venezuela
{martinez,mcastro}@ldc.usb.ve, carlos@gia.usb.ve

Abstract. A main concern in the simulation of adaptive behaviors is the characterization of organizational principles or architectures of adaptive behaviors in animals and synthetic animats. These characterizations are made through experimentation and analysis over well-defined models. In this work, we present a model to study the Vertical Cultural Transmission (**VCT**), as a catalytic factor over the interaction between individual learning and population evolution. Our model is based on the incorporation of advice, in the form of suggestions, as a way of information transmission between agents. An evolutionary reinforcement learning technique called classifier systems is used as the mechanism for individual learning. In particular, a recent variant based on the accuracy of the predictions made by the rules, called XCS, is applied. In order to control the environmental complexity, the Latent Energy Environments model, LEE, is adopted.
Finally, we present experimental results comparing three populations that are differentiated by their adaptation mechanisms: VCT learning, individual learning and evolution. For analise our results, we used self-organizing maps to clusterize two phenotypical traits that characterize our advise VCT model, belief and self-confidence.

Keywords: Animats, learning, evolution, cultural transmission, Baldwin Effect, genetic classifier systems, Latent Energy Environments, self-organizing map.

1 Introduction

A main influence factor over a species survival is its capacity to develop adaptation mechanisms to its environment. These mechanisms could operate at genetic and phenotypic levels. We call genetic adaptations those developed from changes to the genome over evolutionary time. Phenotypic adaptations are those that occur via plasticity, *i.e.*, learning and maturation, during an organism lifetime span. Since both genetic and phenotypic adaptations can act simultaneously, questions about how the interactions between them affect the individual adaptation and the species survival, arise in a natural way.

Fernando Moura Pires, Salvador Abreu (Eds.): EPIA 2003, LNAI 2902, pp. 89–100, 2003.

The first hypothesis to address these questions was proposed by Lamarck [12]. His hypothesis states that characteristics acquired during an individual lifetime are passed to its heirs, having a direct influence over the evolution of the species.

Even when strong scientific evidences invalidate Lamarck's model [24], it has been applied computationally to accelerate the solution of several problems by means of evolutionary computation [2,21].

In 1896 Baldwin [3], Morgan [19] and Osborn [20], independently, proposed a set of mechanisms by means of which the characteristics acquired by the individuals through learning are inherited in an indirect way. These mechanisms are known as the *Baldwin Effect.*

The Baldwin Effect is *the tendency of organisms that learn or acquire useful characteristics to be successful, leading to a higher probability of their reproduction and a fixation of their useful characteristics in the population despite the absence of direct inheritance of these characteristics* [4].

From the work made by Hinton and Nowlan [10] on modeling the relationship between learning and evolution using the Baldwin Effect, this effect began to be the object of great interest for evolutionary computation, adaptive behavior and artificial life communities.

Some evolutionary biologists state that human beings have reached a greater level of cognitive development than other animals due to the fact that they coexists with their ancestors a quarter of their expected lifetime [5], having a greater exposition to their ancestors' behavioral characteristics. This coexistence would facilitate the acquisition of these characteristics via imitation, in a broad sense of the word: *Memes propagate themselves in the meme pool by leaping from brain to brain via a process which, in the broad sense, can be called imitation* [8].

The ability of learning from others in its diverse manifestations, from social learning [1] to cultural Transmission [6] and memetics [8], introduce a new source of learning that can reduce the learning cost for the individual. Then this ability could modify the form, in which phenotypic adaptations influence genetic adaptations.

In 1995 Cecconi, Menczer and Belew [7] introduced indirect learning by imitation in a Baldwinian model. They showed experimentally how the maturation age is delayed when organisms are able to learn from the behavior of their parents by imitation. The idea of taking advice or suggestions in learning was introduced by McCarthy and worked by several authors [13], but until this moment it had not been considered from the point of view of the Vertical Cultural Transmission as a source of phenotypic plasticity and its effect over population evolution.

From the hypothesis that cultural transmission influences positively the population adaptation, we considered the creation of a baldwinian model for studying the effects of the familiar coexistence, and the information transmission implied by it, on an agent adaptation to its environment, and the evolution of the community to which it belongs. This model allows us to study the interactions between learning and evolution with the incorporation of Cultural Transmission, in its vertical modality, from parents to children, as a learning source [6].

To achieve our goal we have compared the performance of two kinds of individuals. The first ones, agents whose actions are only product of an internal decision and their learning is made via direct reinforcements. The second ones, individuals whose actions are influenced by suggestions of their ancestors. In other words, these agent's learning are reinforced in an observational, indirect way, *i.e.*, they have social learning capacity [15]. Learning within each individual is implemented by using the learning classifier systems called XCS [25], a derivation of those developed by Holland [11].

2 Proposed Model

The description of our decentralized model is made by characterizing the individuals and the interrelations between them. Russell [22] states that in order to characterize an agent, it is necessary to describe its perceptions, actions, objectives, and environment. At this point we present the description based on Russell's terms of the model's agents.

2.1 Agents

Agents are **animats**, *simulated animals or real robots whose rules of behavior are inspired by those in animals. They are usually equipped with sensors, with actuators, and with a behavioral control architecture that allow them to react or respond to variations in its environment* [17].

2.2 Perception

An Animat will sense its environment through a vision organ. This will allow the animat to determine accurately, *i.e.*, without noise, the content of v units of measurement (cells) of the world in the direction of its vision (front), v cells to its left, and v to its right. In addition, agents can sense the nutritional elements contained in their "stomach". Figure 1 illustrates one of the possible results of sensing the environment by an agent.

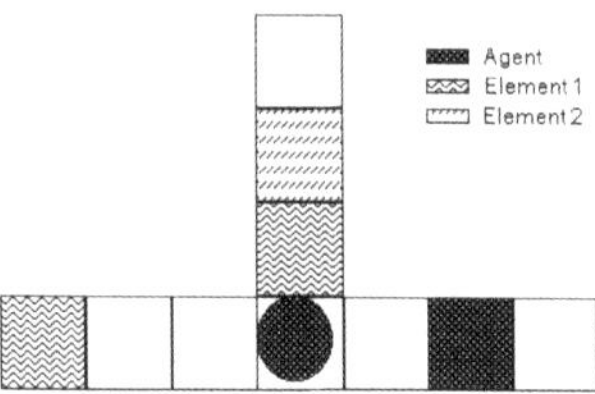

Fig. 1. Example of vision of an agent, agent has vision range $3 (v = 3)$.

The agent of figure 1 has vision range 3, $v = 3$, and perceives the presence of an *Element*1 in its third cell to the left and in its first front cell; it also sees an *Element*2 in its second cell in front, and another *Agent* in its second cell to the right. The third cell to the right is not visible because agents are opaque obstacles. This agent also sense that it has an *Element*1 in its stomach.

Perceived elements are translated into an input *message* to the behavioral control architecture. The length of the messages is fixed and depends on the agent's vision range and the number of elements types of the environment. The general structure of a message for agents with vision range three for two types of elements is shown in figure 2. This figure also shows the binary translation of figure 1's perceptions.

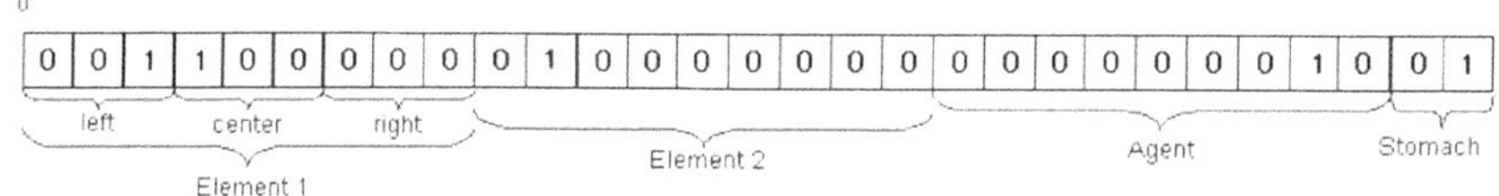

Fig. 2. Structure of a message, $v = 3$, *numberelements* $= 2$.

2.3 Actions

Animats can act over the environment by making some of the following actions: advance (move 1 cell forward), turn right (turn 90° clockwise), turn left (turn 90° counter clockwise), eat, and reproduce. Motion actions (advance, turn right and turn left), will produce a reduction of the animat's energy level.

If in the position resulting from these actions the animat finds a resource that can be digested, *i.e.*, can be combined with one of the resources stored in the animat's stomach, automatically the eat action is triggered. Agents' stomach capacity is fixed, currently they can store two elements of each kind. Eating would produce a change in the animat's energy level according to a certain table of reactions, as shown in table 1.

Table 1. LEE Reactions table. B_1 and B_2 are elements types, $\beta = 0$ is a negative reinforcement constant, and $E = 5$ is a reward constant.

	B_1	B_2
B_1	$-\beta E$	E
B_2	E	$-\beta E$

If the animat achieves certain energy level, $\alpha = 100$ and has reached its sexual maturation age, $MA = 50$, it will reproduce in an asexual manner.

2.4 Goal

The animat's objective is to survive, that is, to maintain its energy level over 0. In order to maintain or increase their energy level agents must learn which combinations of environment elements give them a greater amount of energy.

2.5 Environment

The environment is based on the model of Latent Energy Environments, LEE, proposed by Menczer and Belew [16]. The LEE model has been used because it allows the construction of environments of "measured complexity." The environment complexity is measured through a careful definition of the energy consumed by organisms and the work they need to invest in order to obtain it.

Our animats, as well as those proposed in LEE, live in a shared environment, consisting of a rectangular grid (25×25) with toroidal edge conditions. Each cell of the grid can hold an animat or a nutritional element.

In the LEE model the idea of food that should be consumed to increase the animat's energy is replaced by the notion of "atomic elements" that must be combined by the organisms to obtain the energy necessary to survive. Let $B_1, ..., B_n$ be the possible elements in the environment. A reaction has the form: $B_i + B_j \rightarrow E_{ij} + R_{ij}$. Where E_{ij} is the energy resulting from the reaction between elements B_i and B_j; and R_{ij} is the residual product. Our model doesn't consider residual products.

The maximum quantity of organisms that can be sustained in an environment, or *carrying capacity*, can be determined from the amount of available resources and the energy produced by the reactions: $p_{max} = rE/c$, where c is the agents' motion action cost ($c = 0.1$), E is the energy that can be gained according to the reactions table ($E = 5$) (see table 1) and r is the nutritional elements' growing rate ($r = 3$). For the current model values, $p_{max} = 150$.

The expected size of a population ($K = 75$) with a random walk behavior can be determined by means of the equation: $K = rE(1 - \beta)/2c$.

3 Control Model

3.1 XCS Agents

Initially an action selection decision, given an environment state, will be made by means of a *XCS*, genetic classifier systems based on accuracy [25].

The XCS classifier systems, as well as Holland's, are domain independent adaptive learning systems. Its main distinguishing features are the basing of classifier fitness on the accuracy of classifier reward prediction instead of the prediction itself, and the use of a niche genetic algorithm, i.e., a GA (genetic algorithm) that operates on a subset of the classifier population.

A classifier is a compact representation of a complex set of environment states. Rules have the form $< condition > \rightarrow < action >$. Conditions are strings of length l in the alphabet $\{0, 1, *\}$. Their structure corresponds to those of the messages that appear in figure 2. A classifier's condition satisfies a message if its condition matches the input message. A condition c match message m if and only if: $\forall i, (1 \leq i \leq l) \rightarrow \Pi_i(c) = \Pi_i(m) \vee \Pi_i(c) = '*'$. Actions are also fixed-length strings in the alphabet $\{0, 1\}$.

XCS are composed by three subsystems: a performance system, an evaluation system, and a rule discovery system.

The performance system takes an input from the environment, selects an action and transforms it in an output message. Structurally a performance system consists of a finite population $[P]$ of classifiers. The basic execution cycle of the performance system is as follows[25]:

1. Obtain the single input string from the environment.
2. Form the match set $[M]$ of classifiers whose condition matches the input string.
3. Select an action based on the prediction of the classifiers in $[M]$.
4. Form the action set $[A]$ of classifiers in $[M]$ which advocated the action selected in 3.
5. Translate the selected action into the output of the system.

The learning system takes feedback signals from the environment and updates the values of the four parameters (prediction, prediction error, accuracy, and fitness) that replace the traditional fitness of a tradidional Classifier System (CS). This change allows a more complete $State \times Actions \rightarrow Prediction$ mapping than traditional CSs.

The rule discovery system uses a genetic algorithm in order to create new rules. XCS's rule discovery system has two operations: niche genetic algorithm and covering. The niche genetic algorithm acts over the Action Set $[A]$, choosing random parents in proportion to the rules' fitness. Offsprings are copies of the parents, modified by crossover and mutation. Covering is triggered when the matches set is empty or its media prediction is a small fraction of the population [P] average prediction. Covering creates a new classifier whose condition matches the current input message. Its action is generated randomly.

3.2 VCT Agents

Vertical Cultural Transmission agents (**VCT agents**) ask for/receive suggestions of their ancestors. Action selection for VCT agents will not only depend on the XCS proposed action, but also takes into account suggestions from their ancestors using the following mechanism:

1. The agent proposes an action, A_1, with force F_1, where F_1 is the product of the action prediction, P_{A_1}, by the "self confidence", *sc*, of the agent.
2. The ancestor proposes an action A_2 with a force F_2, where F_2 is the "belief" of the agent in his ancestor, *bel*.
3. An action is selected from A_1 and A_2, ramdomly, proportional to the forces of those actions.

4. If A_1 is selected, the agent's XCS reinforcement algorithm is executed and its *self confidence*, sc, is updated using this equation:

$$sc = \begin{cases} sc + \delta' \Delta E & \text{if } \Delta E > 0 \\ sc - \delta & \text{otherwise.} \end{cases}$$

Where δ is a penalty constant, $0 < \delta << 1$, δ' is a reward constant ($\delta' > \delta$), and ΔE is the animat's energy variation.
5. If A_2 is selected, the animat's *belief* in his ancestor, bel, is updated using the following equation:

$$bel = \begin{cases} bel + \delta' \Delta E & \text{if } \Delta E > 0 \\ bel - \delta & \text{otherwise.} \end{cases}$$

The *belief* (bel) is a value that allows an agent to estimate how good the actions suggested by his ancestor have been. The *self confidence* (sc) is an estimate of how good the self-proposed actions have been. The values of bel and sc vary between 0 and 1.

4 Self-Organizing Maps

The Kohonen self-organizing map (SOM) is an unsupervised learning algorithm that creates a set of prototype vectors representing the data set and carries out a topology preserving projection of the prototypes from a high-dimensional input space onto a low-dimensional space [23].

In our case, each unit of the Kohonen map is associated with two time series (*belief(t)* and *self confidence(t)*) that represent parameters that characterize observational learning in these VCT agents. With self organizing maps we expect to observe serveral classes of emergent behaviors of the VCT agents. In particular these parameters modify the use that is given to parental advices.

The SOM consists of a regular two-dimensinal grid of map units. Each unit i is represented by a prototype vector $m_i = [m_{i1}, ..., m_{ik}]$, where k is the input vector dimension, in our case 40. The units are conected to adjacent ones by neighborhood relation.

The SOM is trained iteratively. At each iteration, a reference vector x is randomly chosen from the input data set. Distances between x and all the prototype vectors are computed. The best-matching unit, which is denoted by b, is the map unit with prototype closest to x.

$$||x - m_d|| = min_i ||x - m_i||$$

The update rule for the prototype vector of unit i is

$$m_i(t+1) = m_i(t) + \eta(t) h_{bi}(t) [||x - m_i(t)||]$$

where t is the time, $\eta(t)$ is the adaptation coefficient, and $h_{bi}(t)$ is the neighborhood kernel centered on the winner unit:

$$h_{bi} = exp\left(-\frac{||r_b - r_i||^2}{2\sigma^2(t)}\right)$$

where r_i and r_b are the position of unit b and i on the SOM grid. Both $\sigma(t)$ and $\eta(t)$ decrease monotonically with time.

For a complete survey of self-organizing maps see [9].

The number of clusters in the Kohonen algorithm is chosen through the observation of the homogeneity of the clusters.

5 Experiments

We have developed a software application, *VCTApp*, over the Swarm platform for multiagent systems [18].

We made experiments with 4 types of agents, according to their behavior control's architecture: random, individual learners (**XCS**), non learning XCS, and Vertical Cultural Transmission enabled agents (**VCT**). Results correspond to an average over 10 runs for each experimental group. For all experimental groups the initial population size is 300.

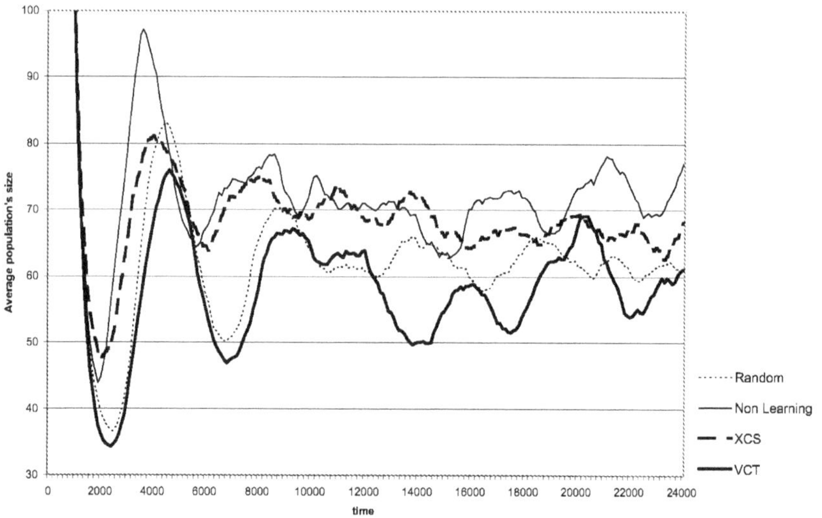

Fig. 3. Average number of individuals graph.

Figure 3 shows the temporal evolution of the average number of individuals for the 4 populations considered. The population size provides an initial measurement of the population's quality (the one proposed by LEE).

Other measures like energy average, explain some particularities observed in the population's graph, as described in [14].

It can be observed that all populations go through a transient period, characterized by harmonic fluctuations. These stages are surpassed around time 8000.

The XCS and non-learning XCS populations are better than the populations of random agents, even though all of them oscillate below the theoretical estimation for random populations.

The size of the populations of non-learning XCS agents improves more rapidly because its genotypic adaptation is faster, since only those organisms with a good genetic composition are able to reproduce.

The incorporation of individual learning causes a decrease of the variations of the populations size, since learning increases the number of agents capable of surviving in their environment.

5.1 Beliefs and Self Confidences

The proposed VCT learning algorithm is based on suggestions. An agent takes these suggestions into account depending in its belief on its predecessor's suggestions and the confidence on its own actions. An agent uses these two decision parameters *belief* and *self confidence* to decide the action to be executed. If his *belief* is greater than his *self confidence* the agent will tend to execute the action suggested by his predecessor. We use *belief(t)* to denote the value of the parameter *belief* at time t and $sc(t)$ to denote the value of the *self confidence* at time t. The value of both parameters at t_0 is 0.5.

It is expected that during the first "epochs" of life of an agent, the suggestions of its predecessor accelerate the adaptation of the agent. And after a certain time the agent's self confidence stabilizes at a "high" value. This means that the agent becomes more independent of parental suggestions.

We expect to find several classes of emergent behaviors of the *belief* and *self confidence* values. Then we need a clusterization algorithm to obtain an insight into the cluster structure of the data.

We used here a Kohonen map algorithm for finding prototype behaviors of beliefs and self confidences. Each prototype can be interpreted as a common behavior of the parameters. The prototypes are local averages of the data and, therefore, less sensitive to random variations than the original data. Each cluster prototype will allow us to understand how the suggestions are used by agents, and to obtain information about the effects of vertical cultural transmission.

The number of clusters in the Kohonen algorithm is chosen through the observation of the homogeneity of the clusters by visual inspection of prototypes. Figure 4 shows the prototypes obtained for a 3×3 Kohonen map.

The number of hits, i.e, individual with beliefs and self confidence behaviors similar to the prototype, in each map unit is showed in figure 5.

In figure 4 clusters (b) and (g) have beliefs over self confidence, these two classes account for 15.7% of the population. This kind of agents mainly base their actions on their predecessor's suggestions all their observed lifetime. This is not a common pattern, compared to the group of the populations (77%) (clusters (a),(c),(d),(f),(h), and (i)) that have a self confidence over 0.9 before epoch 4000.

Clusters (a),(c),(d),(f),(h), and (i), reach an stable value of self confidence, then they barely use their parents suggestion.

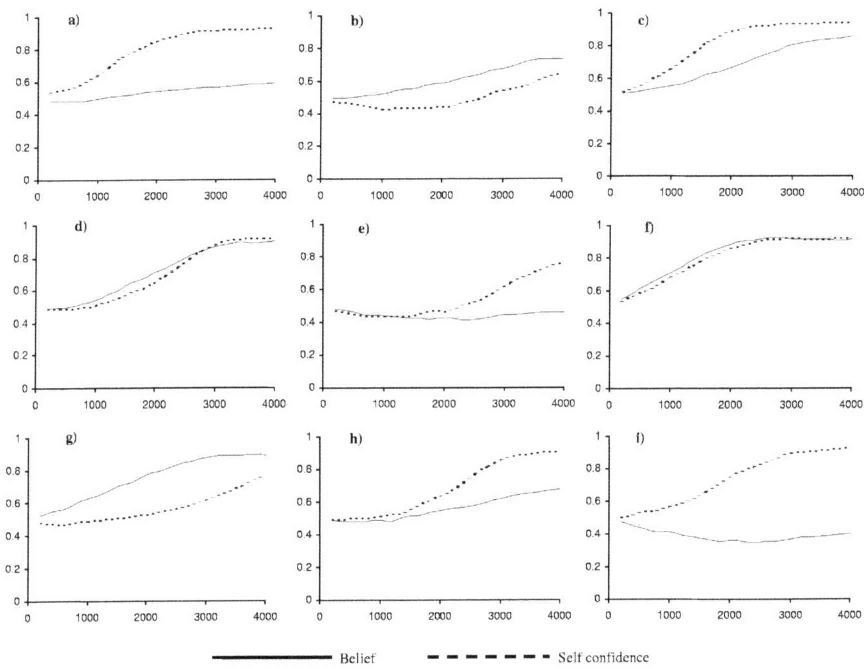

Fig. 4. Prototypes obtained from the population using a 3x3 Kohonen map.

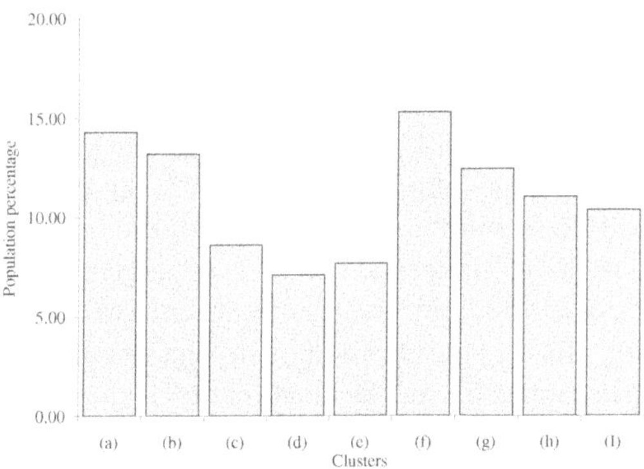

Fig. 5. Percentages of the population that belong to the clusters of fig 4.

Individuals in clusters (d) and (f) have similar values for self confidence and belief and account for 24.2% of the population. For these clusters, agents and their predecessors have a high level of success in their decisions. These individuals are descendants of parents with good performance and good genes.

6 Conclusions

In this work we have proposed a model for studying the effects of vertical cultural transmission on the adaptation of agents to the environment as well as the evolution of the populations to which these agents belong.

This model is characterized by the use of an adaptive mechanism of advice as the mechanism for modeling the vertical cultural transmission. It is also charaterized by the use of latent energy environments, *LEE*, to control the environment's complexity. Agents' individual learning is implemented by means of an adaptive learning system, *XCS*, that have generalization capacities and allow to make complete mappings of pairs $(states, action)$ in *prediction*. An indirect relation between individual learning and population evolution also differentiates the model, as proposed by the Baldwin Effect.

Experiments showed that, in this particular environment, individual as well as social learning decelerates populations evolution.

These results seem to indicate that individual learning as much as social learning does not guarantee a greater genetic diversity, since they diminish the size of the populations, contradicting one of the assumptions on which Baldwin Effect is based, the one that states that individual plasticity favors population plasticity.

As future work, we will study the influence of both individual an social learning over genetic diversity of the populations. We also want to study other fitness measures as individual's energy levels and reproduction rates. Finally we propose the incorporation of other ways of social learning like the oblique cultural transmission and horizontal cultural transmission.

References

1. E. Avital and E. Jablonka. Social Learning and the evolution of behavior. *Animal Behavior*, 48:1195–1999, 1994.
2. R.L. Axtell, R. Axelrod, and M. Epstein, J.and Cohen. Aligning Simulation Models: A case Study and Results. *Computational and Mathematical Organization Theory*, 1(2), 1996.
3. J. Baldwin. A new factor in evolution. *American Naturalist*, 30:441–451, 1896.
4. R Belew and M. Mitchel, editors. *Adaptative Individuals in Evolving Populations: Models and Algorithms*, volume XXIII of *SFI Studies in Sciences of Complexity*. Addison Wesley, 1996.
5. S. Blackmore. *The meme machine.* Oxford University Press, 1999.
6. L. Cavalli-Sforza and M. Feldman. *Cultural Transmision and evolution: A quantitative approach.* Princeton University Press, 1981.
7. F. Cecconi, F. Menczer, and R. Belew. Maturation and the evolution of imitative learning in artificial organisms. *Adaptative Behaviour*, 4:29–50, 1996.
8. R. Dawkins. *The Selfish Gene.* Oxford University Press, Oxford, 1976.
9. B. Fritzke. Some competitive learning methods, 1997.
10. G. Hinton and S. Nowlan. How learning can guide evolution. *Complex Systems*, 1:495–502, 1987.

11. J.H. Holland. *Adaptation in Natural and Artificial Systems*. MIT Press, Cambridge, MA, 1975.
12. J. B. Lamarck. *Zoological Philosophy*. Chicago University Press, 1809, 1984.
13. R. Maclin and J. Shavlik. Incorporating advise into agents that learn from reinforcements. In *Proceedings of the Twelve National Conference on Artificial Intelligence*, pages 694–699, 1994.
14. I. C. Martinez. Un modelo descentralizado de la transmisión cultural vertical. Master's thesis, Universidad Simón Bolívar, 1999.
15. M. Matarić. Learning to behave socially. In D. Cliff, P. Husbands, J. A. Meyer, and S. W. Wilson, editors, *From Animals to Animats 3: Proceedings of the Third International conference on Simulation of Adaptative Behavior (SAB 94)*. MIT Press/Bradford Books, 1994.
16. F. Menczer and R. Belew. Latent energy environments. In Belew and Mitchel [4].
17. J. Meyer and A. Guillot. From sab90 to sab94: Four years of animat research. In D. Cliff, S. Husbands, J. Meyer, and S. Wilson, editors, *From Animals to Animats 3: Proceedings of the Third International Conference of Adaptative Behavior*. MIT Press/Bradford Books, 1994.
18. N. Minar, R. Buckhart, C. Langton, and M. Askenazi. The swarm simulation system: A toolkit for building multi-agents systems. Working Paper 96-046-042, Santa Fe Institute, Santa Fe, NM, 1996. Disponible como: http://www.santafe.edu/projects/swarm/swarmdocs/swarmdoc.html.
19. C Morgan. On modification and variation. *Science*, 4:786–789, 1896.
20. H. Osborn. Ontogenic and phylogenic variation. *Science*, 4:786–789, 1896.
21. Brian J. Ross. A lamarckian evolution strategy for genetic algorithms. In Lance D. Chambers, editor, *Practical Handbook of Genetic Algorithms: Complex Coding Systems*, volume 3, pages 1–16. CRC Press, Boca Raton, Florida, 1999.
22. S. Russell and P. Norvig. *Artificial Intelligence. A modern Approach.* Prentice Hall, 1995.
23. J. Vesanto and E. Alhoniemi. Clustering of the self-organizing map. *IEEE-NN*, 11(3):586, May 2000.
24. A. Weissman. *The Germ-Plasm: A Theory of Heredity*. Scribners, New York, 1893.
25. S. W. Wilson. Classifier fitness based on accuracy. *Evolutionary Computation*, 3(2):149–175, 1995.

Solving Set Partitioning Problems with Global Constraint Propagation*

Ricardo Saldanha and Ernesto Morgado

Instituto Superior Técnico, www.ist.utl.pt
SISCOG – Sistemas Cognitivos, Lda., www.siscog.pt

Abstract. We propose a constraint-based approach for solving set partitioning problems. We show that an efficient, open and easily modifying model is obtained by using a constraint propagator that is: *global*, in the sense that it enforces consistency between local knowledge (such as variable domains) and global knowledge (such as the optimisation goal); and *dynamic*, in the sense that it propagates the decisions taken during the search process. This propagator derives new constraints based on the existing ones by efficiently chaining a set of propagation rules that we present here and demonstrate. This propagator can be used not only to prune efficiently the search space, but also to prove in certain cases that a given solution is optimal. This approach was tested with five crew duty scheduling problems supplied by two operators from the railway and bus domains. Results were compared with the ones obtained with an approach that is a good representative of the industrial state-of-the-art.

1 Introduction

The set partitioning problem (SPP) is a well-known problem in discrete mathematics and it can be stated as follows:

Definition 1. *Given a set of elements* $\mathbf{E}$ *and a set of predefined parts* $\overline{\mathbf{E}} \subseteq 2^{\mathbf{E}}$ *(where* $2^{\mathbf{E}}$ *stands for the powerset of* $\mathbf{E}$*), find a partition* $\mathbf{\Pi}$ *of* $\mathbf{E}$ *such that each* $x \in \mathbf{\Pi}$ *is in* $\overline{\mathbf{E}}$ *and* $|\mathbf{\Pi}|$ *is minimal.*

By assigning different meanings to $\mathbf{E}$ and $\overline{\mathbf{E}}$, the SPP can model many real-life problems, such as crew scheduling, vehicle routing and logistics. For instance, if $\mathbf{E}$ represents a set of transportation activities and if $\overline{\mathbf{E}}$ represents a set of duties, the SPP becomes the crew duty scheduling problem (CDSP). A *duty* is a set of activities that can be performed by a crewmember during a labour period, that is, a period of time inside which a lot of physical, operational and labour constraints apply, such as: the period must start and end in the same station, it should not be too large, it must include a meal break, there must be enough gap between each two consecutive activities, etc. In formal terms, a duty is any

* This research was supported by Fundação para a Ciência e a Tecnologia in cooperation with the European Social Fund, by Instituto Superior Técnico and IDMEC.

Fernando Moura Pires, Salvador Abreu (Eds.): EPIA 2003, LNAI 2902, pp. 101–115, 2003.

set of activities x such that $\pi(x)$ is true, where π is a predicate, called *duty predicate*, that returns true *iff* its argument satisfies all the physical, operational and labour constraints.

As shown in Balas & Padberg [1], the SPP was first solved with integer linear programming (ILP) techniques, traditionally used in operations research (OR). More recent developments (see Caprara *et al.* [4] and Kroon & Fischetti [10]) show that large crew scheduling instances of the SPP can be solved efficiently with these techniques.

Heuristic search techniques were also applied to crew scheduling instances of the SPP by Morgado & Martins [12,13]. They developed a crew scheduling system called CREWS^{TM}, which uses hierarchical abstract operators, a modified version of the beam search algorithm (see Bisiani [2]), and a non-traditional problem definition given by:

Definition 2. *Given a set of elements* $\mathbf{E}$ *and a part predicate* π*, find a partition* $\mathbf{\Pi}$ *of* $\mathbf{E}$ *such that each part* $x \in \mathbf{\Pi}$ *satisfies* $\pi(x)$ *and* $|\mathbf{\Pi}|$ *is minimal.*

This definition becomes the statement of the CDSP if $\mathbf{E}$ and $\pi(x)$ represent respectively a set of transportation activities and the duty predicate. Comparing Definitions 1 and 2, the main difference is that the former receives $\mathbf{E}$ and $\overline{\mathbf{E}}$ as explicit inputs, and the part predicate π as an implicit input (as long as $\pi(x) \equiv x \in \overline{\mathbf{E}}$); and the latter receives $\mathbf{E}$ and π as explicit inputs, and the $\overline{\mathbf{E}}$ as an implicit input (as long as $\overline{\mathbf{E}} \equiv \{x \subseteq \mathbf{E} \mid \pi(x)\}$).

By using Definition 2, the CREWS^{TM} system does not have to separate the computation in the two traditional phases: the *part generation* phase, where $\overline{\mathbf{E}}$ is generated; and the *part selection* phase, where the space of different combinations of parts is explored until a solution is found.

Constraint-based (CB) techniques were first applied to the SPP by Guerinik & Van Caneghem [8] and later by Müller [14] and Curtis *et al.* [5]. Differences and similarities caracterize the three approaches.

The traditional problem definition given in 1 is adopted in all cases. This means that the process of obtaining a solution is devised in the two traditional phases: part generation and part selection.

Different ways of modelling the problem were considered: while in Guerinik & Van Caneghem [8] and Müller [14] the variables represent parts and the values *yes/no* decisions, in Curtis *et al.* [5] the variables represent elements (of $\mathbf{E}$) and the values parts.

All the three approaches perform constraint propagation, but in a way we characterise as non-global, because it does not enforce consistency between local knowledge (such as variable domains) and global knowledge (such as the optimisation goal treated as a soft constraint). This propagation regards only set partitioning constraints (i.e. each element should be covered by exactly one part) and it is performed either statically before the part selection phase (Guerinik & Van Caneghem [8] and Müller [14]) or dynamically during the part selection phase (Curtis *et al.* [5]).

In order to compensate the limitations of a non global constraint propagation, Guerinik & Van Caneghem [8] and Curtis *et al.* [5] use mathematical programming techniques to obtain global knowledge to guide the search process and prune the search space further. They create a "shadowing" ILP model equivalent to the constraint programming model. During the search process, this ILP model is updated dynamically, to reflect the decisions taken in each partial solution, and its linear programming (LP) relaxation is solved. If the relaxation is infeasible, a dead end is detected. If an optimal solution exists, it can be used to reduce further the variable domains and to implement efficient variable and value ordering heuristics.

The introduction of the "shadowing" ILP model brings the possibility of solving considerable larger problems in a reasonable amount of time, but it also brings some limitations. Since ILP models behave like black box systems, part of the solving process becomes opaque to the common end user. Since ILP models are less expressive than CB models and since adding a new constraint implies changing coherently the two models (otherwise they will not cooperate properly), the type of constraints that can be added to the overall model becomes more limited and the process of changing the model more complicated.

In order to overcome this limitations we propose a pure CB approach centred on global and dynamic constraint propagation.

2 The CSP Model

We propose a constraint satisfaction problem (CSP) model based on the non-traditional problem statement given in Definition 2. As in Morgado & Martins [13], this model formulates the SPP as the following assignment problem: given a set of elements $\mathbf{E} = \{e_1, ..., e_E\}$ and a set of part labels $\mathbf{P} = \{p_1, ..., p_P\}$, find an assignment between $\mathbf{E}$ and $\mathbf{P}$ such that each element is assigned to one part label, the set of elements assigned to each part label satisfies π and the number of part labels with assigned elements is minimum. Notice that the number P of part labels available can be as large as necessary to ensure the problem is solvable. Since part label and part are strictly related concepts we will address both of them with the term "part".

The variables $\mathbf{V} = \{v_1, ..., v_E\}$ of the model are associated with the elements (as in Curtis *et al.* [5]). Each variable v_i is associated with the element $e_i \in \mathbf{E}$ and has $\mathbf{P}$ as its initial domain. The instantiation of v_i with p_j is denoted by $\bar{v}_i = p_j$ and represents the assignment between the element e_i and the part p_j.

When distinction is not important, we will use the term "element" to designate either an element in itself or its corresponding variable. When that distinction is important we will use functions $v(x)$ and $e(x)$ which return respectively the variable associated with a given element and the element associated with a given variable. We also define functions $\mathbf{V}(x) \equiv \{v(y) \mid y \in x\}$ and $\mathbf{E}(x) \equiv \{e(y) \mid y \in x\}$.

The variables $\mathbf{V}$ are related by a set $\mathbf{C}$ of constraints originally formed by a single global constraint denoted by $c(v_1, ..., v_E)$. This constraint is consistent with instantiations assigning parts to elements in such a way that each set of elements assigned to the same part satisfies π. This corresponds to the following definition of the constraint's predicate:

$$\widehat{c}(\bar{v}_1, ..., \bar{v}_E) = \bigwedge_{p \in \mathbf{P}} \pi(\{e(x) \mid \bar{x} = p, x \in \mathbf{V}\}) \ . \tag{1}$$

We will assume that π is regular, that is:

Definition 3. *A part predicate π is regular iff for every $x, y \subseteq \mathbf{E}$:*

$$\pi(x \cup y) \Rightarrow \pi(x) \ . \tag{2}$$

When π is regular the following proposition applies:

Proposition 1. *For any instantiation such that $\bar{x}_1 = \cdots = \bar{x}_n$ (i.e. assigns the elements $e(x_1), ..., e(x_n)$ to the same part), the following implication holds if π is regular:*

$$\widehat{c}(\bar{v}_1, ..., \bar{v}_E) \ \wedge \ \bar{x}_1 = \cdots = \bar{x}_n \Rightarrow \pi[\mathbf{E}(\{x_1, ..., x_n\})] \ . \tag{3}$$

Proof. Applying the proposition $a \wedge b \Rightarrow a$ to the righthand side of 1, we have $\widehat{c}(\bar{v}_1, ..., \bar{v}_E) \Rightarrow \pi(\{e(x) \mid \bar{x} = \bar{x}_1, x \in \mathbf{V}\})$. Since $\bar{x}_1 = \cdots = \bar{x}_n$, the righthand side of the implication can be written in the form $\pi[\mathbf{E}(\{x_1, ..., x_N\}) \cup \mathbf{E}']$. According to 2 we obtain $\pi[\mathbf{E}(\{x_1, ..., x_N\}) \cup \mathbf{E}'] \Rightarrow \pi[\mathbf{E}(\{x_1, ..., x_N\})]$, which proves the proposition. □

The variables $\mathbf{V}$, the values $\mathbf{P}$ and the constraints $\mathbf{C}$ form a constraint hypergraph, which we denote by $H \equiv (\mathbf{V}, \mathbf{P}, \mathbf{C})$ and represent graphically as shown in Fig. 1 for the case where $\mathbf{V} = \{v_1, v_2, v_3\}$, $\mathbf{P} = \{p_1, p_2\}$ and $\mathbf{C} = \{c(v_1, v_2, v_3)\}$.

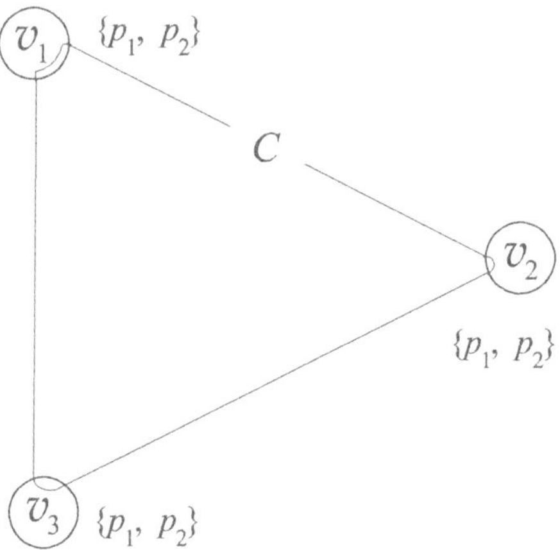

Fig. 1. Hypergaph representing the problem of assigning three elements to two parts.

With respect to the problem statement 2, the proposed model contains symmetries because the space of alternative instantiations is much larger than the space of alternative partitions of **E**. For each partition of size n there are $P!/(P-n)!$ different instantiations representing the same partition. We will see later how to avoid generating symmetrical solutions.

3 Solving the Optimisation Problem

Since our global constraint propagation framework was designed to solve satisfaction problems, the first step is to decompose the optimisation problem into a sequence of satisfaction problems. This is easily done by using a well-known technique which Marriott & Stuckey [11] called *optimistic partitioning*. The following algorithm is an application of this technique:

1. Set $P_1 = 0$ and $P_2 = E$ as an initial lower and upper bound for the optimal number of parts;
2. find a solution with a number of parts no greater than $P_{12} = (P_1 + P_2) \div 2$;
3. if a solution is found, then set $P_2 \leftarrow P_{12}$; otherwise, set $P_1 \leftarrow P_{12} + 1$;
4. if $P_1 = P_2$, return P_1 as the optimal solution; otherwise, go back to 2.

The number of iterations of this algorithm is $O(\log E)$, which means that the global complexity depends mostly on the complexity of the procedure used to solve each satisfaction problem.

4 Solving the Satisfaction Problems

Our approach consists of exploring step-by-step different ways of building sets of parts until a feasible set is found. In each step we decide whether two (or more) particular elements will or not be combined in the same part. Instead of representing these two options in terms of variable instantiations, we represent them in terms of constraints that are added to the constraint hypergraph: equality constraints in the first option, and difference constraints in the second one. It can be shown (see Saldanha [17]) that by solving the problem in this way we are able to avoid the symmetries that we mentioned above.

We decompose our approach in three modules: the decision operator, the constraint propagator and the search strategy. The first determines the composition of the decision tree and typically concerns variable and value ordering heuristics, the second prunes the decision tree and the latter determines how that tree is traversed.

While in traditional CSP approaches the decision operator instantiates variables and the constraint propagator reduces domains, in this approach they both add new constraints to the constraint hypergraph: the decision operator adds *heuristic constraints*, and the constraint propagator *derived constraints*. Unlike the latter, the former may be inconsistent with the rest of the other constraints, since they are not generated based on exact knowledge. Both heuristic and derived constraints are chosen from two families of constraints: n-ary differences and n-ary equalities.

The n-ary differences are denoted by $\neq(x_1, ..., x_n)$ (where $n \geq 2$) and express the fact that the elements $e(x_1), ..., e(x_n)$ must be assigned to exactly n different parts. Also denoted as `alldifferent` (see Régin [15]), this constraint is consistent with the instantiations satisfying the following predicate:

$$\widehat{\neq}(\bar{x}_1, ..., \bar{x}_n) \equiv \bigwedge_{j=1}^{n} \bigwedge_{k=j+1}^{n} \bar{x}_j \neq \bar{x}_k \ . \tag{4}$$

The n-ary equalities are denoted by $=(x_1, ..., x_n)$ (where $n \geq 2$) and state that the elements $e(x_1), ..., e(x_n)$ must share the same part. This corresponds to the following constraint predicate definition:

$$\widehat{=}(\bar{x}_1, ..., \bar{x}_n) \equiv \bar{x}_1 = \cdots = \bar{x}_n \ . \tag{5}$$

Since equality and difference constraints are both symmetrical relations, in order to avoid redundancies, we force them to be written in canonical form, which means that the corresponding arguments must be sorted by increasing value of the variable subscript (e.g. $\neq(v_1, v_2)$ is canonical, but $\neq(v_2, v_1)$ is not). In order to convert any constraint (canonical or not) into a canonical one we use an asterisk. For instance, $c(v_2, v_1, v_3)^*$ and $c(v_1, v_3, v_2)^*$ are exactly the same as $c(v_1, v_2, v_3)$.

In the next sections we describe in detail each of the three above mentioned components.

5 The Constraint Propagator

The constraint propagator is the key element of this approach. Based on the existing constraints it produces derived constraints by forward chaining a set of propagation rules. As far as the authors are aware, these rules and the way they are chained are original material. Once added to the constraint hypergraph, the derived constraints increase its consistency level, making it more backtrack free.

5.1 Propagation Rules

The first rule derives binary differences and follows directly from Proposition 1.

Rule 1 *The following inference is valid for $x, y \in \mathbf{V}$:*

$$c(v_1, ..., v_E) \in \mathbf{C} \ \wedge \ \neg\pi(\{e(x), e(y)\}) \vdash \neq(x, y)^* \ ,$$

Proof. Either $\neq(x, y)^*$, $=(x, y)^*$ or both are consistent with the premise. According to Proposition 1, $\neg\pi(\{e(x), e(y)\})$ implies that $=(x, y)^*$ is inconsistent with the global constraint. Since only $\neq(x, y)^*$ is consistent with the premise, it can be derived. □

Binary constraints are the arcs of the *incompatibility graph*, an important subgraph of H which we denote by $G \equiv (\mathbf{V}, \mathbf{P}, \{\neq(x,y) \mid \neq(x,y) \in \mathbf{C}\})$.

The second rule infers P-ary differences from binary differences and follows directly from 4.

Rule 2 *The following inference is valid for* $x_1, ..., x_n \in \mathbf{V}$*:*

$$\{\neq(x_i, x_j)^* \mid 1 \leq i < j \leq n\} \subseteq \mathbf{C} \quad \wedge \quad n = P \vdash \neq(x_1, ..., x_P)^* \ ,$$

$$\{\neq(x_i, x_j)^* \mid 1 \leq i < j \leq n\} \subseteq \mathbf{C} \quad \wedge \quad n > P \vdash \mathbf{C} \text{ is inconsistent} \ ,$$

Proof. According to 4, the set of binary differences $\{\neq(x_i, x_j)^* : 1 \leq i < j \leq n\}$ is equivalent to the n-ary difference $\neq(x_1, ..., x_n)^*$. When $n > P$, this constraint (and therefore $\mathbf{C}$) is inconsistent because there are not enough values to instantiate each variable in a different way. □

The following inference

$$\{\neq(v_1, v_2), \neq(v_1, v_4), \neq(v_2, v_4)\} \subseteq \mathbf{C} \quad \wedge \quad P = 3 \quad \vdash \quad \neq(v_1, v_2, v_4)$$

exemplifies the application of this rule for $P = 3$, and it can be shown graphically in Fig. 2. Notice that the three binary differences, where the P-ary difference is implicit, form a graphical clique of size 3 represented in grey.

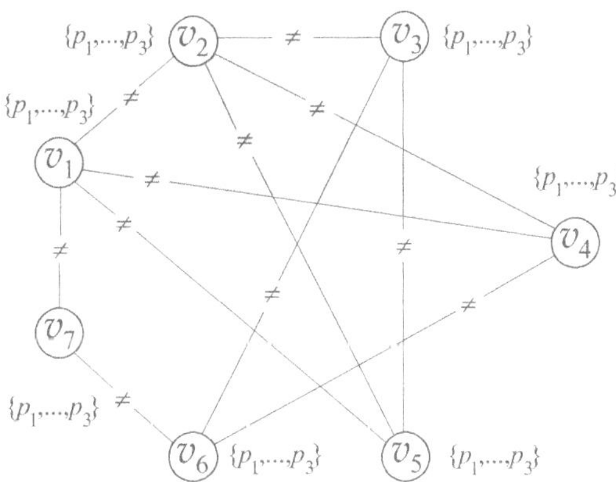

Fig. 2. A P-ary difference entailed by three binary differences.

Based on two P-ary differences we can infer binary equalities by using the following propagation rule:

Rule 3 *The following inference is valid for* $z_1, ..., z_{P-1}, x, y \in \mathbf{V}$*:*

$$\begin{array}{c} \{\neq(z_1, ..., z_{P-1}, x)^*, \neq(z_1, ..., z_{P-1}, y)^*\} \subseteq \mathbf{C} \wedge \\ c(v_1, ..., v_E) \in \mathbf{C} \ \wedge \ \pi(\{e(x), e(y)\}) \end{array} \vdash =(x,y)^* \ ,$$

$$\begin{array}{c} \{\neq(z_1, ..., z_{P-1}, x)^*, \neq(z_1, ..., z_{P-1}, y)^*\} \subseteq \mathbf{C} \wedge \\ c(v_1, ..., v_E) \in \mathbf{C} \ \wedge \ \neg\pi(\{e(x), e(y)\}) \end{array} \vdash \mathbf{C} \text{ is inconsistent} \ .$$

Proof. Either $=(x, y)^*$, $\neq(x, y)^*$ or both are consistent with the premise, otherwise **C** is inconsistent. According to Proposition 1, $\neg\pi(\{e(x), e(y)\})$ implies that $=(x, y)^*$ is inconsistent with the global constraint, therefore $=(x, y)^*$ is inconsistent with the second premise. Both premises are inconsistent with $\neq(x, y)^*$ because if they were, based on the two P-ary differences, we could infer $\neq(z_1, ..., z_{P-1}, x, y)^*$, which is inconsistent due to the fact that there are not $P+1$ different parts to instantiate the $P+1$ variables. □

The following inference

$$\{\neq(v_1, v_2, v_4), \neq(v_1, v_2, v_5), c(v_1, ..., v_7)\} \subseteq \mathbf{C} \ \wedge \ \pi(\{e_4, e_5\}) \ \vdash \ =(v_4, v_5)$$

exemplifies the application of this rule for $P = 3$, and it can be shown graphically in Fig. 3. Notice that the two triangles in grey represent the two P-ary differences and the doted arc between variables v_4 and v_5 the derived binary equality.

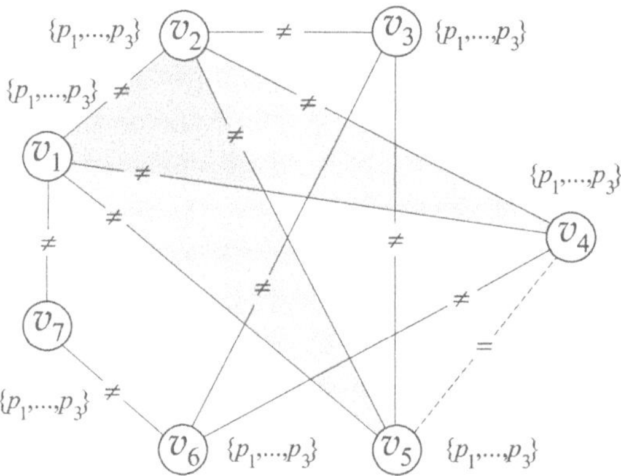

Fig. 3. A binary equality entailed by two P-ary differences.

Based on n-ary equalities, larger n-ary equalities can be derived by using the following propagation rule:

Rule 4 *The following inference is valid for* $x_1, ..., x_m, y_1, ..., y_n, z \in \mathbf{V}$*:*

$$\begin{array}{l} \{=(x_1, ..., x_m, z)^*, =(y_1, ..., y_n, z)^*\} \subseteq \mathbf{C} \wedge \\ \qquad c(v_1, ..., v_E) \in \mathbf{C} \wedge \ \vdash \ =(x_1, ..., x_m, y_1, ..., y_n, z)^* \ , \\ \pi[\mathbf{E}(\{x_1, ..., x_m, y_1, ..., y_n, z\})] \end{array}$$

$$\begin{array}{l} \{=(x_1, ..., x_m, z)^*, =(y_1, ..., y_n, z)^*\} \subseteq \mathbf{C} \wedge \\ \qquad c(v_1, ..., v_E) \in \mathbf{C} \wedge \ \vdash \ \mathbf{C} \text{ is inconsistent } . \\ \neg\pi[\mathbf{E}(\{x_1, ..., x_m, y_1, ..., y_n, z\})] \end{array}$$

Proof. The derived equality is entailed by the two equalities in the premise due to the transitiveness of the equality relation. According to Proposition 1,

$\neg\pi[\mathbf{E}(\{x_1, ..., x_m, y_1, ..., y_n, z\})]$ implies that the derived equality is inconsistent with the global constraint, therefore the second premise is inconsistent. □

Based on equality constraints we can infer more binary differences by using the following propagation rules.

Rule 5 *The following inference is valid for* $x_1, ..., x_m, y \in \mathbf{V}$*:*

$$\begin{array}{r} \{=(x_1, ..., x_m)^*, c(v_1, ..., v_E)\} \subseteq \mathbf{C} \wedge \\ \neg\pi[\mathbf{E}(\{x_1, ..., x_m, y\})] \end{array} \vdash \{\neq(x_k, y)^* \mid k = 1, ..., m\} \ .$$

Proof. For every $1 \leq k \leq m$, either $\neq(x_k, y)^*$, $=(x_k, y)^*$ or both are consistent with the premise. According to Proposition 1, $\neg\pi[\mathbf{E}(\{x_1, ..., x_m, y\})]$ implies that $=(x_1, ..., x_m, y)^*$ (or $=(x_k, y)^* \wedge =(x_1, ..., x_m)$) is inconsistent with the global constraint. Since only $\neq(x_k, y)^*$ is consistent with the premise, it can be inferred for every $1 \leq k \leq m$. □

Rule 6 *The following inference is valid for* $x_1, ..., x_m, y_1, ..., y_n \in \mathbf{V}$*:*

$$\begin{array}{r} \{=(x_1, ..., x_m), =(y_1, ..., y_n)\} \subseteq \mathbf{C} \wedge \\ c(v_1, ..., v_E) \in \mathbf{C} \wedge \\ \neg\pi[\mathbf{E}(\{x_1, ..., x_m, y_1, ..., y_n\})] \end{array} \vdash \{\neq(x_i, y_j)^* \mid i = 1, ..., m, j = 1, ..., n\} \ .$$

Proof. For every $1 \leq i \leq m$ and $1 \leq j \leq n$, either $\neq(x_i, x_j)^*$, $=(x_i, x_j)^*$ or both are consistent with the premise. According to Proposition 1, if $\neg\pi[\mathbf{E}(\{x_1, ..., x_m, y_1, ..., y_n\})]$ is true, then $=(x_1, ..., x_m, y_1, ..., y_n)$ (or $=(x_1, ..., x_m) \wedge =(y_1, ..., y_n) \wedge =(x_i, y_j)^*$) is inconsistent with the global constraint. Since only $\neq(x_i, y_j)^*$ is consistent with the premise, it can be inferred for every $1 \leq i \leq m$ and $1 \leq j \leq n$. □

5.2 Propagation Loop

The propagation rules previously described can only produce interesting results if they are chained in a propagation loop like the one presented on Fig. 4.

The propagation loop starts with the application of Rule 1 to derive binary differences and add them to $\mathbf{C}$. Based on those constraints, P-ary differences can then be derived trough the application of Rule 2. Based on these last constraints, n-ary equalities can be inferred with Rules 3 and 4 (one after another). Based on these new constraints, more binary differences can be inferred through the application of Rules 5 and 6. Based on these last constraints, new P-ary differences can be derived through the reapplication of Rule 2. The loop proceeds repeating the same sequence of steps until some rule is incapable of adding new constraints to $\mathbf{C}$ (i.e. $\Delta\mathbf{C} = \emptyset$) or until an inconsistency is detected on $\mathbf{C}$.

The most critical step of the propagation loop is the application of Rule 2. This is because matching the premise of Rule 2 with $\mathbf{C}$ requires finding maximum cliques in a graph (as we have shown in Fig. 2), which is an NP-complete problem (see Bomze *et al.* [3]). We developed an algorithm that performs well on the type of problems we are interested in (see Saldanha [17]). It is based on a lower and an upper bound for the size of the maximum clique.

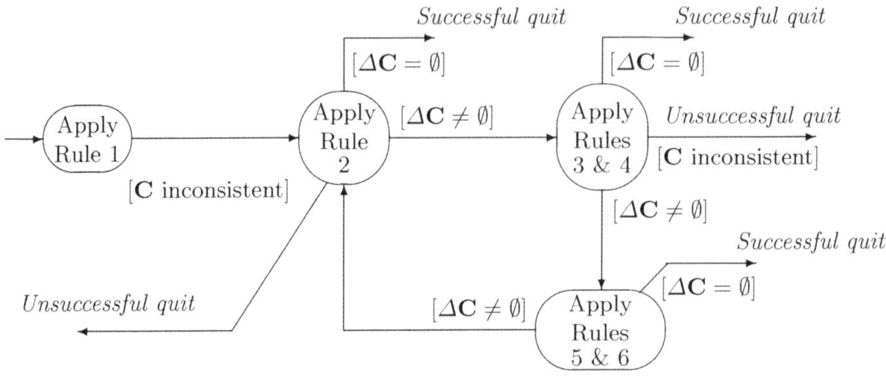

Fig. 4. Propagation loop

5.3 A Lower Bound for the Optimum Number of Parts

The constraint propagator above described can not only be used to enforce consistency over the constraint hypergraph but also to provide a lower bound for the optimum number of parts P^{opt}. By invoking repeatedly the propagator for increasing or decreasing values of P, once we find a value $\underline{P}^{\text{opt}}$ satisfying the following condition:

$$\mathbf{C} \text{ is consistent for } P = \underline{P}^{\text{opt}} \;\wedge\; \mathbf{C} \text{ is inconsistent for } P = \underline{P}^{\text{opt}} - 1 \ ,$$

we conclude that $\underline{P}^{\text{opt}}$ is the best lower bound for P^{opt}. This lower bound provides a sufficient condition of optimality since if a solution with $\underline{P}^{\text{opt}}$ parts is found, then it is optimal.

6 The Decision Operator

The decision operator takes the same kind of decisions as the one described in Curtis *et al.* [5]. When applied to a node n of the decision tree, it produces an ordered set $\{n_1, ..., n_m\}$ of m successor nodes corresponding to alternative ways of incorporating a new part in the set of solved parts. The incorporated parts are all extensions of a base set with a single element called the base element. In formal terms each part is given by $\mathbf{E}(\mathbf{V}_k) = \mathbf{E}(\{v, v_{k1}, ..., v_{kn}\})$, where $e(v)$ and v are respectively the base element and the base variable. This latter is given by the variable ordering heuristic, while the order in which the successors will be explored in the decision tree is given by the value ordering heuristic.

In Curtis *et al.* [5] incorporating part $\mathbf{E}(\mathbf{V}_k)$ in the solved parts means assigning all variables in $\mathbf{V}_k$ to the same value. In our approach it means adding the following heuristic constraints to $\mathbf{C}$:

$$\{=(v, v_{k1}, ..., v_{kn})^*\} \cup \{\neq(x, y)^* \mid x \in \mathbf{V}_k, y \in \mathbf{V} - \mathbf{V}_k\} \ . \tag{6}$$

Each equality $=(v, v_{k1}, ..., v_{kn})^*$ is consistent with $\mathbf{C}$ if the following conditions are met:

$$\pi[\mathbf{E}(\mathbf{V}_k)], \tag{7}$$

$$\bigwedge_{=(x_1,...,x_n)\in\mathbf{C}} \{x_1, ..., x_n\} \subseteq \mathbf{V}_k \vee \{x_1, ..., x_n\} \cap \mathbf{V}_k = \emptyset \ , \tag{8}$$

$$\bigwedge_{\neq(x_1,...,x_P)\in\mathbf{C}} \{x_1, ..., x_P\} \cap \mathbf{V}_k \neq \emptyset \ . \tag{9}$$

Condition 7 assures consistency with the global constraint by forcing $\mathbf{E}(\mathbf{V}_k)$ to satisfy the part predicate. Condition 8 guarantees consistency with all n-ary equalities in $\mathbf{C}$ by not allowing each equality to have their variables partially covered by $\mathbf{V}_k$. Finally, Condition 9 assures consistency with all P-ary differences by forcing $\mathbf{V}_k$ to intersect all P-ary differences. This condition is necessary because, if $\mathbf{V}_k$ does not intersect for instance $\neq(x_1, ..., x_P)$, then it is possible to infer $\neq(v, x_1, ..., x_P)$, which is inconsistent.

Both Conditions 8 and 9 show that the decision operator is guided by the global knowledge contained in the constraints derived by global constraint propagation.

For the variable ordering heuristic we use a dynamic version of the *Max-cardinality* heuristic (see Dechter & Meiri [6,7] and Sadeh & Fox [16]). In our context this means choosing as the base variable the one that participates in more binary differences (i.e with maximum degree in G) among the variables $\mathbf{V}'$ not belonging to any solved part:

$$v = \arg\max\{\text{degree of } x \text{ in } G \mid x \in \mathbf{V}'\} \ . \tag{10}$$

The fact that this heuristic is re-evaluated in each node of the decision tree makes it dynamic and more adaptive to the changes suffered by the constraint graph as the problem is being solved.

We use a value ordering heuristic that is suitable for crew scheduling problems and depends only on the incorporated part. It uses the following criterion to sort the successors: the more promising is the incorporated part the earlier the successor should be explored with respect to the others; the promise of a part (duty) is defined as the duration of its elements (activities). In formal terms this corresponds to:

$$\bigwedge_{i=1}^{m} \bigwedge_{j=i+1}^{m} \text{promise of } \mathbf{V}_i \geq \text{ promise of } \mathbf{V}_j \ , \tag{11}$$

$$\text{promise of } x \equiv \sum_{v \in x} \text{duration of } e(v) \ . \tag{12}$$

Since the set of parts is not an input data to our model, each set $\mathbf{V}_k$ must be generated. This is accomplished by an algorithm that iterates over all independent sets of G including variable v and selects the ones satisfying Conditions 7, 8 and 9.

In real life problems, the number m of successors is typically large. It can easily originate decision trees with a branching factor of $O(100)$ and a depth of $O(100)$, which is totally intractable. The only way to obtain a solution in a reasonable amount of time is to limit the number of successors returned by the decision operator. We do this by generating successors only for the most promising generated parts (i.e. $\mathbf{E}(\mathbf{V}_1)$ and some more), which means forcing each generated part $\mathbf{E}(\mathbf{V}_k)$ to satisfy the following additional conditions:

$$k \leq M \vee (\text{ promise of } \mathbf{V}_k = \text{ promise of } \mathbf{V}_M) \ , \tag{13}$$

$$\text{promise of } \mathbf{V}_k \geq \mu(\text{ promise of } \mathbf{V}_1) \ , \tag{14}$$

where M and μ are input parameters. The former is the maximum number of parts in the non-strict sense, i.e. the number of parts may be $M+n$ but the last n parts must have exactly the same promise as the least promising of the first M parts. The latter is the minimum relative promise allowed.

7 The Search Strategy

We use a look-ahead approach inspired on the *Forward checking* algorithm (see Haralick & Elliott [9]), mixing constraint propagation with chronological back-tracking. Each time a node n is expanded, the following steps are taken:

1. the constraint propagator is invoked to determine the consequences of the most recent decisions incorporated in n; this means adding new derived constraints to n;
2. the decision operator is invoked to generate the successors of n; each successor has all the constraints of n plus a set of heuristic constraints corresponding to the decisions incorporated in the successor.

8 Experimental Results

In order to test our approach we developed a prototype that integrates the three modules described above: the constraint propagator, the decision operator and the search strategy. This prototype was coded in C++ and does not use any existing constraint solver package.

We tested our prototype with the five crew duty scheduling problems shown on Table 1. They are based on real data and their size is of a typical problem assigned to a single human planner.

The first four problems were supplied by NS Reizigers, the Dutch railway company (to whom we are very grateful). They refer to the scheduling of drivers from multiple depots for the timetable period between 1998/08/31 and 1999/05/29. The activities (elements) in each problem are mainly intercity services between the home depots.

The fifth problem was supplied by an European urban bus company which we will call AnonyBUS. It refers to the scheduling of drivers from a single depot

Table 1. Characterisation of the problems p.

p	$\|\mathbf{E}\|$	Depots	$\underline{P}^{\text{opt}}$	Arcs in G
NS1	287	5	37	16378
NS2	242	4	28	11822
NS3	436	6	37	40428
NS4	697	10	75	105167
AnonyBUS1	519	1	59	18266

operating in two bus lines. Together with the input data we received a solution made by human planners with 59 duties (parts).

The problem data includes: the network specified with its home depots, stations and restaurant facilities; the road and vehicle knowledge of the drivers; the timetable of each service; the vehicle schedule; and a set of operation an labour constraints concerning transfer times, signing on and signing off, road and driving knowledge, meal breaks, duty duration, etc.

In order to evaluate our prototype we tested it with the chosen problems and compare the results with the ones obtained with CREWS^{TM} (version 6.3.0), which we consider a good representative of the industrial state-of-the-art. Our prototype was tested under a unique configuration, i.e. all tests where performed with the following parameter values: $M = 10$ and $\mu = 0.8$. On the other hand, several configurations of CREWS^{TM} were tested because the configuration that obtains the best solution for one problem may not be the configuration that obtains the best solution for another problem. In CREWS^{TM} each configuration corresponds to a certain combination of a state transition operator, an evaluation function and a beam search parameterisation.

Table 2 shows the best solutions obtained with both systems in a PC equipped with an INTEL PENTIUM III running at 533 MHz, with 128 Mb of RAM. For each problem solved and system used we show: the configuration used, the number P of parts (duties) found in the solution, the search time in seconds, and the number of nodes visited in the decision tree. An asterisk after the number of parts (duties) indicates that the solution is optimal because $P = \underline{P}^{\text{opt}}$. Solutions with a few more duties were found in a much shorter time. For instance, for problems NS1, NS2, NS3 and NS4 our prototype found solutions with 42, 29, 40 and 89 duties in 217, 295, 9104 and 78578 seconds.

These results show that our prototype returns better solutions and is more robust. In fact, it not only obtains solutions with fewer parts, but is also capable of proving that some of them are optimal, which is something that CREWS^{TM} cannot do without exploring all the decision tree (which is often impossible in a reasonable amount of time). Our prototype is also more robust because it uses a unique configuration, while CREWS^{TM} uses different configurations for different problems. Since there is no way to know a priori which configuration is better for a given problem, many configurations must be tested before a conclusion

Table 2. Comparison of results for each problem p.

	CREWS^{TM}				Our prototype			
p	Config	P	Time	Nodes	Config	P	Time	Nodes
NS1	B(2)	41	8040	7138	A(10,0.8)	41	25717	249826
NS2	C(2,16,3,10)	30	76740	1292	A(10,0.8)	28*	627	5040
NS3	A(3,10)	44	16440	13249	A(10,0.8)	39	810554	1395294
NS4	A(3,10)	92	53340	19498	A(10,0.8)	86	617543	1643292
AnonyBUS1	A(4,50)	59*	22260	18497	A(10,0.8)	59*	34	270

is reached, and this may consume a considerable amount of time (which is not included in Table 2).

9 Conclusions

We described a constraint-based approach for solving set partitioning problems that is simultaneously efficient, open and easy to modify, something that earlier approaches were not capable of. This goal was achieved by using global and dynamic constraint propagation. By enforcing consistency between local knowledge (such as variable domains) and global knowledge (such as the optimisation goal treated as a soft constraint) thrashing due to global inconsistencies is considerably reduced. By performing constraint propagation during the search process the consequences of the decisions can be anticipated and used to guide the search process and prune the decision tree.

This propagator derives new constraints based on the existing ones by chaining efficiently a set of propagation rules. These rules and the way they are chained were presented here as original material. We have seen also how to prove in certain cases that a given solution is optimal.

We tested this approach with five crew scheduling problems supplied by two operators from the railway and bus domains. The results showed that our approach outperforms CREWS^{TM} a good representative of the industrial state-of-the-art, by obtaining better solutions in a more robust way.

References

1. E. Balas and M.W. Padberg. Set Partitioning: A Survey. *SIAM Review*, 18:710–760, 1976.
2. R. Bisiani. Beam Search. In S. C. Shapiro, editor, *Encyclopedia of Artificial Intelligence*, pages 56–58. Wiley, New York, 1987.
3. I. Bomze, M. Budinich, P. Pardalos, and M. Pelillo. The Maximum Clique Problem. In D.-Z. Du and P. M. Pardalos, editors, *Handbook of Combinatorial Optimization*, volume 4. Kluwer Academic Publishers, Boston, MA, 1999.
4. A. Caprara, M. Fischetti, P. Toth, D. Vigo, and P. L. Guida. Algorithms for Railway Crew Management. *Mathematical Programming*, 79:125–141, 1997.

5. S. Curtis, B. Smith, and A. Wren. Forming Bus Driver Schedules Using Constraint Programming. In *Proceedings of the First International Conference on the Practical Applications of Constraint Technologies and Logic Programming*, pages 239–254, 1999.
6. R. Dechter and I. Meiri. Experimental Evaluation of Preprocessing Techniques in Constraint Satisfaction Problems. In *Proceedings of the Eleventh International Joint Conference on Artificial Intelligence*, pages 271–277, 1989.
7. R. Dechter and I. Meiri. Experimental Evaluation of Preprocessing Algorithms for Constraint Satisfaction Problems. *Artificial Intelligence*, 68:211–241, 1994.
8. N. Guerinik and M. Van Caneghem. Solving Crew Scheduling Problems by Constraint Programming. In *Lecture Notes in Computer Science*, volume 976, pages 481–498. Springer-Verlag, 1995.
9. R. M. Haralick and G. L. Elliott. Increasing Tree Search Efficiency for Constraint Satisfaction Problems. *Artificial Intelligence*, 14:263–313, 1980.
10. L. Kroon and M. Fischetti. Crew Scheduling for Netherlands Railways "Destination: Customer". In S. Voss and J. R. Daduna, editors, *Computer-Aided Scheduling of Public Transport*, volume 505 of *Lecture Notes in Economics and Mathematical Systems*, pages 181–201. Springer, 2001.
11. K. Marriott and P. J. Stuckey. *Programming with Constraints: An Introduction.* MIT press, Cambrige, Massachusetts, 1999.
12. E. Morgado and J.P. Martins. Crews_NS: Scheduling Train Crew in The Netherlands. In *Proceedings of the Fourteenth National Conference on Artificial Intelligence and Ninth Innovative Applications of Artificial Intelligence Conference*, pages 893–902. AAAI Press, 1997.
13. E. Morgado and J.P. Martins. Crews_NS: Scheduling Train Crew in The Netherlands. *AI Magazine*, 19(1):25–38, 1998.
14. T. Müller. Solving Set Partitioning Problems with Constraint Programming. In *Proceedings of the Sixth International Conference on the Practical Application of Prolog and the Fourth International Conference on the Practical Application of Constraint Technology (PAPPACT'98)*, pages 313–332, London, UK, The Practical Application Company Ltd., 1998.
15. J.-C. Régin. A Filtering Algorithm for Constraints of Difference in CSPs. In *Proceedings of the Twelfth National Conference on Artificial Intelligence*, volume 1, pages 362–367. American Association for Artificial Intelligence, 1994.
16. Norman M. Sadeh and Mark S. Fox. Variable and Value Ordering Heuristics for the Job Shop Scheduling Constraint Satisfaction Problem. *Artificial Intelligence Journal*, 86(1):1–41, 1996.
17. R. L. Saldanha. *Planeamento de Tripulações: Um Propagador de Restrições Global para a Geração de Turnos.* PhD thesis, Instituto Superior Técnico, Lisboa, 2003. Submited for aproval.

Heuristic-Based Backtracking for Propositional Satisfiability

A. Bhalla, I. Lynce, J.T. de Sousa, and J. Marques-Silva

Technical University of Lisbon,
IST/INESC-ID, Lisbon, Portugal
{ateet,ines,jts,jpms}@sat.inesc.pt

Abstract. In recent years backtrack search algorithms for Propositional Satisfiability (SAT) have been the subject of dramatic improvements. These improvements allowed SAT solvers to successfully solve instances with thousands of variables and hundreds of thousands of clauses, and also motivated the development of many new challenging problem instances, many of which still too hard for the current generation of SAT solvers. As a result, further improvements to SAT technology are expected to have key consequences in solving hard real-world instances. The objective of this paper is to propose heuristic approaches to the backtrack step of backtrack search SAT solvers, with the goal of increasing the ability of a SAT solver to search different parts of the search space. The proposed heuristics are inspired by the heuristics proposed in recent years for the branching step of SAT solvers, namely VSIDS and some of its improvements. Moreover, the completeness of the new algorithm is guaranteed. The preliminary experimental results are promising, and motivate the integration of heuristic backtracking in state-of-the-art SAT solvers.

1 Introduction

Propositional Satisfiability is a well-known NP-complete problem, with theoretical and practical significance, and with extensive applications in many fields of Computer Science and Engineering, including Artificial Intelligence and Electronic Design Automation.

Current state-of-the-art SAT solvers incorporate sophisticated pruning techniques as well as new strategies on how to organize the search. Effective search pruning techniques are based, among others, on nogood learning and dependency-directed backtracking [16] and backjumping [5], whereas recent effective strategies introduce variations on the organization of backtrack search. Examples of such strategies are weak-commitment search [17], search restarts [9] and random backtracking [10].

Advanced techniques applied to backtrack search SAT algorithms have achieved remarkable improvements [2,8,11,12], having been shown to be crucial for solving hard instances of SAT obtained from real-world applications. Moreover, and from a practical perspective, the most effective algorithms are *complete*,

Fernando Moura Pires, Salvador Abreu (Eds.): EPIA 2003, LNAI 2902, pp. 116–130, 2003.

and so able to prove unsatisfiability. Indeed, this is often the objective in a large number of significant real-world applications.

Nevertheless, it is also widely accepted that local search can often have clear advantages with respect to backtrack search, since it is allowed to start the search over again whenever it gets *stuck* in a locally optimal partial solution. This advantage of local search has motivated the study of approaches for relaxing backtracking conditions (while still assuring completeness). The key idea is to *unrestrictedly* choose the point to backtrack to, in order to avoid thrashing during backtrack search. Moreover, one can think of combining different forms of relaxing the identification of the backtrack point.

In this paper, we propose to use heuristic knowledge to select the backtrack point. Besides describing the generic heuristic backtracking search strategy, we establish backtracking heuristics inspired in the most promising branching heuristics proposed in recent years, namely the VSIDS heuristic used by Chaff [12] and BerkMin's branching heuristic [8]. Moreover, completeness conditions for the resulting SAT algorithm are established.

The remainder of this paper is organized as follows. The next section presents definitions used throughout the paper. Afterwards, we briefly survey backtrack search SAT algorithms. In Section 4 we introduce heuristic backtracking. Then, we describe unrestricted backtracking algorithms for SAT, and explain how heuristic backtracking can be regarded as a special case of unrestricted backtracking. In addition, we address completeness issues. Next, Section 6 gives preliminary experimental results. Finally, we describe related work and conclude with directions for future research work.

2 Definitions

This section introduces the notational framework used throughout the paper. Propositional variables are denoted $x_1, \ldots, x_n$, and can be assigned truth values 0 (or F) or 1 (or T). The truth value assigned to a variable x is denoted by $\nu(x)$. (When clear from context we use $x = \nu_x$, where $\nu_x \in \{0, 1\}$). A literal l is either a variable x_i or its negation $\neg x_i$. A clause ω is a disjunction of literals and a CNF formula φ is a conjunction of clauses. A clause is said to be *satisfied* if at least one of its literals assumes value 1, *unsatisfied* if all of its literals assume value 0, *unit* if all but one literal assume value 0, and *unresolved* otherwise. Literals with no assigned truth value are said to be *free literals*. A formula is said to be *satisfied* if all its clauses are satisfied, and is *unsatisfied* if at least one clause is unsatisfied. A *truth assignment* for a formula is a set of pairs of variables and their corresponding truth values. The SAT problem consists of deciding whether there exists a truth assignment to the variables such that the formula becomes satisfied.

SAT algorithms can be characterized as being either *complete* or *incomplete*. Complete algorithms can establish unsatisfiability if given enough CPU time; incomplete algorithms cannot. Examples of complete and incomplete algorithms are backtrack search and local search algorithms, respectively. In a search context, complete algorithms are often referred to as *systematic*, whereas incomplete algorithms are referred to as *non-systematic*.

3 Backtrack Search SAT Algorithms

Over the years a large number of algorithms have been proposed for SAT, from the original Davis-Putnam procedure [4], to recent backtrack search algorithms [2,8,11,12] and to local search algorithms [15], among many others.

The vast majority of backtrack search SAT algorithms build upon the original backtrack search algorithm of Davis, Logemann and Loveland [3]. The backtrack search algorithm is implemented by a *search process* that implicitly enumerates the space of 2^n possible binary assignments to the n problem variables. Each different truth assignment defines a *search path* within the search space. A *decision level* is associated with each variable selection and assignment. The first variable selection corresponds to decision level 1, and the decision level is incremented by 1 for each new decision assignment [1]. In addition, and for each decision level, the *unit clause rule* [4] is applied. (The iterated application of the unit clause rule is often referred to as Boolean Constraint Propagation (BCP)). If a clause is unit, then the sole free literal must be assigned value 1 for the formula to be satisfied. In this case, the value of the literal and of the associated variable are said to be *implied*. Consequently, assigned variables can be distinguished between *decision variables* and *implied variables*.

In chronological backtracking, the search algorithm keeps track of which decision assignments have been toggled. Given an unsatisfied clause (i.e. a *conflict* or a *dead end*) at decision level d, the algorithm checks whether at the current decision level the corresponding decision variable x has already been toggled. If not, the algorithm erases the variable assignments which are implied by the assignment on x, including the assignment on x, assigns the opposite value to x, and marks decision variable x as toggled. In contrast, if the value of x has already been toggled, the search backtracks to decision level $d - 1$.

Recent state-of-the-art SAT solvers utilize different forms of non-chronological backtracking [2,11,12], in which each identified conflict is analyzed, its causes identified, and a new clause (*nogood*) created to explain and prevent the identified conflicting conditions. Created clauses are then used to compute the backtrack point as the *most recent* decision assignment from all the decision assignments represented in the recorded clause. Moreover, some of the (larger) recorded clauses are eventually deleted. Clauses can be deleted opportunistically whenever they are no longer *relevant* for the current search path [11].

Figure 1 illustrates the differences between chronological backtracking (CB) and non-chronological backtracking (NCB). On the top of the figure appears a generic search tree (either possible in the context of CB or NCB). The search is performed accordingly to a depth-first search, and therefore the non-dashed branches define the search space explored so far. On the one hand, and when

[1] Observe that all the assignments made before the first decision assignment correspond to decision level 0.

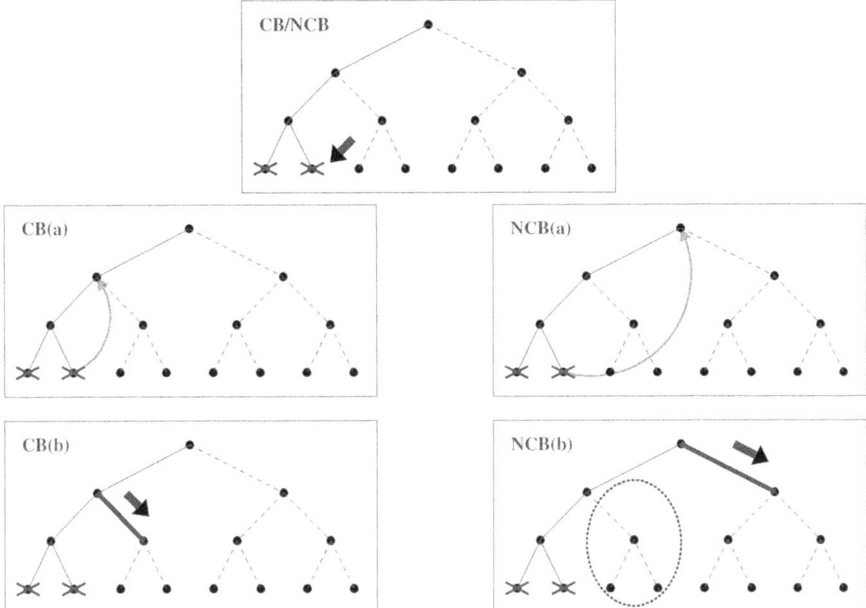

Fig. 1. Chronological Backtracking (CB) *vs* Non-Chronological Backtracking (NCB)

a conflict if found, the chronological backtracking algorithm makes the search backtrack to the most recent yet untoggled decision variable (see CB(a)). On the other hand, when non-chronological backtracking is applied, the backtrack point is computed as the *most recent* decision assignment from all the decision assignments represented in the recorded clause. In this case the search backtracks to a higher level in the search tree (NCB(a)), skipping portions of the search tree that are found to have no solution (see NCB(b)). From the final figures (CB(b) and NCB(b)) it is plain to conclude that the number of nodes explored by NCB is always equal or smaller than the number of nodes explored by CB [2]. (Observe that nogoods can also reduce the search space, since *similar* conflict paths of the search space are avoided to be searched.)

4 Heuristic Backtracking

Heuristic backtracking consists of selecting the backtrack point in the search tree as a function of variables in the most recently recorded clause. Different heuristics can be envisioned for applying heuristic backtracking. In this work we implemented three different heuristics:

1. One heuristic that decides the backtrack point given the information of the most recently recorded conflict clause.

[2] Assuming that a fixed order branching heuristic is used.

2. Another heuristic that is inspired in the VSIDS branching heuristic, used by Chaff [12].
3. Finally, one heuristic that is inspired by BerkMin's branching heuristic [8].

In all cases the backtrack point is computed as the variable with the largest heuristic metric.

Next, we describe how the three different approaches are implemented in the heuristic backtracking algorithm.

4.1 Plain Heuristic Backtracking

Under the plain heuristic backtracking approach the backtrack point (i.e. decision level) is computed by selecting the decision level with the largest number of occurrences in the just recorded clause. After a conflict (i.e. an unsatisfied clause) is identified, a *conflict clause* is created. The conflict clause is then used for *heuristically* deciding which decision assignment is to be toggled. This contrasts with the usual non-chronological backtracking approach, in which the most recent decision assignment variable is selected as the backtrack point.

4.2 VSIDS-Like Heuristic Backtracking

The second approach to heuristic backtracking is based on the Variable State Independent Decaying Sum (VSIDS) branching heuristic [12]. VSIDS was the first of new generation of decision heuristics. This new heuristic has been used in *Chaff*, a highly optimized SAT solver. More than to develop a well-behaviored heuristic, the motivation in Chaff has been to design a fast heuristic. In fact, one of the key properties of this strategy is the very low overhead, due to being independent of the variable state. As a result, the variable metrics are only updated when there is a conflict.

Similarly to Chaff, in VSIDS-like heuristic backtracking a metric is associated with each literal, which is incremented when a new clause containing the literal; after every k decisions, the metric values are divided by a small constant. With the VSIDS-like heuristic backtracking, the assigned literal with the highest metric is selected as the backtrack point.

4.3 BerkMin-Like Heuristic Backtracking

The third approach for implementing heuristic backtracking is inspired in BerkMin's branching heuristic [8]. This heuristic was inspired in the VSIDS heuristic used in Chaff, but the process of updating the metrics of the literals differs. On the one hand, Chaff's authors compute the activity of a variable v by counting the number of occurrences of v in conflict clauses. On the other hand, BerkMin's authors take into account a wider set of clauses involved in conflict making for computing each variable activity. This procedure avoids overlooking some variables that do not appear in conflict clauses while actively contributing to conflicts.

In our implementation of BerkMin-like heuristic backtracking, the metrics of the literals of all clauses that are directly involved in producing the conflict, and so in creating the newly recorded clause, are updated when a clause is recorded. As in the cases of the VSIDS-like backtracking heuristic, the assigned literal with the highest metric is selected as the backtrack point.

5 Unrestricted Backtracking

Heuristic backtracking can be viewed as a special case of unrestricted backtracking [10], the main difference being that while in unrestricted backtracking any form of backtrack step can be applied, in heuristic backtracking the backtrack point is computed from heuristic information, obtained from the current and past conflicts.

Unrestricted backtracking algorithms allow the search to *unrestrictedly* backtrack to *any* point in the current search path whenever a conflict is reached. Besides the freedom for selecting the backtrack point in the decision tree, unrestricted backtracking entails a *policy* for applying different backtrack steps in sequence. Each backtrack step can be selected among chronological backtracking, non-chronological backtracking or incomplete forms of backtracking (e.g. search restarts, weak-commitment search, random backtracking, heuristic backtracking, among many others). More formally, unrestricted backtracking (UB) consists of defining a sequence of backtrack steps $\{\mathrm{BSt}_1, \mathrm{BSt}_2, \mathrm{BSt}_3, \ldots\}$ such that each backtrack step BSt_i can either be a chronological (CB), a non-chronological (NCB) or an incomplete form of backtracking (IFB).

Interestingly, the definition of unrestricted backtracking allows capturing the backtracking search strategies used by current state-of-the-art SAT solvers [2,8, 11,12]. Indeed, if the unrestricted backtracking strategy specifies always applying the chronological backtracking step or always applying the non-chronological backtracking step, then we respectively capture the chronological and non-chronological backtracking search strategies.

Finally, observe that unrestricted backtracking gives a unified representation for different backtracking strategies. Consequently, unrestricted backtracking further allows establishing general completeness conditions for *classes* of backtracking strategies and not only for each individual strategy, as it has often been done [14,17].

In what follows, we will further relate unrestricted backtracking with heuristic backtracking. In addition, we will describe completeness conditions established for unrestricted backtracking. We should note that the completeness conditions established to *all* organizations of unrestricted backtracking may obviously be applied to any special case of unrestricted backtracking (e.g. heuristic backtracking).

5.1 Unrestricted Backtracking and Heuristic Backtracking

As mentioned above, heuristic backtracking can be viewed as a special case of unrestricted backtracking. In unrestricted backtracking any form of backtrack

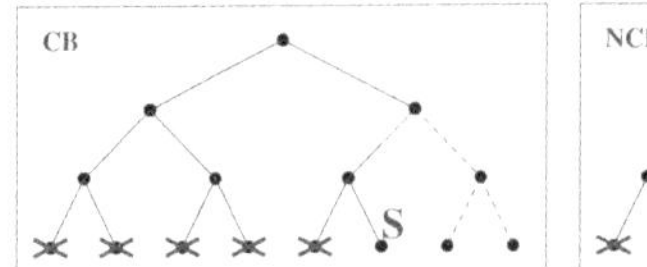

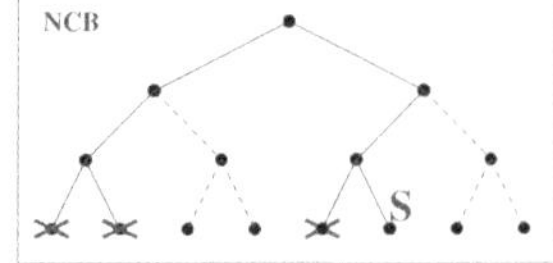

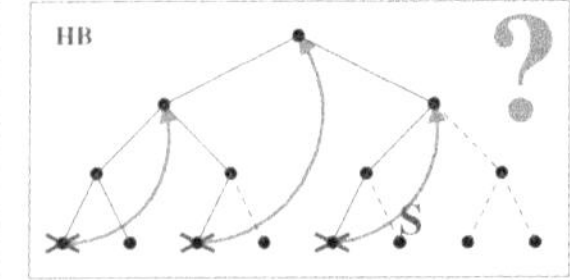

Fig. 2. Comparing Chronological Backtracking (CB), Non-Chronological Backtracking (NCB) and Heuristic Backtracking (HB)

step can be applied (CB, NCB or IFB), while in heuristic backtracking the backtrack point is heuristically selected.

Figure 2 exemplifies how heuristic backtracking can lead to incompleteness. Figure 2 illustrates the subsequent search of Figure 1, for both chronological (CB) and non-chronological backtracking (NCB). In addition, an example is given for heuristic backtracking (HB). The search path that leads to the solution is marked with letter **S**. For CB and NCB the solution is easily found. However, since with heuristic backtracking the search backtracks heuristically, the search space that leads to the solution is simply skipped. Hence, what has to be done in order to assure the correctness and completeness of the heuristic backtracking algorithm? First, and similarly to local search, we have to assume that the variable toggling in heuristic backtracking is *reversible*. For the given example, this means that the solution can be found in a subsequent search, although the solution would have been skipped if variable toggling was not reversible.

However, and exactly as with unrestricted backtracking, a number of techniques can be used to ensure completeness. These techniques are analyzed in [10] and will be reviewed in what follows of this section. Completeness techniques for unrestricted backtracking can be organized in two classes:

- Marking recorded clauses as non-deletable. This solution may yield an exponential growth in the number of recorded clauses [3].
- Increasing a given constraint (e.g. the number of non-deletable recorded causes) in between applications of different backtracking schemes. This solution can be used to guarantee a polynomial growth of the number of recorded clauses.

5.2 Completeness Issues

In this section we address the problem of guaranteeing the completeness of SAT algorithms that implement some form of unrestricted backtracking (e.g. heuristic backtracking). It is clear that unrestricted backtracking can yield incomplete algorithms. Hence, for each newly devised SAT algorithm, that utilizes some form of UB, it is important to be able to apply conditions that guarantee the completeness of the resulting algorithm.

The results presented in this section generalize, for the unrestricted backtracking algorithm, completeness results that have been proposed in the past

[3] In practice this situation hardly ever arises.

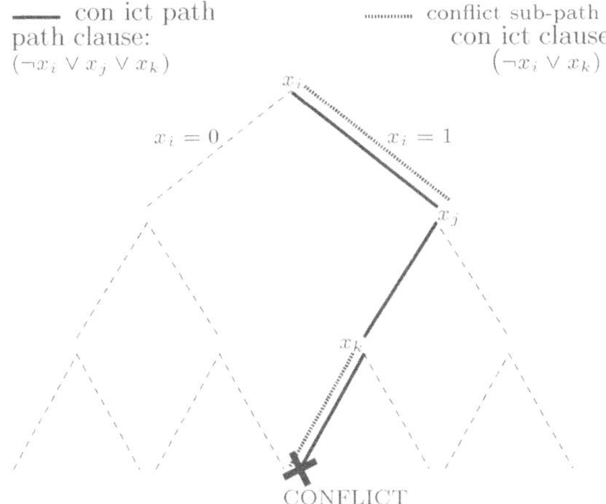

Fig. 3. Search tree definitions

for specific backtracking relaxations. We start by establishing, in a more general context, a few already known results. Afterwards, we establish additional results regarding unrestricted backtracking.

In what follows we assume the organization of a backtrack search SAT algorithm as described earlier in this paper. The main loop of the algorithm consists of selecting a variable assignment (i.e. a *decision assignment*), making that assignment, and propagating that assignment using BCP. In the presence of an unsatisfied clause (i.e. a *conflict*) the algorithm backtracks to a decision assignment that can be toggled [4]. Each time a conflict is identified, all the current decision assignments define a *conflict path* in the search tree. (Observe that we restrict the definition of conflict path solely with respect to the decision assignments.) After a conflict is identified, we may apply a *conflict analysis* procedure [2,11, 12] to identify a subset of the decision assignments that represent a sufficient condition for producing the same conflict. The subset of decision assignments that is declared to be associated with a given conflict is referred to as a *conflict sub-path*. A straightforward conflict analysis procedure consists of constructing a clause with *all* the decision assignments in the conflict path. In this case the created clause is referred to as a *path-clause*. Figure 3 illustrates these definitions. We can now establish a few general results that will be used throughout this section.

Proposition 1. *If an unrestricted backtracking search algorithm does not repeat conflict paths, then it is complete.*

Proof. Assume a problem instance with n variables. Observe that there are 2^n possible conflict paths. If the algorithm does not repeat conflict paths, then it must necessarily terminate.

[4] Without loss of generality, we assume that NCB also uses (binding) variable toggling as the result of backtracking. In some recent algorithms this is not the case [12].

Proposition 2. *If an unrestricted backtracking search algorithm does not repeat conflict sub-paths, then it does not repeat conflict paths.*

Proof. Observe that if a conflict sub-path is not repeated, then no conflict path can contain the same sub-path, and so no conflict path can be repeated.

Proposition 3. *If an unrestricted backtracking search algorithm does not repeat conflict sub-paths, then it is complete.*

Proof. Given the two previous results, if no conflict sub-paths are repeated, then no conflict paths are repeated, and so completeness is obtained.

Proposition 4. *If the number of times an unrestricted backtracking search algorithm repeats conflict paths or conflict sub-paths is upper-bounded by a constant, then the backtrack search algorithm is complete.*

Proof. We prove the result for conflict paths; for conflict sub-paths, it is similar. Let M be a constant denoting an upper bound on the number of times a given conflict path can be repeated. Since the total number of distinct conflict paths is 2^n, and since each can be repeated at most M times, then the total number of conflict paths the backtrack search algorithm can enumerate is $M \times 2^n$, and so the algorithm is complete.

Proposition 5. *For an unrestricted backtracking search algorithm the following holds:*

1. *If the algorithm creates a path clause for each identified conflict, then the search algorithm repeats no conflict paths.*
2. *If the algorithm creates a conflict clause for each identified conflict, then the search algorithm repeats no conflict sub-paths.*
3. *If the algorithm creates a conflict clause (or a path clause) after every M identified conflicts, then the number of times an unrestricted backtracking search algorithm repeats conflict sub-paths (or conflict paths) is upper-bounded.*

In all of the above cases, the search algorithm is complete.

Proof. Recall that the search algorithm always applies BCP after making a decision assignment. Hence, if a clause describing a conflict has been recorded, and not deleted, BCP guarantees that a conflict is declared, without requiring the same set of decision assignments that yields the original conflict. As a result, conflict paths are not repeated. The same holds true respectively for conflict clauses and conflict sub-paths. Since either conflict paths or conflict sub-paths are not repeated, the search algorithm is complete (from Propositions 1 and 3). With respect to creating (and recording) a conflict clause (or a path clause) after every M identified conflicts, clearly the number of times a given conflict sub-path (or conflict path) is repeated is upper-bounded. Hence, using the results of Proposition 4 completeness is guaranteed.

Observe that Proposition 5 holds *independently* of which backtrack step is taken each time a conflict is identified. Hence, as long as we record a conflict for each identified conflict, *any* form of unrestricted backtracking yields a complete algorithm. Less general formulations of this result have been proposed in the recent past [6,17,14].

The results established so far guarantee completeness at the cost of recording (and keeping) a clause for each identified conflict. In this section we propose and analyze conditions for relaxing this requirement. As a result, we allow for some clauses to be deleted during the search process, and only require some specific recorded clauses to be kept [5]. (We should note that clause deletion does not apply to chronological backtracking strategies and that, as shown in [11], existing clause deletion policies for non-chronological backtracking strategies do not compromise the completeness of the algorithm.) Afterwards, we propose other conditions that do not require specific recorded clauses to be kept.

Proposition 6. *An unrestricted backtracking algorithm is complete if it records (and keeps) a* conflict-clause *for each identified conflict for which an IFB step is taken.*

Proof. Observe that there are at most 2^n IFB steps that can be taken, because a conflict clause is recorded for each identified conflict for which an IFB step is taken, and so conflict sub-paths due to IFB steps cannot be repeated. Moreover, the additional backtrack steps that can be applied (CB and NCB) also ensure completeness. Hence, the resulting algorithm is complete.

Moreover, we can also generalize Proposition 4.

Proposition 7. *Given an integer constant M, an unrestricted backtracking algorithm is complete if it records (and keeps) a* conflict-clause *after every M identified conflicts for which an IFB step is taken.*

Proof. The result immediately follows from Propositions 5 and 6.

As one final remark, observe that for the previous conditions, the number of recorded clauses grows linearly with the number of conflicts where an IFB step is taken, and so in the worst-case exponentially in the number of variables.

Other approaches to guarantee completeness involve increasing the value of some constraint associated with the search algorithm. The following results illustrate these approaches.

Proposition 8. *Suppose an unrestricted backtracking strategy that applies a sequence of backtrack steps. If for this sequence the number of conflicts in between IFB steps strictly increases after each IFB step, then the resulting algorithm is complete.*

---

[5] We say that a recorded clause is *kept* provided it is prevented from being deleted during the subsequent search.

Proof. If only CB or NCB steps are taken, then the resulting algorithm is complete. When the number of conflicts in between IFB steps reaches 2^n, the algorithm is guaranteed to terminate.

We should also note that this result can be viewed as a generalization of the completeness-ensuring condition used in search restarts, that consists of increasing the backtrack cutoff value after each search restart [1] [6]. Finally, observe that in this situation the growth in the number of clauses can be made polynomial, provided clause deletion is applied on clauses recorded from NCB and IFB steps.

The next result establishes conditions for guaranteeing completeness whenever large recorded clauses (due to an IFB step) are opportunistically deleted. The idea is to increase the size of recorded clauses that are kept after each IFB step. Another approach is to increase the life-span of large-recorded clauses, by increasing the relevance-based learning threshold [2].

Proposition 9. *Suppose an unrestricted backtracking strategy that applies a specific sequence of backtrack steps. If for this sequence, either the size of the largest recorded clause kept or the size of the relevance-based learning threshold is strictly increased after each IFB step is taken, then the resulting algorithm is complete.*

Proof. When either the size of the largest recorded clause reaches value n, or the relevance-based learning threshold reaches value n, all recorded clauses will be kept, and so completeness is guaranteed from Proposition 5.

Observe that for this last result the number of clauses can grow exponentially with the number of variables. Moreover, we should note that the observation regarding increasing the relevance-based learning threshold was first suggested in [12].

One final result addresses the number of times conflict paths and conflict sub-paths can be repeated.

Proposition 10. *Under the conditions of Proposition 8 and Proposition 9, the number of times a conflict path or a conflict sub-path is repeated is upper-bounded.*

Proof. Clearly, the resulting algorithms are complete, and so known to terminate after a maximum number of backtrack steps (that is constant for each instance). Hence, the number of times a conflict path (or conflict sub-path) can be repeated is necessarily upper-bounded.

6 Experimental Results

This section presents the experimental results of applying heuristic backtracking to different classes of problem instances. In addition, we compare heuristic backtracking with other forms of backtracking relaxations, namely search restarts [9]

[6] Given this condition, the resulting algorithm resembles iterative-deepening.

and random backtracking [10]. Our goal here has been to test the feasibility of the heuristic backtracking algorithm using three different heuristics: a plain heuristic, the VSIDS heuristic and the BerkMin's heuristic. Experimental evaluation of the different algorithms has been done using the JQUEST SAT framework, a Java framework for prototyping SAT algorithms. All the experiments were run on the same P4/1.7GHz/1GByte of RAM/Linux machine. The CPU time limit for each instance was set to 2000 seconds, except for instances from Beijing family, for which the maximum run time allowed was 5000 seconds. In all cases where the algorithm was unable to solve an instance it was due to memory exhaustion.

The total run times for solving different class of benchmarks are shown in Table 1 and Table 2. In both tables, *#I* denotes the number of problem instances, *Time* denotes the CPU time and *X* denotes the number of aborted instances. In addition, each column indicates a different form of backtracking relaxation:

- RST indicates that the search restart strategy [9] is applied with a cutoff value of 100 backtracks and is kept fixed. All recorded clauses are kept to ensure completeness.
- RB indicates that random backtracking [10] is applied at each backtrack step.
- HB(P) indicates that plain heuristic backtracking is applied at each backtrack step.
- HB(C) indicates that the Chaff's VSIDS-like heuristic backtracking is applied at each step.
- HB(B) indicates that the BerkMin-like heuristic backtracking is applied at each step.

Table 1. Performance of different algorithms on every backtrack step.

Benchmarks	#I	RST		RB		HB(P)		HB(C)		HB(B)	
		Time	X	Time	X	Time	X	Time	X	Time	X
bmc-galileo	2	1885.93	0	3052.19	1	1575.97	0	1570.48	0	1553.83	0
bmc-ibm	11	3486.17	1	5781.31	1	4326.73	1	4340.53	1	4318.04	1
Hole	5	317.35	0	2318.71	1	245.69	0	244.27	0	240.27	0
Hanoi	2	2208.09	1	3560.72	1	2113.51	1	2113.02	1	2111.94	1
BMC-barrel	8	4764.22	2	7498.39	3	4505.44	2	4504.73	2	4505	2
Beijing	16	1190.09	2	5751.29	3	4539.51	2	4513.11	2	4520.41	2
Blocksworld	7	937.45	0	1312.18	0	324.07	0	325.73	0	320.41	0
Logistics	4	11.9	0	31.09	0	12.73	0	12.27	0	12.13	0
par16	10	972.39	0	1968.87	0	256.89	0	251.34	0	250.4	0
ii16	10	39.19	0	102.1	0	120.22	0	119.64	0	118.62	0
ucsc-ssa	102	29.89	0	37.59	0	29.41	0	29.56	0	29.48	0
ucsc-bf	223	78.1	0	106.57	0	85.05	0	78.93	0	79.78	0

Table 2. Performance of different algorithms on every 100 backtracks.

Benchmarks	#I	RST		RB		HB(P)		HB(C)		HB(B)	
		Time	X	Time	X	Time	X	Time	X	Time	X
bmc-galileo	2	1833.57	0	2242.93	0	527.14	0	359.22	0	414.57	0
bmc-ibm	11	4553.88	1	4585.39	1	4796.98	1	3989.88	1	4166.41	1
Hole	5	356.44	0	284.9	0	355.71	0	356.6	0	338.57	0
Hanoi	2	2122.98	1	2058.92	1	2183.49	1	2239.5	1	2235.25	1
BMC-barrel	8	4824.22	2	4742.33	2	7521.81	3	6840.03	3	7402.13	3
Beijing	16	5768.92	2	3822.52	2	3555.38	2	3369.57	2	4642.97	2
Blocksworld	7	933.18	0	526.19	0	613.31	0	1092.62	0	1448.54	0
Logistics	4	14.76	0	14.27	0	10.98	0	10.47	0	11.82	0
par16	10	895.83	0	829.68	0	292.77	0	334.4	0	382.55	0
ii16	10	38.3	0	55.49	0	135.86	0	132.85	0	138.61	0
ucsc-ssa	102	33.9	0	46.79	0	36.17	0	35.25	0	49.02	0
ucsc-bf	223	90.7	0	112.01	0	87.23	0	64.67	0	111.95	0

In Table 1, the different forms of backtracking are performed at every backtrack step. In addition, completeness is ensured by marking the recorded clauses as non-deletable. In Table 2, the different forms of backtracking are performed after every 100 backtracks, and an increment of 10 backtracks is applied. In this case, completeness is ensured by marking clauses recorded whenever a relaxed backtrack step is performed as non-deletable.

As can be concluded from the experimental results, heuristic backtracking can yield significant savings in CPU time, and also allow for a smaller number of instances to be aborted. This is true for several of the classes of problem instances analyzed.

7 Related Work

Dependency-directed backtracking and nogood learning were originally proposed by Stallman and Sussman in [16] in the area of Truth Maintenance Systems (TMS). In the area of Constraint Satisfaction Problems (CSP), the topic was independently studied by J. Gaschnig [5] and others (see for example [13]) as different forms of backjumping.

The introduction of relaxations in the backtrack step is also related with dynamic backtracking [6]. Dynamic backtracking establishes a method by which backtrack points can be moved deeper in the search tree. This allows avoiding the unneeded erasing of the amount of search that has been done thus far. The objective is to find a way to directly "erase" the value assigned to a variable as opposed to backtracking to it, moving the backjump variable to the end of the partial solution in order to replace its value without modifying the values of the variables that currently follow it. More recently, Ginsberg and McAllester combined local search and dynamic backtracking in an algorithm which enables arbitrary search movement [7], starting with *any complete assignment* and evolving by flipping values of variables obtained from the conflicts.

In weak-commitment search [17], the algorithm constructs a consistent partial solution, but commits to the partial solution *weakly*. In weak-commitment search, whenever a conflict is reached, the *whole* partial solution is abandoned, in explicit contrast to standard backtracking algorithms where the most recently added variable is removed from the partial solution.

Moreover, search restarts have been proposed and shown effective for hard instances of SAT [9]. The search is repeatedly restarted whenever a cutoff value is reached. The algorithm proposed is not complete, since the restart cutoff point is kept constant. In [1], search restarts were jointly used with learning for solving hard real-world instances of SAT. This latter algorithm is complete, since the backtrack cutoff value increases after each restart. One additional example of backtracking relaxation is described in [14], which is based on attempting to construct a complete solution, that restarts each time a conflict is identified. More recently, highly-optimized complete SAT solvers [8,12] have successfully combined non-chronological backtracking and search restarts, again obtaining remarkable improvements in solving real-world instances of SAT.

8 Conclusions and Future Work

This paper proposes the utilization of heuristic backtracking in backtrack search SAT solvers. The most well-known branching heuristics used in state-of-the-art SAT solvers were adapted to the backtrack step of SAT solvers. The experimental results illustrate the practicality of heuristic backtracking.

The main contributions of this paper can be summarized as follows:

1. A new heuristic backtrack search SAT algorithm is proposed, that heuristically selects the point to backtrack to.
2. The proposed SAT algorithm is shown to be a special case of unrestricted backtracking, and different approaches for ensuring completeness are described.
3. Experimental results indicate that significant savings in search effort can be obtained for different organizations of the proposed heuristic backtrack search algorithm.

Besides the preliminary experimental results, a more comprehensive experimental evaluation is required. In addition, future work entails deriving conditions for selecting among search restarts and heuristic backtracking.

References

1. L. Baptista and J. P. Marques-Silva. Using randomization and learning to solve hard real-world instances of satisfiability. In R. Dechter, editor, *Proceedings of the International Conference on Principles and Practice of Constraint Programming*, volume 1894 of *Lecture Notes in Computer Science*, pages 489–494. Springer Verlag, September 2000.

2. R. Bayardo Jr. and R. Schrag. Using CSP look-back techniques to solve real-world SAT instances. In *Proceedings of the National Conference on Artificial Intelligence*, pages 203–208, July 1997.
3. M. Davis, G. Logemann, and D. Loveland. A machine program for theorem-proving. *Communications of the Association for Computing Machinery*, 5:394–397, July 1962.
4. M. Davis and H. Putnam. A computing procedure for quantification theory. *Journal of the Association for Computing Machinery*, 7:201–215, July 1960.
5. J. Gaschnig. *Performance Measurement and Analysis of Certain Search Algorithms*. PhD thesis, Carnegie-Mellon University, Pittsburgh, PA, May 1979.
6. M. Ginsberg. Dynamic backtracking. *Journal of Artificial Intelligence Research*, 1:25–46, 1993.
7. M. Ginsberg and D. McAllester. GSAT and dynamic backtracking. In *Proceedings of the International Conference on Principles of Knowledge and Reasoning*, pages 226–237, 1994.
8. E. Goldberg and Y. Novikov. BerkMin: a fast and robust sat-solver. In *Proceedings of the Design and Test in Europe Conference*, pages 142–149, March 2002.
9. C. P. Gomes, B. Selman, and H. Kautz. Boosting combinatorial search through randomization. In *Proceedings of the National Conference on Artificial Intelligence*, pages 431–437, July 1998.
10. I. Lynce and J. P. Marques-Silva. Complete unrestricted backtracking algorithms for satisfiability. In *Proceedings of the International Symposium on Theory and Applications of Satisfiability Testing*, pages 214–221, May 2002.
11. J. P. Marques-Silva and K. A. Sakallah. GRASP-A search algorithm for propositional satisfiability. *IEEE Transactions on Computers*, 48(5):506–521, May 1999.
12. M. Moskewicz, C. Madigan, Y. Zhao, L. Zhang, and S. Malik. Engineering an efficient SAT solver. In *Proceedings of the Design Automation Conference*, pages 530–535, June 2001.
13. Patrick Prosser. Hybrid algorithms for the constraint satisfaction problems. *Computational Intelligence*, 9(3):268–299, August 1993.
14. E. T. Richards and B. Richards. Non-systematic search and no-good learning. *Journal of Automated Reasoning*, 24(4):483–533, 2000.
15. B. Selman and H. Kautz. Domain-independent extensions to GSAT: Solving large structured satisfiability problems. In *Proceedings of the International Joint Conference on Artificial Intelligence*, pages 290–295, August 1993.
16. R. M. Stallman and G. J. Sussman. Forward reasoning and dependency-directed backtracking in a system for computer-aided circuit analysis. *Artificial Intelligence*, 9:135–196, October 1977.
17. M. Yokoo. Weak-commitment search for solving satisfaction problems. In *Proceedings of the National Conference on Artificial Intelligence*, pages 313–318, 1994.

On the BEAM Implementation*

Ricardo Lopes[1], Vítor Santos Costa[2], and Fernando Silva[1]

[1] DCC-FC and LIACC, Universidade do Porto, Portugal
{rslopes,fds}@ncc.up.pt
[2] COPPE-Sistemas, Universidade Federal do Rio de Janeiro, Brasil
vitor@cos.ufrj.br

1 Introduction

Logic Programming is based on the idea that computation is controlled inference. The Extended Andorra Model provides a very powerful framework that supports both co-routining and parallelism [3]. In this work we report on the design of the first sequencial implementation for the Extended Andorra Model with Implicit Control, the BEAM [2]. The emphasis is put on the low-level infrastructures that support the implementation, that is the memory organisation and objects representation. A novel scheme for classifying variables in an EAM environment is described and the rules for the unification of variables is presented.

A BEAM *computation* is a series of rewriting operations, performed on And-Or Trees. And-Or Trees contain two kinds of nodes: *and-boxes* represent a conjunction of positive literals; and *or-boxes* represent alternative clauses for a selected literal. A variable is said to be *external* to an and-box when not defined in the current and-box, and *local* otherwise. Moreover, a box is said to be *suspended* if the computation on it can not progress deterministically and the box is currently waiting for an event that will allow it to resume computation.

BEAM support four main rewrite rules: **Reduction**, **Promotion**, **Propagation** and **Splitting**. Moreover, it includes additional simplification rules to generate compact And-Or trees and to optimise the computation process. A full description of the EAM framework is given in [1].

2 BEAM Memory Areas and Object Representation

Memory usage is much more complex on the BEAM than in standard WAM implementations due to the fact that the EAM scheduler does not necessarily follow a stack discipline. In contrast, WAM-based Prolog manages a simple stack where space can be recovered after backtracking.

The external state of the BEAM, stored in memory, is divided into two main areas: the *Code_Space* and the *Global_Memory*. The *Code_Space* holds the database, including the compiled logic program, information on predicates, and a

* The work presented in this paper was partially supported by project APRIL (Project POSI/SRI/40749/2001) and funds granted to *LIACC* through the *Programa de Financiamento Plurianual, Fundação para a Ciência e Tecnologia* and *Programa POSI.*

Fernando Moura Pires, Salvador Abreu (Eds.): EPIA 2003, LNAI 2902, pp. 131–135, 2003.

symbol-table. The use of this area is similar to traditional Prolog systems. The *Global_Mem* maintains the and-or-tree that will be created during the execution of the Prolog programs. This area subdivides into the *Heap* and the *Box Memory*.

The *Heap* holds lists and structures, that is Prolog's compound terms. The use of the Heap is very similar to the WAM's Heap, with the difference that on the BEAM Heap memory can not be recovered after backtracking. A Garbage Collector is thus necessary to recover space in this area (see [1]).

The *Box Memory* satisfies memory requests for the creation of and-boxes, or-boxes, local variables, external variables, and suspension structures. This memory must both deal with intensive requests efficiently, and recover memory after the boxes are removed. A more detailed explanation on these routines can be found in [1]. In the next sections we describe how the BEAM represents or-boxes, and-boxes, local variables and external references to local variables.

Or-boxes represent open alternatives for a goal. Each or-box refers to its parent and-box through the `parent` pointer and the call in the parent and-box that created this or-box, `id_call`. `nr_all_alternatives` gives the number of alternatives available. Last, the box points to a list of `alternatives`, where each element in the list includes:

- a pointer to a corresponding and-box, `alternative`, initially empty; it is initialized only when the alternative is explored;
- a pointer to the goal arguments, `args`; The first alternative creates the arguments vector. The last alternative to execute, after performing head unification, recovers the `args` vector as free memory.
- a pointer to the code for the alternative, `code`; and,
- the `state` of the alternative. Initially, alternatives are in the `ready` state. They next move to the `running` state, from where they may reach the `success` or `fail` states, or they may enter the `suspend` state. Suspended alternatives will eventually move to the `wake` state. As an optimization, if no more goals need to be executed for the goal but the alternative is suspended, the alternative enters a special `suspended_on_end` state.

Note that if *nr_all_alternatives* is one, then there is no need to keep the or-box. Furthermore the determinate promotion rule can be applied to the single alternative. If *nr_all_alternatives* equals zero, the box has failed and we can remove the box and propagate the failure.

And-boxes represent active clauses. And-boxes require a more complex structure than or-boxes, as they store information on what goals are active as well as on external and internal variables associated with the clause.

Access to the parent node is performed through the `parent` pointer and through the `id_alternative` field. The first points back to the parent and-box. The second indicates to which alternative the and-box belongs. Subgoal management requires knowing the number of subgoals in the clause `nr_all_calls`. Each and-box maintains a `depth_level` counter that is used to classify variables. The `list_locals` field maintains a list of vectors containing the variables local to this and-box. A list of bindings to external variables is accessed through the `externals` field. The and-box may have been suspended trying to bind some variables, if so this is registered in the `suspended` field. The `stability` field is used to identify if the box is stable. If side-effects predicates are present in the goals of this and-box, they are registed on the `side_effects` field. Last, each subgoal or call requires separate information:

- a pointer to a corresponding or-box, `call`, initially empty; it is initialized when the call is open;
- a pointer to the `locals` variables vector. Each goal needs an entry to the `locals` variables because the *promotion* rule may add other goals and other variables to the and-box. Still each goal needs to be able to identify its own local variables;
- a pointer to the `code` for the subgoal;
- `State` information says whether the goal is `ready` to enter execution, is `running`, or has entered the `success` or `fail` states. Goals may also be `suspended` or `waiting` on some variable, upon which they will enter the `wake` state.

Initially each and-box has one vector of local variables. However, the number of vectors of local variables in an and-box may increase since the promotion rule allows one to promote local variables to a different and-box. We discuss local variables next.

Local variables either belong to a single subgoal in an and-box, or are shared between subgoals. The `value` field stores the current working value for a variable. Unbound variables are represented as self-referencing pointers. Variables also maintain a list of and-boxes suspended on them, and point back to their `home` and-box. The `home` field of a variable structure points directly to its home and-box. However this field is not sufficient to completely determine if a variable is local or not to an and-box, since a variable can be local to several boxes. The problem arises in the case where an and-box is a single alternative and includes pruning operators. The promotion rule can be applied but the and-boxes must be kept separate, even if sharing the same variables, since moving the pruning operators to an upper level in the tree may lead to an incorrect state.

Having the `home` field of the variable structure pointing to a list of and-boxes would allow us to know all and-boxes where the variable is local. We have not used this solution because having to search through a list every time one needs to classify a variable would be very inefficient. Instead, the BEAM uses a depth-counter associated to an and-box to classify variables. We can now precisely define *local variable* as follows:

> A variable is said to be local to a and-box G if the `depth` counter of the and-box G equals the `depth` counter of the variable's `home`. Otherwise the variable is said to be external to the and-box G.

Using this scheme, the classification of variables becomes very simple and efficient since one only needs a simple comparison.

External Variables save bindings for variables older than the current and-box. Each such binding is represented as a data-structure that includes a pointer to the variable definition, `local_var`, and to its new value, `value`. Whenever a goal binds an external variable, the assignment is recorded both in the current and-box as an external reference and at the local variable itself. This way, whenever a descendent and-box wants to use the value of the external reference, it can simply access the local variable. The `external_reference` data-structure generalizes the Prolog's trail, allowing unwinding of bindings performed in the current and-box.

Suspension List is a doubly linked list that keeps information on all suspended boxes. Each entry in the list maintains a pointer to the suspend and-box, `and_box`, and information on why the and-box is suspended, `reason`. Goals may be suspended for trying to bind external variables, or they can be waiting for some event to occur such as, waiting to be leftmost or waiting for a variable to be bounded so that it can be used in a builtin operation.

BEAM uses the same list to maintain information on suspended and awoken and-boxes. The `SU` pointer marks the beginning of the suspension list (that can be empty). Whenever an and-box suspends, an entry is added to the end of the suspension list. If a suspended and-box receives a wake signal, the and-box entry is moved to the beginning of the list. Thus, if there are awaken boxes, they are immediately accessed by the `SU` pointer. Also note that we always want to work with awoken boxes before working with the suspended ones. By default, the order in which suspended boxes are chosen to be split is determined not by the order in which they are in the suspension list, but for being the leftmost in the And-Or Tree. The BEAM finds the leftmost suspended box by performing explicit depth-search on the And-Or Tree.

3 Unification of Two Variables

In this section we discuss in more detail the algorithm that performs the unification of two variables. One important consideration is that an and-box only suspends when trying to bind one or more external variables. Some of these bindings can be generated when unifying two variables.

The original proposal for the EAM did not present details on variable to variable unification. In fact, the BEAM, as the WAM, has an optimal form to unify two different variables in an EAM environment. Making an arbitrary choice may affect performance by forcing unnecessary suspensions as we explain next.

In the BEAM a variable can belong to an and-box: *permanent* variables, or may be stored in the Heap: *temporary* variables. Thus, there are three possible cases of variable to variable binding:

1. *temporary variable* to *permanent variable*: in this case the unification should make the temporary variable refer to the permanent variable. An immediate advantage is that the computation may not suspend. Moreover, unifying in

the opposite direction may lead to an incorrect state, since future dereferencing of the permanent variable would reference a temporary variable that can unify without suspending the computation.
2. *temporary variable* to *temporary variable*: this case may never occur. Temporary variables are only created when constructing compound terms in the Heap. Moreover, whenever these variables are created they immediately unify with a permanent variable. Thus, using the previous rule, a temporary variable is always guaranteed to reference a permanent variable.
3. *permanent variable* to *permanent variable*: the permanent variable that has its home box at a lower level of the tree should always reference the permanent variable that has its home box closest to the root of the tree. As an example, consider a computational tree with three and-boxes `A`, `B`, and `C` where each box contains a single local (permanent) variable: `X`,`Y`, and `Z` respectively. Suppose that `A` is the root of the tree, and that `B` and `C` are the only available alternatives for `A`. Consider that the computation is processing the and-box `B` and that it becomes necessary to unify the variables `X` and `Y`. If the variable `Y` is made to reference the variable `X`, no suspension is necessary since the variable `Y` is local to the and-box `B`. Moreover, if the and-box `B` fails or if the computation continues to the and-box `C` no reset would be necessary in the `X` variable. On the other hand, if `X` is made to reference the variable `Y`, the computation would need to suspend since `X` is not local to the and-box `B`. Moreover, if the and-box `B` fails or if the computation continues to the and-box `C`, the `X` variable would necessarily have to be reset.

By following these unification rules one can often delay the suspension of an and-box and thus delay the application of the splitting rule.

4 Conclusions

We have presented details on the implementation of BEAM, a system for the efficient execution of logic programs based on David H. D. Warren's work on the Extended Andorra Model with implicit control. Our work was motivated by our interest in studying how the EAM with Implicit Control can be effectively implemented and how it can perform versus other execution strategies. Our results show that the BEAM performs well, even when just using implicit control (see [1]). This finding was very encouraging considering the extra complexity of the Extended Andorra Model.

References

1. R. Lopes. *An Implementation of the Extended Andorra Model.* PhD thesis, Universidade do Porto, http://www.dcc.fc.up.pt/Pubs/Teses/teses.html , September 2001.
2. R. Lopes, V. S. Costa, and F. Silva. A novel implementation of the extended andorra model. In *PADL01*, volume 1990 of *LNCS*, pages 199–213. Springer-Verlag, 2001.
3. D. H. D. Warren. The Extended Andorra Model with Implicit Control. Presented at ICLP'90 Workshop on Parallel Logic Programming, Eilat, Israel, June 1990.

YapDss: An Or-Parallel Prolog System for Scalable Beowulf Clusters

Ricardo Rocha, Fernando Silva, and Rolando Martins

DCC-FC & LIACC
University of Porto, Portugal
{ricroc,fds,rolando}@ncc.up.pt

Abstract. This paper discusses the design of YapDss, an or-parallel Prolog system for distributed memory parallel machines, such as the Beowulf PC clusters. The system builds on the work of YapOr, an or-parallel system for shared memory machines, and uses the distributed stack splitting binding model to represent computation state and work sharing among the computational workers. A new variant scheme of stack splitting, the diagonal splitting, is proposed and implemented. This scheme includes efficient algorithms to balance work load among computing workers, to determine the bottommost common node between two workers, and to calculate exactly the work load of one worker. An initial evaluation of the system shows that it is able to achieve very good speedups on a Beowulf PC cluster.

Keywords: Parallel Logic Programming, Or-Parallelism, Stack Splitting.

1 Introduction

Prolog is arguably the most popular Logic Programming language used by researchers in the areas of Artificial Intelligence (AI), such as machine learning and natural language processing. For most of the AI applications, performance is a fundamental issue, and therefore the ability to speedup Prolog execution is a relevant research topic. The development of parallel Prolog systems have further contributed to excel performance. These systems exploit implicit parallelism inherent to the language and therefore do not impose extra work to application developers.

There are two main sources of implicit parallelism in logic programs, *or-parallelism* and *and-parallelism*. Or-parallelism arises from the parallel execution of multiple clauses capable of solving a goal, that is from exploring the non-determinism present in logic programs. And-parallelism arises from the parallel execution of multiple subgoals in a clause body. Of interest to us here is the implementation of or-parallelism. One basic problem with implementing or-parallelism is how to represent, efficiently, the multiple bindings for the same variable produced by the parallel execution of the alternative matching clauses.

Fernando Moura Pires, Salvador Abreu (Eds.): EPIA 2003, LNAI 2902, pp. 136–150, 2003.

Two of the most prominent binding models that have been proposed, *binding arrays* and *environment copying*, have been efficiently used in the implementation of Or-Parallel Prolog systems on, mostly, *shared memory platforms* (SMP) [10, 1,12,13]. Other proposals have also been put forward addressing the other major type of parallel architectures - *distributed memory platforms* (DMP), also known as *massively parallel processors* [3,15,16].

In this paper we are concerned with the implementation of an Or-Parallel Prolog system, the YapDss, for a new type of DMP, namely Beowulf PC clusters. These systems are built from off-the-shelf components and have turned into a viable high-performance, low-cost, scalable, and standardized alternative to the traditional parallel architectures. We take an approach similar to PALS [16], that is we use stack splitting [8] as the main technique to exploit or-parallelism. Stack splitting is a refined version of the environment copying model that is particularly suited for distributed architectures. Environment copying allows computational agents (or workers, or engines, or processors or processes) to share work by copying the state of one busy worker (with unexplored work) to another idle worker. This operation requires further synchronization among the workers to avoid redundant work. Stack splitting introduces a heuristic that when sharing work, the sharing worker completely divides its remaining work with the requesting worker. The splitting is in such a way that both workers will proceed, each executing its branch of the computation, without any need for further synchronization.

Substantial differences between YapDss and PALS resulted in several contributions from our design. The YapDss system builds from a previous efficient Or-Parallel Prolog system, the YapOr [12], based on the environment copying model and the Yap Prolog compiler [14]. YapDss implements a variant stack splitting scheme, the *diagonal splitting*, different from PALS's vertical splitting scheme [16], which, in our view achieves a better work load balance among the computing workers. It uses a simple, yet very efficient, scheme to determine the bottommost common node between the branches of two workers. The work load of a worker is calculated exactly; it is not an estimate. YapDss implements a number of scheduling strategies without having to resort to explicit messages to propagate system work load to workers. Performance analysis showed that YapDss is able to achieve very good performance on a number of common benchmark programs.

The remainder of the paper is organized as follows. First, we introduce the general concepts of environment copying and stack splitting. Next, we describe the diagonal splitting scheme and discuss the major implementation issues in YapDss. We then present an initial performance analysis for a common set of benchmarks. Last, we advance some conclusions and further work.

2 The Multiple Environments Representation Problem

Intuitively, or-parallelism seems simple to implement as the various alternative branches of the search tree are independent of each other. However, parallel execution can result in several conflicting bindings for shared variables. The environments of alternative branches have to be organized in such a way that conflicting bindings can be easily discernible. A binding of a variable is said to be *conditional* if the variable was created before the last choice point, otherwise it is said *unconditional*. The main problem in the management of multiple environments is that of efficiently representing and accessing conditional bindings, since unconditional bindings can be treated as in normal sequential execution.

2.1 Environment Copying

Essentially, the multiple binding representation problem is solved by devising a mechanism where each branch has some private area where it stores its conditional bindings. A number of approaches have been proposed to tackle this problem [7]. Arguably, *environment copying* is the most efficient way to maintain or-parallel environments. Copying was made popular by the Muse or-parallel system [1], a system derived from an early release of SICStus Prolog. Muse showed excellent performance results [2] and in contrast to other approaches, it also showed low overhead over the corresponding sequential system. Most modern parallel logic programming systems, including SICStus Prolog [6], ECLiPSe [17], and Yap [12] use copying as a solution to the multiple bindings problem.

In the environment copying model each worker maintains its own copy of the environment, but in an *identical address space*, that is, each worker allocates their data areas starting at the same logical addresses. An idle worker gets work from a busy worker, by copying all the stacks from the sharing worker. Copying of stacks is made efficient through the technique of *incremental copying*. The idea of incremental copying is based on the fact that the idle worker could have already traversed a part of the search tree that is common to the sharing worker, and thus it does not need to copy this part of stacks. Furthermore, copying of stacks is done from the logical addresses of the sharing worker to exactly the same logical addresses of the idle worker, which therefore avoids potential relocation of address values.

As a result of copying, each worker can carry out execution exactly like a sequential system, requiring very little synchronization with other workers. When a variable is bound, the binding is stored in the private environment of the worker doing the binding, without causing binding conflicts. Synchronization is only needed to guarantee that no two workers explore the same alternative from a shared choice point. Each shared choice point is thus associated with a new data structure, the *shared frame*, that is used to guarantee mutual exclusion when accessing the untried alternatives in such choice points. This works well on SMP, where mutual exclusion is implemented using *locks*. However, mutual exclusion for shared data structures on DMP leads to frequent exchange of messages, which can be a considerable source of overhead and bottleneck.

Nevertheless the shared nature of choice points, environment copying has been recognized as one of the best approaches to support or-parallelism in DMP platforms [5,4,3]. This is because, at least all the other data structures, such as the environment, the heap and the trail do not require synchronization. Moreover, practice has showed that the best policy to dispatch work for or-parallel execution is *scheduling on bottommost choice points*. The bottommost policy turns public the whole private region of a worker when it shares work. This maximizes the amount of shared work and possibly avoids that the requesting worker runs out of work too early and therefore invokes the scheduler too often. This is especially important for an environment copying approach because it minimizes the potential number of copying operations.

2.2 Stack Splitting

In order to avoid shared frames, while keeping stack copying with scheduling on bottommost choice points, Gupta and Pontelli proposed a novel technique, called *stack splitting* [8], to ensure that no two workers can pick the same alternative from shared choice points. The basic idea is to split untried alternatives between the workers sharing a choice point. The splitting should be in such a way that each private copy of the choice point in a worker's environment has its own untried alternatives. Several schemes for splitting the set of untried alternatives in shared choice points can be adopted. Figure 1 illustrates three different splitting schemes, that we name *horizontal*, *vertical* and *diagonal* splitting. Other schemes are still possible.

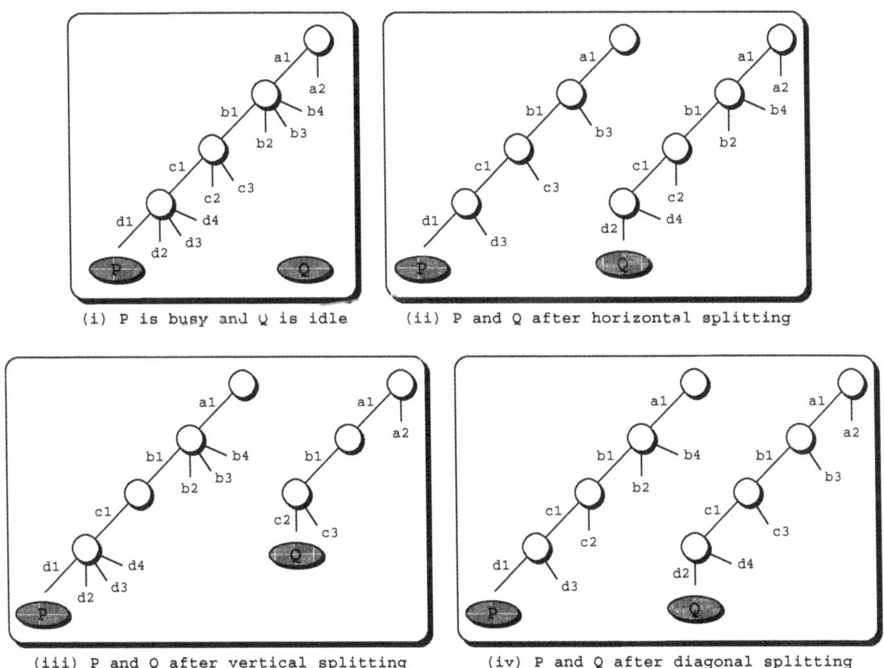

Fig. 1. Splitting of choice points

In horizontal splitting, the untried alternatives in each choice point are alternatively split between the requesting worker Q and the sharing worker P. In vertical splitting, each worker is given all the untried alternatives in alternate choice points, starting from worker P with its current choice point. By observing the figure, it is clear that horizontal and vertical splitting may lead to unbalanced partitioning of the set of untried alternatives between the workers. Despite this fact, the PALS system [16] showed good results by adopting vertical splitting to implement or-parallelism in DMP.

Diagonal splitting uses a more elaborated scheme to achieve a precise partitioning of the set of untried alternatives. It is a kind of mixed approach between horizontal and vertical splitting, the set of untried alternatives in all choice points are alternatively split between both workers. When a first choice point with odd number of untried alternatives (say $2n + 1$) appears, one worker (say Q, the one that starts the partitioning) is given $n + 1$ alternatives and the other (say P) is given n. The workers then alternate and, in the upper choice point, P starts the partitioning. When more choice points with an odd number of untried alternatives appear, the split process is repeated. At the end, Q and P may have the same number of untried alternatives or, in the worst case, Q may have one more alternative than P.

As a result of applying stack splitting, synchronization through shared frames disappears, environments become completely independent of each other and workers can execute exactly like sequential systems. Workers only communicate when sharing work or when detecting termination. This makes stack splitting highly suitable for distributed execution.

3 The YapDss System

YapDss is an or-parallel Prolog system that implements stack splitting to exploit or-parallelism in DMP. As previous systems, YapDss uses a multi-sequential approach [10] to represent computation state and work sharing among the computational workers. Distributed execution of a program is performed by a set of workers, that are expected to spend most of their time performing useful work. When they have no more alternatives to try, workers search for work from fellow workers. YapDss uses a bottommost policy to dispatch work for or-parallel execution. Work is shared through copying of the execution stacks and diagonal splitting is used to split the available work. Communication among the workers is done using explicit message passing via the LAM implementation [9] of the MPI standard. Our initial implementation does not support cuts or side-effects.

3.1 Splitting Work

A fundamental task when sharing work is to decide which untried alternatives each worker is assigned to. As we have already mentioned, YapDss uses the diagonal scheme to split work among workers. In order to implement that scheme and thus avoid the execution of possible duplicate alternatives, we extended choice points with an extra field, the CP_OFFSET. This field marks the offset of the next untried alternative belonging to the choice point. When allocating a choice point, CP_OFFSET is initialized with a value of 1, meaning that the next alternative to be taken is the next alternative in the list of untried alternatives. This is the usual behavior that we expect for private choice points.

With this mechanism, we can easily implement the splitting process when sharing work. We simply need to double the value of the CP_OFFSET field of each shared choice point. This corresponds to alternatively split the set of previous available alternatives in the choice point. To better understand this mechanism, we next illustrate in Fig. 2 a situation where a worker P shares a private choice point with two different workers, first with worker X and later with worker Y.

Fig. 2. Using an offset to split work

Initially, in Fig. 2(i), we have P with a private choice point with five untried alternatives: $a2$, $a3$, $a4$, $a5$ and $a6$. CP_OFFSET is 1 and CP_ALT, which holds the reference to the next untried alternative to be taken, refers $a2$. If backtracking occurs, P will successively try each of the five available alternatives. After loading an alternative for execution, P updates CP_ALT to refer to the next one. Because CP_OFFSET is 1, the next alternative to be taken is the next one in the list.

Moving to Fig. 2(ii), consider that P shares its private choice point with X. This can be done by doubling the value in the CP_OFFSET field of the choice point. Moreover, to avoid that both workers execute the same alternatives, the worker that do not start the partitioning of alternatives (please refer to the previous section), X in the figure, updates the CP_ALT field of its choice point to refer to the next available alternative. With this scenario, when backtracking, P will take alternatives $a2$, $a4$ and $a6$ and X will take alternatives $a3$ and $a5$. This happens because they will use the offset 2 to calculate the next reference to be stored in CP_ALT. Finally, in Fig. 2(iii), P shares the choice point with another worker, Y. The value in CP_OFFSET is doubled again and P is the worker that updates the CP_ALT field of its choice point. Within this new scenario, when backtracking, P will take alternative $a4$ and Y will take alternatives $a2$ and $a6$.

When sharing work, we need to know if the number of available alternatives in a choice point is odd or even in order to decide which worker starts the partitioning in the upper choice point. Note that this is not a problem for horizontal or vertical splitting because that kind of information is not needed. A possibility is to follow the list of available alternatives and count its number, but obviously this is not an efficient mechanism. YapDss uses a different approach, it takes advantage of the compiler. All the first instructions that represent the WAM compiled code of a given alternative were extended to include two extra fields in a common predefined position. We will use the names REM_ALT and NEXT_ALT to refer to these fields. Figure 3 shows an example for a predicate with four alternatives: *alt_1*, *alt_2*, *alt_3* and *alt_4*.

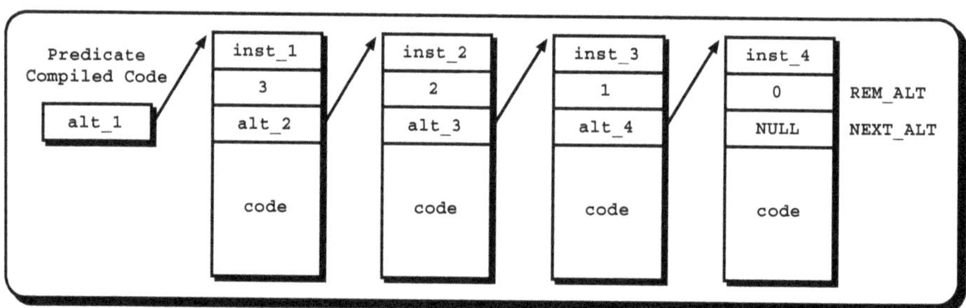

Fig. 3. Compiled code for a predicate in YapDss

The REM_ALT field gives the number of remaining alternatives starting from the current alternative. As we will see next, this allows us to solve the problem of deciding which worker starts the partitioning in a shared choice point. This field was inherited from YapOr.

The NEXT_ALT field is an explicit reference to the compiled code of the next alternative. Note that most of the first instructions that represent the WAM compiled code of a given alternative already contain a reference to the compiled code of the next alternative. The problem is that such references are not positioned in a common predefined position for all instructions. Thus, for these instructions, instead of introducing an extra field we simply make the position uniform. This is extremely important because, when updating the CP_ALT field in a shared choice point (see Fig. 4), we can navigate through the alternatives by simply using the NEXT_ALT field, and therefore avoid testing the kind of instructions they hold to correctly follow the reference to the next alternative.

```
update_alternative(choice point CP) {
  offset = CP_OFFSET(CP)
  next_alt = CP_ALT(CP)
  if (offset > REM_ALT(next_alt))
    next_alt = NULL
  else
    while (offset--)
      next_alt = NEXT_ALT(next_alt)
  CP_ALT(CP) = next_alt
}
```

Fig. 4. Pseudo-code for updating the CP_ALT field in a choice point

The CP_ALT field is updated when a worker backtracks to a choice point to take the next untried alternative or when a worker splits work during the sharing work process. Figure 5 shows the pseudo-code for diagonal splitting. Note that the two workers involved in a sharing operation execute the splitting procedure.

```
diagonal_splitting(bottom choice point BCP, top choice point TCP) {
  if (requesting worker) starts = TRUE  % the requesting worker
  else starts = FALSE                   % starts the partitioning
  current_cp = BCP
  while (current_cp != TCP) {
    alt = CP_ALT(current_cp)
    if (alt != NULL) {
      offset = CP_OFFSET(current_cp)
      if (starts == FALSE)
        update_alternative(current_cp)
      if ((REM_ALT(alt) / offset) mod 2 == 0)  % workers alternate
        starts = !starts
      CP_OFFSET(current_cp) *= 2
    }
    current_cp = CP_B(current_cp)  % CP_B points to the upper choice point
  }
}
```

Fig. 5. Pseudo-code for splitting work using the diagonal scheme

3.2 Finding the Bottommost Common Node

The main goal of sharing work is to position the workers involved in the operation at the same node of the search tree, leaving them with the same computational state. For an environment copying approach, this is accomplished by copying the execution stacks between workers, which may include transferring large amounts of data. This poses a major overhead to stack copying based systems. In particular, for DMP implementations, it can be even more expensive because copying is done through message passing.

To minimize this source of overhead, Ali and Karlsson devised a technique, called *incremental copying* [1], that enables the receiving worker to keep the part of its state that is consistent with that of the giving worker. Only the differences are copied, which permits to reduce considerably the amount of data transferred between workers. However, to successfully implement incremental copying, we need a mechanism that allows us to quickly find the bottommost common node between two workers. For SMP, this is achieved by using the shared frames to store additional information about the workers sharing a choice point [1]. For DMP, we do not have shared data structures where to store that information. To overcome this limitation, in [16], Villaverde and colleagues devised a labeling mechanism to uniquely identify the original source of each choice point (the worker which created it). By comparing private labels from different workers they detect common choice points.

In YapDss we take a similar but simpler approach. We used a private *branch array* to uniquely represent the position of each worker in the search tree. The depth of a choice point along a branch identifies its offset in the branch array. The alternative taken in a choice point defines its value in the branch array. By comparing the branch array of two workers we can easily find the bottommost common node.

Initially, the branch array is empty. When a new choice point is allocated, the top position of the array is marked with the number corresponding to the first alternative to be executed. We take advantage of the `REM_ALT` field to number the alternatives. For example, consider allocating a choice point for the predicate in Fig. 3, the branch array will be initialized with 3 (the `REM_ALT` value of the first alternative). When a worker backtracks, the corresponding entry in the branch array is updated with the new `REM_ALT` value of the next available alternative. Figure 6 shows an example. For simplicity, it considers that all choice points in the figure correspond to predicates with four alternatives, as illustrated in Fig. 3.

Worker P is executing on branch $< a3 : b1 : c2 : d1 >$ and worker Q is executing on branch $< a3 : b3 : c4 >$. Their branch arrays are respectively $< 1 : 3 : 2 : 3 >$ and $< 1 : 1 : 0 >$, which differ in the second entry. We can therefore conclude that the two topmost choice points are common to both workers. They have the same computational state until the bottommost common choice point, and differ bellow such choice point, P is executing alternative $b1$ and Q is executing alternative $b3$. With the branch array data structure, implementing incremental copying for DMP can now be easily done. Moreover, as it uniquely represents the position of each worker in the search tree, we argue that it has good properties that we can take advantage of to extend YapDss to support cuts and side-effects.

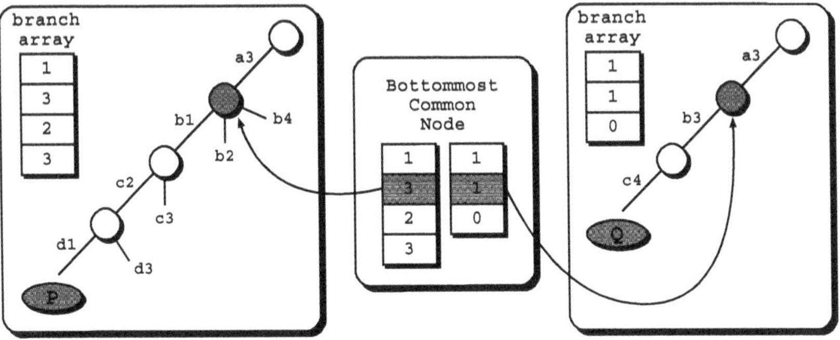

Fig. 6. Using the branch array to find the bottommost common node

3.3 Sharing Work

The sharing work process takes place when an idle worker Q makes a sharing request to a busy worker P and receives a positive answer. In YapDss, the process is as follows. When requesting work, Q sends a message to P that includes its branch array. If P decides to share work with Q, it compares its branch array against the one received from Q in order to find the bottommost common choice point. P then applies incremental copying to compute the stack segments to be copied to Q. It packs all the information in a message and sends it back to Q. If receiving a positive answer, Q copies the stack segments in the message to the proper space in its execution stacks. Meanwhile, P splits the available alternatives in the choice points shared with Q using diagonal splitting. After finishing copying, Q also performs diagonal splitting. While doing diagonal splitting, both workers also update their branch arrays. As an optimization, P can avoid storing its private choice points in the branch array until sharing them.

Note that to fully synchronize the computational state between the two workers, worker Q further needs to install from P the conditional bindings made to variables belonging to the common segments. To solve that, when packing the answering message, P also includes a buffer with all these conditional variables along with their bindings so that Q can update them.

Another point of interest, is how the receiving worker Q can obtain access to the untried alternatives in the choice points of P that are common to both workers [16]. Consider, for example, the situation in Fig. 6. Assuming that P shares work with Q, it will send to Q the stack segments corresponding to its current branch starting from the bottommost common node, that is, branch $< b1 : c2 : d1 >$. Therefore, Q will not be able to access the available alternatives $b2$ and $b4$ in the bottommost choice point because the CP_ALT field in its choice point is NULL. This can be solved by having P to include in the answering message all the CP_ALT fields with available alternatives between the bottommost choice point and the root node [16]. YapDss still does not supports this optimization. Currently, to share untried alternatives from common choice points, P has to explicitly include such segments in the answering message as if they were not common.

3.4 Scheduling

The scheduler is the system component that is responsible for distributing the available work between the various workers. The scheduler must arrange the workers in the search tree in such a way that the total execution time will be the least possible. The scheduler must also minimize the overheads present in synchronization and communication operations such as requesting work, sharing nodes, copying parts of the stacks, splitting work and detecting termination.

An optimal strategy would be to select the busy worker that simultaneously holds the highest work load and that is nearest to the idle worker. The *work load* is a measure of the amount of untried alternatives. *Being near* corresponds to the closest position in the search tree. This strategy maximizes the amount of shared work and minimizes the stacks parts to be copied. Nevertheless, selecting such a worker requires having precise information about the position and work load of all workers. For a DMP based system, maintaining this information requires considerable communications during execution. We thus have a contradiction, to minimize overheads we need more communications. One reasonable solution is to find a compromise between the scheduler efficiency and its overheads. We use a simple but effective strategy to implement scheduling in YapDss.

Each worker holds a private *load register*, as a measure of the exact number of private untried alternatives in its current branch. To compute this exact number we take again advantage of the `CP_OFFSET` and `REM_ALT` fields. The load register is updated in three different situations: when allocating a new choice point, it is incremented by the number of untried alternatives left in the choice point; when backtracking, it is decremented by one unit; and when splitting work, it can be incremented (if receiving work) or decremented (if giving work) by the number of alternatives being split.

Besides, each worker holds a private *load vector* as a measure of the estimated work load of each fellow worker. The load vector is updated in two situations: when sharing work and when receiving a termination token. YapDss does not introduce specific messages to explicitly ask for work load information from a worker, and instead it extends the existing messages to include that information. A trivial case occurs when a worker receives a sharing request, a zero work load can be automatically inferred for the requesting worker. When sharing work, the answering message is extended to include the work load of the giving worker. When detecting termination, the termination tokens are extended to include the work load of all workers in the system.

Termination detection is done using a simple algorithm from [11]. When an idle worker Q suspects that all the other workers are idle too, it initializes a termination token with its work load (zero in this case) and sends it to the next worker on rank. When receiving a token, a worker updates its load vector with the load information already in the token, includes its work load and sends it to the next worker on rank. The process repeats until reaching the initial worker

Q. If, when reaching Q, the token is clean (zero load for all workers) then Q broadcasts a termination message. Otherwise, Q simply updates its load vector and starts scheduling for a busy worker.

When scheduling for a busy worker, we follow the following strategies. By default, an idle worker Q tries to request work from the last worker, say L, which has shared work with it in order to minimize the potential stacks parts to be copied. However, if the work load for L in Q's load vector is less than a threshold value `LOAD_BALANCE` (6 in our implementation), a different strategy is used, Q starts searching its load vector for the worker with the greatest work load to request work from it (note that L can be the selected worker).

When a worker P receives a sharing request, it may accept or refuse the request. If its current work load is less than `LOAD_BALANCE`, it replies with a negative answer. Otherwise, it accepts the sharing request and, by default, performs stack splitting until the bottommost common node N. However, if the available work in the branch until node N is less than `LOAD_BALANCE`, it may extend the splitting branch to include common choice points (please refer to the last paragraph in section 3.3). In both cases (negative or positive answers), P includes in the answering message its current work load. If receiving a negative answer, Q updates its load vector with the value for P and starts searching for the next worker with the greatest work load. Meanwhile, if Q finds that all entries in its load vector are zero, it initializes a termination token.

4 Initial Performance Evaluation

The evaluation of the first implementation of YapDss was performed on a low-cost PC cluster with 4 dual Pentium II nodes interconnected by Myrinet-SAN switches. The benchmark programs are standard and commonly used to assess other parallel Prolog systems. All benchmarks find all solutions for the problem. We measured the timings and speedups for each benchmark and analyzed some parallel activities to identify potential sources of overhead.

To put the performance results in perspective we first evaluate how YapDss compares against the Yap Prolog engine. Table 1 shows the base running times, in seconds, for Yap and YapDss (configured with one worker) for the set of benchmark programs. In parentheses, it shows YapDss's overhead over Yap running times. The results indicate that YapDss is on average 16% slower than Yap. YapDss overheads mainly result from handling the work load register, the branch array, and from testing operations that check for termination tokens or sharing request messages.

Table 2 presents the performance of YapDss with multiple workers. It shows the running times, in seconds, for the set of benchmark programs, with speedups relative to the one worker case given in parentheses. The running times correspond to the best times obtained in a set of 5 runs. The variation between runs was not significant.

The results show that YapDss is quite efficient in exploiting or-parallelism, giving effective speedups over execution with just one worker. The quality of

Table 1. Running times for Yap and YapDss with one worker

Programs	Yap	YapDss
nsort	188.50	218.68(1.16)
queens12	65.03	72.80(1.12)
puzzle4x4	54.61	67.91(1.24)
magic	29.31	30.90(1.05)
cubes7	1.26	1.31(1.05)
ham	0.23	0.30(1.32)
Average		(1.16)

Table 2. Running times and speedups for YapDss with multiple workers

Programs	Number of Workers			
	2	4	6	8
queens12	38.93(1.99)	19.63(3.94)	13.36(5.80)	10.12(7.66)
nsort	124.24(1.98)	63.14(3.90)	42.44(5.80)	33.06(7.45)
puzzle4x4	34.00(1.99)	17.34(3.91)	11.83(5.73)	9.41(7.20)
magic	15.50(1.99)	7.88(3.92)	5.58(5.53)	4.38(7.05)
cubes7	0.67(1.96)	0.40(3.26)	0.33(3.90)	0.23(4.80)
ham	0.17(1.75)	0.10(2.81)	0.09(3.13)	0.10(2.95)
Average	(1.94)	(3.62)	(4.98)	(6.19)

the speedups achieved depends significantly on the amount of parallelism in the program being executed. The programs in the first group, *queens12*, *nsort*, *puzzle4x4* and *magic*, have rather large search spaces, and are therefore amenable to the execution of coarse-grained tasks. This group shows very good speedups up to 8 workers. The speedups are still reasonably good for the second group, programs *cubes7* and *ham*, given that they have smaller grain tasks.

We next examine the main activities that take place during parallel execution in order to determine which of them are causing a decrease in performance. The activities traced are:

Prolog: percentage of total running time spent in Prolog execution and in handling the work load register and branch array.

Search: percentage of total running time spent searching for a busy worker and in processing sharing and termination messages.

Sharing: percentage of total running time spent in the sharing work process.

Reqs Acp: total number of sharing request messages accepted.

Reqs Ref: total number of sharing request messages refused.

Recv Load: total number of untried alternatives received from busy workers during splitting.

Table 3 shows the results obtained with 2, 4 and 8 workers in each activity for two of the benchmark programs, one from each class of parallelism.

The results show that when we increase the number of workers, the percentage of total running time spent on the *Prolog* activity tends to decrease and be

Table 3. Workers activities during execution

	Activities					
Programs	**Prolog**	**Search**	**Sharing**	**Reqs Acp**	**Reqs Ref**	**Recv Load**
queens12						
2 workers	99%	0%	1%	8	3	296
4 workers	98%	1%	1%	99	208	3568
8 workers	93%	6%	1%	160	6630	5592
ham						
2 workers	80%	19%	1%	6	3	64
4 workers	53%	45%	2%	15	87	135
8 workers	25%	74%	1%	18	346	195

moved to the *Search* activity. This happens because the competition for finding work leads workers to get smaller tasks. This can be observed by the increase in the *Recv Load* parameter. If workers get smaller tasks, they tend to search for work more frequently. This can be observed by the increase in the *Reqs Acp* and *Reqs Ref* parameters. The time spent in the *Sharing* activity is almost constant, suggesting that the splitting process is not a major problem for YapDss performance.

5 Concluding Remarks

In this paper we proposed a new variant scheme of the stack splitting scheme, the diagonal splitting, and described its implementation in the YapDss or-parallel Prolog system. This scheme includes efficient algorithms to balance work load among computing workers, to determine the bottommost common node between two workers, and to calculate exactly the work load of one worker.

YapDss showed good sequential and parallel performance on a set of standard benchmark programs, running on a PC cluster parallel architecture. It was able to achieve excellent speedups for applications with coarse-grained parallelism and quite good results globally. This may be a result of the low communication overheads imposed by the scheduling schemes implemented.

Future work include more detailed system evaluation and performance tuning, in particular we intend to evaluate the system on a recently built PC cluster with 4 dual AMD XP 2000+ nodes, with 2 GBytes of main memory per node, interconnected by Giga-Ethernet switches. We also plan to extend YapDss to better support all builtins, support speculative execution with cuts, and integrate the system in the Yap distribution.

Acknowledgments. We are grateful for the insightful comments received from Vítor Santos Costa. This work has been partially supported by APRIL (POSI/SRI/40749/2001), and by funds granted to LIACC through the *Programa de Financiamento Plurianual, Fundação para a Ciência e Tecnologia* and *Programa POSI.*

References

1. K. Ali and R. Karlsson. The Muse Approach to OR-Parallel Prolog. *International Journal of Parallel Programming*, 19(2):129–162, 1990.
2. K. Ali, R. Karlsson, and S. Mudambi. Performance of Muse on Switch-Based Multiprocessor Machines. *New Generation Computing*, 11(1 & 4):81–103, 1992.
3. L. Araujo and J. Ruz. A Parallel Prolog System for Distributed Memory. *Journal of Logic Programming*, 33(1):49–79, 1997.
4. V. Benjumea and J. M. Troya. An OR Parallel Prolog Model for Distributed Memory Systems. In *Proceedings of the 5th International Symposium on Programming Language Implementation and Logic Programming*, number 714 in Lecture Notes in Computer Science, pages 291–301. Springer-Verlag, 1993.
5. J. Briat, M. Favre, C. Geyer, and J. Chassin de Kergommeaux. OPERA: Or-Parallel Prolog System on Supernode. In *Implementations of Distributed Prolog*, pages 45–64. Wiley & Sons, New York, USA, 1992.
6. M. Carlsson and J. Widen. SICStus Prolog User's Manual. SICS Research Report R88007B, Swedish Institute of Computer Science, 1988.
7. G. Gupta and B. Jayaraman. Analysis of Or-parallel Execution Models. *ACM Transactions on Programming Languages*, 15(4):659–680, 1993.
8. G. Gupta and E. Pontelli. Stack Splitting: A Simple Technique for Implementing Or-parallelism on Distributed Machines. In *Proceedings of the 16th International Conference on Logic Programming*, pages 290–304. The MIT Press, 1999.
9. Open Systems Laboratory. LAM/MPI Parallel Computing, 2003. Available from `http://www.lam-mpi.org`.
10. E. Lusk, R. Butler, T. Disz, R. Olson, R. Overbeek, R. Stevens, D. H. D. Warren, A. Calderwood, P. Szeredi, S. Haridi, P. Brand, M. Carlsson, A. Ciepielewski, and B. Hausman. The Aurora Or-Parallel Prolog System. In *Proceedings of the International Conference on Fifth Generation Computer Systems*, pages 819–830. ICOT, Tokyo, 1988.
11. F. Mattern. Algorithms for Distributed Termination Detection. *Distributed Computing*, 2(3):161–175, 1987.
12. R. Rocha, F. Silva, and V. Santos Costa. YapOr: an Or-Parallel Prolog System Based on Environment Copying. In *Proceedings of the 9th Portuguese Conference on Artificial Intelligence*, number 1695 in Lecture Notes in Artificial Intelligence, pages 178–192. Springer-Verlag, 1999.
13. R. Rocha, F. Silva, and V. Santos Costa. On a Tabling Engine that Can Exploit Or-Parallelism. In *Proceedings of the 17th International Conference on Logic Programming*, number 2237 in Lecture Notes in Computer Science, pages 43–58. Springer-Verlag, 2001.
14. V. Santos Costa. Optimising Bytecode Emulation for Prolog. In *Proceedings of Principles and Practice of Declarative Programming*, number 1702 in Lecture Notes in Computer Science, pages 261–267, Paris, France, 1999. Springer-Verlag.
15. F. Silva and P. Watson. Or-Parallel Prolog on a Distributed Memory Architecture. *Journal of Logic Programming*, 43(2):173–186, 2000.
16. K. Villaverde, E. Pontelli, H. Guo, and G. Gupta. PALS: An Or-Parallel Implementation of Prolog on Beowulf Architectures. In *Proceedings of the 17th International Conference on Logic Programming*, number 2237 in Lecture Notes in Computer Science, pages 27–42. Springer-Verlag, 2001.
17. M. Wallace, S. Novello, and J. Schimpf. ECLiPSe: A Platform for Constraint Logic Programming. Technical report, IC-Parc, Imperial College, London, 1997.

Experimental Evaluation of a Caching Technique for ILP*

Nuno Fonseca[1], Vitor Santos Costa[3], Fernando Silva[1], and Rui Camacho[2]

[1] DCC-FC & LIACC, Universidade do Porto
R. do Campo Alegre 823, 4150-180 Porto, Portugal
{nf,fds}@ncc.up.pt
[2] COPPE/Sistemas, Universidade Federal do Rio de Janeiro
Centro de Tecnologia, Bloco H-319, Cx. Postal 68511 Rio de Janeiro, Brasil
vitor@cos.ufrj.br
[3] Faculdade de Engenharia & LIACC, Universidade do Porto
Rua Dr. Roberto Frias, s/n 4200-465 Porto, Portugal
rcamacho@fe.up.pt

Keywords: Inductive Logic Programming, Coverage Caching

1 Introduction

Inductive Logic Programming (ILP) is a Machine Learning technique that has been quite successful in knowledge discovery for relational domains. ILP systems implemented in Prolog challenge the limits of Prolog systems due to heavy usage of resources such as database accesses and memory usage, and to very long execution times. The major reason to implement ILP systems in Prolog is that the inference mechanism implemented by the Prolog engine is fundamental to most ILP learning algorithms. ILP systems can therefore benefit from the extensive performance improvement work that has taken place for Prolog. On the other hand, ILP is a non-classical Prolog application because it uses large sets of ground facts and requires storing a large search tree.

One major criticism of ILP systems is that they often have long running times. A technique that tries to tackle this problem is coverage caching [5]. Coverage caching stores previous results in order to avoid recomputation. Naturally, this technique uses the Prolog internal database to store results. The question is: does coverage caching successfully reduce the ILP systems running time? To obtain an answer to this question we evaluated the impact of the coverage caching technique using the April [1] ILP system with the YAP Prolog system. To understand the results obtained we profiled April's execution and present initial results. The contribution of this paper is twofold: to an ILP researcher it provides an evaluation of the coverage caching technique implemented in Prolog using well known datasets; to a Prolog implementation researcher it shows the need of efficient internal database indexing mechanisms.

* The work presented in this paper has been partially supported by project APRIL (Project POSI/SRI/40749/2001) and funds granted to *LIACC* through the *Programa de Financiamento Plurianual, Fundação para a Ciência e Tecnologia* and *Programa POSI*. Nuno Fonseca is funded by the FCT grant SFRH/BD/7045/2001.

Fernando Moura Pires, Salvador Abreu (Eds.): EPIA 2003, LNAI 2902, pp. 151–155, 2003.

To a brief introduction to some concepts and terminology used in ILP we refer to [2,3]. An extended version of this paper available as a technical report [4].

2 Coverage Caching

The objective of an ILP system is the induction of logic programs. As input an ILP system receives a set of examples E, divided in positive (E^+) and negative examples (E^-), of the concept to learn, and some prior knowledge B, or *background knowledge*. Both examples and background knowledge are usually represented as logic programs. An ILP system tries to produce a theory (logic program) where positive examples succeed and the negative examples fail. To find a satisfactory theory, an ILP system searches through a search space of the permitted clauses.

The coverage of a clause h_i is computed by testing the clause against the positive and negative examples. This is done by verifying for each example e in E if $B \wedge h_i \vdash e$. Coverage caching aims at reducing the computation time spent in coverage tests by storing the coverage lists (the set of positive and negative examples covered by the clause) for each clause generated.

The coverage lists are used as follows. An hypothesis S is generated by adding a literal to a hypothesis G. Let $Cover(G) = \{all\ e \in E\ such\ that\ B \wedge G \models e\}$. Since G is more general than S then $Cover(S) \subseteq Cover(G)$. Taking this into account, when testing the coverage of S it is only necessary to consider examples of $Cover(G)$, thus reducing the coverage computation time. Cussens [5] extended this scheme by proposing what is designated as coverage caching. The coverage lists are permanently stored and reused whenever necessary, thus coverage computation of a particular clause is performed only once. Coverage lists reduce the effort in coverage computation at the cost of significantly increasing memory consumption.

In order to reduce execution time the cache must be very efficient, by this we mean that insertions and retrievals of elements in the cache should be done very fast. The April system uses the YAP Prolog internal and clausal database to store clauses's coverage, the only solution available within the Prolog language.

3 Experiments and Results

To analyze the impact of the coverage caching technique on both memory usage and execution time, we conducted a series of experiments using datasets from the Machine Learning repositories of the Universities of Oxford[1] and York[2]. The experiments were made on an AMD Athlon(tm) MP 2000+ dual-processor PC with 2GB of memory, running the Linux RedHat (kernel 2.4.20) operating system. We used version 0.5 of the April ILP system and version 4.3.24 of the YAP Prolog. A more complete description of the experiments can be found in [4].

[1] `http://www.comlab.ox.ac.uk/oucl/areas/machlearn/applications.html`
[2] `http://www.cs.york.ac.uk/mlg/index.html`

Note that in order to speedup the experiments we limited the search space on some datasets. This reduces the total memory usage and execution time needed to process the dataset at the cost of finding possible worst theories. However, since we are comparing the memory consumption and execution time when using coverage caching or not using it, the estimate we obtain will still give a good idea of the impact of the cache.

Table 1 presents the impact of activating coverage caching in April. It shows the total number of hypotheses generated ($| H |$), the execution time, the memory usage, and the impact in performance for execution time and memory usage (given as a ratio between using coverage caching and not using coverage caching). The memory values presented correspond to the total memory used by April.

Table 1. Impact of coverage caching

Dataset	$\mid H \mid$	Time (sec.)		Memory (bytes)		yes/no(%)	
		no	yes	no	yes	Time	Memory
amine uptake	66933	58.37	357.4	3027460	11255228	612.30	371.77
carcinogenesis	142714	616.38	506.65	7541316	13542528	82.19	179.57
choline	803366	1840.25	13596.07	5327052	32537788	738.81	610.80
krki	2579	3.78	1.15	2225176	2318084	30.42	104.17
mesh	283552	637.34	3241.73	7255884	25733376	508.63	354.65
multiplication	478	8.87	8.93	4261768	4422080	100.67	103.76
pyrimidines	372320	915.95	5581.91	5659544	27856496	609.41	492.20
proteins	433271	7837.96	794.4	27075788	27495636	10.13	101.55

As expected, the results indicate a significant increase in memory usage when coverage caching is activated. However, unexpectedly the use of coverage caching also increased the execution time, in some cases more than 5 times, for larger datasets (i.e. datasets with larger number of examples and $| H |$). The `proteins` dataset shows a reduction of around 90% in the execution time which is what one would like to observe when employing a caching mechanism.

The overheads in execution time were somehow unexpected and prompted us to further investigate the reasons for this behavior. We decided to activate YAP's profiling and then rerun the April system for all datasets previously considered.

One first issue that we would like to clarify is whether coverage caching reduced the number of goal invocations executed. Table 2 shows the total number of calls and retries performed by YAP with the cache activated and deactivated. The result values represent the aggregate number of calls and retries for all datasets. Note that the number of retries shown, with the cache deactivated, is lower than the real value because in some datasets the YAP counters overflowed. In these cases the maximum value possible was used instead. The use of cache reduced the number of calls by 90% and reduced the number of retries by at least 15%. This shows that the use of caching clearly achieves the goal of reducing computation but surprisingly the execution time increased by 56%. Note that the number of calls were reduced by 30 billions approximately.

Table 2. Total number of calls and execution time

Module	cache=yes	cache=no	yes/no
Calls	3,141,742,379	33,508,263,954	0.09
Retries	26,112,058,881	>30,730,206,551	0.84
Time (sec.)	38731.23	24718.04	1.56

We analyzed the profiling logs trying to identify the predicates that were causing the inefficiency problems. Table 3 presents a summary of the number of calls for the predicates considered more relevant. Since the number of calls for most of the predicates decreased with the use of cache, we selected those predicates whose number of calls were still very high, or increased, or operate the Prolog database.

Table 3. Number of calls for some predicates. The `idb_cache::idb_keys` predicate is a dynamic predicate used to store cache keys, and value in parenthesis is the number of recalls.

Predicate	cache=yes	cache=no	Variation
prolog:abolish/1	13,304	17,204	-3,900
prolog:assert/1	98,362	5,663	+92,699
prolog:assertz/1	1,592,288	2,049,054	-456,766
prolog:numbervars/3	5,265,269	4,349	+5,260,920
prolog:eraseall/1	5,902,918	7,734,758	-1,831,840
prolog:recordz/3	5,665,526	7,562,647	-1,897,121
prolog:copy_term/2	5,677,883	515,905	+5,161,978
prolog:call/1	6,396,015	8,314,571	-1,918,556
prolog:erase/1	20,674,230	24,155,488	-3,481,258
prolog:recorda/3	25,866,551	23,760,276	+2,106,275
prolog:ground/1	110,305,158	90,361,520	+19,943,638
idb_cache:idb_keys	5,166,049 (789,534)	0	+5,166,049

Table 3 shows that in the `prolog` module the number of calls increased only for the `assert`, `recorda`, `numbervars`, `copy_term`, and `ground` predicates. The increase of calls in the `idb_cache` module was most felt in the `idb_keys` predicate. All the other predicates in the `idb_cache` make calls to the predicates in the `prolog` module, in particular to the `recorded` predicate that YAP could not show in the profile statistics. From the profile results we estimated that the number of calls to the `recorded` predicate increased by around 22 millions when using coverage caching.

Since YAP does not provide the time spent computing each predicate, we did further experiments to measure the impact of each of those predicates in the execution time. We observed that the predicates that deal with the internal database and clausal database are the main source of execution time overhead. In particular, the dynamic predicate `idb_keys` and the database predicate `recorded` are those with biggest impact. These two heavily used predicates are the main cause for coverage caching inefficiency. Since the reduction or elimination of Prolog database operations is not possible, a solution to cope with this problem is the improvement of the indexing mechanism of YAP Prolog internal database. Moreover, we find that it would be very much useful the support of an efficient indexing mechanism using multiple keys.

4 Conclusions

ILP systems are non-classical Prolog applications because of the use of large sets of ground facts and high resource consumption (memory and CPU). We provided results showing the impact on memory usage and execution time of an ILP technique called coverage caching. This technique uses intensively the internal database to store results in order to avoid recomputation. An empirical analysis of the coverage caching technique using the April ILP system with Yap Prolog showed a degradation of the execution time although it significantly reduced the number of Prolog calls and retries. To pinpoint this unexpected behavior we profiled April using YAP Prolog. The analysis of the profile data lead us to conclude that the use of YAP's database is the cause for performance degradation. Improving the indexing mechanism of YAP Prolog internal database, moreover including efficient support for indexing with multiple keys, will certainly improve April's performance as well as other applications that use the database intensively. It is our hope that these findings will motivate Prolog implementors to further excel their implementations.

References

1. Nuno Fonseca, Fernando Silva, Rui Camacho, and Vitor S. Costa. Induction with April - A preliminary report. Technical report, DCC-FC & LIACC, UP, 2003.
2. S. Muggleton and L. De Raedt. Inductive logic programming: Theory and methods. *Journal of Logic Programming*, 19/20:629–679, 1994.
3. S.-H. Nienhuys-Cheng and R. de Wolf. *Foundations of Inductive Logic Programming*, volume 1228 of *Lecture Notes in Artificial Intelligence*. Springer-Verlag, 1997.
4. Nuno Fonseca, Vitor S. Costa, Fernando Silva, and Rui Camacho. On the implementation of an ilp system with prolog. Technical report, DCC-FC & LIACC, UP, 2003.
5. James Cussens. Part-of-speech disambiguation using ilp. Technical Report PRG-TR-25-96, Oxford University Computing Laboratory, 1996.

jcc: Integrating Timed Default Concurrent Constraint Programming into JAVA

Vijay Saraswat[1], Radha Jagadeesan*[2], and Vineet Gupta[3]

[1] CSE Department, Penn State University, University Park, Pa 16802
[2] School of CTI, De Paul University, Chicago Il 60604
[3] Google, Inc, Mt View, Ca 94043.

Abstract. This paper describes jcc, an integration of the timed default concurrent constraint programming framework [16] (Timed Default cc) into JAVA [7]. jcc is intended for use in education and research, for the programming of embedded reactive systems, for parallel/distributed simulation and modelling (particularly for space, robotics and systems biology applications), and to support the development of constraint-based program analysis and type-checking tools.
In fully implementing the Timed Default cc framework, jcc supports the notion of (typed) logical variables (called "promises", after [5]), allows the programmer to add his/her own constraint system (an implementation of the Herbrand constraint system is provided), implements (instantaneous) defaults via backtracking, implements a complete renewal of the constraint-store at each time instant, and implements bounded-time execution of the Timed cc control constructs.
jcc implements the notion of *reactive vats* [5] as single threads of execution within the JVM; a vat may be thought of as encapsulating a single synchronous, reactive Timed cc computation. A computation typically consists of a dynamically changing collection of interacting vats (some of which could potentially be located at different JVMs), with dynamically changing connectivity.
jcc programs fully inter-operate with JAVA programs, and compile into standard JVM byte-code. jcc programs fully respect the JAVA type system; logical variables are typed. jcc is compatible with the Generic Java [3] extensions, thereby allowing the use of parameterized types. Indeed, jcc may be viewed as an extension of JAVA which replaces JAVA's notoriously difficult imperative thread-based concurrency with the notion of reactive vats interacting via constraints on logical variables.
jcc source code is available under the Lesser GNU licence through SourceForge.[1]

1 Introduction and Overview

While JAVA [7] has been remarkably successful as a new programming language, its treatment of concurrency remains extremely problematic from a conceptual point of view, and extremely difficult from a practical point of view. To a fairly traditional core of strongly-typed class-based object-oriented programming, JAVA adds threads and synchronization based on locking mutable objects in a heap shared between all the threads,

* Research supported in part by NSF CCR 0244901
[1] The authors wish to thank Daniel Burrows, Lav Rai, Avanti Nadgir and Guilin Chen for their feedback and contributions to the jcc system.

Fernando Moura Pires, Salvador Abreu (Eds.): EPIA 2003, LNAI 2902, pp. 156–170, 2003.

together with rules that govern the flow of information between thread-specific data-structures (stack, heap cache) and the shared store [7, Chapter 17]. Surprisingly, the requirement that some seemingly natural properties should hold (e.g. coherence) leads to significant performance penalties [13]. Worse, some intuitively obvious properties (e.g. the thread-safety of immutable objects such as `Strings`, double-checked locking [4] etc) do not hold. The originators of JAVA have commissioned a working group (JSR 133[2]) to fix these problems. While this work is still in progress (e.g. see [10]), clearly the development of alternate models of concurrency for JAVA seems called for.

A particularly insidious problem in reasoning about JAVA programs is that every line of JAVA code, *particularly* code not using any explicit concurrency or synchronization construct, could be executed in parallel by multiple threads on the same object, leading to potentially serious synchronization problems. That is, concurrent execution in JAVA is the default. This makes reasoning about the correctness of any piece of JAVA code extremely difficult – there is no clear separation between "sequential" JAVA and multi-threaded JAVA. One must explicitly consider all possible interleavings of method calls on an object in order to guarantee safety.

In this paper we propose jcc, a new concurrency model for loosely-coupled concurrent programming in JAVA based on the ideas of synchronous reactive programming [2, 16] (sometimes called "event-loop concurrency"). The model and the implementation are intended to support applications in education and research, for the programming of embedded reactive systems, for parallel/distributed simulation and modelling (particularly for space and systems biology applications), and to support the development of constraint-based program analysis and type-checking tools. In future work we expect to extend jcc to the richer setting of Hybrid cc (supporting a notion of continuous change, [8]), thereby opening up many more areas of application, particularly in the realm of modelling and simulation of physical, engineered and biological systems.

Vats and Ports. Fundamentally, we propose that *both* the stack and the heap (the location for objects) are private to a thread, so that *by default* mutable objects do not need to be synchronized since they can be operated on only by a single thread. Following [5], we call such a self-contained thread of execution a *vat*. (Vats are closely related to the new JAVA notion of *isolates* [19]; one may think of vats as single-threaded isolates.) A single Java Virtual Machine (JVM) instance may now be thought of as consisting of multiple vats together with a shared heap of *immutable objects*.[3] Vats communicate with each other through a few, shared, mutable "gatekeeper" objects called *ports*. Each port is located at a vat and may be "read" only by (code running in) that vat; it may be written into by any vat referencing a related immutable object called the *teller* for the port. Objects written into a port are (deep) copied from the source vat to the target vat, with the copying bottoming out on immutable objects (e.g. tellers). Ports are considered primitive objects in jcc; they cannot be written in jcc, though they can be subclassed by

[2] See `http://jcp.org/en/jsr/detail?id=133`, particularly the discussion of how the current specification is broken "Unfortunately the current specification has been found to be hard to understand and has subtle, often unintended, implications.... Several important issues [...] simply aren't discussed in the existing specification."

[3] An object is said to be immutable in JAVA if all its fields are `final`: that is, they must be assigned at the time of object creation and never again thereafter.

jcc code (cf `Thread` in JAVA).[4] Thus a port represents a single-reader, multiple-writer queue of objects. We say that a vat A *sends a message* to vat B if it writes an object into a port of B; jcc guarantees, using ideas from *wait-free synchronization* [9], that sending vats are never blocked. The *environment* $e(A)$ of a vat A may be defined as the union of the set $f(A)$ of vats that posses tellers for ports in A and the converse set $t(A)$ of vats for whose ports A possesses tellers.[5]

With such an architecture, it is natural to require that a vat A process a single message from its environment at a time, and process it to completion before receiving the next message. In processing a message, the vat may create new objects (in its local heap), invoke methods on the objects in its heap, and send messages to vats in $t(A)$. None of these operations may block; therefore if each vat may be guaranteed to execute a bounded number of operations in response to each input message, it is guaranteed to complete the processing of each input message in a bounded amount of time.

Time. We now make the observation that the receipt of a message from the world, and the computation of a response, imposes a total order on the execution of the vat. This total order is called *time* (cf. Berry's synchrony hypothesis, [12]). Note that the notion of time here is *logical* as opposed to physical – the "next" message is not required to occur at the next "second" or "millisecond". However, a particular implementation (e.g. on a real-time operating system) may guarantee that a message arrives at a vat at every chosen physical time instant, e.g. millisecond. (For such programs it must be guaranteed that the vat is able to respond, with the available compute cycles, before the arrival of the next message.) Thus the techniques in this paper can be used to program physical real-time systems as well.

The explicit introduction of time allows us to introduce a host of control structures that make it possible to describe behaviors *across time*, as we now discuss.

In JAVA-like languages, one may think of each object o as participating in an *object flow*. The elements of this flow are the objects which are communicated as arguments in message invocations on o, or returned as the result of a method invocation by o, or created by o. Immutable objects can only redirect the flow to other objects. Mutable objects can sample the flow, record it in their finite state (their set of fields), and predicate their responses to subsequent flows on this memory (= record of past state).

JAVA-like languages only allow objects to store *data* from past interactions. The methods defined on an object may be thought of as specifying the *instantaneous response* of an object to a stimulus (= method invocation) from its environment. All and only the code in the body of the method (and the code it calls, transitively) is executed on the presentation of this stimulus.

We now introduce the idea of allowing objects to store *programs* (or *agents*) from past interactions. That is, we allow an object to specify, based on current interactions, code that should be executed in the *future* (to compute the response of this object to future stimuli). To enable this, we introduce the notion of *time-based control constructs*. The statement `next {S}` is executed at the current time instant and records that the

[4] Subclassing may specify, for instance, how received messages are ordered before being de-queued.

[5] Because we allow tellers to be communicated in messages, these sets vary dynamically.

statement S should be executed at the next time instant (that is, the next time that the enclosing vat processes a message from its environment). Thus actions at any given instant depend not only on the particular method invocation at that time instant, but also on such agents from the past. Since there may be several such agents, and they may have been independently generated (and at different instants in the past) it becomes very convenient for us to think of them as executing (logically) in *parallel*. This is referred to as *intra-vat logical parallelism*.

How should these agents be organized so that the result of executing them is independent of their order of execution? Here we may appeal to the theory of *determinate concurrency* as developed in concurrent constraint programming [14,16]. We view these agents as concurrent constraint programs that interact with each other by imposing and checking constraints on shared (logical) variables. (We allow both *positive* and *negative* forms of checking or asking. A positive ask suspends until a particular item is entailed by the store; a negative ask can be fired if it can be established that a particular item will never be entailed by the store for the duration of this time instant. This may require lookahead or backtracking.) We can make these agents sensitive to the data generated in the current interaction by posting that data in the constraint store at the beginning of the interaction. So as to allow the programmer to precisely define the temporal extent of items in the constraint store, we adopt the rule that by default all items in the store are dropped at the end of a time instant; therefore at the start of the next time instant only those items will be available which occur explicitly within the scope of `next` (or which are added by the environment at the beginning of that step).

Timed Default CC. Concretely, jcc may be thought of as arising from the integration of the Timed Default cc framework into (Sequential) JAVA. The Timed Default cc framework extends the CCP framework with a notion of *defaults* and *time*. To the *tell*, *(positive) ask*, concurrency as conjunction and hiding as existential idea of CCP, defaults add the idea of *negative asks*: agents may be specified that fire based on the *absence* of information (for the duration of the computation).[6] Time introduces the idea of *phased execution*: a time instant is identified with the receipt of a stimulus from the environment and the execution of a default CCP (Default cc) program to determine *both* the instantaneous response and the computation to be executed at the next time instant.

While time and defaults are conceptually completely orthogonal (i.e. the semantics of one is defined independently of the other); past work has shown that the extensions are particularly synergistic. In particular, defaults allow various *instantaneous pre-emption* control constructs (such as `do...watching`) to be expressed in the language. Indeed defaults may be used to express arbitrarily sophisticated patterns of interruption, resumption and evolution across time.

Desiderata for jcc. One of our goals is to introduce Timed Default cc in the mainstream of programming practice. One pathway to this goal is the design of a completely new programming system (c.f. Oz [18]) organized around constraints and communication.

[6] It is necessary to insist that negative information be stable so as to retain the notion that the result of the computation should be independent of scheduler delays or the order of execution of agents.

However, our experience in leading several engineering teams in industry that have designed, implemented and released commercial products and services in the Internet space points to the enormous value of integrating these ideas into existing languages and environments such as C++, JAVA, and C#.

We thus set up the following design goals for jcc:

1. jcc programs should completely inter-operate with JAVA: they should be able to use JAVA class libraries (that do not explicitly use threads), and be callable from JAVA class libraries.
2. jcc programs should be strongly typed, and the type system should inter-operate with the JAVA type system, including the Generic Java extension [3].
3. jcc programs should compile to standard JVM byte codes.
4. A simple API should be provided to allow the programmer to add new constraint systems.
5. To support reflective meta-programming, jcc should provide an abstraction type for agents, and classes for each of the additional built-in control constructs for agents (e.g. `Always`, `Next` etc).
6. The implementation should be usable for small to medium-sized programs.

1.1 Comparison with Other Work

The conceptual framework of vats and promises has been borrowed from the programming language E [5], which itself has been influenced by a long line of concurrent logic programming languages. Unlike the designers of E, we have sought to realize these ideas incrementally within JAVA rather than create a new language from whole cloth.

The treatment of defaults and temporal control constructs in Timed Default cc is closely related to ESTEREL. Just as for ESTEREL, several compilation techniques for defaults and the temporal constructs are possible (e.g. compilation to finite state machines, compilation to BDDs or circuits etc). In the current version of the jcc system (described in this paper) we have chosen to implement the control constructs directly. Vats may be thought of as quite similar to the Communicating Reactive Processes of [1]. They differ in that we use a very simple form of concurrent constraint programming (ports) for inter-vat communication, instead of using the framework of CSP. This fragment is quite similar to the asynchronous π-calculus and permits dynamic collection of processes, and dynamically changing connectivity between processes.

The JAVA community has recently introduced the notion of *isolates* to enable multiple independent computations to run within a JVM [19]. Vats may be thought of as *singly-threaded* isolates that communicate declaratively with each other (via ports).

Rest of This Paper. In the next section we discuss the core language design in more detail. The design is presented in two phases. The first phase introduces vats and ports. This level is analogous to the design of a concurrent logic programming language such as Janus [17] (albeit in an object-oriented context). This language is completely usable in its own right. The second phase introduces the notion of promises, time and defaults. Next we present several simple examples of jcc programs.

The jcc system has been produced under the LGPL open source code licence. The current system, version 0.2, is available for download from SourceForge. All the features discussed in this paper have been completely implemented, except for front-end syntax processing. Instead programmers today have to use the "agent-based syntax" described below. The implementation has been used in two graduate courses, in which several hundred line long jcc programs have been developed (e.g. variations on the ESTEREL Reflex and Wrist-watch programs).

The current implementation is a few thousand lines long.

2 Language Design

Syntactically, the language is obtained from JAVA by adding the constructs given in Table 1.[7] jcc may be thought of via the "equation":

$$\text{jcc} = \text{JAVA} - \text{Threads} + \text{Vats} + \text{Promises} + \text{Agents}$$

2.1 Vats

A vat is a unit of concurrent execution with its own local stack and heap. (It is associated with a JAVA thread in the current implementation.) Vats function very much like *containers* for components known as `Agents`, the analogous notion in jcc to JAVA's Enterprise Java Beans (EJBs).

Vats may be thought of as executing `Agents` and communicate with other vats through `Ports`.

Agents. A vat may be created with an instance of `Actor` or `ActiveAgent`.[8] The class `Actor` extends `Port` and implements `Runnable`, and may be thought of as a component that is accessible from the vat's context (through the port) and that can be executed by the vat (very much like an EJB). An `ActiveAgent` extends `Port` and provides a method to return an `Agent`.

`Agent` is the key meta-abstraction in jcc. It objectifies an agent whose behavior extends across time. Agents allow for meta-programming: Agents are objects that can be constructed on the fly (e.g. based on incoming data), and scheduled for execution. Agents can be built from other agents. Agents allow for reactive synchronous programming within conventional JAVA syntax (that is, without the use of the control constructs described in Table 1), since built-in `Agent` classes are provided for each of the control constructs. For simplicity one may assume that every jcc computation is implemented by associating an `Agent` with a `Vat`; this `Agent` is built dynamically by executing the pure JAVA code obtained by translating jcc control constructs into invocations of constructors on the appropriate `Agent` classes. Therefore in the following we describe the

[7] Many other temporal constructs are provided, not all are listed.

[8] All the classes mentioned in this section live in the package `jcc.lang`. We use the annotation `/*filled*/` to indicate that a variable must have a non-null value. One may use an extended static checker for JAVA (e.g. [6]) to check these annotations at compile time.

Table 1. Syntactic Additions in jcc

jcc *contains* JAVA *less threads.* All syntactic constructs in JAVA (1.3) are permitted in jcc (including inner classes), except as indicated here. jcc programs may not use the classes `Thread` or `ThreadGroup` (from the `java.lang` package) or the `synchronized` and `volatile` keywords from JAVA.

`realized` *method keyword.* Methods defined on subclasses of `Promise` with return type `void` may be annotated with the keyword "`realized`". Such a method invocation on an object *o* suspends until *o* is realized. If the method has a return type of (a subclass of) `Promise` an unbound variable of that type is returned; this variable will be equated to the result of the actual method call made when *o* is realized

Additional control constructs. jcc supports the following control constructs. Below, let `p` range over promises, and S over *jump-closed* statements, that is, statements which are such that any jumps from within S (for instance, occurrences of `break`, `continue` or `return`) are directed at locations within S. Any variables occurring in S that are bound outside S should also be declared `final`.

`when (p) {S}`	*Run* S *once* `p` *is realized.*
`next {S}`	*Run* S *in the next instant.*
`always {S}`	*Run* S *at every instant.*
`every (p) {S}`	*Run* S *at every instant* `p` *is realized.*
`whenever (p) {S}`	*Run* S *at the first instant* `p` *is realized.*
`unless (p) {S}`	*Run* S *once it can be established that* `p` *cannot be realized.*
`watching (p) {S}`	*Run* S, *aborting it at the instant in which* `p` *is realized.*
...	
`effect {S}`	*Run* S *at the end of the current time instant.*

`jcc.lang` *classes.* User code may use the classes in Table 2, Table 3 as well as the class `Abort`:

```
public class Abort extends Exception {
    public Abort() { ...}
    public Abort( final Exception z ) {...}
    public Abort( final String z ) {...}}
```

behavior how a `Vat` executes its associated `Agent`, and the behavior of these built-in `Agent` classes; this suffices to provide a description of how a `Vat` executes an `Actor`.

An `Agent` has three methods, all of which may be implemented by instantaneous code (that is, JAVA code not containing any of the jcc control constructs of Table 1). It is the responsibility of the vat (discussed in more detail below) to invoke these methods in a manner consistent with interpreting the code as a specification of a Timed Default cc agent whose behavior extends across time.

The vat invokes the method `now()` in order to execute the code associated with the agent for the current time instant. Agents support logical concurrency. Through the notion of *promises* and *watchers* (discussed further below), it is possible for pieces of computation in a vat to be suspended until the associated promise is *realized*. Therefore a vat also has a *scheduler* responsible for scheduling these pieces of computation. jcc

Table 2. Basic Promises in jcc

```
abstract public class Promise implements Backtrackable {
   // Call with false to create a new unbound variable.
   public Promise(boolean realized){...}
   public final Promise /*filled This*/ dereference(){...}
   public final void equate(/*filled This*/ Promise other){
      ...}
   public boolean known( ) {...} // Is this realized?
   public void ensureKnown() throws Abort {...}
   public void runWhenRealized(/*realized*/ Now call)
       throws Abort {...}
   public void abortWhenRealized( ) throws Abort {...}
   public boolean equals(/*filled This*/ Object o ) {...}
   public int hashCode() {...}
   public void print(/* filled */ PrintStream o) {...}
   //Subclasses define how to equate two realized promises.
   abstract protected
    void equateBothDerefedAndRealized(/*filled*/ Promise o)
    throws Abort;}
public class Atom extends Promise {
   public final static Atom NIL = new Atom( null);
   /** Create an unbound Atom. */
   public Atom() {...}
   /** Create an atom that contains the object o. */
   public Atom( Object o) {...}
   /** Return the value associated with this atom. */
   public Object getValue() {...}
   protected void equateBothDerefedAndRealized ...}
public class Integer  extends Atom {
   public Integer() {...}
   public Integer(int o) {...}
   public Integer(/*filled*/ java.lang.Integer o) {...}
   public int intValueDeref() {...}
   public int intValue() {...}
   // this= a + b. Suspend until any two are realized.
   public void plus(/*filled*/ Integer a,
                    /*filled*/ Integer b){...}
  ... // Similarly for times.}
public class List extends Promise {
   final public Promise head;
   final public List /*This*/ rest;
   public static final List NULL = new List( null, null);
   /** Return a new promise for a list. */
   public List() {...}
   /** Return a new realized list. */
   public List(Promise head, List rest ) {...}
   public boolean isNull() {...}
   protected void equateBothDerefedAndRealized ...}
```

makes no guarantees of the scheduler, other than a watcher will eventually be executed (within the current time instant) if the variable it is watching is realized. jcc does guarantee *single-threaded* execution for watchers: agents may assume they have exclusive access to all objects they reference (other than ports). No other thread may be modifying or accessing these objects at the same time.

Execution of this code may involve backtracking in order to resolve defaults. During this phase, the agent should not attempt to invoke any side-effects, since the code may be backtracked over, and these side-effects will not be undone. Once the agent has quiesced – note that an agent may have several concurrent sub-agents; an agent is considered to have quiesced only if all subagents have quiesced – the vat will invoke `effect()` on it to give it an opportunity to execute any side-effects (e.g. writing to various streams, sending messages to other vats).

The notion of effects is reflected in jcc syntax through the `effect` control construct. When such a control construct is encountered during execution of code by the vat, the construct is added to a list of effects (and not executed). Additions to this list are undone on backtracking. Once backtracking is complete and computation has quiesced, the list of effects is examined and executed.

Ports. Vats communicate with the outside world through a collection of *ports* created by the code running inside the vat. The port is said to be located at (or owned by) the vat. A `Port` maintains an internal buffer for messages received from the *tellers* of the port; these messages may be read through the *promise* for the port. A *teller* to a port is an object that possesses the ability to send a message to the port. Messages received on a port are buffered if the receiving vat is active; otherwise the vat is activated with the port and receives the message by performing a `get` operation on the port.

Vat Life-Cycle. We now describe the life-cycle of a vat. The vat executes in an infinite loop. At the top of the loop it suspends, waiting for a message on any one of its ports. The receipt of such a message triggers an "instantaneous interaction" with the code running in the vat. The message is equated with the promise associated with the port, and the `now` method associated with the current agent is executed. Once this terminates, the `effect` method is executed. Once this terminates, the `next` method is executed to determine the agent to be executed at the next time instant, and a counter tracking the time instant (as an integer) is incremented. The vat now returns to the top of the loop.

If the store becomes inconsistent at any time instant, or the agent throws an `Abort` exception, the vat terminates its execution abruptly, after *poisoning* all of its ports. The poison ultimately propagates to all the tellers of these ports, causing local exceptions to arise whenever an attempt is made to send a message through a poisoned teller. However, a poisoned vat does not automatically poison other vats; each vat has a separate constraint store.

2.2 Promises

The class `Promise` plays the same role in jcc as the class `java.lang.Object` plays in JAVA. The class is intended to be the base class subclassed by programmers to define new data-types.

A promise is a *typed logical variable*. As far as users of promise are concerned, a promise may be in one of four states: *realized, bound, unrealized and watched*, or *unrealized and unwatched*.

Typically, instances are created at subtypes of `Promise`. They may be created either as *variables* (using the nullary constructor), or as (top-level) *constants* (using any other constructor). A (top-level) constant is an instance which is not a variable but which has components (fields) that may be variable; such an object is also said to be *realized*. A variable `o` is an instance that has no data associated with it. Rather, its state changes as a result of invocations of the method `o.equate(p)`, where `p` is another promise (`o` is then said to be *bound* to `p`). Invoking the method `o.equate(p)` corresponds to posting the constraint `o=p` to the store.

If an object is neither realized nor bound, it is said to be *unrealized*.

Note that it is possible to equate a constant to another. If the two constants are different, one has a contradiction. This is handled by throwing a `FailureError`. With this version of jcc there is no support for recovering from this error. The vat is said to be *poisoned*, and a new vat must be started with a fresh agent. Poisoned vats cease to process input. Attempts to send a message to the vat through a teller raise an exception which may be caught by the teller code.

In effect, equatings represent equations imposed on the concerned variables, and the above process describes a simple *unification* algorithm (with suspension).

Suspension of Computation. We now discuss two fundamental properties of promises.

First, computations may suspend on a promise until the promise is realized. This is accomplished by a new control construct in jcc. If `S` is a statement and `p` is a promise, then jcc admits the statement `when (p) do {S}`.

Such a control construct is defined as follows. If `p` is realized, `S` is executed immediately. Otherwise, `S` is *suspended* on `p`; `p` is now said to be *unrealized and watched*, and `S` is said to be a watcher for `p`. (A promise may have multiple watchers.) A subsequent invocation of `p.equate(q)` will cause `S` to be scheduled for execution if `q` is realized. If `q` is unrealized, then its watchers, if any, are merged with the watchers (if any) for `p`, and one of `p` and `q` is bound to the other. (Thus they have the same set of watchers.) If a promise is not realized, bound or watched, it is said to be *unrealized and unwatched*. (Such a promise corresponds to an unconstrained logical variable.)

Thus, as a result of `equate` method invocations (called equatings), a promise may be bound to another promise, which may be bound to another one, and so on. The *dereferenced value* of a promise is the promise that lies at the end of this binding chain. This promise may be either realized or unrealized (it may not be bound).

Automatic Dereferencing. The second important property of promises is that method invocation respects promise equatings. Methods invoked on promise `p` are *forwarded* down the chain of equatings: first the promise `p` is dereferenced to the promise `q` at the end of the chain, and then the method is invoked on `q`. Thus, any references to `this` in the code for the method on `q` refer to `q` and not `p`. By uniformly dereferencing promises before invoking methods, we maintain the invariant that the holder of a promise cannot distinguish between the promise and the value realizing the promise. This is central to the idea that promises are first-class values in jcc: a method may accept a promise as an argument, store it in a data-structure, read a value from it, place in it a value that has been separately computed.

The `realized` *Keyword on Methods.* jcc adds the `realized` keyword for methods of subclasses of `Promise`. The method must be `void` or must return a `Promise`. An invocation of such a method on an object returns immediately if `o` is unrealized, suspending the body of the method on `o`. In case the method returns a `Promise` a new variable of the type of `Promise` is returned. If `o` is realized, then the body is executed immediately and the value returned.

2.3 Pre-specified Agents

Table 3 enumerates the constructors for the prespecified agents. These classes objectify the Timed Default cc combinators: their constructors take arbitrary agents as arguments (and return agents). The code for these classes contains the core default and time-dependent implementation of jcc.

3 Programming in jcc

All the idioms for programming in Timed cc [15] are available in jcc. The publicly available download has several Timed cc programs.

One may also program in jcc just as one would in JAVA – using standard JAVA idioms (classes, inheritance, state, assignment, multiple methods) for system modelling. However, for public methods one should use `Promises` as arguments and as return values. This allows the computation to be structured using data-flow synchronization rather than control-flow synchronization.

Fundamentally, promises are used to model *logical concurrency*. Often it is desired to perform a certain computation on an object *o* (e.g. invoke a certain operation), but the object is not yet in a state in which this operation can be performed successfully. Therefore it is desired to wait until such time as some other source of change (e.g. another stimulus from the outside world) causes the object to arrive in a state in which the previous operation can be completed successfully. Promises allow such computations to be expressed directly. The first method may return immediately with a promise for the result. The invoking context may continue execution with the returned promise, blocking (using `when` or `whenever` as appropriate) only as and when it needs the returned value. In the meantime, *o* has recorded a computation to be performed in the future to complete this request. Thus promises allow the programmer to structure the computation in such a way that small pieces of code may remain suspended on certain events happening (certain promises becoming realized) and may produce certain other events (cause other promises to become realized). Indeed, the entire computation can be structured as lots of such small pieces – tens of thousands of such pieces. The correctness of each of these pieces is usually much simpler to check.

The semantics of ports and promises (as opposed to shared mutable objects) make them much more suitable for distributed concurrency. Here one may think of a vat running on one machine communicating with a vat running on another, through ports.

Table 3. Public constructors for pre-specified agents

```
public class Always extends BasicAgent {
  // Run a at every time instant.
  public Always(/*filled*/ Agent a){...}}
public class ElseNext extends BasicAgent {
  // Run a at the next instant unless p is realized now.
  public ElseNext(/*filled*/ Promise p, /*filled*/ Agent a){
  ...}}
public class Every extends BasicAgent {
  // Run a at every instant in which p is realized.
  public Every(/*filled*/ Promise p, /*filled*/ Agent a){
  ...}}
public class Next extends BasicAgent {
  // Run a at the next instant.
  public Next(/*filled*/ Agent a){...}}
public class Par extends BasicAgent {
  // Run each of the argument agents in parallel.
  public Par(/*filled*/ Agent[] a){...}
  // and other similar constructors, for i=2...10.}
public class Send extends BasicAgent {
  // Send this promise on this teller.
  public Send(/*filled*/ Teller t, /*filled*/ Promise p){
  ...}}
public class Tell extends BasicAgent {
  // Equate the two promises now.
  public Tell(/*filled*/ Promise p, /*filled*/ Promise q){
  ...}}
public class Unless extends BasicAgent {
  // Run a unless p holds in the current time instant.
  // May backtrack.
  public Unless(/*filled*/ Promise p, /*filled*/ Agent a){
  ...}}
public class When extends BasicAgent {
  // Run a if p is realized now.
  public When(/*filled*/ Promise p, /*filled*/ Agent a){
  ...}
  // Run a if p is equated to q now.
  public When(/*filled*/ Promise p, /*filled*/ Promise q,
              /*filled*/ Agent a){...}}
public class WhenEver extends BasicAgent {
  // Run a at the first instant in which p is realized.
  public WhenEver(/*filled*/ Promise p, /*filled*/ Agent a){
  ...}}
public class Watching extends BasicAgent {
  // Run a; abort at the first instant when p is realized
  public Watching(/*filled*/ Agent a, /*filled*/ Promise p){
  ...}}
```

This allows the two vats to continue normal operations, with a place-holder for the result, without having to suspend waiting for a response from the other.

A Bank Account Example. Consider for example a bank account. One may wish it to be programmed in such a way that it accepts method invocations to withdraw and deposit money. In both cases it should return confirmations. However, if there is not enough money to cover a withdrawal, then the withdrawal should be repeated after each of the next n deposits, and if it is still not possible to withdraw then a negative confirmation should be sent. The typical way to do this in JAVA is to synchronize on some lock object and implement the conditional wait by using `wait/notifyAlls`. Instead, we may use `Promises` as the arguments and return values. The caller of the deposit/withdraw method may proceed, leaving behind code that waits for the result to be realized. The withdraw method will realize its result at some future indeterminate point in time only when it has succeeded, or failed to do so after n tries[9].

```
public class BankAccount {
    int balance = 0;
    Boolean balanceUpdated = new Boolean();
    List pendingW = new ArrayList();
    public BankAccount() {
        every (balanceUpdated) {
          effect {
            if (! pendingW.isEmpty()) {
              for (ListIterator e = pendingW.listIterator();
                                      e.hasNext();) {
                if (((Withdrawal) e.next()).tryWithdrawal())
                e.remove();
              }}}}}
    private class Withdrawal(int amount, Confirmation c) {
        public int count = 10;
        public boolean tryWithdrawal() {
            if (amount <= balance) {
                    balance -= amount;
                    confirmation.equate(new Success(genId()));
                    return true;
                }
            if (count <= 0) {
                confirmation.equate(new Failure(genId()));
                return true;
            }
            count--;
            return false;
        }}
```

[9] In this program, `Boolean` and `List` are from the `jcc.lang` package; for brevity we have omitted the `import` declarations. jcc supports Pizza style [11] implicit constructor declarations via syntax such as `class Shifter(int i) extends ...`. Such syntax is assumed to define `int i` as a private field in the class `Shifter`, and also define a constructor `Shifter(int i)` which initializes the field.

```
int id;
private int genId() {
    return id++;
}
public Confirmation deposit(Integer amount) {
  Confirmation result = new Confirmation();
    when (amount) {
        balance +=amount.intValue();
        balanceUpdated.equate(true);
        confirm.equate(new Success(genId()));
    }
    return result;
}
public Confirmation withdraw (final Integer amount) {
  Confirmation result = new Confirmation();
    when (amount) {
        int value = amount.intValue();
        if (balance <= value) {
            balance -= value;
            result.equate(new Success(genId()));
        } else {
            pendingW.add(
                    new Withdrawal(value, result));
        }
    }
    return result;
}}
```

Thus one can think of jcc as a general purpose language, like JAVA, differing from it only in its treatment of concurrency. Of course for modelling physical systems further restrictions may be placed, e.g. disallowing mutable state.

Conclusion. We have presented the design of the language jcc which extends JAVA by replacing its concurrency model, based on ideas from synchronous reactive programming. A number of new time-based control constructs are added. The basic operations of Timed Default cc are supported.

References

1. G. Berry, S. Ramesh, and R.K. Shyamsundar. Communicating reactive processes. In *Proceedings of the 20th ACM Symposium on Principles of Programming Languages (POPL'93), Charleston, South Carolina.* ACM Press, New York (NY), USA, 1993.
2. Gerard Berry. The Esterel v5 Language Primer Version 5.21 Release 2.0. Technical report, INRIA, April 1999.
3. Gilad Bracha, Martin Odersky, David Stoutamire, and Philip Wadler. Making the future safe for the past: Adding Genericity to the Java Programing Language. In *OOPSLA*, 1998.
4. David Bacon et al. "The double checked locking is broken" declaration. http://www.cs.umd.edu/ pugh/java/memoryModel/DoubleCheckedLocking.html, 2000.

5. Mark S. Miller et al. E: Open source distributed capabilities, 1998. http://www.erights.org.
6. C. Flanagan, K. Leino, M. Lillibridge, C. Nelson, J. Saxe, and R. Stata. Extended static checking for Java, 2002.
7. James Gosling, Bill Joy, Guy Steele, and Gilad Bracha. *The Java Language Specification.* Addison Wesley, 2000.
8. Vineet Gupta, Radha Jagadeesan, and Vijay Saraswat. Computing with continuous change. *Science of Computer Programming*, 30(1–2):3–49, January 1998.
9. Maurice Herlihy. Wait-free synchronization. *ACM Transactions on Programming Languages and Systems*, 13(1):124–149, January 1991.
10. Jeremy Manson and William Pugh. A new approach to the semantics of Multithreaded Java. http://www.cs.umd.edu/ pugh/java/memoryModel/, January 2003.
11. M. Odersky and P. Wadler. Pizza into Java: Translating theory into practice. In *Proceedings of the 24th ACM Symposium on Principles of Programming Languages (POPL'97), Paris, France*, pages 146–159. ACM Press, New York (NY), USA, 1997.
12. Gordon Plotkin, Colin Stirling, and Mads Tote, editors. *Proof, Language and Interaction: Essays in Honour of Robin Milner*, chapter The Foundations of Esterel, pages 425–454. Foundations of Computing. MIT Press, 2000.
13. William Pugh. The JAVA memory model is fatally flawed. *Concurrency:Practice and Experience*, 12(1):1–11, 2000.
14. Vijay Saraswat. *Concurrent Constraint Programming.* Doctoral Dissertation Award and Logic Programming. MIT Press, 1993.
15. Vijay Saraswat, Radha Jagadeesan, and Vineet Gupta. Programming in timed concurrent constraint languages. In B. Mayoh, E. Tyugu, and J. Penjaam, editors, *Constraint Programming: Proceedings 1993 NATO ASI Parnu, Estonia*, pages 361–410, Berlin, Germany / Heidelberg, Germany / London, UK / etc., 1994. Springer Verlag.
16. Vijay Saraswat, Radha Jagadeesan, and Vineet Gupta. Timed default concurrent constraint programming. *Journal of Symbolic Computation*, 22(5–6):475–520, November–December 1996. Extended abstract appeared in the *Proceedings of the 22nd ACM Symposium on Principles of Programming Languages*, San Francisco, January 1995.
17. Vijay Saraswat, Kenneth Kahn, and Jacob Levy. Janus: A step towards distributed constraint programming. In *North American Logic Programming Conference*, October 1990.
18. Gert Smolka. The Oz programming model. In Jan van Leeuwen, editor, *Computer Science Today: Recent Trends and Developments*, volume 1000 of *Lecture Notes in Computer Science*, pages 324–343. Springer-Verlag, Berlin, 1995.
19. Peter Soper. The Application Isolation API, 2001. JSR 121, http://www.jcp.org/en/jsr/detail?id=121.

BAYES-NEAREST: A New Hybrid Classifier Combining Bayesian Network and Distance Based Algorithms*

Elena Lazkano and Basilio Sierra

Department of Computer Science and Artificial Intelligence
University of the Basque Country
P.O. Box 649
E-20080 Donostia-San Sebastián
Basque Country, Spain
{ccpsiarb, ccplaore}@si.ehu.es
http://www.sc.ehu.es/ccwrobot

Abstract. This paper presents a new hybrid classifier that combines the probability based Bayesian Network paradigm with the Nearest Neighbor distance based algorithm. The Bayesian Network structure is obtained from the data by using the K2 structural learning algorithm. The Nearest Neighbor algorithm is used in combination with the Bayesian Network in the deduction phase. For those data bases in which some variables are continuous valued, automatic discretizations of the data are performed. We show the performance of the new proposed approach compared with the Bayesian Network paradigm and with the well known Naive Bayes classifier in some standard databases; the results obtained by the new algorithm are better or equal according to the Wilcoxon statistical test.

1 Introduction

During the last years an extensive development has been produced in hybrid classifiers, that is, in classifiers that are implemented taking the ideas of various standard classifiers. This research has the potential to apply accurate composite classifiers to real world problems by intelligently combining known learning algorithms.

Classifier combination falls within the *supervised learning* paradigm in the Machine Learning area (Mitchell, 1997). This task orientation assumes that we have been given a set of training examples, which are customarily represented by feature vectors. Each training example is labelled with a class target, which is a member of a finite, and usually small set of class labels. The goal of supervised learning is to predict the class labels of examples that have not been seen.

Combining the predictions of a set of component classifiers has been applied for many supervised classification problems (Xu et al., 1992; Ho and Srihati, 1994; Lu, 1996; Dietterich, 1997; Sierra et al., 2001b.).

* This work was supported by the University of the Basque Country and by the Gipuzkoako Foru Aldundi Txit Gorena under OF147/2002 grant.

Fernando Moura Pires, Salvador Abreu (Eds.): EPIA 2003, LNAI 2902, pp. 171–183, 2003.

Classifier combination can fuse together different information sources to utilize their complementary information. The sources can be multi-modal, such as speech and vision, but can also be transformations (Kohavi, 1996) or partitions (Cowell et al., 1999; Murphy and Aha, 1994; Pearl, 1987) of the same signal. In each case, combination can produce appreciable gains, even when individual classifiers exhibit widely varying accuracies.

Underlying the hybrid approach is the concept of reductionism, where complex problems are solved through stepwise decomposition (Sierra et al., 1999). Intelligent hybrid systems involve specific (hierarchical) levels of knowledge defined in terms of concept granularity and corresponding interfaces. Specifically, the hierarchy would include connectionist and symbolic levels, with each level possibly consisting of an ensemble architecture by itself, and with proper interfaces between levels. As one moves upward in the hierarchical structure, we witness a corresponding degree of data compression allowing more powerful ('reasoning') methods to be employed on reduced amounts of data.

In this paper, we present a new hybrid classifier based on two families of well known classification methods; the first one is a probabilistic classifier used to obtain the first model, a Bayesian network (Pearl, 1988; Cowell et al., 1999), and the second one is a distance based classifier (Dasarathy, 1991) which is combined with the Bayesian network in the classification process. We show the results obtained of the new approach and compare it with two probabilistic classifiers: Naive Bayes and Bayesian Networks.

The rest of the paper is organized as follows. Section 2 to 5 review the different concepts needed to understand the new hybrid classifier. Section 6 introduces the new proposed approach and the results obtained are presented in section 7. Last section is dedicated to give conclusions and to point out the future work.

2 Bayesian Networks

Bayesian networks (BN) are probabilistic graphical models represented by directed acyclic graphs in which nodes are variables and arcs show the (in)dependencies among the variables (Castillo et al., 1997; Jensen, 1996).

There are different ways of establishing the Bayesian network structure (Heckerman et al., 1995). It can be the human expert who designs the network taking advantage of his/her knowledge about the relations among the variables. It is also possible to learn the structure by means of an automatic learning algorithm. A combination of both systems is a third alternative, mixing the expert knowledge and the learning mechanism.

Within the supervised classification area, learning is performed using a training datafile but there is always a special variable, namely the class, i.e. the one we want to deduce (Sierra et al., 2000). Some structural learning approaches take into account the existence of that special variable (Friedman et al., 1997; Sierra and Larrañaga, 1998), but most of them – and it is the case of the K2 algorithm explained bellow – do consider all the variables in the same manner and make use of an evaluation metric to measure the appropriateness of a net given the data. Hence, a structural learning method needs two components: the learning algorithm and the evaluation measure (score+search).

The algorithm used in the experimentation here described is the K2 algorithm (Cooper and Herskovits, 1992). This algorithm assumes an order has been established for the variables so that the search space is reduced. The fact that $X_1, X_2, \cdots, X_n$ is an ordering of the variables implies that only the predecessors of X_k in the list can be its parent nodes in the learned network. The algorithm also assumes that all the networks are equally probable, but because it is a greedy algorithm it can not ensure that the net resulting from the learning process is the most probable one given the data. Figure 1 shows the pseudo-code of the algorithm.

```
Input: Ordering, Database + metric.
Output: net structure
for i = 1 to n do
  π_i = ∅
  p_old = g(i, π_i)
  ok_to_proceed = true
  while ok_to_proceed and |π_i| < max_parents do
    z ∈ pred(i) where z = argmax_k g(i, π_i ⋃{k})
    p_new = g(i, π_i ⋃{k})
    if p_new > p_old then
      p_old = p_new
      π_i = π_i ⋃ z
    else
      ok_to_proceed = false
    end if
  end while
end for
```

Fig. 1. Pseudo-code of the K2 structural learning algorithm

The original algorithm used the K2 Bayesian metric to evaluate the net while it is being constructed:

$$P(D|S) = \log_{10}\left(\prod_{i=1}^{n}\prod_{j=1}^{q_i}\left(\frac{(r_i-1)!}{(N_{ij}+r_i-1)!}\prod_{k=1}^{r_i} N_{ijk}!\right)\right) \tag{1}$$

where:

- $P(D|S)$: is a measure of the goodness of the S Bayesian net defined over the D dataset.
- n: is the number of variables

- r_i: represents the number of values or states that the i-th variable can take.
- q_i: is the set of all possible configurations for the parents of variable i
- N_{ijk}: the frequency with whom variable i takes the value k while its parent configuration is j
- $N_{ik} = \sum_{j=1}^{q_i} N_{ijk}$.
- N: is the number of entries in the database

In addition to this metric, we have tried one more measure in combination with the algorithm, the well known entropy metric which measures the disorder of the given data:

$$P(D|S) = \sum_{i=1}^{n} \sum_{j=1}^{q_i} \frac{N_{ij}}{N} \left(- \sum_{k=1}^{r_i} \frac{N_{ijk}+1}{N_{ij}+r_i} \ln \frac{N_{ijk}+1}{N_{ij}+r_i} \right) \qquad (2)$$

2.1 Propagating the Evidence

Evidence propagation or probabilistic inference consists of, given an instantiation of some of the variables, obtaining the a posteriori probability of one ore more of the non-instantiated variables (Henrion, 1988). It is known that this computation is a NP-hard problem, even for the case of a unique variable.

There are different alternatives to perform the propagation methods. Exact methods calculate the exact a posteriori probabilities of the variables and the resulting error is only due to the limitations of the computer where the calculation is performed. The computational cost can be reduced looking over the independence of the nodes in the net.

Approximated propagation methods are based on simulation techniques that obtain approximated values for the probabilities needed. (Pearl, 1987) proposes a stochastic simulation method known as the *Markov Sampling Method*. It first assigns the evidence to the evidential nodes and then simulates the values for the rest of the nodes in the net. Initially, a realization is performed, i.e. values are assigned to the nodes based in their probabilities, and afterwards the non-evidential variables are simulated using an arbitrary order. Then, a value is generated for the selected variable using its conditional probability function and the simulated values.

In the case all the Markov Blanquet[1] of the variable of interest is instantiated, and therefore in many of the supervised classification tasks where there is no missing values, there is no need of the simulation process to obtain the values of the non-evidential variables and thereby, $P(Y = y_i|X1 = x_1, ..., X_n = x_n)$ can be calculated using only the probability tables of the parents and children of the node, i.e. using the parameters saved in the model specification. The method becomes for that particular case an exact propagation method. Figure 2 shows an example of a BN structure specifically obtained for a classification task, in which the special variable (Cl) appears in the center of the structure.

[1] The Markov Blanquet of a node is the set of nodes formed by its parents, its children and the parents of those children

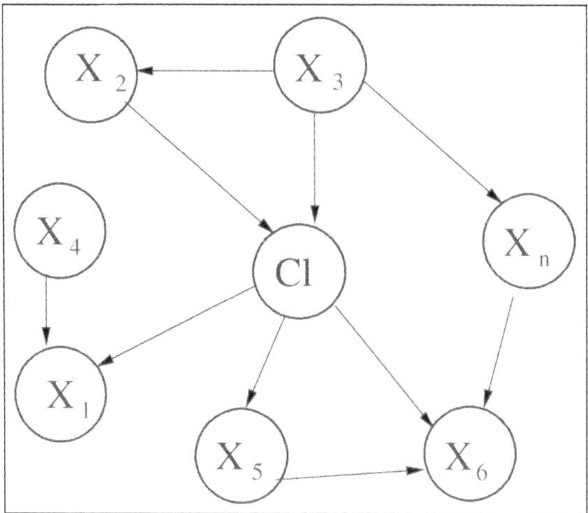

Fig. 2. An example of a Bayesian Network structure. The Class node is associated with the class variable

3 Naive Bayes Classifier

Theoretically, Bayes' rule minimizes error by selecting the class y_j with the largest posterior probability for a given example $\mathbf{X}$ of the form $X =< X_1, X_2, ..., X_n >$, as indicated below (equation 3):

$$P(Y = y_j|X) = \frac{P(Y = y_j)P(\mathbf{X}|Y = y_j)}{P(\mathbf{X})} \tag{3}$$

Since $\mathbf{X}$ is a composition of n discrete values, one can expand this expression to equation 4:

$$P(Y = y_j|X_1 = x_1, ..., X_n = x_n) = \frac{P(Y = y_j)P(X_1 = x_1, ..., X_n = x_n|Y = y_j)}{P(X_1 = x_1, ..., X_n = x_n)} \tag{4}$$

where $P(X_1 = x_1, ..., X_n = x_n|Y = y_j)$ is the conditional probability of the instance $\mathbf{X}$ given the class; y_j. $P(Y = y_j)$ is the a priori probability that one will observe class y_j; and $P(\mathbf{X})$ is the prior probability of observing the instance $\mathbf{X}$. All these parameters are estimated from the training set. However, a direct application of these rules is difficult due to the lack of sufficient data in the training set to reliably obtain all the conditional probabilities needed by the model. One simple form of the previous diagnose model has been studied that assumes independence of the observations of feature variables $X_1, X_2, ..., X_n$ given the class variable Y, which allows us to use the next equality (equation 5):

$$P(X_1 = x_1, ..., X_n = x_n|Y = y_j) = \prod_{i=1}^{n} P(X_i = x_i|Y = y_j) \tag{5}$$

where $P(X_i = x_i|Y = y_j)$ is the probability of an instance of class y_j having the observed attribute value x_i. In the core of this paradigm there is an assumption of independence between the occurrence of features values, that is not true in many tasks; however, it is empirically demonstrated that this paradigm gives good results in medical tasks.

This model is equivalent to the Bayesian network shown in figure 3. Note that the structure is fixed, and the variable to be predicted is parent of all predictor variables.

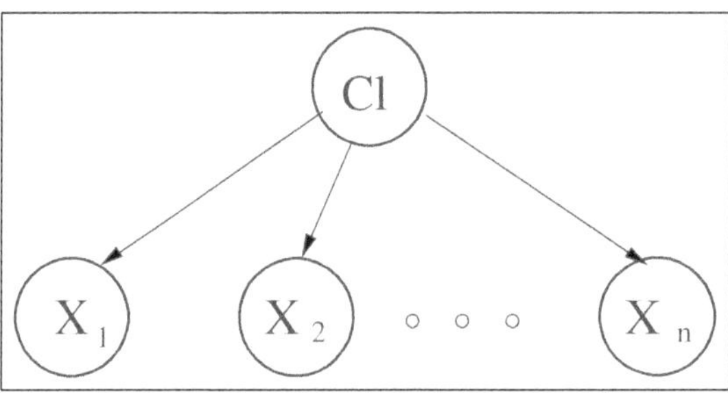

Fig. 3. Naive Bayes structure

In our experiments, we use this Naive Bayes (NB) classifier (Kohavi, 1996) in order to compare the results obtained by using the BN approach and the new proposed method Bayes-Nearest.

4 The *k*-NN Classification Method

The operation process of the Nearest Neighbor algorithm is as follows: A new pair (X, Y) is given, where only the measurement X is observable, and it is desired to estimate Y by utilizing the information contained in the set of correctly classified points. We shall call

$$X'_p \in X_1, X_2, ..., X_n$$

the nearest neighbor of X if

$$\min d(X_i, X) = d(X'_p, X) \qquad i = 1, 2, ..., n$$

The NN classification decision method gives to X the category y'_p of its nearest neighbor X'_p. In case of tie for the nearest neighbor, the decision rule has to be modified in order to break it. A mistake is made if $y'_p \neq y$.

An immediate extension to this decision rule is the so called k-NN approach (Dasarathy, 1991; Aha et al., 1991; Sierra and Lazkano, 2002), which assigns to the candidate X the class which is most frequently represented in the k nearest neighbors to X.

5 Discretization of Continuous Attributes

Many classification algorithms require the classifying variables to be discretized, either because they need nominal values, or in order to reduce the computational cost and to accelerate the induction process. Discretization of the variables does not necessarily affect negatively the learning process, even more, the performance of a classifier can be improved with the discretization. (Dougherty et al., 1995) makes a comparison of several discretization methods over 16 databases and two classifiers, Quinlan's C4.5 (Quinlan, 1993) and the Naive Bayes classifier. The results show that for most of the cases the discretization process improves the performance of the classifiers.

Discretization methods can be classified according to three criteria:

- Global/Local: local discretization produces partitions of the data that are applied to local regions of the space of instances. On the other side, global discretization produces a net in the n-dimensional space of instances, in which each variable is partitioned in regions independently of the rest of the attributes.
- Supervised/Non-supervised: the "class" variable is used while discretizing the data in a supervised manner. This does not happen in the non-supervised discretization.
- Static/Dynamic: static discretization performs in each step one discretization for each variable. The number of regions k may be an input to the process, or it can also be determined independently for each variable. Dynamic discretization searches for the possible values of k simultaneously for all the variables, capturing the interdependencies during the discretization method.

Below some discretization methods found in the literature are presented.

The easiest way to make a discretization is to fix a number of intervals k, and to divide the range of values of a variable in k intervals of the same length. This method is known as the *equal width interval binning*. The *equal frequency intervals* method consists of dividing the set of values on k intervals or regions, each interval containing $\frac{m}{k}$ adjacent instances (m being the total number of instances).

Those methods do not consider the class when determining the intervals. Thereby, they are non-supervised methods and the classification information contained within the original database can be lost if the discretization combines cases tightly associated to different classes.

Entropy-based discretization methods have proved to be very effective for different problems. This methods pretend to divide the set of data in k subsets of minimal entropy. Given a dataset and a variable to discretize, the entries are ordered according to the values of the variable and the value that minimizes the entropy in the generated subsets is selected as a breakpoint. This criterion is applied recursively in each of the new subsets (Catlett, 1991; M. and Irani, 1993).

6 Proposed Approach: Bayes-Nearest

In this section a new classification algorithm that combines the Bayesian Network paradigm with the Nearest Neighbor algorithm is presented. A general overview of the learning phase of the Bayesian Network part of the new approach can be seen in Figure 4. The Bayesian Network structure is obtained from the database in an automatic form by using the K2 structural learning algorithm. In order to better evaluate the classification power of the Bayesian Network approach, we use two different net evaluation metrics in the learning process (the so called K2 metric and the entropy metric), and compare the results obtained by using each of them.

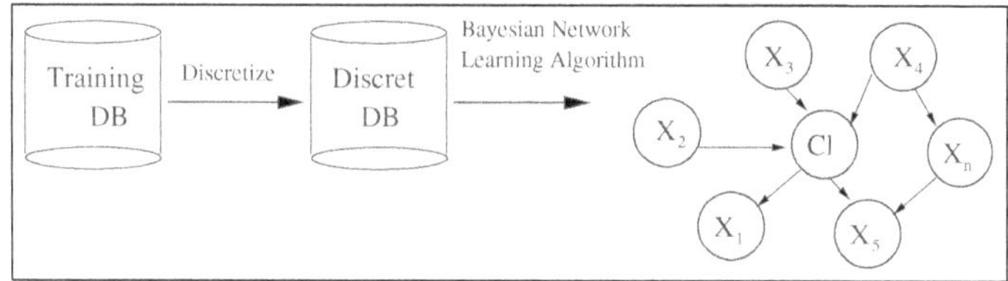

Fig. 4. A general schemata of the BN model learning process

Input: samples file, containing n cases $(X_i, Y_i), i = 1, ..., n$ and a new case (X, Y) to be classified. Output: Class for the new case Select the nearest neighbor to x from the sample file cases Propagate this nearest case using the previously learned BN Output the class C_i which a posteriori probability P_i is maximal among all the classes

Fig. 5. The pseudo-code of the Bayes-Nearest Algorithm.

The classification process carried out by our new algorithm is showed in algorithmic form in Figure 5. As explained before, the classification process is done by looking for the nearest case to the new case to be classified in the Training Database, and by propagating the evidence of this nearest case in the previously learned BN. Figure 6 shows a schemata of this new method.

The BN propagation algorithm does not take into consideration the fact that, for a new case, the parent combination values for some variables does not appear

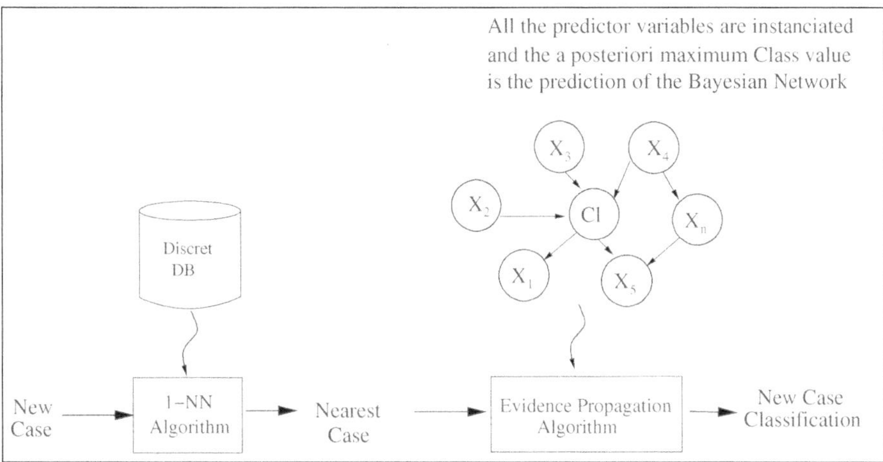

Fig. 6. A general schemata of the new cases classification method. Notice that the class of the nearest example is, of course, not passed to the BN

in the training database and, due to the application of the Laplace corrector factor those parent combination value probabiliti values will be minimal. In this new Bayes–nearest method, we cope with that fact using the K-NN alforithm. Once the BN is learned, the nearest case in the training database is used during the deduction phase.

7 Experimental Results

Six databases are used to test our hypothesis. All of them are obtained from the *UCI Machine Learning Repository* (Murphy and Aha, 1994). These domains are public at the Statlog project WEB page (Michie et al., 1995). The characteristics of the databases are given in table 1. As it can be seen, we have chosen different types of databases, selecting some of them with a large number of predictor variables, or with a large number of cases and some multi-class problems.

In order to give a real perspective of applied methods, we use 10-Fold Cross-validation (Stone, 1974) in all experiments. All databases have been randomly separated into ten sets of training data and its corresponding test data. Obviously all the validation files used have been always the same for the five algorithms shown.

It agrees to indicate, on the other hand, that the used databases have been discretized previously when the values of the predicting variables required it. The discretization has been made using an equal frequency interval method. But in order to give a more sound comparison among the different classifiers, the discretization has been the same for all the databases. This fact allows us to outline the effect of the classifying method on the obtained accuracy, as we have not tried to look for a specific discretization method for each database, which would benefit the presented new approach.

Table 1. Details of experimental domains (ten same size but different train and test file for each domain)

Domain	*Training cases*	*Test cases*	*Num. of classes*	*Num. of attributes*
Breast	614	69	10	11
Letters	15,000	5,000	26	16
Pendigit	7,494	3,493	10	16
satimage	4,435	2,000	7	36
shuttle	43,500	14,500	7	9
Vote	300	135	2	16

The class distribution of the training databases can be seen in figure 7. Different distributions appear, some of them are uniformly distributed while in other cases the distribution is bowed.

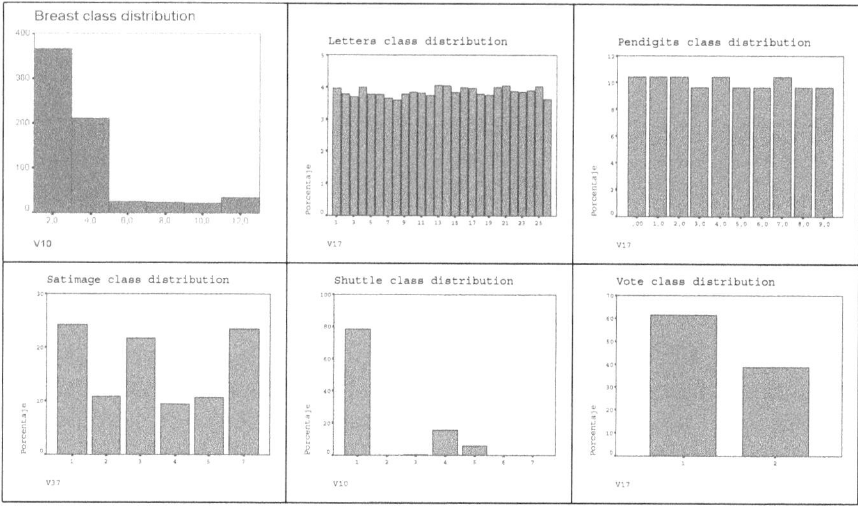

Fig. 7. Class distributions of the training databases

Table 2 shows the results obtained for the different learning mechanisms and the different databases. This table shows that the new algorithm presents better classification percentages for five of of the six standard databases that have been utilized. For the "vote" database the results are poorer. We have used the Wilcoxon Rank-Sum (Wilcoxon, 1945) test with $\alpha = 0.05$ in order to compare the results obtained by each of the probabilistic classifiers in the databases, and we have obtained as result that the new proposed approach outperforms the others for the "Breast" and "Pendigits" databases, while it is not possible to reject the null hypothesis of equal accuracy between the Bayesian Network and the Bayes-Nearest methods in the rest four databases used.

Table 2. Well classified validated results obtained for each datafile by each of the tested paradigms

		K2		*Entropy*	
Datafile	*Naive Bayes*	K2-BN	K2-BN-nearest	Entr-BN	Entr-BN-nearest
Breast	61.79 ± 13.97	65.20 ± 18.54	57.33 ± 17.81	59.08 ± 19.14	$\mathbf{66.95 \pm 19.78}$
Letters	72.88 ± 1.69	71.94 ± 3.50	$\mathbf{74.50 \pm 3.50}$	69.97 ± 4.67	72.59 ± 4.21
Pendigits	84.37 ± 1.74	89.36 ± 1.23	$\mathbf{90.67 \pm 1.06}$	89.29 ± 0.96	90.53 ± 1.13
Satimage	72.31 ± 9.57	78.13 ± 6.85	78.07 ± 6.68	78.06 ± 6.62	$\mathbf{78.44 \pm 6.36}$
Shuttle	78.60 ± 0.55	98.17 ± 1.57	98.17 ± 1.57	98.46 ± 0.98	$\mathbf{98.49 \pm 0.98}$
Vote	90.11 ± 3.26	$\mathbf{94.26 \pm 4.63}$	91.74 ± 4.62	93.79 ± 4.88	91.73 ± 5.01

The main hypothesis we are working with is that this new approach gives to the BN classifier more powerful results, and this idea could be used to outperform Bayesian classifiers. It is not the same when speaking about the K-NN paradigm, since it is not a probabilistic one and the obtained results could be quite different (for example, it is well known that the K-NN approach obtains an accuracy of about 62% with the Breast datafile, which is poorer than the one obtained by the presented new paradigm, but it is also known that K-NN obtains a 95% performance by using the Letters database, which is better than the obtained with the new algorithm.

8 Conclusions and Further Work

In this paper a new hybrid classifier that combines Bayesian Networks with distance-based algorithms is presented. The main idea is to perform the evidence propagation in the Bayesian Network not for the case that is being classified at each moment, but for its nearest case in the training database.

The results obtained show that the new hybrid algorithm performs better for most of the used databases. But the distance metric used in the nearest neighbor algorithm does not give good results when the number of values of the predictor variables take is small.

It seems that the more possible combinations of values exist for the predictor variables and minor is the proportion reflected in the training database for each of the classes, better behaves the new algorithm with respect to the Bayesian Networks. Although this fact must be further analyzed, the experimental done shows that the new approach can outperform the other probabilistic classifiers in the so called sparse databases – databases with a large number of variables or a high number of classes and few number of cases.

Looking to the computational load, this classification technique allows us to pre-propagate all the cases in the database and thereby, to classify a new case, it is only needed to look for its nearest case and select the class with the maximum a posteriori probability previously obtained. This allows to reduce the time needed to predict a new case and thereby makes the new method suitable for real-time applications.

An extension of the presented approach is to select among the feature subset that better performance presents by the classification point of view. A Feature Subset Selection (Inza et al., 2000, 2001; Sierra et al., 2001a) technique can be applied in order to select which of the predictor variables should be used. This could take advantage in the hybrid classifier construction, as well as in the accuracy.

References

[Aha et al., 1991] Aha, D., Kibler, D., and Albert, M. (1991). Instance-based learning algorithms. *Machine Learning*, 6:37–66.

[Castillo et al., 1997] Castillo, E., Gutiérrez, J., and Hadi, A. (1997). *Expert Systems and Probabilistic Network Models*. Springer-Verlag.

[Catlett, 1991] Catlett, J. (1991). On chanching continuous attributes into ordered discrete attributes. In Verlag, S., editor, *Proceedings of the European Working Session on Learning*, pages 164–178.

[Cooper and Herskovits, 1992] Cooper, G. F. and Herskovits, E. A. (1992). A bayesian method for the induction of probabilistic networks from data. *Machine Learning*, 9:309–347.

[Cowell et al., 1999] Cowell, R. G., Dawid, A. P., Lauritzen, S., and Spiegelharter, D. J. (1999). *Probabilistic Networks and Expert Systems*. Springer.

[Dasarathy, 1991] Dasarathy, B. V. (1991). Nearest neighbor (nn) norms: Nn pattern recognition classification techniques. *IEEE Computer Society Press*.

[Dietterich, 1997] Dietterich, T. G. (1997). Machine learning research: four current directions. *AI Magazine*, 18(4):97–136.

[Dougherty et al., 1995] Dougherty, J., Kohavi, R., and Sahami, M. (1995). Supervised and unsupervised discretization of continuous features. *International Conference on Machine Learning*, pages 194–202.

[Friedman et al., 1997] Friedman, N., Geiger, D., and Goldszmidt, M. (1997). Bayesian network classifiers. *Machine Learning*, 19(4):131–163.

[Heckerman et al., 1995] Heckerman, D., Geiger, D., and Chickering, D. M. (1995). Learning bayesian networks: The combination of knowledge and statistical data. *Machine Learning*, 20:197–243.

[Henrion, 1988] Henrion, M. (1988). Propagating uncertainty in bayesian networks by probabilistic logic sampling. In *Proceedings of the Fourth Conference on Uncertainty in Artificial Intelligence*, pages 149–163.

[Ho and Srihati, 1994] Ho, T. K. and Srihati, S. N. (1994). Decision combination in multiple classifier systems. *IEEE Transactions on Pattern Analysis and Machine Intelligence*, 16:66–75.

[Inza et al., 2000] Inza, I., Larrañaga, P., Etxeberria, R., and Sierra, B. (2000). Feature subset selection by bayesian networks based optimization. *Artificial Intelligence*, 123(1-2):157–184.

[Inza et al., 2001] Inza, I., Larrañaga, P., and Sierra, B. (2001). Feature subset selection by bayesian networks: a comparison with genetic and sequential algorithms. *International Journal of Approximate Reasoning*, 27(2):143–164.

[Jensen, 1996] Jensen, F. V. (1996). *Introduction to Bayesian networks*. University College of London.

[Kohavi, 1996] Kohavi, R. (1996). Scaling up the accuracy of naive-bayes classifiers: a decision-tree hybrid. In *Proceedings of the Second International Conference on Knowledge Discovery and Data Mining*.

[Lu, 1996] Lu, Y. (1996). Knowledge integration in a multiple classifier system. *Applied Intelligence*, 6:75–86.

[M. and Irani, 1993] M., F. U. and Irani, K. B. (1993). Multi-interval discretization of continuous-valued attributes for classification learning. In Kauffman, M., editor, *Proceedings of the 13th International Joint Conference on Artificial Intelligence*, pages 1022–1029.

[Michie et al., 1995] Michie, D., Spiegelhalter, D., and Taylor, C. e. (1995). Machine learning, neural and statistical classification.

[Mitchell, 1997] Mitchell, T. (1997). *Machine Learning*. McGraw-Hill.

[Murphy and Aha, 1994] Murphy, P. M. and Aha, D. W. (1994). Uci repository of machine learning databases.

[Pearl, 1987] Pearl, J. (1987). Evidential reasoning using stochastic simulation of causal models. *Artificial Intelligence*, 32(2):245–257.

[Pearl, 1988] Pearl, J. (1988). *Probabilistic Reasoning in Intelligent Systems: Networks of Plausible Inference*. Morgan Kaufmann.

[Quinlan, 1993] Quinlan, J. R. (1993). *C4.5: Programs for Machine Learning*. Morgan Kaufmann Publishers, Los Altos, California.

[Sierra et al., 2000] Sierra, B., Inza, I., and Larrañaga, P. (2000). Medical bayesian networks. *Lecture Notes in Computer Science*, 1933:4–14.

[Sierra and Larrañaga, 1998] Sierra, B. and Larrañaga, P. (1998). Predicting survival in malignant skin melanoma using bayesian networks automatically induced by genetic algorithms. an empirical comparision between different approaches. *Artificial Intelligence in Medicine*, 14:215–230.

[Sierra and Lazkano, 2002] Sierra, B. and Lazkano, E. (2002). Probabilistic-weighted k nearest neighbor algorithm: a new approach for gene expression based classification. In *KES02 proceedings*, pages 932–939. IOS press.

[Sierra et al., 2001a] Sierra, B., Lazkano, E., Inza, I., Merino, M., Larrañaga, P., and Quiroga, J. (2001a). Prototype selection and feature subset selection by estimation of distribution algorithms. a case study in the survival of cirrhotic patients treated with tips. *Artificial Intelligence in Medicine*, pages 20–29.

[Sierra et al., 2001b] Sierra, B., Serrano, N., Larrañaga, P., Plasencia, E. J., Inza, I., Jiménez, J. J., Revuelta, P., and Mora, M. L. (2001b). Using bayesian networks in the construction of a bi-level multi-classifier. *Artificial Intelligence in Medicine*, 22:233–248.

[Sierra et al., 1999] Sierra, B., Serrano, N., Larrañaga, P., Plasencia, E. J., Inza, I., Jiménez, J. J., Revuelta, P., and Mora, M. L. (1999). Machine learning inspired approaches to combine standard medical measures at an intensive care unit. *Lecture Notes in Artificial Intelligence*, 1620:366–371.

[Stone, 1974] Stone, M. (1974). Cross-validation choice and assessment of statistical procedures. *Journal Royal of Statistical Society*, 36:111–147.

[Wilcoxon, 1945] Wilcoxon, F. (1945). Individual comparisons by ranking methods. *Biometrics*, 1:80–83.

[Xu et al., 1992] Xu, L., Kryzak, A., and Suen, C. Y. (1992). Methods for combining multiple classifiers and their applications to handwriting recognition. *IEEE Transactions on SMC*, 22:418–435.

A Data Mining Approach to Credit Risk Evaluation and Behaviour Scoring

Sara C. Madeira[1,2], Arlindo L. Oliveira[1,3], and Catarina S. Conceição[3]

[1] Inesc-ID/IST,
1049-001 Lisbon, Portugal, aml@inesc-id.pt
[2] Universidade da Beira Interior,
6200-001 Covilhã, Portugal, smadeira@di.ubi.pt
[3] Link Consulting SA,
1000-138 Lisbon, Portugal, catarina.conceicao@link.pt

Abstract. *Behaviour scoring* is used in several companies to score the customers according to *credit risk* by analyzing historical data about their past behaviour. In this paper we describe a *data mining* approach to credit risk evaluation in a Portuguese telecommunication company.

1 Introduction

Mobile telecommunications companies need to evaluate the credit risk of their current customers and of potential new customers. Before accepting a new customer, or in order to re-calculate the credit limit of an existing customer, it is necessary to estimate his risk class, and classify him in one of the potential risk classes. This scoring process is largely based on scorecards [6], obtained using non exact models and specific knowledge from business, and whose doubtful precision can lead to a high number of classification problems.

The company where this project was developed was not an exception in what relates to the use of scorecards: a scorecard was used to determine the credit risk of potential customers. Each potential customer was scored using a scorecard, classified in one of several risk classes, and then assigned a reference credit limit, and an initial customer segment ("Low", "Medium" or "High"). Every six months, the customers' risk class, and consequently their customer segment and credit limit were re-calculated. This is when *behaviour scoring* begins. Every customer with a sufficient number of invoices was analyzed using the last N invoices and the delays observed in their payments. The average payment delay of each customer calculated using a weighted average of the observed delays in the payment of the invoices considered, was used as the basis for this re-classification process.

Several criticisms were made by the business experts to the existing credit risk evaluation system. The main two were related with the lack of possibility to anticipate the risk and the high number of invoices needed to re-classify accurately the customers.

Facing this scenario, the use of standard machine learning techniques came out as a innovative and credible alternative to perform behaviour scoring without using a behaviour scorecard. Multiple logistic regression, decision trees and

Fernando Moura Pires, Salvador Abreu (Eds.): EPIA 2003, LNAI 2902, pp. 184–188, 2003.

neural networks were used to test the potential explanatory value of hundreds of variables, define the target concept of this real world machine learning problem, and, finally construct the inference models needed to implement a credit risk evaluation and behaviour scoring approach based on Data Mining [2].

2 Inference Models: Time Window and Target Concept

The models derived should infer the customer segment based on historical data, and enable the anticipation of the risk class three months in the future using six months of historical data. In order to do this, nine months of historical data should ideally be used to derive the models: the *training examples* should be obtained using six months of data to characterize the customers' past behaviour, while the remaining three months should be used to calculate the customer segment three months after the *eyeball.* The eyeball is defined as the date when the inference model is used to predict the customer segment (see Fig. 1).

In order to enable the re-classification of recent customers, the *model set* should be constructed using examples of customers with a minimum of four invoices. Assuming that the last three months of historical data are used to simulate the customers' future behaviour, and consequently, their future risk, the customer segment can be re-calculated after the due date of the customers' first invoice, without having to wait six months to re-evaluate their credit risk.

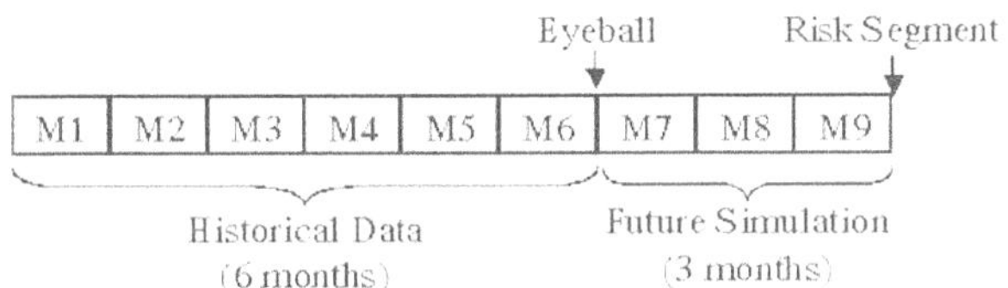

Fig. 1. Time Window

Inferring the customer segment is a *concept learning* task [1], where the concept is a three-value function defined over all customers: H when the customer segment is "High", M when the customer segment is "Medium" and L when the customer segment is "Low". The learning problem can be defined as follows: let $\{\mathrm{X}_1, \ldots, \mathrm{X}_N\}$ be a set of N data objects, which can be represented as a $N \times n$ data matrix, $\mathcal{X}$, where n is the number of attributes used to describe each instance X_k. This means that $\mathcal{X}$ is the set of instances over which the concept is defined and each customer is an instance represented by the vector $\mathrm{X}_k = (\mathrm{x}_1, \ldots, \mathrm{x}_n)$, $\mathrm{x}_i \in \mathcal{D}_i$ and $\mathcal{D}_i$ is the domain of the attribute x_i, which can be real, in the case of real-valued attributes, or discrete, in the case of nominal attributes. The *target concept*, denoted by c, is in this case a function defined over the set of instances $\mathcal{X}$ that corresponds to the customer segment:

$$c : \mathcal{X} \rightarrow \{H, M, L\} \tag{1}$$

3 Using a Proxy to Obtain the Target Concept

Most data mining techniques, and particularly the ones we intended to use, accept a set of training examples (ordered pairs $< X_k, c(X_k) >$), each consisting of an instance X_k from $\mathcal{X}$ and its target concept value $c(X_k)$. However, the business experts did not provide us with a set of examples of customers already classified as "Low", "Medium" or "High" from whose behaviour and history the machine learning algorithms could learn. They could only identify the maximum days delay observed in the payment of the customers' last invoices as a very informative attribute about the customers' probability of default. This value could easily quantify the credit risk of a given customer and his probability to suffer extreme dunning actions, like deactivation. Having this in mind, we decided to study the relation between the maximum payment delay observed in the payment of the last nine invoices of the customer and his probability of default, which is, in this case, a synonym of probability of dunning deactivation.

The approach used to compute the customer segment was based on the following assumption: a customer whose probability of default is greater than the profit margin of the company should definitely be classified as a "Bad" customer, since he/she will, on the average, be a liability for the company. Assuming this, a statistical study was made in order to find out which maximum value of payment delay implied a probability of default of approximately 65%, the estimated average margin. The entire population of customers was analyzed in order to find out the probability of default of a customer three months in the future, given his maximum payment delay observed to date. The probability of default, *pd*, associated with a given value of maximum payment delay, *mpd*, was computed as follows:

$$pd = \frac{\mathcal{B}}{\mathcal{C}} \times 100 \tag{2}$$

where $\mathcal{B}$ is the number of dunning deactivations observed in the future for the group of customers whose maximum payment delay was greater than *mpd* at time t, and $\mathcal{C}$ is the number of customers with maximum payment delay greater than *mpd* at time t. The distinction between the segments "High" and "Medium" was also made using the probability of default.

During the previous statistical study we noticed that below a certain number of maximum days delay, the probability of default did not change, and was for this reason independent from the maximum days delay. This means that the probability of default of a customer who has always paid in time is in fact as high as that of the customers whose maximum payment delay has never exceed a certain number of days. The value of the probability of default of a customer of the segment "High" was set to approximately 2%, and consequently the segment "Medium" included all customers whose probability of default was between 2% and 65%. The probability of default was estimated from the maximum delay observed in the payment history of the customer.

4 A Two Level Approach to Inference of Models

In the information system of the company, the data was organized in several levels. The top two were legal entity and payment responsible. Each legal entity can have several payment responsible. The great majority of data, and the potentially explanatory variables were concentrated at the payment responsible level. This data included all the historical data related to the customers' payment behaviour. However, the business experts were also interested in evaluating the customer risk at the top level data: legal entity. Facing the fact that aggregating the existing data from the level payment responsible to the top level would not be optimal in terms of model precision, it was decided to use a two level approach to the inference of models. Four models were derived at the payment responsible level, one for each customer class considered.

After deriving the models at the payment responsible level, the predicted customer segments of each payment responsible are used together with other attributes found relevant at the legal entity level to construct another data set that was labelled by a business expert. This data set was then used to derive a model at the legal entity level, as shown in Fig. 2.

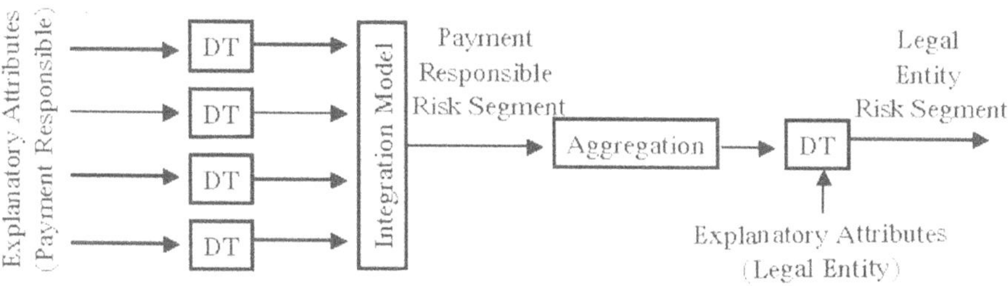

Fig. 2. Two Level Models.

5 Analyzing the Precision of the Inference Models

Several models were derived at the payment responsible level using three well known data mining techniques: multiple logistic regression, decision trees [3,4] and neural networks [5]. Regression models and neural networks were not competitive with decision trees in what concerns to precision. Furthermore, deriving human interpretable models was preferable, and we could easily obtain them from the decision trees. The derived decision trees had between 10 and 60 nodes and could for this reason be easily converted into understandable if-then rules.

Assuming that the labels computed for each instance (see Sect.3) model exactly the credit risk of the customers, it is interesting to compare the performance of the data mining approach at the payment responsible level with the base segmentation model, used previously. The base segmentation model classifies a customer in accordance with the maximum payment delay observed until

Table 1. Confusion Matrices: Base Segmentation Model and Decision Trees.

% classified as →	Low	Medium	High
Low	**41.10**	3.60	0.16
Medium	8.24	**10.84**	6.47
High	1.82	4.81	**22.96**

% classified as →	Low	Medium	High
Low	**35.41**	0.56	0.00
Medium	5.24	**22.14**	1.16
High	0.54	2.66	**32.29**

the eyeball. In order to perform this comparison we computed the differences between the classification obtained by the base segmentation model and the true customer segments observed three months later.

Table 1 shows that the total error of the base segmentation model was 25.10% in the test set, compared with the 10.16% of the decision trees. This represents a positive gain of 15% in the precision of the behaviour scoring approach.

These results translate into increased precision at the legal entity level, not reported here for lack of space.

6 Conclusions

We presented an approach that uses machine learning techniques to perform behaviour scoring and infer the credit risk of the customers. Predictive models were trained to infer the credit risk of the customers three months in the future given six months of historical data. The final models were derived using decision trees, which were chosen for their precision and human interpretability.

The capability of anticipating the customer segmentation three months in the future gives the business experts the possibility to act in advance, by revising the credit limits in order to decrease substantially the probability of default of the customers. The two level approach followed gives the company two customer segments, one for the payment responsible and another for their legal entity, enabling the flexibility to act at the level most adapted to the specific situation.

References

1. Mitchel, T. M.: Machine Learning. McGraw-Hill Internacional Editions, Computer Science Series. Singapore (1997)
2. Han, J., Kamber, M.: Data Mining. Concepts and Techniques. Morgan Kaufman Publishers, San Francisco, U.S.A. (2001)
3. Breiman, L., Friedman, J.H., Olsen, R. A., Stone, C. J.: Classification and Regression Trees. Pacific Grove, Wadsworth (1984)
4. Quinlan, J. R.: Induction of decision trees. Machine Learning, 1:81–106 (1986)
5. Rumelhart, D.E., McClelland, J.L., PDP Research Group: Parallel Distributed Processing, MIT Press, Cambridge (1986)
6. Banks, W.J., Leonard, K.J:Credit Scoring and mathematical models. Credit and Financial Managment Review, Volume 1 (1995)

Influence of kNN-Based Load Forecasting Errors on Optimal Energy Production

Alicia Troncoso Lora[1], José C. Riquelme[1], José Luís Martínez Ramos[2], Jesús M. Riquelme Santos[2], and Antonio Gómez Expósito[2]

[1] Department of Languages and Systems, University of Sevilla, Sevilla, Spain
{ali,riquelme}@lsi.us.es
[2] Department of Electrical Engineering, University of Sevilla, Sevilla, Spain
{camel,jsantos,age}@us.es

Abstract. This paper presents a study of the influence of the accuracy of hourly load forecasting on the energy planning and operation of electric generation utilities. First, a k Nearest Neighbours (kNN) classification technique is proposed for hourly load forecasting. Then, obtained prediction errors are compared with those obtained results by using a M5'. Second, the obtained kNN-based load forecast is used to compute the optimal on/off status and generation scheduling of the units. Finally, the influence of forecasting errors on both the status and generation level of the units over the scheduling period is studied.

Keywords. Nearest neighbours, load forecasting, optimal energy production.

1 Introduction

The prediction of future loads is crucial for the economic and secure operation of electrical power systems. In the short, medium and long term, generation scheduling comprises a set of interrelated optimization problems that require a load forecasting procedure. Consequently, accurate forecasting techniques are crucial for the electric power industry to reduce the uncertainty of the load and to compute an optimal and realistic generation scheduling.

Nowadays, forecasting methods for load estimation can be classified in two main groups: classical statistical methods and techniques based on machine learning. Classical statistical methods [1,2] aim at estimating the current load from the values of past load. The relationships between the load and other relevant factors (e.g., temperature) are used to determine the underlying model of the load time series, the main advantage of classical methods being their inherent simplicity. However, as the relationships between load and factors which have influence on load are nonlinear, it is not an easy task to identify realistic and accurate models using classical methods.

In the last years, techniques based on machine learning such as Artificial Neural Networks (ANN) [3,4] have been applied to one day-ahead load forecasting. The ANNs are trained to learn the relationships between the input variables

Fernando Moura Pires, Salvador Abreu (Eds.): EPIA 2003, LNAI 2902, pp. 189–203, 2003.

(mainly preceding loads and actual temperature) and historical load patterns. The main disadvantage of ANNs is the required learning procedure.

More recently, classification techniques based on the nearest neighbours have been successfully applied in different areas from the traditional pattern recognition such as medical diagnosis tools, game theory expert systems or time series forecasting. Several papers have been published on the application of nearest neighbours techniques to the electricity market price forecasting [6,7], but applications to load forecasting problems are missed.

This paper presents a study of the effects of the accuracy of hourly load forecasting on the generation planning and operation of an electric utility. First, a kNN classification technique is proposed for load forecasting. Then, the hourly load forecasting errors are compared with those obtained results by using a M5'. Second, the obtained kNN-based load forecasts are used to compute the optimal on/off status and generation scheduling of the units. Then, the influence of forecasting errors on both the status and generation level of the units over the scheduling period is studied.

2 One Day-Ahead Load Forecasting

The one day-ahead load forecasting problem aims at predicting the load for the twenty-four hours of the next day. To solve this problem two schemes can be considered:

1) Iterative Scheme: This scheme aims at predicting the load of one hour and the obtained prediction is used as an input for the load forecasting of the next hour. The process is repeated until the load forecasting of the next 24 hours is obtained. The iterative prediction has the disadvantage that the errors are accumulated throughout the prediction horizon.
2) Direct Scheme: This scheme aims at predicting the next twenty-four hours from the same input data. The direct prediction does not take into account the relationships between the load of one hour and the load of successive hours.

Test results have shown similar accuracy for both schemes, and, consequently, the direct scheme has been adopted in this study.

2.1 Description of the Proposed Approach

In this section, an algorithm based on kNN [8] for hourly load forecasting is described. kNN algorithms are techniques for pattern classification based on the similarity of the individuals of a population. The members of a population coexist surrounded of similar individuals which have similar properties. This simple idea is the learning rule of the kNN classifier. Thus, the nearest neighbours' decision rule assigns to an unclassified sample point the classification of the nearest of a set of previously classified points. In contrast to statistical methods that try to identify a model from the available data, the kNN method uses the training set as the model.

A particular kNN algorithm is characterized by issues such as the number of neighbours, type of distance used, etc.

In the method used in this paper, each individual is defined by the 24-hours load of a day. Thus, the kNN classifier finds the daily load curve that is "similar to" the load curve of previous days.

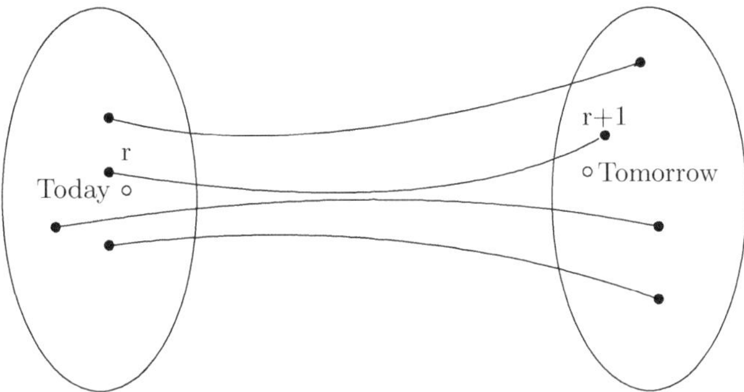

Fig. 1. Learning rule of the proposed approach.

The basic algorithm for the prediction of the electric energy demand for day $d+1$ can be written as follows:

1. Calculate the distances between the load of the day d, D_d, and the preceding points $\{D_{d-1}, D_{d-2}, ...\}$ using a metric $dist$. Let v_1,...,v_k be the k nearest days to the day d, sorted by closeness.
2. The prediction is:

$$\widehat{D}_{d+1} = \frac{1}{\alpha_1 + ... + \alpha_k} \sum_{j=1}^{k} \alpha_j \cdot D_{v_j+1} \tag{1}$$

where

$$\alpha_j = \frac{dist(D_d, D_{v_k}) - dist(D_d, D_{v_j})}{dist(D_d, D_{v_k}) - dist(D_d, D_{v_1})} \tag{2}$$

Notice that $0 \leq \alpha_j \leq 1$, i.e., the weight is equal to zero when the considered day is the most distant and one when the considered day is the nearest.

Once the forecasted load of the day $d+1$ has been obtained, the actual load of the day $d+1$ is used as an input for the load forecasting of the day $d+2$.

Notice that the prediction aims at estimating the load for a certain day from a linear combination of the load of the days that follow the nearest neighbours days.

If the k nearest neighbours for a vector D_d are $[D_{v_1}, ..., D_{v_k}]$, where v_i is the ith nearest neighbour, the set of points $[D_{v_1+1}, ..., D_{v_k+1}]$ will usually be the nearest to D_{d+1} for noise-free time series.

Figure 1 shows the geometric idea of the kNN classifier when the considered number of neighbours is equal to one. Today's hourly load and the unknown load of tomorrow are represented by circumferences. The four black points are the neighbours of today's load. The point r is the nearest neighbour. Then, a possible estimation for tomorrow's load is the load of the day $r + 1$.

In the classical kNN, the nearest neighbours of tomorrow's load are used for the prediction for tomorrow's load, but this is not possible. Thus, the method presented in this section is the adapted kNN algorithm.

Some key issues of the proposed technique are the following:

- **Choice of a metric:** A time series Y can be considered as a point in a n-dimensional space. Given a sequence query, q, a sequence of Y with the same length as q is searched out, z, such that the distance between the sequences is minimum. The choice of the metric to measure the similarity between two time series depends mainly on the specific features of the considered series. The most common metric is the square of the Euclidean distance, although other metrics can be used [9,10].
- **Number of neighbours:** The accuracy of hourly load forecasting can be influenced by this parameter. In practice, the optimal value of k is usually small for noise-free time series, since only a small number of different values for k must to be considered to find the optimal value. In this paper, k is determined by minimizing the mean relative, absolute and square errors for the training set.

2.2 Numerical Results

The kNN algorithm described in the previous section has been applied in several experiments to obtain the forecast of the Spanish electric energy demand. The working days of the period January 2000-May 2001 have been used to determine the optimal number of neighbours and the distance to measure the similarity between two curves.

The available period of June-November 2001 (Summer-Autumn seasons) has been chosen as a test set to check the forecasting errors and to validate the proposed method.

Figure 2a and 2b show the influence of the number of neighbours used for the next-day load forecasting on the mean relative, absolute and square errors for the considered training set, the distance to evaluate the similarity between a previous day and the historical data being the Euclidean and Manhatan distance, respectively.

From Figure 2, the following conclusions can be stated for the load time series:

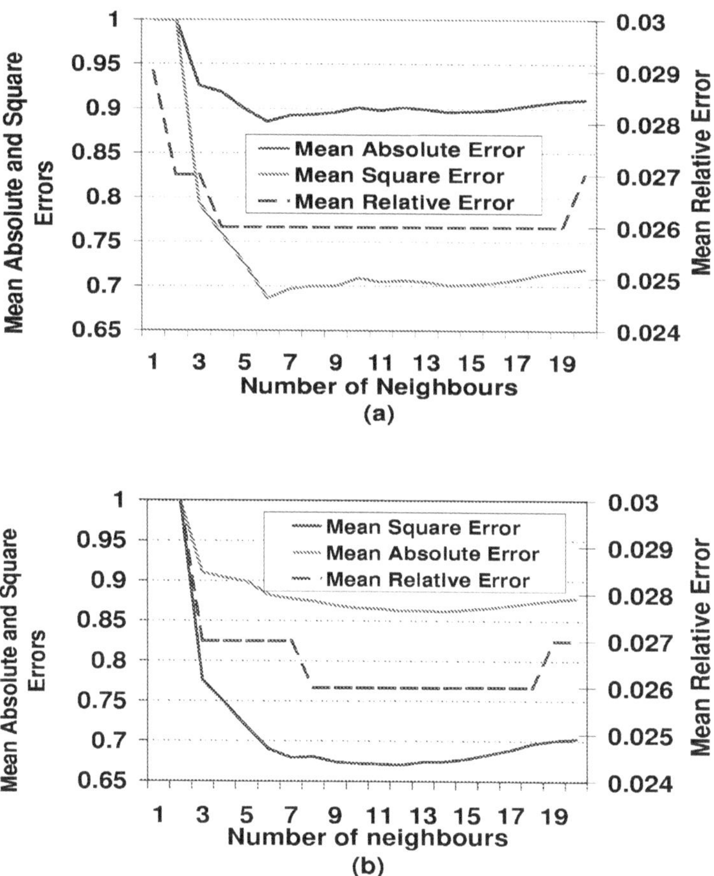

Fig. 2. Optimal number of neighbours using **a)** the Euclidean Distance, **b)** the Manhatan Distance.

1. The optimal number of neighbours is equal to six using the Euclidean distance while it is equal to thirteen using the Manhatan distance. Consequently, this number depends on the type of norm used to compute the distance.
2. The optimal number of neighbours is independent of the type of error used like objective function to minimize. For example, the optimal number of neighbours is six for all type of errors (relative, absolute and square error) when the Euclidean distance is considered.

Test results have shown the same average error for the training set when two distances have been considered: the Euclidean and Manhatan distance. Thus, the Manhatan distance is only considered in the sequel.

Figure 3a shows the hourly average of the real and forecasted load for the working days from June 2001 to November 2001, being the mean error 2.3%. A

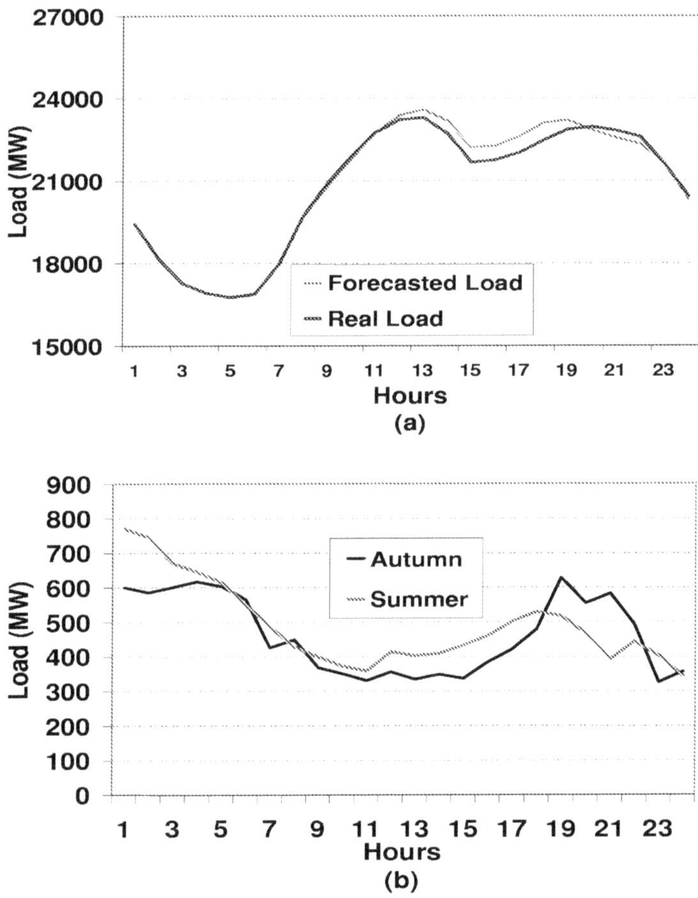

Fig. 3. a) Hourly average of real and forecasted load; **b)** Absolute-value hourly average of the forecasted load error.

good performance of the prediction method based on kNN can be observed. Note that the results obtained applying this method are similar than those carried out using other techniques such as ANNs [5].

Figure 3b presents the hourly average absolute value of the error of the forecasted load for the Autumn and Summer seasons. Note that the forecasting errors are larger during valley hours. However, it is more important to obtain an accurate prediction during peak hours because the electric energy is more expensive during these hours.

Figure 4a and 4b present the forecasted load for the two weeks that lead to the largest and smallest average errors, along with the actual load for the test set. The weeks with the largest and smallest errors correspond to Tuesday September 11th until Monday September 17th, and Monday October 22nd until

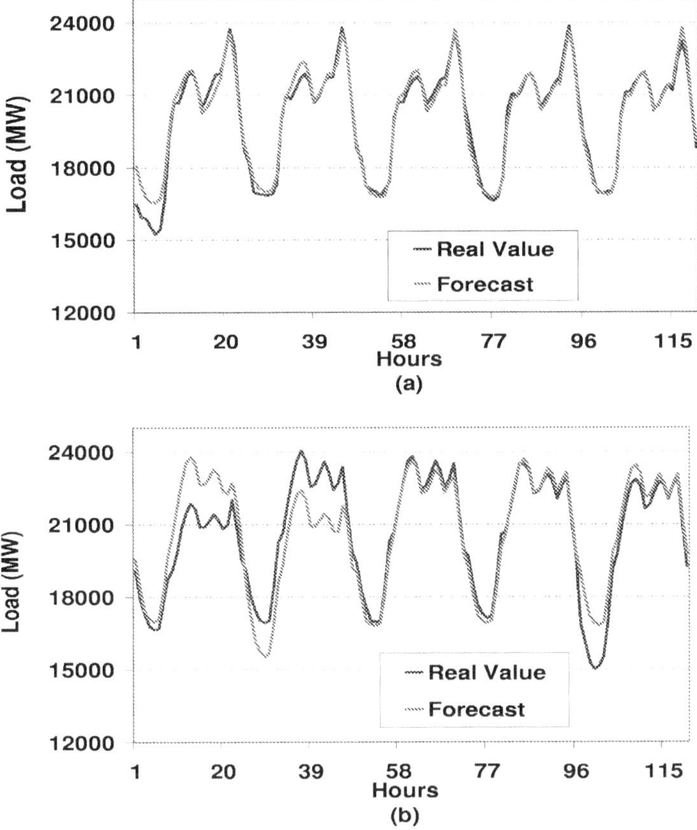

Fig. 4. a) Best weekly forecasts; **b)** Worst weekly forecasts.

Friday October 26th, respectively. It can be observed that the week with the higher prediction errors is the one that corresponds to the terrorist assault of the New York Twin Towers. Notice that the prediction errors corresponding to September 12th are rather high due to the anomalous load of the day before.

Table 1. Daily mean errors of the best and worst weekly forecasts.

Days	1	2	3	4	5	Mean (%)
October 22th-October 26th	3.13	1.25	1.11	0.08	0.07	1.4
September 11th-September 17th	5.88	6.73	1.18	1.13	4.55	3.9

The five working-day mean errors for the best and worst weeks are shown in Table 1. The weekly mean errors are 1.4% and 4%, respectively.

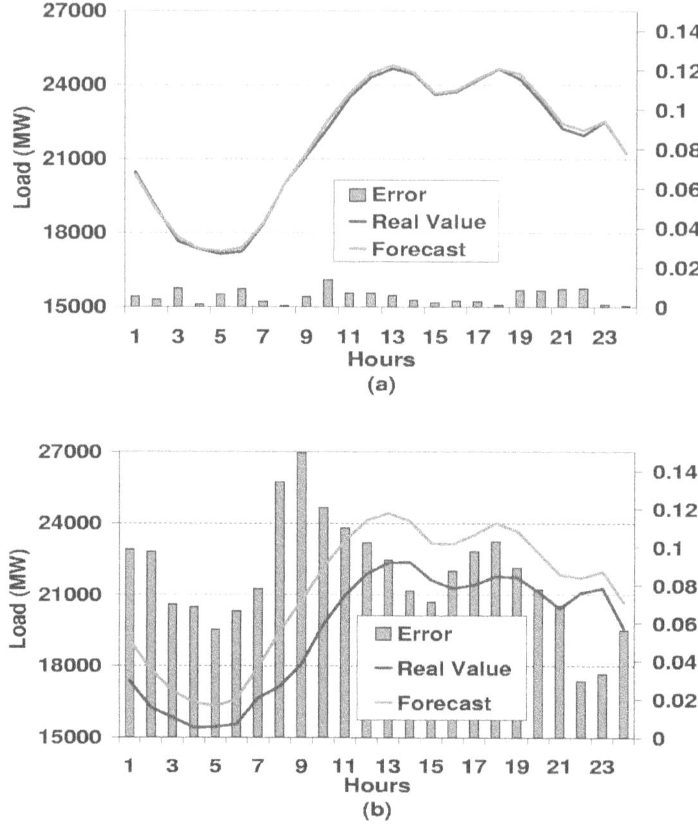

Fig. 5. a) Best daily forecasts; **b)** Worst daily forecasts.

Figure 5a and 5b present the forecasted load for the two days that lead to the largest and smallest average relative errors, along with the actual load for the test set. The days with the largest and smallest errors correspond to Monday August 6th and Tuesday July 17th, respectively. It can be observed that the day with the higher prediction errors is the one that corresponds to the first Monday of August, the day of the beginning of the Summer holiday for most of Spanish people.

The results obtained applying this method are compared with those carried out using the classifier M5' described in the Appendix.

Table 2 presents the mean relative value of forecasting errors and the maximum and minimum daily errors for the test set. Fifty-three rules of the dependent variables are found by M5' for the load forecasting problem. Note that the obtained results applying the kNN are better than those carried out using the M5' algorithm. The average error is 11% when the M5' is used, while the obtained average error using a kNN is 2.3%.

Table 2. Comparison of predicted daily demand for both methods.

	June-November 2001	
	kNN	M5'
Minimum daily errors (%)	0.5	7
Maximum daily errors (%)	8.5	16.5
Average Relative errors (%)	2.3	11

3 The Optimal Energy Production Problem

Once the forecasted demand profile has been obtained, the optimal status on/off and hourly generation level of the units must be determined in order to minimize the expected total cost satisfying the system load forecasting.

This module computes the optimal solution of the classical short-term Unit Commitment and Economic Dispatch (UC-ED) problem [11]. The goal is to obtain, for every hour, the optimal on/off status and generated power of each generating unit so that the total demand is satisfied in the presence of technical constraints.

3.1 Objective Function

The total generation cost of the scheduling period, given the on/off status of the thermal units, $U_{i,t}$, is defined by

$$C_T = \sum_{t=1}^{n_t} \sum_{i=1}^{n_g} \{C_{i,t} \cdot U_{i,t} + SU_i \cdot U_{i,t} \cdot (1 - U_{i,t-1}) + SD_i \cdot (1 - U_{i,t}) \cdot U_{i,t-1}\} \quad (3)$$

where n_t is the number of hours of the scheduling period, n_g is the number of thermal units, each having a cost function $C_{i,t} = C_i(P_{i,t})$ of the generated power $P_{i,t}$, and SU_i, SD_i are respectively the start-up and shut-down cost of generator i.

3.2 Constraints

The minimization of the objective function is subject to the following constraints:

- Upper and lower generation limits of thermal generators:

$$P_i^m \leq P_{i,t} \leq P_i^M \qquad i = 1, \ldots, n_g \quad t = 1, \ldots, n_t \quad (4)$$

  where P_i^M, P_i^m are respectively the maximum and minimum power output of generator i.
- Maximum up and down ramps of thermal units:

$$-DR_i \leq P_{i,t} - P_{i,t-1} \leq UR_i \qquad i = 1, \ldots, n_g \qquad t = 1, \ldots, n_t \quad (5)$$

  where UR_i, DR_i are respectively the maximum up and down ramp of thermal unit i.

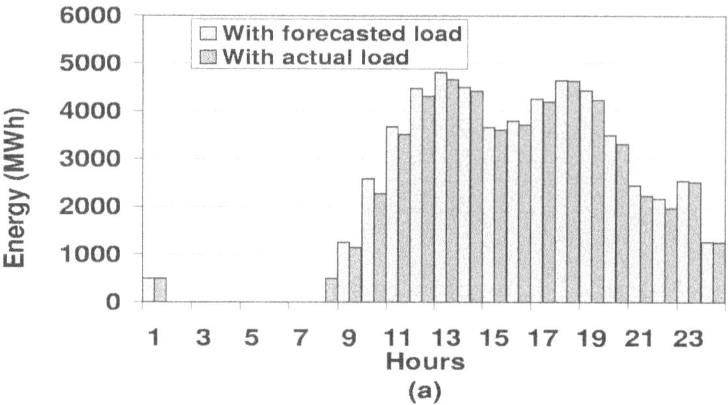

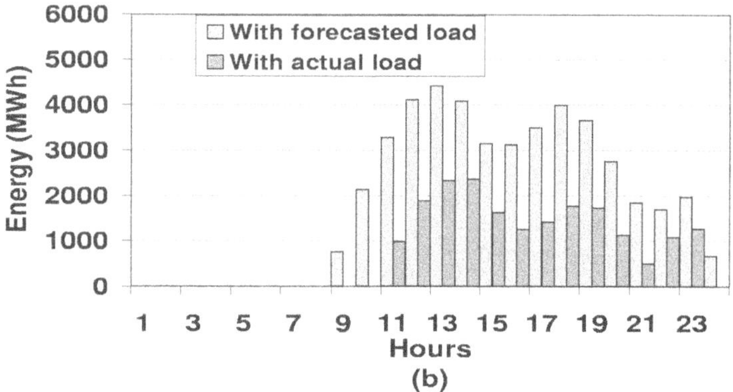

Fig. 6. Optimal scheduling of gas-turbine units for **a)** July 17th, **b)** August 6th.

- Power balance constraints:

$$\sum_{i=1}^{n_g} P_{i,t} \cdot U_{i,t} = D_t \qquad t = 1, ..., n_t \tag{6}$$

  where D_t is the system load forecasting at hour t that must be satisfied by thermal units.
- Spinning reserve constraints:

$$\sum_{i=1}^{n_g} P_i^M \cdot U_{i,t} \geq D_t + R_t \qquad t = 1, ..., n_t \tag{7}$$

  where R_t is the spinning reserve requirement at hour t.

The above model is solved by using a combined Interior Point (IP) optimization technique and a Genetic Algorithm (GA) [12]. The GA is used to compute the optimal on/off status of thermal units, while the IP module deals with the optimal solution of the short term economic dispatch, given the on/off status of the units.

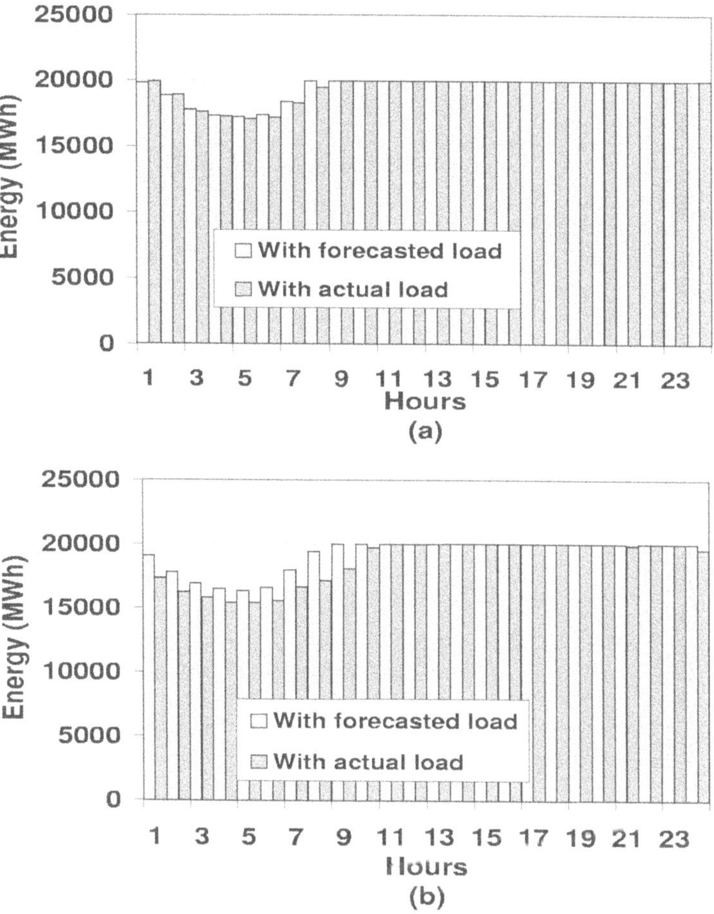

Fig. 7. Optimal scheduling of coal-fired units for **a)** July 17th, **b)** August 6th.

4 Test Results

The optimization model described in the former section is used in conjunction with the kNN-based forecasted load to assess the hourly scheduling of a test generation system comprising two generation technologies: conventional coal-fired generators and gas-turbine generators. Both generation technologies are modeled by equivalent generators with the corresponding technical characteristics.

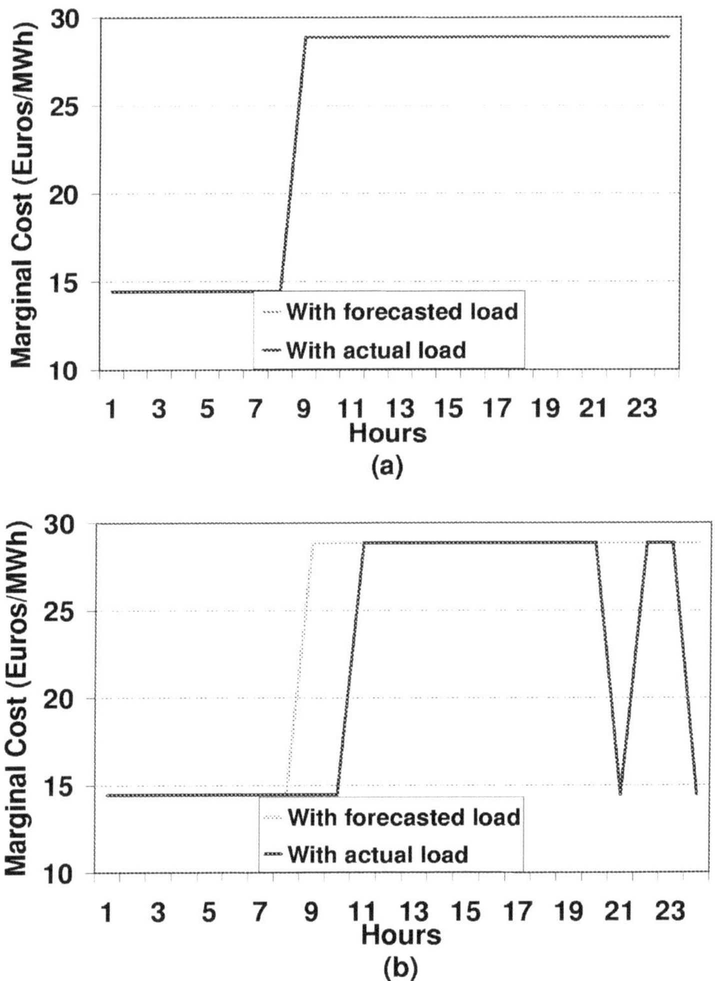

Fig. 8. Marginal price during the scheduling period for **a)** July 17th, **b)** August 6th.

The scheduling horizon embraces 24 hours. Coal-fired units take several hours to fully start and, consequently, this unit usually works at rated power. Besides, gas-turbine units are quite fast in response, and can be used to satisfy the demand at peak hours.

Figure 6a and 6b present the optimal scheduling of the gas-turbine generators attained with forecasted load and that obtained if exact load were available the day before for two selected days: July 17th and August 6th, respectively.

As discussed in the first part of the paper, these days correspond to the smallest and largest average relative errors. Note that the values of the generated power and the status on/off with forecasted and real load are very similar on July 17th, but rather different on August 6th.

Figure 7a and 7b compare the optimal scheduling of coal-fired generators obtained with forecasted load with those that would have been obtained if the actual load had been known in advance for July 17th and August 6th, respectively. As expected, coal-fired units always generate the maximum power except during the valley hours. Notice that the energy production scheduling with forecasted and actual load is almost the same on July 17th and August 6th. Thus coal-fired generators have not influence on the difference between the real total cost (when the actual load has been considered) and the approximate total cost (when the forecasted load has been considered).

Figure 8a and 8b show the optimal hourly energy cost of the generation system obtained with forecasted load and the actual load for July 17th and August 6th, respectively. It can be observed that the marginal cost with forecasted and actual load is almost the same on July 17th, with an increase on the total daily cost of only a 0.7%. However, on August 6th, the marginal cost obtained with forecasted load is larger than that obtained with the actual load at hours 9am, 10am, 9pm and 24 pm due to the gas-turbine units being started-up at these hours when the forecasted load is considered and shut-down if the actual load were used. A total cost increase of a 13.4% can be attributed to forecasting errors. It can be observed how relevant the forecasting errors are, as far as the cost of a realistic generation scheduling is concerned.

5 Conclusions

This paper addresses the influence of the accuracy of a kNN-based hourly load forecasting algorithm on the energy scheduling of a generation system. First, a kNN classification technique is proposed for load forecasting and the hourly load forecasting errors are compared with those obtained results by using a M5'. Secondly, kNN-based forecasted load profiles have been used to compute the optimal energy scheduling of a real system, and the influence of forecasting errors on the generation scheduling and the expected cost increase have been presented. The proposed algorithm based on kNN reveals much lower forecasting errors for the energy demand that the M5'. This fact is due to the M5' builds linear models and the energy demand time series is mainly nonlinear.

Acknowledgments. The authors would like to acknowledge the financial support of the Spanish Government under projects ACC-1021-TIC-2002, DPI2001-2612 and TIC2001-1143-C03-02.

References

1. A. D. Papalexopoulos and T. C. Hesterberg: A Regression-Based Approach to Short-Term System Load Forecasting. IEEE Trans. on Power System, Vol. 5, pp. 1535–1547. 1990.

2. F. J. Nogales, J. Contreras, A. J. Conejo and R. Spínola: Forecasting Next-Day Electricity Prices by Time Series Models. IEEE Trans. on Power System, Vol. 17, pp. 342–348. 2002.
3. A. S. Alfuhaid and M. A. El-Sayed: Cascaded Artificial Neural Network for Short-Term Load Forecasting. IEEE Trans. on Power System, Vol. 12, pp. 1524–1529. 1997.
4. J. Riquelme, J.L. Martínez, A. Gómez and D. Cros Goma: Load Pattern Recognition and Load Forecasting by Artificial Neural Networks. International Journal of Power and Energy Systems, Vol. 22, pp. 74–79. 2002.
5. R. Lamedica, A. Prudenzi, M. Sforna, M. Caciotta, V. Orsolini Cencellli: A Neural Network Based Technique for Short-Term Forecasting of Anomalous Load Periods. IEEE Transaction on Power Systems, Vol. 11, pp. 1749–1756. 1996.
6. A. Troncoso Lora, J. C. Riquelme Santos, J. M. Riquelme Santos, J. L. Martínez Ramos, A. Gómez Expósito: Electricity Market Price Forecasting: Neural Networks versus Weighted-Distance k Nearest Neighbours. DEXA Database Expert Systems and Applications, Aix Provence, 2002.
7. A. Troncoso Lora, J. M. Riquelme Santos, J. C. Riquelme Santos, A. Gómez Expósito, J. L. Martínez Ramos: Forecasting Next-Day Electricity Prices based on k Weighted Nearest Neighbours and Dynamic Regression. IDEAL Intelligent Data Engineering Autamitized Learning, Manchester, 2001.
8. B.V. Dasarathy : Nearest neighbour (NN) Norms: NN pattern classification techniques. IEEE Computer Society Press, 1991.
9. R. D. Short, K. Fukunaga: The Optimal Distance Measure for Nearest Neighbour Classification. IEEE Transaction on Information Theory, 1981.
10. K. Fukunaga, T. E. Flick: An Optimal Global Nearest Neighbour Metric. IEEE Transaction on Pattern Analysis and Machine Intelligence, 1984.
11. A.J. Wood and B.F. Wollenberg, *Power Generation, Operation and Control.* John Wiley & Sons, 1996.
12. J. L. Martínez Ramos, A. Troncoso Lora, J. Riquelme Santos, A. Gómez Expósito: Short Term Hydro-thermal Coordination Based on Interior Point Nonlinear Programming and Genetic Algorithms. IEEE Porto Power Tewch Conference, 2001.
13. G. Holmes, M. Hall, E. Frank: Generating Rule Sets from Model Trees. Australian Joint Conference on Artificial Intelligence, 1999.
14. J. R. Quinlan: Learning with Continuous Classes. Australian Joint Conference on Artificial Intelligence, 1992.
15. Y. Wang, I. H. Witten: Induction of Model Trees for Predicting Continuous Classes. European Conference on Machine Learning, 1997.

Appendix: Continuous Class Prediction

This appendix briefly presents the M5' [13,14] learning algorithm used in the present work to establish a comparison between the results of the application of this algorithm and the proposed kNN classification technique on the next day energy demand forecasting problem.

In machine learning, it is important to present results that can be easily interpreted. Decision trees based on If-Then rules are one of the most popular description languages used in machine learning.

Basically, M5' builds a tree-based piecewise linear model. Model trees are decision trees with linear models at the leaf nodes. Thus, this method obtains ordered sets of If-Then rules for time series prediction that produces understandable models.

In general, the rule learning procedure for classification techniques can be stated in two steps:

1. Initially, rules are induced.
2. Rules are improved solving a global optimization problem.

The M5' algorithm builds a tree by splitting the data based on the values of predictive attributes. Once the tree has been constructed, this method computes a linear model for each node. Then the tree is pruned from the leaves while the estimated error decreases. The error for each node is the mean of the absolute difference between the predicted and the actual value of each example of the training set that reaches the node. This mean is multiplied by a weight that takes into account the number of examples that reach the node. The process is repeated until all examples are covered by one o more rules.

The M5' described is implemented in the WEKA Library [15].

Creating User-Adapted Design Recommender System through Collaborative Filtering and Content Based Filtering

Kyung-Yong Jung[1], Young-Joo Na[2], and Jung-Hyun Lee[1]

[1] Department of Computer Science & Engineering, Inha University, Inchon, Korea
kyjung@gcgc.ac.kr, jhlee@inha.ac.kr

[2] Department of Clothing and Textiles, Inha University, Inchon, Korea
youngjoo@inha.ac.kr

Abstract. Information filtering is an important technology for the creation of recommender system, which are adapted to the user's needs. In this paper we identify collaborative filtering and content-based filtering as independent technologies for information filtering. We propose the user-adapted design recommender system of textile design applying both technologies as one of methods in the material development centered on customer's sensibility and preference. Ultimately, this paper suggests empirical applications to verify the adequacy and the validity on this system with the development of design recommender system.

1 Introduction

The diversity of the audiences and the need of customer retention require active recommender systems, which expose themselves in a customized or personalized way: We call those recommender systems called the user-adapted design recommender system. New technologies are necessary to personalize and customize content. Information filtering can be used for the discovery of important content and is therefore a key technology for the creation of user adapted recommender systems. We focus on the application of collaborative filtering for user-adapted recommender system[1]. We studied techniques for combining content-based filtering with collaborative filtering in order to address typical problems in collaborative filtering system and to improve the performance.

2 System Overview

The user-adapted design recommender system is a project that aims at study how the combination of collaborative filtering and content-based filtering can be used to build user-adapting recommender system. Figure 1 shows system overview for user-adapted

Fernando Moura Pires, Salvador Abreu (Eds.): EPIA 2003, LNAI 2902, pp. 204–208, 2003.

design recommender system. We use filtering techniques to create a user-adapting textile design, in which the hypertext structure is created for each specific user, based on prediction of what this user should prefer. The system then selects textiles similar to textiles with high ratings during user login. Collaborative filtering is also used to make prediction based on the rating that other users have provided during previous visits. For collaborative filtering based on textile, Representative-Attribute Neighborhood of age, gender and zipcode[5] is adapted to determine the number of neighbors that will be used for preferences.

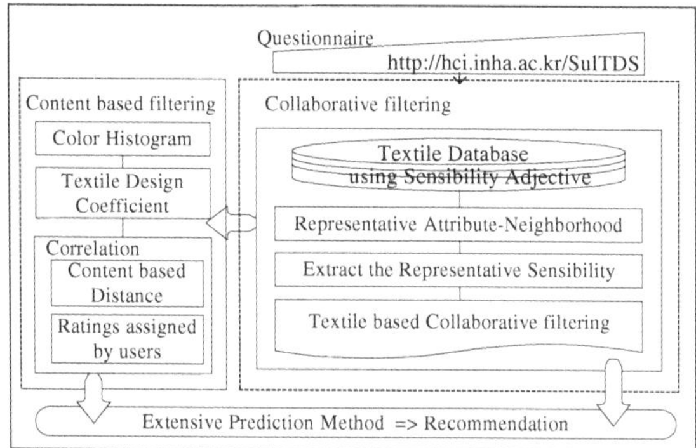

Fig. 1. System overview for user-adapted design recommender system

3 Collaborative Filtering Framework

Most collaborative filtering systems collect the user opinions as ratings on a numerical scale, leading to a sparse matrix rating (*user*, *item*) in short $r_{u,i}$. Collaborative filtering technique then uses this rating matrix in order to derive predictions[2,3,5]. In our recommender system, we apply a commonly used algorithm, proposed in the *GroupLens* project[4,6] and also applied in *Ringo*[2,3], which is based on vector correlation using the Pearson correlation coefficient. Usually the task of a collaborative filtering technique is to predict the rating of a particular user u for a textile i. The system compares the user u's rating with the rating of all other users, who have rated the considered textile i. Then a weighted average of the other users rating is used as a prediction. If I_u is set of textiles that a user u has rated then we can define the mean rating of user u. Collaborative filtering algorithms predict the rating based on the rating of similar users. The value of $w(u,a)$ measures the similarity between the two users' rating vectors. A high absolute value signifies high similarity and low absolute value dissimilarity. The general predict formula is based in the assumption that the prediction is a weighted average of the other users rating. The weights refer to the amount of similarity between the user u and the other users by Equation (1). The factor k normalizes the weights.

$$p^{collab}(u,i) = \overline{r_u} + \left(1 / \sum_{a \in U_i} w(u,a) \right) \times \sum_{a \in U_i} w(u,a)(r_{a,i} - \overline{r_a}) \qquad \overline{r_u} = \frac{1}{|I_u|} \sum_{i \in I_u} r_{u,i} \tag{1}$$

4 Content-Based Filtering

In our prototype, we have currently implemented two feature extraction components, derived from the work described in color histograms and textile design coefficients. We project these values in the HSV space which models more accurately the human perception of colors. The HSV coefficients are quantized to yield 166 different colors. For each textile, the histogram of these 166 colors is computed (proportion of pixels with a given quantized color). While color histograms do not take into account the arrangement of pixel, textile design coefficients can be computed to characterize local properties of the textile. We are using a wavelet decomposition using Haar transform, by which a number of sub-textiles corresponding to frequency decomposition are generated. These sub-textiles are quantized to binary values, so that each pixel of the original textile is associated with binary vector of length 9. The histogram of these vectors is the feature vector associated to analysis of the textile. We use a linear estimated for the content-based prediction, which is illustrated in the following Equation (2). P^{color} represents the prediction for textile i for user u.

$$p^{color}(u,i) = \sum_j \lambda_j \frac{\sum_{a \in C_j(i)} r_{u,a}}{|C_j(i)|} \qquad d^{color}(k,l) = L_1(h_k, h_l) = \sum_j |h_k(j) - h_l(j)| \tag{2}$$

5 Creating User-Adapted Design Recommender System

Figure 2 shows the user-adapted design recommender system that uses extensive prediction method through collaborative filtering and content based filtering.
We combine the content-based filtering predictors with the collaborative filtering predictor $p^{collab}(u,i)$, as described in section 3, linearly using the following formula.

$$p^{comb}(u,i) = \mu^{collab} p^{collab}(u,i) + \mu^{color} p^{color}(u,i) + \mu^{textile} p^{textile}(u,i) \qquad \sum \mu = 1$$

The weights $\mu^{\{collab,color,textile\}}$ are estimated by the use of linear regression with a set-aside subset of the rating.

[Sensibility adjective] is the part that the users enter his/her preferred sensibility in the order and its degree by moving the control bar. The user has the 18 adjective pairs shown in drop-down list. The selected 5 adjectives are each given weights: first weight, 100%; second weight, 50%; third weight, 30%; fourth weight, 15%; and fifth weight, 5%. Our system runs its engine to recommend the five textiles as fitting the preferred sensibility to the user. If there is no proper textiles in database, [Combined prediction] will recommend 5 textiles according to the sensibility adjectives of others based on collaborative predictor on the user's attributes, through the content-based predictor.

The determination of user's attributes includes the process which let him/her evaluate the sensibility on 3 textiles among 60 textiles. Though this step, similar class of database showing the similar evaluation to his/her will be referred to predict the sensibilities on other 57 textiles using collaborative predictor and determine the user's attributes. The users can control the textile design with view factor control window,

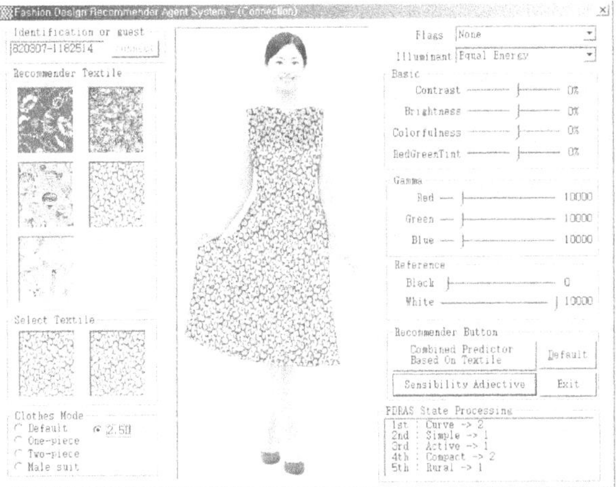

Fig. 2. User-Adapted Design Recommender System

this input will change the textile of apparel on visual model to approach the sensibility preferred by him/herself. View factor control includes Illuminant, Flags[None, Negative, Logarithmic Filter, Negative & Logarithmic Filter], Basic[Contrast, Brightness, Colorfulness, RedGreenTint], Reference[Black, White], Gamma[Red, Green, Blue]. This gives the tool controlling in detail on the hue, chroma, value and texture of textile design. Therefore, design recommender system will become the referencing tool on planning sensibility product to the merchandisers or buyers of textiles and apparel industry.

6 Evaluation

After the questionnaire based on web has been online for 3 months (2002.1~2002.4), 31232 ratings by 512 users (259 males and 253 female) were collected. Table 1 lists the measured precision for the previously discussed predictors.

Table 1. Prediction precision of collaborative, content-based, sensibility adjective, and combined predictor

Prediction method	MAE	DEV	COR
Collaborative filtering	0.704	1.397	0.353
Content-based filtering	0.735	1.405	0.477
Sensibility adjective	0.709	1.301	0.395
Combine	0.681	1.159	0.383

Here, it is interesting to note the improvements of the combined approach compared to the collaborative, content based, and sensibility adjective approach. An improvement of mean absolute prediction error is the combined prediction over the collaborative prediction can be identified. Further, an improvement of standard deviation of the absolute error (DEV) can be observed indicating, that the predictions are more robust using the combination, i.e. large prediction errors are likely avoided. The increase of the mean correlation (COR) indicates that the overall ordering of the textiles in the test-set is more respected by the prediction when the combination is used instead of collaborative prediction by itself.

7 Conclusion

It is important for the strategy of product sales to investigate the customer's sensibility and preference degree in the environment that the process of material development has been changed focusing on the customer center. In this paper we have identified filtering, especially collaborative filtering, as a key technology for the creation of user-adapted recommender systems, which allow users to access information more efficiently by exposing a personalized structure of the recommender system. And we identify collaborative filtering and content-based filtering as independent technologies for information filtering. However, information filtering is a hard problem, and cannot be addressed by one filtering technology alone. Due to limitations of both collaborative filtering and content-based filtering, it is useful to combine these independent approaches to achieve better filtering results and therefore better the recommender system. In the future, we plan evolve the extension algorithm to achieve better performance.

Acknowledgements. This work was supported by grant No. R04-2003-000-10177-0 from the Basic Research Program of the Korea Science & Engineering Foundation.

References

1. M. Balabanovic, and Y. Shoham, "*Fab*: Content-based, Collaborative Recommendation," Communication of the Association of Computing Machinery, 40(3), pp. 66–72, 1997.
2. J. S. Breese, D. Heckerman, C. Kadie, "Empirical Analysis of Predictive Algorithms for Collaborative Filtering," Proc. of the 14th Conference on Uncertainty in AI, 1998.
3. J. Herlocker, et al., "An Algorithm Framework for Performing Collaborative Filtering," In Proc. of ACM SIGIR'99, 1999.
4. Badrul M. Sarwar, Joseph A. Konstan, Al Bochers, Jon Herlocker, Bral Miller, and John Riedl, "Using filtering agents to improve prediction quality in the grouplens research collaborative filtering system," In Proc. of ACM CSCW'98, 1998.
5. K. Y. Jung, J. H. Lee, "Prediction of User Preference in Recommendation System using Association User Clustering and Bayesian Estimated Value," LNAI 2557, 15th Australian Joint Conference on Artificial Intelligence, pp. 284–296, 2002.
6. P. Resnick, et. al., "GroupLens: An Open Architecture for Collaborative Filtering of Netnews," Proc. of ACM CSCW'94, pp. 175–186, 1994.

Is the UCI Repository Useful for Data Mining?

Carlos Soares

LIACC/Fac. of Economics, University of Porto
Rua do Campo Alegre, 823, 4150-180 Porto, Portugal
csoares@liacc.up.pt

Abstract. We propose a methodology to investigate the relevance for the real world of repositories of benchmark problems like the one commonly known as the UCI repository. It compares the distribution of relative performance of algorithms in data sets from a given repository and from the "real world". If the distributions are different, the knowledge about the relative performance of algorithms obtained from the repository in question is mostly useless. In the case of the UCI repository, this would mean that a significant proportion of published results would be of little practical use. However, this is not what our results indicate. We also propose an adaptation of this method to test whether tool developers are "overfitting" repositories, which also yields negative results in the UCI repository.

1 Introduction

I once got the following one line review to a paper submitted to the Knowledge Discovery in Databases (KDD) Conference:

> UCI is not KDD.

The other reviewers gave more detailed reasons for rejecting the paper, but this particular comment has puzzled me ever since and it is the central issue of the work presented in this paper. The main goal is to identify some of the questions that should be answered to assess the value of problem repositories for the corresponding problem domains. Afterwards, we need to develop methods to answer those questions. Although we will focus on KDD and on the Machine Learning (ML) repository at the University of California at Irvine (UCI-R) [2], this kind of issue is also relevant in other fields where empirical research is used, like optimization and planning.

In the next section we summarize some of the work analyzing the relevance of the UCI-R. In Section 3 we present some arguments in favor of the usefulness of UCI-R for KDD, namely as a source of meta-knowledge to support the step of algorithm/parameter selection in data mining tasks. We also describe a methodology to test whether problem repositories potentially contain that kind of meta-knowledge and we apply it to the UCI-R. In Section 4, we adapt the same methodology to test whether developers of algorithms are overfitting a problem repository and, again, we apply it to the UCI-R. In KDD, the issue

Fernando Moura Pires, Salvador Abreu (Eds.): EPIA 2003, LNAI 2902, pp. 209–223, 2003.

of the size of the data is also frequently raised. We analyze the issue briefly in Section 5, based on the methodologies above. We discuss the results presented (Section 6) and then conclude (Section 7).

2 Related Work

The lack of relevance of the UCI-R data sets for the real world is often taken for granted, as it is clear from the review mentioned above and some papers, like [27]. On the other hand, the same authors also argue that UCI-R problems can be used to find relationships between classes of problems and the performance of algorithms. However, to the best of our knowledge, no attempts have been made to investigate thoroughly the real world relevance of the UCI-R or any other problem repository.

Furthermore, the most important problems that are usually raised concerning the role of the UCI-R in research are not its (presumed) lack of relevance. Firstly, most empirical work using UCI-R data sets focuses on determining which algorithm is the "best" rather than trying to understand under which conditions an algorithm works well or not [27,17,1]. The possibility of overfitting, i.e., obtaining good results by chance, is also high, given the number of experiments performed on a relatively small number of data sets [28]. A third drawback is that the majority of the problems in the UCI-R are concerned with supervised learning, which has driven ML researchers to focus on small improvements to existing algorithms rather than developing new ones or addressing different tasks [1]. Finally, the problem domain is usually treated as a "random variable over which to average results, rather than interesting on its own right" [17] and thus the utility of the extracted knowledge is rarely evaluated. However, this is mostly due to an unsolvable problem, which is the unavailability of the corresponding end user to analyze that knowledge [27].

Despite its (presumed) lack of relevance, the usefulness of the UCI-R is generally acknowledged, namely to enable repetition of results, for preliminary assessment of new ideas and to gain understanding into classes of problems for which algorithms perform well [27,28,1]. The need for repositories of problems has been recognized for other classes of problems, like time series prediction [15].

3 To Be or Not to Be Useful

I guess that the main point of the reviewer who made the comment above was that in real-world problems — KDD problems — the majority of the effort is spent preparing the data for the algorithms,[1] i.e., understanding the business objectives, selecting the data sources and collecting, cleaning and transforming

[1] In [3] it is estimated that more than 70% of the total time of a KDD project is spent in data preparation. Although this is not a very recent paper, we do not expect the situation to have changed significantly.

the data. Given that all of this work has been already carried out in the UCI-R problems, it may seem that these are not useful for KDD.

Next, we argue that data set repositories like the UCI-R may contain meta-knowledge that is useful in the algorithm selection step of the KDD process. The arguments presented motivate the methodology to assess whether a problem repository potentially contains such meta-knowledge, presented in Section 3.2. Section 3.3 discusses an important issue concerning the validity of the methodology. Before applying the methodology (Section 3.7), we describe the experimental setup, with particular emphasis on the description of some of the new data sets used (Sections 3.4, 3.5 and 3.6).

3.1 On the Relevance of the UCI Repository for KDD

There comes a time in every KDD task when the problem has been clearly defined and the data has been selected, cleaned, transformed and is ready to be processed by a learning algorithm. In other words, the problem looks exactly like a data set in the UCI-R. At that point the data analyst must select one or more algorithms to try out. Additionally, algorithms often have parameters that must be set. Some algorithms are reasonably robust to parameter settings (e.g., decision trees) while others depend heavily on adequate choices (e.g., Neural Networks and Support Vector Machines). Usually, the process of selecting algorithms and parameters[2] combines expertise from the data analyst with extensive trial-and-error.

There are a number of drawbacks with this approach. Relying on the data analysts' expertise to select algorithms may be unreliable for a number of reasons. Firstly, not many people are experts on more than a limited number of algorithms. This is an important drawback because there are many alternatives and new ones are frequently released. Secondly, in dynamic domains the best algorithm may change with time. This is true for problems that are currently very relevant in the KDD field, like problems with streaming data (e.g., intrusion detection, e-commerce, web mining and stock analysis [31]). Finally, human expertise is expensive. On the other hand, trial-and-error is a costly process. It consumes a lot of computational resources, especially with large amounts of data, as frequently happens in KDD applications, and it significantly delays the delivery of results.

The need for "automatic, data-dependent selection of data mining parameters and algorithms" has been recognized as an important research issue in a recent KDD panel [11]. Automatic support for algorithm selection requires *meta-knowledge*, i.e., knowledge that relates the performance of algorithms to characteristics of problems. Meta-knowledge may be of theoretical (e.g., obtained from experts [6]) or empirical nature (e.g., obtained from experimental studies [4]). This work is concerned with empirical meta-knowledge. It can be generated by analysis of the behavior of algorithms [12], comparative studies [18] and meta-learning [5]. To be reliable, it must be based on a sufficient number of data

[2] In the rest of the paper, the term *algorithms* will also be used represent different configurations of the parameters of algorithms.

sets. Such an amount of problems is only publicly available in data repositories, like the UCI-R [2] or the KDD repository. The KDD repository mostly contains problems at a stage of the KDD process earlier than the algorithm selection step. The UCI-R is more suitable for this work because, as mentioned above, data is already prepared in most of the cases. Note that the generation of empirical meta-knowledge requires a large amount of computational resources, just like the trial-and-error approach to algorithm selection. However, given that there is no rush to obtain the results, experiments can be performed when resources are not being used for anything else.

3.2 Methodology to Assess Relevance of Problem Repositories

The main problem with empirical meta-knowledge is that it can only be obtained if the data sets are a representative sample of the population of real world data sets. To investigate whether this is true, we must define which *population* is this. We define the population of real world data sets, as the set of data sets that a data analyst may encounter when dealing with KDD applications. Although this is certainly an enormous and very complex population, we can approach it from a simplified perspective, if we take into account that our focus is on the algorithm selection step. So, our target population is defined by the *relative performance* of algorithms on real world data sets, i.e., whether an algorithm has better, worse or equivalent performance when compared to other algorithms. Despite being simpler, we still do not know anything about this population.[3] However, we can sample from it. This happens when new data sets originating from KDD problems become available. Then, we can estimate the relative performance of algorithms on these data sets by running them. This leads us to our first claim:

Claim 1. *Given a set of algorithms, a data repository and a new sample of data sets originating from KDD processes, we claim that the data repository is useful for KDD if the distributions of the relative performance, i.e. the ranks, of the algorithms on the data repository and on the new data sets are similar.*

Note that we assume that by determining the relative performance of algorithms we can construct a ranking of those algorithms. Given that we can only obtain estimates of the true performance of algorithms on data sets, we must take the statistical significance of the differences in estimated performance into account. The rank of algorithm i is defined as 1 + the number of algorithms that have significantly better performance than i. We believe that this definition is more appropriate to deal with ties in the setting of ranking classification algorithms than the definition commonly used in Statistics. In Statistics, ties are usually dealt with by assigning average ranks. Suppose an extreme case were all 10

[3] The No-Free-Lunch (NFL) theorem [30] does not necessarily apply to this population because we are only dealing with data sets that users may be faced with. This is a very small subset of the population that NFL applies to, which includes, among others, all random data sets.

algorithms are tied. They would all be assigned rank 5.5. It is more natural to assign all of them the 1st rank, especially when operations with several rankings are being performed, as is our case. Important properties of this definition are:

- Ranks are integers.
- Two algorithms that are tied may have different ranks.[4]

The rankings can be used to calculate the distribution of the ranks for each algorithm, separately for repository and for real world data sets. We can compare general characteristics of two distributions using statistical tests for general differences. As we do not have information about the shape of the distributions, we must use distribution-free tests, like the Kolmogorov-Smirnov test. We will not describe this test here because it can be found in many Statistics textbooks (e.g., [22]) and it is commonly available on Statistical packages (e.g., R [13]). The test should be two-sided because we are trying to detect general differences.

Note that this test represents a *necessary* but not *sufficient* condition for the relevance of a repository for the corresponding problem domain. If the null hypothesis is rejected, than the two samples do not come from the same population. Thus, we can conclude that the repository is not relevant. However, if the test fails, this does not necessarily mean that the samples do come from the same population and, thus, that the repository is relevant. Nevertheless, it does provide an important indication in that direction.

3.3 On the Representativeness of the Sample of New Problems

The methodology presented above assesses the relevance of a repository of problems to a given problem domain by assessing whether the distribution of the relative performance of a set of algorithms on those problems is the same as on a sample of problems drawn from the corresponding domain.

The issue of representativeness can be raised for the sample of new problems as for the repository problems. However, there are a few rules of thumb that can be followed to maximize the quality of the sample of new data sets. First, we must ensure that the data comes from the desired population. The data set should be obtained in the process of tackling a data mining application. Generally, this will also ensure that the data set was not used to fine tune any algorithm during its development, which would certainly affect the corresponding rank distribution. We should also try to ensure that there is no bias in the selection of problems. This can mainly be done by varying the sources. Additionally, we should also try to obtain as many problems as possible. However, mostly for confidentiality reasons, this is rather difficult, especially in the KDD setting.

The reliability of the conclusions of the methodology proposed also depends on an adequate choice of of algorithms. The computational cost of estimating the performance of algorithms limits the size of the set to be considered. Therefore,

[4] Suppose algorithm A is tied with algorithm B and B with C. However, A is better than C. A and B will be assigned rank 1 and C will be assigned rank 2. So, although B and C are tied, they have different ranks.

it should at least be guaranteed that algorithms representing representing a wide variety of learning biases is included.

3.4 Repository Data Sets

We have applied the methodology proposed earlier to evaluate the usefulness of the UCI repository [2] for the algorithm recommendation step of the KDD process. We focused on the most frequent type of problems in UCI-R, which is classification.

After analyzing the information files included we have selected 136 problems. In some cases it was not easy to identify the type of problem and in others it was difficult to identify the class attribute. Furthermore, creating the data sets from the files in the repository required considerable preparation.[5] We tried to minimize disruption by using the information files although these are often incomplete and unclear. The most important hurdle was the difficulty in identifying attribute types (e.g., numeric fields coding a set of unordered symbols). Some of the operations performed were:

- Joining all data files into a single one.
- Constructing/adapting the description file.
- Eliminating identifier attributes (attributes with a different value for each case) and attributes with only one value.
- Data cleaning (correcting case of attribute values; removing cases with missing class; removing "control" attributes which may, for instance, provide information about the class; scaling attributes with very small values).
- Ignoring costs, when available.

3.5 New Data Sets

The sample of new data sets contained 23 problems. It was gathered during the course of the METAL project [20], mostly through one of the outcomes, the Data Mining Advisor (www.metal-kdd.org). The data sets cover a large variety of sources, which, as mentioned in Section 3.3, is important to ensure that it is representative of the corresponding problem domain. These domains include automotive industry, insurance business, biology and finance, among others. Here we provide details concerning a few of the data sets and the corresponding KDD applications.

Two data sets were donated by DaimlerChrysler. One is concerned with the KDD process of predicting faulty behavior of cars [19]. The data come from the Quality Information System of DaimlerChrysler, which stores information about all Mercedes vehicles that are built, including information about their maintenance. The database contained over 40GB of data, at the time the data set was generated. It is expected to contain noise given that the data come from various sources, including complaints that are submitted by the repair

[5] In many cases, we reused the data sets prepared as part of the METAL project [20].

shops. The particular data set used here was generated in one of the iterations of the knowledge discovery process performed. This process was guided by the CRISP-DM model [7], with particular emphasis on the steps of data selection and transformation (including sampling, clustering and transformation of attributes). More details can be found in [19].

The second DaimlerChrysler data set is concerned with the design of engine intake ports [14]. The data come from the Passenger Cars Database, which contained information about over 20.000 different engine intake port designs, at the time the data set was generated. In the knowledge discovery process that generated the data set used here, particular attention was devoted to the selection and transformation steps. More details can be found in [14].

The Sisyphus data from Swiss Life [29] was used to generate three data sets. These data come from the MASY data warehouse system containing information about the private life insurance business of Swiss Life insurance company. The data is organized into eight tables, ranging from 500 to over 100.000 examples, contains missing values and probably also noise. It was prepared by the Information Systems Research group of the company, who defined two different prediction tasks. In the METAL project, this data was used to prepare three data sets, two of them concerning the first task and the other concerning the second one. The knowledge discovery process that generated those data sets included the steps of data selection, cleaning and transformation. The two data sets generated for the first task can be regarded as two different iterations of the KDD process. In one of them, the data were selected from two tables while in the other, four tables were used. We note that, although this data has been available for sometime, it is multirelational and we believe that the specific propositional data sets we have generated have not been widely used.

A data set concerning the prediction of the variation of the value of IBM stock was kindly provided by Mário Oldemiro. It is based on the same data that was used in [23]. The attributes are indicators based on past values of the stocks. The University of Geneva provided a data set concerning the prediction of the structure of proteins from their sequence of aminoacids. It was prepared by the Department of Biology of that university. The last data set we will mention is a pattern recognition data set describing byzantine musical notes that was provided by the University of Athens.

3.6 Algorithms and Estimation of Performance

The set of algorithms used represents several different approaches to classification: two decision tree classifiers, C5.0 [26] and Ltree [10], which is a decision tree that can introduce oblique decision surfaces; two neural networks from the SPSS Clementine package (Multilayer Perceptron and Radial Basis Function Network); the IB1 instance-based and the Naive Bayes classifiers from the MLC++ library [16]; a local implementation of the multivariate Linear Discriminant [21]; two rule-based systems, C5.0 rules and RIPPER [8]; and an ensemble method, boosted C5.0. The variety of biases included is important to ensure that the results of the methodology proposed in this paper are reliable, as explained in Section 3.3.

The results were obtained with MLEE [24]. The measure of performance used was classification error. It was estimated using 10-fold stratified cross-validation using default parameters on all algorithms. In some cases the algorithms crashed or exceeded the time limit of 12 hours established for each fold. In both cases, the algorithms were ignored in the corresponding data sets. We were unable to obtain any results on two data sets, `shuttle-landing-control` and `trains`, due to an insufficient number of cases (<20).

The statistical significance of the differences in performance of algorithms was assessed with the McNemar test, applied to each pair of algorithms [9]. Given that several pairwise comparison tests are performed for each data set, the significance level used must be corrected to account for the increased probability that a null hypothesis is rejected by chance [28]. To achieve a nominal significance level of 5% we have used a significance level of $5\%/\frac{n(n-1)}{2}$ in each of the tests, obtained with the Bonferroni correction [22], where n is the number of algorithms compared.

The top row of Figure 1 presents histograms of the mean number of ties per data set for increasing number of examples, both for UCI-R and new data sets. As expected, the power of the test is higher for larger data sets. Indeed, for data sets with less than 500 cases, ties occur in more than half of the pairwise comparisons. Therefore, we have decided to ignore those data sets because they contain little information about relative performance, which is the focus of this analysis. In the bottom row of Figure 1 we present the histogram of the proportion of data sets again for increasing number of examples, again separating UCI-R and new data sets. We observe that approximately half of the UCI-R data sets and one third of the new ones will be removed.

3.7 Is the UCI Repository Useful for KDD?

After removing data sets with less than 500 cases, as described in the previous section, we obtained two samples with 62 UCI-R data sets and 16 new ones, respectively. We have calculated the corresponding distributions of the ranks for each algorithm (first two columns of Figure 2). A quick analysis of the graphs gives some information about the overall performance of the algorithms. In the UCI-R data sets, the rank distributions for the three variations of C5.0 and Ltree are "L"-shaped, with a predominance of higher ranks. As for the other algorithms, the distributions are mostly spread over all ranks. The rank distribution shapes for the new data sets are generally similar to the corresponding shapes in the UCI-R data sets. Thus, it seems that data repositories are indeed representative of KDD data sets. The similarities are not so obvious in the case of C5.0 rules, C5.0 tree, MLP and RBFN. In the case of the two C5.0 variations, the majority of the ranks moves from 1st to 2nd. As for the two Clementine algorithms, the distribution is relatively flat in the UCI-R while they are mostly in the lower ranks in the new data sets. In all of these cases, the algorithms may

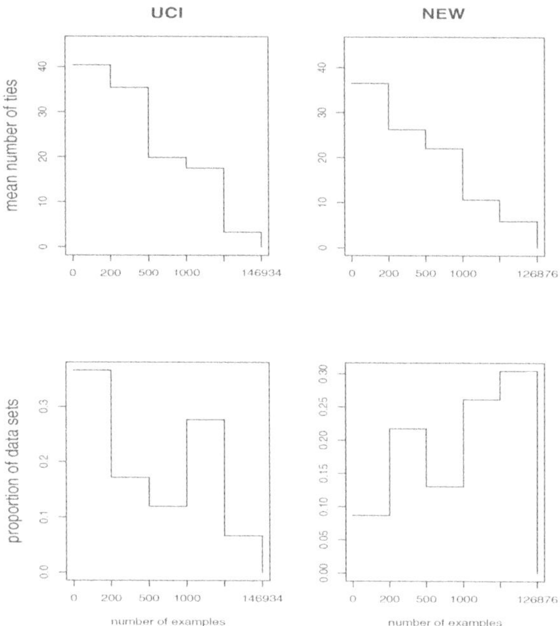

Fig. 1. Mean number of ties and proportion of data sets for different data set sizes both for the UCI data sets and the new ones.

Table 1. Results of the Kolmogorov-Smirnov and Wilcoxon tests to assess general differences between the distributions of algorithm ranks and to compare the distributions of algorithm ranks in repository and new data sets with less than 500 cases (p values).

	C5-B	C5-R	C5-T	MLP	RBFN	LD	Lt	IB1	NB	RIP
K-S	0.723	0.070	0.010	0.117	0.100	0.607	0.971	0.984	0.763	0.271
W	0.051	0.026	0.009	0.067	0.030	0.854	0.633	0.424	0.775	0.239

be "overfitting the UCI-R", i.e., they perform better in the repository data sets than in the new ones. We will investigate this issue further in the next section.

The application of the Kolmogorov-Smirnov test confirms our general impression that the distributions are similar (Table 1). Again, if we take into account that multiple tests are being performed by making the Bonferroni adjustment for a nominal significance level of 5%, we obtain a significance level to use in each of the tests of $5\%/10 = 0.5\%$. At this significance level, we are not able to reject the null hypothesis that the distributions have the same shape for any of the algorithms. This is true even in the cases in which a visual inspection was not so conclusive. However, our doubts are confirmed by the fact that the four algorithms considered have the lowest p values.

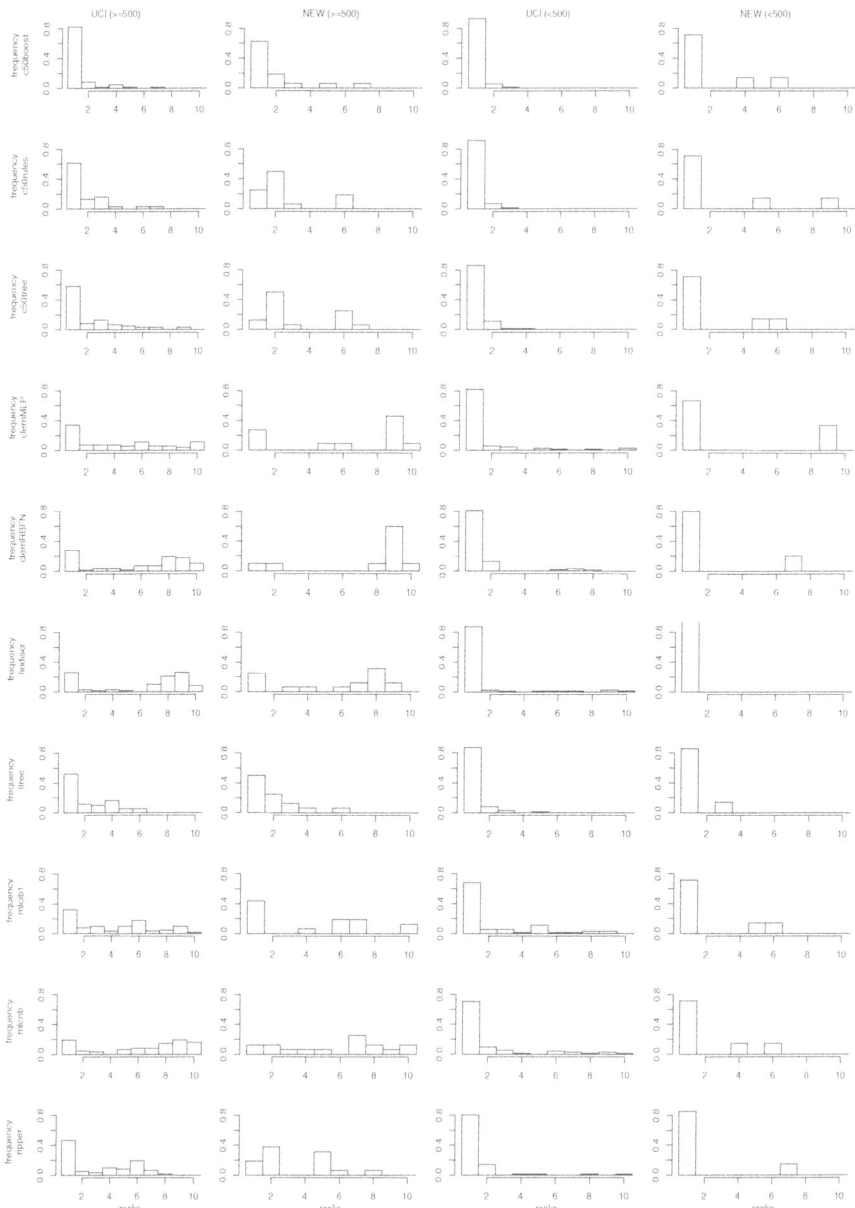

Fig. 2. Distribution of ranks of ten algorithms on UCI and new data sets. The first two columns represent data sets with 500 or more cases and the last two columns represent data sets with less than 500 cases.

Furthermore, the outcome of these tests must be interpreted carefully. The fact that the p values are larger than the significance level used means that there is no evidence in the samples that the distributions are different. This cannot be interpreted as proof that the distributions are the same, i.e. that the samples are drawn from the same population. It is, however, an indication in favor of this hypothesis and, as in any other data analysis problem, we must assume that the sample is representative of the population, until proof in contrary.

4 To Overfit or Not to Overfit

With a large amount of experimentation performed on a limited number of data sets, it is probable that some of the good results are simply obtained by chance. In other words, it is probably that ML and DM research is overfitting the UCI-R. However, to the best of our knowledge, this issue has never been investigated thoroughly. Next, we propose a method to assess whether it is true. It shares the same philosophy as the method presented above to assess whether repository data sets are representative of real world data sets.

Our second claim addresses the issue of testing if an algorithm is overfitting a data repository, assuming, as in Section 3, that we are concerned with the relative performance of algorithms.

Claim 2. *Given a set of algorithms and a data repository, we claim an algorithm is overfitting the data repository if its relative performance, i.e. its ranks, are systematically higher in the data repository than in the sample of KDD data sets.*

For this purpose, we can use statistical tests for differences in location that assess whether two samples come from distributions with different average ranks. Again, since we do not have information about the shape of the distributions, we must use distribution-free tests, like the Mann-Whitney test or Wilcoxon test. Again, we do not describe these tests which are commonly used in Statistics (e.g., see [22], which also shows that the two tests are equivalent). The test should be one-sided because we are trying to detect if one average rank is larger than the other.

We note that if no significant differences are detected by the Kolmogorov-Smirnov test for general differences, as happened in the previous section, it may still make sense to apply the Mann-Whitney test for differences in location. In fact, given that the latter tests a more specific hypothesis, it has more power than the former [22]. Therefore, it may be the case that no significant differences are found in the distributions of ranks for an algorithm in the repository and new data sets but the algorithm is shown to overfit the former, in the sense that it obtains better performance in the repository data sets than in the new ones.

4.1 Are Commercial Tool Developers Overfitting the UCI?

In Section 3.7 we observed that C5.0 rules, C5.0 tree, MLP and RBFN seem to be overfitting the UCI-R. However, the Kolmogorov-Smirnov did not detect any

Table 2. Results of the Kolmogorov-Smirnov and Wilcoxon tests to assess general differences between the distributions of algorithm ranks and to compare the distributions of algorithm ranks in repository and new data sets (p values).

	C5-B	C5-R	C5-T	MLP	RBFN	LD	Lt	IB1	NB	RIP
K-S	0.675	0.675	0.675	0.679	1	1	1	1	0.999	1
W	0.194	0.031	0.099	0.129	0.432	0.824	0.423	0.512	0.483	0.585

significant difference in the shapes of the rank distributions on UCI-R and new data sets for any of those algorithms, although they were the ones with lowest p value, as would be expected. As explained in the previous section, it may still make sense to test whether there is a difference in the mean ranks.

Using an adjusted significance level of 0.5% as in Section 3.7, the Wilcoxon test does not reject any of the null hypotheses again, confirming the results obtained with the Kolmogorov-Smirnov test (Table 1). As would be expected once more, the four algorithms have low p values, which in the case of C5.0 tree is close to significance.

5 Does Size Matter?

In the analysis performed so far, we have ignored data sets with less than 500 cases due to the high number of ties in the pairwise comparisons performed on those data sets. This was done to prevent those ties to dominate the analysis, possibly invalidating the corresponding results. Nevertheless, a separate analysis was performed. The two columns on the right of Figure 2 present the graphs with the rank distributions for data sets with less than 500 cases. Visually it seems that clemMLP and all variations of C5.0 obtain lower ranks in the new data sets than in the ones from the UCI-R. However, the tests do not confirm this impression (Table 2). Note that this may happen due to the small sample size, which, in the case of new data sets only contains seven points.

The distributions for "large" and "small" data sets are quite different. However, the difference seems to be due to the lack of power of the McNemar test used for pairwise comparisons. Therefore, we cannot draw any conclusion regarding size.

6 Discussion

In this paper we have proposed methods to test the relevance of repositories of data sets for "real world" KDD. We have focused on data sets that are already pre-processed. Therefore, their relevance concerns the step of the KDD process where this is also true, namely modelling and algorithm selection [7]. This also implies that we also focus on the relative performance of algorithm performance, i.e., their ranking.

The methods proposed require that a reasonable number of new problems is gathered and experiments to obtain performance information for the algorithms under consideration are carried out. Therefore, they are essentially aimed for data repository administrators, which should execute them periodically, given a sufficient number of new problems. Thus they will only indirectly be useful to data analysts. A periodic assessment of the representativeness of data repositories in relation to the population of "real world" data sets will provide indication of whether meta-knowledge based on those repositories (e.g., results of comparative studies or meta-learning systems) is probably[6] useful for the KDD problem currently being tackled by a given data analyst. This would also enable the continuous growth of data repositories, by integrating the new problems after their use as samples of real world KDD data sets. This growth has been identified as an important issue to avoid the overfitting of repositories [28].

The most important problem with the methods proposed is the gathering of new data sets. The fewer the number of data sets, the less the probability that the null hypotheses of the statistical test used will be rejected, and, thus, it will be more difficult to show that repositories are not representative of new data sets or that an algorithm is over or underfitting a data repository. The power of the test may be also affected by the fact that our basic data consists of ranks and not continuous values, although their application is still valid and expected to be useful [22]. However, our experiments were performed with a reasonable number of new problems and the results of the tests confirmed the hypotheses we defined by visual inspection of the distributions of ranks.

In this paper we have focused on classification problems and the evaluation criterion used was error. However, the methodology only assumes that algorithms can be ranked. Therefore, it is independent of the type of problem. It may also be applied to regression, clustering, planning, optimization, etc. Additionally, it is independent of the evaluation criterion. Given that the suitability of error to compare algorithms is often questioned (e.g., [25]), we could use instead the Area Under the ROC Curve. Other criteria are often important in KDD problems, like the complexity or the understandability of the models or the time required by the algorithms. They may also be used as long as the relative performance of algorithms can be assessed.

7 Conclusions

The usefulness of problem repositories like the one at UCI is subject to extreme positions: some people use them blindly without taking into account their limitations, while others simply reject them completely without trying to make adequate use of them. However, to the best of our knowledge, this issue has always been treated rather superficially.

In this paper we first argue that, in principle, data repositories can be useful for KDD, namely to support the algorithm selection step. Next, we propose methods to assess the usefulness of a given data repository from that perspective, i.e., in terms of the relative performance of algorithms. We apply those

[6] As explained above, we cannot be sure due to the nature of the statistical tests used.

methodologies to the UCI repository. The results show no reason to believe that the UCI repository does not contain knowledge that is potentially useful for the algorithm selection step of the KDD process.

Acknowledgments. Thanks to all who have provided data sets, without which this work would not have been possible. I have also received many useful comments which helped improve this work, especially from Pavel Brazdil and João Gama. The financial support from ESPRIT project METAL, project ECO under PRAXIS XXI, FEDER, Programa de Financiamento Plurianual de Unidades de I&D and from the Faculty of Economics is gratefully acknowledged.

References

[1] S. Bay, D. Kibler, M. Pazzani, and P. Smyth. The UCI KDD archive of large data sets for data mining research and experimentation. *Information Processing Society of Japan Magazine*, 42(5), 2001.
[2] C. Blake and C. Merz. Repository of machine learning databases, 1998. http:/www.ics.uci.edu/~mlearn/MLRepository.html.
[3] R. Brachman, T. Khabaza, W. Kloesgen, G. Piatetsky-Shapiro, and E. Simoudis. Mining business databases. *Communications of the ACM*, 39(11):42–48, 1996.
[4] P. Brazdil, J. Gama, and B. Henery. Characterizing the applicability of classification algorithms using meta-level learning. In F. Bergadano and L. de Raedt, editors, *Proceedings of the European Conference on Machine Learning (ECML-94)*, pages 83–102. Springer-Verlag, 1994.
[5] P. Brazdil, C. Soares, and J. Costa. Ranking learning algorithms: Using IBL and meta-learning on accuracy and time results. *Machine Learning*, 50(3):251–277, 2003.
[6] C. Brodley. Addressing the selective superiority problem: Automatic Algorithm/Model class selection. In P. Utgoff, editor, *Proceedings of the Tenth International Conference on Machine Learning*, pages 17–24. Morgan Kaufmann, 1993.
[7] P. Chapman, J. Clinton, R. Kerber, T. Khabaza, T. Reinartz, C. Shearer, and R. Wirth. *CRISP-DM 1.0: Step-by-Step Data Mining Guide.* SPSS, 2000.
[8] W. Cohen. Fast effective rule induction. In A. Prieditis and S. Russell, editors, *Proceedings of the 11th International Conference on Machine Learning*, pages 115–123. Morgan Kaufmann, 1995.
[9] T. Dietterich. Approximate statistical tests for comparing supervised classification learning algorithms. *Neural Computation*, 10(7):1895–1924, 1998. ftp://ftp.cs.orst.edu/pub/tgd/papers/nc-stats.ps.gz.
[10] J. Gama. Probabilistic linear tree. In D. Fisher, editor, *Proceedings of the 14th International Machine Learning Conference (ICML97)*, pages 134–142. Morgan Kaufmann, 1997.
[11] J. Gehrke. Report on the SIGKDD 2001 conference panel "new research directions on KDD". *SIGKDD Explorations*, 3(2), 2002.
[12] M. Hilario and A. Kalousis. Building algorithm profiles for prior model selection in knowledge discovery systems. In *Proceedings of the IEEE SMC'99 International Conference on Systems, Man and Cybernetics.* IEEE Press, 1999.

[13] R. Ihaka and R. Gentleman. R: A language for data analysis and graphics. *Journal of Computational and Graphics and Statistics*, 5(3):299–314, 1996.
[14] J. Keller, I. Holzer, and S. Silvery. Using data envelopment analysis and case-based reasoning techniques for knowledge-based engine intake port design. In *Proceedings of the International Conference on Engineering Design (ICED99)*, 1999.
[15] E. Keogh and S. Kasetty. On the need for time series data mining benchmarks: A survey and empirical demonstration. In *Proceedings of the Eight ACM SIGKDD International Conference on Knowledge Discovery and Data Mining*, pages 102–111. ACM, 2002.
[16] R. Kohavi, D. Sommerfield, and J. Dougherty. Data mining using MLC++: A machine learning library in c++. *International Journal on Artificial Intelligence Tools*, 6(4):537–566, 1997. Available at
`http://robotics.stanford.edu/users/ronnyk/mlcj.ps.gz`.
[17] P. Langley. Crafting papers on machine learning. In P. Langley, editor, *Proceedings of the Seventeenth International Conference on Machine Learning*, pages 1207–1212. Morgan Kaufmann, 2000.
[18] T.-S. Lim, W.-Y. Loh, and Y.-S. Shih. A comparison of prediction accuracy, complexity, and training time of thirty-three old and new classification algorithms. *Machine Learning*, 40:203–229, 2000.
[19] G. Lindner and R. Studer. Forecastig the fault rate behavior for cars. In *Proceedings of the "From Machine Learning to Data Mining and Knowledge Discovery" ICML 99 Workshop*, 1999.
[20] METAL Consortium. Esprit project METAL (#26.357). 2002.
[21] D. Michie, D. Spiegelhalter, and C. Taylor. *Machine Learning, Neural and Statistical Classification*. Ellis Horwood, 1994.
[22] H. Neave and P. Worthington. *Distribution-Free Tests*. Routledge, 1992.
[23] M. Oldemiro and L. Torgo. Predicting daily returns for the ibm stock. In L. Torgo, editor, *Proceedings of the Workshop on Artificial Intelligence Techniques for Financial Time Series Analysis*. Available from
http://www.liacc.up.pt/~ltorgo/AIFTSA, 2001.
[24] J. Petrak. *MLEE: Machine Learning Experimentation Environment*. OFAI, 2002. http://www.ai.univie.ac.at/~johann/mlee.html.
[25] F. Provost and R. Kohavi. On applied research in machine learning. *Machine Learning*, 30(2/3):127–132, 1998.
[26] R. Quinlan. *C5.0: An Informal Tutorial*. RuleQuest, 1998.
http://www.rulequest.com/see5-unix.html.
[27] L. Saitta and F. Neri. Learning in the "real world". *Machine Learning*, 30(2/3):133–163, 1998.
[28] S. Salzberg. On comparing classifiers: Pitfalls to avoid and a recommended approach. *Data Mining and Knowledge Discovery*, 1:317–327, 1997.
http://www.cs.jhu.edu/~salzberg/critique.ps.
[29] M. Staudt, J.-U. Kietz, and U. Reimer. A data mining support environment and its application on insurance data. In D. Heckerman, H. Mannila, D. Pregibon, and R. Uthurusamy, editors, *Proceedings of the Fourth International Conference on Knowledge Discovery in Databases & Data Mining*, pages 105–111. AAAI Press, 1998.
[30] D. Wolpert. The lack of a priori distinctions between learning algorithms. *Neural Computation*, 8:1341–1390, 1996.
[31] M. Zaki. Editorial: Online, interactive and anytime data mining. *SIGKDD Explorations*, 3(2), 2002.

Improving the Efficiency of ILP Systems*

Rui Camacho

LIACC, Rua do Campo Alegre, 823, 4150 Porto, Portugal
FEUP, Rua Dr Roberto Frias, 4200-465 Porto, Portugal
rcamacho@fe.up.pt
http://www.fe.up.pt/~rcamacho

Abstract. Inductive Logic Programming (ILP) is a promising technology for knowledge extraction applications. ILP has produced intelligible solutions for a wide variety of domains where it has been applied. The ILP lack of efficiency is, however, a major impediment for its scalability to applications requiring large amounts of data. In this paper we propose a set of techniques that improve ILP systems efficiency and make then more likely to scale up to applications of knowledge extraction from large datasets. We propose and evaluate the *lazy evaluation* of examples, to improve the efficiency of ILP systems. *Lazy evaluation* is essentially a way to avoid or postpone the evaluation of the generated hypotheses (coverage tests).
The techniques were evaluated using the IndLog system on ILP datasets referenced in the literature. The proposals lead to substantial efficiency improvements and are generally applicable to any ILP system.

Keywords: Inductive Logic Programming, Efficiency

1 Introduction

Inductive Logic Programming (ILP) has achieved considerable success in a wide range of domains. It is recognised however that efficiency is a major obstacle to the use of ILP systems in applications requiring large amounts of data. Relational Data Mining applications are an example where efficiency is an important issue. In this paper we address the problem of efficiency in ILP systems by proposing a technique to speedup the evaluation of hypotheses.

A typical ILP system carries out a search through an ordered hypothesis space. During the search hypothesis are generated and their quality estimated against the given examples. Improving the efficiency of such search procedure may be done by avoiding to generate useless hypothesis or/and improving the evaluation procedures.

* The work presented in this paper has been partially supported by Universidade do Porto, project APRIL (Project POSI/SRI/40749/2001), funds granted to *LIACC* through the *Programa de Financiamento Plurianual, Fundação para a Ciência e Tecnologia* and *Programa POSI*.

Fernando Moura Pires, Salvador Abreu (Eds.): EPIA 2003, LNAI 2902, pp. 224–228, 2003.

Avoiding to generate useless hypotheses may be achieved with the specification of language bias limiting therefore the size of the search space ([1]). An alternative approach considers the study of refinement operators that allow to efficiently navigate through a hypothesis space ([2]).

The problem of efficient testing of candidate hypotheses has been tackled by the following techniques. Work of a stochastic nature (see [3,4]). These reduce the evaluation effort at the cost of being correct only with high probability. A study on exact transformations of queries when evaluating hypotheses may be found in [5] and [6]. In [5], the authors illustrated that query execution was a very high percentage of total running time.

In this paper we address the problem of ILP system efficiency by avoiding or reducing the computational cost in the evaluation of the hypotheses using the examples. The proposed techniques are globally called *lazy evaluation* of examples and reduce considerably the amount of examples necessary to evaluate each hypothesis. The proposed techniques may be adopted in any ILP system.

The structure of the rest of the paper is as follows. In Section 2 we present the *lazy evaluation* of examples techniques. The experiments that empirically evaluate our proposals are described in Section 3. The last section draws the conclusions.

2 Lazy Evaluation of Examples

Language bias may be used to avoid the generation, and therefore, the evaluation of a significant number of hypotheses. However, once an hypothesis has been generated the problem then is how to evaluate it efficiently using the available data (examples and background knowledge). This problem is specially critical if either the number of examples is large, like in Data Mining applications, or the evaluation of individual hypothesis (theorem proving effort) is hard [7]. The second problem has been addressed recently by means of techniques like query packs [8] or query transformations [5] and [6]. To handle the first situation, a probabilistic evaluation has been proposed [3] with the advantage of avoiding the use of all of the examples. This approach however prevents the system from having a correct measure of the hypothesis value.

We propose *lazy evaluation of examples* as a way to avoid unnecessary use of examples and therefore speed up the evaluation of each hypothesis. As the probabilistic approach we do not use all the examples to evaluate each hypothesis. Contrary to the probabilistic approach we get an exact count but only when it is absolutely necessary to do so. We can still profit from improvements due to query transformations and therefore combine the two technique for increasing speedup. We distinguish between lazy evaluation of positive examples, lazy evaluation of negative examples and positive evaluation avoidance. The techniques are now described.

Some systems like Progol [9], Aleph[1] or IndLog [10] rely on heuristics to guide the search during refinement. If the search is complete then the role of the heuristic is to improve speed. The final hypothesis should be the same. For some heurstics it is important to determine the exact number of examples covered. However, an hypothesis will only be accepted if it is consistent with the negative examples. A partial clause[2] must be specialised otherwise the search for further refinements of the partial clause terminates there. In this circumstances "lazy" evaluation of the negative examples is useful. When using the *lazy evaluation of negatives* we are only interesting in knowing if the hypothesis covers more than the allowed number of negative examples. We are not really interesting in knowing how much above the noise level the hypothesis is. Testing stops as soon as there are no more negative examples to be tested or the number of negative examples covered exceeds the allowed number for consistency (noise level). The noise level is quite often very close to zero and therefore the number of negative examples used in the test of each clause is very small. If the heuristic does not use the negative counting then this produces exactly the same results (clauses and accuracy) of the non-lazy approach but with a very significant speedup. It is also very common that the negative examples outnumber the positives. We may still use heuristics based on length and on positive cover.

IndLog also allows the positive cover to be evaluated lazily. A partial clause must be either specialised (if it covers more positives that the best consistent clause found so far) or is justifiably pruned away otherwise. When using lazy evaluation of positives it is relevant only to determine if an hypothesis covers more positives or not than the current best consistent hypothesis. We might then evaluate the positive examples just until the best cover so far is exceeded. If the best cover is exceeded we retain the hypothesis (either accept it as final is consistent or refine it otherwise) if not we may justifiably discard it. Only when accepting a consistent hypothesis we need to evaluate its exact positive cover.

We may go a bit further and simply do not evaluate the positive cover at all of partial clauses. The advantage of the first version of lazy evaluation of positives is that we may discard hypotheses that are worse than the best consistent so far, while in the second version we may keep around some partial clauses with very poor positive cover. The advantage of the second version however is that for each hypothesis we only test it on the negatives until it covers at least the noise level. Generating hypotheses is very efficient and although we may generate more hypotheses we may still gain by the increase in speed of their evaluation process. This technique may be very useful in domains where the evaluation of each hypothesis is very time-consuming.

When performing lazy evaluation of positive and negative examples we may use a breadth-first search strategy for example. This is not a too bad choice if, like in most applications, one is looking for short clauses that are very close to the top of the subsumption lattice.

---

[1] Available from http://web.comlab.ox.ac.uk/oucl/research/areas/machlearn/Aleph/
[2] A clause that covers more than the allowed number of negative examples.

Lazy evaluation of either negative or positive examples cannot be used when the technique called *lazy evaluation of literals* [11] is used. To compute the constant values all of the positive and negative coverage has to be computed exactly. It is also not applicable in data sets with positives only examples and the use of compression measure ([9]) or a user defined cost function like Aleph and IndLog might use ([11]).

3 The Experiments

To empirically evaluate our proposals we run IndLog [10] encoded in Yap Prolog [12] (version 4.21) and run on a PC. For each dataset the induced clause(s) are the same with and without lazy evaluation. Therefore the accuracy of the induced theories does not change by adopting any of the proposed techniques. The datasets used in the experiments were downloaded from the Oxford[3] and York[4] Universities Machine Learning repositories.

In the experiments the IndLog settings were such that all lazy evaluations for the same dataset produce the same final theory and construct the same set of hypotheses. For the *lazy evaluation of negatives* we measured the number of theorem proving calls used to evaluate the negative examples and also the CPU time spent. For the *lazy evaluation of positives* we measured the number of theorem proving calls used to evaluate the positive examples and also the CPU time needed. For the *no positive evaluation* form of lazy evaluation we measured the number of theorem proving calls used to evaluate both the negative and positive examples, the spent CPU time and the number of nodes constructed during the search. The results are shown in Table 1.

Table 1. Percentage of theorem proving calls and CPU time savings when using lazy valuation of examples (lazy / no lazy × 100%).

Dataset	lazy negs		lazy pos		no pos			
	negs calls (%)	cpu time (%)	pos calls (%)	cpu time (%)	nodes (%)	negs calls (%)	pos calls (%)	cpu time (%)
amine uptake	25	75	69	99	146	56	14	97
carcinogenesis	27	79	80	115	105	76	23	68
choline	27	74	54	92	100	44	13	46
mesh	86	99	93	99	105	125	77	81
multiplication	31	99	91	104	152	95	44	127
mutagenesis	40	99	66	101	100	48	10	98
pyrimidines	38	76	63	99	120	62	13	58
triazines	8	56	39	77	148	55	26	48

Table 1 shows the percentage of the measured values when compared with the run when not using any kind of lazy evaluation. Except for the small (number of examples) datasets there is significant gain in using the lazy evaluation technique.

[3] URL: http://www.comlab.ox.ac.uk/oucl/groups/machlearn/
[4] URL:http://www.cs.york.ac.uk/mlg/index.html

4 Conclusions

We proposed and evaluated a set of techniques globaly called *lazy evaluation* of examples that improve the efficiency of ILP systems. As shown by the empirical results the *lazy evaluation* may produce substantial improvements to an ILP system.

References

1. Nédellec, C. and Rouveirol, C. and Adé, H. and Bergadano, F. and Tausend, B. *Declarative Bias in ILP* ed. De Raedt, L., in Advances in Inductive Logic Programming, 82–103, 1996, IOS
2. Patrick van der Laag and Shan-Hwei Nienhuys-Cheng *Completeness and Properness of Refinement Operators* Journal of Logic Programming, 34, 3, 201–226, 1998
3. A. Srinivasan *A study of two sampling methods for analysing large datasets with ILP* Data Mining and Knowledge Discovery,vol. 3, N. 1, 95–123, 1999
4. M. Sebag and C. Rouveirol *Tractable induction and classification in first-order logic via stochastic matching* (IJCAI97) Proceedings of the 15th International Joint Conference on Artificial Intelligence, 888–893, 1997
5. Santos Costa, Vítor and Srinivasan, Ashwin and Camacho, Rui, *A note on two simple transformations for improving the efficiency of an ILP system* Proceedings of the 10th International Conference on Inductive Logic Programming, LNAI, vol 1866, ed. J. Cussens and A. Frisch, 225–242, 2000
6. Vítor Costa and Ashwin Srinivasan and Rui Camacho and Hendrik Blockeel and Bart Demoen and and Gerda Janssens and Jan Struyf and Henk Vandecasteele and Wim Van Laer *Query Transformations for Improving the Efficiency of ILP Systems* Journal of Machine Learning Research, 2002
7. M. Botta and A. Giordana and L. Saitta and M. Sebag *Relational learning: hard problems and phase transitions* Proc. of the 6th Congress AI*IA, LNAI 1792, 178–189, 1999
8. Blockeel, Hendrik and Dehaspe, Luc and Demoen, Bart and Janssens, Gerda and Ramon, Jan and Vandecasteele, Henk *Executing Query Packs in ILP* Proceedings of the 10th International Conference on Inductive Logic Programming,LNAI 1866, ed. J. Cussens and A. Frisch, 60–77, 2000
9. Muggleton, S. *Inverse Entailment and Progol* New Generation Computing, Special issue on Inductive Logic Programming, vol. 13, N. 3-4, 245–286, 1995
10. R. Camacho, *Inducing Models of Human Control Skills using Machine Learning Algorithms* PhD thesis,Department of Electrical Engineering and Computation, Universidade do Porto, 2000
11. A. Srinivasan and R.C. Camacho *Numerical reasoning with an ILP program capable of lazy evaluation and customised search* Journal of Logic Programming, vol. 40, N. 2-3, 185–214, 1999
12. Costa, V. and Damas, L. and Reis, R. and Azevedo, R., *YAP Prolog User's Manual* Universidade do Porto, 1989

Reorganizing News Web Pages for Mobile Users

Woncheol Kim[1], Eenjun Hwang[1], and Wonil Kim[2]

[1] The Graduate School of Information and Communication, Ajou University,
San 5, Wonchon-dong, Paldal-gu, Suwon 442-749, Korea
{wc323, ehwang}@ajou.ac.kr

[2] College of Electronics & Information Engineering, Sejong University,
Gunja-Dong, Gwangjin-Gu, Seoul, 143-747, Korea
wikim@sejong.ac.kr

Abstract. Today the fastest growing communities of web users are mobile visitors who browse web pages using wireless PDAs and cellular phones. However, most web pages are optimized exclusively for desktop clients on the broadband network and are inconvenient to users with small screen mobile devices. They display only a few lines of text and cannot run client-side programs or scripts due to lack of system resources. Even worse, their connections are usually too slow to support most of the data-intensive applications. To address this problem, in this paper, we propose a *newslet* scheme that makes it feasible to browse ordinary news web pages on small screen mobile devices. It first extracts news sections of user preference from news web pages and then automatically reorganizes them for convenient browsing on the mobile devices.

1 Introduction

Recently, with the wide spread of mobile devices such as PDAs(Personal Digital Assistants) and wireless network technology, there has been tremendous increase of the web page accesses using mobile browsing devices on the wireless connection. Most existing web pages are written in HTML and optimized for the desktop computers. Even though computing power and screen resolution of mobile devices have been improved, they are still not as capable as desktop computers. They inherently have small screens, low network bandwidth and weak computing power. These impose serious restrictions when users browse web pages on the small screen devices. For example, it needs multiple scrolling and takes much longer time to access any desired contents. There have been many researches to solve this problem and they can be categorized into two types; personalized service for each user and trimmed service for unimportant contents. In order to provide personalized service, user's action should be predicted from the past usage pattern. However, it is not easy to acquire the profile of each user's interests. On the other hand, in the trimmed service, a particular user may lose wanted information, if the trimming process does not identify each user's preference. In this paper, we propose a *newslet* scheme that automatically reorganizes web pages according to the individual user preference for personalized news service.

Fernando Moura Pires, Salvador Abreu (Eds.): EPIA 2003, LNAI 2902, pp. 229–243, 2003.

The *newslet* scheme makes it feasible to navigate web pages through mobile devices even on the low bandwidth wireless connection. Especially, instead of restricting each web page to have only one topic, we divide each page into multiple sections according to the topic.

The rest of this paper is organized as follows. Section 2 and 3 provides previous works and web mining techniques. Section 4 describes personalized news reorganizer. Section 5 describes our *newslet* extraction technique. Section 6 describes the overall system structure. Section 7 reports some of the experiment results. Section 8 presents main conclusion of our work.

2 Previous Approaches

So far, there have been many researches for efficient navigation of web pages on a small display device. Pda++ [1] was proposed to zoom on the display and CZ web [2] and Widgets [3] have been proposed in order to summarize web pages. WEST [4] proposed a scheme called "focus + context" that provides an overview of a web page. Power Browser [5] divides a web page into semantic textual units and composes a summary based on the unit. Digestor [6] proposed an accordion style summarization by using structural page transformations and sentence elision. Trevor et al. [7] proposed a new user interface that splits current mode of integrating "link following" and "reading" into separate modes, namely, navigating and acting.

One of the current trends in the web design is how to display as much information as possible in a page. As a result, it is getting more complicated to find relevant information on the mobile devices. Furthermore, those previous researches did not consider personalized services, although every visitor has different needs. In order to provide personalized services, many works have considered web mining methods. The web contains useful collection of hyperlinks and usage information for data mining. People want to discover useful knowledge by searching, integrating, mining and analyzing the web. Web mining can help people discover useful information and improve the web sites.

WebWatcher [8] assists users by giving them advices on the navigation. While the user browses web pages, WebWatcher assesses the hypertext links contained in the pages, and then recommends those links that are considered promising in matching the goal of the session. Letizia [9] is an intelligent agent that works with a conventional web browser such as Netscape. It tracks users' browsing behavior and tries to infer their goals. While a user is reading a page, Letizia conducts a resource-limited search based on the goals deduced. Relevant pages found during the search will be recommended to the user upon request. The goal of Letizia is to automatically perform some of the web exploration on behalf of the user to anticipate future page accesses. Besides intelligent systems, another area of interest is discovering useful access patterns from user access logs in distributed information systems. Yan [10] proposed how to automatically classify users of a web page according to their access pattern. User access logs are examined to discover clusters of users that access similar pages. This technique can discover categories of web pages that might be useful in the application such as designing online catalogues for electronic commerce. Chen [11] suggests that the browsing movement between web pages can be captured in a directed graph called traversal path graph. A set of maximal forward references which represent different browsing sessions are first extracted from the directed graph. These frequent paths are the most common traversal patterns of the users. Finally, they were several works that have analyzed web log of the server and grasped the behavior patterns of users. They are used for adaptive web pages [12] according to the user's behavior pattern.

In this paper, we use web usage mining [13, 14, 15] method to adapt mobile devices, in order to support personalized services to mobile users.

3 Web Usage Mining

The Web mining consists of web content mining, web usage mining and web structure mining.

Web Content Mining is the process of information discovery from the sources across the World Wide Web. The lack of structure that permeates the information sources on the web makes automated discovery of web-based information difficult. In recent years these factors have prompted development of more intelligent tools for information retrieval.

Web Structure Mining aims at developing techniques to take advantage of the collective judgment of web page quality, which is available in the form of hyperlinks. Since many hyperlinks contain high quality semantic clues, web structure mining is beneficial to make good use of such semantic information in order to acquire crucial information by performing web linkage analysis.

Web Usage Mining is the mining process for analyzing user browsing and access patterns. Analyzing web log may also help build customized web services for each user. Usage mining usually involves cleansing, identifying, integrating and transforming log files. It is because typical log files contain a lot of unnecessary data in them. Web usage mining consists of data preprocessing, pattern discovery, and pattern analysis.

Usage preprocessing is the most difficult task in the usage mining due to the incompleteness of available data. Unless a client side tracking mechanism is used, only the IP address, agent, and server side click-stream are available to identify users and server session. In order to discover the pattern or interest of users, pattern discovery methods such as statistical analysis, clustering, classification, sequential patterns and dependency modeling can be used.

The goal of pattern analysis is to filter out uninteresting rules or patterns from the set found in the pattern discovery phase. The general form of pattern analysis consists of a knowledge query mechanism such as SQL. Another method is to load usage data into a data cube in order to perform OLAP operations. Content and structure information can be used to filter out patterns containing pages of a certain usage type, content type, or pages that match a certain hyperlink structure.

Usage patterns extracted from web data have been applied to a wide range of applications including personalization, system improvement, site modification, business intelligence and usage characterization. Web usage mining has been used in many applications including:

- **Personalization:** Web usage mining is an efficient tool for achieving this goal. Both WebWatcher and Letizia have concentrated on providing web site personalization based on usage information. This approach usually utilizes web server log analysis to discover user access patterns, and uses proxy server in order to easily track the user session across multiple web sites.
- **System improvement:** Performance and other service attributes are crucial to user satisfaction. Web usage mining provides the key to the understanding of web traffic behavior, web caching policies and web-based services.
- **Site modification:** Web usage mining provides detailed feedback on user behavior which in turn provides the web site designer useful information for the web site reorganization. Adaptive web site project focuses on automatically changing the structure of a site based on usage patterns discovered from server log files.
- **Business intelligence:** In the e-business applications, one of the crucial information is how customers use their web sites. Many previous works have showed how to discover such knowledges from user's usage pattern. They used web server logs to find out users' access patterns at the given web site.
- **Usage characterization:** While most works that utilize usage, content, and structure of the web don't necessarily consider themselves to be engaged in data mining, there is a large amount of overlap between web characterization and web usage mining. A model was proposed to predict the probability distribution of various pages that a user might visit.

4 Personalized News Service

Basically, our news reorganizer performs personalized news services depending on user's interest and usage pattern. To provide personalized news services, we extract user's interest or preference on the news pages from user access patterns and then reorganize them.

4.1 User Preference Analysis

Depending on the location where user behavior information is collected, user's retrieval pattern analysis can be classified as follows.

- **Server-side analysis:** This plays an important role in performing web mining because server log explicitly records the browsing behavior of site visitors. However, the data recorded in the server log may not be entirely reliable due to the presence of caching within the web environment. Cached histories are not recorded in the server log.

- **Client-side analysis:** This can be performed by a remote agent such as JavaScript or Java applet. Client-side analysis has an advantage over server-side analysis in that it improves both the caching and the session identification. However, it requires user cooperation and can only collect single-user, single-site browsing behavior.
- **Proxy-side analysis:** This behaves like the server-side analysis. But this approach does not suffer from the caching problem. Furthermore, proxy is easier to insert modules. For the efficient communication, proxy server is located between client and server, and performs reconstruction as in the previous approaches. Since navigating web pages by mobile devices can be affected by many factors such as battery capacity, network bandwidth, and small display, our prototype system resides in the proxy server located between client and server.

4.2 *Newslet* Scheme

In order to extract user's interest area, we propose a segmentation scheme called *newslet*. A *newslet* can be defined as a meaningful area that represents a function or a topic in the news page. We first identify various topics of a news page, and then consider each news section as a *newslet*. This means that a web page is divided into several *newslets*. More specifically, *newslet* scheme consists of following three steps.

- **User interest extraction:** In this step, various browsing behaviors of mobile web visitors are collected. Previous interactions with the web site are analyzed for the visiting patterns. Those patterns are used to provide personalized web contents for each individual visitor. Here, we will apply the web mining technique to extract user behavior patterns, which use the link information to find traversal patterns of web page.
- **Page transformation:** In this step, we analyze web pages and transform them into a collection of *newslets*. A *newslet* is an semantically independent unit that has one distinct topic or function in the original news page. During the web page analysis, we extract topic areas from each page using weights of keywords and the number of the links in the HTML element. Whenever a user navigates a specific page, our system analyzes its HTML document.
- **Reconstruction:** In this step, we reorder the web pages appropriately for the mobile devices. Those sections in which users have more interest should be displayed before the one that users have less interest on the screen. Consequently, users with a small display and low bandwidth mobile device can browse news very efficiently.

Newslet scheme can automatically personalize the contents of a web page based on individual user's preference, and just requires low network bandwidth. Moreover, it can present the whole contents of a web page on the small screen. This will improve the readability and understandability of web pages via small display devices.

5 Extraction of User Preference

In order to extract user preference, keywords are first extracted from news pages. And then sequences are identified and extracted from user sequence pattern. Finally, news pages are decomposed into a collection of *newslets* by the topic or function.

5.1 Keyword Extraction from News Page

A news page contains many topics that can be divided into categories such as sports, economics and politics. In order to decide the category to which a given *newslet* belongs, we need to check the weight of selected keyword in the *newslet*. To do that, we first have to know how to extract related keywords from the news page. While extracting keywords from the page, extracting too many keywords might cause an ambiguity in the decision of the news section boundary. Therefore, we assign weights to the important sentences. The sentence rank itself is decided by the sum of other keywords' weights and scores. In addition, in order to choose important sentences from the web page, we use the Luhn's Keyword Cluster technique [16], the frequencies of the keyword in the <Title> tag and the keyword weight.

First of all, we have to decide whether a sentence is important or not, For example, if the sum of keyword weights in the sentence becomes bigger than a certain threshold value, we consider it to be a significant sentence. We define the weight of a sentence as follows:

$$SW_1 = \frac{SK^2}{TK} \qquad \text{where} \begin{cases} SW_1 = & \text{the sentence weight score} \\ SK = & \text{the number of significant keywords} \\ TK = & \text{the total number of keywords} \end{cases}$$

Then we extract important sentences using keyword frequency in the <Title> tag. Keywords in <Title> tag of the web page often express the subject of the web page. We decide the rank of each sentence using the keywords in the <Title> tag and extract keywords of the important sentence in the web page. The weight of a significant sentence is determined by the frequency of keywords in a <Title> tag as follows:

$$SW_2 = \frac{NTT}{TNT} \qquad \text{where} \begin{cases} SW_2 = & \text{the sentence weight score} \\ NTT = & \text{the number of title terms found} \\ TNT = & \text{the total number of terms in a title} \end{cases}$$

For the more accurate measurement, we include different font size, color and thickness. Since web page authors are generally decorating keywords to emphasize the sentence, the sentence with the decorated keywords is more important than the other sentences. We define the sentence weight score as follows:

$$SW_3 = \frac{MW^2}{TW} \qquad \text{where} \begin{cases} SW_3 = & \text{the sentence weight score} \\ MW = & \text{the number of modified words} \\ TW = & \text{the total number of words} \end{cases}$$

Now the significant sentence weight score is the summation of all the three values above, that is, $SSW = SW_1 + SW_2 + SW_3$, where SSW = Significant Sentence Weight Score.

5.2 Sequence Extraction from User Sequence Patterns

In this paper, user access patterns in the web environment are analyzed using traversal pattern algorithm from the previous news page access behavior [17].

In the web environment where pages are linked together, users tend to traverse pages back and forth in accordance with the link. As a result, some pages might be revisited because of its location rather than its content. For example, in a web page with tree structure, to reach a sibling web page, a user usually tends to use backward icon and then go to the sibling page instead of using a new URL. Consequently, to extract significant user access pattern from the log file, such backward reference behavior should be taken into consideration.

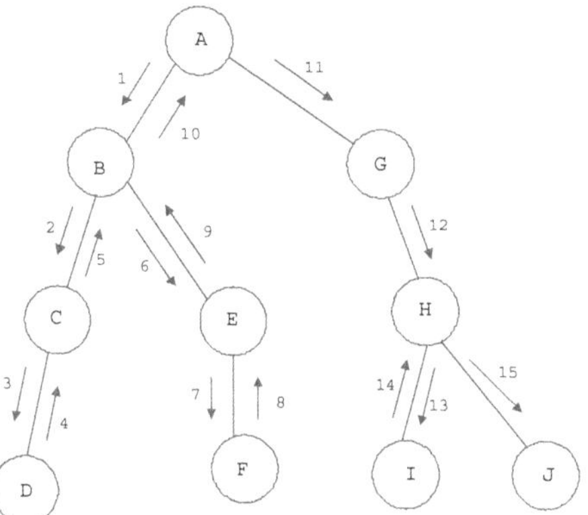

Fig. 1. Traversal pattern example

In this paper, we assume that backward reference is used not for browsing but for traveling, and focus on the discovery of forward reference patterns. When a backward reference occurs, a forward reference path is terminated. This forward reference path is called maximal forward reference.

Suppose the log file contains the following traversal path (A, B, C, D, C, B, E, F, E, B, A, G, H, I, H, J) as shown in Figure 1. The algorithm in the Figure 2 then extracts the following maximal forward references: ABCD, ABEF, AGHI, AGHJ. Here, we use link anchor text, which appears between the <a> tags in a link. For example <a href="http://adtl.ajou.ac.kr">ajou univ, database lab</a>, "ajou univ, database lab" is the link anchor text. We call keywords of link anchor text link anchor keywords (LAKs). Link anchor texts contain important information about the link, and we use the LAKs to classify each news section.

```
FindNewsPath(L)

make traversal sequence such as {(s1, d1),(s2, d2)....(sn, dn)}
set i = 1 and string y to null for initialization, where string y is used to store the current forward
reference path.                                        // setp1
set the flag F = 1 to indicate a forward traversal.

while(the sequence is not completed scanned)
{
  Let A = si and B = di                        //step2
  if (A is equal to null)
    Write out the current string Y to the database Df
    Set string Y = B
    Goto step5
  end if
  if (B is equal to some reference in string y)   //step3
   if (F is equal to 1)
     write out string Y to database Df
     using keyword matching between K and decide K's news section
     append decided news section to the end of string Ns
   end if
   discard all the references after the j-th one in string Y
   F = 0;
   goto step5
  end if
  append B to the end of string Y              // step4
  fetch anchor text and store it to K
  if (F is equal to 0)
   F = 1
  end if
  set i = i + 1                                // step5
}
make Ns's path to section path's graph
```

Fig. 2. Extracting user preference algorithm

After extracting maximal forward references, LAKs are created as a sequence of links. For example, if a user visits links in the order of A, B, C and D, then LAKs such as {stock, bank, market, creditor} are extracted from a link in the business news section. After that, LAKs of a maximal forward reference are stored into an K-dimensional array sequentially. We will decide the category of a news section by comparing the keyword with these keywords. This step will repeat iteratively for the remaining maximal forward reference.

As mentioned before, we use the log file to discover user access pattern. Typical log file contains various kinds of information. That includes IP address of a visitor, user identifier, access time, methods of request, URL of the requested page, used protocol, any possible error codes and the number of transmitted bytes. Here, irrelevant information such as image file, error code and protocol is removed during the preprocessing.

Figure 3 shows how to extract user's preferred news sections using the link information. LAKs are obtained from the link information and then preferred news sections are identified from LAKs. Assume that a user accesses pages in the sequence P→B→E→T→M→S as shown in Figure 3. Then our proposed system would reorganize the web pages and send them. One possible reorganized sequence would be P→B→E→T→M→S. We represent state diagram about user

Link information	LAKs (Link anchor keywords)	News section
~/ newsArticle.jhtml?type=politicsNews&storyID=2844205	Congress, Try, Solve ,Medicare Problems	Politics (P)
~/ newsArticle.jhtml?type=politicsNews&storyID=2844971	Israel, Palestinians, Peace, Steps	
.....	.....	
~/_tsclsii/markets/marketstory/10090182.html	Stocks, Turn, Mixed,	Business (B)
~/financeNewsArticle.jhtml?type=businessNews&storyID=2845238	Jobless, Claims, Fall, Continued, Claims, Up	
.....	.....	
~/ newsArticle.jhtml?type=entertainmentNews&storyID=2844570	Thanks, Memory, Americans, Rock	Entertainment (E)
~/ newsArticle.jhtml?type=entertainmentNews&storyID=2842373	Idol, Fox, Pop, Albums, Charts	
.....	.....	
~/ newsArticle.jhtml?type=technologyNews&storyID=2843665	Computer, European Broad-band, mobile	Technology (T)
~/ newsArticle.jhtml?type=technologyNews&storyID=2837894	Microsoft, Windows, Linux	
.....	.....	
~/ newsArticle.jhtml?type=internetNews&storyID=2842114	Matrix, Reloaded, radio, television,	Movie (M)
~/ newsArticle.jhtml?type=internetNews&storyID=2839697	X-Men, United, Hulk, Movie	
.....	.....	
~/newsArticle.jhtml?type=politicsNews&storyID=2840773	Bush, G8, Iraq, Debate	Politics (P)
~/ newsArticle.jhtml?type=politicsNews&storyID=2843578	Anti-War, Polish, Mayor, Bush Visit	
.....	.....	
~/newsArticle.jhtml?type=golfNews&storyID=2820132	Leading, prize-money, winners, U.S., PGA, tour,	Sports (S)
~/newsArticle.jhtml?type=baseballNews&storyID=2820183	Language, Police, baseball, homerun	
.....	.....	

Fig. 3. Finding news sequence

access pattern after storing news section to Ns. Therefore user preference can be extracted from comparing with user access pattern during user session.

5.3 Newslet Extraction from News Page

In this paper, to identify topic areas of a page, we used weights of keywords and the number of the links in the HTML element.

Whenever the user navigates a specific page, our system looks into the HTML document. extracts the HTML element and then constructs its parse tree. After that, the first node of the parse tree, namely, the root element of the tree is stored in the queue.

Next, for a node element in the queue, if the number of the child node's links is larger than or equal to a threshold value, then it is considered to represent some different topic. We define such node as a *newslet* and store it to the *newslet* queue; otherwise, it is more likely to be integrated into its parent. This process is repeated until there is no element in the queue. Figure 4 shows the *newslet* extraction algorithm. The keywords in the selected *newslet* area are extracted and the meaning of the *newslet* should be given according to the news topic. After analyzing the *newslets*, we calculate the rank of user interests based on SessionTime and BranchTime. SessionTime and BranchTime are the time spent

```
NewsletPartition (p)
 parse HTML page
 construct Parse tree
 Queue Parse Tree
  while ( Queue is not empty)
 {
    if (top element in Queue has a child with at least k links)
    push all the children of top element to Queue
    else
    declare it as a newslet
          if ( user click is included in this newslet)
              return newslet
          end if
  end if
   }
```

Fig. 4. Newslet extraction algorithm

by the user to browse the news pages and the time spent for browsing one news section, respectively.

Then, we calculate accumulated user's interest for the field in the news page and identify the field of interest based on the calculation.

$$\mathrm{TUI} = \sum_{k=1}^{s} \frac{UI_i \times func(time)}{TS - ST_i} \text{ where } \begin{cases} TUI = & \text{Total User Interests per each topic} \\ UI = & \text{User Interests per each topic} \\ func(time) = & \text{function of date} \\ TS = & \text{Total Session Time} \\ ST = & \text{SessionTime} \\ S = & \text{count of each UI} \end{cases}$$

The function *func(time)* and SessionTime are used to extract total user interest. User pattern is predictable because web site visitors generally follow the same set of links, view the same set of pages, and tend to view pages with similar contents viewed in the past.

6 System Overview

Since the navigation of web pages using mobile devices can be affected by many factors such as battery capacity, network bandwidth and small display, our prototype system is located in the proxy server between the client and the server. We implemented the proxy server as an extension to the HTTP proxy server, and put all the relevant functions for reconstructing web pages into the proxy server. Figure 5 shows the overall system architecture. When a mobile user requests a news page, the target web page will be displayed by the following sequence.

1. When a user accesses the web page using a mobile device, the extracting engine module identifies the user using login information and analyzes user patterns. In addition, the extracting engine module stores extracted user interests into the database.
2. When the User Analyzer module of the proxy server receives a request from the WWW server, it identifies the user and acquires user information through

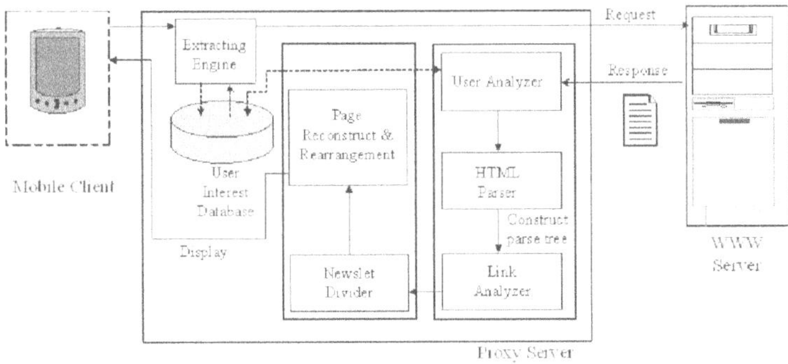

Fig. 5. System Overview

the user interest database. Then it transmits user information and the web page to the HTML parser module.
3. When the HTML parser module receives the web page, it constructs a parse tree from the web page. After that Link Analyzer module extracts link information in order to make a *newslet*.
4. The *newslet* Divider module analyzes the number of linked HTML nodes in order to identify function areas and construct a *newslet* for the web page.
5. Page Reconstruct and Rearrangement module reorder the *newslets* in order to find news sections of user interest. Those sections in which the user has more interest should be displayed on the top part of the screen.

7 Simulation and Analysis

While most web pages have at least 800 x 600 or 1024 x 768 resolution, small devices usually have 320 x 240 resolution. We construct *newslet* that can fit into 320 x 240 resolution device.

7.1 Simulated Device

We have simulated a prototype system that supports browsing of HTML web pages using embedded Visual Basic 3.0 with a mobile emulator. It is equipped with small display with web capability.

7.2 Evaluation

To evaluate the efficiency of our system, we have performed several experiments for various news pages. We evaluate the performance by two categories. They are the number of scrolling and the page size.

The number of scrolling. Table 1 shows the number of scrolling without reorganization. The usual six sections of news paper, Politics, Technology, Business, Sports, Entertainment, and Movies are indicated as P, T, B, S, E, and M respectively. We assume a typical section order of a news page is P, B, T, S, E and M and the mobile screen can show only three news sections at one time.

First of all, we calculate the number of up/down scroll to check whether the reorganized pattern is adequate or not.

Table 1. The number of scrolling without reorganization

User	Display sequence	User sequence	The number of scrolling	total number of scrolling
A		P,B,E,T,M,P,E	0,0,2,0,1,3,2	8
B		M,B,E,P,B,M,B	3,2,1,2,0,3,2	13
C	P,B,T,S,E,M	M,E,B,P,S,T,S	3,0,2,1,1,0,0	7
D		M,T,S,M,E,T,M	3,1,0,1,0,1,1	7
E		E,M,S,T,P,B,P	2,1,0,1,2,0,0	6
F		P,B,S,E,T,M,T	0,0,0,1,1,0,1	3

The fixed display sequence of news sections is P, B, T, S, E and M in case of non-reorganized mobile device. Suppose a user A accesses news pages in the order of P, B, E, T, M, P and E. Since the simulated device can show three sections at a time on the display, the user can only see P, B and T. When the user accesses news section P, he/she does not need to scroll to see P. He/she does not need to scroll to access B either. Next, the user accesses news section E, and in this case the user needs to scroll up twice to access E, which will show T, S and E at the screen. Now, the user does not need to scroll because next news section is T from the user access pattern. In order to see news section M, the user should do scroll just one time; the mobile screen now shows S, E and M. Finally a user scrolls down five times to see news section P and E. The total number of scrolling for user A in this case is eight (2+1+3+2).

Table 2 shows the case where the web page reorganization was performed. Now, the personalized display sequence is P, B, E, T, M and S. The user A can see P, B and E. because the simulated device can show three sections on the display as in the earlier case. The user accesses news pages in the order of P, B, E, T, M, P and E. When the user accesses news section P, he/she does not need to scroll to see P. He/she does not need to scroll to access B and E either. Next, when the user accesses news section T, now the user needs to scroll up once to access T, watching (B, E, T) at the screen. In order to see news section M, the user should do scroll up just once; with mobile screen of (E, T, M). Finally, the user scrolls down twice to see news section P. The user does not need scrolling because mobile screen shows (P, B, E). Therefore, the user A needs only 4 scrolls in total; 1 down scroll for accessing T, 1 down for accessing M and 2 ups for P

Table 2. The number of scrolling with reorganization

User	Display sequence	User sequence	The number of scrolling	total number of scrolling
A	P,B,E,T,M,S	P,B,E,T,M,P,E	0,0,0,1,1,2,0	4
B	M,B,E,P,S,T	M,B,E,P,B,M,B	0,0,0,1,0,1,0	2
C	M,E,B,P,S,T	M,E,B,P,S,T,S	0,0,0,1,1,1,0	3
D	M,T,S,E,P,B	M,T,S,M,E,T,M	0,0,0,0,1,0,0	1
E	E,M,S,T,P,B	E,M,S,T,P,B,P	0,0,0,1,1,1,0	3
F	P,B,S,E,T,M	P,B,S,E,T,M,T	0,0,0,0,1,1,0	2

again. Consequently, reorganized scheme by user preference is more convenient to user with small screen mobile devices.

Reduced size of page size. Table 3 compares the file size and display size before and after the page reconstruction.

Table 3. Page file of web pages after rebuilding

Page	Original page size	Newslet size
CNN	122.4 Kb	25.5 Kb
BBC	110.6 Kb	23.2 Kb
MSNBC	123.4 Kb	25.6 Kb
ABCNews.com	115.8 Kb	22.5 Kb
Google news	118.2 Kb	30.7 Kb
USATODAY	128.1 Kb	28.1 Kb
CBS SportsLine	117.4 Kb	27.2 Kb
CNET news.com	114.3 Kb	29.7 Kb
TechWeb	126.6 Kb	27.0 Kb

Table 3 shows that our proposed scheme has reduced the file size or display size a lot because pop-up windows, advertisement windows, script, and so on were removed and web pages were reconstructed for a small display. The average file size and display size were decreased by 72% and 74%, respectively.

From the experiment, we show that the decreased file size relieves the low bandwidth limitation of current mobile devices and the reduced display size relieves the small display limitation and scrolling.

Results. The different sequences of user interests are shown in Fig 6. Fig 6 depicts display screen showing user interests in the order of Politics, Business, Entertainment, etc and Business, Entertainment, Technology, etc, respectively.

Consequently, contents on the small screen are personalized according to the user interest.

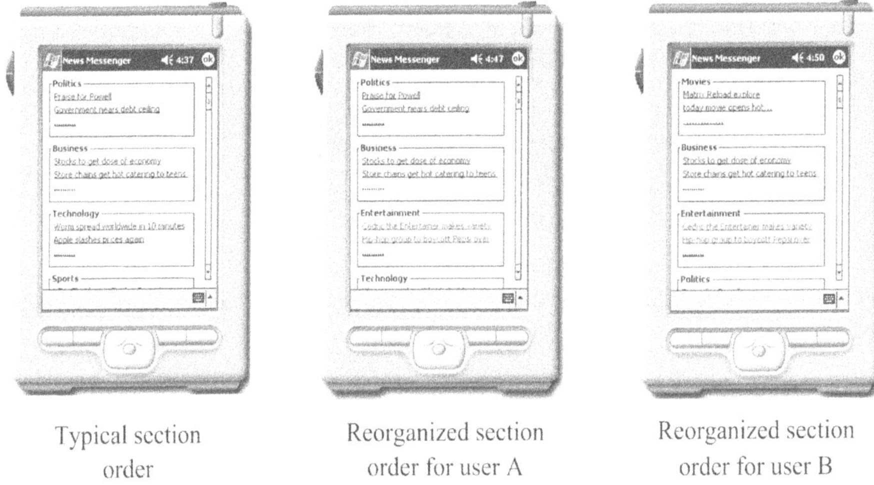

Fig. 6. Reconstruction of news page

8 Conclusion

In this paper, we proposed a new scheme for reorganizing news pages for mobile devices based on the user preference. We have developed a simulated prototype system and divided a web page into a set of *newslets*. This makes it feasible to browse ordinary news web pages on the small screen mobile devices. It extracts sections of preference from news web pages and automatically reorganizes them using those extracted sections. We evaluated the efficiency of our proposed scheme by measuring two categories. They are the number of scrolling and the file size. Reduced scrolling makes it convenient to browse news pages. A *newslet* is much smaller in file size compared to the original page, which helps to relieve network bandwidth limitation of wireless connection.

Acknowledgement. This work was supported by a grant (M1-0219-24-0000) from the National Research and Development Program funded by the Ministry of Science and Technology, Republic of Korea

References

1. B. B. Bederson, J. D. Hollan: Pda++: A Zooming Graphical Interface for Exploring Alternate Interface Physics. ACM Symposium on user Interface Software and Technology (1994)

2. B.Fisher, M. Agelidis, J. Dill, P. Tan, G. Collaud, and C. Jones: CZWeb: Fish-eye Views for Visualizing the World-Wide Web. Proceedings of the 6th International World Wide Web Conference (1997)
3. T. Kamba, S. A. Elson, T. Harpold, T. Stamper, and P. Sukaviriya: Using small screen space more efficiently. Proceedings of CHI'96, ACM Press (1996)
4. S. Bjrk, L.E. Holmquist, J. Redstrm, I. Bretan, R. Danielsson, J. Karlgren, and K. Franzn: WEST: A Web Browser for small Terminals. ACM Sysmposium on User Interface Software and Technology (1999)
5. Buyukkokten, H. Garcia-Molina, A. Paepcke, and T. Winograd: Power Browser: Efficient Web Browsing for PDAs. Proceedings of CHI'2000, ACM Press, Amsterdam (2000)
6. T. W. Bickmore, B. N. Schilit: Digestor: Device-independent Access to the World Wide Web. Proceedings of the 6th international World Wide Web Conference, Santa Clara, CA (1997)
7. J. Trevor, D. M. Hilbert, B. N. Schilit and T. K. Koh: From Desktop to Phonetop: A UI For Web Interaction On Very Small Devices. ACM Symposium on User Interface Software and Technology (2001)
8. Armstrong et al.: WebWatcher: A Learning Apprentice for the World Wide Web. Working Notes of the AAAI Spring Symp: Information Gathering from Heterogeneous, Distributed Environments. AAAI Press. (1995) 6–12.
9. Henry Lieberman: etizia: An Agent That Assists Web Browsing. In Proc. of the 1995 International Joint Conference on Artificial Intelligence, Montreal, Canada. (1995)
10. T.W. Yan et. al.: From User Access Patterns to Dynamic Hypertext Linking. Proceeding of the Fifth International World-Wide Web Conference (1996)
11. M.S. Chen, J.S. Park and P.S. Yu: Data mining for Path Traversal Patterns in a Web Environment. Proceedings of the 16th International Conference (1996)
12. Mike Perkowitz, Oren Etzioni: Adaptive Web Sites: Conceptual Cluster Mining. In Sixteenth International Joint Conference on Artificial Intelligence, Stockholm, Sweden. (1999)
13. Baldonado Lizhen Liu, Junjie Chen, and Hantao Song: The research of Web mining. Intelligent Control and Automation, Proceedings of the 4th World Congress on, Volume: 3. (2002) 2333–2337
14. Jaideep Srivastava, Robert Cooley, Mukund Deshpande, Pang-Ning Tan: Web Usage Mining: Discovery and Applications of Usage Patterns from Web Data. SIGKDD Explorations. (2000)
15. F. Masseglia, P. Poncelet and R. Cicchetti: WebTool: An Integrated Framework for Data Mining (PS). Proceedings of the 10th International Conference on Database and Expert Systems Applications (DEXA'99), Florence, Italy, LNCS, (1999) 892–901
16. De Bra and R.D.J. Post: Information retrieval in the World-Wide Web: making client-based searching feasible. Proceedings of the First International World-Wide Web Conference. (1994)
17. Ming-Syan Chen, Jong Soo Park, Philip S. Yu: Efficient Data Mining for Path Traversal Patterns. IEEE Transactions on Knowledge and Data Engineering, Vol 10, No, 2, 209–221.

Learning Semi Naïve Bayes Structures by Estimation of Distribution Algorithms

V. Robles[1], P. Larrañaga[2], J.M. Peña[1], M.S. Pérez[1], E. Menasalvas[1], and V. Herves[1]

[1] Department of Computer Architecture and Technology, Technical University of Madrid, Madrid, Spain, {vrobles,jmpena,mperez,emenasalvas}@fi.upm.es, vherves@datsi.fi.upm.es

[2] Department of Computer Science and Artificial Intelligence, University of the Basque Country, San Sebastián, Spain, ccplamup@si.ehu.es

Abstract. Recent work in supervised learning has shown that a surprisingly simple Bayesian classifier called naïve Bayes is competitive with state of the art classifiers. This simple approach stands from assumptions of conditional independence among features given the class. Improvements in accuracy of naïve Bayes has been demonstrated by a number of approaches, collectively named semi naïve Bayes classifiers. Semi naïve Bayes classifiers are usually based on the search of specific values or structures. The learning process of these classifiers is usually based on greedy search algorithms. In this paper we propose to learn these semi naïve Bayes structures through estimation of distribution algorithms, which are non-deterministic, stochastic heuristic search strategies. Experimental tests have been done with 21 data sets from the UCI repository.

Keywords. Naïve Bayes, semi Naïve Bayes, heuristic search, estimation of distributions algorithms.

1 Introduction

The naïve Bayes classifier [5,12] is a probabilistic method for classification. It can be used to determine the probability that an example belongs to a class given the values of the predictor variables. The naïve Bayes classifier guarantees optimal induction given a set of explicit assumptions [3]. However, it is known that some of these assumptions are not compliant in many induction scenarios, for instance, the condition of variable independence respecting to the class variable. Improvements of accuracy has been demonstrated by a number of approaches, collectively named semi naïve Bayes classifiers, which try to adjust the naïve Bayes to deal with a-priori unattended assumptions.

Previous semi naïve Bayes classifiers can be divided into three groups, depending on different pre/post-processing issues: (i) to manipulate the variables to be employed prior to application of naïve Bayes induction [16,18,23], (ii) to select subsets of the training examples prior to the application of naïve Bayes classification [14,17] and (iii) to correct the probabilities produced by the standard naïve Bayes [8,10,26].

The learning process of the semi naïve Bayes classifiers is usually based on greedy search algorithms. In this paper we propose to learn these semi naïve Bayes structures

Fernando Moura Pires, Salvador Abreu (Eds.): EPIA 2003, LNAI 2902, pp. 244–258, 2003.

through estimation of distribution algorithms, which are non-deterministic, stochastic heuristic search strategies.

All the algorithms evaluated in this paper are shown on table 1. In the left column we have the greedy based algorithms, which are: *Iterative Bayes* [10], Pazzani [23] and *Adjusted Probability naïve Bayes* (APNBC) [26]. In the right column we have their corresponding heuristic based algorithms, which are: *Interval Estimation Naïve Bayes* IENB [24], Pazzani-EDA and APNBC-EDA. These last two algorithms have been developed as part of the contribution of this paper.

Table 1. Evaluated algorithms

Greedy algorithm	Corresponding heuristic algorithm
Iterative Bayes [10]	Interval Estimation Naïve Bayes [24]
Pazzani [23]	Pazzani-EDA
APNBC [26]	APNBC-EDA

The outline of this paper is as follows: Section 2 presents the naïve Bayes classifier. Section 3 is a brief introduction to estimation of distribution algorithms. Section 4 presents the algorithms evaluated in this paper. Section 5 illustrates the experimental results obtained with the UCI datasets. To conclude, section 6 gives the conclusions and discusses further future work.

2 Naïve Bayes

The naïve Bayes classifier [5,12] is a probabilistic method for classification. It performs an approximate calculation of the probability that an example belongs to a class given the values of predictor variables. The simple naïve Bayes classifier is one of the most successful algorithms on many classification domains. In spite of its simplicity, it is shown to be competitive with other more complex approaches in several specific domains.

This classifier learns from training data the conditional probability of each variable X_k given the class label c. Classification is then done by applying Bayes rule to compute the probability of C given the particular instance of $X_1, \ldots, X_n$,

$$P(C = c|X_1 = x_1, \ldots, X_n = x_n)$$

Naïve Bayes is based on the assumption that variables are conditionally independent given the class. Therefore the posterior probability of the class variable is formulated as follows,

$$P(C = c|X_1 = x_1, \ldots, X_n = x_n) \propto P(C = c) \prod_{k=1}^{n} P(X_k = x_k|C = c) \quad (1)$$

This equation is highly appropriate for learning from data, since the probabilities $p_i = P(C = c_i)$ and $p_{k,r}^i = P(X_k = x_k^r|C = c_i)$ may be estimated from training data. The result of the classification is the class with highest posterior probability.

3 Estimation of Distributions Algorithms

3.1 Introduction

EDAs [22,20] are non-deterministic, stochastic heuristic search strategies that form part of the evolutionary computation approaches, where number of solutions or individuals are created every generation, evolving once and again until a satisfactory solution is achieved. In brief, the characteristic that differentiates most EDAs from other evolutionary search strategies such as GAs is that the evolution from a generation to the next one is done by estimating the probability distribution of the fittest individuals, and afterwards by sampling the induced model. This avoids the use of crossing or mutation operators, and the number of parameters that EDAs require is considerably reduced.

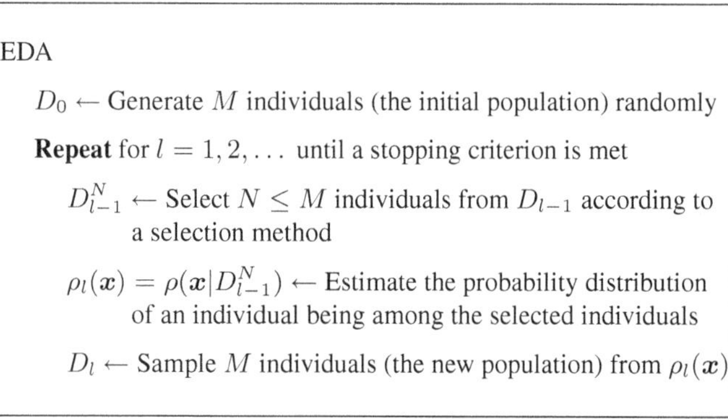

Fig. 1. Pseudocode for the EDA approach

In EDAs, individuals are not said to contain genes, but variables which dependencies have to be analyzed. Also, while in other heuristics from evolutionary computation the interrelations between the different variables representing the individuals are kept in mind implicitly (e.g. building block hypothesis), in EDAs the interrelations are explicitly expressed through the joint probability distribution associated with the individuals selected at each iteration. The task of estimating the joint probability distribution associated with the database of the selected individuals from the previous generation constitutes the hardest work to perform, as it requires the adaptation of methods to learn models from data developed in the domain of probabilistic graphical models.

Figure 1 shows the pseudocode of a generic EDA algorithm, in which we distinguish four main steps in this approach:

1. At the beginning, the first population D_0 of M individuals is generated, usually by assuming an uniform distribution (either discrete or continuous) on each variable, and evaluating each of the individuals.
2. Secondly, a number N ($N \leq M$) of individuals are selected, usually the fittest.
3. Thirdly, the n–dimensional probabilistic model that better expresses the interdependencies between the n variables is induced.

4. Next, the new population of M new individuals is obtained by simulating the probability distribution learnt in the previous step.

Steps 2, 3 and 4 are repeated until a stopping condition is verified. The most important step of this new paradigm is to find the interdependencies between the variables (step 3). This task will be performed using techniques from the field of probabilistic graphical models.

3.2 EDAs in Discrete Domains

In the particular case where every variable is discrete, the probabilistic graphical model is called *Bayesian network*.

All the EDAs are classified depending on the maximum number of dependencies between variables that they accept (maximum number of parents that any variable can have in the probabilistic graphical model):

- Without interdependencies
  The Univariate Marginal Distribution Algorithm (UMDA) [21] is the most representative example of this category.
- Pairwise dependencies
  An example of this category is the greedy algorithm called MIMIC (Mutual Information Maximization for Input Clustering) [2]. The main idea in MIMIC is to describe the true mass joint probability as closely as possible by using only one univariate marginal probability and $n - 1$ pairwise conditional probability functions.
- Multiple interdependencies
  EBNA (Estimation of Bayesian Network Algorithm) will be used as an example of this category. The EBNA approach firstly introduced in [6], where the authors use the Bayesian Information Criterion (BIC) as the score to evaluate the goodness of each structure found during the search.

3.3 EDAs in Continuous Domains

In the particular case where every variable in the individuals are continuous and follows a gaussian distribution, the probabilistic graphical model is called *Gaussian network*, and the EDA algorithms are named CEDAs *Continuous EDAs*.

Next, an analogous classification of continuous EDAs as for the discrete domain is done, in which these continuous EDAs are also classified depending on the number of dependencies they take into account:

- Without dependencies
  In this case, the joint density function is assumed to follow a n–dimensional normal distribution, and thus it is factorized as a product of n unidimensional and independent normal densities. UMDA_c [19] is an example of continuous EDAs.
- Bivariate dependencies
  MIMIC_c^G [19] is a representative example of this type of algorithms, which is basically an adaptation of the MIMIC algorithm [2] to the continuous domain.

- Multiple dependencies
  Algorithms in this section are approaches of EDAs for continuous domains in which there is no constraint in the learning of the density function every generation. EGNA$_{BGe}$ (Estimation of Gaussian Network Algorithm) [19] is a clear example of this category. The method used to find the Gaussian network structure is a Bayesian score+search. In EGNA$_{BGe}$ a local search is used to search for good structures.

4 Algorithms

In this section all the algorithms evaluated in the next section are described.

4.1 Iterative Bayes and Interval Estimation Naïve Bayes

The *Iterative Bayes* [10] algorithm begins with the a priori conditional probabilities obtained by naïve Bayes. Those probabilities are iteratively updated in order to improve the probability class distribution associated with each training example.

The iterative procedure uses a hill-climbing algorithm. At each iteration, all the examples in the training set are classified using the current conditional probabilities. The evaluation of the actual set of conditional probabilities is done by the next expression:

$$\frac{1}{n}\sum_{i=1}^{n}(1.0 - argmax_j\; p(C = c_j|X_1 = x_1, \ldots, X_n = x_n)) \tag{2}$$

where n represents the number of instances and j the number of classes. The iterative procedure proceeds while the evaluation function decreases till the maximum of 10 iterations.

To update the conditional probabilities, it is used the following heuristic:

1. The value of each conditional probability never goes below 0.01.
2. If an example is correctly classified then the increment is positive, otherwise it is negative. The value of the increment is $1.0 - p(Predict|X_1 = x_1, \ldots, X_n = x_n)/num.classes$. That is, the increment is a function of the confidence on predicting class $Predict$ and the number of classes.
3. For all attribute-values observed in the given example, the increment is added to all the entries for the predicted class and half of the increment is subtracted to the entries of all the other classes.

The conditional probabilities are incrementally updated each time a training example is presented. This implies that the order of the training examples could influence the final results.

Iterative Bayes tries to improve the conditional probabilities of naïve Bayes in an iterative way with a hill-climbing strategy. On the other hand, we have the algorithm *Interval Estimation naïve Bayes* (IENB) [24], that belongs to the approaches that correct the probabilities produced by the standard naïve Bayes.

In this approach, instead of calculating the point estimation of the conditional probabilities from data, as simple naïve Bayes makes, confidence intervals are calculated. After that, by searching for the best combination of values into these intervals, it is aimed to relieve the assumption of independence among variables the simple naïve Bayes makes. This search is carried out by EDAs and is guided by the accuracy of the classifiers.

There are three main important aspects in IENB algorithm:

1. **Calculation of Confidence Intervals**
   Given the dataset, the first step is to calculate the confidence intervals for each conditional probability and for each class probability. For the calculation of the intervals first the point estimations of these parameters must be computed.
   This way, each conditional probability $p^i_{k,r} = P(X_k = x^r_k | C = c_i)$, that has to be estimated from the dataset must be computed with the next confidence interval.

   For $k = 1, \ldots, n; i = 1, \ldots, r_0; r = 1, \ldots, r_k$ the next formula:

$$\left(\hat{p}^i_{k,r} - z_\alpha \sqrt{\frac{\hat{p}^i_{k,r}(1 - \hat{p}^i_{k,r})}{N_i}} ; \hat{p}^i_{k,r} + z_\alpha \sqrt{\frac{\hat{p}^i_{k,r}(1 - \hat{p}^i_{k,r})}{N_i}} \right) \tag{3}$$

   denotes the interval estimation for the conditional probabilities $p^i_{k,r}$, where,
   r_k denotes the possible values of variable X_k
   r_0 represents the possible values of the class
   $\hat{p}^i_{k,r}$ denotes the point estimation of the conditional probability $P(X_k = x^r_k | C = c_i)$
   z_α denotes the $(1 - \frac{\alpha}{2})$ percentil in the $\mathcal{N}(0,1)$ distribution
   N_i is the number of cases in dataset where $C = c_i$

   Also, in a similar way, the probabilities for the class values $p_i = P(C = c_i)$, are estimated with the next confidence interval,

$$\left(\hat{p}_i - z_\alpha \sqrt{\frac{\hat{p}_i(1 - \hat{p}_i)}{N}} ; \hat{p}_i + z_\alpha \sqrt{\frac{\hat{p}_i(1 - \hat{p}_i)}{N}} \right) \tag{4}$$

   where, $\hat{p}^i_i$ is the point estimation of the probability $P(C = c_i)$
   z_α is the $(1 - \frac{\alpha}{2})$ percentil in the $\mathcal{N}(0,1)$ distribution
   N is the number of cases in dataset

2. **Search Space Definition**
   Once the confidence intervals are estimated from the dataset, it is possible to generate as many naïve Bayes classifiers as needed. The parameters of these naïve Bayes classifiers must only be taken inside theirs corresponding confidence intervals.
   In this way, each naïve Bayes classifier is going to be represented with the next tupla of dimension $r_0(1 + \sum_{i=1}^{n} r_i)$

$$(p^*_1, \ldots, p^*_{r_0}, p^{*1}_{1,1}, \ldots, p^{*r_0}_{1,1}, \ldots, p^{*r_0}_{1,r_1}, \ldots, p^{*r_0}_{n,r_n}) \tag{5}$$

   where each component in the tupla p^* represents the selected value inside its corresponding confidence interval.

Thus, the search space for the heuristic optimization algorithm is composed of all the valid tuplas. A tupla is valid when it represents a valid naïve Bayes classifier. Formally,

$$\sum_{i=1}^{r_0} p_i^* = 1; \forall k \forall i \sum_{r=1}^{r_k} p_{k,r}^{*i} = 1 \tag{6}$$

Finally, each generated individual must be evaluated with a fitness function. This fitness function is based on the percentage of successful predictions on each dataset, which means that we are carrying out one wrapper approach.

3. **Heuristic Search for the Best Individual**
   Once the individuals and the search space are defined, one heuristic optimization algorithm is ran in order to find the best individual.

4.2 Pazzani and Pazzani-EDA

Pazzani [23] tries to improve the naïve Bayes classifier by searching for dependencies among attributes. He proposes two algorithms for detecting dependencies among attributes: *Forward Sequential Selection and Joining* (FSSJ) and *Backward Sequential Elimination and Joining*.

The FSSJ algorithm initializes the set of attributes to be used by the naïve Bayes classifier to the empty set. A naïve Bayes with no attributes simply classifies all examples to the most frequent class that occurs in the training data. Next, two operators are used to generate new classifiers:

1. To add a given attribute (not used by the current classifier) as a new attribute conditionally independent of all the others attributes (used by the classifier).
2. To join a given attribute (not used by the current classifier) with another possible attribute (currently used by the classifier).

At each step in the classifier, every addition and every joining of an unused attribute with a used attribute is considered and evaluated using leave-one-out on the training data. If no change makes an improvement, the current classifier is returned. Otherwise, the change that makes the most improvement is retained and the process of modifying the classifier is repeated.

The BSEJ algorithm initially creates a naïve Bayes classifier treating all attributes as conditionally independent. It uses two operators for considering new hypotheses:

1. To replace a given pair of attributes (used by the classifier) with a new attribute that joins the pair of attributes.
2. To delete one attribute (used by the classifier).

Like the FSSJ algorithm, the BSEJ algorithm considers all possible single-step operators, evaluates these using leave-one-out cross validation in the training data and permanently makes the change with the greatest improvement. If no changes results in an improvement, the current classifier is returned.

In this paper, we propose to make a heuristic search of the Pazzani structure with the target of maximize the percentage of successful predictions. We will do this heuristic search with EDAs.

The figure 2 contains two Pazzani structures and their corresponding individuals.

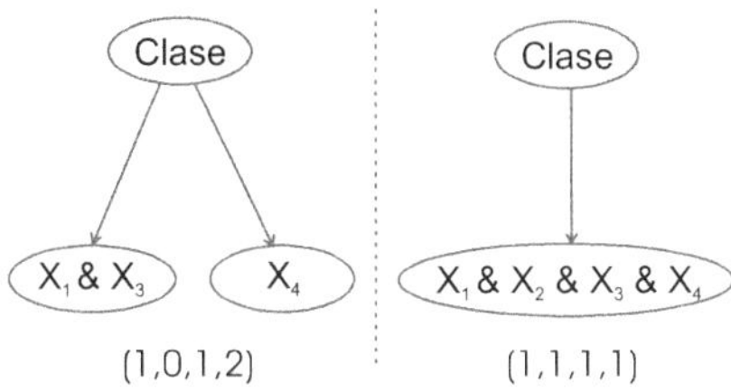

Fig. 2. Two Pazzani structures and their corresponding individuals

Thus, for a dataset with n attributes, individuals will have n genes, each one with a integer value between 0 an n. The value 0 represents that the corresponding attribute is not part of the Pazzani structure. A value between 1 an n means that the corresponding attribute belongs to that group in the Pazzani structure.

4.3 APNBC and APNBC-EDA

Adjusted probability naïve Bayes induction (APNBC) [26] is just a simple extension to the naïve Bayes classifier. A numeric weight is inferred for each class. During discriminative classification, the naïve Bayes probability of a class is multiplied by its weight to obtain an adjusted value. The lineal adjust proposed by the authors can be expressed as:

$$P(C = c_i|X_1 = x_1, \ldots, X_n = x_n) \propto w_i P(C = c_i) \prod_{k=1}^{n} P(X_k = x_k|C = c_i) \quad (7)$$

In a two class case, it is only necessary to find an adjustment value for one of the classes. This is because for any combination of adjustments a_1 and a_2 for the classes c_1 and c_2, the same effect will be obtained by setting the adjustment for c_1 to a_1/a_2 and the adjustment for c_2 to 1. In the multiple class case, the search for suitable adjustments is similar, setting one value to 1 and making a search for the rest of the other values. In this context, a simple hill-climbing search is employed. All adjustment values are initialized to 1, and a single adjustment that maximizes resubstitution accuracy is found. It is important to emphasize that the APNBC approach can achieve worsen results than naïve Bayes classifiers.

In the case of the use of CEDAs (*continuous EDAs*) for the search of the adjustment values, it is necessary to define the individuals format. In CEDAs, for each gen, we must define a maximum (real) value and a minimum (real) value. The search will be made between these values. In APNBC, for a dataset of n classes, we will use an individual with $n-1$ genes –the last class will be adjusted to 1– and each individual gen will have a

Table 2. Description of the data sets used in the experiments

Name	Attributes			Classes	Instances	
	Total	**Continuous**	**Nominal**		**Learning**	**Validation**
breast	10	10	-	2	699	-
chess	36	-	36	2	3196	-
cleve	13	6	7	2	303	-
corral	6	-	6	2	128	-
crx	15	6	9	2	692	-
flare	10	2	8	2	1066	-
german	20	7	13	2	1000	-
glass	9	9	-	7	214	-
glass2	9	9	-	2	163	-
hepatitis	19	6	13	2	155	-
iris	4	4	-	3	150	-
lymphography	18	3	15	4	148	-
m-of-n-3-7-10	10	-	10	2	300	1024
pima	8	8	-	2	768	-
satimage	36	36	-	6	6435	-
segment	19	19	-	7	2310	-
shuttle-small	9	9	-	7	5800	-
soybean-large	35	-	35	19	683	-
vehicle	18	18	-	4	846	-
vote	16	-	16	2	435	-
waveform-21	21	21	-	3	300	4700

value between 0 and 5. Besides, each individual will be validated with the *leave-one-out* method.

5 Experimentation Results

5.1 Datasets

Results are compared for 21 classical datasets –see table 2–, also used by other authors [9]. All the datasets belong to the UCI repository [1], with the exception of *m-of-n-3-7-10* and *corral*. These two artificial datasets, with irrelevant and correlated attributes, were designed to evaluate methods for feature subset selection [13].

5.2 Experimental Methodology

To estimate the prediction accuracy for each classifier our own implementation of a naïve Bayes classifier has been implemented. This implementation uses the Laplace correction for the point estimation of the conditional probabilities [11,13] and deals with missing values as recommended by [3].

However, our new algorithm does not handle continuous attributes. Thus, a discretization step with the method recommended in [4] has been performed using MLC++

Table 3. Experiment results for Iterative Bayes and IENB

Dataset	*NB*	*IENB*	*Improvement*	*Iterative Bayes Improvement*
breast	97.14	97.71 ± 0.00 †	0.57	-0.16
chess	87.92	93.31 ± 0.10 †	5.39	
cleve	83.82	86.29 ± 0.17 †	2.47	0.1
corral	84.37	93.70 ± 0.00 †	9.33	
crx	86.23	89.64 ± 0.10 †	3.41	
flare	80.86	82.69 ± 0.13 †	1.83	
german	75.40	81.57 ± 0.10 †	6.17	-0.05
glass	74.77	83.00 ± 0.20 †	8.23	-1.19
glass2	82.21	88.27 ± 0.00 †	6.06	
hepatitis	85.16	92.60 ± 0.34 †	7.44	1.41
iris	94.67	95.97 ± 0.00 †	1.30	1.4 †
lymphography	85.14	94.56 ± 0.00 †	9.42	
monf-3-7-10	86.33	95.31 ± 0.00 †	8.98	
pima	77.73	79.84 ± 0.09 †	2.11	
satimage	82.46	83.88 ± 0.32 †	1.42	3.59 †
segment	91.95	96.38 ± 0.08 †	4.43	1.5 †
shuttle-small	99.36	99.90 ± 0.00 †	0.54	
soybean-large	92.83	95.67 ± 0.10 †	2.84	
vehicle	61.47	71.16 ± 0.25 †	9.69	4.39 †
vote	90.11	95.07 ± 0.19 †	4.96	1.45 †
waveform-21	78.85	79.81 ± 0.10 †	0.96	

tools [15]. This discretization method is described by Ting in [25] that is a global variant of the method of Fayyad and Irani [7].

Nineteen of the datasets have no division between training and testing sets. On these datasets the results are obtained by a *leave-one-out* method inside of the heuristic optimization loop.

On the other hand, two out of these twenty one datasets include separated training and testing sets. For these cases, the heuristic optimization algorithm uses only the training set to tune the classifier. A *leave-one-out* validation is performed internally inside of the optimization loop, in order to find the best classifier. Once the best candidate is selected, it is validated using the testing set.

All the heuristic experiments were ran in a Athlon 1700+ with 256MB of RAM memory. The parameters used to run EDAs or CEDAs were: population size 500 individuals, selected individuals for learning 500, new individuals on each generation 1000, learning type $UMDA$ (*Univariate Marginal Distribution Algorithm*) or $UMDA_C$ (*UMDA continuous*) [21], depending on the algorithm, and elitism. Each experiment has been ran 10 times.

5.3 Results

This section present the experimental results of the evaluation of the different semi naïve Bayes approaches presented above.

Table 4. Experimental results for APNBC-EDA and APNBC

Dataset	*NB*	*APNBC-EDA*	*Eval.*	*Improvement*	*APNBC Improvement*
breast	97.14	97.57 ± 0.00 †	2600	0.43	-0.20
chess	87.92	88.14 ± 0.00 †	11300	0.22	
cleve	83.82	84.16 ± 0.00 †	7500	0.34	-1.00
corral	84.37	90.63 ± 0.00 †	1500	6.26	
crx	86.23	86.96 ± 0.00 †	10400	0.73	-0.20
flare	80.86	83.77 ± 0.00 †	4000	2.91	
german	75.40	75.90 ± 0.00 †	30600	0.50	
glass	74.77	79.44 ± 0.00 †	7500	4.67	
glass2	82.21	88.34 ± 0.00 †	2200	6.13	
hepatitis	85.16	88.39 ± 0.00 †	3300	3.23	
iris	94.67	96.00 ± 0.00 †	3200	1.33	0.60
lymphography	85.14	86.49 ± 0.00 †	3500	1.35	1.40
monf-3-7-10	86.33	98.24 ± 0.04 †	5500	11.91	
pima	77.73	79.43 ± 0.00 †	5500	1.70	-0.50
satimage	82.46	85.19 ± 0.00 †	25500	2.73	
segment	91.95	92.68 ± 0.00 †	11400	0.73	
shuttle-small	99.36	99.47 ± 0.00 †	6500	0.11	
soybean-large	92.83	93.70 ± 0.00 †	13700	0.87	-1.50
vehicle	61.47	65.25 ± 0.17 †	6600	3.78	
vote	90.11	90.57 ± 0.00 †	5400	0.46	
waveform-21	78.85	80.21 ± 0.05 †	3100	1.36	5.00

Iterative Bayes vs. IENB. Results for IENB and *Iterative Bayes* approaches are shown in table 3. In IENB the results are calculated for the 0.95 percentile ($z_\alpha = 1.96$). Columns in the table (as they appear from left to right) are: first, the value obtained by the simple naïve Bayes algorithm, second, the mean value ± standard deviation from IENB, third, the improvement respect to naïve Bayes (*IENB-Naïve Bayes*) and finally the improvement respect to naïve Bayes obtained by *Iterative Bayes* (*Iterative Bayes-Naïve Bayes*).

Results are really interesting. Respect to naïve Bayes, using IENB, we obtained an average improvement of 4.30%. Besides, although this is not always true, better improvements are obtained in the datasets with less number of cases, as the complexity of the problem is lower. *Iterative Bayes* is not so good, being better than IENB only in one dataset, *satimage*.

The non-parametric tests of Mann-Whitney were used to test the null hypothesis of the same distribution between these approaches and naïve Bayes. This task was done with the statistical package S.P.S.S. release 11.50. The results for the tests applied to all the algorithms are:

- Respect to naïve Bayes algorithm:
  - Naïve Bayes vs. IENB. Fitness value: $p < 0.001$ for all datasets.
  - Naïve Bayes vs. Iterative Bayes. Fitness value: $p < 0.001$ only in 5 of 10 datasets.

Table 5. Experimental results for Pazzani FSSJ and BSEJ algorithms

			FSSJ				*BSEJ*	
Dataset	*FSSJ*	*Eval.*	*(Att,Groups)*	*Impr*	*BSEJ*	*Eval.*	*(Att,Groups)*	*Impr*
breast	97.42	80	(3 , 2)	0.28	97.56	200	(10 , 9)	0.42
chess	94.33	396	(5 , 1)	6.41	97.06	14256	(35 , 26)	9.14
cleve	85.10	169	(4 , 3)	1.28	85.43	676	(12 , 10)	1.61
corral	74.80	18	(1 , 1)	-9.57	93.70	108	(6 , 4)	9.33
crx	86.79	195	(5 , 2)	0.56	88.10	1125	(14 , 11)	1.87
flare	84.04	90	(3 , 2)	3.18	84.04	500	(6 , 6)	3.18
german	77.18	500	(7 , 3)	1.78	77.68	2400	(19 , 15)	2.28
glass	76.53	153	(5 , 3)	1.76	76.53	162	(9 , 8)	1.76
glass2	87.04	99	(4 , 2)	4.83	87.04	162	(9 , 8)	4.83
hepatitis	91.56	456	(7 , 3)	6.40	88.96	1083	(18 , 17)	3.80
iris	95.97	12	(1 , 1)	1.30	95.97	32	(3 , 3)	1.30
lymphography	84.35	252	(4 , 3)	-0.79	90.48	972	(18 , 16)	5.34
monf-3-7-10	77.32	30	(1 , 1)	-9.01	88.27	200	(9 , 9)	1.94
pima	79.79	72	(4 , 1)	2.06	79.79	192	(6 , 6)	2.06
satimage	86.17	828	(7 , 3)	3.71	86.84	12914	(36 , 22)	4.38
segment	96.32	589	(7 , 4)	4.37	95.89	3971	(18 , 10)	3.94
shuttle-small	99.74	72	(3 , 2)	0.38	99.90	324	(9 , 6)	0.54
soybean-large	93.40	3010	(13 , 8)	0.57	94.57	7350	(34 , 30)	1.74
vehicle	70.77	162	(4 , 1)	9.30	72.66	3240	(17 , 9)	11.19
vote	96.77	128	(3 , 2)	6.66	94.47	1792	(15 , 10)	4.36
waveform-21	69.65	189	(4 , 1)	-9.20	79.70	89	(21 , 19)	0.85

These results show that the differences between naïve Bayes and Interval Estimation naïve Bayes are significant in all the datasets, meaning that the behavior of selecting naïve Bayes or IENB is very different. On the other hand, results for Iterative Bayes are statistically significant only in 5 of 10 datasets.

The symbols † in the table show that the result is statistically significant respect to naïve Bayes.

APNBC vs. APNBC-EDA. The experimental results of APNBC –extracted from the original paper [26]– and the results of APNBC-EDA are shown on table 4. The column contents are (from left to right): first, the percentage of correct classification using naïve Bayes; second mean and standard deviation of classification accuracy using APNBC-EDA; third, average number of evaluations to reach the solution; fourth, improvement compared to naïve Bayes classifier; fifth and last columns represent the classifier accuracy and solution improvement using either APNBC-EDA or standard APNBC (the last one has been taken from the original source mentioned above).

There are only eight out of the twenty-one cases with results for APNBC algorithm. In six of these problems APNBC-EDA clearly outperforms APNBC, in one (*lymphography*) results are almost the same. In *waveform-21* APNBC improves 5,00% while APNBC-EDA only reaches 1,36%.

It is remarkable to emphasize that in the eight datasets APNBC-EDA gets a mean improvement of 1.01%, and APNBC only achieves 0.45%. Considering all the twenty-

Table 6. Experimental results for Pazzani-EDA

Dataset	*Pazzani-EDA*	*Eval.*	*(Att,Groups)*	*Impr*
breast	97.82 ± 0.06 †	20650	(10 , 7)	0.68
chess	97.93 ± 0.24 †	44900	(26 , 15)	10.01
cleve	86.98 ± 1.18 †	49600	(9 , 5)	3.16
corral	100.00 ± 0.00 †	7400	(5 , 3)	15.63
crx	89.23 ± 0.07 †	80200	(12 , 7)	3.00
flare	84.04 ± 0.00	9700	(5 , 4)	3.18
german	78.41 ± 0.06 †	90900	(17 , 11)	3.01
glass	77.93 ± 0.00 †	40200	(7 , 5)	3.16
glass2	87.04 ± 0.00	7700	(6 , 5)	4.83
hepatitis	93.64 ± 0.29 †	55800	(11 , 7)	8.48
iris	95.97 ± 0.00	3600	(1 , 1)	1.30
lymphography	93.88 ± 0.00 †	48900	(15 , 7)	8.74
monf-3-7-10	100.00 ± 0.00 †	39600	(8 , 2)	13.67
pima	79.82 ± 0.28	7300	(7 , 4)	2.09
satimage	86.94 ± 0.12	105300	(12 , 7)	4.48
segment	96.15 ± 0.06 †	24300	(14 , 7)	4.20
shuttle-small	99.90 ± 0.00	30200	(7 , 5)	0.54
soybean-large	95.67 ± 0.17 †	32	(20 , 15)	2.84
vehicle	76.50 ± 0.32 †	61300	(12 , 7)	15.03
vote	96.77 ± 0.13 †	30200	(7 , 4)	6.66
waveform-21	79.72 ± 0.07 †	89200	(17 , 9)	0.87

one problems APNBC-EDA performs an average of 2.46% better than naïve Bayes. It is very significative that APNBC only gets better accuracy than naïve Bayes in three out of the eight cases experimented by [26], APNBC-EDA improves in all of the datasets. These results show a clear difference for APNBC-EDA against standard APNBC.

As well as in the previous experimentation a non-parametric Mann-Whitney test has been performed to evaluate the significance of the improvements. The values obtained are:

- Respect to naïve Bayes algorithm:
  - Naïve Bayes vs. APNBC-EDA. Fitness value: $p < 0.001$ for all datasets.

These values show a significative difference between naïve Bayes and APNBC-EDA results for all the datasets.

Pazzani (FSSJ/BSEJ) vs. Pazzani-EDA. The experimental results achieved by the greedy algorithms FSSJ and BSEJ are presented on table 5. The four columns on the left-hand side show the results of FSSJ and the four on the right-hand side show the results of BSEJ. Results of Pazzani-EDA algorithm are shown on table 6. Each of the algorithms have the following values: percentage of instances classified correctly, number of necessary evaluations, number of selected attributes and groups of attributes; and the improvement comparing to naïve Bayes.

Considering all the datasets, FSSJ algorithm shows an average improvement of 1.25% (comparing to naïve Bayes), BSEJ 3.61% and Pazzani-EDA improves 5.51%.

Labelled with the symbol † on table 6 in 15 of the 21 datasets the difference between Pazzani-BSEJ and Pazzani-EDA is statistically significative.

As a summary, another benefit in using heuristic search with EDAs is that Pazzani structures are simpler: less number of attributes (recall, Pazzani performs an attribute selection strategy) and few groups of attributes. BSEJ uses 15 attributes and 12 groups (in average), Pazzani-EDA uses only 12 attributes and 7 groups.

6 Conclusion and Further Work

The experimental results presented on this paper show a clear advantage in the use of heuristical search methods, rather than greedy approaches, as an optimization tool for semi naïve Bayes classifiers.

The better improvements have been achieve using Pazzani-EDA (5.50%) and IENB (4.65%). Both strategies can be combined in the following way: (a) looking for the best Pazzani structure and (b) tuning the probabilities of each group using the IENB approach.

The only drawback of this approach is the increment of the number of tentative naïve Bayes classifier required to find the optimal parameters. For large problems with significative evaluation times each of the individuals could take several seconds to be computed. As a solution for this problem a parallel implementation of these algorithms is an open issue we are working on.

References

1. C. L. Blake and C. J. Merz. UCI repository of machine learning databases. http://www.ics.uci.edu/~mlearn/, 1998.
2. J. S. De Bonet, C. L. Isbell, and P. Viola. MIMIC: Finding optima by estimating probability densities. *Advances in Neural Information Processing Systems*, Vol. 9, 1997.
3. P. Domingos and M. Pazzani. Beyond independence: conditions for the optimality of the simple Bayesian classifier. In *Proceedings of the 13th International Conference on Machine Learning*, pages 105–112, 1996.
4. J. Dougherty, R. Kohavi, and M. Sahami. Supervised and unsupervised discretization of continuous features. In *Proceedings of the 12th International Conference on Machine Learning*, pages 194–202, 1995.
5. R. Duda and P. Hart. *Pattern Classification and Scene Analysis*. John Wiley and Sons, 1973.
6. R. Etxeberria and P. Larrañaga. Global optimization with Bayesian networks. In *II Symposium on Artificial Intelligence. CIMAF99. Special Session on Distributions and Evolutionary Optimization*, pages 332–339, 1999.
7. U. Fayyad and K. Irani. Multi-interval discretization of continuous-valued attributes for classification learning. In *Proceedings of the 13th International Conference on Artificial Intelligence*, pages 1022–1027, 1993.
8. J.T.A.S. Ferreira, D.G.T. Denison, and D.J. Hand. Weighted naïve Bayes modelling for data mining. Technical report, Deparment of Mathematics, Imperial College, May 2001.
9. N. Friedman, D. Geiger, and D.M. Goldszmidt. Bayesian network classifiers. *Machine Learning*, 29(2-3):131–163, 1997.
10. J. Gama. Iterative Bayes. *Intelligent Data Analysis*, 4:475–488, 2000.
11. I.J. Good. *The Estimation of Probabilities: An Essay on Modern Bayesian Methods*. MIT Press, 1965.

12. D.J. Hand and K. Yu. Idiot's Bayes - not so stupid after all? *International Statistical Review*, 69(3):385–398, 2001.
13. J. Kohavi, B. Becker, and D. Sommerfield. Improving simple Bayes. Technical report, Data Mining and Visualization Group, Silicon Graphics, 1997.
14. R. Kohavi. Scaling up the accuracy of naïve-Bayes classifiers: a decision-tree hybrid. In *Proceedings of the Second International Conference on Knowledge Discovery and Data Mining*, pages 202–207, 1996.
15. R. Kohavi, G. John, R. Long, D. Manley, and K.Pfleger. MLC++: A machine learning library in C++. *Tools with Artificial Intelligence. IEEE Computer Society Press*, pages 740–743, 1994.
16. I. Kononenko. Semi-naïve Bayesian classifier. In *Sixth European Working Session on Learning*, pages 206–219, 1991.
17. P. Langley. Induction of recursive Bayesian classifiers. In *European Conference on Machine Learning. Berlin: Springer-Verlag*, pages 153–164, 1993.
18. P. Langley and S. Sage. Induction of selective Bayesian classifiers. In Morgan Kaufmann, editor, *Proceedings of the Tenth Conference on Uncertainty in Artificial Intelligence*, pages 399–406, Seattle, WA, 1994.
19. P. Larrañaga, R. Etxeberria, J.A. Lozano, and J.M. Peña. Optimization in continuous domains by learning and simulation of gaussian networks. In *Proceedings of the Workshop in Optimization by Building and Using Probabilistic Models. A Workshop within the 2000 Genetic and Evolutionary Computation Conference, GECCO 2000*, pages 201–204, 2000. Las Vegas, Nevada, USA.
20. P. Larrañaga and J. A. Lozano. *Estimation of Distribution Algorithms: A New Tool for Evolutionary Computation.* Kluwer Academic Publisher, 2001.
21. H. Mühlenbein. The equation for response to selection and its use for prediction. *Evolutionary Computation*, 5:303–346, 1998.
22. H. Mühlenbein and G. Paaß. From recombination of genes to the estimation of distributions I. Binary parameters. In *Lecture Notes in Computer Science 1411: Parallel Problem Solving from Nature - PPSN IV*, pages 178–187, 1996.
23. M. Pazzani. Searching for dependencies in Bayesian classifiers. In *Proceedings of the Fifth International Workshop on Artificial Intelligence and Statistics*, pages 239–248, 1996.
24. V. Robles, P. Larrañaga, J.M. Peña, E. Menasalvas, and M.S. Pérez. Interval Estimation Naïve Bayes. In *Lecture Notes in Computer Science*, 2003.
25. K.M. Ting. Discretization of continuous-valued attributes and instance-based learning. Technical Report 491, University of Sydney, 1994.
26. G.I. Webb and M.J. Pazzani. Adjusted probability naive Bayesian induction. In *Proceedings of the 11th Australian Joint Conference on Artificial Intelligence*, pages 285–295, 1998.

Learning Action Theories with Ramifications

David Lorenzo

Computer Science Dept., Univ. Coruña
15071 A Coruña (Spain)
lorenzo@dc.fi.udc.es

Abstract. A logic programming formalization of action domains has been well-studied and some work exists on the combination with learning methods. We extend previous work to deal with the indirect effects of actions and to solve the problems derived from cyclic dependences.

1 Introduction

Machine Learning methods have been used to learn the domain specific knowledge from observed time traces of property values of an existing dynamic system. In most cases the inferred model corresponds to a set of STRIPS-like operators. Furthermore, these approaches force the explicit representation of all the effects of an action as direct effects, producing the so-called *Ramification problem*, which makes encodings based on STRIPS operators increasingly complex. We focus on theories of actions based on logic programming since the representation of properties of actions is easier with logic programs due to the non-monotonic character of negation as failure. The system *LRAC* [1] learns action theories in the form of logic programs under the stable models semantics based on a narrative-based implementation of the Situation Calculus, where situations are represented by non-negative integers (0 denotes the initial situation). So-called *effect axioms* are clauses of the form $caused(f, v, s) \leftarrow happens(a, s), \pi$ where the *holds/2* literals in π are only of the form $[\neg]holds(f', s\text{-}1)$. We have the following predicates:

- $caused(F, V, T)$: fluent F is caused to have value V (true or false) at time T.
- $holds(F, T)$: fluent F holds at time T.
- $happens(A, T)$: action A occurs at time T.

Observations are in the form of *narratives* of actions, consisting of the values of fluents at the initial situation represented with the predicate *holds/2*, the actions executed and the effects produced, represented with the predicate *happens/2* and *caused/3* respectively. Multiple narratives are provided as separate models, one for each narrative. This corresponds to the "learning from interpretations" paradigm of ILP where examples consist of multiple interpretations and not just one interpretation as it is usual in ILP. *LRAC* includes the universal inertia axiom as part of the input data so that observations need only be explicitly given for the effects of actions, whereas the inertia axiom propagates non-affected truth values from one situation to the next one. Once narratives are encoded this way, *LRAC* applies conventional ILP methods and *extensional coverage* testing that consists of using the (ground) positive examples for the coverage testing

Fernando Moura Pires, Salvador Abreu (Eds.): EPIA 2003, LNAI 2902, pp. 259–263, 2003.

instead of the rules previously learned. Despite the learned theory is tested differently from the way in which it is effectively used, the learned theory is also a solution for entailment under the stable models semantics provided the input narratives are completely specified.

2 Learning Ramifications of Actions

Ramification is the problem of dealing, not just with the direct effects of an action, but also with the cascade of changes brought about by events triggered by the direct effects. In most cases, it is very difficult to describe such effects by using a condition on the starting state from which the action is executed, which makes descriptions increasingly complex and consequently harder to learn since they need to anticipate the ramifications of the executed action, Most solutions that have been proposed for the ramification problem require *effect axioms* to specify the most significant effects of an action and rely on *ramification constraints* for specifying additional changes that are due to the action. A ramification constraint is a clause $caused(f, v, s) \leftarrow \pi$ where the *holds/2* literals in π are only of the form $[\neg]Holds(f', s)$. Ramification constraints represent that some effects are derived from other effects not matter the actions that are executed.

Since *LRAC* can now learn two types of axioms, it uses a compression measure to determine whether a fluent should be learned as a direct or an indirect effect. The insight is that ramification constraints make programs sensibly shorter, given that they may subsume the effect axioms of several actions. This has a positive influence in their learnability as the difficulty of learning a logic program is very much related to its length. A summary of results for some representative domains are shown in table 1. The fourth column shows the number of narratives and length of each narrative, and the fifth column shows the number of effect axioms and ramification constraints. Though these domains are toy-problems, they are very similar to real-life problems in the sense that essentially the same representational problems arise.

Table 1. Summary of training data for some domains

Domain	actions	fluents	examples	rules	time	runs	nodes/run
blocks world	1	2	(10,20)	(4,2)	209.12	6	662.5
blocks world (rec)	2	3	(18,9)	(5,3)	363.68	9	1256.33
hanoi towers	1	2	(7,6)	(2,2)	69.47	4	1017.25
relay circuit	1	2	(10,4)	(6,7)	0.32	13	11.30
double relay circuit	1	2	(10,5)	(20,7)	55.97	28	209.53
logistics (AIPS)	6	2	(10,20)	(6,3)	267.62	9	13.55
robot (AIPS)	3	3	(24,10)	(5,2)	6.79	8	188.75
grid (AIPS)	4	3	(4,19)	(4,3)	61.58	7	56.14
gripper (AIPS)	3	4	(2,27)	(5,3)	7.55	8	11.25
rocket (AIPS)	3	3	(2,17)	(5,2)	8.86	7	64.14
shakey world	8	3	(4,16)	(12,3)	648.64	24	419.33
mystery (AIPS)	3	4	(3,20)	(8,4)	845.91	15	230.2
bulldozer (AIPS)	4	3	(6,8)	(11,3)	170.17	14	830.642
sokoban (AIPS)	2	2	(2,15)	(4,4)	175.39	14	125.71

In all cases, the introduction of ramification constraints produced a smaller theory (and more comprehensible). Without them, *LRAC* learns theories that are unnecessarily complex and thereby also less reliable and accurate or at least require additional examples and higher training times. We will now comment on the results obtained in some well-known domains focusing on how *LRAC* managed the indirect effects of actions.

In most domains *LRAC* learned ramification constraints only for the negative value of predicates. For instance, the negative value of *clear*/1 and the negative value of *on*/2 in the blocks world can be indirectly inferred from the positive value of *on*/2 (Fig. 1).

The ramification constraint for the negative value of *on*/2 represents that a block cannot be at two locations. It produces a shorter theory since otherwise two effect axioms would be needed to deal separately with the cases where a block is moved onto other block or onto the table. *LRAC* did not learn another possible constraints, e.g., $clear(x) \supset \neg on(y, x)$, because it does not cover those examples where x represents the table. The ramification constraint for the negative value of *clear*/1 represents that a block is not clear provided another block is stacked on it. This constraint does not produce a benefit as to coverage, however, since it produces a smaller theory. Actually the positive value of *clear*/2 is also an indirect effect ($\neg on(y, x) \supset clear(x)$), however, *LRAC* learned two effect axioms because of the limited quantification of logic programs (variable y is universally quantified).

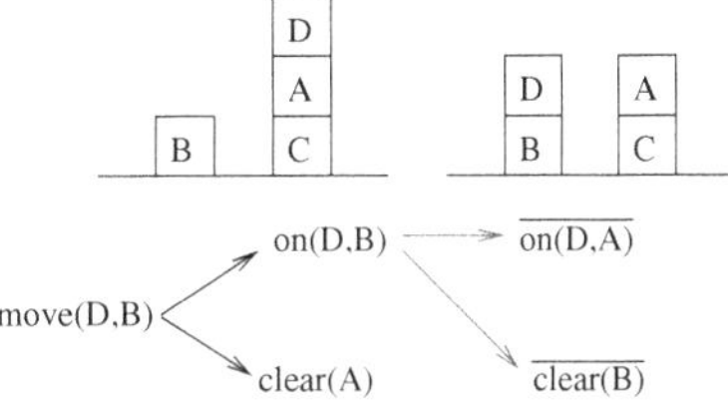

Fig. 1. The blocks world

We considered a modified scenario of the blocks world by adding a predicate *at*/2 to represent the current room of a block and the action *push*/2 so that blocks can be pushed to a different room. This domain illustrates the ability to learn *recursive* effects since a stack of blocks can be pushed to a different room. One of the ramification constraints learned by *LRAC* asserts that the current room of a block is the room of the block on which it is stacked, so that the block on the ground determines the room of the stack of blocks above it. This ramification constraint covers also those cases where the current room of a block changes (indirectly) when it is stacked onto another block that is in a different room, hence, the ramification constraint replaces also the corresponding effect axiom for *move*/2. In this domain, handling indirect effects is strictly needed for achieving generalization, given that the number of affected blocks *varies at each situation*. Note that no complete set of effect axioms can be found for action *push*/2, otherwise we should have as many effect axioms as the number of blocks piled in the highest tower.

Let us consider the circuit of Fig. 2. This circuit is used as a benchmark domain for the ramification problem in the literature. There is only a type of action in this domain that toggles the position of switches. *light* and *relay* are considered indirect effects so that the *relay* is active whenever both sw_1 and sw_3 hold simultaneously. Similarly for *light* with sw_1 and sw_2.

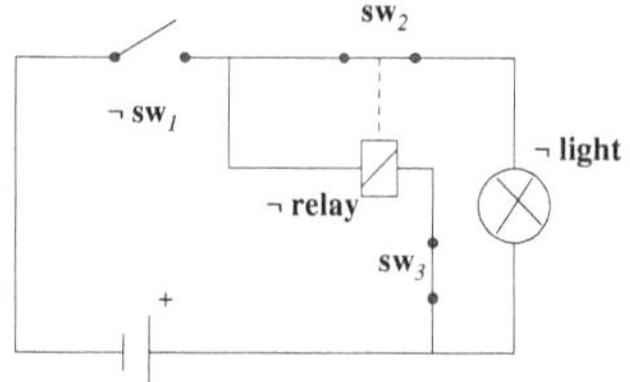

Fig. 2. Relay circuit

The ramification constraint for the positive value of *relay* (resp. *light*) produces a significantly shorter theory, otherwise two effect axioms would be needed since *relay* is affected by the actions that affect sw_1 and sw_3. The positive value of sw_2 is always a direct effect of $toggle(sw_2)$, whereas the negative value of sw_2 is in some cases a direct effect of $toggle(sw_2)$ and in other cases an indirect effect of $toggle(sw_1)$ and $toggle(sw_3)$. In the latter case, *LRAC* learned a ramification constraint ($relay \supset \overline{sw_2}$) where the relay opens sw_2 when activated through $toggle(sw_1)$ and $toggle(sw_3)$. On the other hand, *LRAC* did not learn other possible (and correct) constraints like $light \supset sw_1$ which do not correspond to a causal relationship of the circuit, since that constraint does not cover those examples where sw_1 is closed when sw_2 was open[1]). And similarly for $relay \supset sw_1$ and so on.

3 Cyclic Ramifications

Programs learned by *LRAC* are guaranteed to have a finite recursion, however, care must be taken to ensure that the addition of ramification constraints does not cause a *non-finite recursion*[2], where fluents may use one another in their definitions. *LRAC* explicitly disregards cyclic dependences so that the resultant program is still acyclic. Cycle detection requires the computation of the stable model of $B \cup H$ for each partial theory H and for each narrative. To avoid the cost of such computation we consider the graph of ground recursive dependences between the already covered positive examples. After each new clause is learned, *LRAC* looks for cycles in this graph. If a cycle is identified, the last clause that was learned is removed and remembered to avoid that *LRAC* goes into a loop of continuously generating and retracting the same clause and the learning process is resumed. Then *LRAC* can learn an alternative definition. In extreme cases, *LRAC* will learn only effect axioms since these do not introduce new cycles.

Let us consider the circuit of Fig. 3. According to the description found in the literature, we have the following state constraints:

$$\begin{array}{llll} s_1 \equiv re_1 & re_1 \supset s_2 & li \equiv s_3 & li_2 \equiv s_2, s_2' \\ s_2 \equiv re_2 & re_2 \supset s_3 & li_1 \equiv s_1, s_1' & li_3 \equiv s_3, s_3' \end{array}$$

The cycles above do not arise in practice provided additional domain-specific knowledge called *influence information* of how fluents may affect each other is available.

However, without such information, *LRAC* learned alternative definitions for some fluents. In some cases the use of effect axioms and ramification constraints achieved the same compression and *LRAC* is biased to prefer effect axioms to

[1] In those situations, there are no simultaneous changes.

[2] Under the stable models semantics, such a cycle produces an undefined value for the predicates involved.

minimize the possibility of cycles. For instance, *LRAC* learned two effect axioms for the positive value of s_2 instead of one effect axiom and the ramification constraint $re_1 \supset s_2$, since they achieved the same compression. Similarly, re_1 is actually a derived effect of s_1 and however *LRAC* learned effect axioms for both fluents. On the other hand, relays re_1 and re_2 in case of activation attract the switches located above (s_2 and s_3 respectively). However, since s_2 and re_2 (resp. s_3 and li) are apparently equivalent, *LRAC* learned the cycles $s_3 \equiv li$ and $s_2 \equiv re_2$ which were broken by learning an alternative definition for s_2 and s_3. Note that it would be also possible to learn an alternative definition for re_2 and li whereas s_2 and s_3 would be considered indirect effects, which, however, do not correspond to the causal relationships of the domain. However, *LRAC* learned the correct description for s_3 since there are more actions affecting it, so that the constraint $re_2 \supset s_3$ subsumes the corresponding effect axioms for $toggle(s_1)$ and $toggle(s_2)$. Despite these differences, the resulting theory is still a correct description of the domain[3].

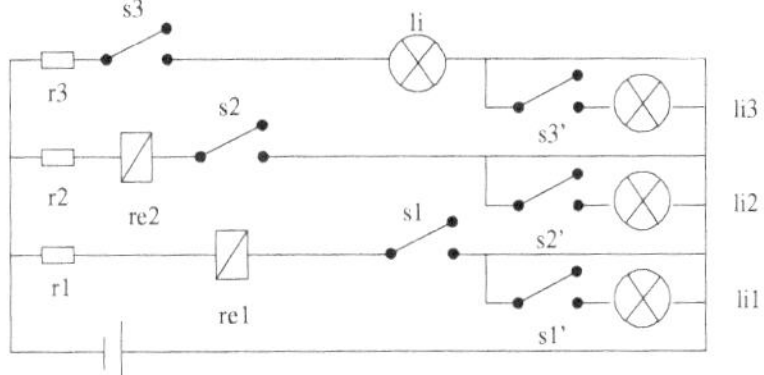

Fig. 3. Double relay circuit

There are, however, some perfectly normal, well-behaved physical systems where cyclic definitions can appear in the description. Let us consider two connected gear wheels with actions *start* and *stop* for each wheel that make a wheel start (resp. stop) turning. In this example, every wheel has an action associated, such that any force causing a wheel to start or stop turning propagates to the other wheel (and vic.). *LRAC* learned 4 ramification constraints where every wheel is both an effect and a cause instead of the 8 effect axioms that would be needed. *LRAC* broke the cycles by retracting 2 ramification constraints and learning the corresponding effect axioms for one of the wheels. As a result $turn(wheel_1)$ is considered always a direct effect and $turn(wheel_2)$ always as an indirect effect. Other solutions may be possible depending on the order at which *LRAC* learns the ramification constraints but none includes the positive cycle. There is a correct description (including the 4 ramification constraints) where $turn(wheel_1)$ is a direct effect of $start(wheel_1)$ and an indirect effect of $start(wheel_2)$ –and similarly for $turn(wheel_2)$. However, it provides no gain in terms of compression, on the contrary, the solution with the cycle requires 4 effect axioms apart from the 4 ramification constraints, whereas the one learned by *LRAC* includes 4 effect axioms and 2 ramification constraints. However, it is still unclear to us if allowing cycles leads to a better theory in terms of compression.

References

1. D. Lorenzo. Learning causal action theories from narratives of actions. In S. Benferhat and E. Giunchiglia, editors, *Proceedings of the 9th International Workshop on Non-monotonic Reasoning*, pages 349–355, 2002.

[3] In this domain, the difference in the size of the theory when only direct effects are considered is notable, specially for s_3 and li_3 which are in the highest level in the dependency graph.

Mining Low Dimensionality Data Streams of Continuous Attributes

Francisco J. Ferrer-Troyano, Jesús S. Aguilar-Ruiz, and José C. Riquelme

Department of Computer Science, University of Seville
Avenida Reina Mercedes s/n, 41012 Seville, Spain
{ferrer, aguilar, riquelme}@lsi.us.es

Abstract. This paper presents an incremental and scalable learning algorithm in order to mine numeric, low dimensionality, high–cardinality, time–changing data streams. Within the Supervised Learning field, our approach, named SCALLOP, provides a set of decision rules whose size is very near to the number of concepts to be extracted. Experimental results with synthetic databases of different complexity degrees show a good performance from streams of data received at a rapid rate, whose label distribution may not be stationary in time.

Keywords: Classification, decision rules, incremental learning, scalable learning algorithms, data streams.

1 Introduction

In recent years, designing scaling–up and scalable algorithms has consolidated as an important challenge within data mining research community. Memory and time limitations compel make such system to give an approximate answer from few scans (ideally only one) assuring that both result and performance are not adversely affected by the order of the examples. In addition, when the distribution is not stationary (records are collected over months), algorithms based on data partitioning techniques (instance/feature sampling) are oversensitive to both underfitting and overfitting. Many scalable learning algorithms are based on decision trees, modelling the whole search space hierarchically as disjointed hypercubes. The large and complex trees given by these systems cast doubts on its capabilities as suitable knowledge representation due to the user need to explore paths of several dozen of levels to know interesting patterns. In addition, mining time–changing data streams may involve to check an *out–of–date* sub–tree, increasing the computational cost. A common approach in these systems consists in repeatedly applying the learner to a sliding window of w examples. The main goal in these systems is then to find the value for w that optimizes the performance as a function of the input data. So interactive and user–controlled data mining systems are becoming increasingly developed. Such approaches trade accuracy for simplicity providing more meaningful and understandable models.

This paper introduces a scalable classification algorithm named SCALLOP (SCALabLe classification algorithm tO learning Patterns) that provides a model

Fernando Moura Pires, Salvador Abreu (Eds.): EPIA 2003, LNAI 2902, pp. 264–278, 2003.

on demand from several user–defined parameters. Using a window of size 1, our approach obtains hypercubic decision rules sorted in a relevance order according to the regions whose characteristics interest the user. In the next sections we describe our approach and discuss its major drawbacks. Next we present experimental results on synthetic data of different degrees of complexity which show its usefulness and effectiveness to mine numerical, low–dimensionality, high–speed, time–changing data steams.

2 Related Work

There has been many recent works on mining very large databases and data streams. Domingos and Hulten introduce VFDT [7] and CVFDT [14] which build a decision tree using constant time and memory per example. Their approach is based on Hoeffding bounds, which guarantee that the output is asymptotically nearly identical to that given by a batch conventional learner from enough examples. They also apply Hoeffding's inequalities to build a scaling–up method that is applicable to any induction algorithm based on discrete search [15]. Decision tree based classifiers are also Gehrke et al.'s BOAT [10] and Agrawal et al.'s SPRINT [20]. BOAT obtains an approximate tree through a subsample of fixed size. Previous approaches based on subsampling methods are also proposed by Catlett [4]. In contrast, SPRINT [20] is disk–based learner that use all the examples and focus on optimizing sequential access to disk.

Garofalakis et al. [17,9] propose several algorithms for building decision trees under size and accuracy constraints in order to give an meaningful model for the user. Dobra and Gehrke's SECRET [6] is a regression tree based algorithm providing a more easy to interpret output than that given by decision trees. SECRET uses EM clustering algorithm for Gaussian mixtures to generate leaves as linear transformation from found close clusters.

There is also large literature on scaling–up algorithms [19,11,3], model maintenance [8,16,5,2], and scalable clustering algorithms [18,12,13,21].

3 The SCALLOP Algorithm

Classification is generally defined as follows. An input finite data set of training examples is given. Every training example is a pair $e = (x, y)$ where x is a vector of m attribute values (each of which may be numeric or symbolic) and y is a class discrete value named label. The goal is to obtain a model $y = f(x)$ to classify or decide the label for new non–labelled test examples named queries. Henceforth, the next notation is used to describe our approach. Let m be the number of continuous attributes. Let $Y = \{y_1, \ldots, y_z\}$ be the set of class labels. Let $e_i = (x_i, y_i)$ be the ith training example to be read, where x_i is a normalized vector in $\mathcal{R}^m$ and y_i is a discrete value in Y. SCALLOP builds a model formed by z sets of decision rules, one set per label.

In order to achieve a balanced performance between the running time and the classification accuracy, each rule R is a data structure that comprises twelve elements:

- Definition limits I: set of m closed intervals $[I_{jl}, I_{ju}]$, one per numerical attribute ($j \in \{1, \ldots, m\}$). l denotes lower bound and u upper bound.
- Centroid C: vector in $\mathcal{R}^m$ generated as weighted mean from the examples covered by R.
- Central vector N: vector of the nearest example to C from all those examples covered by R.
- Delimiters D: set of the most distant β vector to each other from all examples covered by R. β is an user–defined parameter.
- Markers M: set of the nearest β examples to N that have been covered by R. M, D, and C are used to modify a wrong rule.
- Overlapping rules O: set of links that reference others rules with which R shares a sub–region belonging to the region defined by I. Only rules belonging to the same set can make non-empty intersections among themselves.
- Growth limits B: set of m open intervals (B_{jl}, B_{ju}) (one per numerical attribute) so that: $B_{jl} < I_{jl} \leq I_{ju} < B_{ju}$; $\forall j \in [1, m]$. These limits play an important role since by knowing where a rule can extend to, the algorithm makes stable the model faster. Furthermore, this information is very helpful to classify new queries with few rules by voting.
- s is the support or number of examples covered by R which are associated with the same label.
- d is the number of different labelled examples covered by R. The maximum value of d is computed as a function of s and the user parameter γ, so that: $\frac{s-d}{s} \geq \gamma$.
- f is a boolean value that indicates if R was split ever.
- r is the index of the last example covered by R.
- u is a boolean value that indicates if R was extended with some of the last δ read records. δ is an user parameter.

In addition, the search space is modelled according to five user–defined parameters: the maximum number of rules per label α, the minimum support λ, the minimum confidence γ, the minimum update frequency μ, and the pruning frequency δ. Every δ read examples, if the number of rules for a label is greater than α then SCALLOP attempts to simplify the model by joining similar rules and by removing *uninteresting* rules: those ones with a support smaller than λ per cent of the number of read examples and those ones that were not updated with the latest μ read examples.

The algorithm starts with α rules per label generated from the first α read examples of each label. These rules are not hypercubes but points. We name these rules *point–rules*. When there have been read more than α examples for a certain label y_i, three situations are differentiated with every new example $e_i = (x_i, y_i)$:

- ***Correct covering***: x_i is covered by one or several rules associated with the same label y_i.

Algorithm 1 updateModel

```
Input:e: Example; i, α, β, γ: integer;
Output:covered: boolean
Input/Output:model: Array of (List of DecisionRule)
< x,y >⇐< normalize(e.vector()),e.label() >
if received[y] < α then
  model[y].add(new DecisionRule(x))
  {a new point-rule is generated, basic case}
else
  covered ⇐ checkCover(γ,i,y,x,model)
  if NOT covered then
    aRule⇐ findExpandibleRule(β,x,y,model)
    if aRule ≠ null then {case 2}
      extendRule(aRule,x,model[y])
    else
      if model[y].size() < α then {basic case}
        model[y].add(new DecisionRule(x))
      end if
    end if
  end if
end if
received[y]++
```

Fig. 1. Three cases are differentiated by updating the model with a new example. The label distribution is stored for using it in the classification phase, if necessary.

- ***Possible expansion***: x_i is not covered by any rule in the model but there is at least one rule associate with the same label that can be extended to cover it without overlapping with a different labelled rule.
- ***Possible split***: x_i is covered by one or several rules associated with a different label $y' \neq y_i$.

Cases 1 and 3 take turns to be firstly checked. If none of them come true, then the actions associated with the case 2 are run. After each pruning (every δ read examples), SCALLOP counts how many times the cases 1 and 3 come true. For the next δ examples SCALLOP will check firstly that case with the highest count according to the preceding δ read examples.

Correct covering: every rule that covers x_i increases its positive support by one unit, updates the index of the last covered example and moves its centroid (procedure *checkCover* in Figure 1). When the first rule R_c that covers the new example is found, the other rules that may also cover it are found thanks to the links of R_c to them ($R_c.O$). All the rules that also cover x_i are updated with the same three operations.

One rule out of R_c and those linked by $R_c.O$, the rule R_n whose centroid $R_n.C$ is the nearest to x_i, may be updated with respect to $R_n.M$ and $R_n.N$.

If x_i is nearer to $R_n.C$ than $R_n.N$, then x_i replaces $R_n.N$, and $R_n.N$ is checked to be in $R_n.M$. If the size of $R_n.M$ is smaller than β, then x_i (or the previous $R_n.N$ if the replacement was done) is directly added to $R_n.M$. If the size of $R_n.M$ is equal to β but x_i is nearer to $R_n.N$ than the *marker* z most distant from $R_n.N$, then z is replaced by x_i.

Possible expansion. When no rule covers x_i, SCALLOP looks for rules R_e associated with the same label y_i which can extend to cover x_i. A rule R_e can be expanded to seize the point x_i if fulfills two conditions:

1. x_i is not beyond the growth–bounds $R_e.B$, that is:

$$\forall j \in \{[1, \ldots, m\} \cdot \; x_{ij} \in (R_e.B_{jl}, R_e.B_{ju})$$

2. The resulting extended rule does not intersect with any rule associated with a label different to y_i.

Only one rule, out of all the candidate rules that can extend to cover the new example, is able to grow: that one whose *growth* or volume increase is the smallest when covering x_i (see Figure 2).

Definition 1 (Growth of a rule) *Let R be a rule in $\mathcal{R}^m$. Let x be a point in $\mathcal{R}^m$. It is defined the growth G of the rule R in order to cover the point x_i as:*

$$G(R, x_i) = \prod_{j=1,\; g_j>0}^{m} 10^{\phi} g_j \; - \prod_{j=1,\; r_j>0}^{m} 10^{\phi} r_j;$$

$$g_j = u_j - l_j; \; u_j = \max(x_{ij}, R.I_{ju}); \; l_j = \min(x_{ij}, R.I_{jl}); \\ r_j = R.I_{ju} - R.I_{jl}; \; \phi \in \mathcal{N}$$

In order to measure only the new region that is taken when a rule R extends to cover a new example x_i, the *growth* takes into account only those dimensions for which there is an expansion.

Since SCALLOP normalizes each attribute value in [0,1] before processing an example, the term 10^{ϕ} is used to avoid that a rule R_a without expansion in a certain dimension k ($R_a.I_{kl} = R_a.I_{ku}$) has greater *growth* than a rule R_b that has expansion in such a dimension and the same intervals in the rest of dimensions ($R_a.I_j = R_b.I_j \; ; \forall \; j \neq k$). Consider two rules in $\mathcal{R}^2$, R_a and R_b, which can be extended to cover a new point $x = \{0.5, 0.5\}$, so that: $R_a.I = \{[0.1, 0.4]; [0.5, 0.5]\}$ (a segment) and $R_b.I = \{[0.1, 0.4]; [0.6, 0.7]\}$ (a surface). Without the term 10^{ϕ}, it results in: $G(R_a, x) = 0.4 - 0.3$; $G(R_b, x) = 0.4 \cdot 0.2 - 0.3 \cdot 0.1$. That is, contrary to expected, R_a grows more than R_b. We have used $\phi = 3$ in our experiments.

A rule can extend to cover a point if it does not overlap with any rule associated with a different label. If this rule R_e is found, it is updated with six operations:

- $R_e.r \leftarrow i$
- $R_e.u \leftarrow$ **true**
- $R_e.s \leftarrow R_e.s + 1$
- $R_e.I_{jb} \leftarrow Min(R_e.I_{jb}, x_{ij})$;

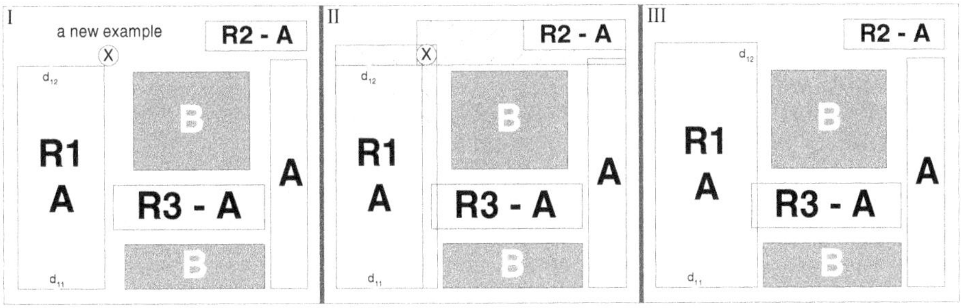

Fig. 2. Case ***Possible expansion.*** (1) A new A–example x is not covered by any rule. (2) The rules *R1* and *R2* do not intersect with any rule associated with a different label when are extended to cover x. (3) Because of the *R2's growth* is greater than *R1's*, this latter rule extends to cover x. The set *R1.D* is updated with x, and the rules *R1* and *R3* are linked each other through *R1.O* and *R3.O*, respectively.

- $R_e.I_{ju} \leftarrow Max(R_e.I_{jb}, x_{ij})$;
- $R_e.C_j \leftarrow \frac{R_e.C_j \cdot R_e.s + x_{ij}}{R_e.s+1}$; $\forall j \in \{1, \dots, m\}$

When a rule R_e is extended, it may overlap with other rules associated with the same label, so that SCALLOP updates the set of links in both directions. In addition, its set of *delimiters* $R_e.D = \{d_{e1}, \dots, d_{en}\}$ may be updated. If the number of *delimiters* at the current time (n) is smaller than β, then x_i is added to $R_e.D$. When n is equal to β, a delimiter d_{ek} may be replaced by x_i. Let d_{ek} be the nearest delimiter to x_i. Let d_{eq} be the nearest delimiter to d_{ek}. If the Euclidean distance between x_i and d_{eq} is greater than the Euclidean distance between d_{ek} and d_{eq}, then d_{ek} is replaced by x_i (see Figure 2).

In a first prototype of SCALLOP the rule selected to cover a new example x_i was that one with the nearest centroid to x_i. With this approach we searched for a smaller number of rules by attempting to obtain regions greater than the regions covered by the current rules. But this approach was not a good choice when noise is present in data. *Clean* streams are unlikely since the nonstop traffic of high dimensionality and high cardinality in the attribute values gives rise to noise, missing, and inconsistencies frequently.

With the *growth* introduced, the model will have a greater number of rules, and these rules will have smaller volume. Nevertheless, by generating more reduced hypercubes, the likelihood that noisy examples are located inside will be smaller than by trying to generalize rules as large as possible. To compact scarcely crowded and dispersed rules, the procedure *refineModel* is called every δ read examples. This means an extra computational cost only at the beginning of the process, as when the model reaches stability, such a refining is almost unnecessary.

Algorithm 2 checkEnemyCover

```
Input:γ, y: integer; x: Vector
Output:covered: boolean
Input/Output:model: Array of (List of DecisionRule)
{Called by the procedure checkCover (in Figure 1)}
if exists a rule R of a label y' ≠ y that covers to x then
  covered ← true
  R' ⇐ nearestRule(R, R.O, x)
  confidence ← (R.s − R.d − 1)/R.s
  if confidence≥ γ then
    R.d ← R.d + 1
  else
    reducedRules ⇐ splitRule(R, x)
    removeWrongRule(R, model[y'])
    addNewRules(reducedRules, model[y'])
    model[y].add(new DecisionRule(x))
  end if
else
  covered ⇐ false
end if
```

Fig. 3. A rule R is split when its confidence is smaller than γ. In this case, several derived rules based on $R.N$,$R.D$, and $R.M$ are generated.

Possible split: when x_i is covered by a rule generated for a different label y', the covering rule R' with the nearest centroid to x_i is founded as in the first case.

If the new confidence of R' $((R'.s - R'.d - 1)/R'.s)$ is still greater than or equal to the minimum γ given by the user, then the number of enemies $(R'.d)$ covered by R' is increased by one unit.

If the new confidence is smaller than γ, then a new *point–rule* R_p for x_i is added to the model. Next the support of R' resolves two new subcases. If $R'.s$ is smaller than $\lambda\%$ examples received, then R' is directly removed. On the contrary, if $R'.s$ is greater than or equal to $\lambda\%$ examples read, then R' is replaced by several derived rules that are built using an iterative procedure from $R'.N$, $R'.D$, and $R'.M$ (procedure *splitRule* in Figure 3):

1. $R'.N$, the delimiters of $R'.D$, and the markers of $R'.M$ are sorted in a list LS by the Euclidean distance to x_i in a decreasing order. Let sd and sm be the size of $R'.D$ and $R'.M$, respectively.
2. A new *point–rule* R'' is created for the first element in LS, the most distant vector to x_i with respect to the vectors of LS. Then $R''.f$ is initialized as *true* and such a generating vector is removed from LS. While it is possible, SCALLOP attempts to extend R'' with the first vector in the list. R'' can be extended when the resulting region does not cover x_i. If R'' is extended, the first element in LS is removed again. If the vector that creates or extends R'' is a delimiter, then $R''.s$ is initialized to or increased by one unit. If such

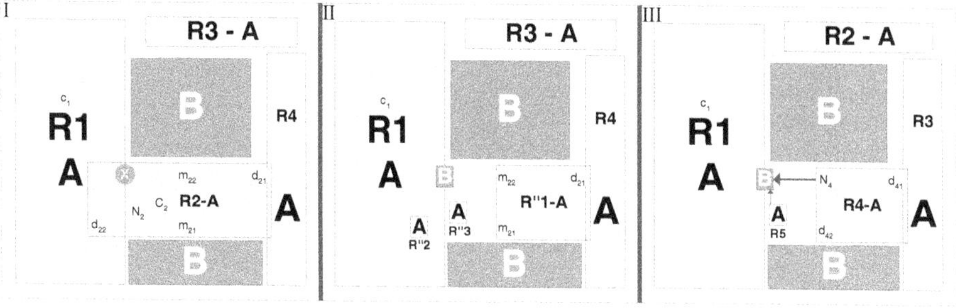

Fig. 4. Case ***Possible split.*** (1) A new B–example x is covered by two rules (*R1* and *R2*) associated with the label A. (2) The rule whose centroid is the nearest to such an example (*R2*) results in three new reduced rules (*R"1*, *R"2*, and *R"3*) that are generated according to *R2.N*, *R2.D* and *R2.M*. (3) *R"1* overlaps with a previous rule so that both rules updates their set of links. Moreover, *R"2* is removed since is totally covered by *R1*. Because of *R2* was never split, *R"1 R"3* update their growth bounds by x. *R1* is not changed.

a vector is $R'.N$ or belongs to $R'.M$, then $R''.s$ is initialized to or increased by $(R'.s - sd)/(sm + 1)$.

3. When R'' can not be extended, $R''.B$ is updated with $R'.B$ (see Figure 6). If $R'.f$ is *true*, then $R''.B$ may be updated with x_i: when R'' covers exactly $m-1$ attribute values of x_i, then the value not covered means either an upper growth bound or a lower growth bound (procedure *updateGrowthBounds* in Figure 5). Finally, R'' is added to the list *reducedRules*. If LS is not empty, the procedure repeats the loop (2) again.

A new rule R'' generated by the procedure *splitRule* might be partially or totally covered by a previous rule $R_c \neq R'$, which must is linked through $R'.O$.

If a rule R'' is totally cover by R_c, then R'' is not included in the model (rule *R"2* in Figure 4–II). Moreover, R_c is not updated by R'' because the examples covered by R' and located inside R'' they updated $R_c.r$, $R_c.C$, and $R_c.s$ when they were read (case ***Correct covering***).

If R'' is partially covered by R_c (rule *R"1* in Figure 4–II, *R4* in Figure 4–III), then both rules update to each other the sets of links $R''.O$ and $R_c.O$, respectively.

If a new rule R'' is disjointed with all the rules associated with its same label (rule *R"3* in Figure 4–II, *R5* in Figure 4–III), then is directly added to the model.

Although the new example x_i may be covered by several rules associated with a different label (rules *R1* and *R2* in Figure 4), only the rule whose centroid is the nearest to x_i is split. We have decided on this criterion under the assumption that if the example x_i belongs to a pattern, then near examples associated with the same label y_i must be read shortly later, and wrong rules will be corrected.

Algorithm 3 updateGrowthBounds

```
Input:x: Vector; R1: DecisionRule
Input/Output:R2: DecisionRule
if R1.f then
  OverlappedDims(x, R2,numOD,attNO)
  {numOD is the number if dimensions in which x and R2 overlap}
  {attOD is a dimension in which x and R2 do not overlap}
end if
for all j = 1 to m do
  if numOD= m − 1 AND j =attOD then
    R2.B_jl ⇐ max(x_j, R1.B_jl)
    R2.B_ju ⇐ min(x_j, R1.B_ju)
  else
    R2.B_jl ⇐ R1.B_jl
    R2.B_ju ⇐ R1.B_ju
  end if
end for
```

Fig. 5. Updating the growth bounds of the rule $R2$ based on the growth bounds of the split rule $R1$ and the attribute values of the example x that split $R1$.

Every time a noisy example x is read, dividing only one rule instead of all the rules that cover x avoids an unnecessary computational cost. In addition, the subsequent updating of the model is hardly harmed as the number of new rules scarcely increases (only the rules from a split that have enough support are included in the model). If x_i is noisy or belongs to a minority pattern, then R_p will be removed in the next pruning. Furthermore, the number of overfitting–errors in the final classification phase will be smaller since the probability of covering a new query will be higher. Owing to data streams present a high sensitivity to noise, to make sure a rule is wrong before splitting involves a decisive issue to quickly attain the stability of the model.

With a similar criterion, only the nearest rule that covers a new example x_i could be updated instead of all the rules for the same label. Nevertheless we have decided on the second option because the centroid associated to each rule will tend to the centroid of an equal solid hypercube with the same spatial location and with uniform mass density. It may benefit the splitting of a rule and the computation of its delimiters and markers, in that it will tend to be more accurate. In addition, the computational cost is not adversely affected.

When no rule associated with the label y_i can cover x_i, a new *point–rule* is generated provided the number of rules associated with y_i is smaller than α (*basic case*). This happens when every expansion causes a non–empty intersection among rules associated with different labels.

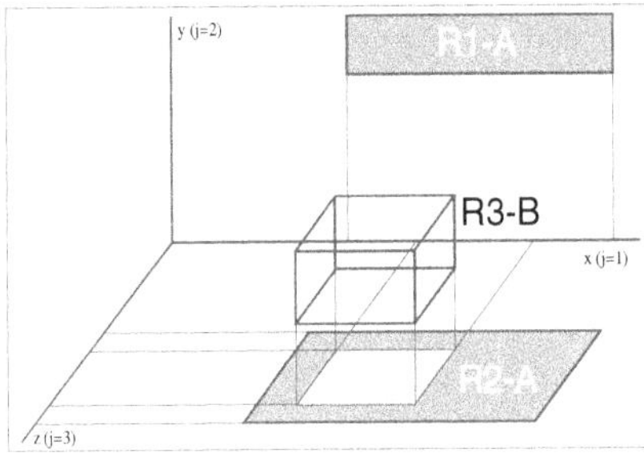

Fig. 6. Updating the growth bounds of a rule in $\mathcal{R}^3$. The rules $R2$ and $R3$ overlap in two dimensions (x, z), whereas $R1$ and $R3$ overlap only in one dimension. $R2.B_{3u}$ is updated with $R3.I_{3l}$ and $R3.B_{3l}$ is updated with $R2.I_{3u}$ $(= R2.I_{3l} = 0)$, respectively. $R1.B$ is not changed.

3.1 Refining the Model

The set of rules is refined every δ new examples in order to achieve a simpler and more accurate model. This periodical attempt of improving consists of three phases.

First, an iterative procedure is run to join rules associated with the same label. When no union is possible the procedure ends. In every iteration, the two nearest rules to each other whose union is possible are analyzed. The two nearest rules are those whose resulting volume is the smallest in relation to the volume of the rest of the possible unions. The union R_u from two rules R_a and R_b of the same label is done if two conditions are fulfilled:

1. R_u does not intersect with any rule associated with a different label.
2. The resulting hypercube is located inside the hypercube obtained from the growth bounds of R_a and R_b. That is, the growth bounds of R_u and R_b allow such a joint, so that:
   $rl_j, ru_j \in (bl_j, bu_j)$;
   $rl_j = \min(R_a.I_{jl}, R_b.I_{jl})$;
   $ru_j = \max(R_a.I_{ju}, R_b.I_{ju})$;
   $bl_j = \max(R_a.B_{jl}, R_b.B_{jl})$;
   $bu_j = \min(R_a.B_{ju}, R_b.B_{ju})$; $\forall j \in \{1, \ldots, m\}$

When two rules R_a and R_b are joined as R_u, R_a and R_b are removed and R_u is added to the model, so that:

- $R_u.u \leftarrow R_a.u$ **OR** $R_b.u$
- $R_u.f \leftarrow R_a.f$ **AND** $R_b.f$
- $R_u.r \leftarrow \max(R_a.r, R_b.r)$
- $R_u.s \leftarrow R_a.s + R_b.s$ - Intersection(R_a, R_b)
- $R_u.C_j \leftarrow \frac{R_a.C_j \cdot R_a.s + R_b.C_j \cdot R_b.s}{R_u.s}$; $\forall j \in \{1, \ldots, m\}$

- $R_u.I_{jl} \leftarrow min(R_a.I_{jl}, R_b.I_{jl})$;
- $R_u.I_{ju} \leftarrow max(R_a.I_{ju}, R_b.I_{ju})$;
- $R_u.B_{jl} \leftarrow max(R_a.B_{jl}, R_b.B_{jl})$;
- $R_u.B_{ju} \leftarrow min(R_a.B_{ju}, R_b.B_{ju})$;
- $R_u.D \leftarrow$ **selectFrom**$(R_a.D, R_b.D)$
- $R_u.M \leftarrow$ **selectFrom**$(R_a.N, R_a.M, R_b.N, R_b.N)$
- $R_u.N \leftarrow$ **selectFrom**$(R_a.N, R_a.M, R_b.N, R_b.N)$

In a second step every rule has to satisfy two conditions to stay in the model: 1) must cover at least one of the last δ read examples; 2) the positive support must be greater than or equal to the minimum given by the user (as percentage of the total number of examples read at that time). δ is another user parameter. If noise is present in data, those *wrong* rules that stem from noise are likely to have a low support and a variable update rate. If after this prune the number n of rules is still greater than α, then they are sorted by both the positive support and the index of the last covered example, in a decreasing order, so that the last $n - \alpha$ rules are directly removed. Every rules that stay in the model reset its number of enemies ($R.d \leftarrow 0$) and its expansion ($R.u \leftarrow$ **false**).

Before removing a rule R_r, some rules associated with a different label may update their growth bounds. If R_r was extended with one of the last δ read examples and was not split ever, then SCALLOP takes it as a valid minority rule (not noise). Therefore, the rules of different label that will remain in the model should not extend across the region given by the definition limits of R_r (Figure 6). To avoid a wrong expansion that may involve a splitting shortly after, SCALLOP updates the growth bounds of every different labelled rule R_s that overlaps with R_r in all dimensions except one j, so that:

$$\textbf{if } R_r.I_{jl} > R_s.I_{ju} \textbf{ then } R_s.B_{ju} \leftarrow \min(R_s.B_{ju}, R_r.I_{jl})$$
$$\textbf{if } R_r.I_{ju} < R_s.I_{jl} \textbf{ then } R_s.B_{jl} \leftarrow \max(R_s.B_{jl}, R_r.I_{ju})$$

3.2 Classifying New Queries by Voting

If a new query Q is covered by a rule R_q, then Q is directly classified as the label associated with R_q. If there is no rule covering the new query, SCALLOP tries to infer which labels are not possible for Q and it is classified by voting. Figure 7 shows this procedure. If the query is beyond the growth bounds of all the rules associated with a certain label l, then l is rejected to classify Q. If Q is beyond the growth bounds of a rule R_y with label y, then the votes against y are increased in one unit. If a rule R_t of label t can be extended to cover Q (it is inside the growth bounds of R_t and the resulting expansion does not intersect with any rule associated with a label different to y), then the votes for t are increased in one unit. Thus, the label assigned is that with the highest number of votes. When two labels have the same number of votes, the label distribution (*received*) decides which is the class value for the new query.

Algorithm 4 classifyQuery

```
Input:Q: Vector in R^m;
Output:label: Discrete;
if there is a rule R_q that covers Q then
  label ← the label associated with R_q
else
  for all label y_k ∈ Y do {Y = {y_1, ..., y_z}}
    validLabel[k] ← false
    for all rule R associated with the label y_k do
      if Q is beyond the growth limits of R then
        votesAgainst[k] ← votesAgainst[k] + 1
      else
        if R can extend to cover Q then
          validLabel[k] ← true
          votesFor[k] ← votesFor[k] + 1
        end if
      end if
    end for
  end for
  label ← decide(validLabel,votesFor,votesAgainst,received)
end if
```

Fig. 7. Algorithm to classify new queries.

4 Empirical Evaluation

We have run all our experiments on an AMD x86/1.4Ghz and 256Mb DDR RAM PC running Windows XP. SCALLOP have been tested for 15 continuous attributes using a method similar to [7]. The concepts to be learned are created by randomly generation of decision trees with 8 levels (128 concepts to be learned). Each leaf is randomly assigned a class label between only two possible values, 0/1. The tree was grown in each internal node with a random pair (attribute,value) that is consistent with the path from the root to such a node. For every example of the training stream, the 15 attribute values are generated with a simple uniform number generator as a stream of pseudo–random numbers in the real interval [0,1]. The class label associated with each training example is then assigned according to the target tree. As in [7], we carried out all tests without ever writing the training examples to disk (i.e., generating them on the fly and passing them directly to the algorithm).

We have evaluated three aspects of the performance given by SCALLOP: the prediction accuracy, the stabilization speed, and the running time. They have been measured for different sizes of the training stream. We have added a class label noise level of 1% so that every 100 examples, one of them was passed with a random label. For each training set, 10% of examples were used for testing. We have carried out ten evaluations for each training and ten training for each size. The values used for the parameters of the algorithm were: $\alpha = 100$, $\beta = 3$, $\gamma = 0.9$, $\delta = 10^4$, $\lambda = 0.01$, $\mu = 2 \cdot 10^4$, and $\sigma = 10^6$.

Table 1. Performance given by SCALLOP learning 128 concepts of 15 continuous dimensions. NE is the number of examples; CA is the classification accuracy; TC is the percentage of test examples covered by the ruleset; AC is the accuracy obtained by direct covering; NR is the final number of rules; NS is the total number of rules split during the process; and RP is the number of new rules generated before α examples of each label are read.

NE	%CA	%TC	%AC	NR	NS	RP
$5 \cdot 10^4$	66.0 ± 0.70	29.3	28.8	190	780	480
$1 \cdot 10^5$	74.0 ± 0.40	45.5	45.4	185	1400	1000
$2 \cdot 10^5$	84.0 ± 0.17	64.5	64.4	185	2150	2050
$3 \cdot 10^5$	91.5 ± 0.15	73.6	73.5	185	2550	3080
$4 \cdot 10^5$	93.0 ± 0.11	81.8	81.7	185	3150	4180
$5 \cdot 10^5$	94.0 ± 0.11	84.9	84.9	185	3225	5380
$1 \cdot 10^6$	95.3 ± 0.02	90.4	90.4	170	3330	12370
$5 \cdot 10^6$	95.8 ± 0.02	90.3	90.3	137	4000	72200

Table 2. Running time to build the model and classify 10% test examples. NE is the number of examples; TL is the time needed to built the model (in seconds); TC is the time to classify the test examples (in seconds); and %UE is the percentage of examples that are not used to update the model.

NE	TL	TC	%UE
$5 \cdot 10^4$	65	0.4	42
$1 \cdot 10^5$	115	0.6	33
$2 \cdot 10^5$	165	1.0	24
$3 \cdot 10^5$	210	1.3	18
$4 \cdot 10^5$	250	1.6	16
$5 \cdot 10^5$	290	1.6	15
$1 \cdot 10^6$	340	2.2	6
$5 \cdot 10^6$	925	10.8	1

Table 1 shows the results obtained with respect to the accuracy and the stability given by SCALLOP. The last row shows the results for a changing–tree, so that every million example the target tree was replaced making SCALLOP to reject the generated rules. From 5 million examples, the tree was stationary. The accuracy becomes stable from one million examples like the number of covered examples. It is important the high percentage of test examples correctly classified without direct cover for $5 \cdot 10^4$ tests (almost 37% of correctly classified) and for 10^5 (almost 30%). The number of split rules does not increase under a linear trend but from one million examples tend to be asymptotic bounded. From five million examples, the number of final rules is very near to the number of concepts to be learned.

Table 2 shows the results obtained in running time (seconds). Column TL shows that the running time to update the model is proportionally decreasing as the number of examples increases, so that the system's stability increases as the number of examples. Column UE shows that the quality of the rules is increasingly nearer to the real concepts to be extracted. These results lead us to think that SCALLOP is a good choice to mine major patterns from continuous data streams.

5 Conclusions

A scalable classification learning algorithm based on decision rules and prototypes has been introduced in this paper. Providing a model on demand, which improves its simplicity and helpfulness for the user, we have developed a system for mining numerical, low–dimensionality, high–speed, time–changing data streams that updates the model with each new example. With a refining method as part of the algorithm, SCALLOP is able to remove *out–of–date* rules that have become uninteresting for the user and wrong rules caused by noise. This periodical pruning does not adversely affect the computational cost but rather speeds up its subsequent updating by helping to make the model more stable.

The strong point of our algorithm is that the generated rules *know* where can extend to, what provides few rules to classify new queries without decreasing the accuracy. This approach is different to decision tree based algorithms in that the whole search space is not modelled and the new queries are classified by voting.

Our future research directions are oriented to drop irrelevant dimensions, and recover dropped attributes turned relevant later (there is no much literature on feature selection from data streams). We are also studying to deal with nominal attributes in order to be able to compare SCALLOP with another classification algorithms, as CVFDT [14] and SPRINT [20].

Acknowledgements. The research was supported by the Spanish CICYT under grant TIC2001-1143-C03-02.

References

1. R. Agrawal and R. Srikant. Fast algorithms for mining association rules. In Jorge B. Bocca, Matthias Jarke, and Carlo Zaniolo, editors, *Proc. 20th International Conf. on Very Large Data Bases, VLDB*, pages 487–499. Morgan Kaufmann, 12–15 1994.
2. P.L. Bartlett, S. Ben-David, and S.R. Kulkarni. Learning changing concepts by exploiting the structure of change. In *Computational Learing Theory*, pages 131–139, 1996.
3. P.S. Bradley, U.M. Fayyad, and C. Reina. Scaling clustering algorithms to large database. *Knowledge Discovery and Data Mining*, pages 9–15, 1998.
4. J. Cattlet. *Megainduction: machine learning on very large databases.* PhD thesis, Basser Department of Computer Science, University of Sydney, Australia, 1991.
5. D. Wai-Lok Cheung, J. Han, V. Ng, and C. Y. Wong. Maintenance of discovered association rules in large databases: An incremental updating technique. In *ICDE*, pages 106–114, 1996.

6. A. Dobra and J. Gehrke. Secret: A scalable linear regression tree algorithm. In *Proc.* 8th *ACM SIGKDD International Conf. on Knowledge Discovery and Data Mining*, Edmonton, Canada, 2002. ACM Press.
7. P. Domingos and G. Hulten. Mining high-speed data streams. In *Proc.* 6th *ACM SIGKDD International Conf. on Knowledge Discovery and Data Mining*, pages 71–80, Boston, MA, 2000.
8. V. Ganti, J. Gehrke, and R. Ramakrishnan. Mining data streams under block evolution. *ACM SIGKDD Explorations*, 3(2):1–10, 2002.
9. M. Garofalakis and R. Rastogi. Scalable data mining with model constraints. *ACM SIGKDD Explorations*, 2(2):39–48, 2000.
10. J. Gehrke, V. Ganti, R. Ramakrishnan, and W.Y. Loh. BOAT – optimistic decision tree construction. In *ACM SIGMOD Conference*, pages 169–180, Philadelphia, Pennsylvania, 1999.
11. J. Gehrke, R. Ramakrishnan, and V. Ganti. Rainforest – a framework for fast decision tree construction of large datasets. In *Proc.* 24th *Int. Conf. Very Large Data Bases, VLDB*, pages 416–427 , 1998.
12. S. Guha, N. Mishra, R. Motwani, and L. O'Callaghan. Clustering data streams. In *IEEE Symposium on Foundations of Computer Science*, pages 359–366, 2000.
13. S. Guha, R. Rastogi, and K. Shim. CURE: an efficient clustering algorithm for large databases. In *ACM SIGMOD International Conference on Management of Data*, pages 73–84, June 1998.
14. G. Hulten, L. Spencer, and P. Domingos. Mining time-changing data streams. In *Proc.* 7th *ACM SIGKDD International Conf. on Knowledge Discovery and Data Mining*, pages 97–106, San Francisco, CA, 2001. ACM Press.
15. G. Hulten, L. Spencer, and P. Domingos. Mining complex models from arbitrarily large databases in constant time. In *Proc.* 8th *ACM SIGKDD International Conf. on Knowledge Discovery and Data Mining*, Edmonton, Alberta, Canada, 2002. ACM Press.
16. M. Kelly, D. Hand, and N. Adams. The impact of changing populations on classier performance, 1999.
17. R. Rastogi M. Garofalakis, D. Hyun and K. Shim. Scalable data mining with model constraints. In *Proc.* 6th *ACM SIGKDD International Conf. on Knowledge Discovery and Data Mining*, pages 335–339, Boston, MA, 2000.
18. L. O'Callaghan, N. Mishra, A. Meyerson, and S. Guha. High–performance clustering of streams and large data sets. In *Proc.* 18th *International Conf. on Data Engineering*, pages 359–366, 2000.
19. F. Provost and V. Kolluri. A survey of methods for scaling up inductive algorithms. *Data Mining and Knowledge Discovery*, 3(2):131–169, 1999.
20. J.C. Shafer, R. Agrawal, and M. Mehta. SPRINT: A scalable parallel classifier for data mining. In *Proc.* 22th *International Conf. Very Large Databases, VLDB*, pages 544–555, 1996.
21. T. Zhang, R. Ramakrishnan, and M. Livny. BIRCH: an efficient data clustering method for very large databases. In *ACM SIGMOD International Conf. on Management of Data*, pages 103–114, Montreal, Canada, June 1996.

Adaptation to Drifting Concepts

Gladys Castillo[1,2], João Gama[1,3], and Pedro Medas[1]

[1] LIACC, University of Porto, Portugal
[2] Department of Mathematics, University of Aveiro, Portugal
[3] FEP, University of Porto, Portugal
gladys@mat.ua.pt, {jgama,pmedas}@liacc.up.pt

Abstract. Most of supervised learning algorithms assume the stability of the target concept over time. Nevertheless in many real-user modeling systems, where the data is collected over an extended period of time, the learning task can be complicated by changes in the distribution underlying the data. This problem is known in machine learning as *concept drift*. The main idea behind *Statistical Quality Control* is to monitor the stability of one or more quality characteristics in a production process which generally shows some variation over time. In this paper we present a method for handling concept drift based on Shewhart P-Charts in an on-line framework for supervised learning. We explore the use of two alternatives P-charts, which differ only by the way they estimate the target value to set the center line. Experiments with simulated concept drift scenarios in the context of a user modeling prediction task compare the proposed method with other adaptive approaches. The results show that, both P-Charts consistently recognize concept changes, and that the learner can adapt quickly to these changes to maintain its performance level.

1 Introduction

User modeling systems are basically concerned with making inferences about the user's assumptions (e.g. preferences, goals, interests, etc.) from observations of the user's behavior during his/her interaction with the system. On the other hand Machine Learning deals with the formation of models from observations. In recent years a growing number of applications of machine learning techniques to user modeling systems have been developed (e.g. information filtering). Observations of the user's behavior can provide data (training examples) that a machine learning system can use to induce a model designed to predict future actions [13]. Nevertheless, for many user modeling systems where data is collected over an extended period of time, the machine learning task can be complicated by changes in the distribution underlying the data. This problem is known as *concept drift* in machine learning. Depending on the rate of these changes we can distinguish *concept drift* (when changes occur gradually) of *concept shift* (when changes occur abruptly). Concept drift scenarios require on-line, incremental learning algorithms, able to adapt quickly to drifting concepts.

Fernando Moura Pires, Salvador Abreu (Eds.): EPIA 2003, LNAI 2902, pp. 279–293, 2003.

In the last few years several methods to cope with *concept drift* have been developed (e.g. [6,7,9,14]). The goal of this paper is to consider yet another method to handle concept drift in an on-line framework for supervised learning. Our method is based on *Statistical Quality Control.* In order to detect that a change has occurred, usually, a process that monitors the value of some indicators, such as performance measures, must be implemented. The benefit of our method, compared to the other approaches, is that this monitoring process is explicitly modelled using P-charts, an attribute *Shewhart control chart.* In this paper, we explore how two alternatives P-Charts can be used to detect concept changes. These two P-Charts differ only by the way they estimate the target value to set the center line on the chart. We present a general algorithm to handle concept drift based on P-Chart, which is broadly applicable to a range of domains and learning algorithms. Experiments with simulated concept drift scenarios in the context of a student modeling task compare our method with other approaches. The results show that both P-charts consistently recognize concept changes, and that, the learner can adapt quickly to these changes in order to maintain its performance level.

In the next section, we review other work on adaptation to drifting concepts. In section 3 we introduce some notions of Statistical Quality Control, and then, explain how P-Chart can be used in the monitoring process to detect concept drift. Further, we present the general algorithm to handle concept drift based on P-Chart. In section 4 we describe a user modeling prediction task in an adaptive educational system, and in section 5 we present experiments to evaluate the proposed method in the context of this user modeling task. Finally, section 6 contains the conclusions and future work.

2 Related Work

In machine learning drifting concepts are often handled by time windows or weighted examples according to their age or utility. In general, approaches to cope with concept drift can be classified into two categories: *i)* approaches that adapt a learner at regular intervals without considering whether changes have really occurred; *ii)* approaches that first detect concept changes, and next, the learner is adapted to these changes. Examples of the former approaches are *weighted examples* and *time windows* of fixed size. Weighted examples are based on the simple idea that the importance of an example should decrease with time (references about this approach can be found in [6],[7],[8], [9],[14]). When a time window is used, at each time step the learner is induced only from the examples that are included in the window. Here, the key difficulty is how to select the appropriate window size: a small window can assure a fast adaptability in phases with concept changes but in more stable phases it can affect the learner performance, while a large window would produce good and stable learning results in stable phases but can not react quickly to concept changes. In the latter approaches,with the aim of detecting concept changes, some indicators (e.g. performance measures, properties of the data, etc.) are monitored over time (see [6] for a good overview of these indicators). If during the monitoring process a concept drift is detected, some actions to adapt the learner to these changes can be taken. When a time window of adaptive size is used these actions usually lead to adjusting the window size according to the extent of concept drift [6]. As a general rule, if a concept drift is detected the window size decreases, otherwise the window size increases. An example of work relevant to this approach is the FLORA family of algorithms developed by Widmer and Kubat [14]. For instance, FLORA2 includes a window adjustment heuristic for a rule-based classifier. To detect concept changes the accuracy and the coverage of the current learner are monitored over time and the window size is adapted accordingly.

Other relevant works, which are served as base for this paper, are the works of R.Klinkenberg and C.Lanquillon, both of them in information filtering. For instance, Klinkenberg and Renz in [6], in order to detect concept drift, they propose monitoring the values of three performance indicators: *accuracy*, *recall* and *precision* over time, and then, comparing it to a confidence interval of standard sample errors for a moving average value (using the last M batches) of each particular indicator. Although these heuristics seem to work well in their particular domain, they have to deal with two main problems: *i*) to compute performance measures, user feedback about the true class is required, but in some real applications only partial user feedback is available; *ii*) a considerable number of parameters are needed to be tuned. Afterwards, in [7] Klinkenberg and Joachims present a theoretically well-founded method to recognize and handle concept changes using support vector machines. The key idea is to select the window size so that the estimated generalization error on new examples is minimized. This approach uses unlabeled data to reduce the need for labeled data, it doesn't require complicated parameterization and it works effectively and efficiently in practice. However, it is not independent of the hypothesis language (a support vector machine) and therefore it is not generally applicable.

On the other hand, Lanquillon [8] employs *Statistical Quality Control* to detect changes in document stream with either little or no user feedback. Three alternative performance measures: *sample error rate* (it requires only some user feedback per batch), *expected error rate* and *virtual rejects* (the two last measures don't require any user feedback) are monitored over time. A representative training set is maintained through storage of new examples for which the true class labels have been provided by the user. If the monitor has detected some change, the filtering system is adapted based on the current training set by running through the entire learning process from scratch.

3 Exploring the Use of Two P-Charts to Cope with Drifting Concepts

Similarly to Lanquillon, the underlying theory we propose to use to deal with concept drift is *Statistical Quality Control*. In the section following we will introduce some notions of this theory (a deeper discussion can be found in [12]).

3.1 Notions of Statistical Quality Control

The main idea behind *Statistical Quality Control* is to monitor the stability of one or more quality characteristics in production processes [2]. The values of the quality characteristic generally show some variation, which can be caused by either some "*natural causes*" inherent in the production process or by some "*special causes*" that can be traced to a particular problem. "*Natural causes*" are presented all the time while "*special causes*" occur at unpredictable times. A process can be run in either of two mutually exclusive states: an *in-control* state or an *out-of-control* state. An *in-control* state means that the successive values of the quality characteristic, as they are observed over time, show a stable random variation about a target value (variations caused by "*natural causes*"). Otherwise a process is *out-of-control.* A process is in statistical control if "*special causes*" have been detected and removed, so these sources of variability will not influence the process in the future [2].

The Shewhart controls charts are a useful tool to distinguish whether a process is *in-control* or *out-of-control.* The values of the quality characteristic are plotted on the chart in time order and connected by a line. Some *control limits* are established. If a value falls outside the control limits, it is assumed that the process is *out-of-control*, i.e.,some "*special causes*" have shifted the process off target, and therefore, some actions will be required to remove them. If the distribution of the quality characteristic is Normal (or approximately Normal) there is some statistical arguments for using the 3 *sigma control limits* (*sigma* is the standard deviation around the mean). It is well-known that, if the distribution of a statistic is Normal,then approximately 99.7% of the observations will fall within three *standard deviations* of the *mean* of the statistic. In addition to control limits, we can also use *warning limits.* These limits are usually set a bit closer to the mean than the control limits. For instance, if two consecutive values fall outside the *warning limits* some actions can also be taken.

If the mean μ and the standard deviation σ of the statistic of interest (the values of the quality characteristic) are known, then these values are used to set up the parameters of the control chart, as follows:

$$CL = \mu, \tag{1}$$

$$LCL = \mu - 3\sigma; UCL = \mu + 3\sigma, \tag{2}$$

$$LWL = \mu - k\sigma; UWL = \mu + k\sigma; 0 < k < 3. \tag{3}$$

where CL represents the center line, LCL and UCL - the upper and lower control limits, and LWL and UWL - the upper and lower warning limits. However, in most cases μ and σ are unknown and these values must be estimated from previously observed data.

The control charts are often classified according to the type of quality characteristic that they monitor: *variables* or *attributes.* Attribute data is also known as *count attribute.* For the purpose of this paper, we focus on the P-Chart - a control chart for the *proportion nonconforming* (the ratio of the number of *nonconforming* items in a population to the total number of items in that population) where: *i*) a dichotomous attribute with only two mutually exclusive and exhaustive outcomes is measured (e.g. each unit produced is classified either *conforming* or *nonconforming* to some specifications); *ii*) the successive observations are independent over time; *iii*) for a random sample of n items the count of units that are *nonconforming* is registered; *iv*) the quality characteristic to be monitored is the sample proportion *nonconforming*; *v*) the sample size can vary.

The count of *nonconforming* items follows a Binomial distribution with parameters n and p, where p is the probability that any unit will *nonconforming* (the population proportion). The distribution of the sample proportion *nonconforming* can also be obtained from the binomial with parameters:

$$\mu = p \; ; \; \sigma = \sqrt{\frac{p(1-p)}{n}} \tag{4}$$

Moreover if the sample sizes are large ($n \geq 30$), the *sample proportion nonconforming* is approximately Normal (a well-known result derived by the Central Limit Theorem). As we have stated before, when p is not known, then it must be estimated from observed data. Suppose that the estimate $\hat{p}$ of p is obtained from previous data by some estimator. Then, from equations (1)–(4), the parameters of the P-Chart for each individual t-th sample with size n_t would be:

$$CL = \hat{p} \; , \tag{5}$$

$$UCL = \hat{p} + 3\sqrt{\frac{\hat{p}(1-\hat{p})}{n_t}} ; LCL = max\left\{0, \hat{p} - 3\sqrt{\frac{\hat{p}(1-\hat{p})}{n_t}}\right\} , \tag{6}$$

$$UWL = \hat{p} + k\sqrt{\frac{\hat{p}(1-\hat{p})}{n_t}} ; LWL = max\left\{0, \hat{p} - k\sqrt{\frac{\hat{p}(1-\hat{p})}{n_t}}\right\} , 0 < k < 3 \tag{7}$$

The usual procedure to compute the estimate $\hat{p}$ is by the weighted average of m preliminary sample proportions (as a rule, m should be 20 or 25)

$$\hat{p} = \overline{p} = \frac{1}{\sum_{i=1}^{m} n_i} \sum_{i=1}^{m} n_i p_i = \frac{1}{\sum_{i=1}^{m} n_i} \sum_{i=1}^{m} (count)_i \tag{8}$$

where p_i is the sample proportion of the i-th sample with size n_i. Further we call the estimate $\hat{p}$ the target value.

3.2 Using P-Chart for Detecting Concept Drift

In this section we explore the use of two alternatives P-Charts for detecting concept drift in an on-line framework for supervised learning. Data arrives to the learner over time in batches. For each batch, the examples are classified using the current learner. The quality characteristic to be monitored is the *sample error rate*, a sample proportion of the misclassified examples. Following is a more formal definition of the sample error rate:

Definition 1. *The* sample error rate *of a learner $h_{\mathcal{L}}$ with respect to target concept f and sample D with n examples is the proportion of misclassified examples by $h_{\mathcal{L}}$, i.e.,*

$$Err(D, h_{\mathcal{L}}) \equiv error(D, f, h_{\mathcal{L}}) = \frac{1}{n} \sum_{x \in D} \delta(f(x), h_{\mathcal{L}}(x)) \tag{9}$$

where $\delta(f(x), h_{\mathcal{L}}(x)) = \begin{cases} 1, when f(x) \neq h_{\mathcal{L}}(x) \\ 0, otherwise \end{cases}$ *is the* one-zero loss *function.*

In order to evaluate the *sample error rate* for each batch, user feedback about the correct class for the examples is required. If the monitoring process detects concept drift, the learner must be adapted accordingly. Next, the adapted learner can be used to predict the class labels of the examples of the next batch.

In classical *Shewhart control charts* it is assumed that the successive sample proportions should exhibit a stable random variation around the target value over time. Such behavior is not observed in the learning tasks where, we know, concept changes are likely to occur. It is well known that the learner's goal is to minimize the *zero-one loss* function. Consequently, while the learner has not learned enough about the underlying target concept, the error rate should exhibit a downward trend that reflects the desired improvement of the performance. At once a concept change occurred, an opposite trend in the error rate is immediately observed. In principle, a learning process is *in-control* only when the learner is extremely stable. Therefore, in learning tasks we need to dynamically estimate the target value taking into account the actual performance level of the learner.

The two alternatives P-Charts, we propose to use, differ only by the way they estimate the target value. To distinguish them, we denote one chart PAVG-chart and the other PMIN-chart. For the PAVG-chart at each time t the target value $\hat{p}$ is estimated by the weighted average of the sample errors on the M previous batches, i.e., the estimate $\hat{p}$ can be computed from equation (8) for $i = t - M$ to $t - 1$. Here M is a required parameter that must be tuned. Similarly, Lanquillon in [8] propose to estimate the target value by the weighted average of the sample errors on recent batches only if they are within the warning limits of the chart.

The way in which we estimate the target value of the PMIN-chart is based on the exposed facts related to the dynamic behavior of the learning task and also on the method to detect concept drift presented in [10]. Let us introduce the following definition:

Definition 2. *A* context *S corresponds to a set of examples from the data stream where the distribution underlying the examples is stationary (without drifts).*

In general, the problem of handling drifting concepts can be viewed as the problem of the detection of the last moment when a concept drift occurred. Thus, the data stream can be analyzed as a sequence of different contexts over time, i.e. the detection and extraction of stable concepts between drifts. Suppose that at time t a new context begins to be processed. At the beginning, while the learner has not learned enough, the error rate for this context should exhibit a downward trend. This means that for the current context, all the time when a lower error rate is achieved, the learner will try to improve, or at least, to maintain its performance level. Based on these facts, we propose to maintain a *minimum value* for the error rate for the current context and set the target value to this minimum value instead of using some average of previous observed values. Taking into account the way we estimate the target value, we can state that PMIN-chart is not a typical statistical P-chart since it does not use a statistical well-founded estimator (we will try to explore these issues in future works).

Suppose that $Err_S^{(t)}$ is the error rate for the context $S^{(t)}$ at time t and $SErr_S^{(t)}$ its standard deviation. From equations(9),(4) these values can be computed by:

$$Err_S^{(t)} \equiv Err(S^{(t)}, h_{\mathcal{L}}); \; SErr_S^{(t)} = \sqrt{\frac{Err_S^{(t)}(1 - Err_S^{(t)})}{n_S^{(t)}}} \tag{10}$$

where $n_S^{(t)}$ is the number of examples of the actual context S at time t. Let Err_{min} denote the *minimum-error rate*. Initially, Err_{min} is set to some predefined value (a big number). Next, at each time step, if $Err_S^{(t)} + SErr_S^{(t)} < Err_{min}$ then Err_{min} is set to $Err_S^{(t)}$.

3.3 A General Algorithm for Handling Concept Drift in Online Supervised Learning Based on Control P-Chart

We have developed a general algorithm for handling *concept drift* in an on-line framework for supervised learning based on P-Chart. This is presented in Figure 1. In each time step, the algorithm begins by determining the *sample error rate* for the current batch. Next, the target value is estimated by the *mean_estimator* procedure (how it is estimated depends on the method that is used: weighted average, minimum error, etc.). After estimating the target value, all the chart parameters are computed by the equations (5)–(7). Since a low sample error rate is desirable, we don't need to use the low limits here. If the current sample error Err_t is above the upper control limit, a *concept shift* is suspected, and it is assumed that a new context is beginning. In this case, only the examples from this new context are used to re-learn the learner, thus forgetting all the previous data. If the last alert occurred at the previous time step (LastAlert=t-1), we assume, that the new context began at the time indicated in FirstAlert. If the current sample error is above the upper warning limit and it occurred at two or more consecutive times a *concept drift* is suspected. In this case, the examples of the current batch are not used to update the learner (it allows that the monitoring process will more quickly recognize a concept shift). If neither, a *concept shift* or *concept drift* is suspected, the learner is updated to combine the current learner with the examples of the current batch.

The precise way in which a learner can be updated in order to include new data depends basically on the learning algorithm employed. In principle, there are two main approaches: *i*) re-build the learner from scratch; *ii*) update the learner combining the current model with the new data. For instance, updating a Naïve Bayes classifier is simple: the counters required for calculating the prior probabilities can be increased as new examples arrives. For other learners, updating can be more difficult (e.g. support vector machines). May be, in this case it would be easier to relearn from scratch. A deeper discussion about these issues can be found in [8].

```
procedure HandleConceptDriftWithPChart
                 (data,learner,k,mean_estimator())

 for t=1 to N  //for each batch with size n_t at time t
  Errt:=Err(Batch_t,Learner);
  CL:= mean_estimator();
  Sigma:=sqrt(CL*(1-CL)/n_t);
  UCL:=CL+3.Sigma; WCL:=CL+k.Sigma;
  If Errt > UCL then          /* concept shift suspected
  {If LastAlert=t-1 then t_ini:=FirstAlert else t_ini:=t;
     learner:=ReLearnFrom(learner,t_ini)}
  else
   If Errt > WCL then         /* concept drift suspected
    If LastAlert=t-1 then     /* consecutive alerts
      LastAlert:=t
      else                   /* it can be a false alarm
        {learner:= UpdateWith(learner,Batch_t)
         FirstAlert:=t, LastAlert:=t}
    else                     /* no changes was detected
      learner:= UpdateWith(learner,Batch_t);
 Next t;
 return: learner
End
```

Fig. 1. General algorithm for handling concept drift using P-Chart.

4 The User Modeling Prediction Task

The proposed algorithm to handle concept drift was tested for a user modeling prediction task in the context of GIAS, an adaptive authoring tool to support learning and teaching (see [1] for more details). In GIAS, the authors (teachers) can define a course and associate to each course topic a set of existing online learning resources. Whenever a student requests the learning resources of a selected topic, a topic generator must decide which resources are '*appropriate*' or *'not appropriate'* for the student, thus partitioning the set of available resources into these two classes. The choice of the appropriate set of resources for a particular student depends on the *resource's characteristics* and on the student's *cognitive state,learning style* and *preferences.*

Learning style can be defined as the different ways a person collects, processes and organizes information. This kind of information helps more effectively adaptive learning systems, to decide how to adapt its navigation and its presentation, thus enhancing the student learning. On the other hand a *learning resource* can be viewed as the implementation of a learning activity in a multimedia support. By matching a *learning style* with the characteristics of the *learning resources*, in principle, it is possible to determine what types of resources are more appropriate to a particular student. Nevertheless, it is a fact that the student preferences of certain types of multimedia resources or learning activities can change over time. Since, an adaptive learning model is desirable. Therefore, the prediction task that consists in determining whether a learning resource is or is not appropriate for a particular student taking into account his/her learning style and preferences and the resource's characteristics, can be related with the *concept drift problem* for a concept learning task. Moreover, in some aspects, this task is related to the task of information filtering.

We use the Felder-Sylverman model [4] of learning style which classifies students in five dimensions: *visual/verbal, sensing/intuitive, sequential/global, inductive/ deductive, active/reflective* (we use only the first three dimensions). In order to acquire the initial learning style we employ the Index of Learning Styles Questionnaire (ILSQ) [3]. It helps to classify the preference for one or the other category in each dimension as *mild, moderate* or *strong.*

In our learning task, the examples are described through 5 attributes: the first three characterizing the *student's learning style* and the last two characterizing the *learning resource.* The possible values for each attribute are presented in the Table 1.

Table 1. Establishing attributes and their possible values

Attribute	Values
Characterizing the student's learning style	
VISUALVERBAL	$VVi, VV \in \{Visual, Verbal\}, i \in \{mild, moderate, strong\}$
SENSINGCONCEPTUAL	$SCi, SC \in \{Sensing, Conceptual\}, i \in \{mild, moder., strong\}$
GLOBALSEQUENTIAL	$GSi, GS \in \{Global, Sequential\}, i \in \{mild, moderate, strong\}$
Characterizing the learning resource	
LEARNING ACTIVITY	Lesson objectives/Explanation/Example/Conceptual Map /Synthesis Diagram/Glossary /Summary /Bibliography/ Historical Review /Inter.Activity
RESOURCE TYPE	Text/HTML Text/Picture/Animated Picture/ Animated Picture with Voice/ Audio /Video /Software

For instance, suppose the following example:
VISUALVERBAL: *Verbalmoderate*; SENSINGCONCEPTUAL:*Sensingmild*; GLOBALSEQUENTIAL:*Globalmild*; LEARNING ACTIVITY:*explanation*; RESOURCE TYPE :*audio*.

The induced learner must predict if a learning resource implementing a learning activity such as '*explanation*' in a multimedia support of type '*audio*' would be appropriate for a student with a *moderate* preference for VERBAL category, a *mild* preference for SENSING category and a *mild* preference for a GLOBAL category.

For each student an *individual predictive model* is maintained. First, the model is initialized from some initial training data taking into account the acquired information about the student's learning style. Whenever a student selects a topic, the student's current predictive model is used to classify the available resources.

We choose the Naïve Bayes (NB) classifier, one of the learning algorithms most used in user modeling, as our predictive model because: *i*) it is simple; *ii*) it learns quickly (it doesn't require large amount of data to learn); *iii*) low computations to make decisions are needed; *iv*)its results as probabilities are easy to apply. Moreover, we propose to employ Adaptive Bayes [5], an adaptive version of the Naïve Bayes. The main difference between these two algorithms is that Adaptive Bayes includes an updating scheme, that makes it possible to better fit the current model to new data: after seeing each example, first, the counters are incremented, and then, they are again updated in order to increase the confidence on the correct class (the amount of adjustment is proportional to the discrepancy between the predicted class and the correct class).

Since the NB classifier returns probabilities, all the resources of a same class can be ranked. As a result, a page is sent to the student including two separated ranked lists with the resource's links: a "*resources suggested for study*" list with the links for those resources classified as '*appropriate*' and "*other resources for study*" list with the links for those resources classified as '*not appropriate*'. Whenever possible, the correct class is obtained based on the observations about the user's choice of links: visited links are taken as positive examples. Obtaining a relevant set of negative examples is more difficult. To obtain more examples we suggest to the students to rate the resources explicitly. The obtained examples are used to evaluate the sample error and update the predictive model.

5 Experiments

In order to test the two P-Charts proposed in section 3 we have conducted experiments simulating *concept drift* scenarios in the context of the described prediction task using artificial datasets.

5.1 Dataset Generation and Experimental Setup

The artificial datasets were generated to simulate the changes in the user's preferences, which can conduce to further adjustments in the initial learning style.

To simplify the experiments we don't discriminate the preferences for a learning style category. Hence, the number of different learning styles is equal to 2^3, which corresponds to the number of different datasets evaluated for each algorithm. Note, that the underlying concept is different for each learning style. The basic idea enclosing in the simulation of *concept drift* is based on the following facts that really exist in this learning task: for instance, suppose that a student is initially classified as VERBAL. Learning resources that match with a verbal learner (e.g. a learning resource that implements a learning activity such as "*Historical Review*" in a "*HTML Text*" support) should be appropriate for this verbal student. Hence, the underlying target concept can be represented by the following logical rule:

```
IF LearningStyle Is Verbal AND
 (ResourceLearningActivity OR ResourceType) matches Verbal
 THEN Resource is Appropriate
```

Nevertheless, during the further interaction with the system, the student can change his/her preferences for another kind of learning resource that no longer matches with his/her learning style. This means that the underlying concept has changed and, consequently, the previous rule can be replaced with another one, like this:

```
IF LearningStyle Is Verbal AND
  (ResourceLearningActivity OR ResourceType) matches Visual
 THEN Resource is Appropriate
```

Moreover, these changes in the student's preferences lead to further adjustments in the student learning style, i.e., the underlying data distribution can also change. Thus, to simulate concept drift scenarios, for each learning style, datasets with 1600 examples were generated randomly. Each example was classified according to the current concept, which changes after every 400 examples (a sequence of four logical rules was defined). All the examples were grouped into 32 batches of equal size with 50 examples each. Moreover, in order to initialize the learner, a training dataset with 200 examples according to the first concept was also generated.

The experiments were performed according to the on-line framework for supervised learning described in the section 3.2. The two learning algorithms: Naïve Bayes (NB) and Adaptive Bayes (AB) were evaluated in combination with each of the following approaches: a non-adaptive approach (the *baseline* approach), Fixed Size Window (WFS) and the HandleConceptDriftWithPChart algorithm described in the Figure 1 (the parameter k is set to 1) using PAVG-chart (we denote this approach PAvg) and using PMIN-chart (we denote this approach PMin).

5.2 Experimental Results and Analysis

In Figure 2 you can see an illustration of the two P-charts. In each time step, the chart lines are adjusted according to the method employed to estimate the target value and to set the center line. Both charts detected the three concept shifts that really are in the data. The two first concept shifts (after $t = 8$ and after $t = 16$) were detected immediately by the two P-charts (as you can see, the point representing the sample error fall above the current control limit). The third concept shift (after $t = 24$) was also detected immediately by PAvg-Chart, while it was detected with a little delay by PMin-Chart. However, beginning at $t = 25$, this chart started signaling a concept drift (the points that fall outside the warning limits). This means, that an upward trend of the sample error was detected. When further, at $t = 27$ the concept shift was detected, all the examples beginning at $t = 25$ are considered to belong to the same context and consequently they are all used to re-learn the learner.

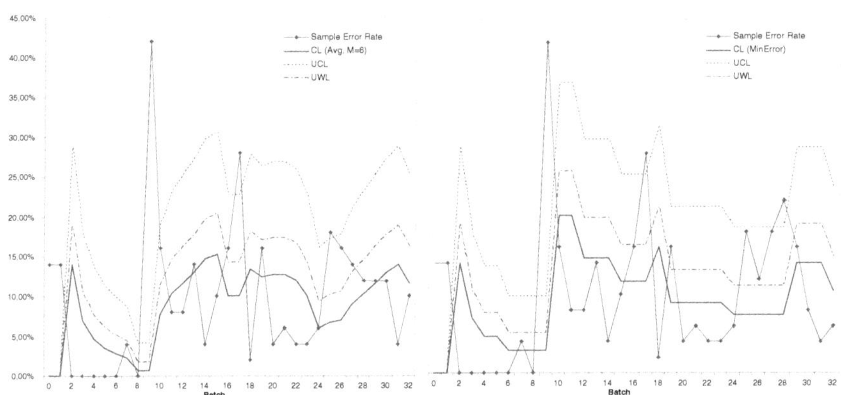

Fig. 2. The PAvg-Chart(left) and PMin-Chart(right)

Table 2 shows the accuracy of all combinations of learning algorithms and the different approaches averaged over 10 runs for each learning style. The results shown in column "Acc. Avg" were obtained by averaging over the accuracy of the eight learning styles for each approach. These averaged values are used to construct the learning curves on the Figure 3. As you can see, at first, while there is no concept drift, the performance of all approaches is good enough; however, those approaches that use Adaptive Bayes show a better performance. After the first change has occurred (after $t = 8$), the performance of those approaches without concept drift detection, decreases significantly. Since the fixed size window approach re-learns regularly from the last six batches, it can recover its performance a little, but this adaptive approach could not outperform the P-Chart approaches. Moreover, as you can notice, there are no significant differences on the performance between PAvg and PMin. Both approaches work well and quickly react to concept drift. However, the results that we show for the PAvg in the Figure 3 are the results that we obtained for $M = 6$. Table 3 compares accuracy for different values of M. The results show that the performance is affected by the variation of the parameter M. If the parameter M is tuned

Table 2. Accuracy of the Naïve Bayes and Adaptive Bayes combined with all the explored approaches for the 8 learning styles ($M = 6$ for WFS and PAvg M=6)

	Approaches	LS1	LS2	LS3	LS4	LS5	LS6	LS7	LS8	Acc. Avg
(1)	NB	70.50	64.42	69.59	64.71	77.33	77.27	57.83	60.51	67.77
(2)	NB & WFS	86.86	85.11	83.06	78.81	87.48	85.98	86.66	84.48	84.80
(3)	NB & PAvg	91.52	90.96	91.38	89.37	90.49	88.51	91.14	87.56	90.11
(4)	NB & PMin	91.41	90.96	91.24	89.15	90.27	90.03	90.25	89.30	90.04
(5)	AB	75.73	70.79	73.42	67.01	80.61	80.09	70.38	68.24	73.28
(6)	AB & WFS	89.04	87.39	86.69	82.01	89.33	88.43	89.06	87.12	87.38
(7)	AB & PAvg	91.85	91.81	92.86	90.90	92.14	89.76	92.79	90.19	91.52
(8)	AB & PMin	91.90	91.61	92.62	90.87	91.77	90.60	91.84	89.30	91.31
I	(2) vs. (1)	+16.3	+20.69	+13.46	+14.11	+10.15	+8.71	+28.83	+23.96	+17.03
	(3) vs. (1)	+21.02	+26.54	+21.79	+24.66	+13.16	+11.24	+33.31	+27.04	+22.35
	(4) vs. (1)	+20.91	+26.54	+21.65	+24.44	+12.94	+12.76	+32.43	+28.53	+22.27
II	(6) vs (5)	+13.31	+20.17	+17.96	+22.36	+9.88	+8.42	+20.76	+19.31	+16.52
	(7) vs (5)	+16.12	+21.03	+19.26	+23.89	+11.53	+9.67	+22.42	+21.95	+18.23
	(8) vs (5)	+16.17	+20.83	+19.20	+23.86	+11.16	+10.51	+21.47	+21.06	+18.03
III	(4) vs. (3)	-0.11	0.0	-0.14	-0.22	-0.22	+1.52	-0.89	+0.52	-0.07
	(8) vs (7)	+0.05	-020	-0.06	+0.03	-0.38	+0.84	-0.95	-0.89	-0.20
IV	(5) vs. (1)	+5.23	+6.37	+3.83	+2.30	+3.29	+2.83	+12.55	+7.73	+ 5.51
	(6) vs. (2)	+2.19	+2.28	+3.64	+3.19	+1.85	+2.45	+2.41	+2.64	+2.58
	(7) vs. (3)	+0.33	+0.86	+1.30	+1.53	+1.66	+1.25	+1.66	+2.64	+1.40
	(8) vs. (4)	+0.49	+0.66	+1.37	+1.72	+1.50	+0.57	+1.59	+2.26	+1.27

accordingly, there are no significant differences on the performance of these two P-charts. Therefore, we suggest the use of the PMin instead of the PAvg because: *i*) PMin doesn't depend on any parameter; *ii*) PMin better reflects the behaviour of the learning process.

Table 3. Varying the parameter M of the P-Avg method and its effect on the performance

	NB	AB
PMin	90.04	91.24
PAvg $M = 4$	90.17	91.57
$M = 6$	90.11	91.52
$M = 8$	89.92	91.08
$M = 10$	87.61	89.29

Finally, in the last lines of the Table 2, some comparative studies of the learner performance for a pair of approaches are presented. Studies I and II compare adaptive approaches to deal with concept drift against the baseline non-adaptive approach in combination with Naïve Bayes and Adaptive Bayes, respectively. The results show that a significant improvement is achieved by using any adaptive method instead of the non-adaptive one for both the learning algorithms. However, the gain obtained by using the P-chart methods is superior to the gain obtained by using windows of fixed size. In the latter approach the learner is adapted regularly without considering whether a concept changes has really occurred. Moreover, a more significant improvement is achieved with the Naïve Bayes due to the adaptation scheme included into Adaptive Bayes. The study III compares the performance of the PAvg against PMin: the "(4) vs. (3)" line shows the performance increase obtained by using Naïve Bayes with PMin instead the PAvg, while "(8) vs. (7)" shows the performance increase obtained by using Adaptive Bayes with Pmin instead the Pavg. As we have stated above, if M is set to 6 there are no significant differences on the performance of these two methods. The last study IV compares the two learning algorithms. The results show that Adaptive Bayes outperforms Naïve Bayes for all the approaches. In general, a more significant improvement is achieved when adaptive methods are combined with Adaptive Bayes.

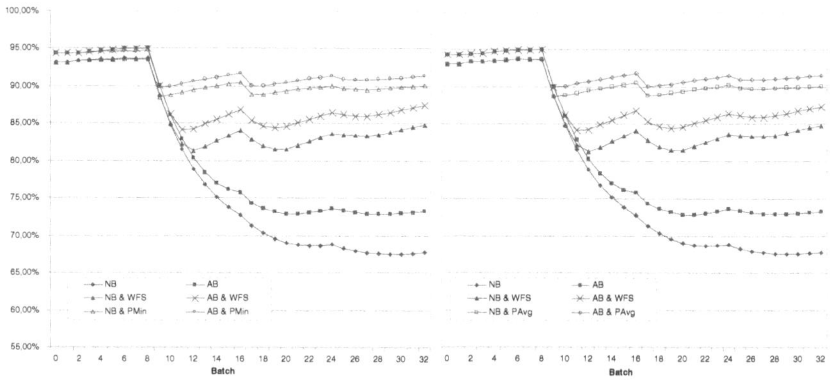

Fig. 3. Comparison of the accuracy using P-Min and P-Avg with M=6

6 Conclusions and Future Work

This paper describes yet another method to handle *concept drift* in an on-line framework for supervised learning based on *Statistical Quality Control.* We present a general algorithm to handle concept drift using P-Charts, which is broadly applicable to a range of domains and learning algorithms. The benefit of our method, compared to the other approaches, is that the monitoring process is explicitly modeled using P-charts. We explore how two alternative P-Charts: PAvg-chart and PMin-chart can be used to monitor the sample error rate in order to detect concept changes. These P-charts differ only by the way they estimate the target value to set the center line on the chart. The experimental results in the context of a user modeling prediction task using Naïve Bayes show that both P-charts consistently recognize concept changes, and that, in general, the proposed method allows the learner to adapt quickly to these changes in order to maintain its performance level. However, for purpose of estimation of the target value it is more convenient to consider PMin than PAvg because: *i)* PMin doesn't require any parameter to be tuned; *ii)* since the learner's goal is to minimize the one-loss function, PMin better follows the natural behaviour of the learning process. In future works we plan to test the proposed method with other concept drift scenarios and other learning algorithms.

Acknowledgments. Gratitude is expressed to the financial support given by the ALES project (POSI/39770/SRI/2001).

References

1. Castillo, G., Gama, J., Breda, A.M.: Adaptive Bayes for a User Modeling Prediction Task based on Learning Styles. In P. Brusilovsky, A. Corbett and F. de Rosis (Eds.). User Modeling 2003. Proceedings of the Ninth International Conference. LNAI **2702**, Springer-Verlag (2003) 328–332.
2. del Castillo, E.: Statistical Process Adjustment for Quality Control, John Willey and Sons, Inc., New York (2002).
3. Felder, R.M., Soloman, B.A.: Index of Learning Style Questionnaire, available online at: http://www2.ncsu.edu/unity/lockers/users/f/felder/public/ ILSdir/ilsweb.html.
4. R.M.: Matters of Style. ASEE Prism **6 (4)**(1996) 18–23.
5. Gama, J., Castillo, G.: Adaptive Bayes. Advances in Artificial Intelligence - IBERAMIA 2002, LNAI **2527**, Springer Verlag (2002) 765–774.
6. Klinkenberg, R., Renz, I., Adaptive Information Filtering: Learning in the Presence of Concept Drifts, Learning for Text Categorization, Menlo Park, CA, USA, AAAI Press (1998) 33–40.
7. Klinkenberg, R., Joachims, T.: Detecting Concept Drift with Support Vector Machines, Proceedings of the Seventeenth International Conference on Machine Learning (ICML), San Franciso, Morgan Kaufman (2000).
8. Lanquillon, C.: Enhancing Test Classification to Improve Information Filtering, PhD. Dissertation (2001), University of Madgdeburg, Germany, available on-line at: http://diglib.uni-magdeburg.de/Dissertationen/2001/carlanquillon.pdf
9. Maloof, M., Michalski, R.: Selecting Examples for Partial Memory Learning, Machine Learning **41** (2000) 27–52.
10. Medas, P., Gama, J.: Aprendizagem com Detecção de Mudança de Conceito, Actas das X Jornadas de Classificação e Análise de Dados, Aveiro (2003) 27–31.
11. Mitchell, Tom. Machine Learning. McGraw Hill, (1997).
12. Montgomery, D.C.: Introduction to Statistical Quality Control (3rd ed.), John Willey & Sons, Inc., New York (1997).
13. Webb, G., Pazzani, M., Billsus, D.: Machine Learning for User Modeling. In User Modeling and User-Adapted Interaction **11** (2001) 19–29.
14. Widmer, G., Kubat, M.: Learning in the Presence of Concept Drift and Hidden Context. Machine Learning **23** (1996) 69–101.

Border Detection on Remote Sensing Satellite Data Using Self-Organizing Maps

Nuno C. Marques and Ning Chen

CENTRIA, Department of Informátion, Faculdade de Ciências e Tecnologia
New University of Lisbon, Quinta da Torre, 2829-516 Caparica, Portugal
nmm@di.fct.unl.pt, ning@fct.unl.pt
http://centria.di.fct.unl.pt/~nmm

Abstract. In this paper, a new approach to Mediterranean Water Eddy border detection is proposed. Kohonen self-organizing maps (SOM) are used as data mining tools to cluster image pixels through an unsupervised process. The clusters are visualized on the SOM internal map. From the visualization, the borders can be detected through an interactive way. As a result, interesting patterns are visible on the images. The proposed SOM approach is tested on Atlantic Ocean satellite data and compared with conventional gradient edge detectors.

Keywords: Remote sensing satellite data, border detection, self-organizing map (SOM), clustering, gradient edge detector

1 Introduction

With the increasing amount of multimedia databases, image retrieval is becoming a very important research area. Recent developments and promising issues on visual-based image retrieval are reviewed in [17]. Satellite data provides a huge resource for image retrieval in diverse fields including weather prediction, water resource, agriculture and environment sciences [11]. Data mining tools could be used to exploit interesting patterns from remote sensing satellite data in the context of image retrieval.

This paper will focus on the detection of Mediterranean Water Eddies (Meddies) on remote sensing satellite thermal images. Meddies allow the spreading of Mediterranean Water in the Atlantic at depth between 800 and 1200 meters, over thousands of kilometers with very little mixing. Due to its high salinity and temperature, the presence of Mediterranean Water influences strongly the hydrology and dynamics of the Atlantic Ocean and plays an important role in the transport of particles, suspended material and live organisms. Recently it was found that the clockwise rotation of the Meddies extends from the depths where they are centered up to the surface layer of the ocean. The identification of the surface signature of Meddies using satellite remote sensing data (sea surface temperature-SST and chlorophyll concentration) could be a key point for a better understanding of the dynamics of the Atlantic Ocean. Active ongoing research on the generation and movement of Meddies requires the inspection of satellite

Fernando Moura Pires, Salvador Abreu (Eds.): EPIA 2003, LNAI 2902, pp. 294–307, 2003.

maps. Until now this has been a mainly visual task [15], involving a large amount of time. Due to the large amount of information received at Oceanographic Institute satellite station, there is an urgent need for an automated analysis of such information. This paper will show how Kohonen self-organizing maps are helpful in the Meddy identification problem.

Kohonen self-organizing maps (SOM) are robust, fast, effective artificial neural networks for unsupervised clustering. SOMs allow us to reduce the amount of data and, simultaneously, project the data nonlinearly onto a lower dimensional grid. SOMs possess unique properties for data reduction, projection, and visualization [10]. Through topology preserving transformations, they project the data to a set of neurons on regular grid maps. The neurons close to each other in the grid space have similar features in the input space. The main advantage of using SOMs over other clustering algorithms for this task is their visualization capabilities. In fact, by visualizing the data projected into SOM's lower dimensional grid we are able to easily discover the cluster structure in data. Although there have been many studies concerning image acquisition using SOM in the literature, its application to the ocean research field for the purpose of border detection remains novel. A method for border detection using SOM will be studied in real world images. The application here presented to Oceanographic studies could be generalized to other application areas where border detection is needed.

In this paper, we develop an approach based on SOM neural networks to cluster image pixels according to color (SST) and spatial information in order to recognize Meddy borders through SOM visualization. Experiments show that SOM networks improve the capability of image analysis over the traditional gradient methods. The remainder of this paper is organized as follows. The research work related to our paradigm is addressed in section 2. A detailed description of the proposed approach is given in section 3. Then, the experimental results are discussed and a few issues are addressed in section 4. Finally, the paper is concluded with contributions and future work in section 5. Future work will be focused on developing a fully automated process for border detection.

2 Related Work

Clustering techniques have a wide range of utilization in remote sensing data processing, particularly, SOMs have been successfully applied to various real world problems, e.g., cloud segmentation [19,22], lineament delineation [20], over-ocean oceanic precipitable water retrieval [6], color compression [4], typhoon analysis and prediction [2], image indexing and thesaurus creation [16]. The usages of SOM in past research on image acquisition varied on data sources, extracted features and mining objectives. From the viewpoint of data, SOMs have been applied to remote sensing satellite data including cloud images [19,22,2], digital maps [16], earth surface [20] and oceanic images [6]. In these tasks, the data extracted in preprocess comes from pixel-level features, e.g., color [12], brightness [9], spatial position [12], or region-level features through texture analysis [13, 19] or other statistical approaches [2]. All these works use SOM as a clustering tool in an unsupervised manner, possibly followed by a fine-tuning and labeling step in a supervised manner.

Image segmentation is a process to partition an image into a set of homogeneous, continuous regions with high intra-similarity and low inter-similarity. The similarity criterion is strongly application-dependent and could be based on color, intensity and texture features. The two main approaches developed for image segmentation are region growing and border (edge) detection. In the former, the pixels are firstly separated into partial blocks and then merged into a number of continuous regions [12] or clusters [14]. In the latter, the main focus is not on finding the best segmentation of regions, but rather on detecting the borders of regions. Border detection plays an important role in many computer vision and image interpretation applications. A common approach to solve this problem is to use gradient edge detectors that record the edge as the location of abrupt changes of intensity to neighbors [18]. Variations of edge detectors have been defined on different gradient operators: Sobel, Prewitt, Roberts, and derivatives based on Gaussian filter, e.g. Laplacian, Zero-cross, Canny [5]. All these methods evaluate the magnitude and directions of edges in a small neighborhood. There have been other border detection algorithms proposed using neural networks. In [1], the authors successfully use the topological location of organized map neurons to simulate the outer shape of human head on gray scale images. A graph-based optimal border detection method is reported in [3], learning from the border tracing examples. Unfortunately, these methods are either single-purpose oriented or knowledge supported. Although the current approach proposed in this paper is human-aided, our final objective is to develop a general approach without a priori knowledge of the detected boundary.

3 Methodology

In the reported research work, the remote sensing data consisted on sea surface temperature images of Portugal received and processed at the Space Oceanography Center of the Instituto de Oceanografia (IO) da Faculdade de Ciências de Lisboa. The data was arranged into image maps, represented as matrices of float point numbers. Each cell of these matrices represents the sea surface temperature of a 1.1km x 1.1km region. With the help of graphical functions, the matrix can be shown as a surface image, where for each pixel, the color value represents water temperature. The surface signature of Meddies vary in terms of shape and size, so it is difficult to characterize them in the absence of known samples. Hence, the proposed approach is not to discover the Meddies directly, but rather to detect their borders. A region inside a border can be characterized by a continuous set of pixels with uniform color. The border of a region could then be used for detecting interesting patterns, namely Meddies. Thus, the purpose of this approach is to recognize the border of regions so that the interesting patterns are easily discovered. The proposed border detection is based on the following idea: a pixel is suitable to be recorded as a border location if its color differs enough from its neighboring pixels, otherwise, the pixel should not represent a border location. SOMs are used to cluster the pixels and recognize the border locations. In contrast to the traditional clustering algorithms resulting in a set of clusters or a hierarchy of clusters, our approach aims at discovering the pixels on the boundary of clusters rather than the clusters themselves.

The general scheme of the proposed methodology is outlined in Figure 1. First, a feature retrieval step executes a preprocess operation that precedes the main analysis, generating a feature vector for each pixel. The constitution of the feature vector depends on a few predetermined parameters such as neighborhood region and weight. Secondly, a SOM is initialized and trained with the extracted feature vectors. After training, each input vector is mapped to the neuron with the closest reference vector. Due to the topological preserving properties of SOM, the distances between neurons reflect the similarity of the projected samples in the input space. In the subsequent step, the inter-neuron distances are visualized on the SOM internal map. Consequently, the neurons on the boundary of clusters could be recognized according to a user defined threshold. Afterwards, the corresponding pixels projected on the boundary neurons are obtained as the border locations. After reducing the isolated points the remaining borders are shown as a new image. Current version allows users to perform the last three steps iteratively by adjusting the threshold until the obtained result is considered satisfactory. However, this process could be easily automatized when the Meddy identification model is available. In fact, the desirable threshold value can be easily acquired through proper interaction with the Meddy classification module (i.e. if Meddy classifier is a probability function, we need to search for the threshold value that returns a local maximum in the classification probability).

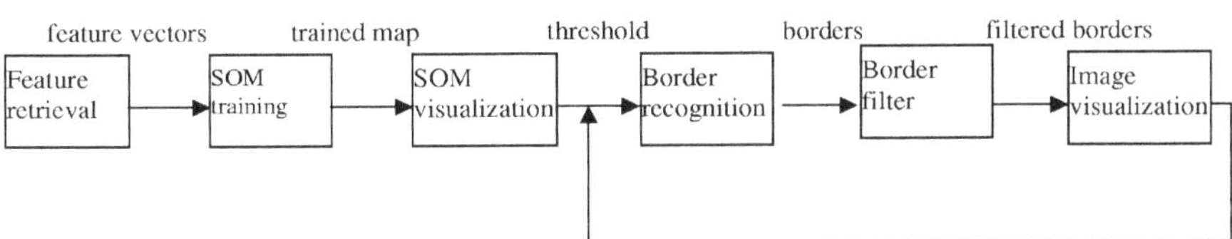

Fig. 1. Procedure of border detection

Feature retrieval is a critical component of image processing, closely related to the objective of mining tasks. For this problem, pixels are characterized by color and spatial features. Intuitively, pixels in similar color should be grouped in the same cluster, meantime, pixels with similar color to neighbors should locate themselves inside the clusters whereas pixels with different color to neighbors should be on the boundary of clusters. Typically, the feature vector is determined by the type and radius of the neighborhood region. In section 4.2, we will study two types of neighborhood region: cross and square. The former uses the neighbors on the same row or column as the current pixel. The latter uses the neighbors inside the square centered at the pixel. A neighborhood of size zero and one was used in our experiments. In Figure 2, the innermost cross or square correspond to a 1-radius region, the second cross or square would correspond to a 2-radius region. When the radius is set as one, a feature vector is composed of 4-neighbors in cross region, and 8-neighbors in square region as well as the central pixel. A weight could be assigned to the center pixel to emphasize the importance of color features over spatial features. The importance of this parameter will be analyzed in section 4.2. After deciding the neighborhood region type, a gliding window scans over the whole matrix from the left to right columns and from top to bottom rows for the same column. For each pixel, a feature vector $[x_{i1}, x_{i2}, \ldots x_{ik}]$ was extracted within the neighborhood region, where k is the dimension of the feature vector. The feature retrieval step ends up with a collection of feature vectors.

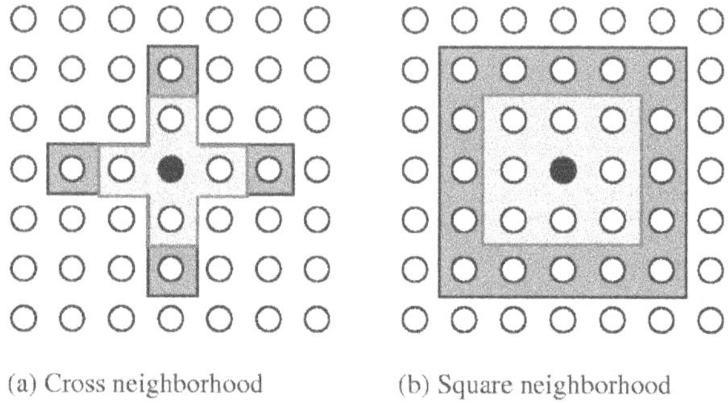

Fig. 2. Neighborhood region of pixel marked with blank dot

In the second step in Figure 1, the extracted feature vectors are sequentially fed to the SOM, where each neuron corresponds to a set of similar pixels. Initially, a 2-dimensional map is created with a lattice of neurons on a topologically regular grid. Each neuron is associated with a reference vector $[m_{i1}, m_{i2}, \ldots m_{ik}]$ reflecting the strength of association to input vectors. A neuron is connected to adjacent neurons by a neighborhood function h. The matching between map neurons and input vectors is measured by Euclidean distance. During the unsupervised training process, the reference vectors are updated according to the input vectors. In this paper, we have applied batch SOM as our training algorithm. Batch SOM algorithms [10] list the input vectors one by one under the best-matching units and update the neurons according to the whole data set at the end of each epoch. The reference vectors are calculated as the weighted mean of the input vectors that are similar either to them or to their topological neighbors:

$$m_p(t+1) = \frac{\sum_{i=1}^{n} h_{c_i p} x_i}{\sum_{i=1}^{n} h_{c_i p}}$$

The batch SOMs have advantages due to order-insensitivity to input data, facilitating the development of parallel processing, and eliminating the influence of learning rate as a coefficient on final result [7].

Regarding SOM visualization in Figure 1 (third step), we just need to examine SOM projection grid. SOM offers a visualized approach to investigate the rough clusters existing in data by a regular grid. For this purpose, the average distance (u-distance) between each neuron and its neighbors is calculated. The neurons with high distances indicate the boundary of clusters, and the neurons with small distances indicate the clusters themselves [21].

After SOM is trained, the input data is mapped to the best matching units (with the closest reference vectors). To recognize the cluster boundary, a typical procedure is to apply a threshold to the map. The neurons with the distances bigger than the threshold are considered as the border neurons. Accordingly, the samples in training data projected on one of such neurons could be found. The pixels corresponding to those samples are considered as border locations. Using different thresholds, multi-solutions of borders could be obtained.

For better image visualization, the obtained borders of previous step could be further processed by a border filter. A simple but effective approach is to reduce the isolated pixels, which is motivated by the continuous property of 'good' borders. Afterwards, an image is generated which is zero for all pixels except the interesting pixels, i.e., the border pixels.

4 Experimental Results

The border detection approach has been applied to the oceanographic data and performed in a machine with 256M memory and intel celeron 1.03 GHz processor running windows XP professional operating system. Typically, the oceanographic images used in our study are 2-dimensional matrices of 700 x 700 pixels. The operations for feature retrieval, border recognition, image visualization, SOM training and SOM visualization are carried out in an adapted version of SOM software [10,23]. For the purpose of comparison, six edge gradient detectors are performed followed by the border filter operation. The parameters are set as below:

- A cross region of 1-radius is used and the weight of center pixel is set as 10 in feature retrieval step.
- The neurons are configured on a hexagonal lattice with the size of 10 x 10 map grid.
- Topological function is defined as 'Gaussian', and the neuron neighborhood radius decreases linearly to stabilize the effect of the input vectors on the map.
- The reference vectors are initialized linearly and trained in batch for 20 epoches.

4.1 Effectiveness

For clarity, we will use two images as case studies to our problem. The first image is a part of the second. Figure 3 (a) shows the original image (image one), where the Meddy is composed of two water vortexes that, in the figure, are similar to up-side-down mushroom shapes. The second image contains several Meddies and will be studied in section 4.3. Figure 3 (b) visualizes the u-distance on the trained map. The resulting detected borders are shown in Figure 3 (c) and (d) at the threshold of 1.0 and 1.12 respectively. As it can be observed, the detected borders match to the actual borders very well. The choice of threshold value is critical to the resulting borders. The threshold value effects on the width and sensitivity of detected borders. Small threshold values obtain weak borders with smooth difference to neighbors as well as strong borders with abrupt difference to neighbors. A too small value of threshold may result in wide borders due to blurred borders in the original image and also lead to many false borders due to nonuniform color inside regions. A too big value of threshold may miss valuable borders. Experiments have also been done using variants of conventional gradient detectors. Canny method is relatively computationally expensive, but effective in processing noise because of the Gaussian smoothing function to remove the isolated noise, nonmaxima suppression to thin the ridges, and double thresholds scheme to reduce the false edge fragments [5]. Since 'Canny' operator performs better than others, the results of 'Canny' method at different thresholds are shown in Figure 3 (e-f). It was observed that the more significant and continuous borders were detected by the proposed SOM algorithm. Correspondingly, 'Canny' either fails to discover all borders (at the high threshold) or produces too much noise (at the low threshold). This indicates that the paradigm of pixel clustering makes the SOM approach more robust to noise and blurred borders. It can be stated that the borders of regions are recognized successfully in the experiments, demonstrating that our approach is practical for this problem.

4.2 Effect of Parameters

The representation of a feature vector depends on the neighbor region, radius and weight. Since we are trying to detect thin borders, for presented results we have used a radius of zero (single point neighborhood region) and one. We have evaluated the results of the algorithms according to the following four criteria. Some experiments have been done on image one by varying the neighborhood region and weight in order to investigate the effect of these parameters on the resultant borders. The criteria used for evaluation include:

- **Noise robustness** reflects the sensitivity to noise and blurred borders.
- **Continuity** means the continuous degree of borders.
- **Definition** concerns the width of borders. A broad border is regarded as badly defined because it does not contain much details, whereas, a thin border is well defined.
- **Threshold detection** evaluates the sensitivity of results to the threshold value and consequently how easy it is to detect the threshold for a human.

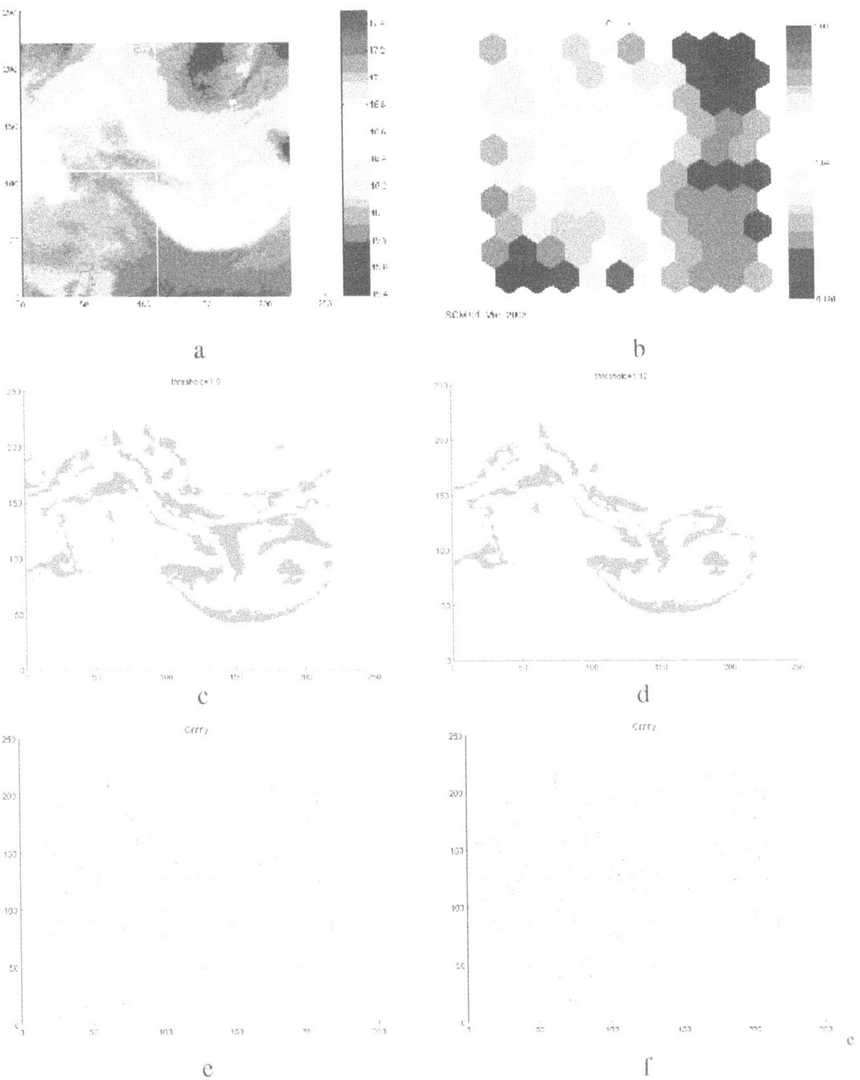

Fig. 3. (a) Original image. (b) U-distance visualization on SOM. (c) Detected borders at threshold of 1.0. (d) Detected borders at threshold of 1.12. (e-f) Borders detected by 'Canny' gradient operator: (e) threshold=0.007, (f) threshold=0.006.

We will consider three neighborhood regions: 'cross', 'square', 'point'. A variant of weights from 1 to 10,000 are assigned to the central pixel. For each set of parameters, the SOM approach is performed on the image and detected borders are evaluated from the viewpoint of the four criteria. Although extensive tests have been performed, for lack of space, only the two images in Figure 4 have been included in this paper. Obviously, the desirable threshold value increases with the weight due to the bigger distance between neurons.

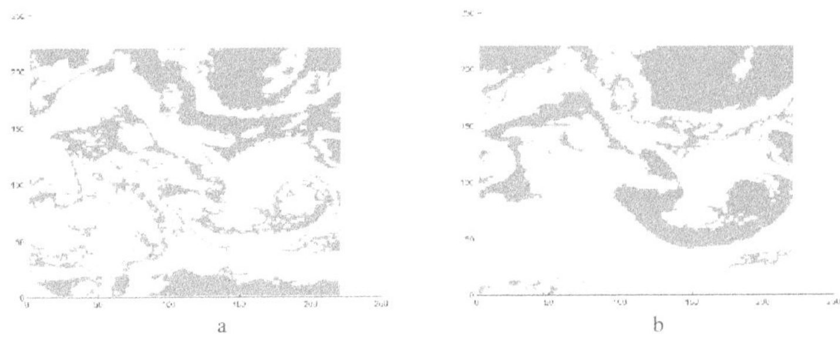

Fig. 4. (a) Detected borders with 'point' region and 1-weight at threshold of 0.05. (b) Detected borders with 'square' region and 90-weight at threshold of 7.

Experiments in Table 1 demonstrate that 'point' region results in rather discontinuous borders with too much noise and difficulty on threshold detection, but quite well defined borders. In this case where only color feature is used for clustering, the pixels in infrequent color, usually on the cluster boundary, are regarded as border locations.

'Square' region has good performance on continuity and robustness, while fails on threshold detection and border definition, possibly because it is morle sensitive to the neighboring pixels. Also, 'cross' neighbor is preferred to 'square' region due to less features used for training. In fact, the computational cost of 'square' region is around 30% more than that of 'cross' region.

Regarding 'cross' region, we find that weights between 6 and 20 get the best results on all the four criteria. Too small values (<6) and too big values (>20) are incapable of finding good borders in all aspects. For small weights (<6), the resultant borders contain much noise and discontinuous fragments. This is possibly due to the nonuniform color inside the regions. A suitable weight on the central pixel makes the color difference between the pixels inside regions and those outside more significant than the difference among the pixels inside. For big weights(>20), the resultant borders are continuous and very robust to noise, but much wider because of blurred borders. In summary, 'cross' region and weights between 6 and 20 will obtain good results with continuous, robust, well-defined, and threshold insensitive borders. According to the empirical knowledge, 1-radius cross region with 10 as the weight of center pixel is a good choice for feature representation.

Because it is impossible to test all values by hand, we take the risk of missing the desirable threshold value. The optimal threshold value search and evaluation on results depend on human subjective judgement without any quantitative analysis. We think that with an automatical process for threshold selection (such as the one referred in section 3) this problem can be solved.

The obtained SOM relies heavily on the initial conditions, e.g., map size and training epoches. Generally, a big size map is needed for a large volume of data to preserve the topological property. Experiments on image one show that a map of size 5x5 does not result in significant performance loss compared to big maps. A map of size 10 x 10 trained by 10 epoches suffices for neuron topological organization on the map.

Table 1. Evaluation of results

Neighborhood region		Noise robustness	Continuity	Definition	Threshold detection
Point		very bad	very bad	good	bad
Square		good	good	bad	bad
	weight<6	bad	bad	good	bad
Cross	6≤weight≤20	good	good	good	good
	weight>20	good	good	bad	good

4.3 Multi-Meddy Detection

When several Meddies are present in the same image, the method here presented is still feasible. The original image (image two) and resultant borders at threshold of 2.3 are shown in Figure 5 (a-b). Despite the huge number of image elements that are present, we are still able to detect several Meddies. However, different threshold values should be used on different Meddies. This is why partial detection is another issue regarding multi-Meddy detection. We have performed partial detection by exploring the local patterns in partial images instead of detecting the global patterns on the whole image directly. For the purpose of partial detection, the whole image is split into a set of partial ones of predefined size and each partial image is processed respectively by the proposed method in the same manner. Figure 5 (c) shows the borders combined by the results of partial detections from another ocean region. In this image the thresholds are chosen manually for each partial image. Unfortunately, results are still unclear due to the manual selection of a different threshold for each partial image. Again, an automatical process for threshold selection should solve this problem.

Another important factor making sense to resulted border is the predetermined size of splitting window. If the window size is too small, the window will separate the continuous borders into fragments. If the window size is too big, the window loses the advantage of image splitting. Again, image splitting raises the difficulty of threshold assignment. Generally, the smaller the size is, the less the difference between samples inside becomes so that a smaller threshold is needed. Again as the number of splits increases, manual selection of threshold value is impractical.

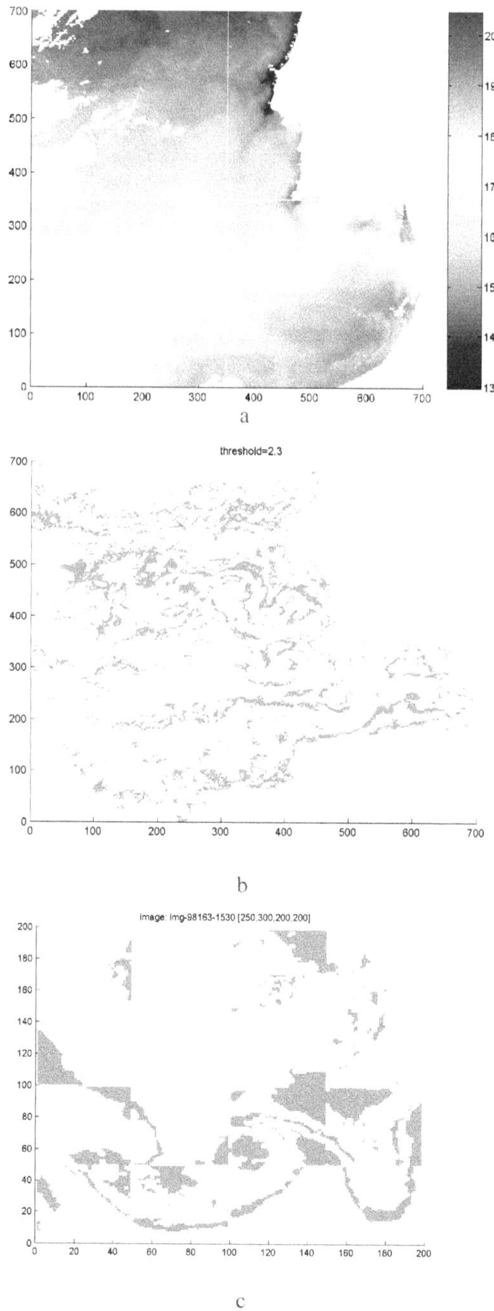

Fig. 5. (a) Original image. (b) Detected borders at threshold of 2.3. (c) Partial detection on a subregion with a splitting window of size 50 x 50.

5 Conclusions

SOMs have been applied as data-driven artificial neural networks for data clustering and visualization to a legion of different applications. Here, SOMs are used for border detection on remote sensing satellite data. The main contributions of the paper include:

- A feature representation is defined on the basis of color and spatial features of pixels.
- A SOM visualized approach is proposed to recognize the borders through an interactive way.
- The performance on Atlantic Ocean satellite data is demonstrated. Experimental results show that the proposed approach works relatively well in terms of effectiveness. The effect of parameters on resultant borders are analyzed.

The results of the proposed approach are encouraging and produce good ground for further research in remote sensing field as a general border detection method. Three interesting problems should be addressed in future work.

The current border detection is not an overall automatic procedure, instead, SOMs provide an interactive way to detect the cluster boundary from visualizations. However, the search for a proper threshold value is difficult and involves multiple trials. A future direction might determine the rough value of the threshold automatically, then adjust it manually until a suitable value is found. Here, u-distance offers a useful heuristic to determine the desirable threshold similar to k-dist in DBSCAN [8]. The u-distances in the grid space estimate the density possibility in the input space. Usually, the density of inner-cluster neurons differ from that of boundary neurons significantly. When sorting the u-distances and displaying them in a graph, the density distribution could be computed to discover the suitable threshold. Also, as it was previously told, after connecting this module with a classification module, the threshold can be automatically detected in a given classification problem. Since this search will be based on all possible threshold values, the methods to select most probable thresholds will also help the computer to automatically preform this search. Namely, we expect to improve the results presented in section 4.3.

Another issue is pattern recognition. Although the detected borders help to find interesting patterns, our final interest maybe identification of valuable patterns, namely Meddies. The automatic shape recognition is the main objective of our future work. For this purpose, some preliminary and extremely important issues will be addressed such as the definition of the image samples and the identification of the set of high-level features characterizing the presence of Meddies in satellite images.

Sequence border detection is the third future direction. Detecting borders from a time sequence of oceanographic images is an attractive topic for tendency analysis which may provide better understanding of those borders to users. Therefore, as a future direction, an interesting thought might be to focus on a promising area discovered from a special image and then perform the border detection operation on the sequence. Thus, the evolution of the borders can be visible from the time series of visualizations.

Clearly the next step regarding Meddy detection will be the systematic application of this algorithm to Meddy border recognition in available images. This will be a dramatic improvement and will allow for the mining of the IO large image database. This work will allow experts to simultaneously identify positive instances of Meddies, a task much easier than to specify domain knowledge. Moreover, high level features such as water vortexes are difficult to translate into pixel-level constraints. As a side result a set of training examples will be available for training a statistical Meddy classifier. This task will be part of a broader project to integrate the advanced AI techniques and expertise into the study of Oceanic phenomena. The ultimate goal of the collaboration with IO is to develop numerical models for the understanding of the Oceanic Mediterranean Undercurrent off the southern coast of Portugal in real time. The creation of the proposed automatic identification system will provide a new and much needed tool for the understanding of the dynamical aspects of Ocean. This could have a strong economic impact in Portugal by allowing a much better understanding of fishing resources, helping to trace sea pollution or even by helping to better predict sea storms.

Acknowledgement. The authors would like to thank the Instituto de Oceanografia, Faculdade de Ciências, Universidade de Lisboa for providing the interesting application problem and suggestions on a first version of the paper. We also thank the Neural networks research center, Helsinki University of Technology for distributing SOM software.

References

1. C. C. Reyes-Aldasoro, A. L. Aldeco: Image segmentation and compression using neural networks. Advances in Artificial Perception and Robotics CIMAT, Guanajuato, Mexico (2000)
2. K. Asanobu: Data mining for typhoon image collection. In Proceedings of the 2nd International Workshop on Multimedia Data Mining (MDM/KDD'2001), in conjunction with ACM SIGKDD Conference, San Francisco, USA (2001) 68–77
3. M. Brejl, M. Sonka: Medical image segmentation: automated design of border detection criteria from examples. Special Issue of Journal of Electronic Imaging **8(1)** (1999) 54–64
4. J. E. Boggess, P. B. Nation, M. E. Harmon: A Kohonen map neural network for data compression of color information in digitized in digitized images. In Proceedings of the 7th Florida AI Research Symposium, Pensacola Beach, FL (1994)
5. J. F. Canny: A computational approach to edge detection. IEEE Trans. Pattern Analysis and Machine Intelligence (1986) 679–698
6. H. Chen, J. Bian, P. Yang, D. Lu: SOM-network-based algorithm for retrieving over-ocean precipitable water from the SSM/I measurements. In Proceedings of SPIE **3502** 149–152
7. Q. Ding, M. Canton, D. Diaz et al.: Data mining survey. `http://midas.cs.ndsu.nodak.edu/~ding/`

8. M. Ester, H. Kriegel, J. Sander, X. Xu: A density-based algorithm for discovering clusters in large spatial database with noise. In Proceedings of Int'l Conference on Knowledge Discovery in Databases and Data Mining (KDD96), Montreal, Canada (1996)
9. I. E. Evangelou, D. G. Hadjimitsis, A. A. Lazakidou, C. Clayton: Data mining and knowledge discovery in complex image data using artificial neural networks. http://citeseer.nj.nec.com/529713.html
10. T. Kohonen: Self-organizing maps. Springer Verlag, Berlin, Second edition (1997)
11. G. Healey, A. Jain: Retrieving multispectral satellite images using physics-based invariant representations. IEEE Trans. Pattern Anal. Machine Intelligence **18** (1996) 842–848
12. Y. Jiang, K. Chen, Z. Zhou: SOM based image segmentation. In G. Wang, Q. Liu, Y. Yao, and A. Skowron (eds.): Lecture Notes in Artificial Intelligence, **2639** (RSFDGrC'03), Berlin, Springer-Verlag (2003), http://cs.nju.edu.cn/people/zhouzh/zhouzh.files/publication/rsfdgrc03b.pdf
13. B. S. Manjunath, W. Y. Ma: Texture features for browsing and retrieval of image data. IEEE Trans. Pattern Anal. Machine Intelligence **18** (1996) 837–842
14. J. Moreira, L. D. F. Costa: Neural-based color image segmentation and classification using self-organizing maps. In Proceedings of Anais do IX SIBGRAPI (1996) 47–54
15. P. B. Oliveira, N. Serra, A. F. G. Fiúza, I. Ambar: A study of meddies using simultaneous in situ and satellite observations. In D. Halpern (ed.), Satellites, Oceanography and Society, Elsevier Oceanography Series **63** (2000) 125–148
16. M. Ramsey, H. Chen, B. Zhu, B. R. Schatz: A collection of visual thesauri for browsing large collections of geographic images. Journal of the American Society of Information Science **50(9)** (1999) 826–834
17. Y. Rui, T. Huang, S. Chang: Image retrieval: current techniques, promising directions and open issues. Journal of Visual Communication and Image Representation **10(4)** (1999) 39–62
18. U. Sangthongpraw, Y. Rangsanseri, P. Thitimajshima: Incorporating cluster information into multispectral image edge detection. In ACRS, Digital Image Processing (1998) http://www.gisdevelopment.net/aars/acrs/1998/ts9/ts9003pf.htm
19. O. Simula, A. Visa: Self-organizing feature maps in texture classification and segmentation. In Proceedings of International Conference on Artificial Neural Networks, Brighton, United Kingdom (1992)
20. N. Vassilasl, S. Perantonis, E. Charou, T. Tsenoglou, M. Stefouli and S. Varoufakis: Delineation of lineaments from satellite data based on efficient neural network and pattern recognition techniques. In Proceeding of Companion Volumn, SETN, the 2nd Hellenic Conference On AI, Tjhessaloniki, Greece (2002) 355–366
21. J. Vesanto, J. Himberg, E. Alhoniemi and J. Parhankangas: Self-organizing map in matlab: the SOM toolbox. In Proceedings of the Matlab DSP Conference, Espoo, Finland (1999) 35–40
22. A. Visa, K. Valkealahti, J. Iivarinen, O. Simula: Experiences from operational cloud classifier based on self-organizing map. In Procedings of SPIE, Orlando, Florida, Applications of Artificial Neural Networks V **2243** (1994) 484–495
23. Laboratory of Computer and information sciences & Neural networks research center, Helsinki University of Technology: SOM Toolbox 2.0. http://www.cis.hut.fi/projects/somtoolbox/

Predicting Harmful Algae Blooms

Rita Ribeiro[1] and Luis Torgo[2]

[1] LIACC, University of Porto, R. Campo Alegre, 823, 4150 Porto, Portugal
[2] LIACC-FEP, University of Porto, R. Campo Alegre, 823, 4150 Porto, Portugal
{rita,ltorgo}@liacc.up.pt,
http://www.liacc.up.pt/~ltorgo

Abstract. In several applications the main interest resides in predicting rare and extreme values. This is the case of the prediction of harmful algae blooms. Though it's rare, the occurrence of these blooms has a strong impact in river life forms and water quality and turns out to be a serious ecological problem. In this paper, we describe a data mining method whose main goal is to predict accurately this kind of rare extreme values. We propose a new splitting criterion for regression trees that enables the induction of trees achieving these goals. We carry out an analysis of the results obtained with our method on this application domain and compare them to those obtained with standard regression trees. We conclude that this new method achieves better results in terms of the evaluation statistics that are relevant for this kind of applications.

Keywords: Outliers, rare events, prediction, regression trees.

1 Introduction

In most prediction problems, the main interest resides in predicting accurately the most frequent cases. Nevertheless, there are some applications where it would be of major importance to predict rare situations. In some of these applications, rare events are associated with extreme values of a variable. Harmful algae blooms rivers are one of these applications. Algae blooms consist in the occurrence of unusually high values of certain algae. Predicting these blooms is a task with strong socio-economic impact. Given that the target variable (the occurrence) is a continuous value, we are facing a regression problem. However, the main difference to standard regression tasks is that our main interest is being accurate at the prediction of occurrences of rare high values of the target variable. The goal of our proposal is not only to anticipate the occurrence of an extreme value but also to be accurate at predicting its concrete value.

In this paper we propose a splitting criterion for regression trees which enables the induction of models that meet our applications requirements. We start with a brief overview of our target application in section 2. In section 3, we formalize our target problems and propose evaluation criteria that should guide the search for the best models. Section 4 describes the details of our proposal. The results obtained with this proposal are presented in section 5. We finish with the conclusions of this work and future research directions.

Fernando Moura Pires, Salvador Abreu (Eds.): EPIA 2003, LNAI 2902, pp. 308–312, 2003.

2 Application Description

In recent years there have been several studies concerning the impact man has on environment and subsequent biological processes. During one of such studies over the state of rivers, numerous reports revealed an excessive summer algae growth in temperate climates across the world. The blooms of these algae reduce the water clarity and the oxygen levels, causing a massive death of river fish and decreasing the water quality. Therefore, the early forecast of these blooms is of extreme importance. From the analysis of a range of measurable chemical concentrations, the objective of this application is to identify the crucial chemical control variables to infer the biological state of the river, in this case the frequence of occurrence of certain algae communities. The data[1] we used was obtained during a related research study. It includes water quality samples from different European rivers during a period of approximately one year. These water samples were submitted to chemical analysis and the resulting 8 measures along with 3 other characteristics (season of the year, river size and river speed), were associated with the frequency of seven different harmful algae found in the water.

The long-term objective of this modelling task is to anticipate the rare occurrence of high concentrations of these seven harmful algae, given the chemical analysis measurements. This would avoid the need of trained manpower to carry out the microscopic analysis necessary to assert the frequency of the algae, which is slower, expensive, and not easily automated.

3 Problem Formulation

In this section we present a general formalization of our problem. Let D be a data set, consisting of n cases $\{\langle \mathbf{x}_i, y_i \rangle\}_{i=1}^n$, where $\mathbf{x}_i$ is a vector of p discrete or continuous variables, and y_i is a continuous target variable value. As we have mentioned before, we are interested in models that are able to predict accurately rare extreme values of Y. To achieve this goal we need to formalize the notion of rare extreme values. Box plots are visualization tools that are often used to identify extreme-valued outliers. Extreme values are defined in these plots as values above or below the so-called adjacent values. Let r be the interquartile range defined as the difference between the 3rd and 1st quartiles of the target variable. The upper adjacent value, adj_H, is defined as the largest observation that is less or equal to the 3rd quartile plus $1.5r$. Equivalently, the lower adjacent value, adj_L, is defined as the smallest observation that is greater or equal to the 1st quartile minus $1.5r$. We can define our rare extreme values as,

$$O = \{y \in D \mid y > adj_H \vee y < adj_L\} \quad O_H = \{y \in D \mid y > adj_H\} \tag{1}$$
$$O_L = \{y \in D \mid y < adj_L\}$$

Having described the main features of our target applications we need to define some evaluation criteria to guide the search for the best models. Typical performance measures used in regression settings, such as the mean squared error,

[1] http://www.erudit.de/erudit/competitions/ic-99/

are inadequate as they do not stress the fact that we are only interested in the performance in extreme values.

In the information retrieval literature (e.g. [3]) the notion of relevance seems particularly adequate to our needs. Relevance is defined as the value or utility of a system output as a result of a user search. Relevance is most of the times assessed using two measures: *precision* and *recall*. Our proposal consists of adapting these two measures to our problem setup with the goal of developing a learning tool that maximizes the relevance of the induced model to our application goals.

We define recall in the context of our target applications as the proportion of extreme-valued outliers in our data that are predicted as such.

$$recall = \mid \{\hat{y} \in \hat{Y}_O \mid (y \in O_H \wedge \ \hat{y} > adj_H) \vee (y \in O_L \wedge \hat{y} < adj_L)\} \mid / \mid O \mid \tag{2}$$

where $\hat{Y}_O$ is the set of $\hat{y}$ predictions of the model for the outlier cases (i.e. O).

With respect to precision, we could not use the classical definition. As we are looking to be accurate at predicting the rare extreme values, we had to adapt it to a regression context. The new definition of precision ($precision_{regr}$) takes into account the distance between the predicted and true values and, at the same time, maintains the scale of the measure within the 0..1 interval so that we are able to integrate recall and precision into a single measure using standard approaches. Our proposed definition of $precision_{regr}$ is the complement of $NMSE_O$, i.e., normalized squared error of the model for the outliers,

$$precision_{regr} = 1 - \sum_{y_i \in O} (\hat{y}_i - y_i)^2 / \sum_{y_i \in O} (\bar{Y} - y_i)^2 \tag{3}$$

Using the F-measure [3], we can obtain an overall evaluation measure from the values of recall and $precision_{regr}$, providing a global preference criterion that can be used to guide the search for the models. It is defined as,

$$F = \left((\beta^2 + 1) \cdot precision \cdot recall\right) / \left(\beta^2 \cdot precision + recall\right) \tag{4}$$

where β controls the relative importance of recall to precision. This is definition we use replacing precision by our proposed $precision_{regr}$.

4 An Approach Using Regression Trees

Standard regression trees are obtained using a procedure that minimizes the mean squared error. This means that the best splits for each tree node are chosen to minimize the weighed squared error between the two branches. As mentioned by Buja and Lee [2] this criterion is not adequate for several data mining applications. That is also the case of our target problems.

The main idea of our proposal (*c.f.* [4] for full details) to avoid the problems of minimizing the weighed squared error, is to use the F-measure presented in Equation (4) to guide the split selection procedure used to grow the trees. The best split is chosen according to the maximum F-measure value achieved by one of its partitions, left or right branch.

In order to obtain the F-measure for the branches of a candidate split we need to obtain the values of precision and recall. Let $\bar{y}_t$ be the average Y value in the node t. The precision in that node is given by the complement of the $NMSE_O$, taking $\bar{y}_t$ as the predicted value. Depending on this value $\bar{y}_t$, being above or below the global median Y, we consider this branch as a tentative to predict high or low outliers, and calculate its precision accordingly.

Regarding the recall of a node t we define it as the proportion of high outliers (O_H) if the y_t lies above adj_H and as the proportion of low outliers (O_H) if the y_t lies below adj_H. When a trial split leads to a branch having an average target value that is not an outlier, the respective recall is zero. This would lead to an F value of zero according to Equation (4). To avoid this undesirable situation we have added a small threshold to the value of recall in Equation (4) so that the value of F is not zero even when the recall is null. A more detailed definition of precision and recall assigned to a node t, is given in [4].

Another important question that needs to be addressed when developing a tree-based system, is the tree growth stopping criteria, as mentioned in [4]. Currently, our method obtains a tree model in a single stage, stopping the tree growth when one of the following conditions arise: the F-measure of the node is above a certain user-definable threshold; the node does not contain any extreme value (i.e. $D_t \cap O = \phi$).

5 Experimental Results

In this section we describe the results of our method with the algae data. We compare our proposal to its base paradigm, standard regression trees.

Given that we have to predict the frequency of seven different algae, we have divided this task in seven different multivariate regression problems. Table 1 gives the number of high extreme-valued contained in the datasets for each algal.

We have carried out 5 repetitions of a 10-fold cross validation experiment using the 200 water samples. These experiments were designed with the goal of estimating the average difference in $precision_{regr}$, recall, and F-measure, between a standard regression tree and our proposed method. For the standard method we have used the package *rpart* of R, using the best tree obtained based on cross validation error-complexity, according to the 0-SE rule method described in [1]. The statistical significance of the observed differences was asserted through paired t-tests. Differences that are significant at the 95% level were marked with one sign, while differences significant at 99% have two signs. Plus (+) signs are used to mark differences favorable to standard regression trees, while minus (−) signs are used to indicate the significant wins of our method. Differences that are not significant at these confidence levels have no sign. The F-measure was calculated with $\beta = 1$, meaning that the same weight was given to $precision_{regr}$ and recall (*c.f.* Equation (4)).

The results of our experiments are shown on Table 1. This table shows an overall advantage of our method, though not too significant. In terms of the

Table 1. Standard regression trees vs our method.

Datasets	extreme outliers	$precision_{regr}$			$recall$			$Fmeasure$		
		CART	Our method	Signif	CART	Our method	Signif	CART	Our method	Signif
algal1	12	0.2787366	0.4261633		0.0000000	0.3500000	−−	0.0000000	0.3479222	−−
algal2	10	0.1258636	0.1455305		0.0066667	0.0700000		0.0058272	0.0667674	
algal3	22	0.0654252	0.1559563	−	0.0933333	0.1980000	−	0.0714700	0.1656287	−
algal4	16	0.1049812	0.1358873		0.1416667	0.1973333		0.0954843	0.0985749	
algal5	13	0.0884105	0.1438035		0.0400000	0.0966667		0.0399061	0.0596241	
algal6	19	0.0934455	0.1100473		0.1276667	0.1266667		0.0848333	0.0935813	
algal7	21	0.1037794	0.0905430		0.0950000	0.1083333		0.0960736	0.0863567	

F-measure we generally achieve better results. The exception is algal 7, where a poor $precision_{regr}$ penalizes the F measure. The value of zero recall, obtained by *rpart* for algal 1, is a consequence of models that do not predict any of the outliers as such, which occurs when a tree does not have any leaf with an average value that is an outlier.

6 Conclusions

We have described a new splitting criteria for regression trees with the goal of addressing the problem of predicting harmful algae blooms. This problem belongs to a specific class of data mining applications, where the main goal of modeling is to predict accurately outlier values in the target variable. Our proposal obtains regression trees designed to maximize the number of extreme-valued outliers that are captured and the precision at predicting their values.

Regarding future work we plan to investigate further this application problem, trying to overcome the failure of our models in terms of $precision_{regr}$ in some situations. Our current explanation lies on the tree growth stopping criteria and we intend to explore other alternatives to the current user settable threshold on the F-measure value. We also intend to improve recall in order to minimize the algae blooms missed by our models.

Acknowledgements. This work is partially supported by project MODAL, POSI/FEDER/FCT and PRAXIS XXI plurianual support to LIACC.

References

1. L. Breiman, J. Friedman, R. Olshen, and C. Stone. *Classification and Regression Trees.* Statistics/Probability Series. Wadsworth & Brooks/Cole Advanced Books & Software, 1984.
2. A. Buja and Y.-S. Lee. Data mining criteria for tree-based regression and classification. In *Proceedings of ACM SIGKDD International Conference on Knowledge Discovery and Data Mining*, pages 27–36, 2001.
3. C. Van Rijsbergen. *Information Retrieval.* Dept. of Computer Science, University of Glasgow, 2nd edition, 1979.
4. L. Torgo and R. Ribeiro. Predicting outliers. In *Proceedings of the seventh Europena Conference on Principles and Practice of Knowledge Discovery in Databases (PKDD 2003)*, LNAI. Springer, 2003. To appear.

Improving Progressive Sampling via Meta-learning

Rui Leite and Pavel Brazdil

LIACC/FEP, University of Porto
Rua do Campo Alegre, 823
4150-180 Porto
{rleite,pbrazdil}@liacc.up.pt

Abstract. We present a method that can be seen as an improvement of standard progressive sampling method. The method exploits information concerning performance of a given algorithm on past datasets, which is used to generate predictions of the stopping point. Experimental evaluation shows that the method can lead to significant time savings without significant losses in accuracy.

1 Introduction

The existence of large datasets creates problems for many data mining algorithms that are readily available. Memory requirements and processing times are often rather excessive. Besides, using all the data does not always lead to marked improvements. The models generated on the basis of a part of the data (sample) are often precise enough for the given aim, and the computational cost involved is incomparably lower.

These problems have motivated research in different data reduction methods. In this paper we are concerned with one particular data reduction method, which is oriented towards reducing the number of examples to be used, and is often referred to as sampling.

The aim of the sampling methods is, in general, to determine which proportion of the data should be used to generate the given model type (e.g. a decision tree). At the same time, we want the model to be comparable to the model that would be generated using all the available data. The existing methods can be divided into two groups: Static sampling methods and dynamic sampling methods [JohnLang96]. As for the first group, the aim is generate a sample by examining the data, but without considering the particular machine learning algorithm to be used afterwards. Some researchers refer to this method as a *filter approach*.

In contrast to this the *dynamic sampling methods* take the machine learning algorithm into account. The final sample is determined by searching though the space of alternatives. The system explores the alternatives in a systematic manner and the performance of the machine learning algorithm is used to guide the future search. Some researchers refer to this method as a *wrapper approach*. It was shown that the dynamic (wrapper) methods obtain in general better results than the static (filter) methods, although they tend to be slower [JohnLang96].

Fernando Moura Pires, Salvador Abreu (Eds.): EPIA 2003, LNAI 2902, pp. 313–323, 2003.

One particular dynamic method that can be used in conjunction with large datasets is called *efficient progressive sampling* [Prov99]. The method starts with a small data sample and in each subsequent step uses progressively larger sample to generate a model and to check its performance. This continues until no significant increase in accuracy is observed. One important characteristic is the size of the samples used in each subsequent step. The sizes follow a geometric progression. Another important aspect is how convergence is detected. The authors use a method referred to as LRLS (linear regression with local sampling). Supposing the algorithm is examining sample ni, LRLS uses 10 samples of similar size to generate models and estimate their accuracies. These estimates are supplied to linear regression algorithm and the inclination of the resulting line is examined. If it is about horizontal (i.e. the inclination is sufficiently near to zero), the process of sampling is terminated. As it was shown by the authors, this method worked well with the large datasets considered. However, a question arises when exactly this method is useful.

We have re-implemented a similar method and used it on a mixture of both large and medium size datasets. We have verified that in many medium size datasets the method required more time than a simple scheme that would learn from all the data. This is easy to explain. The method constructs a succession of models using progressively increasing samples. However, in many cases the accuracy will simply keep increasing and hence the stopping condition will not be satisfied. This means that the algorithm will process all the data, but with an additional overhead of using a succession of increasing samples beforehand.

Our aim was to improve the method so that it could be applied to any dataset, no matter what its size is. The basis strategy relies on eliminating some samples from consideration. We use previous knowledge about the algorithm itself, that is, meta-learning on past results. This is justified by quite good previous results with this technique [BrazdilEtal03].

The rest of the paper is organized as follows. Section 2 describes the proposed method in detail. Section 3 describes the evaluation method and experimental results obtained. Finally, we present the conclusions.

2 Predicting the Stopping Point in Sampling

Dynamic sampling methods use a succession of models generated by a given learning algorithm on the basis of a sequence of progressively increasing samples. The aim is to determine the point in which the accuracy does not increase any more. We call this point a stopping point. Fig. 1 shows a typical learning curve and the stopping point is represented by p^*.

Our aim is to predict the point p^* using an initial segment consisting of np points. Let us examine again the learning curve represented in Fig. 1. Suppose the points p_1, p_2, p_3 and p_4 constitute the initial segment. So, our aim is to estimate the stopping point using these four points, without considering the points further on.

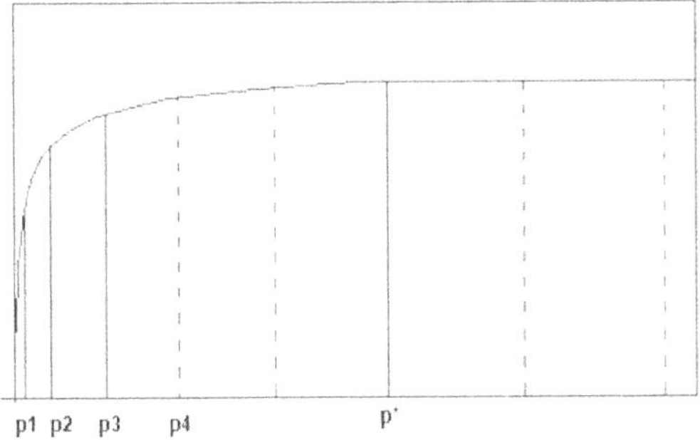

Fig. 1. Learning Curve

The prediction of p^* is done on the basis of previous knowledge about the algorithm in question. The knowledge used is in the form of learning curves obtained before on other (similar) datasets. The aim is to use these curves to predict the stopping point on a curve that is only partly known (we have information about the initial segment only).

The details of this method are described in the following. First, we will discuss how the learning curves are represented. Then, we will show how certain learning curves are identified on the basis of existing information for the purpose of prediction. Finally, we show how the prediction of the stopping point is generated. The reader can consult Fig. 2. for an overview of the method.

```
Algorithm
Parameters:
    i (dataset in question), np (size of the initial segment)
    n (number of datasets), k (number of neighbors), ε (tolerance)

Run given algorithm on dataset i
    while varying samples from m=1 to np.
Calculate accuracies A_{i,m}
Analyze the learning curves stored and
    calculate distances d_{i,j}(j = 1..n ∧ j ≠ i)
Identify k curves with the smallest distance
    (indices n_1, ..., n_k)
Combine predictions of stopping points p*_{n_1} ...p*_{n_k}
    to obtain p*_i and return this value
```

Fig. 2. The basic algorithm for predicting stopping points

2.1 Representation of Learning Curves and Identifying the Stopping Point

Suppose we have datasets $\{D_1, D_2, ..., D_n\}$ and for each one we have a learning curve available (later we will discuss a variant of this basic method which uses N learning curves per dataset). Each learning curve is represented by a vector $< A_{i,1}, A_{i,2}, .., A_{i,z} >$, where $A_{i,m}$ represents the accuracy of the given algorithm on dataset D_i on m-th sample in the sequence. Following Provost et al. [Prov99] the sizes follow a geometric progression. The sequence spans across the whole dataset.

The particular stopping point p_i^* can be readily identified. This is done as follows. First, we identify the global maximum. Then, given a tolerance ϵ, we identify the earliest point in the sequence whose accuracy is within the tolerance limit of the global maximum. This can be formulated as follows:

$$p_i^* = min\{p_m : |max(A_{i,m}) - A_{i,m}| < \epsilon\} \quad (1)$$

2.2 Identification of Appropriate Learning Curves for the Purpose of Prediction

Suppose we are interested in dataset D and we have information about the initial segment of the learning curve (e.g. the first np=4 point). Following earlier work [BrazdilEtal03] we employ a nearest neighbor algorithm (k-NN) to identify similar datasets and retrieve the appropriate learning curves. Here the k-NN algorithm represents a meta-learner that helps us to resolve the issue of predicting the stopping point. As k-NN uses a distance measure to identify similar cases, we need to adapt the method to our problem. Here we just use the information concerning the initial segment. The distance function between datasets D_i and D_j is defined by

$$d(i,j) = \sum_{m=1}^{np} (A_{i,m} - A_{j,m})^2 \quad (2)$$

where m spans across the initial segment. Further on we will discuss some possible enhancements of this method.

2.3 Generating the Prediction Concerning the Stopping Point

Once k learning curves have been identified, we can generate the prediction regards the stopping point on a new curve. This is done by retrieving the stopping points associated with k learning curves and generating a prediction using this information. Let us see how this is done in detail.

Suppose the associated indexes of the k-learning curves are $n_1, n_2, ..., n_k$. Then let the stopping points of each curve be $p_{n_1}^*, p_{n_2}^*, ..., p_{n_k}^*$. In general, the values can differ. One obvious way to estimate the stopping point p_i on the basis of this information is by calculating the *mean* value. Another possibility is to use the *minimum* value and this way bias the predictions towards small values. As we will see later, this has certain advantages. There are obviously other possibilities, but here we have decided to limit our attention just to these two possibilities.

2.4 Enhanced Method That Uses Several Learning Curves per Dataset

It is a well known fact that the performance of many algorithms may vary substantially, as data is drawn from a given source. This phenomenon is usually referred to as variance [Breiman96]. The problem is even more apparent if we use small samples. As a consequence, the learning curves do not always look like the one shown in Fig. 1. The curve shown is monotonically increasing, but some curves may include points that violate this condition. This has an adverse affect on the method described earlier.

To minimize this problem we have decided to adopt an enhanced version of the basic method, which uses N learning curves per dataset. Each learning curve is generated using a different portion of the data. Here we will use a method similar to N cross-validation. That is, we leave one portion of the data out and use the rest to generate the learning curve.

This enhancement has minor repercussions on the description of the basic method. First, the distance between the new dataset D_i (dataset for which we want to predict the stopping point) and an existing dataset D_j is defined by:

$$d(i,j) = \frac{1}{N} \sum_{f=1}^{N} \sum_{m=1}^{np} (A_{i,m} - A_{f,j,m})^2 \tag{3}$$

where $A_{f,j,m}$ represents the accuracy of the given algorithm on dataset D_j, on m-th sample in the sequence on f-th learning curve (f stand for "fold"). So, in effect we try to identify cases which are most similar to the initial segment, but each case is represented by N learning curves.

Once the learning curves have been identified, we need to determine the stopping point. This is done in two steps. First, we process the learning curves for each dataset to calculate means:

$$\overline{A}_{i,m} = \frac{1}{10} \sum_{f=1}^{10} A_{f,i,m} \tag{4}$$

The point $\overline{A}_{i,m}$ represents a mean and can be used to construct a smoothed-out learning curve. This curve is then used to identify the stopping point.

$$p_i^* = min\{p_m : |max(A_{i,m}) - A_{i,m}| < \epsilon\} \tag{5}$$

In all other aspects, the enhanced method is equivalent to the method described in previous sections (2.1 - 2.3).

In the following the method described in this section is referred to shortly as MPS (meta-learning + progressive sampling).

3 Empirical Evaluation

To evaluate the method MPS proposed above we have used the leave-one-out evaluation strategy. We identify a dataset, say D_i, and the aim is to predict the stopping point for this dataset. All other datasets except D_i (and with the associated initial segments) are used to generate the prediction $\hat{p}_i^*$, in the way described earlier. The predicted stopping point is compared to the true stopping point (retrieved from our database). Besides, we also compare the errors associated with the two stopping points and the times used to obtain each solution.

We have used 60 datasets in the evaluation. Some come from UCI [BlakMerz98], others were used within project METAL [MetaL]. All datasets used are shown in Table 1.

Table 1. Datasets used

dataset	n cases	dataset	n cases
acetylation	1511	connect.4	67557
Adult	32560	covtype	581012
Byzantine	17750	dis	3772
contraceptive	1473	heart.disease.cleveland.new	1541
dna.splice	3186	hypothyroid	3163
ibm.stock.val	8087	isolet	7797
injury.severity	7636	krkopt	28056
internetad	3279	kr.vs.kp	3196
led24	3200	letter.recognition	20000
led7	3200	mfeat	2000
mushrooms	8124	musk.clean2	6598
mushrooms.exp	8416	nettalk	146934
musk	6598	nursery	12960
parity	1024	optdigits	5620
quisclas	5891	page.blocks	5473
recljan2jun97	33170	pendigits	10992
task1	111077	pyrimidines	6996
taska.part.hhold	17267	quadrupeds	5000
taska.part.related	18254	sat	6435
taskb.hhold	12934	segmentation	2310
ad	3279	shuttle	58000
adult	48842	sick	3772
agaricus.lepiota	8124	sick.euthyroid	3163
allbp	3772	spambase	4601
allhyper	3772	splice	3190
allhypo	3772	thyroid0387	9172
allrep	3772	triazines	52264
ann	7200	waveform21	5000
car	1728	waveform40	5000
cmc	1473	yeast	1484

The samples are generated using a geometric progression as follows. The size of n_i-th sample is set to the rounded value of $2^{6+0.5 \times n_i}$. Thus the size of the first sample is $2^{6.5}$, giving 91 after rounding, and the second sample is 2^7, giving 128 etc. So the sample sizes were 91, 128, 181, 256 etc.

We have used C5.0 [Quin98] as the base algorithm. That is, our aim was to predict the stopping point of C5.0 on the basis of the initial segment. In the experiments reported here the initial segment included 4 points (np=4). The tolerance limit ϵ was set to 0.001. For each dataset we have retrieved N=10 learning curves which was used to generate a smoothed-out curve.

Regards the meta-learning method, we have used k-NN. In the experiments reported here k was set to 3 [1]. The predictions were combined by calculating the mean, or alternatively, by using the minimum value.

3.1 Results Concerning Savings and Losses

The results obtained using the mean as the combination function are shown in Fig. 3. As we can see, there is on the whole quite good agreement between the predicted stopping point and the true value. The points can be divided into three groups. The first one includes perfect predictions ($\hat{p}_i = p_i^*$). The second group includes all cases for which $\hat{p}_i < p_i^*$. This group includes, for instance, the prediction for adult dataset, which is explicitly identified in the figure. That is, if we followed the prediction, the sampling process would terminate somewhat prematurely. In general, one would expect that this would affect the error of the base algorithm (in general the error will be a bit larger than it would be, if it terminated at the right point). The third group all cases for which $\hat{p}_i = p_i^*$. This group includes, for instance, the prediction for mushrooms dataset, which is explicitly marked in the figure. In general, this will have not effect the error, unless of course, the base algorithm suffers from overfitting.

We can analyse the situation in Fig. 3 more closely and examine the differences between the predicted and the true value and calculate The Mean Absolute Error (MAE). This calculation gives the value 1.53. In other words, our predictions are about 1.53 steps off the ideal value.

Let us now see what would happen if we used a fixed prediction throughout. The best fixed prediction is the mean of the true stopping points. If we used this, the Mean Absolute Error (MAE) would be 2.74. This value is substantially larger than the value obtained using the method MPS.

We can analyse the computational savings achieved. We compare two situations. One involves using the traditional progressive sampling method and trying to identify the true stopping point. In general we need to run through at least p_i^* points. In fact, if we want to safeguard ourselves against local minima, the number of points may be substantially larger.

The second situation includes training the base algorithm on np=4 points to be able to carry out the prediction. In addition, having obtained the prediction we need to train the base algorithm on this sample. So we can compare, how

[1] determined by a simple tuning procedure

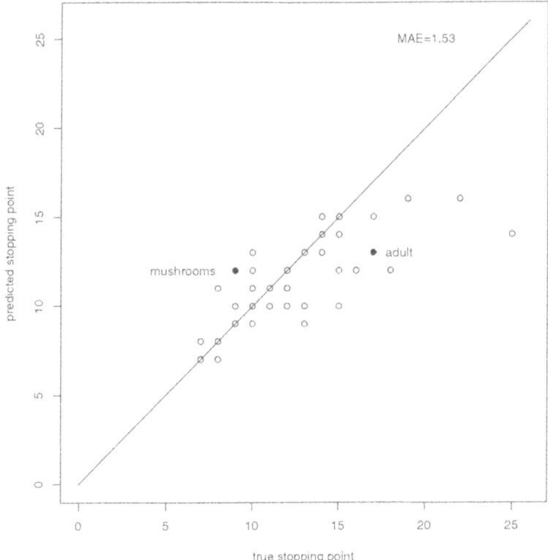

Fig. 3. Comparison between predicted and true stopping points (combination using mean)

many points we do effectively skip and this gives some indication of the computational savings. If we carry out the calculations, we see that on average the savings is 6.16 points (varying between 2 and 11). That is, our method avoids constructing and evaluating at least 6 classifiers on average when compared to the progressive sampling method.

3.2 Biasing the Method towards Larger Time Saving

Earlier (in Section 2.3) we have pointed out that the stopping points of k learning curves can be combined in different ways, such as using a mean or *minimum* value. Using the minimum biases the method towards stopping early and hence leads to larger savings in time. The disadvantage is, of course, certain drop in accuracy. We have decided to examine this alternative in more detail to see whether the advantages outweigh the disadvantages. The first result is shown in Fig. 4.

In this figure the values were combined using the function minimum. We note that the predictions have on the whole moved towards lower values. As would be expected, there are many more cases in the category $\hat{p}_i^* < p_i^*$. Conversely, relatively fewer cases fall in the category $\hat{p}_i^* > p_i^*$.

The Mean Absolute Error (MAE) of predicted stopping points, when compared to true values, is 2.93. That is, the error increased, when compared to the previous alternative using a mean. Despite this, this method has lead to certain savings. If we compare how many points we effectively skip, we get the mean saving of 4.6 (the value varies between 2 and 9 for different datasets). This means that we still avoid constructing about 4-5 classifiers on average, if we use this method when compared to the baseline (simple progressive sampling method).

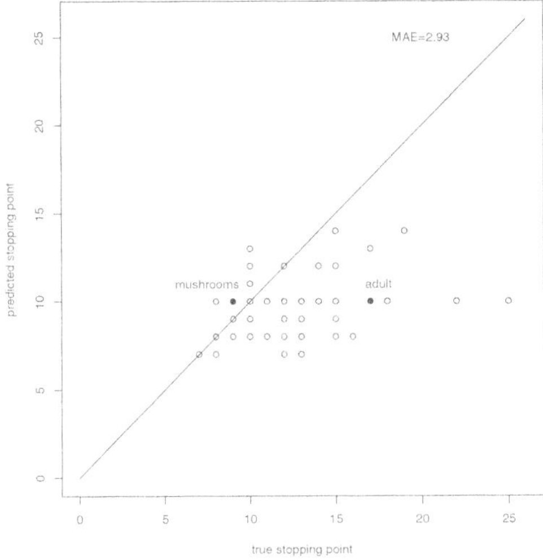

Fig. 4. Comparison between predicted and true stopping points (combination using minimum)

3.3 Results Concerning Actual Times and Accuracies

The analysis presented so far was oriented towards comparing the predicted stopping point with the actual one. In this section we will provide figures concerning actual times, and also, analyse the impact of being off target on accuracy of the base algorithm. All the results presented here are relative to one of the two combination functions used for combining the stopping points - the mean.

In Fig. 5 we compare the times of two approaches. The first one is our method (MPS), which requires training np+1classifiers (vertical axis). The second one is the baseline method (simple progressive sampling method) (horizontal axis). As can be seen in practically all datasets the method leads to time significant savings. On closer analysis we would see that our method is 9.92 faster on average.

The comparison of accuracies of the two methods for various datasets is shown in Fig.6 .

The first observation we can make is that the differences in accuracies for the two methods are relatively small. However, as could be expected the accuracy of our method is a bit lower than the accuracy of the baseline method. On average the difference is 1.4%. This could be considered as the price to pay for the speedup.

On closer analysis we can see that for 29 datasets the difference is zero. On the other hand, in few datasets there is a noticeable difference (e.g. *adult* dataset). This is due to the fact that the method identified a stopping point which is in fact premature.

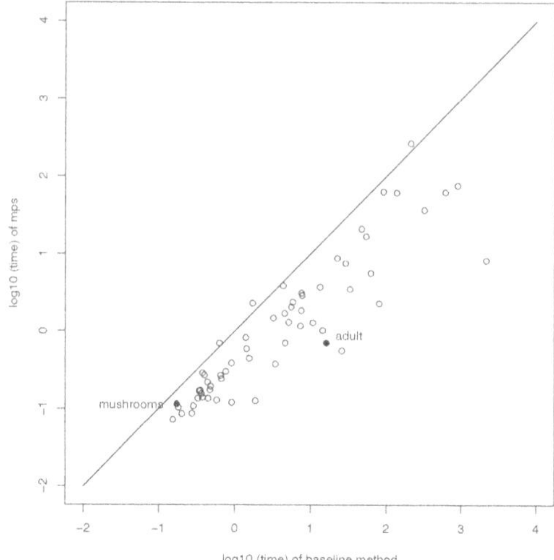

Fig. 5. Comparison of total training times

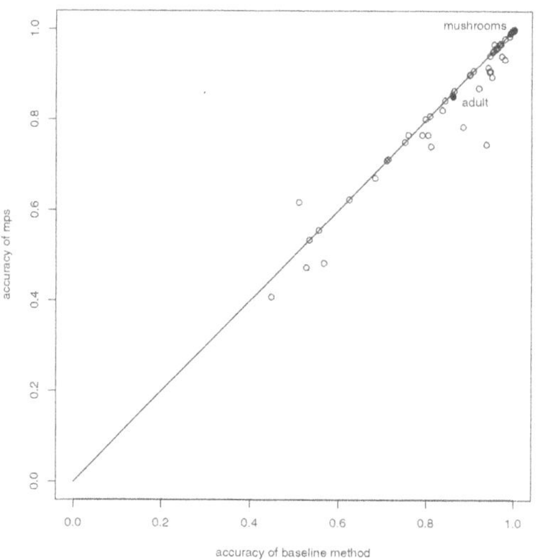

Fig. 6. Comparison of accuracies

4 Conclusions and Discussion

We have presented a method that can be seen as an improvement of standard progressive sampling method. The method exploits information concerning performance of a given algorithm on past datasets, which is used to generate predictions of the stopping point. Experimental evaluation shows that the method can lead to significant time savings without significant losses in accuracy.

Acknowledgments. The authors gratefully acknowledge the financial support from Multi-annual Funding (Financiamento Pluriannual) of Portuguese R&D Units and earlier support from ESPRIT project METAL.

References

[BrazdilEtal03] Brazdil, P., Soares, C., Costa, J. (2003). Ranking Learning Algorithms: Using IBL and Meta-Learning on Accuracy and Time Results, *Machine Learning*, Vol. 50, 251–277.

[Breiman96] Breiman,L. (1996). "Bias, Variance, and Arcing Classifiers" Technical Report 460, Statistics Department, University of California

[BlakMerz98] Blake, C.L. & Merz, C.J. (1998). UCI Repository of machine learning databases [http://www.ics.uci.edu/ mlearn/MLRepository.html]. Irvine, CA: University of California, Department of Information and Computer Science.

[JohnLang96] John, G. and Langley, P. (1996). Static versus dynamic sampling for data mining. In Proc. of *2nd Intl. Conf. Knowledge Discovery and Data Mining*, AAAI Press.

[Prov99] Provost, F., Jensen, D., Oates, T. (1999). Efficient Progressive Sampling. In Proc. of *Fifth Int l Conf. on Knowledge Discovery and Data Mining.* AAAI Press.

[Quin98] Quinlan, R. (1998). C5.0 "An Informal Tutorial". RuleQuest. http://www.rulequest.com/see5-info.html

[MetaL] Metal Project site. http://www.metal-kdd.org/

[WeisIndur98] Weiss, S., Indurkhya, N. (1998). *Predictive Data Mining* Morgan Kaufmann.

Distributed Learning Agents in Urban Traffic Control

Eduardo Camponogara and Werner Kraus Jr

Departamento de Automação e Sistemas,
Universidade Federal de Santa Catarina,
Caixa Postal 476,
Florianópolis, SC 88040-970, Brasil,
camponog@das.ufsc.br,
http://www.das.ufsc.br

Abstract. Automatic learning techniques stand as promising tools to respond to the need of higher efficiency of traffic network, even more so at times of mounting pressure from economic and energy markets. To this end, this paper looks into the operation of a traffic network with distributed, intelligent agents. In particular, it casts the task of operating a traffic network as a distributed, stochastic game in which the agents solve reinforcement-learning problems. Results from computational experiments show that these agents can yield substantial gains with respect to the performance achieved by two other control policies for traffic lights. The paper ends with an outline of future research to deploy machine-learning technology in real-world traffic networks.

1 Motivation

In the past decade, the number of motor vehicles and the volume of transportation have reached unprecedented levels, raising concerns about the level of carbon-dioxide emissions and incurring discomfort to drivers in terms of prolonged travel times, traffic jams, and excessive fuel consumption. To some extent, the problems thereof have been aggravated by the slow speed at which new, improved traffic management and control technology have been deployed. Today, the vast majority of traffic control devices operate according to pre-defined control policies, which do not adapt themselves to the prevailing traffic conditions, while on the other hand, early studies show that real-time strategies can reduce traffic-light waiting time up to 15% [7]. The pressure from today's energy markets and the access to fast, cheaper electronic equipment are changing governmental policies and increasing investment in research and development.

It is our belief that machine-learning techniques can play a major role in improving the existing traffic-control technology. The opportunities for development abound, ranging from intelligent modeling and prediction of traffic flow, through network planning, to real-time control of traffic devices. In particular, the intense research on reinforcement learning and the success of its application in robotics, decision-making, and control have prompted its use in management

Fernando Moura Pires, Salvador Abreu (Eds.): EPIA 2003, LNAI 2902, pp. 324–335, 2003.

and control of traffic networks. To this end, this paper is a step towards extending reinforcement learning techniques to the real-time control of traffic networks.

Section 2 presents the overall traffic-control problem as a reinforcement-learning task and, to account for subtleties of traffic networks, it recasts the problem as a distributed stochastic game, which is a variation of the stochastic games proposed in [3]. In distributed games, there are multiple control agents spread over the network, each with a partial view of the network state and with partial authority over its decision variables. By solving their local reinforcement-learning problems, the agents compete with one another but they could in principle be induced to collaborate, this way promoting convergence to solutions that yield improved network performance.

Section 3 uses the framework of the preceding section to model a small, but prototypical traffic network. The principal features of the experimental scenario are provided along with details of the simulation software, which is being developed to facilitate numerical analyses. For a host of experimental scenarios, Q-learning was applied to solve the agents' reinforcement-learning problems and their performance was contrasted with those attained by random and baseline control policies. The results demonstrate that distributed Q-learning outperforms the other policies, yielding considerable gains.

Section 4 outlines a number of research directions that seem essential to further the application of machine-learning technology in the domain of traffic networks.

2 Traffic Control as a Distributed, Stochastic Game

In principle, the task of operating a traffic network can be conveniently cast as a reinforcement learning problem, naturally accounting for the stochastic and time-varying nature of traffic dynamics. The potential benefits are enticing—for one, the task would be specified in terms of what is deemed to be correct, rather than having to spell out the actions that induce optimal performance; for another, the control system would learn continually from experience and adapt itself to unanticipated events. More formally, the reinforcement learning model [8] consists of:

- a discrete set of the traffic network states, S, invariably comprising the number of vehicles in each road, or otherwise some estimate;
- a discrete set of control actions, A, including the feasible commands to traffic lights and other traffic control devices;
- a set of reinforcement signals, R, corresponding to penalties for undesired behavior, such as jams and excessive delay at junctions; and
- the dynamic model of traffic flow, T, expressing how the network moves from one state to the next in response to actions at each time step; T could be a Markov decision process, given as a set of transition probabilities $\{T(s, a, s')\}$, or implemented by means of a simulator.

The problem is to find a policy π, a stochastic mapping from states to actions, that maximizes some long-run function of the reinforcement signals, such as the expected discounted reward $E[\sum_{t=0}^{\infty} \gamma^t r_t]$, where $0 \leq \gamma \leq 1$ and r_t is the reinforcement signal during the t-th step. There are of course a number of issues and subtleties not addressed in the above model: for instance, the network state may not be fully observable, the reinforcement signals may have multiple dimensions to capture conflicting goals, such as reduced fuel consumption and short travel time, and the state space may be infinite. Herein, we shrug off these issues and concentrate on what we believe is more limiting to the application of reinforcement learning in traffic networks, namely the combinatorial explosion of the state space and the impossibility, as well as undesirability of centralized control. In a more practical setting, the network operation can be viewed as a distributed, stochastic game:

- a set of N distributed agents or controllers;
- a discrete set of the traffic network states, S;
- a set of functions $\Theta = \{\Theta_n\}$, where Θ_n determines how agent-n observes the state s of the network; in the case of a traffic light, Θ_n would provide access only to the information in its vicinity;
- a set of actions $A = A_1 \times \ldots \times A_N$, where A_n is the set of actions available to agent-n;
- a transition function T, $T : S \times A \times S \rightarrow [0, 1]$, such that $\forall s \in S$ and $\forall a \in A$ we have $\sum_{s' \in S} T(s, a, s') = 1$, mapping state and actions to probabilities of reaching other states; and
- a set of reinforcement functions $R = \{R_n\}$, $R_n : S \times A \times S \rightarrow \Re$, which return to the agents their reinforcement signals attributed to the state transitions.

Not unlike the standard problem, each agent-n seeks a policy π_n that maximize some measure of its reward in the long-run, such as the agent's discounted reward $E[\sum_{t=0}^{\infty} \gamma^t r_{n,t}]$, where $r_{n,t}$ is agent-n's reinforcement signal during the t-th state transition and $0 \leq \gamma \leq 1$. This framework is a variation of the stochastic games proposed by [3], differing mainly with respect to the partial state-observation from the part of the agents. Henceforth we assume that a distributed, stochastic game is defined by the tuple $\Gamma = (N, S, \Theta, A, T, R)$. Under not so stringent conditions, a host of algorithms can reach the optimal policy π for the single agent case, that is, the policy that maximizes reward in the long-run. For the multiple agent case, it is not clear whether there exists a set of policies $\pi = \{\pi_1, \ldots, \pi_N\}$ that are simultaneously optimal to their respective problems, let alone an algorithm that can converge to π. Of concern as well is the performance induced by π in contrast to the performance yielded by an optimal, centralized policy π^*, that is to say, a policy maximizing the sum of the rewards of the agents in the long-run, which is the principal goal in operating a traffic network.

3 Simulated Experiments

In an effort to investigate the potential of modeling a traffic network with a distributed, stochastic game and to assess the performance attained by distributed agents, this section gives an account of experiments simulated in a small, but representative section of a traffic network.

3.1 Experimental Set-Up

Figure 1 depicts the traffic sub-network, which will be modeled as a distributed stochastic game. It has two intersections with traffic lights and six points where traffic enters and leaves the sub-network. The street segments have limited capacities and vehicles enter the sub-network at points J_k with given probabilities. The two traffic lights operate in the same manner: they allow four, mutually exclusive moves at their intersection; if traffic light I_1 activates traffic flow from J_6, then the traffic from J_1, J_2, and I_2 are blocked while the oncoming vehicles can flow towards J_1, J_2, or I_2 according to probability distributions that approximate the prevailing traffic conditions. The rate at which vehicles enter the sub-network will vary across experiments, being modeled by a probability σ that a vehicle attempts to enter the sub-network at each time step. Traffic approaching I_1 from J_2, J_6, and I_2, have a 90% chance of heading towards J_1, whereas the traffic coming from J_1 has a 50% chance of moving straight ahead, towards I_2. Traffic approaching I_2 from J_3 or J_5 have a 50% chance of advancing towards I_1, whereas the traffic coming from J_4 has a 90% chance. Traffic approaching I_2 from I_1 will go straight through the intersection with 50% probability. More formally, the distributed stochastic game restricted to the sub-network is $\Gamma = (N, S, \Theta, A, T, R)$, where:

- $N = 2$ is the number of control agents;
- S is a set of vectors, one for each street segment, that record the number and location of vehicles;
- Θ is the set of state-observation functions, where Θ_n maps S to the subset of variables that correspond to the number and position of vehicles on the street lanes leading to intersection I_n, but confined to the fraction of lane positions that are closest to I_n;
- A comprises the green and red lights of the traffic signals at intersections I_1 and I_2;
- T is the state-transition function that follows the traffic patterns outlined above; and
- R is the set of reinforcement signal functions, where R_n returns at each time step the negative of the number of vehicles waiting at intersection I_n that can be observed by agent-n.

3.2 Simulation Software

Although software packages for traffic simulation can be found off the shelf, such as Transyt [5] and SITRA-B+, they tend to have a complex interface and embed low-level dynamics that are beyond the needs of the studies herein. To facilitate the experimental investigations, we implemented a prototype, but flexible and relatively general simulator for distributed stochastic games tailored to the domain of traffic networks. The simulator conforms to the specifications given in the preceding section, having as input:

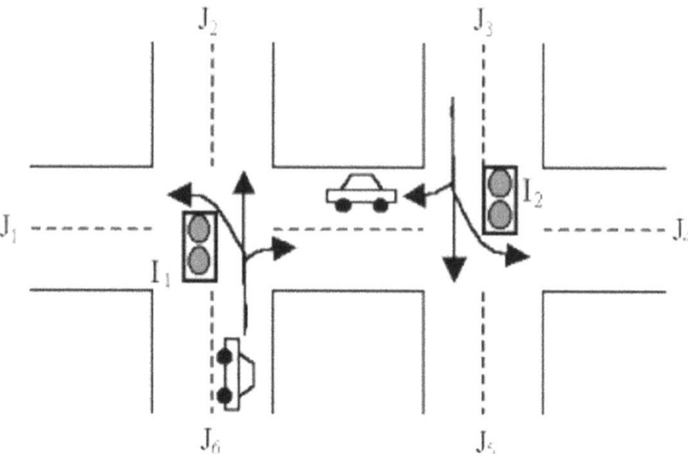

Fig. 1. Section of the traffic network that is object of modeling and control by means of a distributed, stochastic game

- a directed graph $G = (V, E)$ describing the topology of the traffic network—its vertices model intersections and cross-roads, whereas its arcs model the road lanes;
- the set of possible non-concurrent moves at each node of G, specified as pairs of adjacent arcs, along with the probabilities corresponding to the state-transition function T—e.g., intersection I_1 will have four mutually exclusive moves, one of them being $\{(J_6, J_1, P(J_6, J_1)), (J_6, J_2, P(J_6, J_2)), (J_6, J_4, P(J_6, J_4))\}$, where $P(J_n, J_m)$ is the probability that the traffic coming from J_n will move towards J_m;
- parameters for each street lane, specifying its maximum number of vehicles and the number of cells splitting the lane—each cell should accommodate the number of vehicles that can move from one cell to the next in one time step; and
- the initial state of the network, s_0, the number of vehicles in each cell of each street lane.

All of the data of an instance Γ is provided in text files and subsequently fed to the simulator, which was implemented in C/C++ languages and can be compiled in standard Unix boxes. The simulator proceeds by tracing a trajectory of the network state, in iterations, obeying the probabilities of the state-transition function. At this stage, an agent's control policy has to be compiled together with the simulator, but the interface consists of simple yet efficient data structures.

3.3 Distributed Q-Learning Control

From agent-n's standpoint, its control task could be thought of as an ordinary reinforcement problem by regarding the other agents as part of the environment, except that their behavior is not stationary, which is typically dependent on the policy π_n implemented by agent-n. Disregarding these observations at this stage of the research, we can employ standard reinforcement learning algorithms to reach a set of distributed control policies, $\pi = \{\pi_n\}$, that induce satisfactory, if not near-optimal performance. Out of the three elementary solution methods to reinforcement learning problems [10], namely dynamic programming, Monte Carlo methods, and temporal-difference methods, only the latter seems effective.

Dynamic programming (DP) [2] requires precise knowledge of the transition probabilities and reward values, which could be hard to obtain, perhaps unattainable in complex scenarios, such as black-box simulators and the actual traffic network.

Contrary to dynamic programming, Monte Carlo (MC) methods can be applied to environments whose knowledge of their dynamics is incomplete, not necessitating precise information about the state-transition probabilities and rewards, but on the other hand, they have shortcomings such as their typical slow convergence rate and the need of returns over long trajectories in state space.

Temporal-difference (TD) methods, such as Q-Learning, inherit features of Monte Carlo and dynamic programming methods: like MC methods, TD methods can learn optimal policies directly from sample experience, without a model of the network's dynamics; like DP, TD methods update the estimates on the values of state-action pairs from other estimates and the rewards, without having to wait for the outcome of a long sequence of transitions. Another property of TD methods is that they satisfy the principle of certainty equivalence estimate, meaning that they implicitly generate a Markov decision process approximating the dynamics of the environment, for which the decision policy obtained with TD is optimal.

For the purpose of the analyses herein, we assume that the control task is divided in recurring episodes, such as days and weeks. Let π_n be the policy followed by agent-n and let $\gamma_n = \pi - \{\pi_n\}$ be the set with the policies of the other agents. Then, the action-value function $Q_n^{\pi_n,\gamma_n}(s_n, a_n)$ for agent-n, where $s_n \in \{\Theta_n(s) : s \in S\}$ is its observed state and $a_n \in A_n$ is its action, can be defined as follows:

$$Q_n^{\pi_n,\gamma_n}(s_n, a_n) = E_{\pi_n,\gamma_n}\left[\sum_{k=0}^{H} \gamma^k r_{n,t+k+1} : s_{n,t} = s_n, a_{n,t} = a_n\right]$$

where $r_{n,t}$ is the reinforcement signal received by agent-n after the t-th transition, from state $s_{n,t}$ to $s_{n,t+1}$, and H is the length of the episode. The principal goal of an agent-n is to find an optimal policy π_n^* that maximizes the return over the long-run or, alternatively, the optimal action-value function Q_n^*, since any greedy policy with respect to the latter yields the former. More formally, agent-n's optimal action-value function is:

$$\begin{aligned} Q_n^{\pi_n^*,\gamma_n}(s_n, a_n) = \underset{\pi_n}{\text{Maximize}}\ & Q_n^{\pi_n,\gamma_n}(s_n, a_n) \\ \text{Subject to}:\ & \gamma_n \text{ is held constant} \end{aligned}$$

$\forall s_n \in S$ and $\forall a_n \in A_n$. A relevant issue is whether there exists a set of policies π^* that induces optimal policies to all of the agents, in which case:

$$Q_n^{\pi_n^*,\gamma_n^*}(s_n, a_n) = \underset{\pi_n}{\text{Maximize}}\ Q_n^{\pi_n,\gamma_n^*}(s_n, a_n)$$
$$\text{Subject to : } \gamma_n^* \text{ is held constant}$$

for $n = 1, \ldots, N$, $\forall s_n \in S$, and $\forall a_n \in A_n$. Such set π^* of policies is regarded as a set of Nash policies [3,1], meaning that no rational agent-n will deviate from its policy π_n^*, while the other agents stick to the policies in γ_n^*. In general, existence of a set of Nash policies cannot be guaranteed in general, let alone an algorithm that can reach such a set. This paper does not intend to address the issues on existence of and convergence to Nash policies, but rather it focuses on the experimental performance yielded by the agents as they search for Nash policies. A method to search for a set of Nash policies consists in iteratively applying Q-Learning to the distributed agents. This method, herein called distributed Q-Learning control, is outlined below.

Distributed Q-Learning Algorithm

Each agent-n initializes $Q_n(s_n, a_n)$ arbitrarily
Repeat (for each episode)
  Initialize s
  Repeat for each step of the episode
    For each agent-n
      Choose an action a_n based on $Q_n(s_n)$, $s_n = \Theta_n(s)$,
        using a policy derived from Q_n such as ϵ-greedy
      Take action a_n
    End-for

    For each agent-n, observe r_n and $s'_n = \Theta_n(s')$, where s' is the next state
      $Q_n(s_n, a_n) \leftarrow Q_n(s_n, a_n) + \alpha_n[r_n + \gamma_n \max_{a'_n} Q_n(s'_n, a'_n) - Q_n(s_n, a_n)]$,
        where $\alpha_n \in [0, 1]$ is the learning rate and
        $\gamma_n \in [0, 1]$ is the discount rate of agent-n
    End-for
  End-repeat
End-repeat

3.4 Experimental Results

The distributed Q-learning algorithm was applied to the distributed, stochastic game Γ of the traffic network presented above. The episodes were simulated with the aid of our simulation software and consisted of four thousand steps, with each episode starting from the same initial state s_0, this way modeling a full network cycle such as a day. To more accurately measure the quality of the solution methods, the initial state was varied to reflect the traffic conditions, from light to heavy traffic, according to a traffic density parameter σ—that is, σ is the probability that any cell of any street segment is occupied by vehicles in the initial state s_0. A suit of experimental scenarios was obtained by varying σ and applying one of the following fixed policies or policy-learning methods:

Uniformly random policy: it assigns the same probability to all actions available to an agent-n, i.e., $\pi_n(s_n, a_n) = 1/|A_n|$ for all $s_n \in \{\Theta_n(s) : s \in S\}$ and $a_n \in A_n$.

Best-effort policy: it lets traffic flow from the lane with the longest queue.

Q-learning implemented by agent-1: agent-1 applies the Q-learning algorithm to control the traffic signals at intersection I_1, as delineated in Section 3.3, whereas agent-2 follows the uniformly random policy.

Q-learning implemented by agent-2: only agent-2 uses Q-learning.

Q-learning implemented by both agents.

Each experiment consisted of one policy-learning method (or fixed policy) and a traffic density value—about 800 episodes were simulated, each consisting of 4,000 iterations. For the policy-learning methods, the discount rate was $\gamma = 0.95$, the learning rate was fixed at $\alpha = 0.1$, and the parameter for ϵ-greedy policies was decreased gradually with the number of episodes according to the schedule $\epsilon^k = \text{Max}\{0.1, 0.75 \times 0.995^k\}$, where k is the episode number.

Table 1 shows the performance produced by the policy-learning methods and contrasts them with the performance induced by the uniformly random policy. These results show that a reduction of 18% in the average waiting time is induced by agent-1 or agent-2, if either agent implements Q-learning, while a reduction of approximately 38% is obtained if both agents use the Q-learning algorithm. Figure 2 depicts the performance trajectories of the uniformly random and Q-learning policies for the case of traffic density $\sigma = 0.2$.

Table 2 presents the performance yielded by the full policy-learning method and the one produced by the best-effort policy. The results show that a reduction in the waiting time of the order of 43% can be induced if both agents run the Q-learning algorithm. Comparing the data in Tables 1 and 2, we infer that the best-effort policy outperforms the random policy for low traffic densities, but the former incurs higher waiting times under heavy traffic conditions. Figure 3 depicts the performance trajectories induced by the best-effort policy and the full Q-learning policy for the case of traffic density $\sigma = 0.2$.

4 Future Research Directions

The work presented heretofore is in its nascent, leaving great opportunities for further developments and applications to management and control of traffic networks. The results obtained thus far indicate that substantial performance gains can be achieved in addition to greater automation of decision-making processes.

Table 1. Results of experiments simulated for several traffic densities (σ), obtained with the policy-learning methods and confronted against the random policy.

σ	Average Number of Waiting Vehicles				
	Random Policy	Q-learner @ I_1	Q-learner @ I_2	Q-learners @ I_1 and I_2	
				Value	Gain (%)
0.10	1.47	0.79	0.86	0.07	95.23
0.15	2.46	1.32	1.49	0.14	94.30
0.20	3.55	1.81	2.07	0.22	93.80
0.25	4.57	2.32	3.18	0.55	87.96
0.30	7.38	3.77	6.10	1.97	73.30
0.35	8.55	4.48	6.97	2.91	65.96
0.40	14.89	11.21	11.25	8.07	45.80
0.45	16.07	13.67	12.44	10.13	36.96
0.50	18.68	16.53	14.42	12.33	33.99
0.55	21.98	19.61	17.29	15.29	30.43
0.60	22.42	19.89	17.84	15.43	31.17
0.65	22.45	20.23	17.73	15.42	31.31
0.70	26.63	22.94	22.25	18.65	29.96
0.75	29.37	25.25	25.30	21.45	26.96
Mean	14.32	11.70	11.37	8.76	38.56

Table 2. Results of experiments simulated for several traffic densities (σ), obtained with the full policy-learning method and the best-effort policy

σ	Average Number of Waiting Vehicles		
	Best-Effort	Q-learning @ I_1 and I_2	
		Value	Gain (%)
0.10	0.23	0.07	67.88
0.15	0.30	0.14	50.89
0.20	0.65	0.22	66.46
0.25	1.69	0.55	67.25
0.30	6.39	1.97	69.11
0.35	8.75	2.91	66.75
0.40	10.56	8.07	23.55
0.45	12.26	10.13	17.41
0.50	13.16	12.33	6.30
0.55	19.72	15.29	22.48
0.60	24.87	15.43	37.96
0.65	26.81	15.42	42.46
0.70	30.59	18.65	39.03
0.75	32.71	21.45	34.42
Mean	13.48	8.76	43.76

In what follows, we speculate about research directions that could be undertaken to deploy automatic-learning technology to real-world networks.

Accurate modeling of traffic networks: its is necessary to account for the subtleties of traffic dynamics, either extending existing models [6] or employing simulators whose accuracy is satisfactory [5], whereby the algorithms can be validated; this initiative is likely to deal with short-term and long-term prediction of traffic behavior, experimental validation, and the use of feedback information from sensors.

Function approximators: the high-dimensionality of the state-control space of traffic networks, perhaps the principal justification for distributed decision-making, is a recurring theme in the field that has to be addressed for the practical application of reinforcement learning techniques; the estimation of action-value functions for high-dimensional tables poses difficulties to memory allocation as well as computation, which might be circumvented with function approximations that make use of generalization properties, such as artificial neural networks.

Means for collaboration among distributed agents: a feature contrasting this work and that presented in [3] rests on the fact that the former is a collaborative effort of the agents, whereas the latter is intrinsically competitive; the distributed, stochastic game arose from the distribution of the decisions among the agents, this way creating competition between the agents as they do the best for themselves in maximizing their long-run rewards; nevertheless, mechanisms could be conceived to draw the Nash solutions, or their approximations, towards Pareto optimal rewards, such as the distributed value function proposed in [9] and altruistic factors akin to those appearing in [4].

Safeguard procedures against erratic behavior: even after extensive simulation of the network operation with automatic-learning agents, undetected flaws can persist and potentially cause failure; to counter erratic behavior arising from such flaws, it seems wise to devise fault-detection elements that can override the agents and enforce some baseline control strategy, similar to procedures embedded in control systems of manufacturing plants, for instance.

Extensive simulations: the task of operating a large traffic network is pronouncedly complex and it is bound to violate conditions for existence of equilibria [3], not mentioning assumptions made by algorithms with performance guarantees; it is then pertinent to exhaustively simulate the work of automatic-learning control agents, thereby checking for potential flaws, measuring the overall performance, and identifying points for improvement.

Real-world demonstrations: the research effort anticipated above can only be consolidated with a real-world demonstration, which could comprise a few intersections within a small region of a traffic network; to this end, the authors of this paper are participating in a multi-institutional research project whose aim is to advance today's management and control technology of traffic networks; this initiative will extend over a period of four years and it has provisions for designing, implementing, and testing the new technology in a small, but prototypical section of a city's traffic network.

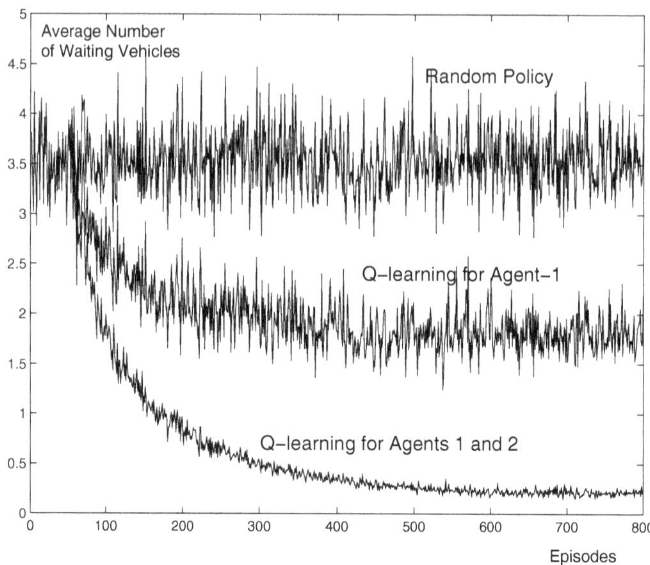

Fig. 2. The performance of Q-learning algorithms and the uniformly random policy for traffic density $\sigma = 0.2$

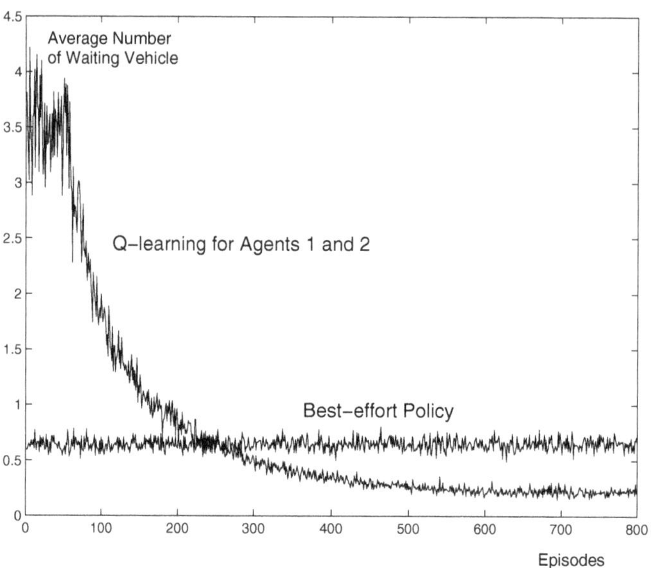

Fig. 3. The performance of the full Q-learning algorithm and the best-effort policy for traffic density $\sigma = 0.2$

5 Closing Remarks

Aiming at improving the performance of today's traffic networks, this work has suggested the deployment of distributed, intelligent agents. It presented the task of operating such networks as a distributed, stochastic game which gives rise to a set of reinforcement-learning problems, one for each of the control agents. The solution of the agents' problems with Q-learning methods proved to be effective in a small, nevertheless representative scenario, outperforming two other control policies. A list of research directions was suggested to further the development and implementation of this technology in real-world traffic systems.

Acknowledgments. This research has been supported in part by Conselho Nacional de Desenvolvimento Científico e Tecnológico (CNPq), Secretaria de Política de Informática (SEPIN), and Financiadora de Estudos e Projetos (FINEP), all from Brazil, under CNPq research grant number 552248/02-9.

References

1. Basar, T., Olsder, G. J.: Dynamic Noncooperative Game Theory. Society for Industrial and Applied Mathematics, Philadelphia, Pennsylvania (1999)
2. Bertsekas, D. P.: Dynamic Programming and Optimal Control. Athena Scientific, Belmont, Massachusetts (1995)
3. Bowling, M., Veloso, M. M.: Existence of multiagent equilibria with limited agents. Technical Report CMU-CS-02-104, Computer Science Department, Carnegie Mellon University, Pittsburgh, Pennsylvania (2002)
4. Camponogara, E.: Altruistic agents in dynamic games. In: Proceedings of the 16th Brazilian Symposium on Artificial Intelligence, LNAI 2507, Springer-Verlag, (2002) 74–84
5. Crabtree, M. R., Vincent, R. A., Harrison, S.: Transyt 10 User's Guide: TRRL Application Guide 28. Technical Report, Transport and Road Research Laboratory, Crawthorne, England (1996)
6. Gazis, D. C.: Traffic Theory. Kluwer Academic Publishers, Boston, Massachusetts (2002)
7. Hunt, P. B., Robertson, D. I., Bretherton, R. D., Winton, R. I.: SCOOT - a traffic responsive method of coordinating signals. Technical Report, Transport and Road Research Laboratory, Crowthorne, England (1981)
8. Kaelbling, L. P., Littman, M. L., Moore, A. W.:, Reinforcement learning: a survey. Journal of Artificial Intelligence Research **4** (1996) 237–285
9. Schneider, J., Wong,W.-W., Moore, A. W., Riedmiller, M.: Distributed value functions. In: Proceedings of the 16th International Conference on Machine Learning, Bled, Slovenia (1999) 371–378
10. Sutton, R. S., Barto, A.: Reinforcement Learning: An Introduction. MIT Press, Cambridge, Massachusetts (1998)

The Chatbot Feeling – Towards Animated Emotional ECAs

Gábor Tatai[1], Annamária Csordás[2], Attila Szaló[2], and László Laufer[3]

[1] Department of Computer Science, University College London
Gower Street, WC1E 6BT, London, UK
g.tatai@cs.ucl.ac.uk
[2] AITIA Inc., 1117 Budapest, Infopark sétány 1. Hungary
{acsordas;aszalo}@aitia.ai
[3] Department of Psychology, ELTE University of Sciences
1064 Izabella utca 46, Budapest, Hungary
notme@izabell.elte.hu

Abstract. We present some aspects of our embodied conversational agent (ECA) that is a chatterbot interface integrated into a website. Our paper highlights only two important attributes of the system: the visualization of the synthetic character and the use of fast emotion generation. We consider several approaches to graphical realization and explain the reasons behind our decision. Also, we briefly describe our emotion generation module from the architectural and theoretical perspectives.

Keywords: Embodied conversational agent, chatterbot, affective computing, visualization

1 Using ECAs on the Internet

E-mail replaced snail-mail, but it did not replace phone calls. The reason why this will never happen is timing. The preference for real-time events, real-time information flow, expresses an innate need of mankind. Internet ECAs have this advantage as opposed to any other on-line customer-company communication method, such as web pages, e-mail, guest books, etc. Even though ECAs and simpler chatterbots may give wrong answers to certain questions, if they react to the customers, if they create some sort of representation of themselves in the customers mind, they win the battle of keeping them.

There is no space to discuss all the features and interesting implementation experiences with our *BotCom* ECA in this paper. Therefore we focus on two highlights where, we think, our ECA is special or when a theoretical or practical observation has proved to be particularly useful, so that others might benefit from these as well.

Fernando Moura Pires, Salvador Abreu (Eds.): EPIA 2003, LNAI 2902, pp. 336–340, 2003.

2 Visual Appearance

Aiko (see Fig. 1.), a female instance of BotCom, running on the users' web interface. The representation of her reactions and emotions is implemented through a 3D pre-rendered, realistic animation. In everyday interactions the secondary communication channels: the partner's face and gestures are accompanying the majority of the important and relevant information [1]. Although the body language also provides some clues for our companion for proper understanding we thought that it is cost worthy to show the upper body only, focusing on the facial expressions and occasionally visualizing the hands as well. To be able to diversify and refine the reactions, the collection of animations can be extended, but the right balance should be kept between the number of animations and system performance. Since we are talking about an Internet-based system where the animations have to be downloaded to the client's computer, the size of the animations is critical.

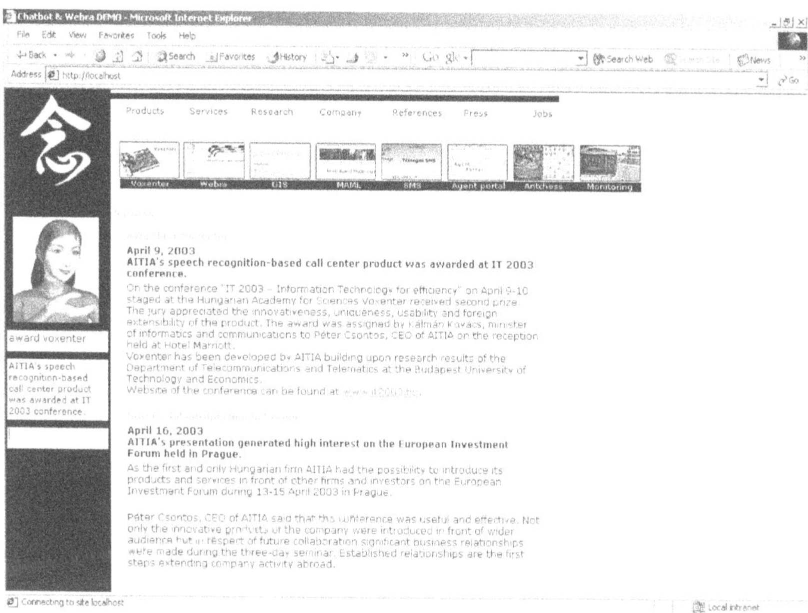

Fig. 1. Aiko, a beautiful instance of BotCom, integrated into a web interface introducing our company

When representations move, they often tend to animate only certain parts of the body (e.g. eyes, lips, eye-brows, chin), the roles of which are considered to be important in communication. Despite the more lifelike and realistic appearance of 3D real-time rendered graphics, there is no underpinning evidence of differences in expressiveness amongst cartoons, photos, movies etc. High-quality animated ECAs are not necessarily intelligent, they only think they are, and users think so as well. Moreover, various studies confirm that users assume high-quality animated ECAs to be more intelligent (e.g. [5]).

There is an important tradeoff here that requires some explanation. We have evaluated many of them according to recent guidelines [2][3][4][5]. We noted that those ECAs use either 2D animations or 2D Flash animations in vector format. But those with 2D animations are not so attractive according to our surveys, not only because of the 2D, but also the tiny size of the faces. It is hard to follow such small-scale lip movements on the screen, especially because these Internet-based ECAs occupy only a fraction of the display. There are also experiments that use 3D models with the VRML 2.0 player, which recognizes the body description language HANIM. However, to play a VRML animation on the client side, one needs to download not only the animation data, but to install a VRML plug-in for the browser as well. In addition a VRML player can hardly be embedded within a website, as it usually requires a separate working space on the screen with its own control panel. An alternative way to provide quality 3D animation would be to embed a 3D real time renderer engine in the web page that could be managed by any close-to-standard body or face controlling language such as HANIM, FACS (Facial Action Coding System) [6] or GESTYLE [7]. This situation would be even worse than with the VRML player, as there is no such standardized engine at present. Thus it would require downloading for each session, not to mention the computing resources that it would consume in rendering a 3D face. The reaction of the face would then be by no means a real-time effect, on an average PC.

As an alternative, therefore, we have chosen to use pre-rendered animation segments that are continuously changing on the visual interface of the chatbot, depending on the chatbot's and the users' answers. The advantages of this approach are clear: economic use of computing resources; looks more life-like than 2D; it is fast, as it can produce real-time reaction and synchronization; flash plug-in is a widely-used *de facto* standard; small animation segments can be downloaded during conversation – hence economic bandwidth usage; complex animation sequences, such as gags, can be played to accompany jokes or other complex communication events. This would be impossible with present technology if one were using a body and emotion description language.

Possible drawbacks are the following: the set of expressions is limited; there is no possibility to combine different facial expressions; the size of preset animations is limited to the accessibility of average bandwidth of the target user group. However, animation size and quality can be increased when transmitting over networks with high-bandwidth coverage.

3 The GALA Hierarchical Emotion Processing Model

In order to create a usable synthetic emotion model for a chatterbot that communicates mainly via text messages, it is essential to design an appropriate mapping scheme between the emotions and the expressions that the chatbot sends or receives.

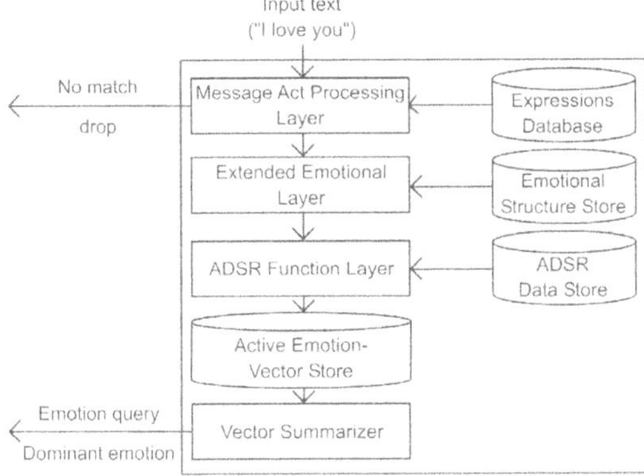

Fig. 2. The architecture of the GALA engine and the processing of a message act

Our goal was to select a sophisticated emotional model complex enough to provide ample workspace, but not bound to a net of cognitive processes. We have found that the model suggested by the psychologist Robert Plutchik is an appropriate starting point [9]. He defined eight basic emotions, each with 3 intensity. A novelty of his proposal is that the emotional space is mapped to an upturned 3D cone, where the positioning of a particular emotion reflects psychological distances and intensity differences between states. The origo is in the apex of the cone expressing neutrality ("no emotion"). This geometrical approach allows easy manipulation of the emotions.

In the first layer of our emotion model the conversational elements (words, expressions, sentences) in the dialogue are assigned to emotional *message acts* [8]: communicational elements, whose effect is described by a set of basic emotions. The mapping of words and expressions into emotions and more complex emotional structures can be found in a database, but users may also build up a complete expression-emotion mapping database by labeling parts of the text (words, expressions or entire sentences) with message acts or basic emotions.

The second layer allows the construction of mixed emotions, the composites of one or more basic emotions, and stores them in an "Emotional Structure Store" (ESS), in the form of vectors, for each basic emotion. Since the amplitude of the emotions changes over time and the characteristics of this change vary according to emotion, we have defined a third layer (ADSR function layer) to describe this change by the ADSR (Attack, Decay, Sustain, Release) curve of each basic emotion individually.

The actual *resulting emotion vector* is the normalized sum of the active vectors stored in the Active Emotion-Vector Store (AEVS) and points to some location within the cone. The *dominant emotion* for a t moment will be that basic emotion (out of 24) which is the closest to the endpoint of the vector sum. (We have described this GALA architecture in more detail in our previous work [11].)

4 Conclusions and Future Work

In this paper we have introduced some features of BotCom, our ECA and its female instance, Aiko who is equipped with most of the beneficial features a chatbot needs for success.

Our future work will concentrate on improving the dialogue quality, and further refinement of the emotions module. We are trying to refine and adjust Plutchik's emotional model to the HCI (Human-Computer Interaction) communicational needs of users. In order to carry out these changes we are experimenting with emotional transmission in both HCI and CMC (Computer Mediated Communication) situations.

References

1. C. Pelachaud (2000): Some considerations about embodied agents. *Proceedings of the Workshop on "Achieving Human-Like Behavior in Interactive Animated Agents"*, Barcelona, Spain.
2. S. Buisine, S. Abrilian, C. Rendu and J-C. Martin (2002): Towards experimental specification and evaluation of lifelike multimodal behavior. *Proceedings of the AAMAS 2002 Workshop on 'Embodied conversational agents – let's specify and evaluate them!'*, Bologna, Italy.
3. K. Isbister and P. Doyle (2002): Design and evaluation of Embodied Conversational Agents: A proposed taxonomy. *Proceedings of the AAMAS 2002 Workshop on 'Embodied conversational agents – let's specify and evaluate them!'*, Bologna, Italy.
4. Zs. Ruttkay, C. Dormann and H. Noot (2002): Evaluating ECAs – What and how? *Proceedings of the AAMAS 2002 Workshop on 'Embodied conversational agents .- let's specify and evaluate them!'*, Bologna, Italy.
5. J. Xiao, J. Stasko and R. Catrambone (2002): Embodied conversational agents as a UI paradigm: A framework for evaluation. *Proceedings of the AAMAS 2002 Workshop on 'Embodied conversational agents – let's specify and evaluate them!'*, Bologna, Italy
6. P. Ekman and W. V. Friesen (1978): Facial action coding system: A technique for the measurement of facial movement. Consulting Psychologists Press, Palo Alto, California, USA.
7. H. Noot and Z. Ruttkay (2003): The GESTYLE language.
8. M. A. Gilbert (1999): Language, words and expressive speech acts. van Eemeren, F., Grootendorst, R., Blair, J. A., Willard, C. A. (eds.): Proceedings of the Fourth International Conference of the International Society for the Study of Argumentation. pp. 231–234.
9. R. Plutchik. 2001. The nature of emotions. *American Scientist* 89(4): 344–350.
10. B. Stronks, A. Nijholt, P. van der Vet and D. Heylen (2002): Designing for friendship: Becoming friends with your ECA. Marriott, A., Pelachaud, C., Rist, T., Ruttkay, Z., Vilhjalmsson, H. (eds.): *Proceedings Embodied conversational agents – let's specify and evaluate them!*, pp. 91–97. Bologna, Italy.
11. G. Tatai, A Csordás, Á. Kiss, L. Laufer and A. Szaló (2003): The Chatbot Who Loved Me. Proceedings of the "Embodied Conversational Characters as Individuals" workshop of the 2nd International Joint Conference on Autonomous Agents and Multi-Agent Systems (AAMAS03), Melbourne, Australia.

Using CLIPS to Detect Network Intrusions

Pedro Alipio, Paulo Carvalho, and José Neves

Departamento de Informática, Escola de Engenharia,
Universidade do Minho, Campus de Gualtar,
4710-057 Braga, Portugal
pal@isep.ipp.pt, {paulo,jneves}@uminho.pt

Abstract. This paper shows how to build a network intrusion detection system by slightly modifying NASA's CLIPS source code, introducing features such as single and multiple string pattern matching, certainty factors and time-stamp operators. Several Snort functions and plugins were adapted and used for packet decoding and preprocessing to provide the basic requirements for such a system. The integration of CLIPS and Snort features allows the specification of complex stateful network intrusion detection heuristics which can model abstract attack scenarios. The results show that CLIPS can be useful to follow and correlate intruder activities by monitoring network traffic.

Keywords: Intrusion detection, CLIPS, SNORT, certainty factors, attack scenarios.

1 Introduction

Network intrusion detection sensors analyze network traffic in real-time scenarios, in search of malicious activities. As a malicious event is detected, adequate responses are issued in order to stop the intruder's activity or to alert the system's administrator. Several strategies have been used to build such a sensor, although the most usual one follows a signature-based approach [1]. A signature-based sensor uses an algorithm that compares captured packets to signatures of known malicious events. This type of algorithms has been evolving very quickly over recent years. On the one hand, systems such as Snort [2] use efficient pattern-matching procedures to detect events, supporting more than a thousand rules without significant performance degradation. On the other hand, simple pattern-matching techniques do not provide the required logics to describe the complete attack scenario in an expressive and flexible manner. Unfortunately, more complex rules cannot be applied to sensors as they are a major cause of performance bottleneck in network traffic real-time analysis.

More expressive rule based systems are needed to specify the complete set of related events defining an attack model. To overcome this limitation, knowledge based systems such as production systems can be used as a detection engine. In this paper, we describe how the general production system tool CLIPS [3] can be used to detect network intrusions using previously captured network traffic. The proposed system can also be applied to real-time network intrusion detection, however it has performance limitations (a high packet drop ratio) specially for high link rates. Despite that, it can be used to

Fernando Moura Pires, Salvador Abreu (Eds.): EPIA 2003, LNAI 2902, pp. 341–354, 2003.

correlate network events creating a complete attack scenario model which can be used to instantiate several attacks performed with different tools on each of its phases.

The packet capture engine was written in C based on the Snort packet decoder. This choice is convenient as rules and plugins are continuously being developed for Snort lightweight network intrusion detection system [2]. Furthermore, using the same packet data structure as Snort allows to adapt any of its preprocessor plugins easily. This is particularly useful for implementing features such as IP defragmentation, TCP stream reassembly, and HTTP URI decode, among others. The CLIPS language was extended with several functions to perform, among others, time-stamp manipulation and Snort like string pattern-matching. By controlling CLIPS agenda, it is possible to introduce multiple string pattern-matching and certainty factors. Multiple string pattern-matching increases the system performance significantly when there are several rules testing the packet payload simultaneously. Certainty factors are very useful to identify and avoid false positive alarms. When the certainty factor of an issued alarm is too low, it is considered unreliable.

To prove the CLIPS production system expressiveness in intrusion detection a simple ruleset to detect the complete attack scenario in DARPA's LLDOS 2.0.2 dataset, is explained.

2 Related Work

There are several contributions focusing on the use of expert systems or knowledge based systems in computer systems intrusion detection.

P-BEST (Production-Based Expert System Toolset) has evolved from a lineage of intrusion detection projects, which include MIDAS [4], IDES [5], NIDES [6], and more recently the EMERALD eXpert [7]. P-BEST is a forward chaining expert system shell, which was applied for both network and host based intrusion detection.

The ASAX (Advanced Security and Audit Trail Analysis on UniX) project [8] uses a rule-based language called RUSSEL (Rule Based Sequence Evaluation Language), which provides a combination of procedural and rule-based programming to reason about activity on Unix systems by analyzing audit trails.

The University of California at Santa Barbara used a slightly different approach in USTAT (Unix State Transition Analysis Tool) [9]. Intrusions were detected using state transition diagrams modeling the sequence of operations and state changes occuring during the attack instead of production rules. A similar approach was used in the IDIOT (Intrusion Detection in Our Time) system. IDIOT's detection engine was also based on a graphical view of the malicious behavior, but using colored petri-nets to model an intrusion signature [10].

Wisdom and Sense [11] and NADIR [12], both from Los Alamos National Laboratory, are further examples of knowledge based systems oriented to malicious activity detection. In the case of Wisdom and Sense, the anomaly detection component is also implemented as a rule-base. The signature analysis component is a combination of site-specific policies, expert penetration rules and other administrative data in the same rule-base. NADIR intrusion signature rule-base uses empirical data resulting from interviews with several security experts.

However, none of those systems used a public domain general purpose expert system shell, and none of those intend to create high level abstract rules to model a complete attack scenario based on captured network traffic.

3 An Overview of CLIPS

CLIPS (C Language Integrated Production System) was developed using C programming language at NASA/Johnson Space Center aiming at high portability, low cost, and easy integration with external systems.

CLIPS is a multiparadigm programming language providing support for rule-based, object-oriented, and procedural programming [13]. The inference engine algorithms and the knowledge representation provided by the rule-based programming language are similar, but more powerful than those used in OPS5 production system [14]. CLIPS rules syntax is similar to rule languages such as ART, ART-IM, Eclipse, and Cognate. Only forward chaining is supported. The object-oriented programming in CLIPS is called COOL (CLIPS Object Oriented Language), which combines features of common object-oriented languages, such as Smalltalk and Common Lisp Object System (CLOS), with some new ideas. The procedural programming language has features similar to C, PASCAL, ADA and others, but it is syntactically similar to LISP. CLIPS source code is available for multiple platforms.

3.1 CLIPS Basic Components

As any other expert system shell, CLIPS has three basic components: a fact list containing data on which inferences are derived; a knowledge base which contains all the rules and an inference engine controling the overall execution.

Facts. In order to resolve a problem, a CLIPS program must have data or information to reason about. A "chunk" of data is called a *fact*. Facts consist of a *relation name* (a string) followed by zero or more *slots* (also strings) and their associated values, as the following example illustrates:

```
(person
    (name "Pedro Alípio") (age 29)
    (eye-color brown) (hair-color dark-brown)
)
```

Before facts can be created, CLIPS must be informed about which slots are valid for a given relation name. Templates are specifications of facts sharing the same relation name and the same structure. A template for fact *person* could be defined as:

```
(deftemplate person "A person template"
    (slot name)
    (slot age)
    (slot eye-color)
    (slot hair-color)
)
```

Slots can be specified as single values or multivalues by placing the keyword *multislot* instead of *slot*. Facts can be added, removed and modified with CLIPS commands *assert*, *retract* and *modify*.

Rules. An expert system needs rules to perform reasoning over facts. In production systems, a rule is defined as a set of conditional elements and a set of actions. If there is a matching in all the conditional elements of the Left-Hand Side (LHS), the rule is placed in the agenda. When the inference engine selects a rule for firing from the agenda, the Right-Hand Side (RHS) is executed. A rule in CLIPS has the following syntax:

```
(defrule <rule name> [<comment>]
    <patterns>* ; Left-Hand Side (LHS) of the rule
=>
    <actions>* ; Right-Hand Side (RHS) of the rule
)
```

Patterns consist of constraints applied to the fact list. Those constraints can be specified on the fact's slots. When a full LHS matching occurs, by using *?var_name* in the pattern slot value or *$?var_name* for multifield values, variables can be bound to fact's slots values. In the pattern *(data (y ?x&:(> ?x 4)))*, CLIPS binds variable *x* to slot *y* on every instance of *data* until it finds an instance where the value of variable *x* is greater than 4. These patterns are very useful since they are simultaneously a constraint and a variable binding. All the variables that have been bound on the LHS can be used in the rule's RHS.

Inference engine. CLIPS uses a forward chaining inference engine, which is a data-driven technique used in constructing goals or reaching inferences derived from a set of facts. To avoid the possibility of infinite loops, CLIPS exhibits a property called *refraction*, which prevents from firing more than once for a specified set of facts. To improve performance in the rule pattern match stage, the *Rete* algorithm is used [15]. The *Rete* algorithm is a fast pattern matcher which compiles information about rules in a network to obtain its speed. Instead of testing all rule's LHSs, it only looks for changes in matches on every cycle. This speeds up the matching process significantly since rules matching unaltered facts will not be tested.

4 Changing CLIPS to Support Network Intrusion Detection

CLIPS was designed to be embedded in other applications. When CLIPS is used as an embedded application the *main.c* file[1] must be changed to meet specific application requirements. This may include calling specific CLIPS statements without any user interaction, such as adding facts, reseting CLIPS, loading rules or running the system.

[1] CLIPS's main file starts the environment, initializes user functions and calls the command line interpreter.

4.1 Structure of the System

The CLIPS network intrusion detection system is conceptually divided in two major components: the packet capture engine and the CLIPS embedded expert system shell. Integration is carried out by decoding captured data into higher abstraction layers and passing it to CLIPS as facts. Figure 1 shows a more detailed view of the systems's architecture.

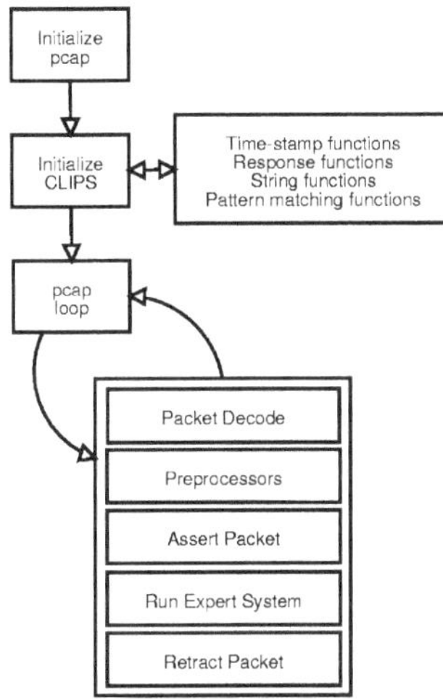

Fig. 1. Systems' structure.

The system is able to operate over two distinct data sources: real-time network traffic or raw packet files previously captured. If a real-time network traffic data source is chosen, the packet capture engine needs to know on which network interface it will be active. BPF filters (Berkley Packet Filters) can also be applied to packets captured from both data sources.

The CLIPS initialization process consists of creating the CLIPS environment, initializing user functions, loading a configuration file and reseting the system. CLIPS environment are several data structures which require memory allocation and are used to maintain the system's current state. User functions (written in C) are mapped into CLIPS functions for several purposes such as packet time-stamp manipulation or pattern matching. The configuration file is used to configure the system, indicating which rule files and preprocessing plugins will be applied to captured packets.

Each time a packet is captured a packet handler is invoked. The packet handler decodes raw packets into higher level data structures. Preprocessor plugins are then applied to network traffic, modifying the contents of those data structures. Packet data is converted into a CLIPS fact and asserted into the fact list. The ruleset is then invoked to perform the detection process. When CLIPS inference engine stops, the current packet is removed from the fact's list.

4.2 Packet Capture Engine

Network traffic is captured using *libpcap*, which is the packet capture library used in *tcpdump*[16]. This allows portability, isolates the application from link technology, and allows the system to read raw packet data files captured by *tcpdump*. Other important advantage of using *libpcap* is that it provides an easy way of applying kernel packet filters (such as BPF) reducing the network traffic and increasing the system real-time performance [17].

Each time a traffic unit is captured a packet handler is called by *libpcap*. The packet handler function, among other operations, has to decode the raw packet into data structures representing the TCP/IP stack. To provide easy integration with Snort's preprocessor plugins and rules, its packet decode functions were adapted. A large data structure called *packet* is then used to integrate simultaneously each packet layer header and data in a higher level format for URIs, TCP options, payload and others.

Adding packet data to CLIPS. Packet data has to be added to CLIPS's fact list before being analyzed. A function which takes the decoded packet as an argument, performs type conversion form C language to CLIPS, so that API functions can be called to assert the packet fact. As it was discussed on section 3.1, a template has to be created before fact assertion. The packet fact template is not created invoking any CLIPS API functions. Instead, during the initialization process, the packet fact template is read and executed from *main.clp*.

```
(deftemplate MAIN::packet
    (slot proto) (slot nproto) (multislot timestamp)(slot srcaddr)
    (slot srcp) (slot dstaddr) (slot dstp) (slot flags) (slot ttl)
    (slot tos) (slot id) (slot ipopts) (slot fragbits) (slot seq)
    (slot ack) (slot itype) (slot icode) (slot icmp_id)
    (slot icmp_seq) (slot ip_proto)(slot fragoffset) (slot dsize)
)
```

In the template definition, *MAIN* stands for the CLIPS module, which will be explained later. Slots *proto*, *nproto* and *timestamp* specify respectively the transport protocol, the network protocol and time-stamp which in turn is a multivalue slot containing two values: seconds and microseconds. The other slots specify packet information and have their equivalent in Snort's rule options [18].

4.3 Payload Pattern Matching

The template structure does not have any slot to store the packet payload data. There are two reasons why this data is not converted into a fact slot: the first is related to performance issues and the second is related to the implementation of multiple pattern matching. As payload data length may be greater than one thousand bytes, passing it to a fact slot would be CPU and memory consuming. Payload single and multiple pattern matching is done using a test function instead of looking up for fact instantiations.

The LHS of rule can also test boolean functions. To avoid a performance decrease when looking for rule instantiations which match packet header constraints and a payload pattern, rules are written using both fact constraints and a boolean test function. Packet header data must be checked in the first place in order to reduce the number of rules that will check the packet payload contents. The payload pattern matching operation is then carried out checking a smaller set of patterns.

Single pattern matching. To perform single pattern matching to packet payload data, a boolean function called *payload* was added to CLIPS. This function takes one, two or three arguments. The first argument is the pattern that will be searched for. The second argument is the search offset in the packet payload area. The third argument is the search depth. Single pattern matching should only be used to test a small number of bytes, and not the whole packet payload data. As in Snort, the Boyer-Moore algorithm is used for single pattern matching [19].

Multiple pattern matching. The multiple pattern matching algorithm allows to test several patterns against the packet payload simultaneously, increasing the detection performance. The problem is how to do this using CLIPS rules. The solution was to add a user function called *m_payload* which takes the rule identification and the pattern to be tested as arguments. The rule identification has to be passed to the function because there is no way of knowing which rule is being tested. Recall that, in the Rete algorithm only when the leaf nodes are reached by the token (fact list change notification), the rules matching all their conditional elements are known. The pattern test is not carried out by the function. In fact, it adds the pattern to an array so that later on, when the whole conflict set is known, all patterns in the array can be simultaneously tested with Aho-Corasick Algorithm [20]. The activations without matching patterns are removed from the agenda.

4.4 Certainty Factors

Certainty factors are used as a measure of trust in the generated alarms. There are two major sources of uncertainty in rule based systems: rule contradiction and rule subsumption. Rule contradiction occurs in the presence of two or more rules with the same LHS and with different RHSs. Rule subsumption occurs when a rule LHS is a subset of another rule LHS.

On a first approach, let $CF = 1/n$ be the expression defining a certainty factor *CF*, where n is the number of rules in conflict on the inference's engine last cycle. If there is only one rule on the agenda, the certainty factor will be one hundred percent, otherwise certainty will decrease as the number of rules in conflict increases. The problem with this expression is that it does not consider subsumption. A rule subsumes another rule if both are in the agenda and one is more complex than the other. Rule complexity is evaluated by counting facts constraints and tests on the LHS of a rule. The expression $CF_i = C_i/(n * C_{Max})$ expresses the certainty factor of rule i on both rule contradiction and rule subsumption, i.e, n reflects the number of rules in conflict, C_i the complexity of the rule i and C_{Max} the maximum complexity of all rules in the agenda. The certainty factor value will be lower for rules with less complexity, i.e. specific rules are more reliable than general ones.

To implement this feature a *callback* function is required. As soon as the conflict set is obtained, a function has to be called to evaluate the maximum complexity and the number of rules in the agenda.

4.5 The Agenda Callback Function

CLIPS has a way of calling a function each time a rule fires. This is particularly interesting to implement multiple pattern matching and certainty factors, since an agenda callback function is required. The CLIPS's API function *AddRunFunction* takes the function to be called whenever a rule is fired as an argument. Unfortunately, this is not enough to create the agenda callback function because the rule RHS is executed, which is not convenient. The solution is to create a special rule in file *main.clp* telling the inference engine to set the focus on a module called *EVENTS* each time a packet is detected.

```
(defrule MAIN:got_traffic "Analyser got a packet"
    (packet)
=>
    (focus EVENTS)
)
```

Module *EVENTS* is where the event signatures are defined. When rule *got_traffic* is fired, the agenda callback function is then automatically invoked.

4.6 Writing CLIPS's Rules for Network Intrusion Detection

CLIPS features, such as modules, can be used to write well structured intrusion detection signatures. Defining the ruleset as a hierarchical structure reduces the number of rules to be checked each time a packet arrives. For example, if a TCP packet is to be analyzed, it does not make sense to apply UDP signature rules to the packet. Therefore, a top level module called *MAIN* is used to define global variables, the packet template and a rule focusing on module *EVENTS* each time a packet is detected.

In module *EVENTS*, actually the main module for all intrusion signatures, the ruleset is divided into several modules according to TCP/IP protocols. If the captured packet is TCP, UDP or ICMP the inference engine should focus on corresponding module *TCP_EVENTS, UDP_EVENTS* or *ICMP_EVENTS*. Three levels were defined so far: level 1, with module *MAIN*; level 2, with module *EVENTS* and level 3, with modules *TCP_EVENTS*, *UDP_EVENTS* and *ICMP_EVENTS*.

One extra level containing rules applied to the application layer protocols was also defined to further reduce the rulesets size (see Figure 2).If the packet is HTTP, it does not make sense to apply FTP rules to it. So, on level 3 several rulesets can be specified according to the packet application protocol. The HTTP application protocol usually takes port 80, but if a proxy server is in use, port 3128 or 8080 can be used instead. Other

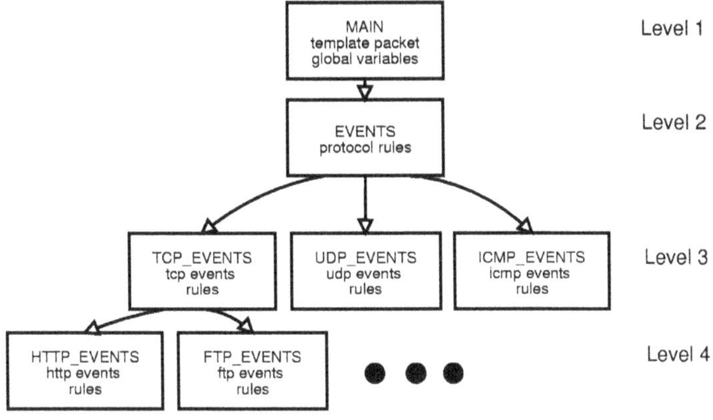

Fig. 2. Module's structure for signatures rulesets.

applications use transient ports, therefore port numbers cannot be used for explicitly divide a ruleset. Transparency is obtained through the definition of global variables. Different configurations can be applied, depending on the location in the network where the traffic was captured, by just changing those variables.

For example, the variables to define HTTP and FTP ports could be written using CLIPS statement *defglobal*:

```
(defglobal MAIN
    ?*http_port* = 3128
    ?*ftp_port* = 21
)
```

where the first argument is the module's name. Variables are then defined and initialized.

This hierarchical module structure leads to a performance increase in real-time network intrusion detection, though some modules tend to be heavy. For instance, the *HTTP_EVENTS* module may have a large number of rules performing packet payload analysis.

5 Results and Its Interpretation

To prove the system's expressive capabilities, a network traffic dump file from DARPA's[2] was used as data source. This data file was collected over a span of approximately one hour, 45 minutes on April 16, 2000, from 14:45 to 16:28. The attacker used a scripted exploit to break into a variety of hosts around the Internet to install the necessary components to run a Distributed Denial of Service (DDoS), and then launch it against a US government site. As part of the attack, he/she first probed for host operating system by doing DNS HINFO queries, then used the Solaris *sadmind* exploit, a well-known Remote-to-Root attack to successfully gain root access to three Solaris hosts at Eyrie

[2] `http://www.ll.mit.edu/IST/ideval/data/2000/LLS_DDOS_2.0.2.html`

Air Force Base. This succeeded due to the relatively poor security model in use, where many services, including the dangerous *sunrpc* service are proxied through the base's firewall from outside to inside. To perform the DDoS, the attacker used the Mstream tool, one of the less sophisticated DDoS tool. Two components are needed to install Mstream: the *server* which actually generates and sends the DDoS attack packets and the *master* which provides the user-interface to control the *server*.

The five phases of the attack scenario are:

1. Probe of mill.eyrie.af.mil, Eyrie's public DNS server, via the HINFO query;
2. Break-into mill.eyrie.af.mil via sadmind exploit;
3. FTP upload of mstream DDoS tool and attack script, to break-into more Eyrie hosts;
4. Telnet to mil.eyrie.af.mil, setup DDoS master and probing and break-into attempts via sadmind exploit;
5. Launching the DDoS: telnet to mil.eyrie.af.mil, telnet to localhost port 6723, connect to the master, and launch attack to www.af.mil.

Phase one and phase two can be easily detected by the use of Snort like packet matching rules. To detect the DNS HINFO probe, a sequence of bytes are sought in the payload of a DNS query packet (UDP, with destination port 53). This sequence of bytes contains the query type DNS field. If the rule matches, a DNS HINFO query is inferred by the system through the assertion of fact *attempt-recon* which specifies the event's class, the source address, destination address and the type of probe. Using CLIPS, such a rule can be specified as:

```
(defrule UDP_EVENTS::dns_hinfo
    (packet
        (proto udp)(timestamp $?ts)
        (srcaddr ?sa)(dstaddr ?da)
        (srcp ?sp)(dstp 53)
    )
    (test (payload "|00 00 0d 00 01|"))
=>
    (assert (attempted-recon ?sa ?da "DNS HINFO")
)
```

CLIPS's rule for phase two was adapted from the Snort rule available at Arachnids web site[3] (IDS546). If the rule matches, the fact *system-attempt* is inferred specifying the event class, the source address, the destination address and the tool used to break-into the system.

```
(defrule UDP_EVENTS:sadmind
    (packet (proto udp)
        (timestamp $?ts)(srcaddr ?sa)(dstaddr ?da)(srcp ?sp)
        (dstp ?dp&:(and (>= ?dp 32771) (<= ?dp 34000) ))
        (dsize ?dz&:(> ?dz 999))
    )
    (test (payload "|9003e05c 92222010 941bc00f ec023ff0|"))
```

[3] http://www.whitehats.com

```
=>
    (assert (system-attempt ?sa ?da "SADMIND"))
)
```

At this stage, it is known that the attacker tried to breakinto the system, although it is not known yet if he/she was successful in the attempt. Therefore, all the network traffic coming from both the attacker host and the attacked host must be considered suspicious. It is possible to monitor these two hosts with the following rules:

```
(defrule EVENTS:watch_activity1
    (system-attempt ?sa ?da)
    (packet
        (proto ?p) (timestamp $?ts)
        (srcaddr ?sa)(dstaddr ?da)
        (srcp ?sp2)(dstp ?dp)
    )
=>
    (printout t "suspicious-activity from " ?sa " : " ?sp2 " to " ?da " : " ?dp
        " proto " ?p crlf)
)
(defrule EVENTS:watch_activity2
    (system-attempt ?sa ?da)
    (packet
        (proto ?p)(timestamp $?ts)(srcaddr ?da)(dstaddr ?sa)
        (srcp ?dp)(dstp ?sp2)
    )
=>
    (printout t "suspicious-activity from " ?sa " : " ?sp2 " to " ?da " : " ?dp
        " proto " ?p crlf)
)
```

If the attacker runs a remote session such as telnet and then attacks other hosts (as it is described in phase 4), all the malicious activity found on the network traffic would be reported as being issued by the telnetd host and not by the host actually doing it. Therefore, this activity can be understood has an attempt to impersonate, or in other words, camouflage. This can be modeled into the following CLIPS rules:

```
(defrule TCP_EVENTS:impersonate_attempt_using_telnet1
    (packet
        (proto tcp)(timestamp $?ts)(srcaddr ?sa)(dstaddr ?da)
        (srcp ?sp)(dstp 23)
    )
    (system-attempt ?sa ?da ?tool)
=>
    (assert (impersonate-attempt ?sa ?da "TELNET"))
)
(defrule TCP_EVENTS:impersonate_attempt_using_telnet2
    (packet
```

```
            (proto tcp)(timestamp $?ts)(srcaddr ?da1)(dstaddr ?da2)
            (srcp ?sp)(dstp 23)
        )
        (impersonate-attempt ?sa ?da1 ?tool)
    =>
        (assert (impersonate-attempt ?sa ?da2 "TELNET"))
    )
```

The second rule is needed because the attacker can perform several remote sessions. The fact *impersonate-attempt* specifies the event class which is the fact name, the source address (of the attacker), the compromised host address and the session type.

In phase 5, the use of mstream DDoS tool can be detected using a CLIPS rule adapted form the Snort rule in the Arachnids web site (IDS529). If the rule is fired we can be sure that the attacker has really broken into the host. The fact *system-success* specifies the event class which is the fact name, the source address, the destination address and the tool used by the attacker.

```
    (defrule UDP_EVENTS:ddos_ddos-mstream-handler_to_agent_newserver
        (packet
            (proto udp)(timestamp $?ts)(srcaddr ?sa)(dstaddr ?da)
            (srcp ?sp)(dstp ?dp)
        )
        (test (payload "newserver"))
    =>
        (assert (system-success ?sa ?da "MSTREAM" $?ts)
    )
```

Finally, to model the complete attack scenario, a higher lever rule is needed.

```
    (defrule ATTACKS:attack_model1
        (attempted-recon ?sa ?da ?tool1)
        (system-attempt ?sa ?da ?tool2)
        (impersonate-attempt ?sa ?ia ?tool3)
        (system-success ?ia ?da2 ?tool4 $?ts)
    =>
        (alarm attack_model1 $?ts ?sa -1 ?da -1
        (str-cat "ATTACK MODEL 1 - Used Tools: "?tool1 "," ?tool2 "," ?tool3
        "," ?tool4)
            "attack" (get_rule_cf)
            (create$ "arachnids,529")
        )
    )
```

There are hundreds of attacks following this scenario. By adding more rules to detect events for each one of the specified classes, several attacks based upon this model would be detected and would have their events correlated. Most of other attack scenarios are based on small variations of this model, therefore writing new rules to describe them is an easy task.

Using the system to detect and correlate events based on network traffic previously captured proves to be a major contribution. The proposed system helps to visualize and follow all the actions performed by the attacker to achieve his malicious intents. Resorting to CLIPS's production rules it is possible to specify both simple network events and complete attack scenarios.

6 Conclusions

Building a low cost network intrusion detection system by using public domain tools and libraries is a possible and feasible solution. In this paper, an example of such a system, developed using NASA's CLIPS production system shell and adapting Snort code and data structures is proposed. The system supports complex heuristics, keeping event related information in a fact list and uses forward chaining reasoning mechanisms to reach a conclusion. If several conclusions are reached, certainty factors are used to assess those conclusions' reliability. Multiple pattern matching was used to improve the payload analysis performance. Unfortunately, there are some bottlenecks when using the system in real-time detection, as a inference engine is much more complex than a simple pattern matching engine. Despite that, events can be correlated through simple CLIPS rules describing complex attack scenarios.

More efficiency could be obtained by changing the CLIPS inference engine to support built-in multiple pattern matching. Although CLIPS is not a high performance tool oriented to real-time use, it works fine with previous Tcpdump captured traffic.

Future work includes improving the system's sensor mode behavior by using a hybrid algorithm for multiple pattern matching as in [21]. CLIPS may be extended just by mapping C language functions into CLIPS functions. Interoperability features can be added by building user functions for IDMEF message manipulation [22] and IDXP protocol implementation so that the alarms can be exchanged with other Intrusion Detection Systems [23] and having alarms received from those systems, mapped into CLIPS facts for higher-level analysis.

References

1. Kumar, S.: Classification and Detection of Computer Intrusions. PhD thesis, Purdue, IN (1995)
2. Roesch, M.: Snort - lightweight intrusion detection for networks. In: Proceedings of LISA '99: 13th Systems Administration Conference. (1999)
3. Riley, G.: CLIPS A tool for building expert systems. (http:// www.ghg.net/ clips/ CLIPS.html)
4. Sebring, M.M., Shellhouse, E., Hanna, M.E., Whitehurst, R.A.: Expert systems in intrusion detection: A case study. In: Proceedings of 11th National Computer Security Conference, Baltimore, Maryland, National Institute of Standards and Technology/ National Computer Security Center (1988) 74–81
5. Javitz, H.S., Valdes, A.: The SRI IDES statistical anomaly detector. In: Proceedings of the 1991 IEEE Symposium on Security and Privacy, Oakland, California, IEEE Computer Society Press (1991) 316–326
6. Anderson, D., Frivold, T., Valdes, A.: Next-generation intrusion detection expert system (NIDES). Technical Report SRI-CSL-95-07, Computer Science Laboratory, SRI International (1995)

7. Lindqvist, U., Porras, P.A.: Detecting Computer and Network Misuse Through the Production-Based Expert System Toolset (P-BEST). In: Proceedings of the 1999 IEEE Symposium on Security and Privacy, Oakland, California. (1999)
8. Habra, N., Charlier, B.L., Mounji, A., Mathieu, I.: ASAX : Software Architecture and Rule-Based Language for Universal Audit Trail Analysis. In: European Symposium on Research in Computer Security (ESORICS). (1992) 435–450
9. Ilgun, K.: USTAT: A real-time intrusion detection system for UNIX. In: Proceedings of the 1993 IEEE Symposium on Research in Security and Privacy, Oakland, CA (1993) 16–28
10. Crosbie, M., Dole, B., Ellis, T., Krsul, I., Spafford, E.: IDIOT - User Guide. Technical report (September 1996)
11. Vaccaro, H.S., E.Liepins, G.: Detection of anomalous computer session activity. In: Proceedings of the 1989 IEEE Symposium on Security and Privacy, Oakland, California, IEEE Computer Society Press (1989) 280–289
12. Jackson, K.A., DuBois, D.H., Stallings, C.A.: An expert system application for network intrusion detection. In: Proceedings of the 14th National Computer Society Conference, Washington, D.C., National Institute of Standards and Technology/National Computer Society Center (1991) 215–225
13. Giarratano, J.C.: CLIPS User's Guide, Volume I - Basic Programming Guide. (2002)
14. Forgy, C.L.: OPS5 User's Manual. Technical Report CMU-CS-81-135, Carnegie Mellon University, Dept. of Computer Science (1981)
15. Forgy, C.: Rete: A Fast Algorithm for the Many Pattern/Many Object Pattern Match Problem. Artificial Intelegence (1982) 17–37
16. Jacobson, V., Leres, C., McCanne, S.: tcpdump. (www.tcpdump.org)
17. McCanne, S., Jacobson, V.: The BSD Packet Filter: A New Architecture for User-Level Packet Capture. In: Proceedings of the 1993 Winter USENIX Conference, San Diego, CA (1993)
18. Roesch, M.: Snort Users Manual, http://www.snort.org. Snort release: 1.9.x edn. (2002)
19. Boyer, R.S., Moore, J.S.: A fast string searching algorithm. Communications of the ACM **20** (1977) 762–772
20. Aho, A., Corasick, M.: Efficient string matching: An aid to bibliographic search. Communications of the ACM **18** (1975) 333–343
21. C. Jason Coit, J., M. McAlerney, S.: Towards Faster String Matching for Intrusion Detection or Exceeding the Speed of Snort. In: Proceedings of the DARPA Information Survivability Conference and Exposition (DISCEX II'01). (2001) 367
22. Curry, D., Debar, H.: Intrusion Detection Message Exchange Format, Data Model and Extensible Markup Language (XML). http://www.ietf.org/internet-drafts/draft-ietf-idwg-idmef-xml-07.txt (2002) (work in progress).
23. Feinstein, B., Matthews, G., White, J.: The Intrusion Detection Exchange Protocol (IDXP). http://www.ietf.org/internet-drafts/draft-ietf-idwg-beep-idxp-05.txt (2002) (work in progress).

Model for Dialogue between Informational Agents

Erika Valencia and Jean-Paul Sansonnet

[1] Wassenaarseweg, 31, 2596 CE Den Haag, Netherlands
[2] LIMSI-CNRS, 91403 Orsay Cedex, France

Abstract. A theoretical model for agents interaction to study semantic heterogeneity is proposed. The context of this study is informational agents with knowledge bases that are heterogeneously interacting in a dialogue. Our problem is then: how does the interaction influence the evolution of the semantic heterogeneity between the agents, and how does this heterogeneity influence the interaction. To study semantic heterogeneity, we define agents that are not embedded in a common task program, they have no common goal and no common domain vocabulary. Our goal is then double:propose a model of dialogue between semantically heterogeneous informational agents, and use it to study semantical heterogeneity (HS) *per se* in a dynamical context in order to propose scenarios for solving this HS.

1 Introduction

Agents are considered here from the informational point of view, and modelled as information based agents: they contain a knowledge base and only exchange information in a dialogue. We provide a formal model of Informational agents in the next section.

For task oriented agents, the opening of a dialogue is dictated by the need to *complete a task*, and this need exists as soon as a task is defined [1,2]. The termination of a dialogue is then automatically reached when the given task is achieved. In other words, for task-oriented agents, the beginning and the termination of a dialogue is measured as a function of an external element: the task. For these reasons, the phase of a dialogue that has been most studied and modelled in the task-oriented multi-agents community is the development phase of the dialogue.

The informational agents we study are not task oriented because they do not interact necessarily through the internet in order to solve a common task. We consider their interaction at a more general level, and we will therefore not define the opening, development and termination of dialogues between informational agents with respect to such a common task. We propose that the opening phase of a dialogue between informational agents is *initiated* by a dissonant state of an agent. This is based on the *Dissonance Theory [4]*; and that the development and termination phases are regulated by *pertinence*.

Fernando Moura Pires, Salvador Abreu (Eds.): EPIA 2003, LNAI 2902, pp. 355–359, 2003.

2 Informational Agents in Dialogue

2.1 Knowledge Base

An informational agent carries A_i a knowledge base KB_i. The formalism used to model the information in the knowledge base is a first order logic with a three values $(true, false, unknown)$ valuating function. The agents are defined in a description language implemented over the Mathematica programming language [6]. Each agent's base KB_i is defined according to the following structure:

- **Facts**: comprising a *symbol* $f_{i,j}$ where i refers to the agent A_i and j is the numbering of the fact in A_i's list of facts; a *body* ${f_{i,j}}^{\beta}$ containing the fact's predicate in terms of first order logics; a *path* ${f_{i,j}}^{\pi}$ that is a *conversational chain* of agents through which the fact came to A_i; and also the *lists* of the agents that agreed ${f_{i,j}}^{\{agree\}}$, rejected ${f_{i,j}}^{\{reject\}}$ or knew ${f_{i,j}}^{\{know\}}$ already the fact $f_{i,j}$. The path ${f_{i,j}}^{\pi}$ and the lists ${f_{i,j}}^{\{\}}$ are build *sequentially* during conversations.
- **Rules**: they are implications in the sense of first order logics, and are noted $r_{i,j}$ where i refers to the agent A_i and j is the numbering of the rule in A_i's list of rules. Like the facts, they are also defined with a path and agree, reject and know lists.
- **Channels** are *unidirectional* structures, noted $ch_{i \to b}$, where i stands for the agent A_i and b stands for its locutor A_b. A new channel is opened *each time* a dialog is opened with a new locutor [1] and is never closed. $ch_{i \to b}$ is composed of a *symbol* b, referring to the agent to which it is connected, the *list* of the facts already told to A_b, $ch_{i \to b}^{tolds}$, the *list* of the facts to tell to A_b, $ch_{i \to b}^{totell}$, selected among the facts that participate into a dissonance, and the integer cumulated counts of all the agrees $ch_{i \to b}^{agree}$, rejects $ch_{i \to b}^{reject}$, and knows $ch_{i \to b}^{know}$, obtained during the dialogues on this channel.

2.2 Informational Heterogeneity: Dissonance

The dissonance theory is based on the hypothesis that humans have a specific *need* to fulfill, called *cognitive consonance* [5]. Whenever this consonance is lost (or a dissonance is provoked), they tend to *act* in order to reach a consistent state again.

We define that an agent is *consonant* when a fact f_a is a logical consequence of a fact f_b, otherwise it is *dissonant*. Any piece of information received during an interaction), and any new deduction from the facts of the knowledge base can provoke such a dissonant state. The *need* to reach a consonant state again leads the agent to provoke new interactions (only actions possible in our model), that is to *start* a new thread of dialogue.

According to the dissonance theory, there are three categories of actions to reach a consonant state after a dissonance occurred:

[1] We will see that channels are used to record contextual information, or trace chronicles, about the streams exchanged between two agents. The viewpoint of an agent on such an exchange stream is called a channel.

- The first S_1, is to not integrate the new information, since it is not compatible with its own knowledge system;
- A second S_2, is to consider that some piece of information it had before and that participates to the incoherence of its new knowledge system is wrong. This means that the agent puts **more confidence degree** in the new information than in his current believes.
- The third S_3, is to suppose that the new piece of information and the old piece of information that the agent possessed before and that participates to the incoherence are only apparently in contradiction, and that some kind of further explanation would explain how they could be compatible. That is then a motivation for opening a dialog.

The logical incoherence is defined as:

$$\{KB_1 \cup i_{new}\} \Longrightarrow \bot$$

2.3 Informational Confidence and Trust

To select which of the above solutions to apply, the agent calculates the degree of confidence in the old pieces of information $f_{1,old}$ or $r_{1,old}$ of KB_1 that are not coherent with i_{new} and in the new piece of information i_{new}, and compares these values.

- If the confidence degree in i_{new} is less than the confidence degree in internal facts and/or rules participating to the dissonance, then the solution S_1 is chosen, and we say that i_{new} is rejected.
- If the confidence degree in i_{new} higher than the confidence degree in internal facts and/or rules participating to the dissonance, then the solution S_2 is chosen and we say that i_{new} is *integrated* to KB_1, while the internal facts and/rules participating in the dissonance are erased from KB_1.
- If the confidence degrees in i_{new} and in the internal facts and/or rules participating to the dissonance are "comparable" in value, then the solution S_3 is chosen. What we mean by comparable is of course relative to the norm chosen for the measures. It is an adjustable parameter of the implemented system, and we will give a numerical example in the next section.

The measure of confidence in an information of KB_1 is the confidence degree C_{1,f_j}, respectively C_{1,r_j}, in any fact $f_{1,j}$, resp. any rule $r_{1,j}$, of its knowledge base KB_1. This measure is a function of the *history* of the acquisition of the information $f_{1,j}$, resp. $r_{1,j}$, by A_1: this history is stored in the path ${f_{1,j}}^{\pi}$, resp. ${r_{1,j}}^{\pi}$.

The path ${f_{1,j}}^{\pi}$ keeps track of the succession of agents through which ${f_{1,j}}^{\pi}$ was transmitted to A_1, each time, together with their own confidence in this information, for example:

$${f_{1,j}}^{\pi} = \{(A_3, C_{3,f}), (A_5, C_{5,f}), (A_9, C_{9,f}), ..., (A_k, C_{k,f})\}$$

where A_3 is the last agent that send $f_{1,j}$ to A_1, and A_k was the first one of the chain. Then, the measure C_{1,f_j} is given by:

$$C_{1,f_j} = ((0.6 \times C_{3,f}) + (0.3 \times C_{5,f}) + (0.1 \times C_{9,f}))$$

which means that only the three last agents of the chain are taken into account, with a weighted sum giving much more weight to the last agent in the chain, here A_3. Of course, this weighted sum $\sum_{k=1}^{n}(w_k \times c_{k,f})$, could take into account more agents of the chain ($n > 3$) and the weights w_k could be decided according to a different repartition function.

The **confidence** degree $C_{1,f_{new}}$ of A_1 in f_{new} does not actually correspond to the actual confidence that the agent A_1 puts in the fact f_{new} *per se*, because $C_{1,f_{new}}$ is merely a preliminary *score* used by the agent to compare it to the confidence of an internal fact $C_{1,f}$ (or/and an internal rule $C_{i,r}$), in order to decide which solution S_1, S_2 or S_3 he should apply to get out from the dissonant state.

The score taken for $C_{i,f_{new}}$ is equal to A_2: $C_{2,f_{2,new}}$ if this fact is send by an agent A_2. Note that if the new fact f_{new} comes from a perceptive experience, we can either give an arbitrary value to $C_{i,f_{new}}$ or give a confidence degree depending on the perceptive *means* through which the fact is perceived by A_i, but this analysis is not within the subject of the current study.

For all practical purposes, the score will then always be the one of the source agent. In the case where the receiver agent A_1 decides to integrate this new information (case of solution S_2), then a confidence degree is given to f_{new}, which now becomes part of KB_1 and is renamed $f_{1,j+1}$. This confidence degree is calculated with the following formula:

$$C_{1,f_{new}} = C_{1,f_{j+1}} = (C_{2,f_{new}} \times t_{1\to 2})$$

where $t_{1\to 2}$ is the trust that A_1 has for A_2, this parameter is defined below.

2.4 Semantical Intersection: Focus and Pertinence

The pursue of a dialogue is based on the *pertinence* of the information exchanged. We define a measure of the pertinence p_f or p_r of a content information. The pertinence is modelled by the lexical semantical intersection defined in the Worldnet project [3]. This pertinence is calculated with respect to the current focus of the dialogue.

The *focus* of a dialogue is dependent on the content information exchanged, and may be different for each agent because they have their viewpoint on a dialogue. In a dialogue between A_i and A_j, these viewpoints are stored in the channel $ch_{i\to j}$ for A_i and in the channel $ch_{j\to i}$ for A_j, for example. For one agent A_i for example, the information exchanged during a dialogue is stored in the lists $ch_{i\to j}^{tolds}$ and $ch_{i\to j}^{totell}$ of his channel. But these lists store the content information exchanged from the very first dialogue and that do not necessarily relate to the actual focus of the present dialogue. Only the three last facts or rules of each list are taken into consideration when defining a focus. Again, this number is chosen for practical purposes and could be different when appropriate testing would dictate so.

The *focus* of a dialogue between A_i and A_j, from the point of view of A_i, is given by:

$$Focus(i \leftrightarrow j, A_i) =$$
$$\cup\{ch_{i \to j}^{tolds'}, ch_{i \to j}^{totell'}\}$$

where $tolds'$ stands for the three most recent elements of the list $tolds$, and $totell'$ stands for the three most recent elements of the list $totell$.

This focus is used by A_i to test the lexical pertinence of each new content information f_{new} sent to it. The pertinence is then the boolean result from the intersection $\cap\{Focus(i \leftrightarrow j, A_i), f_{new}\}$.

The dialogue terminates when the dissonance is solved. The coherence of the knowledge base KB_i is therefore tested each time a new information is added or an old information is deleted.

3 Application and Conclusion

This model for dialogue is an object-oriented program written with a scripting language that we defined over the Mathematica programming language [6].

To model the notion of dissonant state, and the application of solutions to it, we introduced the confidence and trust degrees, that are meta-knowledge of the agents over the information they posses. This *meta-knowledge* is calculated using the history of the dialogue that is recorded in the paths and channels.

Pertinence and trust and measures that are constantly updated after each interaction through the record of the history of the interaction associated with each *channel* of communication opened between each pair of agents. Likewise, the HS is also a measure associated with each channel.

References

1. A. Bond. *Proceedings of the 1990 Conference on Office Information Systems*, chapter Comitment: A computational Model for Organizations of Cooperating Intelligent Agents. Cambridge, 1990.
2. S. Cammarata, D. M. Arthur, and R. Steeb. *Proceedings of the 8th International JOint Conference on Artificial Intelligence*, Strategies of Cooperation in Distributed Problem Solving, pp. 767–770, 1983, Germany.
3. C. Fellbaum. *Breadth and Depth of the Lexicon*. 1999.
4. L. Festinger. *A theory of cognitive dissonance*. Evantson, Peterson, iii edition, 1957.
5. J.-P. Poitou. *La dissonance cognitive*. Armand-Collin, collection u edition, 1974.
6. S. Wolfram. *The Mathematica book*. Wolfram Media. Cambridge University Press, fourth edition, 1999.

A Possibilistic Logic Modeling of Autonomous Agents Negotiation

Leila Amgoud and Henri Prade

Institut de Recherche en Informatique de Toulouse (IRIT)
118, route de Narbonne, 31062 Toulouse, France
{amgoud, prade}@irit.fr

Abstract. Negotiation plays a key role as a means for sharing information and resources with the aim of looking for a common agreement. This paper proposes a new approach based on possibility theory, which integrates both the merits of argumentation-based negotiation and of heuristic methods looking for making trade-offs. This unified setting proves to be convenient not only for representing the mental states of the agents (beliefs possibly pervaded with uncertainty, and prioritized goals), but also for revising the belief bases and for selecting a new offer.

1 Introduction

In most agent applications, the autonomous components need to interact with one another because of the inherent interdependencies which exist between them, and negotiation is the predominant mechanism for achieving this by means of an exchange of offers. Agents make offers that they find acceptable and respond to offers made to them. Works in multi-agents negotiation can be roughly divided into two categories. The first one has mainly focused on the numerical computation of trade-offs in terms of utilities, and the search for concessions which still preserve the possibility of reaching preferred states of affairs e.g.[5, 7]. This type of approaches often uses heuristic strategies and does not incorporate mechanisms for modeling persuasion processes. Recently, a second line of research [6] has focused on the necessity of supporting offers by arguments during a negotiation. Indeed, an offer supported by a good argument has a better chance to be accepted by an agent, and also may lead an agent to revise its goals. These works have mainly introduced a protocol for handling arguments. In [1], a formal model of reasoning shows how arguments are constructed from the knowledge bases of the agents and how these arguments are evaluated. However, these approaches have some limitations. Indeed, the first category of approaches, although effective for finding compromises, does not leave much room for the exchange of arguments and information. On the contrary, in argumentation-based approaches, it is not clear how the goals are handled and updated if necessary, how an agent chooses an offer which of course should satisfy its goals and how a compromise can be searched for. In the following, a unified setting is presented where mental states can be represented and revised, and where choices can be made by the agents on the basis of their beliefs and preferences.

Fernando Moura Pires, Salvador Abreu (Eds.): EPIA 2003, LNAI 2902, pp. 360–365, 2003.

2 The Negotiation Framework

Here negotiation dialogues take place between two agents a and $\overline{a}$. Each negotiating agent is supposed to have a set $\mathcal{G}$ of *goals* to pursue, a knowledge base, $\mathcal{K}$, gathering the information it has about the environment, and finally a base $\mathcal{GO}$, containing what the agent believes the goals of the other agent are. $\mathcal{K}$ may be pervaded with uncertainty (the beliefs are more or less certain), and the goals in $\mathcal{G}$ and $\mathcal{GO}$ may not have equal priority. Levels of certainty are assigned to formulas in $\mathcal{K}$, and levels of priority to the goals. We obtain three possibilistic bases [3] that model gradual knowledge and preferences: $\mathcal{K} = \{(k_i, \alpha_i),\ i = 1, \ldots, n\}$, $\mathcal{G} = \{(g_j, \beta_j),\ j = 1, \ldots, m\}$, $\mathcal{GO} = \{(go_l, \delta_l),\ l = 1, \ldots, p\}$ where k_i, g_j, go_l are propositions or closed first order formulas and α_i, β_j, δ_l are elements of $[0, 1]$. The bases of agent a are denoted by: $\mathcal{K}_a$, $\mathcal{G}_a$, $\mathcal{GO}_a$ and those of $\overline{a}$ by: $\mathcal{K}_{\overline{a}}$, $\mathcal{G}_{\overline{a}}$, $\mathcal{GO}_{\overline{a}}$. A possibility distribution [3] expresses the semantics of each of the three bases: π_K, $\pi_{\mathcal{G}}$ and $\pi_{\mathcal{GO}}$ which are mappings from the set of interpretations ω into $[0, 1]$, which rank-order the interpretations according to their certainty or priority. We assume that an agent is not allowed to change its own goals during a negotiation while it may revise its beliefs in $\mathcal{K}$ or in $\mathcal{GO}$.

Let X be a set of possible offers which can be made during a negotiation process by each agent. Elements x of X are viewed as propositional variables. Let $\mathcal{K}^x$ be the belief state of an agent once x takes place. In fact, $\mathcal{K}^x = \mathcal{K} \cup \{(x, 1)\}$. An agent is supposed to be able to evaluate to what extent it is certain that its set of prioritized goals is satisfied (on the basis of its beliefs about the state of the world) and assuming that an offer x takes place. This is evaluated in the possibilistic setting by the inclusion degree of the fuzzy set of the possible states of the world into the set of interpretations which satisfy the goals at a high degree: $N_{\mathcal{K}^x}(\mathcal{G}) = min_\omega\ max(\pi_{\mathcal{G}}(\omega), 1 - \pi_{\mathcal{K}^x}(\omega))$. Similarly, an agent can compute to what extent it is possible that an offer x is acceptable for the other agent, according to its belief, by $\Pi_{\mathcal{K}^x}(\mathcal{GO}) = max_\omega\ min(\pi_{\mathcal{GO}}(\omega), \pi_{\mathcal{K}^x}(\omega))$.
To capture a negotiation dialogue between these agents we follow [1] in using a variant of the dialogue system DC introduced by MacKenzie. In this scheme, agents make dialogical moves by asserting facts into and retracting facts from *commitment stores* (CSs) which are visible to other agents. At each stage of the dialogue a participant has a set of legal moves: agents are allowed to make offers, to challenge a given offer, to justify an offer by arguments, to accept or to refuse an offer. An agent can also withdraw from the negotiation. Let $\mathcal{M}$ denote the complete set of moves. $\mathcal{M} = \{$Offer, Challenge, Argue, Accept, Refuse, Withdraw$\}$. Each agent maintains a fourth possibility distribution $\pi_{\mathcal{M}}(m_i) = \eta_i$ where $m_i \in \mathcal{M}$. The degree η_i represents to what extent it is possible for an agent to make the move m_i. For each move we specify when it can be made and how it updates the CSs and the mental states of the agents. Moreover, we give the next legal moves which are possible for the other agent. In the following, we suppose that agent a addresses the move to $\overline{a}$.

The basic move in negotiation is an *Offer*. For example, in a bargaining context, an agent can suggest a price. In the tourism example we consider later, an agent can suggest a travel destination. The basic idea here is that an agent

selects an offer x, not already rejected, which maximizes the certainty $N_{\mathcal{K}_a^x}(\mathcal{G}_a)$ of the satisfaction of its important goals and the possibility $\Pi_{\mathcal{K}_a^x}(\mathcal{GO}_a)$ that x may be acceptable for the other agent $\overline{a}$. An offer move may lead the agent which receives it to modify its beliefs about the other agent's goals.
$-Offer(x)$ where x is any formula in X.
Pre-conditions: (1) $X \neq \emptyset$ (there is at least one offer available still), (2) $\pi_{\mathcal{M}_a}(Offer) = 1$ (the move is fully possible), (3) Choose x maximizing $\mu_a(x) = \min(N_{\mathcal{K}_a^x}(\mathcal{G}_a), \Pi_{\mathcal{K}_a^x}(\mathcal{GO}_a))$.
Post-conditions: (1) $CS_i(a) = CS_{i-1}(a) \cup \{x\}$ and $CS_i(\overline{a}) = CS_{i-1}(\overline{a}) \cup \{x\}$. (2) Agent $\overline{a}$ revises $\pi_{\mathcal{GO}_{\overline{a}}}$ into $\pi'_{\mathcal{GO}_{\overline{a}}}$ such that: $max_\omega min(\pi'_{\mathcal{GO}_{\overline{a}}}(\omega), \pi_{\mathcal{K}_{\overline{a}}^x}(\omega)) = 1$. This expresses the consistency of $\overline{a}$'s beliefs about the world and the goals of a once x takes place. If this condition does not hold with $\pi_{\mathcal{GO}_{\overline{a}}}$, a possibilistic revision [4] is performed. (3) $\pi_{\mathcal{M}_{\overline{a}}}(Accept) = \pi_{\mathcal{M}_{\overline{a}}}(Refuse) = \pi_{\mathcal{M}_{\overline{a}}}(Challenge) = \pi_{\mathcal{M}_{\overline{a}}}(Offer) = 1$ and $\pi_{\mathcal{M}_{\overline{a}}}(Argue) = \pi_{\mathcal{M}_{\overline{a}}}(Withdraw) = 0$.
$-Argue(S)$ where $S = \{(k_i, \alpha_i), i = 1, n\} \subseteq \mathcal{K}_a$ represents the support of an argument uttered by agent a (see [1] for a definition of (weighted) argument). Note that in DC players are unable to produce a supporting argument.
Pre-conditions: $\pi_{\mathcal{M}_a}(Argue) = 1$. **Post-conditions:** (1) $CS_i(a) = CS_{i-1}(a) \cup S$ and $CS_i(\overline{a}) = CS_{i-1}(\overline{a})$. (2) If S is acceptable (in the sense of [1]), the agent $\overline{a}$ will revise its base $\mathcal{K}_{\overline{a}}$ into a new base $(\mathcal{K}_{\overline{a}})^*(S)$ (see [4] for the definition of revision under an uncertain input which is forced to hold after revision). (3) $\pi_{\mathcal{M}_{\overline{a}}}(Accept) = \pi_{\mathcal{M}_{\overline{a}}}(Offer) = \pi_{\mathcal{M}_{\overline{a}}}(Challenge) = \pi_{\mathcal{M}_{\overline{a}}}(Argue) = 1$ and $\pi_{\mathcal{M}_{\overline{a}}}(Refuse) = \pi_{\mathcal{M}_{\overline{a}}}(Withdraw) = 0$.
The following are moves which are made in response to offer and argue moves.
$-Accept(x)$ where x is a formula in X. After an offer x, an agent can respond with an explicit acceptance if x is acceptable, i.e. maximizes $N_{\mathcal{K}_a^x}(\mathcal{G}_a)$.
Pre-conditions: $\pi_{\mathcal{M}_a}(Accept) = 1$ and x maximizes $N_{\mathcal{K}_a^x}(\mathcal{G}_a) over X$.
Post-conditions: (1) $CS_i(a) = CS_{i-1}(a) \cup \{x\}$ and $CS_i(\overline{a}) = CS_{i-1}(\overline{a})$, (2) $\pi_{\mathcal{M}_{\overline{a}}}(Refuse) = 0$ and $\forall\ m_i \neq Refuse$, $\pi_{\mathcal{M}_{\overline{a}}}(m_i) = 1$.
$-Accept(S)$ where S is a set of formulae in $\mathcal{L}$. **Pre-conditions:** $\pi_{\mathcal{M}_a}(Accept) = 1$.
Post-conditions: (1) $CS_i(a) = CS_{i-1}(a) \cup S$ and $CS_i(\overline{a}) = CS_{i-1}(\overline{a})$. (2) $\pi_{\mathcal{M}_{\overline{a}}}(Refuse) = 0$ and $\forall\ m_i \neq Refuse$, $\pi_{\mathcal{M}_{\overline{a}}}(m_i) = 1$.
An agent is also allowed to reject a given offer if it is not acceptable for it.
$-Refuse(x)$ where $x \in X$. **Pre-conditions:** $\pi_{\mathcal{M}_a}(Refuse) = 1$ and $\Pi_{\mathcal{K}_a^x}(\mathcal{G}_a) = 0$.
Post-conditions: (1) $CS_i(a) = CS_{i-1}(a) \backslash \{x\}$ and $CS_i(\overline{a}) = CS_{i-1}(\overline{a})$. (2) $\pi_{\mathcal{M}_{\overline{a}}}(Refuse) = 0$ and $\forall m_i \neq Refuse, \pi_{\mathcal{M}_{\overline{a}}}(m_i) = 1$. (3) $X = X - \{x\}$. Any rejected offer is removed from the set of possible offers. We might also think of revising $\mathcal{GO}_{\overline{a}}$ on the basis of the move "Refuse(x)" performed by agent a. This is not done here for the sake of simplicity.
$-Withdraw$ **Pre-conditions:** $\pi_{\mathcal{M}_a}(Withdraw) = 1$ and $\forall x$, $\mu_a(x) = min(N_{\mathcal{K}_a^x}(\mathcal{G}_a), \Pi_{\mathcal{K}_a^x}(\mathcal{GO}_a)) = 0$ or $X = \emptyset$ (There is no acceptable offer to make).
Post-conditions: (1) $CS_i(P) = \emptyset$ and $CS_i(C) = \emptyset$. (2) $\forall m_i \in \mathcal{M}, \pi_{\mathcal{M}_{\overline{a}}}(m_i) = 0$.

The next move allows an agent to elicit a response, especially an argument. An agent asks for an argument when the offer made to it is not acceptable to him and there still remain non rejected offers.
$-Challenge(x)$ where x is a formula in $\mathcal{L}$.
Pre-conditions: $\pi_{\mathcal{M}_a}(Challenge) = 1$ and $N_{\mathcal{K}_a}(\mathcal{G}_a) \neq 0$ but is not maximal over the remaining offers. **Post-conditions:** (1) $CS_i(a) = CS_{i-1}(a)$ and $CS_i(\overline{a}) = CS_{i-1}(\overline{a})$. (2) $\pi_{\mathcal{M}_{\overline{a}}}(Argue) = 1$ and $\forall\ m_i \neq Argue,\ \pi_{\mathcal{M}_{\overline{a}}}(m_i) = 0$.

Definition 1. *A negotiation dialogue is a tuple <Players, Moves, Dialogue, Termination> where:* ***Players*** $= \{a, \overline{a}\}$*,* ***Moves*** *are as defined above, a* ***Dialogue*** $\mathcal{D}$ *is a non-empty sequence of moves* $M_1, \ldots, M_p$ *s.t. (1) An agent cannot address a move to itself. (2) The two agents take turns. (3) Agent a begins the negotiation by making an offer. (4) The commitment stores are empty at the beginning of the dialogue. (3) An agent is not allowed to provide a move which has been already provided by another agent or by itself. This guarantees non circular dialogues.* ***Termination*** *is a function that returns the result of the negotiation:* succeeds *(a compromise is found), or* fails *(one agent withdraws).*

Properties. (i) Any negotiation dialogue between two agents a and $\overline{a}$ will terminate. Moreover, termination takes place with either an *accept(x)* move or a *withdraw* move. (ii) A *compromise* x found by the agents a and $\overline{a}$ maximizes $min(N_{\mathcal{K}_a^x}(\mathcal{G}_a), N_{\mathcal{K}_{\overline{a}}^x}(\mathcal{G}_{\overline{a}}))$, provided that agents do not strongly misrepresent the preferences of the other in $\mathcal{GO}$.

3 Two Illustrative Examples

Inspired from [2], we illustrate the above framework on a bargaining problem with a seller s and a buyer b. Each of them maintains two distributions about possible prices. The first type of distribution, $\pi_{\mathcal{G}_b}$ (resp. $\pi_{\mathcal{G}_s}$) restricts the prices which are more or less acceptable for the buyer (resp. the seller) at a given stage. Preferred interpretations represent the ideal prices for the saler (resp. to the buyer). Similarly, the second type of possibility distributions $\pi_{\mathcal{GO}_b}$ and $\pi_{\mathcal{GO}_s}$) represents the beliefs of agent b (resp. s) about the prices which are more or less acceptable for the other at a given stage. In this simplified example, the knowledge bases $\mathcal{K}_s$ and $\mathcal{K}_b$ are supposed to be empty. As a consequence the only possible moves are: $\{Offer, Accept(Offer), Refuse, Withdraw\}$. In the following we will not present a real dialogue between s and b, but we describe a cycle of negotiation starting with an $Offer(x)$ move made by the seller s.
(1.) s makes the move $Offer(x)$ by choosing an x which maximizes $\mu_s(x)$ over X. $\mu_s(x)$ can be simplified here into $\min(\pi_{\mathcal{G}_s}(x), \pi_{\mathcal{GO}_s}(x)))$.
(2.) The buyer b modifies $\pi_{\mathcal{GO}_b}$ as said in the post-conditions of an offer. It means here that $\pi_{\mathcal{GO}_b}(x)$ is put to "1" if it was not already its level of possibility.
(3.) Agent b has three possibilities: (3.1) to accept x if x maximizes $\pi_{\mathcal{G}_b}$ over X. Then negotiation stops. (3.2) to refuse the offer x if $\pi_{\mathcal{G}_s}(x) = 0$. In this case, x is removed from the set X as well as prices which are above x. The fact that here offers greater than the current offer are also removed from X is peculiar to price

bargaining. In the same way, if the seller s makes the move $refuse(x)$, then X is updated by removing x as well as any price less than x. (3.3) to compute an offer y which maximizes $\mu_b(y) = \min(\pi_{\mathcal{G}_b}(y), \pi_{\mathcal{GO}_b}(y))$. If $y = x$ then b accepts x else it suggests y as a new offer.
(4.) Agent s or b withdraws from the negotiation when it cannot make any further offer (i.e. the maximum of $\mu_s(x)$ over the current X is equal to 0).
As a second illustration of the approach, we consider the example of Peter and Mary who discuss about the place of their next holidays. Peter's goals are a place which is cheap and preferably sunny. This can be encoded by a possibilistic base like: $\mathcal{G}_{Peter} = \{(Cheap(x), 1), (Sunny(x), \alpha)\}$ with $0 < \alpha < 1$. In terms of the associated possibility distribution, this means that any place which is not cheap is impossible for Peter, any cheap but not sunny place is possible only at a level 1 - α, and any cheap and sunny place is is fully satisfactory for him. Peter's beliefs are that Tunisia is certainly cheap and that Italy is likely to be not cheap. This is encoded by the following base: $\mathcal{K}_{Peter} = \{$(Cheap(Tunisia), 1), $(\neg Cheap(Italy), \beta)\}$. Mary definitly wants a sunny place, hopefully cheap and preferably not too warm. This can be encoded by a base like: $\mathcal{G}_{Mary} = \{(Sunny(x), 1)$, (Cheap(x), ϵ), $(\neg Too{-}warm(x), \delta)\}$ such that $\epsilon > \delta$. Mary's beliefs are that Tunisia is sunny and too warm, that Italy is sunny and not too warm. Her belief base is as follows: $\mathcal{K}_{Mary} = \{(Sunny(Tunisia), 1), (Sunny(Italy), 1), (Too - warm(Tunisia), 1),$ $(\neg Too - warm(Italy), 1)\}$. For the sake of simplicity, we suppose that both Peter and Mary know nothing about the preferences of the other. This means that the possibility distributions $\pi_{\mathcal{GO}_{Peter}} = \pi_{\mathcal{GO}_{Mary}} = 1$ for any interpretation. Assume that Mary makes the first offer, say Italy ($Offer(Italy)$). Peter will challenge this offer and Mary will justify her choice by an argument stating that she believes that Italy is sunny and not too warm. At this stage of the dialogue, Peter will integrate the argument of Mary into its belief base and makes a counter argument stating that Italy is likely to be not cheap. Mary integrates this knowledge into her belief base and accepts it. Now, Peter makes a new offer which is Tunisia and Mary will accept it since she now knows that Italy violates a goal which is more important for her than the goal violated by Tunisia. Then the dialogue stops since the two persons find Tunisia as a compromise.

4 Conclusion

As shown above, possibility theory offers a unified setting for not only representing the mental states of the agents (including degrees of beliefs on the world and prioritized goals), but also for revising the belief bases or the set of goals, and for describing the decision procedure for selecting a new offer and also a new move to play, thus describing the whole negotiation process. Note that no strategy has been described here. Strategies could take advantage of non binary possibility distributions for describing the next possible moves.

References

1. L. Amgoud, S. Parsons, and N. Maudet. Arguments, dialogue, and negotiation. In *Proc. of the 14th ECAI*, 2000.
2. Benferhat, Dubois, Kaci, and Prade. Représentation bipolaire et modification de préférences en logique possibiliste. In *13 Cong. RFIA, Angers*, pages 955–964, 2002.
3. D. Dubois, J. Lang, and H. Prade. A brief overview of possibilistic logic. In *Proc. of Symb. and Quanti. Approaches to Uncert., ECSQAU'91. LNCS 548.*, pages 53–57.
4. D. Dubois and H. Prade. A synthetic view of belief revision with uncertain inputs in the framework of possibility theory. *Int. J. Approx. Reasoning*, 17:295–324, 1997.
5. X. Luo, N. Jennings, N. Shadbolt, H. fung Leung, and J. H. man Lee. A fuzzy constraint based model for bilateral, multi-issue negotiations in semi-competitive environments. In *To appear in Artificial Intelligence*, 2003.
6. C. Sierra, N. Jennings, P. Noriega, and S. Parsons. A framework for argumentation-based negotiation. In *4th Workshop ATAL*, pages 167–182, 1997.
7. O. Wong and R. Lau. Possibilistic reasoning for intelligent payment agents. In *Proc. of the 2nd Workshop on AI in Electronic Commerce AIEC*, pages 170–180, 2000.

Towards Individual Power Design
Rediscovering the Will of Acting Agents

Francisco Coelho[1] and Helder Coelho[2]

[1] Departamento de Matemática,
Universidade de Évora
fc@uevora.pt
[2] Departamento de Informática,
Faculdade de Ciências da Universiade de Lisboa
hcoelho@di.fc.ul.pt

Abstract. We started the setup of a virtual laboratory for the study of power struggles where autonomous agents embody different capabilities. The scenario is a caricature of hierarchical production societies which are driven to be structured into different organizational forms. Under the assumption of limited rationality, we look at diverse mechanisms able to *drive the agent choice of action* and to act. In our simple setup, an agent will look to shift to a new leader when placed in a poor individual situation. On the other hand, if the agent is comfortable, it might lower the pression imposed to its subordinates. Our agent models are yet too naive to distinguish motivation from will: the decision procedures aren't sophisticated enough to enable the consideration of reasoning processes running at each deliberation step. Thus we can't identify reasons (or motives) driving action selection. However, there is a causal relation from agent's state and its choosing process (but not its action).
Along the present paper, special care is given to the validation of conjectures, where the data collected from the simulations is subject of statistical analysis towards their infirmation/refutation. Our present research around power will try to highlight new points of view over the architecture of an agent and the inner spot of potency, without loosing rigour on experimentation. Our initial experiments point out that, in these organisations, 1) Life Expectation and Individual Productive Capacity are related with the Hierarchical Rank and 2) If, under certain critical circumstances, agents can change to new leaders – or eventually become ones – Global Productive Capacity reach higher numbers but Life Expectation is lower.

Keywords: Multi-Agent Based Simulations, Social Activity, Agent Mechanisms.

Fernando Moura Pires, Salvador Abreu (Eds.): EPIA 2003, LNAI 2902, pp. 366–378, 2003.

1 Introduction

Power \Pow"er\, n. [OE. pouer, poer, OF. poeir, pooir, F. pouvoir, n. & v., fr. LL. potere, for L. posse, potesse, to be able, to have power. See *Possible*, *Potent*, and cf. *Posse comitatus*.]
1. Ability to act, regarded as latent or inherent; the faculty of doing or performing something; capacity for action or performance; capacity of producing an effect, whether physical or moral: potency; might; as, a man of great power; the power of capillary attraction; money gives power. "One next himself in power, and next is crime." – Milton

Webster's Revised Unabridged Dictionary (1913)

Technology and the breakup of the factory as the traditional work-place have created new social subjects whose value is no longer tied to their skills.

The spread of communication networks and the globalization of production mean that the world has become insecure and totalized, but the possibilities for subversion have correspondently equally increased. A new historical conjuncture was born at the end of the 90's, bringing the formation of new alliances between natural and artificial forces. The contrast between the ineffective individual power –swallowed in the massified population– and the social power of the state –enhanced by rigid norms and regulations over individuals– is even more perceived. Yet, in artificial scenarios, it is possible to organize the autonomy of software agents and embody power to make them act and transform the environment. We may have access to the interior of the mind of the artificial creatures where we can tune their motivation and choice machinery, or even insert will mechanisms.

The old productive forces (land, labor, the accumulation of capital) burst through the obsolete superstructures (juridical and political ones) showing the need to think about new forms of democracy, where science and technology need to be present. The old formula which makes the working class the dynamic motor of capital was destroyed and the economic mechanism of accumulation does not work as the consistent way of controlling antagonisms. The dialectical mediation between the individual and the state, the so-called Hobesian social contract, had come to an end and the Spinoza's politics of the multitude, the composition of the collective subject, was brought to light [6]. The totalizing and fixed dimension of social making is not interesting any more because in the actual world, dominated by communication, *the understanding of overpowering cooperative networks is the key issue.* We pretend to study these new ideas by doing experiments in virtual laboratories.

The choice of building agents with a single utility function was already criticized [1]. The concept of socialized agent is now build on an *adequate theory of values* and on the discovery of other *inner mechanisms* of what attitudes make an agent active at large. Dependence, a very important facet to study social power [3], is now secondary because power is not always disciplined and controlled when we look to autonomous individuals. And also influence is less important, because the knowledge of intervention is built more upon *will* and again on *choice*[1]. The potential of the social agent is not reduced to its autonomy, where rational decisions (based upon deliberation and choice) play a definitive role, but autonomy (motivation and choice) is the real infrastructure of the power to act, *i.e. motivation* and *will* are mixed with *reason* to aid an agent to play primary roles and acting. This is what occurs in an enterprise, where regulations (and norms) try to discipline agent behaviors and to govern the whole structure to accomplish certain tasks. When failures (less productivity and production, lack of work by illness, low budgets and incomes) occur, a shuffle is required by down-sizing the organization and by changing the top leadership and the middle managers. New chiefs appear and new ways to deal with things are introduced. The question is: Are these changes introduced top-down or bottom-up? Are workers the real players?

The awareness of the society complexity is closely linked to the knowledge of its own transformation and this relation focus on what is missed. Every time we are deprived of knowledge, this happens because we are defeated on the terrain of power, and this means that the relationship to knowledge through power is not something trivial. In the beginning there was action, but always action depends on actors, players and interventionists.

In the present paper we enlarge, in a holistic manner, the role of agents in organizational environments in order to think about institutions and change [2], not only from the side of structures and functions (static viewpoint), but trying to introduce dynamic aspects: agents act by themselves, by introducing new schemes of organization and power, and to get better global performances. Our research follows the moto of Allen Newell and Herbert Simon [8], by looking to AI as an empirical science: we try to approach practical problems (economic and enterprise situations) by developing a theory of agents and of action as a step to a new theory of mind, where conceptual descriptions and causal explanations play a definite role [4].

1.1 Two Ideas

The authors wish to pass two ideas. At the *paradigmatic* level, resuming the introductory text of this section and effectively being a paradigm for this work (by giving long-term objectives), the P-idea:

> *Power can't be completely understood without the knowledge of the individual mechanisms driving the choice of action.*

At the *methodological* level, giving short-term goals, the M-idea:

> *Multi-agent based simulations, as a scientific tool, need to be completed with post-mortem analysis.*

[1] The so-called BDI architecture, advanced in the 80's by Bratman, is not able to include several choice hubs in the structure of the mind of an agent.

It is mainly the methodology that is visible in the remaining of this paper. However, the paradigm has a background presence and will be subject to further research.

In section 2 the reader will find a draft of the methodology. It is not well tuned yet, with the excuse that multi-agent based simulations (MABS) is a recent field of research.

Section 3 present a simple economic model [2] were the P-idea and the M-idea find a show-room allowing some progress about a broad understanding of this model and its variations: by doing experiments we may design a road map for further investigations around the mind of an agent. This section follow the main goal of this paper: to show that the P-idea and the M-idea are good (in the *useful* sense) ideas. Indeed, this section ends with a discussion on the roles of these ideas.

At last, section 4 propose the future steps of our work, mainly concerned with the refinement of the P-idea.

2 A Methodological Approach to MAS

The use of computer simulations by observing behaviors of agents is a way to understand reality and complex phenomena, and it has, like any other scientific tool, the danger of misunderstanding. The sources of flaws in multi-agent systems (MAS) include biased inference from the outputs. Very often, and very understandably, the subjectivity of the scientist is entangled with the reading of pure numerical outputs. Once aware of this danger, one can prevent from it by *confronting conjectures to output data by objective and scientific testing procedures.* Statistical Analysis offers this kind of tools. An iterative methodology were conjectures about a system can be built, tested and reformulated would follow these lines:

1. Build a model of the agency in a certain environment;
2. Repeat until satisfied:
    a) Advance Conjectures and Hypothesis;
    b) Select Parameters and Measures;
    c) Run Simulations, Observe Behaviors and Gather Data;
    d) Perform Statistical Tests on Collected Data;
    e) Infirm/Refute Conjectures;

This methodology to face complexity is based upon the constitution of a virtual world (agents and environment), the tuning of their key features (parameters) and properties, the historical observation of the character of the interactions, and the stabilization of the evolution.

2.1 Testing Conjectures

There are two sorts of conjectures one could think about a particular system:

Isolated: Concerning with the dynamics of the system's agents;
Relative: Concerning the performance of the system with respect of other systems;

In the first case, the isolated one, the universe of the observer is a given system. All the questions are in terms of the system's agents, whereas in the relative setting the observer has access to alternative systems and it is concerned with the relative performance of the target system with respect of the alternative ones.

Each run of a simulation usually produce a long table of numbers, each row being a list of the values of the measured variables in each agent, in each time-step. A tested procedure outline [5] to analyze data from simulations is has follows: Suppose that the state of each agent in the system contain the variable[2] x. For each run of the simulation, at each time step *compute over the set of all agents*

$$\overrightarrow{x} = \left(\min x,\, \bar{x},\, \max x,\, \sigma^2 x\right)$$

and

1. Find the transient period[3] of $\overrightarrow{x}$;
2. Forget the data from time-steps before the transient period;
3. When two or more variables have to be considered, take the largest transient period for all the variables.

With this procedure most of the effects of the choice of the initial conditions are dissipated. Thus, the observations are more representative of the system's dynamics and less dependent on the particular choice of the initial conditions.

The choice of measures and the profile of the simulations to be run depend on the conjectures the observer wants to test. There is no limit on its diversity both about isolated or relative conjectures: One can measure a single variable from an agent's state. For graphs (*e.g.* of relations among agents) one can look at their connectivity, cluster number, flow, dimension, etc. At the system level one can think of the average, extremes, variance of agent's variables, entropy[9], many sorts of dimensions, etc.

3 Virtual Economy: One Observatory for Power Struggles

A simple system is the economic toy model CC, described by [2]. Briefly, agents in CC are engaged in the production of a single good. Each agent is described by a 4-tuple

$$\langle n,\, a,\, c,\, d\rangle$$

[2] This supposition of homogeneity on agent's state is not so restrictive as might look: We can always think of the subsystem whose agents' state do contain that variable. It is in this subset that the measurement makes sense.

[3] While a rigorous test isn't available, we simply look at the plot of $\overrightarrow{x}$ and choose the time t_0 such that *after* t_0 the graph is "regular".

where n (for **n**ame) is a unique identifier of the agent, a (**a**ge) is the number of time-steps the agent is active, c (**c**apacity) control the agent's production (its doings) and d (**d**ependent-of) is the name of some agent in the organisation attached to the system (possibly, himself, or its boss).

The d parameter is the *social link*. Notice that it is possible to define a directed graph following the dependent-of pointers. In general this graph is not connected. Call each (weak-) connected component *group*. Groups are graphs with a ring where each node in this ring is the root of a tree. Agents on the trees form an hierarchy leaded by the root. So, groups are hierarchical production units (organisations), leaded by the ring in the top. This is a simple social structure composition, measured by agent's *rank*, the distance the agent is from the ring of its group.

At each time-step the production activity in each group is dependent of its member's capacity and reconverted to updated capacities, according to the agent's rank in the group. If the capacity of an agent falls below a given threshold this agent is replaced by a new one with the same name, age 0, random capacity and random dependent-of. Group's production is designed to be an economy until a given dimension and a dis-economy above that value. The initial configuration is set randomly.

Notice that groups are dynamic organisational structures within this model. In the case of the collapse a given agent, its subtree might be transferred to another group. In the limit, it is possible the occurrence of groups formed by only one agent, pointing to themselves.

3.1 A First Test

The authors of the *CC* model conjectured that:

The locus of old agents tend to be at the top of hierarchies.

This conjecture is about systems with 16 agents and running until time 4000. In order to test it, given the output of one simulation with 16 agents and running until time-step 4000, consider the data from the last 10 steps. For each agent x and each time-step $t \geq 3990$ there is a measurement pair

$$(r_{x,t},\ a_{x,t})$$

recording the rank and age of agent x at time-step t.

Both graphs of $\overrightarrow{r}$ and $\overrightarrow{a}$ are "regular" from almost the initial time. Since the conjecture is about old agents, it is enough to consider the last time-steps of the run. For the last 10 time-steps (i.e. for time ≥ 3990), the plot of Rank vs. Age is depicted in figure 1.

Each dot is the (partial) state of some agent, at some time-step. Every agent travels up (since it is getting older) and eventually sideways, in the case of agent replacements (ploted in the line age $= 0$).

The upper-right corner of the graph is empty, showing that agents with low social rank (and then, with large rank number) don't survive for many cycles.

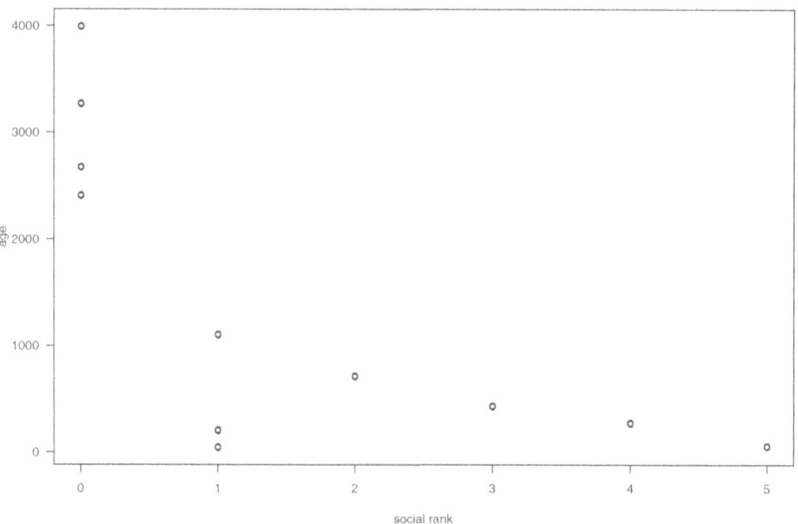

Fig. 1. Looking inside the organisation: rank versus age

In contrast, agents in the top (with rank 0) show the potential of surviving forever. In reality, this strange situation often occurs in bureaucracies where red tape avoid any insurrection!

The methodology requires that the output data should confront the conjecture. A simple statistical measure of relation is the *correlation* of the random variables, in this case rank and age. This measure takes two lists X and Y with the same length and outputs a real number in the interval $[-1, 1]$ with this interpretation:

- $cor\,(X, Y) = 1$ the variables are *positively* related (directly proportional);
- $cor\,(X, Y) = 0$ the variables are *not* related;
- $cor\,(X, Y) = -1$ the variables are *negatively* related (inversely proportional);

For the computed samples, we obtain

$$cor = -0.76882$$

which is a strong indicator that rank and age are inversely proportional: Agents in the top (with small rank) live longer (big age).

However, for a statistician, this might not be enough: one should test if this value is not fruit of hazard. One standard test for correlation correction is the Pearson's Product-Moment Correlation. Again for the computed samples, the output of this test is:

data: rank and age;
values: $t = -15.8592$; $df = 174$; $p - value = 2.2 \times 10^{-16}$;
alternative hypothesis: true correlation is not equal to 0;
95 percent confidence interval: from -0.8231304 to -0.7005716;
sample estimates: $cor = -0.76882$;

and the reading is:

- Assuming that the samples follow independent normal distributions;
- The probability of finding a sample contradicting the conclusions of this test is $p - value = 2.2 \times 10^{-16}$;
- The *cor* value of the *population* is in interval $[-0.8231304, -0.7005716]$ with probability 0.95.

From this test there are two possible conclusions:

extra-cautious: If the samples follow independent normal distributions then older agents of CC live in the top of the hierarchies;
normal: older agents of CC live in the top of the hierarchies.

3.2 A Comparison of Behaviors

In the CC model agents are severely limited on their individual actions and have no impulse to prefer any option: power is only viewed from the social perspective. Returning to the P-idea, agents must have *individual mechanisms driving their choice of actions and pushing them to act.* To start with, there must be some pool of actions. If the agent should be aware of its environment (whatever it is) then it must also have *senses*. In the simplest scenario, agents choose their next action without recourse to the senses.

A first and simple variation, CC_1, of the CC model is obtained by including a reaction mechanism, and by doing so we start a shift from social to individual power. Agents are still described by

$$\langle n, a, c, d \rangle$$

but can *react* to poor capacity values: If capacity fall below a given threshold, the agent change to a new, random, *d*ependent-on, giving away with different forms of organization.

In the second enhancement of the CC model, CC_2, two other mechanisms are embodied, one for attraction and another for fleeing. Each agent can perform two sorts of actions: 1) lower the tax imposed to its dependents or 2) look at the taxes of three agents, randomly chosen, and select the one with lower tax as its new leader and head. These two actions have different activation schemes: If the capacity is above a given threshold, the agent will lower its tax parameter by 10%. The second action is probabilistically activated: The lower hierarchy position, the higher probability to perform it. Thus, agents in the top (with rank 0) stay quiet (with respect to this kind of action). Agents on rank 1 start it with probability $p_1 > 0$; Agents on rank 2, with probability $p_2 > p_1$; etc.

The attentive reader may notice that CC_2 agents need an extra parameter to hold individual taxes. Agents are now described by a 5-tuple:

$$\langle n, a, c, d, t \rangle$$

where t stands for tax. This parameter is set in the initial time-step by a given value. From there on, in each agent, this parameter has its own dynamics.

Notice that the "physical" laws of the "world" remain unchanged in all the three models CC, CC_1 and CC_2.

The differences are isolated inside the agents.

But, with these changes, agents can (potentially) embody behaviors, reactions, strategies and tactics. At this point a natural question is:

How do these features, obviously changing individual trajectories, affect the global performance of the organisation?

In order to perform statistical tests to answer this question –remember the outline for the M-idea in section 2– consider the following procedure :

1. Let T be a fixed time-step after the transient period of all the models, say $T = 9900$;
2. Let X be a set of model variables shared by all the models, say
   a) `aveAGE` (the mean of agent's age at time-step T),
   b) `aveRANK` (the mean of agent's rank at time-step T) and
   c) `aveCAP` (the mean of agent's capacity at time-step T).
3. Run each model N times (say $N = 30$) until time-step T and record the values of these X variables.

The output of this procedure is, for each model (CC, CC_1 and CC_2), a table with $|X|$ columns and N rows. These tables contain the (post-mortem) data ready to suffer statistical analysis. A basic question is:

Is the average value of $x \in X$ in model M_1 equal to the average value of x in M_2?

This question can be tested with the Welch Two Sample t-test. The detail of this test for $x =$ `aveCAP`, $M_1 = CC$, $M_2 = CC_1$ is

data: `aveCAP` of CC and `aveCAP` of CC_1;
values: $t = -6.1125$; $df = 48.946$; p-value $= 1.576 \times 10^{-7}$;
alternative hypothesis: true difference in means is not equal to 0;
95 percent confidence interval: from -0.5357993 to -0.2706565;
sample estimates: `aveAGE` of $CC = 9.044840$; `aveAGE` of $CC_1 = 9.448077$;

The corresponding reading is:

– The probability of finding a sample contradicting the conclusions of this test is $p-value = 1.576 \times 10^{-7}$ (showing a good *representativiness* of the sample);

- $\texttt{aveCAP}(CC) - \texttt{aveCAP}(CC_1) \in]-0.5357993, -0.2706565[$ with probability 0.95 (indicating productivity differences on the two models);

So, since the 95% confidence interval for the difference of means *doesn't contain* 0 and *it is negative*, we can say that

$$\texttt{aveCAP}(CC) < \texttt{aveCAP}(CC_1)$$

or, in plain English:

Claim. The CC_1 model exhibit higher productive capacity that CC does.

One advantage of doing MABS in computer systems is that, once a procedure is fixed, it is easy to repeat it. This is a summary of all the possible comparisons for age, capacity and rank of the CC, CC_1 and CC_2 models. The *conclusive* classifies those comparisons where the confidence interval doesn't contain 0. Bellow we show the importance of the p-value in these tests:

- Capacity:
  - $CC - CC_1 < 0$, conclusive, p-value $= 1.576 \times 10^{-7}$;
  - $CC - CC_2 < 0$, conclusive, p-value $= 3.675 \times 10^{-6}$;
  - $CC_1 - CC_2 < 0$, inconclusive, p-value $= 0.8021$;
- Age:
  - $CC - CC_1 > 0$, conclusive, p-value $= 2.611 \times 10^{-9}$;
  - $CC - CC_2 > 0$, conclusive, p-value $= 1.477 \times 10^{-10}$;
  - $CC_1 - CC_2 > 0$, conclusive, p-value $= 0.003635$;
- Rank:
  - $CC - CC_1 < 0$, inconclusive, p-value $= 0.8406$;
  - $CC - CC_2 < 0$, inconclusive, p-value $= 0.7543$;
  - $CC_1 - CC_2 < 0$, inconclusive, p-value $= 0.9461$;

All the experiments were done with safety because we looked to the agent's internal mechanisms without changing the external environment. Clearly, with respect to CC, both CC_1 and CC_2 have equal advantages and disadvantages: Both reach higher capacities and lower ages. The rank comparisons yield always inconclusive tests, suggesting that these models don't distinguish themselves by agent's ranks. At last, notice that the only conclusive comparison of CC_1 and CC_2 is that agents in CC_1 tend to be older.

The presence of the p-value is also an important indicator for the validation of the conclusion. The CC_1-CC_2 age comparison, here conclusive with p-value = 0.003635 (a high value), with different samples produced an inconclusive test.

Notice that the invalid (with high p-value) tests highlight the need of great care with the data analysis: Indeed, the sample values are never equal. Consider the case of the capacity comparison CC_1-CC_2. The respective means are 9.448077 and 9.432432. With basis only on this data one could (unsoundly) infer that CC_1 is more productive that CC_2. This is the sort of erroneous inference this methodology rules out.

3.3 Discussion

This section shows that the M-idea is

- Feasible: The M-idea required a lot of statistical software [7], but all tests were already available;
- Effective: Some unsound conclusions based on a direct reading of the samples could be ruled out.

Invalid tests highlight the need of objective care on data analysis.

and, about the P-idea, it is the *knowledge* of the differences on the internal design of agents that *explains* the observed –and tested– differences on the social dynamics found on the comparisons of CC, CC_1 and CC_2. Without this knowledge, given that these models differ *only in inner agent design*, it wouldn't be possible to advance an explanation for the observations.

Individual power machinery can subvert social dynamics.

4 Future Work

The work in progress needs a road map to guide the next steps. In the following we propose some topics that are open to further quest.

4.1 Social Structure of CC

This presentation doesn't make justice to the previous work on CC: Rings seem to exhibit a balanced distribution of capacities. There are many other questions on the stability of structures. Indeed, in this paper, the social organization of CC was disregarded: All measures used are independent of group structures.

4.2 Model-Model Comparisons: Entropy

An interesting measure of any agent model within some organisation seem to be the *Shannon Entropy*

$$-\sum_i p_i \log p_i$$

where p_i is the probability of finding the model in state i and the sum ranges over all possible states the model can be in. Recent work [9] point out that this measure might be a good indicator of *coordination* arising among agents placed in an organisation. We are interested to study autonomous agents, without explicit external command, but corporately structured. We want also to investigate how individual local decisions yield coherent global behaviour, how agents with will (energy, information) impose structure and organisation, and, also, how a group of agents tend to disorder (a natural tendency) and, eventually, to take power.

Adding information to a collection of agents can lead to increased organisation, but only if it is added in a certain way: "coordination can arise through coupling the macro level (agent self organisation, with decreasing entropy) to an entropy increasing entropy at a micro level". Power is a key to further research.

4.3 Agent Mentality Reloaded

After the clarification about the required decision machinery for renewing the BDI (Belief-Desire-Intention) architecture [1], we need to introduce some changes concerning the mental states flow. Two topics are urgent: a new state, will, between beliefs and desires is necessary to make a mighty agent, *i.e.* the potency of an agent is only obtained by including anima inside the agent mind; and, the so-called linear flow cause-and-effect sequence of mental states must be opposed to the circular causation, in which effects become their own causes. We know now that the human mind was formed by experience, through the interplay of heredity and environment, and, therefore, a new theory of free will would help artificial agents to become more interventive.

4.4 Power Agents and Bounded Rationality

In principle, there is no bound on the computational costs of agent's activities. This unrealistic feature can –should– be mended. One way to do it is through the assumption of *bounded rationality*:

> *Each agent can only perform a limited amount of operations at each time-step.*

This bound should affect *time*, *resources*, and *actions* but it is not only a matter of better agent management: the crucial feature is to have the power to act, a kind of inner ability to change reality. In this line, since the activity of each agent, at each time step, can be very complex, there is the need of a simple, elegant, solution to the implementation of these bounds.

One such solution might be achieved through the association of an energy-like cost to each action the agent can perform. At the start of each time-step the agent has an energy value to be consumed through its activities in the running time-step. It is now easy to accomplish a resume-action in the case of the available energy drop below low-level thresholds. Notice that this method is effective to bound time, resources and actions.

Acknowledgements. This work has been partially funded by FCT (Portugal) under Project POSI/ 39351 /SRI /2001 MAGO2.

References

1. Luís Antunes, João Faria, and Helder Coelho, *Utility in interacting markets, a position paper*, Proceedings of RASTA'03, June 21 2003.
2. José Castro Caldas and Helder Coelho, *The interplay of power on the horizon*, Proceedings of the II International Conference on Computer Simulation and the Social Sciences (Paris), September 2000.
3. Cristiano Castelfranchi, *All I understand about power (and something more)*, Proceedings of the 2nd SARA workshop (Lisbon), February 11 2000.

4. Milton Corrêa and Helder Coelho, *From mental states and architectures to agent's programming*, Progress in Artificial Intelligence – IBERAMIA98 (Springer-Verlag, ed.), 1998, pp. 64–75.
5. Miguel A. de Avillez and Low Mac, *Mixing timescales in a supernova-driven interstellar medium*, Astrophysical Journal **581** (2002), 1047–1060.
6. Michael Hardt and Antonio Negri, *Empire*, Harvard University Press, 2000.
7. Ross Ihaka and Robert Gentleman, *R: A language for data analysis and graphics*, Journal of Computational and Graphical Statistics **5** (1996), no. 3, 299–314.
8. Allen Newell and Herbert Simon, *Computer science as empirical inquiry: Symbols and search*, Communications of the ACM **19** (1975), no. 3, 113–126.
9. H. Van Dyke Parunak and Sven Brueckner, *Entropy and self-organization in multi-agent systems*, Proceedings of the International Conference on Autonomous Agents (Agents 2001) (2001), 124–130.

An Architecture for a Rational Reactive Agent

Pierangelo Dell'Acqua[1,2], Mattias Engberg[1], and Luís Moniz Pereira[2]

[1] Department of Science and Technology – ITN
Linköping University, 601 74 Norrköping, Sweden
{pier,maten}@itn.liu.se
[2] Centro de Inteligência Artificial – CENTRIA
Departamento de Informática, Faculdade de Ciências e Tecnologia
Universidade Nova de Lisboa, 2829-516 Caparica, Portugal
lmp@di.fct.unl.pt

Abstract. We present an architecture for a rational, reactive agent and describe its implementation. The paper addresses issues raised by the interaction of the rational and reactive behaviour of the agent, and its updating mechanism. We relate it with the work of others.

1 Introduction

In previous work we defined a logical formalization of a framework for multi-agent systems and we defined its semantics [13]. In such a framework, we embedded a flexible and powerful kind of agent that are rational, reactive, abductive, able to prefer and they can update the knowledge base of other agents.

The knowledge state of each agent is represented by an an abductive logic program in which it is possible to express rules, integrity constraints, active rules and priorities among rules. This allows the agents to reason, to react to the environment, to prefer among several alternatives, to update both beliefs and reactions, and to abduce hypotheses to explain observations. We defined a declarative and procedural semantics of this kind of agent [4,14]. These agents are then embedded into a multi-agent system in such a way that the only form of interaction among them is based on the notions of project and update.

The semantics of the agents depends on the query that each agent has to prove at a certain moment in time. In fact, in proving a query G the agent may abduce hypotheses that explain G, and in turn these hypotheses may trigger active rules, and so on. Hypotheses abduced in proving G are not permanent knowledge, rather they only hold during the proof of G. To make them permanent knowledge, an agent can issue an internal project and update its own knowledge base with those hypotheses.

Our approach to agents is an enabling technology for sophisticated Web applications due to their deliberative, reactive and updating capabilities. See [15] for a discussion on the use of preference reasoning in Web applications, and [1] for a discussion on the use of Logic Programming for the Semantic Web.

In this paper we present an architecture for such a kind of agents and outline its implementation. Our aim is to have a simple architecture and to test its

Fernando Moura Pires, Salvador Abreu (Eds.): EPIA 2003, LNAI 2902, pp. 379–393, 2003.

behaviour in different application domains. In particular, we are interested in testing the interaction between the rational/deliberative (D) and reactive (R) behaviour of the agent, and its updating mechanism (U). In fact, the interaction of these components raises a number of issues that are addressed in Section 3.

D-R Can (should?) the deliberative behaviour of the agent influence the reactive behaviour? and vice versa? This is an important issue. For example, if the deliberative mechanism of the agent is performing some planning, and some exogenous event occurs, then the reactive mechanism of the agent can detect the anomaly, suspend the planning and require to start a replanning phase.

D-U If α has a goal to prove and contemporarily some updates to consider, which of the two tasks shall α perform first? The policy of giving priority to goals may decrease the agent performance when a quick reaction is required. In contrast, prioritizing updates can cause unwanted delays of the proof of a goal only to consider unrelevant updates.
Another issue concerns the behaviour of the agent when is proving a goal G (i.e., it is deliberative) and it receives an update. Should α complete the execution of G, and then consider the update? or instead should it suspend the execution of G, consider the update and then relaunch G ?

R-U If α receives several updates, should α consider each update and then trigger its active rules? or should it consider all the updates and only then trigger the active rules?

Two other interesting features of our architecture are the ability (i) to declaratively interrupt/suspend the execution of a query, and (ii) to declaratively self-modify its control parameters. These features are important for example in the context of reactive planning when the agents are situated in dynamic environments. Here, there is often a need to suspend the current execution of a plan due to unexpected exogenous events, and to replan accordingly. Also, the agent must be able to tune its behaviour according to the environment's conditions. For example, in a dangerous situation the agent may decide to become more reactive to quickly respond to changes of the environment. In contrast, in other situations the agent is required to be more deliberative, like when it enters into a planning phase.

The remainder of the paper is structured as follows. Section 2 presents the logical framework, the notion of abductive agents, and the agent cycle. The architecture of the agent is presented in Section 3. Finally, Sections 6 and 7 compare our work with the literature and presents future lines of research work.

2 Preliminaries

In this section we present the language of agents and our conception of abductive agents. The reader is referred to [14] for more details and examples on the language, including its declarative semantics, [4] for the procedural semantics, and [5] for the declarative semantics of update and preference reasoning.

2.1 Logic Programming Framework

In this exposition, we syntactically represent the theories of agents as propositional Horn theories. In particular, we represent default negation *not* A as a standard propositional variable. Propositional variables whose names do not begin with "*not*" and do not contain the symbols ":", "÷" and "<" are called *domain atoms*. For each domain atom A we assume a complementary propositional variable of the form *not* A. Domain atoms and negated domain atoms are called *domain literals*.

Communication is a form of interaction among agents. The aim of an agent β when communicating a message C to an agent α, is to make α update its current theory with C (i.e., to make α accept some desired mental state). In turn, when α receives the message C from β, it is up to α whether or not incorporate C. This form of communication is formalized through the notion of projects and updates. Propositional variables of the form $\alpha{:}C$ (where C is defined below) are called *projects*. $\alpha{:}C$ denotes the intention (of some agent β) of proposing the updating of the theory of agent α with C. Projects can be negated. A negated project of the form *not* $\alpha{:}C$ denotes the intention of the agent of not proposing the updating of the theory of agent α with C. Projects and negated projects are generically called *project literals*.

Propositional variables of the form $\beta \div C$ are called *updates*. $\beta \div C$ denotes an update with C in the current theory (of some agent α), that has been proposed by β. Updates can be negated. A negated update of the form *not* $\beta \div C$ in the theory of some agent α indicates that agent β does not have the intention to update the theory of agent α with C. Updates and negated updates are called *update literals*.

Preference information is used along with incomplete knowledge. In such a setting, due to the incompleteness of the knowledge, several models of a program may be possible. Preference reasoning is enacted by choosing among those possible models, through the expression of priorities amongst the rules of the program. Preference information is formalized through the notion of priority atoms. Propositional variables of the form $n_r < n_u$ are called *priority atoms*. $n_r < n_u$ means that rule r (whose name is n_r) is preferred to rule u (whose name is n_u). Priority atoms can be negated. *not* $n_r < n_u$ means that rule r is not preferred to rule u. Priority atoms and negated priority atoms are called *priority literals*.

Domain atoms, projects, updates, and priority atoms are generically called *atoms*. Domain literals, project literals, update literals, and priority literals are generically called *literals*.

Definition 1. A *generalized rule* is a rule of the form $L_0 \leftarrow L_1, \ldots, L_n$ with $n \geq 0$ where every L_i $(0 \leq i \leq n)$ is a literal.

Definition 2. A *domain rule* is a generalized rule $L_0 \leftarrow L_1, \ldots, L_n$ whose head L_0 is a domain literal distinct from *false* and *not false*, and every literal L_i $(1 \leq i \leq n)$ is a domain literal or an update literal.

Definition 3. An *integrity constraint* is a generalized rule whose head is the literal *false* or *not false*.

Integrity constraints are rules that enforce some condition on states, and they take the form of denials. To make integrity constraints updatable, we allow the domain literal *not false* to occur in the head of an integrity constraint. For example, updating the theory of an agent α with $not\ false \leftarrow relaxConstraints$ has the effect to turn off the integrity constraints of α if *relaxConstraints* holds. Note that the body of an integrity constraint can contain any literal. The following definition introduces rules that are executed bottom-up. To emphasize this aspect we employ a different notation for them.

Definition 4. An *active rule* is a generalized rule whose head Z is a project literal and every literal L_i $(1 \leq i \leq n)$ in its body is a domain literal or an update literal. We write active rules as $L_1, \ldots, L_n \Rightarrow Z$.

Active rules can modify the current state, to produce a new state, when triggered. If the body $L_1, \ldots, L_n$ of the active rule is satisfied, then the project (fluent) Z can be selected and executed. The head of an active rule is a project, either internal or external. An *internal project* operates on the state of the agent itself (self-update), e.g., if an agent gets an observation, then it updates its knowledge. *External projects* instead are performed on other agents, e.g., when an agent wants to update the theory of another agent.

To express preference information in logic programs we introduce the notion of priority rule.

Definition 5. A *priority rule* is a generalized rule $L_0 \leftarrow L_1, \ldots, L_n$ whose head L_0 is a priority literal and every L_i $(1 \leq i \leq n)$ is a domain literal, an update literal, or a priority literal.

Priority rules are also subject to updating.

Definition 6. A *query* takes the form $?\!-\ L_1, \ldots, L_n$ with $n \geq 0$, where every L_i $(1 \leq i \leq n)$ is a domain literal, an update literal, or priority literal.

We assume that for every project $\alpha{:}C$, C is either a domain rule, an integrity constraint, an active rule, a priority rule or a query. Thus, a project can take one of the forms:

$$\alpha{:}(L_0 \leftarrow L_1, \ldots, L_n) \qquad \alpha{:}(L_1, \ldots, L_n \Rightarrow Z)$$
$$\alpha{:}(false \leftarrow L_1, \ldots, L_n, Z_1, \ldots, Z_m) \qquad \alpha{:}(?\!-L_1, \ldots, L_n)$$
$$\alpha{:}(not\ false \leftarrow L_1, \ldots, L_n, Z_1, \ldots, Z_m)$$

2.2 Abductive Agents

The knowledge of an agent can dynamically evolve when it receives new knowledge or when it abduces new hypotheses to explain observations. The new knowledge is presented in the form of an updating program, and the new hypotheses in the form of a (finite) set of domain atoms (abducibles).

An *updating program* U is a finite set of updates. An updating program contains the updates that will be performed on the current knowledge state of the agent. As negated updates are not performed by any agent, negated updates cannot occur in any updating program. To characterize the evolution of the knowledge of an agent we need to introduce the notion of sequence of updating programs. In the remaining, let $S = \{1, \ldots, s, \ldots\}$ be a set of natural numbers. We call the elements $i \in S \cup \{0\}$ *states.* A *sequence of updating programs* $\mathcal{U} = \{U^s \mid s \in S\}$ is a set of updating programs U^s superscripted by the states $s \in S$.

Let $\mathcal{A}$ be a set of domain atoms distinct from *false*. We call the domain atoms in $\mathcal{A}$ *abducibles.* Abducibles can be thought of as hypotheses that can be used to extend the current theory of the agent in order to provide an "explanation" for given queries. Explanations are required to meet all the integrity constraints. Abducibles may also be defined by domain rules as the result of a self-update to adopt an abducible as a fact rule.

Definition 7. Let $s \in S \cup \{0\}$ be a state. An *agent* α *at state* s, written as Ψ^s_α, is a pair $(\mathcal{A}, \mathcal{U})$, where $\mathcal{A}$ is the set of abducibles and $\mathcal{U}$ is a sequence of updating programs $\{U^1, \ldots, U^s\}$. If $s = 0$, then $\mathcal{U} = \{\}$.

An agent α at state 0 is defined by a set of abducibles $\mathcal{A}$ and an empty sequence of updating programs, that is $\Psi^0_\alpha = (\mathcal{A}, \{\})$. At state 1 α is defined by $(\mathcal{A}, \{U^1\})$, where U^1 is the updating program containing all the updates that α has received at state 0 either from other agents or as self-updates. In general, an agent α at state s is defined by $\Psi^s_\alpha = (\mathcal{A}, \{U^1, \ldots, U^s\})$, where each U^s is the updating program containing the updates that α has received at state $s - 1$.

Example 1. Consider a situation where an agent Elizabeth (represented by e) is told by Maria (represented by m) to abduce fire to explain the observation that there is smoke, and to sound the alarm to the fire brigade (represented by f) in case of fire. Later on, Elizabeth is told by Robert (represented by r) that a possible explanation for the presence of smoke is that John is smoking, and in such a case she should scream at him. The theory of Elizabeth can be formalized as $\Psi^2_e = \{\mathcal{A}, \mathcal{U}\}$ where $\mathcal{A} = \{\mathit{fire}, \mathit{smoking(john)}\}$ and $\mathcal{U} = \{U^1, U^2\}$:

$$U^1 = \left\{ \begin{array}{l} m{\div}(\mathit{smoke} \leftarrow \mathit{fire}) \\ m{\div}(\mathit{fire} \Rightarrow f{:}\mathit{alarm}) \end{array} \right\} \quad U^2 = \left\{ \begin{array}{l} r{\div}(\mathit{smoke} \leftarrow \mathit{smoking(john)}) \\ r{\div}(\mathit{smoking(john)} \Rightarrow j{:}\mathit{scream}) \end{array} \right\}$$

Suppose that at state 2 there is smoke. Then, Elizabeth has two hypotheses equally plausible to explain it: *fire* and *smoking(john)*. Things change if later on Elizabeth is told by Maria to prefer the hypothesis *fire* to *smoking(john)* when John is at the pub to explain the presence of smoke:

$$U^3 = \left\{ \begin{array}{l} m{\div}(\mathit{fire} < \mathit{smoking(john)} \leftarrow \mathit{pub(john)}) \\ m{\div}(\mathit{pub(john)}) \end{array} \right\}$$

Now, Elizabeth has one preferred hypothesis to explain smoke, i.e., *fire*.

2.3 Agent Cycle

In this section we briefly sketch the behaviour of an agent. This is carried out from the perspective of an agent α. The basic "engine" of α is an abductive logic programming proof procedure, executed via the cycle represented in Fig. 1.

Cycle(α,s,Ψ_α^s,G), where $\Psi_\alpha^s = (\mathcal{A},\mathcal{U})$ and $\mathcal{U} = \{U^1,\dots,U^s\}$.

1. Observe and record any input in the updating program U^{s+1}.
2. Select a query $?{-}g$ in $G \cup Queries(\alpha, U^{s+1})$ and execute $?{-}g$ wrt. $P = \Gamma(s+1, \mathcal{U} \cup \{U^{s+1}\})$. Let $U^{s+2} = \{\alpha \div ans(g, g\theta, La)\}$ if g is provable with substitution θ and abduced hypotheses $La \subseteq \mathcal{A}$, otherwise (i.e., if g is not provable) let $U^{s+2} = \{\alpha \div ans(g, fail, [\,])\}$ and $La = [\,]$.
3. Execute all the projects in $ExecProj(La, Q, s+2)$, where $Q = \Gamma(s+2, \mathcal{U} \cup \{U^{s+1}, U^{s+2}\})$.
4. Cycle with (α,$s+2$,Ψ_α^{s+2},G'), where $\Psi_\alpha^{s+2} = (\mathcal{A}, \mathcal{U} \cup \{U^{s+1}, U^{s+2}\})$ and $G' = G \cup Queries(\alpha, U^{s+1}) - \{?{-}g\}$.

Fig. 1. The agent cycle

Step 1: The cycle of an agent α starts at state s by observing any inputs, i.e. updates from other agents or from the environment, and by recording them in updating program U^{s+1}.

Step 2: A query $?{-}g$ is selected from $G \cup Queries(\alpha, U^{s+1})$, where G is the set of queries still to be executed and $Queries(\alpha, U^{s+1}) = \{?{-}g \mid \alpha{\div}(?{-}g) \in U^{s+1}\}$ is the set of queries requested to be proved by α. Then, g is executed with respect to the generalized logic program P obtained via a syntactic transformation Γ presented in [4]. Basically, Γ takes into consideration the entire sequence of updating programs $\mathcal{U}$ at state $s+1$ and codes it into an object level generalized logic program P. Thus, any abductive proof procedure, such as ABDUAL [7], can be used in proving from P. The answer $ans(g, g\theta, La)$ of the query $?{-}g$ is then recorded in the updating program U^{s+2}. Note that only the queries issued by the agent α itself are executed. The queries issued by other agents are treated as normal updates[1].

Step 3: The set $ExecProj(La, Q, s+2)$ of projects that are executable at state $s+2$ is computed and all the projects executed. A project is executable at state $s+2$ if it is defined by an active rule in P whose body contains literals that are true at $s+2$ or are abducibles in La. If an executable project takes the form $\beta : C$ (meaning that agent α intends to update the theory of agent β with C),

[1] This way α retains control on deciding which queries (requested by other agents) to execute. For example, the theory of α may contain the active rule: $\beta{\div}(?{-}g), Cond \Rightarrow \alpha{:}(?{-}g)$ which states that if α has been requested to prove a query $?{-}g$ by β and some condition $Cond$ holds, then α will issue the internal project to prove the query $?{-}g$.

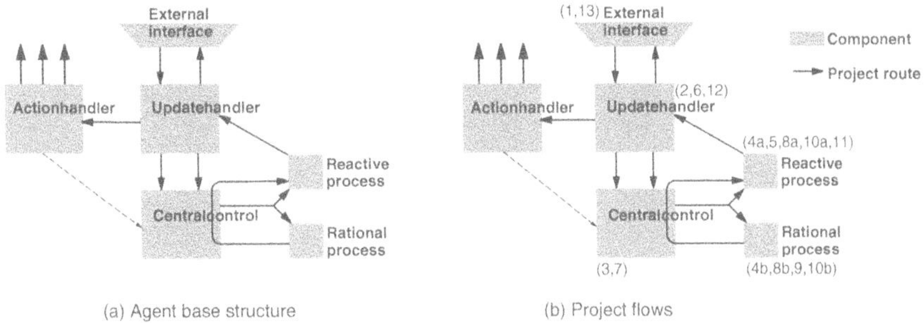

Fig. 2.

then (once executed) the update $\alpha \div C$ will be available as input to the cycle of the agent β.

Step 4: Finally, the agent cycles with state $s+2$, by incorporating the updating programs U^{s+1} and U^{s+2} into $\mathcal{U}$, and with the new list G' of queries.

Initially, the cycle of α is Cycle(α,0,Ψ^0_α,{}) with $\Psi^0_\alpha = (\mathcal{A}, \{\})$.

3 Agent Architecture

The agent framework is implemented as follows: its logical parts (e.g., logical reasoning, preferring, updating, etc.) are implemented in XSB Prolog [11], while its non-logical parts (e.g., agent communication, user interface, etc.) are implemented in Java. We then employ InterProlog [10] to interface Java and XSB Prolog. The next subsections present an overview of the architecture, its components and the flow of projects (for more details consult [16]).

3.1 Overview

The architecture consists of six components, as illustrated in Fig. 2. Each one harbours its own specific task and is implemented in Java to enhance flexibility. Since every component is implemented via a Java thread, the components can run concurrently. Therefore, the behaviour of the agent is not sequential like in Kowalski and Sadri's agent cycle [18]. Rather, the system has the ability to execute at the same time, asynchronously, several tasks differently located in the agent cycle (defined in Section 2.3) . The agent in our implementation is therefore enabled to exhibit both rational and reactive behaviours concurrently. The architecture consists of the following components that form the agent's base structure:

- The *central control*: it controls the behaviour of the entire architecture via a number of control parameters. For example, it determines when a query or an update should be sent to the reactive and/or to the rational processes.

- The *reactive* and the *rational processes*: they characterize the reactive and rational behaviours of the agent, respectively. The rational and reactive processes are implemented by two corresponding XSB Prolog processes whose knowledge bases are kept identical[2].
- The *update handler*: it sorts and forwards the information received from the reactive process and from the surrounding environment.
- The *action handler*: it handles the different tasks (actions) the agent wants executed. It has the ability to affect the environment.
- The *external interface*: it handles the communication between the agent and it's environment, including other agents.

The solid arrows between the components in Fig. 2 (a) illustrate all the possible paths of projects. The dashed arrow indicates that the action handler can change the value of some parameters in the central control. The three arrows exiting the action handler indicate that it can perform several actions to affect the environment,which includes other agents, depending on the situation and tasks at hand.

Between every two components connected by a solid arrow there exists a queue. This is necessary for handling asynchronicity between the threads of the connected components when exchanging information. The queues are not shown in Fig. 2 (a). If a component receives a large workload, the queue collects the information to be exchanged and awaits till the receiving component can handle the new incoming information.

3.2 Project Flow

This section illustrates the flow of projects in the agent architecture. This is narrated from the perspective of an agent α, depicted in Fig. 2 (b). Suppose that an agent β asks agent α to prove a query $?{-}g$ via the external project $\alpha : ?{-}g$. At the next state, the external interface of α receives (step 1) the update $\beta \div ?{-}g$, indicating that β has requested α to prove g.[3] In turn, this update is sent to the update handler (step 2) whose task is to sort the different types of updates. For example, if the update contains an action to be performed, then the update will be sent to the action handler, otherwise to the central control. Since the update contains a query requested by another agent, the update handler sends $\beta \div ?{-}g$ to central control (step 3). Now, central control updates the database of the reactive process (step 4a) and of the rational process (step 4b) with $\beta \div ?{-}g$. Note that when α receives a request to prove a query $?{-}g$ from another agent β (via the update $\beta \div ?{-}g$ in the theory of α), g is not proven directly. Instead, α has the ability to decide whether or not to prove g. Indeed, α proves g only

[2] The use of identical copies of the knowledge base is required by the present unavailability of XSB Prolog threads sharing the same knowledge program. This will be remedied in the near future by ongoing XSB implementation work by colleagues.

[3] An asynchronous transition rule system that characterizes the interactions among agents is presented in [13].

if α itself posts this request via the internal project $\alpha : ?{-}g$. Suppose that the knowledge base of the reactive process contains an active rule of the form:

$$\beta \div ?{-}g \Rightarrow \alpha : ?{-}g$$

saying that, if α receives a request to prove a query $?{-}g$ from an agent β, then α assumes the project to prove g (i.e., $\alpha : ?{-}g$). At the next state of α, the internal project $\alpha : ?{-}g$ will be executed (step 5). This implies that the update handler will receive (step 6) the update $\alpha \div ?{-}g$ from the reactive process, which in turn sends it to central control (step 7). Central control updates again the knowledge bases of the reactive and rational process with $\alpha \div ?{-}g$ (steps 8a and 8b). Since the query is issued by the agent itself, central control will launch the query $?{-}g$ (step 9). Notice that the updating and reasoning phases are considered to be atomic. That is, it is not possible while proving a query to make an update of the knowledge base (unless by relaunching the query itself). If g is provable with substitution θ and list of abduced hypotheses La, central control will update the knowledge bases of the reactive and rational process with the answer $\alpha \div ans(g, g\theta, La)$ of the query $?{-}g$ (steps 10a and 10b). This allows α to eventually send the answer back to β in case its knowledge base contains an active rule of the form:

$$\beta \div ?{-}g, \alpha \div ans(g, ANS, ABD) \Rightarrow \beta : ans(g, ANS, ABD)$$

When this active rule triggers (step 11), the update handler receives the project $\beta : ans(g, ANS, ABD)$ (step 12) which is sent to the external interface (step 13) it being an external project.

3.3 Rational Process

The rational process models the rational ability of agents. It is implemented by an XSB Prolog process. If an agent α is at state s and $\Psi_\alpha^s = \{\mathcal{A}, \mathcal{U}\}$, then the knowledge base of the rational process is the generalized logic program $P = \Gamma(s, \mathcal{U})$ obtained via a syntactic transformation Γ presented in [4]. The ABDUAL procedure [6,7] is employed wrt. P to compute well-founded abductive answers to goals. (This procedure is capable of computing generalized stable models as well.) The rational process receives the queries to be proved from central control. When the rational process proves a query $?{-}g$ with substitution θ and list of abduced hypotheses La, it returns the answer as $ans(g, g\theta, La)$ to central control which in turn updates the knowledge bases of the rational and reactive processes with $\alpha \div ans(g, g\theta, La)$.

3.4 Reactive Process

The reactive process models the reactive behaviour of the agent. It is implemented by an XSB Prolog process whose underlying theory is the generalized logic program $P = \Gamma(s, \mathcal{U})$.[4] The task of the reactive process is to trigger any

[4] Recall that the rational and reactive process have the same knowledge base.

active rule whose body is satisfied by P at the current state s. Triggering an active rule means executing the project occurring in its head. To test which active rules can be triggered central control launches the query $?-exec(La, L)$ to the reactive process, where La is the list of hypotheses abduced by the rational process at state s. Executing $?-exec(La, L)$ returns a list L of executable projects to central control. Basically, the call to $exec(\dots)$ checks the active rules whose body holds in $\Gamma(s, \mathcal{U})$ and returns their heads in the list L. $exec(\dots)$ is defined by a generalized logic program implementing the behaviour of $ExecProj(\dots)$. The definition of $exec(\dots)$ can vary depending on the kind of agent behaviour we want to characterize. The intuition is that P can have several well-founded abductive models, each of which may trigger distinct active rules (and therefore each model will contain distinct projects). If we want to characterize a cautious behaviour for agents, then the executable projects are those occurring in every model. An alternative definition for would be to execute all the projects that occur in some model of P: brave behaviour.

The hypotheses in La assumed to prove a query g remain abduced only during the current cycle of the agent. They can be made permanent knowledge through an internal update. For instance, the active rule $a \Rightarrow \alpha : a$ where $a \in \mathcal{A}$, states to execute the internal update $\alpha : a$ when the hypothesis a is abduced.

Distinguished projects are those defining the predefined predicates *sendInterrupt*, *doAct*, and *stateModify*. For example, the active rule in the theory of an agent α:

$$\beta \div urgentRequest(G) \Rightarrow \alpha : sendIterrupt(G, true)$$

instructs α to interrupt the execution of its current query G', to launch the query G, and to resume the execution of G' once G is proved (since the flag of *sendInterrupt* is true), just in case an agent β has urgently requested it. The active rule:

$$meeting \Rightarrow \alpha : doAct(displayMessage)$$

instructs α to graphically display a message to remind itself of the meeting. An interesting feature of our architecture is that an agent can declaratively change the value of its control parameters. This is achieved through the predicate *stateModify*. The active rule

$$alarmState \Rightarrow \alpha : stateModify(reactiveDelayTime, 100)$$

once triggered allows α to assign the value 100 to the control parameter *reactiveDelayTime*, in case a dangerous situation supervenes. *ReactiveDelayTime* is a parameter in central control that defines the time interval between two distinct tests of which active rules of α that can be triggered. Basically, its value defines the level of reactiveness of α. The list of parameters that control the agent behaviour can be found in [16].

The ability to declaratively interrupt the rational process and to modify the values of the control parameters of the agent architecture is essential to tailor the global behaviour of the agent to its actual needs (cf. [3] for a discussion).

4 Update Handler

The update handler collects both the executable projects coming from the reactive process and the updates coming from the external interface. The task of the update handler is to sort out the projects and updates and to send them to the right destination. Note that to maintain the semantics of updates, all the executable projects of an agent α must be executed at the same time.

A project can be either (i) an external project, (ii) an internal project, or (iii) an internal project containing a predefined atom *sendInterrupt*, *doAct*, or *stateModify*. Updates and external projects are sent to central control and to the external interface, respectively. Regarding internal projects we distinguish among three cases. Those not containing any predefined atom are sent to central control. Those containing the atoms *doAct* or *stateModify* are sent to the action handler, while those containing the atom *sendInterrupt* are sent to central control via a prioritized queue in order to make them executed before regular updates.

5 Central Control

Central control handles all the other components of the architecture by means if its control parameters. Central control has also the ability to interrupt/suspend the execution of a query. To do so, it sends an interrupt $sendInterrupt(g', F)$ to the rational process commanding it to interrupt the execution of the current query g and to execute the query g'. The flag F indicates whether or not the execution of g must be resumed after the proof of g' is completed. The interruption/suspension commands are implemented by XSB Prolog, and can originate externally. They call upon an interrupt handler, whose behaviour is user definable by logic program rules. Its workings are similar in spirit to break interrupts during debugging and, like them, can be embedded.

It comprises two incoming queues: a prioritized queue with updates containing interrupts, and a queue with normal updates. Central control works in cycles. First, it executes the updates with interrupts one by one until the queue is empty. To do so, it suspends the execution of the current query and launches the query associated with the interrupt. Once terminated, the current query can be relaunched or resumed, depending on the flag of the interrupt. Since interrupts cannot contain updates (only queries), the knowledge base remains unchanged after performing an interrupt and therefore the execution of the suspended goal can be resumed. Then the queue with normal updates is given attention by selecting the next update in the queue and by updating the knowledge bases of the rational and reactive process. If it is an internal update of the form $\alpha \div ?{-}g$ (indicating that the agent has posted an update to itself by requiring the execution of a query $?{-}g$), then central control launches the query $?{-}g$ to the rational process, it collects its answer $ans(g, g\theta, La)$ and it updates the knowledge bases of the rational and reactive process with it. Then, it launches the query $exec(La, L)$ to the reactive process and sends the list L of executable projects to the update handler. Finally, central control modifies the value of its control parameters if so requested by the action handler through a *stateModify* command, and cycles again.

Example 2. Consider the situation presented in Example 1. Suppose that at state 3 Elizabeth is proving the query $?-smoke$. This task is carried out as follows. First, central control posts the query to the rational process which proves it by abducing *fire*.[5] After receiving the answer $ans(smoke, smoke, [fire])$ from the rational process, central control posts the update $e \div ans(smoke, smoke, [fire])$ to both the rational and reactive process, and launches the query $?-exec([fire], L)$ to the reactive process. Since the active rule $fire \Rightarrow f{:}alarm$ in U^1 is triggered, the query succeeds with substitution $L = [f{:}alarm]$. Finally, central control posts the list L of executable projects to the update handler to sort them out and send them to the final destination.

6 Related Work

The use of computational logic for modelling multi-agent systems has been widely investigated (e.g., see [2,22] for a roadmap). One approach close to our own is the agent-based architecture proposed by Kowalski and Sadri [18], which aims at reconciling rationality and reactivity. Agents are logic programs that continuously perform the *observe-think-act* cycle. The thinking or deliberative component consists in explaining the observations, generating actions in response to observations, and planning to achieve its goals. The reacting component is defined via a proof-procedure which exploits integrity constraints.

Another approach close to ours is the Dali multi-agent system proposed by Costantini [12]. Dali is a language and environment for developing logic agents and multi-agent systems. Dali agents are rational agents that are capable of reactive and proactive behaviour. These abilities rely on and are implemented over the notion of event.

The Impact system [8] represents the beliefs of an agent by a logic-based program and integrity constraints. Agents are equipped with an action base describing the actions they can perform. Rules in the program generalize condition-action rules by including deontic modalities to indicate, for instance, that actions are permitted or forbidden. Integrity constraints, as in our approach, specify situations that cannot arise and actions that cannot be performed concurrently. Alternative actions can be executed in reaction to messages.

3APL [9] is a programming language for implementing cognitive agents. It provides programming constructs for modelling agent's beliefs and goals, and a number of basic capabilities to revise them.

The BDI approach [21] is a logic-based formalism to represent agents. In it, an agent is characterized by its *beliefs*, *desires* (i.e., objectives it aims at), and *intentions* (i.e., plans it commits to). Beliefs, desires, and intentions are represented via modal operators with a possible world semantics.

[5] Recall that due to the preference expressed on abducibles by Maria, *fire* is preferred to *smoking(john)* when John is at the pub.

Another logic-based formalism proposed for representing agents is Agent0 [23]. In this approach, an agent is characterized by its *beliefs* and *commitments*. Commitments are production rules that can refer to non-consecutive states of the world in which the agent operates. Both the BDI and the Agent0 approach use logic as a tool for representing agents, but rely upon a non-logic-based execution model. This causes a wide gap between theory and practice in these approaches [22].

An example of a BDI architecture is Interrap [20]. It is a hybrid architecture consisting of two vertical layers: one containing layers of knowledge bases, the other containing various control components that interact with the knowledge bases at their level. The lowest control component is the *world interface* that manages the interactions between the agent and its environment. Above the world interface there is the *behaviour-based component*, whose task it is to model the basic reactive capabilities of the agent. Above this component there is a *local planning component* able to generate single-agent plans in response to requests from the behaviour-based component. On top of the control layer there is a *social planning component*. The latter is able to satisfy the goals of several agents by generating their joint plans. A formal foundation of the Interrap architecture is presented in [17].

Sloman et al. [24,25] proposed a hybrid agent whose architecture consists of three layers: the reactive, the deliberative, and the meta-management layer. The layers operate concurrently and influence each other. The deliberative layer, for example, can be automatically invoked to reschedule tasks that the reactive layer cannot cope with. The *meta-management* (reflective) layer provides the agent with capabilities of self-monitoring, self-evaluation, and self-control.

A hybrid architecture, named Minerva, that includes, among others, deliberative and reactive behaviour was proposed by Leite et al. [19]. This architecture consists of several components sharing a common knowledge base and performing various tasks, like deliberation, reactiveness, planning, etc. All the architectural components share a common representation mechanism to capture knowledge and state transitions.

7 Conclusion and Future Work

We have presented an architecture for a type of agent that is able to reason, to react to the environment, to update its knowledge to model the dynamic aspects of the world where it is situated, is able to prefer, and also to abduce hypotheses to explain its observations.

Our aim is to develop a simple architecture and to test its behaviour in different application domains. Currently we are carrying out on an experimental implementation to test our agent in a simple Web site management application.

An interesting line of research is to investigate how to formally describe the behaviour of our agent architecture. This will allow us (i) to formally compare our architecture with other hybrid architectures proposed in the literature, (ii) to verify its logical properties, and (iii) to analyze and expand its architectural design to accommodate other components. Currently, we are investigating whether it is possible to employ/extend the COOP calculus [17] to achieve this goal. In the future, we plan to add more modules to the basic structure, such as a planner, a learning module, etc., modelling other rational abilities and their functionalities, and to test their interactions within the basic architecture.

The design of our architecture allows an agent to tune its behaviour to the environmental needs. Thus, the agent has self-monitoring and self-control capabilities. Regarding self-evaluation, we are exploring the benefits of integrating a meta-management component into the architecture along the lines proposed by Sloman [24]. Our aim is to design an approach to agents where self-evaluation capabilities allow an agent to dynamically reconfigure its architectural components.

At the moment, our agent implementation runs locally on the host machine, but the entire application can be made distributed over internet. This can be achieved via the remote method invocation of Java and by the fact that our XSB subagents keep a mirror copy of the knowledge base of the agent. In this view, the central control component plays the role of a conductor that orchestrates the integration of all the architectural components, and thereby offers an high-level interface for Web services. The advantage of a distributed implementation is that our agents can have their parts spread on the Web. Thus, for instance if a deliberative agent is being developed at one place, several reactive agents may use its deliberations.

Acknowledgements. This work was partially supported by POCTI project 40958 "FLUX – FleXible Logical Updates". We thank David S. Warren for the implementation of break like interrupts in XSB-Prolog, and Miguel Calejo for InterProlog adaptations.

References

1. J. J. Alferes, C. Damásio, and L. M. Pereira. Semantic web logic programming tools. Workshop on Principles and Practice of Semantic Web Reasoning, at 19th Int. Conf. on Logic Programming (ICLP03). To appear in LNAI, 2003.
2. J. J. Alferes, P. Dell'Acqua, E. Lamma, J. A. Leite, L. M. Pereira, and F. Riguzzi. A logic based approach to multi-agent systems. Invited paper in The Association for Logic Programming Newsletter, 14(3), August 2001. Available at http://www.cwi.nl/projects/alp/newsletter/aug01/.
3. J. J. Alferes, P. Dell'Acqua, and L. M. Pereira. Updating, Preferring, and Acting with Abductive Agents – theory and implementation (work in progress).
4. J. J. Alferes, P. Dell'Acqua, and L. M. Pereira. A compilation of updates plus preferences. In S. Flesca, S. Greco, N. Leone, and G. Ianni (eds.), *Logics in Artificial Intelligence*, LNAI 2424, pp. 62–74, 2002.
5. J. J. Alferes and L. M. Pereira. Updates plus preferences. In M. O. Aciego, I. P. de Guzmán, G. Brewka, and L. M. Pereira (eds.), *Logics in AI, Procs. JELIA'00*, LNAI 1919, pp. 345–360, 2000.

6. J. J. Alferes, L. M. Pereira, and T. Swift. Abduction in well-founded semantics and generalized stable models via tabled dual programs. To appear in: J. of Theory and Practice of Logic Programming, 2003.
7. J. J. Alferes, L. M. Pereira, and T. Swift. Well-founded abduction via tabled dual programs. In D. De Schreye (ed.), *ICLP'99*. MIT Press, 1999.
8. IMPACT system. Available at www.cs.umd.edu/projects/impact.
9. 3ALP Web site. Available at www.cs.uu.nl/3apl.
10. InterProlog. Available at www.declarativa.com/InterProlog/default.htm.
11. XSB-Prolog. Available at xsb.sourceforge.net.
12. S. Costantini. Towards active logic programming. Elect. Proc. 2nd Int. Workshop on Component-Based Software Development in Computational Logic, 1999.
13. P. Dell'Acqua, U. Nilsson, and L. M. Pereira. A logic based asynchronous multi-agent system. Computational Logic in Multi-Agent Systems (CLIMA02). Electronic Notes in Theoretical Computer Science (ENTCS), Vol. 70, Issue 5, 2002.
14. P. Dell'Acqua and L. M. Pereira. Preferring and updating in abductive multi-agent systems. In A. Omicini, P. Petta, and R. Tolksdorf (eds.), *Engineering Societies in the Agents' World (ESAW 2001)*, LNAI 2203, pp. 57–73. Springer-Verlag, 2001.
15. P. Dell'Acqua, L. M. Pereira, and A. Vitória. User preference information in query answering. In T. Andreasen, A. Motro, H. Christiansen, and H. L. Larsen (eds.), *5th Int. Conf. on Flexible Query Answering Systems*, LNCS 2522, pp. 163–173, 2002.
16. M. Engberg. *An implementation of a rational, reactive agent.* M. Sc. No LITH-ITN-KTS-EX—03/021–SE, Dept. of Science and Technology (ITN), Linköping University, Norrköping, Sweden, 2003.
17. K. Fischer and C. G. Jung. A layered agent calculus with concurrent, continuous processes. In M. P. Singh, A. Rao, and M. J. Wooldridge (eds.), *Intelligent Agents IV: Agent Theories, Architectures, and Languages*, LNCS 1365, pp. 245–258, 1997.
18. R. A. Kowalski and F. Sadri. Towards a unified agent architecture that combines rationality with reactivity. In D. Pedreschi and C. Zaniolo (eds.), *Logic in Databases, Int. Workshop LID'96*, LNCS 1154, pp. 137–149, 1996.
19. J. A. Leite, J. J. Alferes, and L. M. Pereira. MINERVA - A Dynamic Logic Programming Agent Architecture. In J. J. Meyer and M. Tambe (eds.), *Intelligent Agents VIII*, LNAI 2333, pp. 141–157, 2002.
20. J. P. Müller. *The Design of Intelligent Agents: A Layered Approach.* LNCS 1177, 1997.
21. A. S. Rao and M. P. Georgeff. Modelling rational agents within a BDI-architecture. In R. Fikes and E. Sandewall (eds.), *Proc. of Knowledge Representation and Reasoning (KR&R-92)*, pp. 473–484. Morgan Kaufmann, 1991.
22. F. Sadri and F. Toni. Computational logic and multiagent systems: a roadmap, August 2001. Available at http://www2.ags.uni-sb.de/net/Forum/Supportdocs.html.
23. Y. Shoham. Agent-oriented programming. *Artificial Intelligence*, 60:51–92, 1993.
24. A. Sloman. What sort of architecture is required for a human-like agent. In M. Wooldridge and A. Rao (eds.), *Foundations of Rational Agency*, pp. 35–52. Kluwer Academic Publishers, 1999.
25. A. Sloman and B. Logan. Architectures and tools for human-like agents. In *Proc. 2nd European Conf. on Cognitive Modelling (ECCM98)*, pp. 58–65, 1998.

An Evolvable Rule-Based E-mail Agent

J.J. Alferes[1], A. Brogi[2], J.A. Leite[1], and Luís Moniz Pereira[1]

[1] CENTRIA, Universidade Nova de Lisboa, Portugal
[2] Dipartimento di Informatica, Università di Pisa, Italy

Abstract. The Semantic Web is a "living organism", which combines autonomously evolving data sources/knowledge repositories. This dynamic character of the Semantic Web requires (declarative) languages and mechanisms for specifying its maintenance and evolution. For example, for changing the behaviour of a data source, so that a new rule becomes into effect, one should not be concerned with the complex, interrelated, and dynamically obtained knowledge, and should have a way to simply specify what knowledge is to be changed. This requires the existence of a language for exacting such changes (or updates), which takes in consideration the addition/deletion and changes of rules, thereby automating the task of dealing with inconsistencies arising from those updates. To address this issue, we resort to recent developments in the field of Logic Programming, and show how the framework of EVOLP (EVOlving Logic Programs) can be put to work to model such reactive and updateable rule bases, bringing an important added value to RuleML. We make our case by exhibiting a detailed application example of how EVOLP can be used to express updateable RuleML rule bases, employing it to define an evolving e-mail Personal Assistant Agent.

1 Introduction

The World Wide Web (WWW) is, without a doubt, a great success story, bringing new challenges and opportunities at almost every conceivable level of our existence. While its exponential growth was initially seen as one of its bigger attractive features, it now contributes to one of its major challenges: provide structure and organization to its contents, thus shifting its data and documents from the current human oriented format to a more machine understandable one where a greater level of automation can be achieved. The World Wide Web Consortium's (W3C) [7] Semantic Web Activity [1] was launched to address these concerns. While the eXtensible Markup Language (XML) [20] provides a method to structure documents, and the Resource Description Framework (RDF) [17] one for exposing their meaning, it is widely accepted now the need to reason with, and about, WWW documents. Rules provide the natural and widely accepted mechanism to perform automated reasoning, with available mature theory and technology. The Rule Markup Initiative (RuleML) [13] aims at defining a core format for rule interchange, resorting to XML.

The Logic Programming paradigm, with its well-defined, general, integrative, encompassing, and rigorous framework, together with its recent technolog-

Fernando Moura Pires, Salvador Abreu (Eds.): EPIA 2003, LNAI 2902, pp. 394–408, 2003.

ical and theoretical developments, brings new insights to the above issues, and provides inspiration to this general promising area of investigation [10,11,18].

The Semantic Web is a "living organism", which combines autonomously evolving data sources/knowledge repositories. This dynamic character of the Semantic Web requires (declarative) languages and mechanisms for specifying its maintenance and evolution. For example, for changing the behaviour of a data source, so that a new rule becomes into effect, one should not per force have to be concerned with the complex, interrelated, and dynamically obtained knowledge, and should have a way to simply specify what knowledge is to be changed. This requires the existence of a language for exacting such changes (or updates), which takes in consideration the addition/deletion and changes of rules, thereby automating the task of dealing with inconsistencies arising from those updates. To address this issue, we resort to recent developments in the field of Logic Programming, and show how the framework of EVOLP [2] can be put to work to model such reactive and updateable rule bases, in effect bringing an important added value to RuleML.

The EVOLP framework appeared in the line of development of other existing languages (such as LUPS [4], EPI [8] and KABUL [14]) for specifying and programming the evolution of knowledge bases represented as logic programs. Distinctly from these extant languages, which introduce a lot of new programming constructs, each encoding a high level behaviour of addition and deletion of rules, EVOLP's up front goal was to enable with the evolution of logic programs by adding to traditional logic programming as few constructs as possible, i.e. by staying as close as possible to the usual language of logic programs.

EVOLP can adequately express the semantics resulting from successive updates to logic programs, considered as incremental specifications of knowledge bases, and whose effect may be contextual. It automatically and appropriately deals, via its update semantics (based on Dynamic Logic Programming [3]), with possible potential contradictions arising from successive specification changes and refinements. Furthermore, the EVOLP language can express self-updates triggered by the evolution context itself, present or future. Additionally, foreseen updates not yet executed can automatically trigger other updates, and moreover updates can be nested, so as to (contextually) determine change, both in the next state and in other states further down an evolution strand.

It is the goal of this paper to show that the attending formulation of EVOLP provides a good firm formal basis in which to express, implement, and reason about dynamic RuleML rule bases. To do this, in the ensuing section we recap the formal syntax and semantics of EVOLP. Immediately afterwards we make our case by exhibiting a detailed and protracted application example of how EVOLP can be mustered to express updateable RuleML rule bases, employing it to define an evolving e-mail Personal Assistant Agent, whose executable specification evolves by means of external and of internal dynamic updates, both of which can be made contingent on the evolution context in which they occur. We terminate with a section comprising discussion, comparisons with related application work, open issues, and themes for future development.

2 Evolving Logic Programs

In this section we briefly recall the language and semantics of EVOLP [2]. EVOLP is a logic programming language that caters for the evolution of an agent's knowledge, be it caused by external events, or by internal requirements for change. Moreover, it does so by adding as few new constructs to traditional logic programming as possible.

2.1 Language

What is required to let logic programs evolve? For a start, one needs some mechanism for letting older rules be supervened by more recent ones. That is, one must include a mechanism for deletion of previous knowledge to accompany the agent's knowledge evolution. This can be achieved by permitting default negation not just in rule bodies, as in normal logic programming, but in rule heads as well[1].

Moreover, one needs a means to state that, under some conditions, some new rule or other is to be added to the program. This is achieved in EVOLP simply by augmenting the language with a reserved predicate $assert/1$, whose sole argument is itself a full-blown rule, and so arbitrary nesting becomes possible. This predicate can appear both as rule head (to impose internal assertions of rules) as well as in rule bodies (to test for assertion of rules). Formally:

Definition 1. *Let $\mathcal{L}$ be any propositional language (not containing the predicate $assert/1$). The* extended language $\mathcal{L}_{assert}$ *is defined inductively as follows:*

- *All propositional atoms in $\mathcal{L}$ are propositional atoms in $\mathcal{L}_{assert}$;*
- *If each of $L_0, \ldots, L_n$ is a literal in $\mathcal{L}_{assert}$ (i.e. a propositional atom A or its default negation $not\, A$), then*

$$L_0 \leftarrow L_1, \ldots, L_n$$

  is a generalized logic program rule over $\mathcal{L}_{assert}$ (and dubbed EVOLP rule);
- *If R is a rule over $\mathcal{L}_{assert}$ then $assert(R)$ is a propositional atom of $\mathcal{L}_{assert}$;*
- *Nothing else is a propositional atom in $\mathcal{L}_{assert}$.*

An evolving logic program *over a language $\mathcal{L}$ (or EVOLP program, for short) is a (possibly infinite) set of generalized logic program rules over $\mathcal{L}_{assert}$.*

Besides internal updates, which may be modelled with the above, EVOLP allows too for influence from the outside, where this influence may be: observation of facts (or rules) that are perceived at some state; assertion commands directly imparting the assertion of new rules on the evolving program. Both can be represented as EVOLP rules: the former by rules without the assertion predicate in the head, and the latter by rules having it. Accordingly, outside influence is represented as a sequence of EVOLP programs:

Definition 2. *Let P be an evolving program over the language $\mathcal{L}$. An* event sequence *over P is a sequence of evolving programs over $\mathcal{L}$.*

[1] A known extension to normal logic programs [15], named generalized logic programs.

2.2 Semantics

In general, an EVOLP program describes an agent's initial knowledge base. This knowledge base may already include rules (sporting asserts in heads) that describe the forms of its own evolution. Besides, EVOLP considers sequences of events representing observations and commands arising from the outside. Each event in the sequence is itself a set of EVOLP rules, i.e. an EVOLP program. Thus the semantics issue is that of, when given an initial EVOLP program and a sequence of EVOLP programs as events, to determine what is true and what is false after each event. More precisely, the meaning of a sequence of EVOLP programs is afforded by a set of *evolution stable models*, each of which being a sequence of interpretations or states. The basic compelling idea is that each evolution stable model describes a possible evolution of the initial program along a given number n of evolution steps, taking into account the events in the sequence. Each evolution is represented by a sequence of programs, each corresponding to a knowledge state.

The primordial intuitions for the construction of these program sequences are as follows: Regarding head asserts, whenever the atom $assert(Rule)$ belongs to an interpretation in a given sequence, i.e. belongs to that model according to the stable model semantics of the current program, then $Rule$ must belong to the program in the next state; Moreover, assertion literals in bodies are treated like any other predicate literals. Furthermore, to deal with outside events, i.e. with sequences of EVOLP programs, rules in the i-th event are added on one occasion only to the program of state i.

Sequences of programs are then treated as in DLP (Dynamic Logic programming) [3], where the most recent rules are set in force, and previous rules are valid (by inertia) insofar as possible, i.e. they are kept for as long as they do not conflict with more recent ones. Default negation is treated as in stable models of normal [9] and generalized programs [15]. Formally, a *dynamic logic program* is a sequence $P_1 \oplus \ldots \oplus P_n$ (also denoted $\bigoplus \mathcal{P}$, where $\mathcal{P}$ is a set of generalized logic programs indexed by $1, \ldots, n$), and its semantics is determined by[2]:

Definition 3. *Let $\bigoplus\{P_i : i \in S\}$ be a dynamic logic program over language $\mathcal{L}$, let $s \in S$, and let M be a set of propositional atoms of $\mathcal{L}$. Then:*

$$Default_s(M) = \{not\, A \leftarrow . \mid \nexists A \leftarrow Bdy \in P_i (1 \le i \le s) : M \models Bdy\}$$
$$Reject_s(M) = \{L \leftarrow Bdy \in P_i \mid \exists\ not\, L \leftarrow Bdy' \in P_j, i < j \le s,\ M \models Bdy'\}$$

where A is an atom, $not\, L$ denotes the complement w.r.t. default negation of the head literal L, and both Bdy and Bdy' are conjunctions of literals. $M \models Bdy$ iff for every atom A (resp. literal $not\, A$) in Bdy, $A \in M$ (resp. $A \notin M$).

Definition 4. *Let $\mathcal{P} = \bigoplus\{P_i : i \in S\}$ be a dynamic logic program over language $\mathcal{L}$. A set M of propositional atoms of $\mathcal{L}$ is a stable model of $\mathcal{P}$ at state $s \in S$ iff:*

$$M' = least\left(\left[\bigcup_{i \le s} P_i - Reject_s(M)\right] \cup Default_s(M)\right)$$

[2] For more details on dynamic logic programming the reader is referred to [3].

where $M' = M \cup \{not\_A \mid A \notin M\}$*, and* $least(.)$ *denotes the least (wrt. set inclusion) model of the definite program obtained from the argument program by replacing every default negated literal* $not\, A$ *by a new atom* not_A*.*

Definition 5. *An* evolution interpretation *of length* n *of an evolving program* P *over* $\mathcal{L}$ *is a finite sequence* $\mathcal{I} = \langle I_1, I_2, \ldots, I_n \rangle$ *of sets of propositional atoms of* $\mathcal{L}_{assert}$*. The* evolution trace *associated with an evolution interpretation* $\mathcal{I}$ *is the sequence of programs* $\langle P_1, P_2, \ldots, P_n \rangle$ *where:* $P_1 = P$ *and* $P_i = \{R \mid assert(R) \in I_{i-1}\}$*, for each* $2 \leq i \leq n$*.*

Definition 6. *An evolution interpretation of length* n*,* $\langle I_1, I_2, \ldots, I_n \rangle$*, with evolution trace* $\langle P_1, P_2, \ldots, P_n \rangle$*, is an* evolution stable model *of* P *given a sequence of events* $\langle E_1, E_2, \ldots, E_k \rangle$*, with* $n \leq k$*, iff for every* i $(1 \leq i \leq n)$*,* I_i *is a stable model at state* i *of* $P_1 \oplus P_2 \ldots \oplus (P_i \cup E_i)$*. We say that an atom* A *is true (resp. false) after* n *steps if* A *belongs (resp. does not belong) to the last interpretation of all the (resp. any of the) evolution stable models of length* n*.*

Notice that the rules coming from the outside are treated as events that do not persist by inertia. At any given step i, the rules from E_i are added and the (possibly various) I_i obtained. This determines the programs P_{i+1} of the trace, which are then added to E_{i+1} to determine the models I_{i+1}.

To better understand the definitions, we put them to work on an example.

Example 1. Consider the initial program P:

$$a. \qquad assert(b \leftarrow a) \leftarrow not\, c. \qquad c \leftarrow assert(not\, a \leftarrow). \qquad assert(not\, a \leftarrow) \leftarrow b, d.$$

stating that: a is true; whenever c is false, rule $b \leftarrow a$ is to be asserted; whenever fact $not\, a$ is to be asserted, c is true; and if b and d are true then fact $not\, a$ is to be asserted. Moreover, suppose the following sequence of events was perceived:

$$\langle \{assert(d \leftarrow a)\}, \{e \leftarrow\}, \{\} \rangle$$

The (only) stable model of $P \cup E_1$ is $I_1 = \{a, assert(b \leftarrow a), assert(d \leftarrow a)\}$ and it conveys the information that program P is ready to evolve into a new program $P \oplus P_2$ by adding rules $(b \leftarrow a)$ and $(d \leftarrow a)$ at the next step, i.e. in P_2. In the only stable model I_2 of the new program $P \oplus (P_2 \cup E_2)$, atoms e, b and d are true, as well as atoms $assert(not\, a \leftarrow)$ and c. Thus, $P \oplus P_2$ is ready to evolve into a new program $P \oplus P_2 \oplus P_3$ by adding rule $(not\, a \leftarrow)$ at the next step, i.e. in P_3. Now the negative fact in P_3 conflicts with the positive fact in P, and this older one is rejected. The rules added in P_2 remain valid, but are no longer useful to conclude b and d since a is no longer valid. So $assert(not\, a \leftarrow)$ and c are also no longer true. In the only stable model last in the sequence, I_3, all of a, b, and c are false. Moreover, there being no information on e on any of P_1, P_2 or P_3, e becomes false too. Accordingly, the only evolution stable model is $\langle I_1, I_2, I_3 \rangle$ with the I_is as described above.

Notice that the truth of the event e in the 2nd state does not persist by inertia to later states. Intuitively, in EVOLP, rules coming from the outside, be they observations or assertion commands, are to be understood as events at a state, and so do not persist by inertia. The same holds for the truth of event $assert(d \leftarrow a)$ which also does not persist. However, its truth in the 1st state caused the addition of rule $d \leftarrow a$ to P_2, which itself persists therefrom as per the semantics of DLP.

3 An Evolving E-mail Agent on the Web

Forthwith, EVOLP is employed to specify several features of a Personal Assistant agent for e-mail management on the Web, able to perform a few basic actions such as sending, receiving, and deleting messages, as well as moving them between folders, and to perform tasks such as filtering spam, storing messages in appropriate folders, sending automatic replies, notifying the user, and/or automatically forwarding specific messages, all of which dependant on user specified updatable criteria.

The specification of the policies that trigger agent actions can in general be modelled by a set of logic programming rules, and represented at a Web page by resorting to a Rule Markup Language (RuleML) with reaction rules triggering the actions. This way, all of the interface between the user, the knowledge base with the email messages, and the incoming messages could be achieved via this RuleML rule base: incoming messages would be treated as events given to the RuleML rule base via some Web service, and the user could access the messages via Web services querying the RuleML rule base. All the user would have to do would be to specify his policies in or translate them into RuleML.

If we expect the user to specify once and for all a consistent set of policies, then such a RuleML with reaction rules setting would be all that is required. But reality tells us otherwise: one observes that the user, every now and then, will discover new conditions under which incoming messages should be deleted, and under which messages now being deleted should be kept. If one allows dynamic specification of both the positive rule instances (e.g. *should be deleted*) and negative ones (e.g. *should not be deleted*) of such policies, soon the union of all rules becomes inconsistent. And one cannot expect the user to debug the RuleML rule base so as to invalidate all the old rules that no longer should be available due to more recent countervening ones. We would rather allow the user to simply state whatever new is to be enforced, and let the inference engine associated with the rule base automatically determine the old rules which may persist and those that do not. We are not even presupposing the user is contradictory, but just that he has updated his profile, something quite reasonable. For example, suppose he is tired of receiving spam messages advertising credit and states that all incoming messages whose subject contains the word *credit* are to be deleted. Later he finds out that important messages from his accountant are being deleted because the subject mentions *credit*. He should simply state that such incoming messages from his accountant are not to be deleted, and the inference mechanisms themselves should automatically determine that such messages are not to be deleted, in spite of the previous rule. But if we just evaluate over the union of all specified policies, a contradiction is obtained.

It would also be important for the personal e-mail assistant agent to allow the specification of tasks not so simple as just performing actions whenever their conditions are met. Suppose one is organizing a conference and wants to automate part of the communication with referees and with authors. Basic tasks include automatic replies to authors whenever abstracts are submitted, etc. But more complex tasks can be conceived that we wish the agent to handle, such as: waiting for messages from referees about accepting to review a paper and, once they arrive, forwarding to him a message with the paper if it has already arrived, otherwise waiting till it arrives and then forwarding it; having different policies to deal with papers before and after the deadline; permitting the specification of extensions to the deadline on a case by case manner, and dealing differently with each paper; updating the initial specification for such policies; etc.

Next we show how an EVOLP based markup language, and corresponding inference mechanisms, would deal with the above mentioned contradictions, and automatically solves them with clear and precise semantics, as well as would account for the aforesaid more complex tasks. In the exposition, we concentrate on those features directly concerned with the evolving specification, namely the representation of the dynamic user profile, and of the dynamic specification of its action preconditions and their effects. Methods to specify other common simple tasks can easily be guaged from the exposition.

3.1 The General EVOLP/RuleML Setting

To be able to specify RuleML rule bases using EVOLP as semantics, one first needs some XML schema to write EVOLP rules. This can easily be accomplished and, for the sake of readability, instead of defining that, and using XML notation for writing predicates and rules, here we simply write them as usual in logic programming. The EVOLP framework assumes that sequences of events are given to the evolving knowledge base, each of which is an EVOLP program. Each event causes the addition of an extra program in an evolving sequence $P_1 \oplus \ldots \oplus P_i$ of programs. This means our EVOLP rule bases must be able to cater for sequences of sets of rules, rather than simply for sets of rules. Thus, an appropriate tag (say, `<newProgram/>`) must exist in our schema in order to specify where new programs in the sequence are inserted [6]. We also need some mechanism for sending events, and for adding the new program to the rule base. This is performed via an appropriate Web service (whose description is outside the scope of this paper) that: receives the events; calls the EVOLP inference engine over the existing RuleML rule base in order to compute the new resulting program; and edits the rule base by adding to it the new program in the evolving sequence. Queries to the rule base are also posted via Web services that call the underlying EVOLP inference mechanism.

Our email agent is to be implemented via one such RuleML rule base with the specification of the user policies for his email. New incoming messages are simply viewed as events to the rule base, containing all the contents of the message. More precisely, $newmsg\,(MsgId, From, Subject, Body)$ event are used for incoming message. As for outgoing messages, we presume that a Web service periodically queries the RuleML specification for true predicates of the form $send\,(To, Subject, Body)$, and dispatches corresponding messages.

To simplify the exposition, instead of having the policies stored in a different rule base from that of the (received) messages, we assume that both will be stored in the same rule base. Accordingly, messages will be stored as facts in the same rule base where the policy specifications sit. More precisely, for every message there will be a fact $msg\,(MsgId, From, Subject, Body, Time)$, along with a fact $in\,(MsgId, Folder)$ to represent that the message is in folder $Folder$. Viewing the contents of folders and messages then amounts to appropriately querying the rule base with the specification and messages for those predicates, and displaying the result via a transformed XML page.

3.2 One Concrete Example of Policy Specification

Now we show a concrete example of an email agent specification, and its evolution. We start with a very simple specification stating: all incoming messages are to be stored unless their deletion is explicitly specified; they are to be stored in the inbox folder unless otherwise stated to be automatically moved elsewhere; messages can be moved between folders, and deleted from folders. All this can be represented by the EVOLP program containing rules r_1 through r_{10} below, i.e. $P = \{\langle r_1\rangle, \langle r_2\rangle, \ldots, \langle r_{10}\rangle\}$.

$$r_1 : time\,(1) \leftarrow \qquad r_2 : assert\,(time\,(T+1)) \leftarrow time\,(T)$$
$$r_3 : assert\,(not\,time\,(T)) \leftarrow time\,(T)$$
$$r_4 : assert\,(msg\,(M, F, S, B, T)) \leftarrow newmsg\,(M, F, S, B)\,, time\,(T)\,, not\,delete\,(M)$$
$$r_5 : assert\,(in\,(M, inbox)) \leftarrow newmsg\,(M, \_, \_, \_)\,, not\,move\,(M, F)\,, not\,delete\,(M)$$
$$r_6 : assert\,(in\,(M, F_{to})) \leftarrow newmsg\,(M, \_, \_, \_)\,, move\,(M, F_{to})$$
$$r_7 : assert\,(in\,(M, F_{to})) \leftarrow move\,(M, F_{from}, F_{to})\,, in\,(M, F_{from})$$
$$r_8 : assert\,(not\,in\,(M, F_{from})) \leftarrow move\,(M, F_{from}, F_{to})\,, not\,in\,(M, F_{to})$$
$$r_9 : assert\,(not\,in\,(M, F)) \leftarrow delete\,(M)\,, in\,(M, F)$$
$$r_{10} : assert\,(sent\,(To, S, B, T)) \leftarrow send\,(To, S, B)\,, time(T)$$

The first three rules encode a clock, from now used to time-stamp all incoming messages. Such time-stamping is not really required, and an absolute (system) time could be used instead, but it is useful to show how a local clock can be encoded in EVOLP. Rule r_4 specifies that all incoming messages, when not specified to be deleted, indicated by literal $not\,delete\,(MsgId)$, are to be time-stamped and asserted as a fact along with the message. Rule r_5 specifies that all incoming messages, when not specified to be deleted nor specified to be moved to a specific folder, are to be stored in the folder $inbox$. Rule r_6 specifies the effect of moving an incoming message to a specific folder. Rules r_7 and r_8 encode the effect of moving a message between folders, represented by $move\,(MsgId, Folder_{from}, Folder_{to})$. Note no problem arises in specifying a message to be moved from and to the same folder. Rule r_9 specifies the effect of a delete action, represented by $delete\,(MsgId)$. This action causes a message to be removed from its current folder. Finally, rule r_{10} encodes that sending a message causes the message to have been sent, hereby represented by the assertion of fact $sent\,(To, Subject, Body, Time)$.

At the initial state the stable model contains only $\{time\,(1)\,, assert(time(2)), assert(not\,time(1))\}$. With this initial specification, and since we do not yet have any rules to specify which incoming messages are to be deleted and which are to be moved, every received message is to be moved to folder $inbox$. Also, at every state transition, the clock increases its value. Suppose an event E_1 is received concerning three incoming messages:

$$newmsg\,(1, \text{“a@a”}, \text{“credit”}, \text{“some spam text”})$$
$$newmsg\,(2, \text{“accountant@c”}, \text{“hello”}, \text{“some text”})$$
$$newmsg\,(3, \text{“b@d”}, \text{“freecredit”}, \text{“more spam”})$$

After this event the stable model contains:

$$assert\,(msg\,(1, \text{“a@a”}, \text{“credit”}, \text{“some spam text”}, 1))\,, assert\,(in\,(1, inbox))$$
$$assert\,(msg\,(2, \text{“accountant@c”}, \text{“hello”}, \text{“some text”}, 1))\,, assert\,(in\,(2, inbox))$$
$$assert\,(msg\,(3, \text{“b@d”}, \text{“free credit”}, \text{“more spam”}, 1))\,, assert\,(in\,(3, inbox))$$
$$time\,(1)\,, assert\,(not\,time\,(1))\,, assert\,(time\,(2))$$

From this, program P_2 contains:

$$msg\,(1, \text{“a@a”}, \text{“credit”}, \text{“some spam text”}, 1)\,, in\,(1, inbox)\,, not\,time\,(1)$$
$$msg\,(2, \text{“accountant@c”}, \text{“hello”}, \text{“some text”}, 1)\,, in\,(2, inbox)$$
$$msg\,(3, \text{“b@d”}, \text{“free credit”}, \text{“more spam”}, 1)\,, in\,(3, inbox)\,, time\,(2)$$

indicating that the specification has been updated so as to store all messages, properly time-stamped, in folder $inbox$. Moreover the clock has been updated to its new value.

At this point, the user becomes upset with all the spam messages being received and decides to start deleting them on arrival. With this purpose, he updates the specification by asserting a general rule stating that spam messages should be deleted, encoded as the assertion of rule r_{11}, and he also updates the agent with a definition of what should be considered as spam, in this case simply those whose subject contains the word “credit”, encoded by the assertion of r_{12}.

$$r_{11} : delete\,(M) \leftarrow newmsg\,(M, F, S, B)\,, spam\,(F, S, B)$$
$$r_{12} : spam\,(F, S, B) \leftarrow contains\,(S, \text{“credit”})$$

Throughout, by definition consider literal $contains\,(S, T)$ true whenever T is contained in S, whose specification we omit for brevity. The assertion of these two rules, together with an update so as to delete messages 1 and 3, constitutes event $E_2 = \{assert\,(\langle r_{11}\rangle)\,, assert\,(\langle r_{12}\rangle)\,, delete\,(1)\,, delete\,(3)\}$. After this event, the stable model contains:

$$assert\,(\langle r_{11}\rangle)\,, assert\,(\langle r_{12}\rangle)\,, delete\,(1)\,, delete\,(3)\,, assert\,(not\,in\,(1, inbox))$$
$$assert\,(not\,in\,(3, inbox))\,, assert\,(time\,(3))\,, assert\,(not\,time\,(2))$$

together with those propositions of the form $msg/5$, $time/1$, $in/2$, representing the existing messages, their locations, and the current internal time[3].

From this model program P_3 is constructed, containing r_{11}, r_{12}, together with the facts $time\,(3)$, $not\,time\,(2)$, $not\,in\,(1, inbox)$ and $not\,in\,(3, inbox)$.

Suppose event E_3 is then received with:

newmsg (4, "d@a", "free credit card", "spam spam spam")
newmsg (5, "accountant@c", "credit", "got your credit")
newmsg (6, "girlfriend@d", "hi", "theater tonight?")

After this update, the stable model contains *spam*(*F*, "free credit card", B), *assert*(*in*(6, *inbox*)), *assert*(*msg*(6, "girlfriend@d", "hi", "theater tonight?", 3)), *spam*(*F*, "credit", B), *delete*(4), and *delete*(5).

Since messages 4 and 5 are considered spam messages, they are both set for deletion and thus are not asserted. Only message 6 is asserted. From this model we construct the program P_4 which contains facts *not time* (3), *in* (6, *inbox*), *time* (4), and *msg* (6, "girlfriend@d", "hi", "theater tonight?", 3).

Next we receive an event E_4 containing a single message[4]: *newmsg*(7, "accountant@c", "are you there?", "..."). This message makes the user aware that previous messages from his accountant had been deleted as spam. He then decides to update the definition of spam, to the effect that messages from his accountant are not spam. He achieves this by sending in an event asserting rule r_{13} (below). Note this rule is contradictory with rule r_{12}, for any message from the accountant with the subject containing the word "credit". But EVOLP automatically detects such contradictions and resolves them by taking the newer rule to be an update of any previously existing ones, and we thus expect all such messages not to be deleted. Next the user is appointed conference chair and decides to update his email policy specification to perform some attending tasks. Henceforth, messages with the subject "abstract" are to be moved to folder *abstracts*, encoded by rule r_{14}, those containing the word "cfp" in their subjects should be moved to folder *cfp* (r_{15}). Furthermore, as the user is accustomed to only looking at his inbox folder, he wishes to be notified whenever an incoming message is immediately stored at a folder other than *inbox*. This is accomplished with rule r_{16}, which renders *notify* (*M*) true in every such. Mark that *notify*/1 represents an action with no internal effect on the agent's knowledge base, and that actual notification of the user would require some external program to periodically query the specification. The agent must also send a message acknowledging receipt of every abstract (r_{17}). And since the user will be away from his computer, he decides to forward urgent mail to his temporary new address. This could be enacted by simply stating that urgent messages should be sent to his new address. But he decides to create a new internal action, represented by *forward* (*MsgId*, *To*), whose effect is to forward the newly incoming

[3] From now on we omit all propositions and assertions concerning the clock unless relevant for the presentation.

[4] At this state we omit the model and update.

message $MsgId$ to the address To, thus making it easier to specify future forwarding options. The specification of this action is achieved by asserting rule r_{18}. Then, based on this action, he can specify that all urgent messages be forwarded to his new address, by asserting rule r_{19}. Finally, the user realizes that the messages that have been deleted are not being effectively deleted, but rather only removed from their folders, i.e. $msg(M, F, S, B, T)$ is still true, except that there is no $in(M, \_)$ that is true. He then decides to create another internal action, *purge*, whose effect is that of making false all those messages that have been previously removed from all folders by action *delete*. The specification of this action is obtained via asserting rule r_{20}. The assertion of rules 13–20 constitutes event E_5.

$$
\begin{aligned}
&r_{13}: not\, spam(F, S, B) \leftarrow contains(F, \text{"accountant"}) \\
&r_{14}: move(M, abstracts) \leftarrow newmsg(M, F, S, B), contains(S, \text{"abstract"}) \\
&r_{15}: move(M, cfp) \leftarrow newmsg(M, F, S, B), contains(S, \text{"cfp"}) \\
&r_{16}: notify(M) \leftarrow newmsg(M, F, S, B), not\, assert(in(M, inbox)), \\
&\qquad\qquad assert(in(M, Fldr)) \\
&r_{17}: send(From, S, \text{"Thanks"}) \leftarrow newmsg(M, F, S, B), contains(S, \text{"abstract"}) \\
&r_{18}: send(To, S, B) \leftarrow forward(M, To), newmsg(M, F, S, B) \\
&r_{19}: forward(M, \text{"b@domain"}) \leftarrow newmsg(M, \_, \text{"urgent"}, \_) \\
&r_{20}: assert(not\, msg(M, F, S, B, T)) \leftarrow purge, msg(M, F, S, B, T), not\, in(M, \_)
\end{aligned}
$$

At the subsequent update the agent receives more messages, performs a *purge*, moves message 6 to the private folder, and deletes message 6, all encoded by these facts in E_6:

newmsg(9,'a2@e','abstract','abs...'), *newmsg*(10,'a3@e','abstract','abs...')
newmsg(13,'accountant@c','fwd:credit','...'), *newmsg*(11,'x@d','urgent','...')
move(6, *inbox*, *private*), *delete*(6), *purge*, *newmsg*(8,'a1@e','abstract','abs...')
newmsg(12,'accountant@c','fwd:credit','...')

After this event, the stable model contains, on messages 1 and 3, as a result of the *purge*, $assert(not\, msg(M, F, S, B, T))$; $assert(in(M, abstracts))$ for messages 8, 9 and 10; plus $forward(11, \text{"b@domain"})$ and the corresponding send action, i.e. $send(\text{"b@domain"}, \text{"urgent"}, \text{"..."})$; and, concerning message 6, the stable model contains $assert(in(6, private))$ and $delete(6)$. There are also notifications for messages 8, 9, 10 and 14. Next the user decides that whenever a message is both deleted and moved, the deletion action prevails, i.e. it should not be asserted into the folder specified by the move action. This is encoded by the assertion of rule r_{21} (below). Furthermore, the user decides to update his spam rules to avoid all spam his accountant has been forwarding him (r_{22}). Finally, because he wishes the agent to deal with communication with the referees, he sets up the assignments between referees and submitted papers ($r_{23} - r_{28}$). So, E_7 is $\{assert(\langle r_{21}\rangle), \ldots, assert(\langle r_{28}\rangle)\}$, where:

$$
\begin{aligned}
&r_{21}: not\, assert(in(M, F_{to})) \leftarrow move(M, F_{from}, F_{to}), delete(M) \\
&r_{22}: spam(F, S, B) \leftarrow contains(S, \text{"credit"}), contains(S, \text{"Fwd"}) \\
&r_{23}: assign(\text{"paper1"}, \text{"ref2@b"}) \qquad r_{24}: \mathrm{assign}(\text{"paper2"}, \text{"ref2@b"}) \\
&r_{25}: assign(\text{"paper2"}, \text{"ref3@c"}) \qquad r_{26}: \mathrm{assign}(\text{"paper3"}, \text{"ref3@c"}) \\
&r_{27}: assign(\text{"paper3"}, \text{"ref1@a"}) \qquad r_{28}: \mathrm{assign}(\text{"paper1"}, \text{"ref1@a"})
\end{aligned}
$$

After all have been asserted, at the subsequent state the agent receives a spam message from the accountant, performs a move and a delete of message 12 to test if the new rule is working, and sends messages to the referees inviting them to review the corresponding papers, as encoded by these facts and rules that belong to E_8:

$$newmsg\,(15, \text{"accountant@c"}, \text{"fwd : credit"}, \text{"..."})\,, move\,(12, inbox, folder1)$$
$$delete\,(12) \qquad send\,(R, PId, \text{"invitation to review"}) \leftarrow assign\,(PId, R)$$

At this point, we invite the reader to check that message 15 was rejected and message 12 was indeed deleted. It is important to notice that messages to referees are sent only once. This is because the rule belonging to E_8 is not an assertion and thus never becomes part of the agent's knowledge base. It is just utilized to determine the stable model at this state, and not used again.

Subsequently the user decides to specify the way the email agent should deal with communication with authors and reviewers. Forthwith, we show how some of these tasks can be specified in EVOLP. Upon receipt of a message from a reviewer accepting to review a given paper, the latter should be sent to the referee the moment it arrives. This can be specified by rule r_{29} (below) asserting a rule that sends the paper to the referee, but this assertion should only take place after the referee accepts the task. If the paper has already been received when the reviewer does so, then it should be sent immediately (r_{30}). Of course, papers received after some deadline, unless some extension was granted to a particular one, should be rejected and the author so notified. This is encoded by rules r_{31} and r_{32} which are asserted when the deadline is reached, even though it might not yet been set. Rule r_{31} sends a message to the author while rule r_{32} prevents the paper being sent to the referee. Finally, the user asserts two rules to deal with deadline extensions on a paper by paper basis. Whenever the user includes an event of the form $dline\,(PId, Dur)$ in an update, he is granting an extension of the deadline to paper PId with duration Dur. This immediately causes $ext\,(PId)$ to be asserted, preventing the paper being rejected. Concurrently, by means of rule r_{34}, a rule is asserted that will render $ext\,(PId)$ false once the deadline plus the extension is reached, after which the paper is rejected. Thus, E_9 is $\{assert\,(\langle r_{29}\rangle)\,, \ldots, assert\,(\langle r_{34}\rangle)\}$, where:

$$\begin{aligned} r_{29} : assert(send(R, S, B) \leftarrow newmsg(M, F, S, B), contains(S, PId),&\\ assign(PId, R)\quad)&\\ \leftarrow newmsg(M, R, PId, B), contains(B, \text{`accept'})&\end{aligned}$$

$$\begin{aligned} r_{30} : send(R, PId, B) \leftarrow\ & newmsg(M, R, PId, B_1), contains(B_1, \text{`accept'}),\\ & msg(M_1, F, PId, B, T)\end{aligned}$$

$$\begin{aligned} r_{31} : assert(send(F, S, \text{`too late'}) \leftarrow newmsg(M, F, S, B), contains(S, PId),&\\ not\, ext(PId)\quad)&\\ \leftarrow time(T), deadline(T)&\end{aligned}$$

$$\begin{aligned} r_{32} : assert(not\, send(Referee, S, B) \leftarrow newmsg(M, F, S, B), contains(S, PId),&\\ not\, ext(PId)\quad)&\\ \leftarrow time(T), deadline(T)&\end{aligned}$$

$$r_{33} : assert(ext(PId)) \leftarrow dline(PId, D)$$
$$r_{34} : assert(assert(not\, ext(PId)) \leftarrow time(D+T), deadline(T)) \leftarrow dline(PId, D)$$

Subsequently the user sets the deadline by asserting the fact *deadline* (14)[5], i.e. the event E_{10} contains the fact *assert* (*deadline* (14)).

The remainder of the story goes as follows: at event E_{11} the agent receives both acceptance messages from referee 1; at event E_{12} it receives paper 2; the user grants deadline extensions of two time units to papers 1 and 3, encoded in event E_{13}; at event E_{14} it receives the acceptance messages from referee 2; at event E_{15}, i.e. after the deadline but before the granted extension expires, it receives paper 1; at event E_{16} it receives the acceptance messages from referee 3; at event E_{17}, i.e. after the extension has expired, it receives paper 3. Lack of space prevents us from elaborating further on what folows these events, but we invite the reader to check that: after event E_{14} paper 2 is sent to referee 2; after event E_{15} paper 1 is sent to both referees 1 and 2; after event E_{16} paper 2 is sent to referee 3; since paper 3 arrives after its deadline extension it is rejected, a message being sent to the author, and the paper not sent to any referee.I.e:

$$
\begin{aligned}
E_{11} &= \{newmsg(16, \text{“ref1@a”}, \text{“paper1”}, \text{“accept”}),\\
&\quad newmsg(17, \text{“ref1@a”}, \text{“paper3”}, \text{“accept”})\}\\
E_{12} &= \{newmsg(18, \text{“a2@e”}, \text{“paper2”}, \text{“thepaper”})\}\\
E_{13} &= \{dline(\text{“paper3”}, 2), \text{dline}(\text{“paper1”}, 2)\}\\
E_{14} &= \{newmsg(19, \text{“ref2@b”}, \text{“paper1”}, \text{“accept”}),\\
&\quad newmsg(20, \text{“ref2@b”}, \text{“paper2”}, \text{“accept”})\}\\
E_{15} &= \{newmsg(21, \text{“a1@e”}, \text{“paper1”}, \text{“thepaper”})\}\\
E_{16} &= \{newmsg(22, \text{“ref3@c”}, \text{“paper2”}, \text{“accept”}),\\
&\quad newmsg(23, \text{“ref3@c”}, \text{“paper3”}, \text{“accept”})\}\\
E_{17} &= \{newmsg(24, \text{“a3@e”}, \text{“paper3”}, \text{“thepaper”})\}
\end{aligned}
$$

4 Concluding Remarks

A large number of software products is nowadays available to perform email monitoring and filtering. One example is Spam Agent [19], a recently deployed email monitoring and filtering tool which features a comprehensive set of filters (over 1500) to block spam and unwanted emails. Email monitoring and filtering rules can be defined in terms of message sender, recipient, subject, body, and arbitrary combinations of them. The SpreadMsg software email filtering and forwarding agent [12] provides unattended data capture, scanning, and extraction from a wide variety of data. User rule sets are applied to data and, when criteria are met, data are further parsed and turned into messages that can be delivered to email addresses, text pagers, digital cellular or GSM mobile phones, laptops, PDA's etc.. The SuperScout Email Filter [16], besides supporting similar capabilities to the previously mentioned agents, features a Virtual Learning Agent (VLA). The VLA is a content development tool that can be trained to

[5] Dealing with the synchronisation of external and internal times is outside the scope of this paper. Here, we set the deadline as a value that refers to the agent's internal clock.

understand and recognize specific proprietary content in order to protect confidential and business critical information from the security risks arising from accidental or malicious leakage. Widely used commercial email filtering systems provide SPAM filters and, in some cases, a more general set of email handling rules. Outlook, Netscape, and Hotmail, for instance, all provide means to define email filtering rules. Some systems require the user to write the filtering rules, while others employ learning algorithms or try to extract patterns from examples. An interesting, very recent proposal is the Personal Email Assistant (PEA) [5], which is intended to provide a customizable, machine learning based environment to support email processing. An aspect of PEA is that it relies on combining available open source components for information retrieval, machine learning, and agents. Lack of space prevents us from mentioning other (out of many) email monitoring and filtering agents available. It is worth observing however that, to the best of our knowledge, none of the available agents enjoys the ability of autonomously and dynamically updating its own filtering policies in a way as general as the EVOLP specifications illustrated in the present work.

In this paper, we have illustrated how EVOLP can be employed to specify a personal assistant agent for e-mail management on the Web. More generally, we have shown how EVOLP can be employed to express updateable RuleML rule bases (by means of a suitable XML schema — which we did not illustrate for lack of space). This paves the way for a more general usage of EVOLP in the context of the Semantic Web. In this perspective, EVOLP features an implemented inference engine which can be fruitfully used for querying data and for the rapid prototyping of Web-based agents.

The complexity of the inference engine relates to the possible branching of evolutions of a program. Non-stratified rules for assertions can be used to model alternative updates to the agent's knowledge base, e.g. for stating, under certain conditions, either to move a message to a folder or to delete it but not both. Non-stratification can also be used to model uncertainty in the external observations. In both these cases, EVOLP semantics provides several evolution stable models, upon which reasoning can be made, concerning what happens in case one or other action is chosen. On the other hand, by having various models, EVOLP can no longer be used to actually perform the actions, unless some mechanism for selecting models is introduced. For (static) logic programs, this issue of selecting among stable models has already been extensively studied: either by defining more skeptical semantics that always provide a unique model or by preferring among stable models based on some priority ordering on rules. The introduction of such mechanisms in EVOLP too is the subject of current and future work by the authors, with particular emphasis on defining a well-founded based semantics for EVOLP. Another way to view such a well-founded sematics, is that it is sound, though not complete, wrt. the stable model based semantics of Section 2. However, its complexity, rather than being NP-complete as is the stable models semantics, is polynomial on the size of the EVOLP program.

We began this article by extolling the virtue and promise of Logic Programming, for adumbrating the issues and solutions relative to the (internally and externally) updatable executable specification of agents, and to the study of their evolution by means of a precisely defined declarative semantics with well-defined properties. We have shown, in a concrete web related example, how EVOLP can be used, not only to specify an agent's email policy, but also to dynamically change its specification, and make desired foreseen changes, dependent on dynamic external conditions or events. We have run and tested the example, with an EVOLP implementation available at: http://centria.di.fct.unl.pt/~jja/updates/.

Acknowledgments. This work has been partially supported by project FLUX "Flexible Logical Updates", POSI/SRI/40958/2001, financed by FEDER.

References

1. The Semantic Web Activity. `http://www.w3.org/2001/sw/`.
2. J. J. Alferes, A. Brogi, J. A. Leite, and L. M. Pereira. Evolving logic programs. In *JELIA'02*, volume 2424 of *LNAI*. Springer, 2002.
3. J. J. Alferes, J. A. Leite, L. M. Pereira, H. Przymusinska, and T. Przymusinski. Dynamic updates of non-monotonic knowledge bases. *Journal of Logic Programming*, 45(1–3), 2000.
4. J. J. Alferes, L. M. Pereira, H. Przymusinska, and T. Przymusinski. LUPS : A language for updating logic programs. *Artificial Intelligence*, 138(1–2), 2002.
5. R. Bergman, M. Griss, and C. Staelin. A personal email assistant. Technical Report HPL-2002-236, HP Labs Palo Alto, 2002.
6. H. Boley, S. Tabet, and G. Wagner. Design rationale of ruleml: A markup language for semantic web rules. In *SWWS'01*, 2001.
7. The World Wide Web Consortium. `http://www.w3.org/`.
8. T. Eiter, M. Fink, G. Sabbatini, and H Tompits. A framework for declarative update specifications in logic programs. In *IJCAI'01*. Morgan-Kaufmann, 2001.
9. M. Gelfond and V. Lifschitz. The stable semantics for logic programs. In *ICLP'88*. MIT Press, 1988.
10. B. Grosof. Representing e-business rules for the semantic web: Situated courteous logic programs in ruleml. In *WITS'01*, 2001.
11. B. Grosof and T. Poon. Representing agent contracts with exceptions using xml rules, ontologies, and process descriptions. In *RuleML-BR-SW'02*, 2002.
12. Compuquest Inc. Spreadmsg. www.compuquestinc.com.
13. The Rule Markup Initiative. `http://www.dfki.uni-kl.de/ruleml/`.
14. J. A. Leite. *Evolving Knowledge Bases*. IOS Press, 2003.
15. V. Lifschitz and T. Woo. Answer sets in general non-monotonic reasoning (preliminary report). In *KR'92*. Morgan-Kaufmann, 1992.
16. Caudex Services Ltd. Superscout email filter. www.caudexservices.co.uk.
17. Resource Description Framework (RDF). `http://www.w3.org/RDF/`.
18. M. Schroeder and G. Wagner, editors. *Procs. of RuleML-BR-SW'02*, number 60 in CEUR-WS Publication, 2002.
19. Spam-Filtering-Software.com. Spam agent. www.spam-filtering-software.com.
20. Extensible Markup Language (XML). `http://www.w3.org/XML/`.

Automatic Summarization Based on Principal Component Analysis

Chang Beom Lee[1], Min Soo Kim[2], and Hyuk Ro Park[1]

[1] Department of Computer Science, Chonnam National University, 300 Youngbong-dong, Buk-gu, Kwangju 500-757, Republic of Korea
chblee@empal.com, hyukro@chonnam.ac.kr

[2] AIPR Lab, CS Div, Korea Advanced Institute of Science and Technology, 373-1 Guseong-dong, Yuseong-gu, Daejeon 305-701, Republic of Korea
mskim@ai.kaist.ac.kr

Abstract. This paper describes an automatic summarization approach that constructs a summary by extracting sentences that are likely to represent the main theme of a document. The approach takes advantage of the co-occurrence relationships between words in the document to detect significant sentences. The particular technique used is Principal Component Analysis (PCA) which is one of the multivariate statistical methods. The PCA can quantify both word frequency and co-occurrence in the document on the basis of an eigenvector and its corresponding eigenvalue. We extract thematic words by performing the quantification method, and select significant sentences using the thematic words. Experimental results using newspaper articles show that the proposed method is superior to the methods that use word frequency or lexical chain using a thesaurus.

Keywords: Automatic Summarization; Principal Component Analysis

1 Introduction

Automatic document summarization can be described as a two phase process, i.e. a document interpretation phase and a summary generation phase. The primary goal of a document interpretation phase is to find the main theme of a document and its corresponding thematic words. The thematic words represent collectively the main theme of the document. To find thematic words of a document, previous approaches utilized word frequency information in the document [2,3,4, 5] or lexical chain [1]. The method using word frequency is limited in that co-occurrence relationships between words is not considered at all. The lexical chain method makes good use of word relations such as NT(narrow term), RT(related term) which are represented in a thesaurus. However, such a thesaurus requires a large cost to compile, and often represents too general relations to fit a specific domain.

In this paper, we propose a new summarization method that uses co-occurrence relationships acquired by performing a quantification method called

Fernando Moura Pires, Salvador Abreu (Eds.): EPIA 2003, LNAI 2902, pp. 409–413, 2003.

Principal Component Analysis (PCA). Because the necessary term-relationships can be acquired only from the given document, the proposed method does not need additional information such as WordNet. To produce the summary of a document, we first identify thematic words using term-relationships, and then extract significant sentences from the document based on thematic words.

This paper is organized as follows. Section 2 describes the proposed method. Section 3 reports experiment results. A brief conclusion is given in Section 4.

2 Summarization Based on Principal Component Analysis

2.1 Principal Component Analysis Understanding

PCA is concerned with explaining the *variance–covariance* structure through a few *linear* combinations of the original variables. Its general objective is data reduction and interpretation [6].

PCA uses the covariance matrix instead of the obsevation-variable matrix such as Table 2. An eigenvector and its corresponding eigenvalue can be obtained by applying PCA on the covariance matrix. That is, the covariance matrix can be decomposed into a series of eigenvalue-eigenvector pairs (λ_1, e_1), (λ_2, e_2), ..., (λ_p, e_p) where $\lambda_1 \geq \lambda_2 \geq \ldots \lambda_p$.

The proportion of total population variance due to the kth principal component(PC), ρ_k, is

$$\rho_k = \frac{\lambda_k}{\lambda_1 + \lambda_2 + \ldots + \lambda_p} \quad , where \quad k = 1, 2, \ldots, p \tag{1}$$

If most (ρ_k is $0.8 \sim 0.9$) of the total population variance, for large p, can be attributed to the first one, two, or three components, then these components can "replace" the original p variables without much loss of information [6].

2.2 Extracting Thematic Words by Eigenvalue and Eigenvector

We assume that the thematic words of a document for summarization are confined only to nouns that occur more than 2 times in the document. We also regard the extracted nouns as variables, the sentences as observations, and the value of variables as cumulative frequency in the document.

Table 1 shows the variable list extracted from one of Korean newspaper articles composed of 12 sentences. In our sample article, X1 occurred once in 1st sentence, twice in 2nd sentence, once in 9th sentence. So the column under the head X1 in Table 2 shows the cumulative frequency of X1. In Table 3, the nine PCs are obtained after performning PCA with the nine variables. The most part of the variance of the document can be explained using a few most salient PCs. For example, the first four PCs can justify more than 90% of the given document variance. The cumulative ratio is computed using Eq. (1). The first four PCs justify 90.87% of the total sample variance. Consequently, sample variance is

Table 1. Variable List

variable	value
X1	dae-tong-ryong (president)
X2	mun-je (problem)
X3	guk-ga (nation)
X4	sa-ram (person)
X5	bu-jung-bu-pae (illegality and corruption)
X6	gyong-je (economy)
X7	guk-min (people)
X8	bang-bub (method)
X9	dan-che-jang (administrator)

Table 2. Observation-Variable Matrix

obs \ var	X1	X2	X3	X4	X5	X6	X7	X8	X9
1	1	0	0	0	0	0	0	0	0
2	3	1	0	0	0	0	0	0	0
3	0	0	1	1	0	0	0	0	0
4	0	0	2	2	1	0	0	0	0
5	0	0	0	0	2	2	0	0	0
6	0	0	3	0	0	0	1	0	0
7	0	2	0	0	0	0	2	1	0
8	0	0	0	0	0	0	0	0	0
9	4	3	0	0	0	0	0	0	0
10	0	0	0	0	0	0	0	2	2
11	0	0	0	0	0	0	0	0	0
12	0	0	0	0	0	0	0	0	0

Table 3. Eigenvector and corresponding Eigenvalue

var \ PC	PC1	PC2	PC3	PC4	PC5	PC6	PC7	PC8	PC9
X1	**0.768**	0.274	-0.153	-0.275	-0.129	0.185	0.390	0.178	0
X2	0.494	-0.009	0.307	0.454	0.382	0.273	-0.458	-0.150	0
X3	-0.331	**0.666**	0.308	-0.054	-0.194	0.540	-0.066	0.023	-0.109
X4	-0.158	0.287	-0.053	-0.141	0.828	-0.112	0.149	0.367	0.109
X5	-0.131	-0.008	-0.503	0.302	0.209	0.395	0.403	-0.523	0
X6	-0.071	-0.132	-0.476	0.344	-0.158	0.312	-0.221	0.678	0
X7	-0.042	-0.066	**0.455**	**0.530**	-0.120	-0.066	0.572	0.223	0.329
X8	-0.051	-0.478	0.286	-0.167	0.161	0.327	0.257	0.158	-0.658
X9	-0.058	-0.382	0.119	-0.418	0.050	0.469	-0.064	-0.010	0.658
eigenvalue(λ_i)	3.631	1.439	1.162	0.808	0.384	0.283	0.035	0.004	0
cumulative ratio(%)	46.86	65.44	80.44	**90.87**	95.84	99.49	99.95	100.00	100.00

summarized very well by these four PCs and the data from 12 observations on 9 variables can be reasonably reduced to 12 observations on 4 PCs.

One remaining problem is how to express each selected PC. A PC can be represented by linear combination of variables multiplied by their respective coefficient. For instance,

$$PC1 = 0.768 * X1 + 0.494 * X2 + \ldots + (-0.058) * X9 \tag{2}$$

Because the coefficients represent the degree of relationship between variables and a PC, the variables with coefficient higher than 0.5 is used to represent the PC. When the PC has no search, the variable with the highest coefficient is used to represent the PC. For example, in table 3, the correlation coefficient between PC1 and X1 is 0.768, so X1 is selected for the expression of PC1. As the most part variance of a document justified by some of the PCs, we selected variables which have a strong correlation (≥ 0.5) with one of these PCs as thematic words. In our example, the extracted thematic words from PC1 to PC4 are X1, X3 and X7.

2.3 Extracting Significant Sentences by Thematic Words

To extract the siginificant sentences by means of thematic words, we first compute the score of each sentence in the document. The score of each sentence is computed by repeatedly summing 1 for each occurrence of a thematic word in the sentence. After the scores are computed for each sententce, the sentences are sorted in the order of descending score. This score indicates how important the sentence is in the document. The sentences are included in the summary in the order of their scores. The number of included sentences is depend on compression rate.

3 Experiments

We compared the proposed method with the methods using word frequency and lexical chain using a thesaurus. The thesaurus used consists of 142,682 words and provides the relations between words, including hypernymy, hyponymy and synonymy. We used 100 documents of Korean newspaper articles for the evaluation, which were compiled by KISTI[1]. Each document consists of orginal article and manual summary amounting to 30% of the source text. We selected the thematic words as shown below.

- frequency : selecting the words which occur more than 6 times
- lexical chain : selecting all of the words in the strongest chain
- 1–sentence : observation for PCA is a sentence
- 2–sentence : observation for PCA is two consecutive sentences
- 3–sentence : observation for PCA is three consecutive sentences

[1] Korea Institute of Science & Technology Information

To evaluate the various methods, we measured precision, recall, and F–measure which are defined respectively as follows.

$$Precision = \frac{\#\ of\ the\ correct\ summary\ sentences\ that\ the\ system\ extracts}{\#\ of\ the\ sentences\ that\ the\ system\ extracts}$$

$$Recall = \frac{\#\ of\ the\ correct\ summary\ sentences\ that\ the\ system\ extracts}{\#\ of\ the\ manually\ extracted\ summary\ sentences}$$

$$F{-}Measure = \frac{2*Precision*Recall}{Precision+Recall}$$

Table 4 shows that by means of F-measure, the proposed method has improved the performance by about 9% ∼ 12% over word frequency method, by about 3% ∼ 6% over lexical chain method.

Table 4. Evaluation result

			Proposed		
	Frequency	Lexical Chain	1-Sentence	2-Sentence	3-Sentence
Average Precision	0.2361	0.2976	0.3447	0.3352	0.3611
Average Recall	0.2084	0.2624	0.3034	0.2979	0.3203
F-Measure	0.2214	0.2789	0.3227	0.3154	0.3395

4 Conclusion

We proposed a summarization approach that constructs a summary by extracting sentences. The particular technique used is PCA which can quantify both word frequency and co-occurrence in the document on the basis of an eigenvector and its corresponding eigenvalue. Experimental results using newspaper articles show that the proposed method is superior to the methods that use word frequency or lexical chain using a thesaurus.

References

1. Regina Barzilay, Michael Elhadad : Using Lexical chains for Text Summarization. proc. Association for Computational Linguistics. (1997) 10–17
2. H.P.Luhn : The Automatic Creation of Literature Abstracts. IBM Journal of Research and Development. **2(2)** 1958
3. H.P. Edmundson : New Methods in Automatic Extracting. Journal of the ACM. **16(2)** (1969) 264–285
4. L.C.Tong, S.L.Tan : A Statistical Approach to Automatic Text Extraction. Asian Library Journal
5. J.Kupiec, J.Pedersen, F.Chen : A Trainable Document Summarizer. Proc. 18th ACM-SIGIR Conf. (1995)
6. Richard A. Johnson, Dean W. Wichern : Applied Multivariate Statistical Analysis. Prentice Hall. (1992) 356–395

A Constraint Grammar Based Question Answering System for Portuguese

Eckhard Bick

Institute of Language and Communication,
Southern Denmark University
lineb@hum.au.dk, http://beta.visl.sdu.dk

Abstract. This paper describes a linguistic, NLP based Information Extraction (IE) system for Portuguese text. The system focuses on the natural language Question Answering task (QA) and relies on full syntactic tree parses, exploiting both lexico-semantic information, syntactic pattern matching and named entity subtyping. Context driven Constraint Grammar rules (CG) are used not only for PoS disambiguation, but also to assign word based function tags and semantic categories. Exact QA matches are supplemented by iterative textual and syntactic relaxation of seach phrases and hit sentence chunks.

Keywords: Information Extraction (IE), Question Answering (QA), Constraint Grammar (CG), Named Entity Recognition (NER)

1 Introduction

In the TREC2002 QA track for English "only" 3 systems achieved correctness rates over 50%, while most of the 67 main task runs performed considerably worse (Vorhees 2003). However, no clear correlation between basic strategy and performance seems to hold. Rather, systems employed a multitude of patterning, tagging, subtyping, gazeteer data bases and weighting resources. NLP tools proper are used by a growing number of systems, albeit most resort to probabilistic or automated learning/training techniques, with Hidden Markov Models, the Brill PoS tagger and treebank trained constituent parsers being prototypical techniques. Though such techniques allow, for instance, syntactic function verification of IE hits, or PoS context based weighting for n-grams, it is not clear why rule based linguistic analysis shouldn't provide even better input for the same tasks. Thus, no published MUC or TREC systems seem to have used the Constraint Grammar (CG) approach for NLP, advocated in this paper, which allows *rule based* contextual integration of such information at different levels of analysis, be it morphological, syntactic or semantic. Focusing on Portuguese as the target language for both input and source-data, our own system relies on a pre-existing general CG parser for this language (*PALAVRAS*, Bick 2000), which has been enhanced with an integrated NER module and a pattern based syntactic tree generator, for both question analysis and information retrieval.

Fernando Moura Pires, Salvador Abreu (Eds.): EPIA 2003, LNAI 2902, pp. 414–418, 2003.

PALAVRAS has a high degree of robusticity and text type coverage, and a comparatively low percentage of errors (less than 1% for word class and 3-4% for surface syntax). Tag types are word based and cover PoS, inflexion and syntactic function, as well as dependency markers. After filtering, final output feeds into a number of formats, including standard VISL tree format (http://beta.visl.sdu.dk).

The language data used in this article are drawn from a 1 million word tree bank chunk from the PALAVRAS-annotated *CETEM Público* news text corpus (Santos & Bick, 2000).

2 System Architecture and Strategies

The system draws on the parser module in various ways: On the one hand, the input question is syntactically and lexically analysed, on the other hand, either the data source itself or the sentences extracted from it are annotated with morphosyntactic tags, sentence structure and semantic class information. Finally, a distributed named entity recognizer (Bick, 2003) is used in order to provide additional semantic information and to identify relevant search points. The QA system uses this information in its efforts to match question patterns and question key constituents in its text database in a syntactically and semantically sensitive way. In the following, the working steps of the system will be explained sequentially.

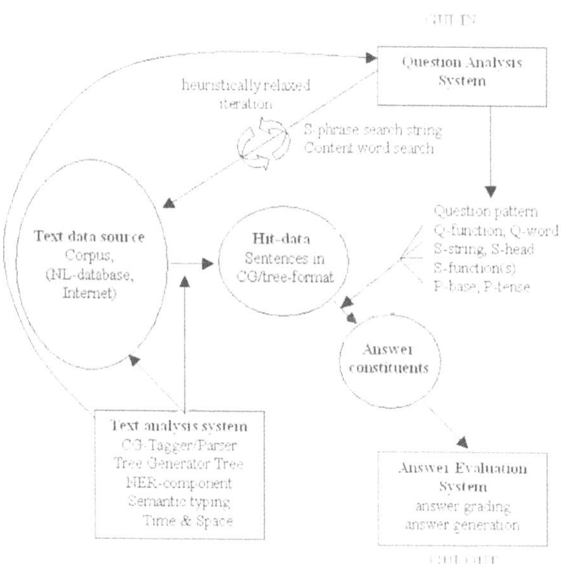

Fig. 1.

2.1 Understanding the User: The Question Analysis Module

Skipping GUI-input/output handling, the first step of a walk-through run produces a full parse of the user's natural language question. From this information, for a question like (Q1a) *Quando nasceu Balladur,* the system fills in a number of variables, like *question pattern* (Atemp-PS), *interrogative constituent:* Q-word ("quando"), Q-function ("ADVL"), *predicator information:* P-base ("nascer"), P-tense ("PS") and *search point constituent:* S-string ("Balladur"), S-function ("SUBJ"), S-head ("Balladur"). Constituents may, of course, be phrases (e.g. nominal, adverbial, verb), as in (Q2) *"Quem é o presidente dos Estados Unidos?"*, and the system also allows for two S-units, fx. when searching for both the object and object complement in a question with the pattern 'S-POaccCo'.

The following are examples of question patterns recognized by the system:

S-PA, S-PCs, S-POacc, S-POpiv, S-POaccCo (Subject interrogative - Quem, que, o=que)
Cs-PS (Que, o=que, qual)
Oacc-PS, Oacc-PSA, Oacc-PSOp (Accusative object interrogative - O=que, ...)
Atemp-PS, Atemp-PSO (Temporal adverbial interrogative - Quando)
Aloc-PS, Aloc-PSO, deAloc-PS, paraAloc-PS (Locative adverbial interrogative - Onde, ...)

If a question consists of a constituent combination not covered by the recognized list of patterns, but still *contains* a recognizable pattern, then the remaining constituents will be filtered away for searching, unless a full text match is possible. A typical Portuguese example are focused questions with pseudo-copula constructions of the type <interr> + "ser" + "que" + P + ..., as in (Q1b): *Quando foi que nasceu Balladur?* Here, the parser's focus recognition rules (which also handles statements with "ser" .... "que" focus brackets) will "wash out" focus particles ("adverbs") of the type 'é=que', 'era=que' or 'foi=que'. Thus, the search pattern will still be 'Atemp-PS', and the Q- and S-variables will be the same as in (1a).

2.2 Searching the Database: From Text Based IR to Syntactic/Semantic Matching

In the first search round, the system extracts sentences (so-called *hit-sentences)* containing the text strings "Balladur" or "o presidente dos Estados Unidos", checks whether the matched search head is, in fact, a subject or a subject head, then looks for a predicator with the same mother node and checks it against the P-base variable and possibly its synonyms (in the second case, for instance, other copula verbs). Finally, if the constituent clause in question contains a daughter with Q-function, and if this daughter satisfies the semantic restrictions of TIME (for the *quando*-question) or HUM (for the *quem*-question), the daughter node will be extracted as an answer candidate. The sentence (H1) is a search hit for "Balladur"-subject and "nascer"-predicator, and the <date>-tag on "1929" fullfils the question's semantic restrictions on the Q-adverbial. Finally, all 3 constituents, SUBJ, P and ADVL, are part of the same mother node, a conjunct finite clause (CJT:fcl).

(H1) Balladur nasceu em Esmirna (Turquia), em 1929, e formou-se na Escola Nacional de Administração, de onde saiu a elite da função pública francesa.

Not all matches are, of course, as syntactically straightforward as in our first example. Consider, for instance, the following question: (Q3) *"Onde Balladur formou-se?"*

Here, the immediate search constituent, Balladur, is syntactically "isolated" from the P-base and place-ADVL matches. Therefore, the syntax matching module has to understand coordination and subject ellipsis (which it does, in this case). A special NER-module helps establishes the place-hood of the ADVL:pp to be matched.

The sentence (H1) will also provide an answer to the question (Q4) *Onde é/fica/situa-se Esmirna?.* However, extracting this information asks for a different technique, since *Esmirna* does not match the S-function of subject, and the answer constituent, *Turquia,* though PLACE-marked, does not match the Q-function of ADVL or ADVS (valency/copula bound adverbial). The strategy used instead, is the same as for *Quem/que/o=que é ...?* copula questions. Here, information is not only extracted from nominal subject complements (SC), but also from appositives and adnominal modifiers. *Turquia* thus carries an N<PRED tag (predicating adnominal), denoting not apposition identity (APP tag), but information *about* its nominal head.

2.3 Search Relaxation Techniques and Answer Evalutation

Both S-string and S-func matches can easily fail, especially with sparse data, if only exact matches are accepted. The S-string match is crucial for the first phase, since without a match, no hit-sentences will be input to the more detailed syntactic and semantic match module. The S-string is therefore iteratively "relaxed", using the strategies of phrase shortening (removal of articles etc), introduction of ".*" dummy chunks between search words and synonym list substitution[1].

Once hit-sentences have been found, matching may still fail at the syntactic/semantic level. Generally, S-*head* matches, rather than complete S-phrase matches, are regarded as sufficient, thus following S-string relaxation. One way of locally relaxing match conditions for a given hit-sentence, is "structural flattening". Consider the sentence:

A guerra civil no Tadjiquistão, que fez mais de 50 mortos, começou em 1992, quando as forças do neo-comunista Rakhmonov derrubaram o governo dos islamistas ...

Given the question (Q5) *Quando Rakhmonov derrubou o governo?,* it is a match problem that *Rakhmonov* in the hit-sentence is three node levels beneath the subject node, i.e. not directly recognized as head of subject. Rather, the unspecific *forças* represents the syntactic subject. Flattening techniques used here are (a) name-np-flattening (appositive-for-np), as in *[o neo-comunista] Rakhmonov*), and (b) toto-pro-pars (semantic heads-for-pp's), as in *[de] Rakhmonov*. Note, that the predicator node is not an exact match either, but rather a base form match (infinitve-normalized) with a P-tense check for past tense.

Finally, answer candidates are fed to the answer evaluation module, which ranks and formats answer strings, using both frequency and a heuristicity index - a counter attached to the individual answer and increased by a specific value (default: +1) every time a match attempt progresses to a new level of match relaxation or syntactic flattening. As a third factor, content word modifiers are weighted in answers to definition

---

[1] Since the systems has a full syntactic analysis of the question at its disposal, search relaxation could also be achieved by combined structural-lexical variation (as suggested in Hermjakob et.al., 2003), including active-passive transformation or V->N word class transformation).

questions, preferring *o Presidente norte-americano* over *o presidente* as the answer to *"Quem é George Bush?"*.

3 Evaluation and Outlook

Due to the pilot-project character of the QA system presented here, and the lack of Portuguese QA-test suits (CG is language-specific), no formal quantitative evaluation had been carried out at the time of writing (May 2003). However, within its restricted range of question patterns, the system was able to extract answers from its text data base even where the information was not accessible to direct text searches, and to narrow down its search space according to syntactic and semantic constraints. Also, it must be born in mind that the QA module itself functions as an add-on to a larger system, the PALAVRAS parser, which *has* been repeatedly evaluated. Thus, the parser's semantic NER module, which is crucial to question answering, has shown promising results when evaluated earlier this year on similar data (Bick, 2003). Here, with a 6-way name category distinction, an overall F-Score of 91.85 was achieved, or an F-score of 93.6 on correctly chunked proper nouns.

Future work should increase the number of question patterns actively recognized, and incorporate a sizable set of synonymity classes for verbs and nouns. Though the current CG has a one-sentence window and does not use entity-ID's explicitly, co-reference resolution should optimally be discourse based and, in a later version, include pronoun anaphora and possibly definite noun phrase subjects, thus involving also paragraph context adjacent to hit-sentences. As a real world application, the system would - for better coverage (and possibly redundancy based frequency ratings) – need to access much larger text data bases, or incorporate internet searches and explicit encyclopedic knowledge.

References

1. Bick, Eckhard: The Parsing System 'Palavras' – Automatic Grammatical Analysis of Portuguese in a Constraint Grammar Framework. Aarhus University Press, Århus (2000)
2. Bick, Eckhard: Multi-Level NER for Portuguese in a CG Framework. In: Proceedings of PROPOR2003, Springer: Faro, forthcoming (2003)
3. Hermjakob, Ulf & Abdessamad Echihabi & Daniel Marcu: Natural Language Based Reformulation Resource and Web Exploitation for QA. In: E.M. Vorhees & L.P. Buckland (eds.): Proceedings of the Eleventh Text REtrieval Conference (2003)
4. Santos, Diana & Bick, Eckhard: Providing Internet access to Portuguese corpora: the AC/DC project. In Gavriladou et al. (eds.): Proc. 2nd International Conf. on Language Resources and Evaluation, LREC2000 (Athens, 2000), pp. 205–10.
5. Vorhees, Ellen M.: Overview of the TREC2002 Question Answering Track. In: E.M. Vorhees & L.P. Buckland (eds.): Proceedings of the 11th TREC (2003)

Mining Generalized Character n-Grams in Large Corpora

Nuno C. Marques and Agnès Braud

CENTRIA, New University of Lisbon, PORTUGAL,
nmm@di.fct.unl.pt, braud@fct.unl.pt

Abstract. In this paper, we study the computational cost of extracting character n-grams from a corpus. We propose an approach for reducing this cost which is relevant especially for text mining and natural language applications. The underlying idea is to take under consideration only n-grams occurring above a given frequency in a corpus. This approach is applied to three different corpora, allowing the extraction of all frequent n-grams in those corpora in reasonable time.

Keywords: Text Mining, APriori algorithm, n-grams, corpus-based algorithms

1 Introduction

Term extraction is an essential problem in text mining and natural language processing. Standard techniques for term extraction usually require word identification followed by some kind of tagging and processing of words. Word identification is the process that aims at identifying basic units of text (or tokens), and is thus usually called tokenization. Term extraction can then be achieved through a tagger (e.g. [1]) followed by parsing (e.g. [2]). However, this kind of approach depends a lot on the linguistic properties of the text under analysis. For example, even something as simple as using spaces to separate tokens has problems (such as punctuation marks attached to some words, e.g. *The U.S.*). We propose an approach for which no domain or linguistic knowledge is required at the earliest steps of the analysis. By selecting all the substrings (character n-grams) that occur in a corpus above a certain threshold, we avoid making any a priori considerations regarding the form of the tokens and the characteristics of the text.

N-gram models are commonly used in statistical natural language processing. Word n-grams are common in the form of bigrams and trigrams. Word trigrams have been used in works like part-of-speech tagging [1] and machine translation [3]. Character based n-grams are common too, although less used (e.g. [4] uses character four-grams for clustering documents in a corpus).

Instead of using a fixed size n, we will vary n from 1 to the size N of the corpus, thus working on the set of all the possible character n-grams appearing in that corpus. We call this the set of *generalized character n-grams*.

Fernando Moura Pires, Salvador Abreu (Eds.): EPIA 2003, LNAI 2902, pp. 419–423, 2003.

The straightforward algorithm for generalized n-gram extraction is expensive, that is one of the reasons why most of the works using n-grams have a fixed value for n. We propose an efficient method for counting all n-grams occurring with high frequency in a corpus, considering that these tend to be relevant terms for an analysis of the text. We will see that, using such a process, no domain or linguistic knowledge is required for the text pre-processing phase.

Recent developments in computational linguistics, namely using improvements on suffix arrays made this generalized hypothesis feasible [5]. Nevertheless, their method is complex and needs to represent all the n-grams so that a lot of space may be required. This can be a problem when we want to represent all the information. The approach presented here has the advantage of storing only frequent enough n-grams. This allows our algorithm to use less space in memory. That way it is possible to extract information from larger corpora. Finally, its simplicity makes this algorithm fairly easy to adapt.

In the following section, we will characterize quantitatively the problem of extracting the n-grams that appear more often than a predetermined threshold, as well as the proposed algorithm. In Sect. 4 we present some experiments that show the ability of this algorithm to extract all frequent n-grams from texts in reasonable time.

2 An Algorithm for Extracting n-Grams from a Corpus

Generally, the total number of possible n-grams increases exponentially with the dimension n. Fortunately language is very restricted in the permutation of elements that have semantic content. This means that only a small fraction of all possible n-grams can be used in a text.

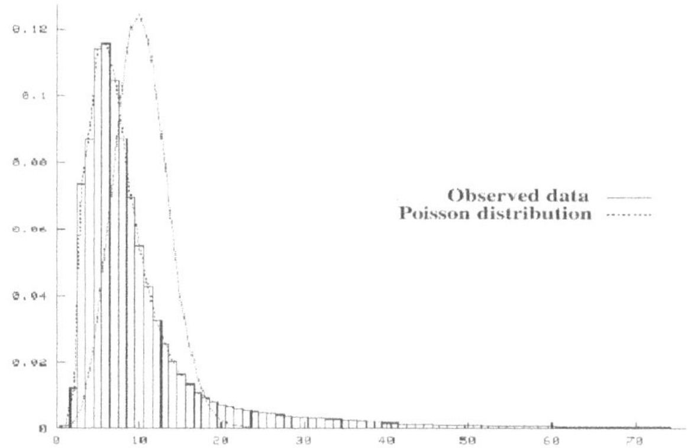

Fig. 1. Observed proportions of distinct n-grams and Poisson distribution with the same mean.

Figure 1 presents a histogram of the observed relative proportions of distinct n-grams that appear more than three times in a small corpus[1] according to n. Similar histograms were observed for several distinct corpora in different languages and for very different corpora sizes.

The algorithm we propose exploits the fact that the number of distinct n-grams starts to decrease for relatively small n-gram lengths ($n \leq 6$). Indeed, we will only consider in our analysis n-grams with a frequency above a certain threshold[2]. This enables us to base ourselves on the following property that is used in the APriori algorithm [6] for the extraction of association rules: if an n-gram contains at least one (n-1)-gram which is not frequent, then that n-gram cannot be frequent and it is not worth keeping it. As the size of the n-grams increases, less and less of them will be considered. Thus computation costs are lower and we can consider longer n-grams than most of the algorithms do. Also, even in a big corpus the number of distinct frequent n-grams reaches zero after a given maximum size (around one hundred letters). This allows us to find all the n-grams in the corpus. We will rerun the process looking for larger and larger n-grams until no more frequent n-gram can be retrieved from the text.

We should also notice that the decrease in the number of possible n-grams is smaller than the one that would be predictable by a purely stochastic process[3]. One probable reason for this is the existence of long multi-word units or terms in text that are used repeatedly. This property stresses the importance of such an extraction process, which allows to search for longer n-grams. Indeed these long n-grams have a number of occurrences that cannot be neglected. In fact this property shows that it is possible to extract some meaningful entries from a corpus, just by counting all frequently occurring character n-grams. This simple approach should then be combined with other information sources for better results ([7]).

The algorithm proposed works incrementally, as the APriori algorithm does, by first computing the frequency of 1-grams and then considering n-grams of increasing length, each time keeping those which occur with a frequency above a threshold $minf$. This algorithm is detailed below.
Let $\mathcal{C}$ be the corpus, $N(G)$ the number of occurrences of the n-gram G in $\mathcal{C}$.

---

[1] We used a 119 news article sample taken from the *Wall Street Journal*

[2] This threshold is usually 3, a value under which any n-gram would be statistically unrepresentative.

[3] Figure 1 also shows a Poisson distribution with the same mean as the data. For long enough n-grams ($n > 15$), the number of occurrences of the observed data is higher than the one predicted by the Poisson process.

Table 1. Quantitative data extracted from two English corpora (WSJ and SUSANNE) and one Portuguese Corpora (LUSA).

Corpus	Corpus Size (bytes)	Minimum frequency	#n-grams	#n-grams w/ repetition	Max. l. n-gram	Time required
WSJ	222647	3	94588	1296406	51	1min10s
SUSANNE	813581	3	327882	5841463	48	3min55s
LUSA	9169473	7	7391240	1901024761	76	1346 min

Input: corpus, minf
Output: the set $\mathcal{S}$ of frequent n-grams

$\mathcal{S}_1$:= {1-grams with frequency>minf}
i:=2
repeat {
  $\mathcal{S}_i := \emptyset$
  for each occurrence of i-grams G in $\mathcal{C}$ {
    if (G $\in \mathcal{S}_i$) {
      increment $N(G)$ }
    else {
      $add := true$
      for the two (i-1)-grams SG of G {
        if (SG $\notin \mathcal{S}_{i-1}$) {
          $add := false$
          exit for } }
      if add {
        $\mathcal{S}_i := \mathcal{S}_i + G$
        $N(G) := 1$ } }
  $\mathcal{S} := \mathcal{S} \cup \{G | G \in \mathcal{S}_i, N(G) > minf\}$
  i:=i+1 }
until $\mathcal{S}_i = \emptyset$

return $\mathcal{S}$

3 The Extracted n-Grams

The algorithm extracts all the n-grams that occur in a corpus with a minimum number of occurrences. This is the only criterion, no linguistic information regarding tokenization, lexical forms or any other linguistic concern is needed.

Table 1 presents results acquired after running our algorithm on three distinct corpora. We have extracted n-grams from two small samples of English text and a fairly big Portuguese corpus. The WSJ corpus is a small sample of news in the *Wall Street Journal*. Susanne corpus is a publicly available corpus. Finally the *LUSA* corpus contains almost two years of news provided by the Portuguese news agency LUSA. The second column of Tab.1 presents the size of these corpora. For each of these corpora we have run our algorithm to extract all the n-grams with frequency above 3 for the small corpora (since the corpora were small we could not use a bigger value) and 7 for the LUSA corpora (a conservative value for meaningfulness). These values are presented in column 3. The total number of distinct character n-grams is presented in column 4 and gives a rough estimate of memory needed in each step of our algorithm. Column 5 shows the total number of n-grams, including repetitions. We can notice that these values are much larger than the total size of the corpora being analyzed. This is due to the inclusion of smaller n-grams in the biggest ones (all frequent n-grams for a given size have been listed). In column 6 we can see that the longest n-gram extracted from the WSJ corpus was "In New York Stock Exchange composite trading Friday,", that corresponds to a very common phrase in our sample. In Susanne the longest n-gram is from a medical text: "bronchial artery + +pulmonary artery anastomoses" (Susanne is a balanced corpus with several kinds of texts considered). In LUSA news text the biggest n-gram has a size of 76, but it corresponds to a sequence of characters used to format the text. The largest meaningful n-grams are then "pretoria-witwatersrand-vereeniging" (corresponding to a proper name used in the news) with 35 characters and "vice-primeiro-ministro do" (vice-prime-minister of) with 26 characters. Finally column 7 presents the user time the extraction process took on a computer with a processor AMD Athlon MP at 2000MHz and 2GB RAM using Linux. These results do indeed show that the proposed approach is feasible even on a fairly large corpora.

4 Conclusions

In this paper we have shown that it is possible to extract frequent generalized character based n-grams from text in an efficient way. The trivial approach for extracting all character n-grams from a large corpus is very expensive in terms of time and space. The proposed approach is based on a principle also used in the APriori algorithm [6]. We have used these n-grams to extract information from text without the need of a tokenization process. Tests show that frequent long enough n-grams include most of the relevant words and multiword units in the corpus [7], leading us to argue that n-grams can be used with advantages over words in many frameworks. The proposed algorithm allows the application of linguistic knowledge in a later (almost final) level of processing, so that we achieve meaningful gains not only in efficiency but also in flexibility. As future work we intend to optimize our algorithm, by taking taxonomies into account. This will allow us to join similar n-grams in the same classes.

References

1. Marques, N.C., Lopes, G.P.: Tagging with small training corpora. Lecture Notes in Computer Science **2189** (2001) 63–72
2. Feldman, R., Fresko, M., Kinar, Y., Lindell, Y., Lipshtat, O., Rajman, M., Schler, Y., Zamir, O.: Text mining at the term level. In Zytkow, J.M., Quafafou, M., eds.: Proceedings of PKDD-98. Volume 1510 of LNAI, Berlin, Springer (1998) 65–73
3. Brown, P., Pietra, V.D., deSouza, P., Lai, J., Mercer, R.: Class-based n-gram models of natural language. Computational Linguistics **18** (1992) 467–480
4. Schütze, H.: Word space. In Hanson, S., Cowan, J., Giles, C., eds.: Advances in Neural Information Processing Systems 5. Morgan Kaufmann Publishers (1993)
5. Yamamoto, M., Church, K.W.: Using suffix arrays to compute term frequency and document frequency for all substrings in a corpus. Computational Linguistics **27** (2001) 1–30
6. Agrawal, R., Imielinski, T., Swami, A.N.: Mining association rules between sets of items in large databases. In Buneman, P., Jajodia, S., eds.: Proceedings of the 1993 ACM SIGMOD International Conference on Management of Data, Washington, D.C. (1993) 207–216
7. Marques, N., Braud, A. (Technical Report DI-FCT/UNL 1/2003)

A Methodology to Create Ontology-Based Information Retrieval Systems

José Saias and Paulo Quaresma

Departamento de Informática,
Universidade de Évora,
7000 Évora, Portugal
{jsaias,pq}@di.uevora.pt

Abstract. Modern information retrieval systems need the capability to reason about the knowledge conveyed by text bases.
In this paper a methodology to automatically create ontologies and class instances from documents is proposed. The ontology is defined in the OWL semantic web language and it is used by a logic programming framework, ISCO, to allow users to query the semantic content of the documents. ISCO allows an easy and efficient integration of declarative, object-oriented and constraint-based programming techniques with the capability to create connections with external databases.

1 Introduction

Modern information retrieval systems need the capability to represent and to reason with the knowledge conveyed by text bases. This knowledge can be represented through the use of ontologies. In fact, ontologies allow the definition of class hierarchies, object properties, and relation rules, such as, transitivity or functionality. Using this knowledge it is possible to define instances of classes, to associate them with documents, and to make inferences about them.

OWL (Ontology Web Language) is a language proposed by the W3C consortium (http://www.w3.org [9]) to be used in the "semantic-web" environment for the representation of ontologies. This language is based in the previous DAML+OIL (Darpa Agent Markup Language - [10]) language and it is defined using RDF (Resource Description Framework - [5]).

In this paper a methodology to automatically create an OWL ontology and OWL class instances from a set of documents is proposed. The methodology is based on natural language processing techniques, namely, a syntactical parser and a semantic analyzer able to obtain a partial interpretation of the documents. Similar approaches aiming to create a daml+oil/owl ontology were presented in [7,8]. These approaches presented preliminary work in this area but they did not propose a general methodology for the creation of OWL ontologies and the enrichment of documents with OWL instances.

After the creation of the OWL ontology, documents are enriched with instances of classes and a logic programming based framework is used to support

Fernando Moura Pires, Salvador Abreu (Eds.): EPIA 2003, LNAI 2902, pp. 424–434, 2003.

inferences over them. The logic programming framework is based on ISCO [1]. ISCO is a new declarative language implemented over GNU Prolog with object-oriented predicates, constraints and allowing simple connections with external databases.

Section 2 describes the natural language processing techniques used to create the OWL ontology. 3 describes the NLP techniques used to create the OWL instances associated with each document. Section 4 describes ISCO, the logic programming framework. Section 5 provides an example of interaction. Finally, in section 6 some conclusions and future work are pointed out.

2 OWL Ontology Creation

In order to be able to deal with documents from different domains, a methodology to automatically create basic ontologies of concepts is proposed. This methodology allows the definition of a base ontology with the relevant concepts but having few hierarchical relations. After having defined this ontology, it may be necessary for human experts to manually rework it in order to fully organize the set of extracted concepts.

The methodology to automatically obtain an ontology of concepts is based on the output of natural language processing tools:

- Text syntactical parsing. The documents are analysed by the parser developed by E. Bick in the domain of the VISL project[1] [2]. This parser is available for 21 different languages, namely for the Portuguese language.
- Partial semantic analysis.
- Entities extraction. From the semantic analysis output, entities are extracted and represented by ontology classes.

2.1 Syntactical Analysis

The syntactical parser developed by E. Bick in the domain of the VISL project is based in the Constraint Grammars formalism and it is able to cover a large percentage of the Portuguese language. However, its output is in a non-standard format and it was necessary to transform it into a structured form, like XML and Prolog terms. A translation tool from the VISL output into XML and Prolog terms was developed and it is available to the VISL users (a detailed description of this tool was presented in [3]).

As an example, suppose the following sentence:

O bombeiro salvou a criança. *The fireman saved the child.*

This sentence has the VISL output:

[1] http://visl.hum.sdu.dk/visl

```
STA:fcl
SUBJ:np
=>N:art('o' M S)        O
=H:n('bombeiro' M S)    bombeiro
P:v-fin('salvar' PS 3S IND)     salvou
ACC:np
=>N:art('a' F S)        a
=H:n('crianca' F S)     crianca
```

As it can be seen, the subject, predicate and direct object were correctly parsed. From this output, the XML translator produces three files:

1. The first file links each word with a *word* tag with a specific *id*.

```
<!DOCTYPE words SYSTEM "words.dtd">
<words>
<word id="word_1">O</word>
<word id="word_2">bombeiro</word>
<word id="word_3">salvou</word>
<word id="word_4">a</word>
<word id="word_5">crianca</word>
<word id="word_6">.</word>
</words>
```

2. The second file associates each *word* with its part-of-speech information.

```
<!DOCTYPE words SYSTEM "wordsPOS.dtd">
<words>
<word id="word_1">
<art canon="o" gender="M" number="S"/>
</word>
<word id="word_2">
<n canon="bombeiro" gender="M" number="S"/>
</word>
<word id="word_3">
<v canon="salvar">
<fin tense="PS" person="3S" mode="IND"/>
</v>
</word>
<word id="word_4">
<art canon="a" gender="F" number="S"/>
</word>
<word id="word_5">
<n canon="crianca" gender="F" number="S"/>
</word>
</words>
```

3. The third file has the parsing structure.

```
<!DOCTYPE text SYSTEM "text_ext.dtd">
<text>
<paragraph id="paragraph_1">
<sentence id="sentence_1" span="word_1..word_6">
```

```
<chunk id="chunk_1" ext="subj" form="np"
                              span="word_1..word_2">
<chunk id="chunk_2" ext="n" form="art" span="word_1">
</chunk>
<chunk id="chunk_3" ext="h" form="n" span="word_2">
</chunk>
</chunk>
<chunk id="chunk_4" ext="p" form="v_fin" span="word_3">
</chunk>
<chunk id="chunk_5" ext="acc" form="np"
                             span="word_4..word_5">
<chunk id="chunk_6" ext="n" form="art" span="word_4">
</chunk>
<chunk id="chunk_7" ext="h" form="n" span="word_5">
</chunk>
</chunk>
</sentence>
</paragraph>
</text>
```

2.2 Semantic Analysis

Each syntactical structure is translated into a First-Order Logic expression. The technique used for this analysis is based on DRS's (Discourse Representation Structures [4]). The partial semantic representation of a sentence is a DRS built with two lists, one with the rewritten sentence and the other with the sentence discourse referents.

At present, we are only dealing with a very restricted semantic analysis and we only try to represent predicates with their subjects and direct objects.

From the XML structure, using XSL transformations, it is possible to obtain the semantic representation of each sentence.

The semantic representation of the example presented in the previous sub-section is:

sentence(doc1, [fireman(A), child(B), save(A,B)], [ref(A), ref(B)]).

This structure represents an instance of a fireman A and an instance of a child B which are related by the action *to save*.

A general tool able to obtain similar semantic partial representations for every sentence was developed and it was applied to the full set of legal documents of the Portuguese Attorney General's Office (7000 documents).

2.3 Entities Extraction

From the sentence semantic representation, entities are extracted and they are the basis for the creation of an ontology of concepts. In fact, for each new concept, a new class, subclass of the *Entity* class, is created.

In the referred example it would be possible to extract the following entities:

– bombeiro *fireman*
– salvar *to save*
– criança *child*

These three entities would cause the creation of correspondent ontology classes.

Figure 1 shows a graphical view of the top-level hierarchy:

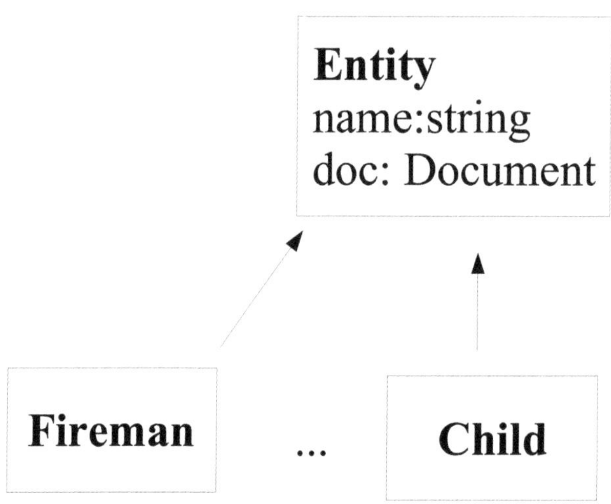

Fig. 1. Top-level entity hierarchy

As it can be seen from the figure, the proposed procedure for the automatic creation of ontologies is only able to obtain a simple two-level hierarchy of concepts. At present, manual intervention is needed to refine this ontology and to represent more complex structures.

As an example, we present the OWL code correspondent to these concepts:

```
<owl:Class rdf:ID="Entity">
</owl:Class>

        <owl:DataTypeProperty rdf:ID="name">
          <rdfs:domain rdf:resource="#Entity"/>
          <rdf:type rdf:resource="&owl;FunctionalProperty"/>
          <rdfs:range rdf:resource="&xsd;String"/>
        </owl:DataTypeProperty>

        <owl:ObjectProperty rdf:ID="entDoc">
          <rdf:type rdf:resource="&owl;FunctionalProperty" />
          <rdfs:domain rdf:resource="#Entity" />
          <rdfs:range rdf:resource="#Document" />
        </owl:ObjectProperty>
```

```
<owl:Class rdf:ID="child">
  <rdfs:subClassOf rdf:resource="&pgr;Entity" />
</owl:Class>

<owl:Class rdf:ID="fireman">
  <rdfs:subClassOf rdf:resource="&pgr;Entity" />
</owl:Class>
```

3 OWL Instance

After having defined an ontology of classes, it is necessary to extract and to represent instances of those classes and to associate them with documents.

This association is presently done via a new class *Action*, which relates subjects, predicates, and direct objects with specific documents. The overall architecture is presented in figure 2.

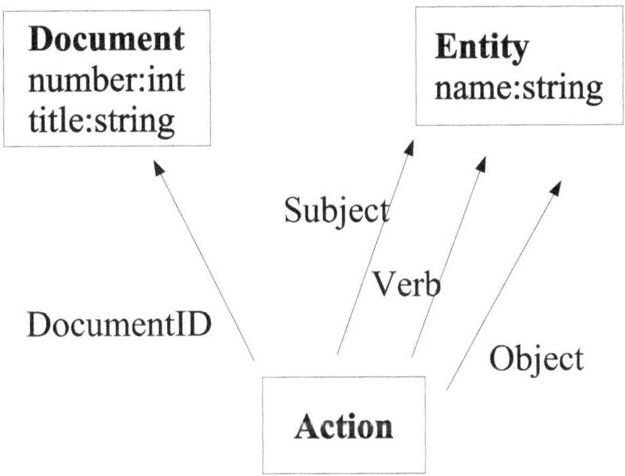

Fig. 2. Top-level classes

The following OWL code defines class *Document* with two properties: *number* and *title*.

```
<owl:Class rdf:ID="Document">
</owl:Class>

        <owl:DataTypeProperty rdf:ID="number">
          <rdfs:domain rdf:resource="#Document"/>
          <rdf:type rdf:resource="&owl;FunctionalProperty"/>
          <rdfs:range rdf:resource="&xsd;integer"/>
        </owl:DataTypeProperty>
```

```
<owl:DataTypeProperty rdf:ID="title">
  <rdfs:domain rdf:resource="#Document"/>
  <rdf:type rdf:resource="&owl;FunctionalProperty"/>
  <rdfs:range rdf:resource="&xsd;string"/>
</owl:DataTypeProperty>
```

This code defines class *Action*:

```
<owl:Class rdf:ID="Action">
</owl:Class>
```

This code relates *Action* and *Entity* through four different object properties: subject, verb, object, documentId. This means that each action is characterized by the document where it appears and by its subject, verb,and object entities.

```
<owl:ObjectProperty rdf:ID="subject">
  <rdf:type rdf:resource="&owl;FunctionalProperty" />
  <rdfs:domain rdf:resource="#Action"/>
  <rdfs:range rdf:resource="#Entity"/>
</owl:ObjectProperty>

<owl:ObjectProperty rdf:ID="object">
  <rdf:type rdf:resource="&owl;FunctionalProperty" />
  <rdfs:domain rdf:resource="#Action"/>
  <rdfs:range rdf:resource="#Entity"/>
</owl:ObjectProperty>

<owl:ObjectProperty rdf:ID="verb">
  <rdf:type rdf:resource="&owl;FunctionalProperty" />
  <rdfs:domain rdf:resource="#Action"/>
  <rdfs:range rdf:resource="#Entity"/>
 </owl:ObjectProperty>

 <owl:ObjectProperty rdf:ID="documentId">
  <rdf:type rdf:resource="&owl;FunctionalProperty" />
  <rdfs:domain rdf:resource="#Action"/>
  <rdfs:range rdf:resource="#Document"/>
 </owl:ObjectProperty>
```

As it was referred, the next step was to add semantic information to each document.

- For each sentence,
  - For each predicate belonging to the entity ontology and relating two concepts,
    - an instance of the correspondent action with its subject and direct object instances is created.

For example, suppose in document 555 the verb *to save* and the entities *fireman* and *child* are related by the already presented sentence:

sentence(doc1, [fireman(A), child(B), save(A,B)], [ref(A), ref(B)]).

Using our methodology, an instance of a new action will be created, relating new instances of concepts *fireman*, *child*, and *to save*.

```
<pgr:Action rdf:ID="a1">
  <pgr:subject rdf:resource="#e142"/>
  <pgr:object rdf:resource="#e21"/>
  <pgr:verb rdf:resource="#e32"/>
  <pgr:documentID rdf:resource="#d2"/>
</pgr:Action>

<pgr:Fireman rdf:ID="e142">
  <pgr:name>fireman</pgr:name>
</pgr:Fireman>

<pgr:Child rdf:ID="e21">
  <pgr:name>child</pgr:name>
</pgr:Child>

<pgr:ToSave rdf:ID="e32">
  <pgr:name>to save</pgr:name>
</pgr:Entity>

<pgr:Document rdf:ID="d2">
  <pgr:number>555</pgr:number>
</pgr:Document>
```

This code means that in document 555 there is an instance of an action with verb *to save* and having a *fireman* as subject and a *child* as direct object.

4 ISCO

After having represented documents through an ontology on concepts and instances of those concepts it is necessary to be able to support inferences about the represented knowledge.

As basic formalism to support knowledge representations and knowledge inferences we propose the use of ISCO. ISCO [1] is a logic based development language implemented over GNU Prolog that gives the developer several distinct possibilities:

- It supports Object-Oriented features: classes, hierarchies, inheritance.
- It supports Constraint Logic Programming. Specifically, it supports finite domain constraints in ISCO queries.
- it gives a simple access to external relational databases through ODBC. It has a back-end for PostgreSQL and Oracle.

- It allows the access to external relational databases as a part of a declarative/deductive object-oriented (with inheritance) database. Among other things, the system maps relational tables to classes – which may be used as Prolog predicates.
- It gives a simple database structure description language that can help in database schema analysis. Tools are available to create an ISCO database description from an existing relational database schema and also the opposite action.

Taking these ISCO features into account, a translator from OWL into ISCO class definitions and Prolog facts and rules was developed. This translator was applied to every OWL class described in the previous section and, as a consequence, correspondent ISCO classes definitions were obtained. Moreover, each OWL class instance was transformed into ISCO logic programming facts.

As an example, the *action* $a1$ presented previously is translated into the following fact:

```
action(ID=a1, subject='#e142', object='#e21',
      verb='#e32', documentID='#d2').

fireman(ID=e142).
child(ID=e21).
tosave(ID=e32).
document(ID=d2).
```

Variables occurring in queries may carry CLP(FD) constraints. For example, suppose variable `X` is an FD variable whose domain is `(1..1000)`, the query

```
document(number = X, title = Y)          (1)
```

will return all pairs `(X, Y)` where `X` is a document number and `Y` is the document's title. `X` is subject to the constraints that were valid upon execution of the query, ie. in the range 1 to 1000.

ISCO class declarations feature inheritance, simple domain integrity constraints and a global integrity constraints.

5 Interaction Example

The interaction is based on the ISCO logic programming framework.

As final goal, we aim to handle the following kind of questions:

- Documents where action A is performed
- Documents where action A is performed having subject S
- Documents where S is the subject of an action

Note that the inference engine needs to be able to deal with the ontology relations. For instance, the question "documents where action A is performed having subject S" means "documents where action A (or any of its sub-classes) is performed having subject S (or any of its sub-classes)".

The translation of natural language queries into correspondent logic forms will not be discussed in this paper (see for instance [6]) and it will be assumed to be handled by some external module.

For the questions presented above, we would have:

- Documents where action A is performed
  - A(id=V), action(verb=V, documentID=ID).
- Documents where action A is performed having subject S
  - A(id=V), S(id=E), action(verb=V, subject=E, documentID=ID).
- Documents where S is the subject of an action
  - S(id=E), action(subject=E, documentID=ID).

5.1 Fireman Example

Suppose the following query:

Quais os documentos em que bombeiros salvaram crianças?
"Which are the documents where firemen saved children?"

This query is transformed into its pragmatic interpretation:

Q = [document(id=A),fireman(id=B), tosave(id=C), child(id=D),
action(subject=B, verb=C, object=D, documentID=A)].

Using this query, the ISCO inference engine is able to constrain variables A, B, C, and D to their possible values accordingly with the existent OWL instances.

$A =_{\#} (123 : 145)$ – A is constrained to the documents that have instances of the correspondent actions

6 Conclusions and Future Work

A methodology to automatically create ontologies and ontology instances from general documents was proposed. The methodology uses a syntactical analyser to obtain sentence parse trees and XSL transformations to obtain partial semantic analysis. From these semantic analysis it is possible to extract triples of subject-verb-objects. These triples are used to define and to create instances of entities and actions. The obtained ontology and the inferred instances are represented in the OWL language and are used to enrich the initial documents.

On the other hand, translators from OWL into ISCO/Prolog were developed and the ISCO/Prolog inference engine may be used to answer queries about the documents content.

At present, the system is in a prototype phase and it needs work in many areas:

- Ontology creation. The ontology was created automatically but it was not possible to create many hierarchical relations between the classes. In order to be able to define these relations we intend to have two approaches:
  - Create connections with existent ontologies
  - Manually define ontologies for specific sub domains
- Normalisation of concepts. The parsing process does not eliminate all duplicate or incorrect entities.
- OWL translation into ISCO/Prolog. A full translation of the OWL language needs to be implemented.
- Evaluation. The system needs to be evaluated and to be tested by users. System performance must be quantified for different sets of documents.

References

1. Salvador Abreu. Isco: A practical language for heterogeneous information system construction. In *Proceedings of INAP'01*, Tokyo, Japan, October 2001. INAP.
2. Eckhard Bick. *The Parsing System "Palavras". Automatic Grammatical Analysis of Portuguese in a Constraint Grammar Framework.* Aarhus University Press, 2000.
3. Caroline Gasperin, Renata Vieira, Rodrigo Goulart, and Paulo Quaresma. Extracting xml syntactic chunks from portuguese corpora. In *TALN'2003 – Workshop on Natural Language Processing of Minority Languages and Small Languages of the Conference on "Traitement Automatique des Langues Naturelles"*, Batz-sur-Mer, France, June 2003.
4. H. Kamp and U. Reyle. *From Discourse to Logic.* Kluwer, Dordrecht, 1993.
5. O. Lassila and R. Swick. *Resource Description Framework (RDF) – Model and Syntax Specification.* W3C, 1999.
6. Paulo Quaresma and Irene Pimenta Rodrigues. A natural language interface for information retrieval on semantic web documents. In E. Menasalvas, J. Segovia, and P. Szczepaniak, editors, *AWIC'2003 – Atlantic Web Intelligence Conference*, Lecture Notes in Artificial Intelligence LNCS/LNAI 2663, pages 142–154, Madrid, Spain, May 2003. Springer-Verlag.
7. José Saias and Paulo Quaresma. Semantic enrichment of a web legal information retrieval system. In T. Bench-Capon, A. Daskalopulu, and R. Winkels, editors, *JURIX'2002 – Fifteenth Annual International Conference on Legal Knowledge and Information Systems*, volume 89 of *Frontiers in AI and Applications*, pages 11–20, London, UK, Dezember 2002. IOS Press.
8. José Saias and Paulo Quaresma. Using nlp techniques to create legal ontologies in a logic programming based web information retrieval system. In *Workshop on Legal Ontologies and Web based legal information management of the 9th International Conference on Artificial Intelligence and Law*, Edinburgh, Scotland, June 2003.
9. Michael Smith, Chris Welty, and Deborah McGuinness. Owl web ontology language guide. Technical report, www.daml.org, 2003. http://www.w3.org/TR/owl-guide/.
10. www.daml.org. *DAML+OIL – DARPA Agent Markup Language*, 2000.

A Preliminary Approach to the Multilabel Classification Problem of Portuguese Juridical Documents

Teresa Gonçalves and Paulo Quaresma

Departamento de Informática,
Universidade de Évora,
7000 Évora, Portugal
{tcg,pq}@di.uevora.pt

Abstract. Portuguese juridical documents from Supreme Courts and the Attorney General's Office are manually classified by juridical experts into a set of classes belonging to a taxonomy of concepts.
In this paper, a preliminary approach to develop techniques to automatically classify these juridical documents, is proposed. As basic strategy, the integration of natural language processing techniques with machine learning ones is used. Support Vector Machines (SVM) are used as learning algorithm and the obtained results are presented and compared with other approaches, such as C4.5 and Naïve Bayes.

1 Introduction

Automatic classification of documents is an important problem in many domains. For instance, it is needed by web search engines and information retrieval systems in order to organize the text bases into sets of semantic categories.

In order to develop better algorithms for document classification it is necessary to integrate research from several areas, such as machine learning, natural language processing and information retrieval.

A methodology for the automatic classification of documents is proposed and applied to a set of documents written in the European Portuguese language. This methodology integrates:

- Machine learning algorithms, namely, a kernel-based learning algorithm – Support Vector Machines;
- Natural language processing techniques, such as, lemmatization (transforming each word inito its lemma without Portuguese symbols) and part-of-speech tagging;
- Information retrieval techniques, such as the use of stop words, the representation of documents as bag-of-words and evaluation procedures.

Since the work of Joachims [4] it is known that Support Vector Machines (SVM) perform quite well compared with other approaches to the text classification problem. In his approach, documents are represented as bag-of-words

Fernando Moura Pires, Salvador Abreu (Eds.): EPIA 2003, LNAI 2902, pp. 435–444, 2003.

(without word order information) [8] and some words are not represented (words belonging to the set of the so called "stop words"). Then, a kernel based learning algorithm is applied (SVM [2]) and the results are evaluated using error measures and information retrieval ones.

In this paper, we follow Joachims' proposal, applying it to the set of Portuguese juridical documents from the Attorney General's Office. This set is composed by 7089 documents and it is being manually classified by juridical experts into a set of concepts from a law taxonomy. However, our proposal is quite distinct from Joachim's work because we aim to prove the importance of linguistic information in the classification problem. At present, we are only using part-of-speech information to eliminate words from the bag-of-words but we intend to use syntactical and semantical information and to propose and evaluate specific kernels (following the ideas of word sequence kernels [1]).

The SVM classification results are analyzed and compared with other machine learning algorithms, such as C4.5 and Naïve Bayes, through the accurate rate (Acc %) and information retrieval measures (K and *true* and *false* F-measures).

In section 2 our classification problem is described and characterized. In section 3 a brief description of the Support Vector Machines theory is presented. Section 4 describes our experiments and evaluates the results. Finally, in section 5, some conclusions and future work are pointed out.

2 Text Classification

Our goal is to automatically classify documents written in the European Portuguese language into sets of concepts. This problem is usually called a multi-label classification because each document can be classified into multiple concepts/topics.

The typical approach to the multi-label classification problem is to divide it into a set of binary classification problems, where each concept is considered independently. In this way, the initial problem is reduced to solve several binary classification problems.

Binary classification problems can be characterized by the inference of a classification rule assigning one of two possible values $(-1, 1)$ to each document. A value of -1 means the document does not belong to the concept and a value of 1 means that it belongs to it.

In this work we are using the set of documents from the Portuguese Attorney General's Office (in portuguese, Procuradoria Geral da República – PGR)[1]. These documents represent the decisions of the Attorney General's Office since 1940 and they define a set with cardinality 7089 and around 96MB of characters. All documents were manually classified by juridical experts into a set of classes belonging to a taxonomy of law concepts with around 6000 terms. However, a preliminary evaluation showed that only around 3000 terms are used in the multi-label classification.

[1] These documents can be found at the PGR site (http://www.pgr.pt)

As final goal we intend to develop a binary classification model for each concept but, for the scope of this work, we have only dealt with the top 50 most used concepts. As an example, we present the top five concepts and its frequency:

- pgr_2572: deficiente das forcas armadas (647)
- pgr_1391: pensao por servicos excepcionais e relevantes (539)
- pgr_744: aposentacao (494)
- pgr_16: funcionario publico (404)
- pgr_1877: competencia (358)

Another important open problem is the representation of the documents. In this preliminary work, we will use the standard vector representation [8], where each document is represented as a bag-of-words and where order information is lost and no syntactical or semantical information is used. As future work, we intend to explore the use of word order and to use syntactic and semantic information in the classification.

Nevertheless, PGR documents were pre-processed in order to obtain the part-of-speech tags for each word (its morpho-syntactical information) and to transform each word in its lemma (for instance, each verb is transformed into its infinitive form and each noun to the singular form). This work is done using the results of a previous project, PGR project, which aimed to develop an intelligent information retrieval system for PGR decisions [6]. In this project, a lexical database – POLARIS – is used to perform the lemmatization and the part-of-speech (POS) tagging is done with this lexical database and a neural network.

Using the POS tags we were able to eliminate words with non relevant information, such as, articles and prepositions, and with the lemmatization procedure it was also possible to reduce the number of distinct words. As final result, we obtained a total of 38703 distinct words. In section 4, some experiments done trying to reduce the number of words (features) are described.

3 Support Vector Machines

In this section a brief introduction to kernel classifiers and support vector machines is presented[2]. More detailed information can be obtained in several specialized books, such as [9,3].

Kernel learning algorithms are based on theoretical work on statistical learning theory, namely the structural risk minimization [11,10].

A binary classifier is a function from an input space X into the set of binary labels $\{-1,+1\}$. A supervised learning algorithm is a function assigning, to each labeled training set, a binary classifier

$$h : X \rightarrow \{-1,+1\} \tag{1}$$

[2] This introduction is based on a similar section in [1]

Whenever X is a vector space, a simple binary classifier is given by:

$$h(x) = sign(< w, x > +b) \tag{2}$$

where $< .,. >$ stands for the vector dot-product.

Learning the linear classifier is equivalent to finding values for w and b, which maximize an evaluation measure.

Linear classifiers fail when the boundary between the two classes is not linear. In this situation the approach followed is to project X into a new feature space F and to try to define a linear separation between the two classes in F. If the projection function is defined by $\phi : X \rightarrow F$ then the linear classifier is:

$$h(x) = sign(< w, \phi(x) > +b) \tag{3}$$

Support Vector Machines (SVM) are specific learning algorithms for linear classifiers, trying to obtain values for w and b. In SVM w is assumed to be defined as a linear combination of the projections of the training data:

$$w = \sum_{i=1}^{l} y_i \alpha_i \phi(x_i) \tag{4}$$

where α_i is the weight of the training example i with input x_i and label y_i.

The optimal weights are the solution of a high dimensional quadratic problem, which can be expressed in terms of the dot product of the projection of the training data $< \phi(x_i), \phi(x_j) >$.

It was proved that it is not necessary to map the input data into the feature space F, as long as it is defined a kernel function $K : X * X \rightarrow R$, such that $K(x, y) =< \phi(x), \phi(y) >$. This is known as the *kernel trick*. On the other hand Mercer's theorem [3] states that any positive semi-definite symmetric function corresponds to some mapping in some space and it is a valid kernel.

In the scope of this work only linear kernels are used and each document is represented by a vector where each dimension value stands for the frequency of a specific word in that document. As future work we intend to propose and evaluate specific kernels trying to take into account linguistic knowledge.

4 Experiments

As it was referred in the previous sections, the SVM learning algorithm was applied to the problem of multi-label classification of the Portuguese Attorney General's Office decisions.

The text base is composed by 7089 documents and the number of existent distinct words was reduced through the application of part-of-speech tagging techniques and through the lemmatization of every word. In this way it was possible to exclude non-relevant words, such as, articles and prepositions and to reduce distinct forms of every word to its lemma (verbal forms to the infinitive form; noun forms to the singular, masculine form). As final result, we obtained a set of 38703 distinct words. After the selection of the relevant words, each document was represented by a vector having 38703 dimensions where each value stands for the occurrence's frequency of the correspondent word in the document.

The 6000 classification labels/concepts were sorted in a decrescent number of occurrences in the documents and the top concepts were selected for the application of learning algorithms (section 2 presents the top five concepts).

4.1 Feature Reduction

The first experiment was to evaluate the overall results of the SVM for the top concepts and to evaluate the impact of the reduction of features/words in the algorithm. The idea behind this reduction was to try to reduce the algorithm complexity without loosing performance. In fact, 38703 attributes is a large number and it creates some computational problems to the learning algorithms.

The reduction was done by eliminating words that appear in less than a specific number of documents. For instance, $R55$ means that all words appearing in less than 55 documents were eliminated.

The results for the top concept were the following (we used a 10-fold cross-validation evaluation procedure and all experiments were done using the WEKA software package [12] from Waikato University[3] with default parameters for all experiments):

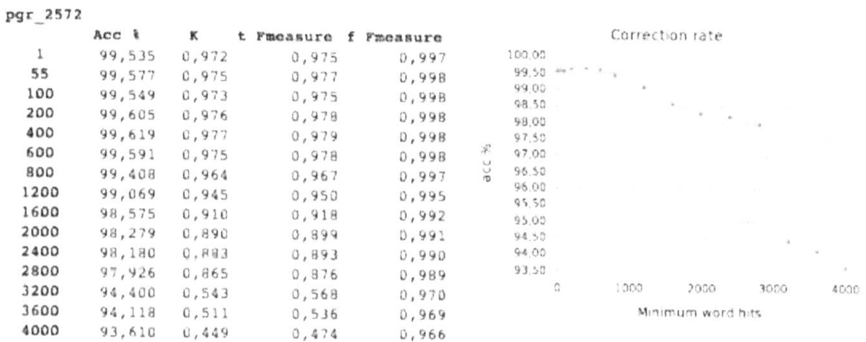

pgr_2572	Acc %	K	t Fmeasure	f Fmeasure
1	99,535	0,972	0,975	0,997
55	99,577	0,975	0,977	0,998
100	99,549	0,973	0,975	0,998
200	99,605	0,976	0,978	0,998
400	99,619	0,977	0,979	0,998
600	99,591	0,975	0,978	0,998
800	99,408	0,964	0,967	0,997
1200	99,069	0,945	0,950	0,995
1600	98,575	0,910	0,918	0,992
2000	98,279	0,890	0,899	0,991
2400	98,180	0,883	0,893	0,990
2800	97,926	0,865	0,876	0,989
3200	94,400	0,543	0,568	0,970
3600	94,118	0,511	0,536	0,969
4000	93,610	0,449	0,474	0,966

Fig. 1. Results for concept *pgr_2572*

Note the high results obtained for the classification – 99.5% accurate classifications. Quite good are also the results for the F-measure of the class *true* and the class *false*. F-measure is a standard information retrieval measure, which combines the precision and the recall measures [8]. Precision and recall are calculated from the contingency table of the classification (prediction vs manual

[3] http://www.cs.waikato.ac.nz/ml/weka

classification). Precision is given by the number of correct classified documents divided by the number of documents classified into the class. Recall is given by the number of correct classified documents divided by the number of documents belonging to the class. K-measure is also an important measure, which tries to obtain the degree of concordance between the two classifiers (manual and SVM). It is commonly accepted that a value of K higher than 0.7 stands for a relevant degree of concordance.

From the analysis of the results it appears that the first 6 experiments had no significant loss of performance. This is a quite interesting and important result because, for instance, $R55$ has only 5388 attributes and $R600$ has only 1518 attributes!

In order to test this hypothesis we performed similar experiments for the next top concepts (we will only show here the results for the next two top concepts).

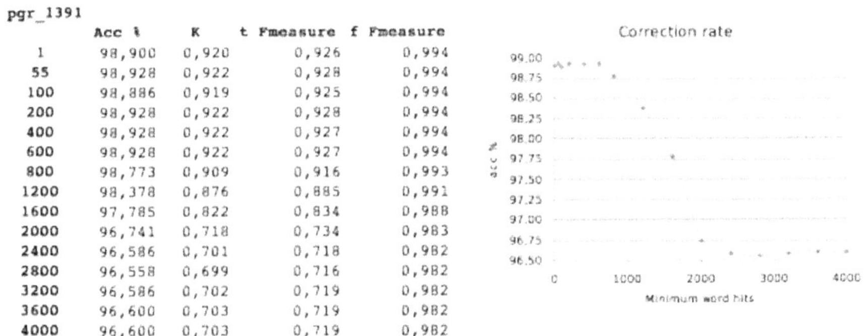

pgr_1391

	Acc %	K	t Fmeasure	f Fmeasure
1	98,900	0,920	0,926	0,994
55	98,928	0,922	0,928	0,994
100	98,886	0,919	0,925	0,994
200	98,928	0,922	0,928	0,994
400	98,928	0,922	0,927	0,994
600	98,928	0,922	0,927	0,994
800	98,773	0,909	0,916	0,993
1200	98,378	0,876	0,885	0,991
1600	97,785	0,822	0,834	0,988
2000	96,741	0,718	0,734	0,983
2400	96,586	0,701	0,718	0,982
2800	96,558	0,699	0,716	0,982
3200	96,586	0,702	0,719	0,982
3600	96,600	0,703	0,719	0,982
4000	96,600	0,703	0,719	0,982

Fig. 2. Results for concept *pgr_1391*

As figure 2 shows, the classifier for concept pgr_1391 has a similar behavior (only after $R600$ decreases performance) but its results are not so good.

Concept *pgr_744* (figure 3) shows a quite different behavior. The percentage of correct classified documents is high (although not so high as the previous concepts) but the K and F_{true} measures are quite low. These results show the importance of these information retrieval measures in the evaluation of document classifiers. One possible origin of these problems is the fact that we have much more negative examples (around 90%) than positive (around 10%). The consequences of this situation is that even the simpler classifier (assigning always the negative class) obtains 90% correct results but it will get a low value for the IR measures.

Figure 4 shows the contingency table for the four top concepts. Table lines show the values for the manual classification and table columns show the values obtained by the classifier. For instance, line 2, column 1, represents the number of documents classified as *true* by the classifier, which belong to the *false* class.

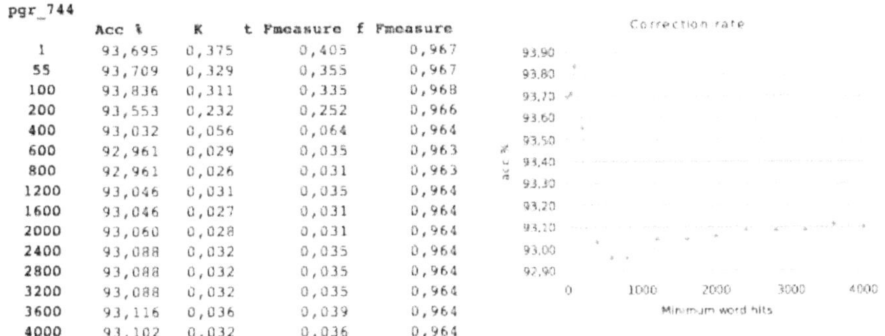

pgr_744	Acc %	K	t Fmeasure	f Fmeasure
1	93,695	0,375	0,405	0,967
55	93,709	0,329	0,355	0,967
100	93,836	0,311	0,335	0,968
200	93,553	0,232	0,252	0,966
400	93,032	0,056	0,064	0,964
600	92,961	0,029	0,035	0,963
800	92,961	0,026	0,031	0,963
1200	93,046	0,031	0,035	0,964
1600	93,046	0,027	0,031	0,964
2000	93,060	0,028	0,031	0,964
2400	93,088	0,032	0,035	0,964
2800	93,088	0,032	0,035	0,964
3200	93,088	0,032	0,035	0,964
3600	93,116	0,036	0,039	0,964
4000	93,102	0,032	0,036	0,964

Fig. 3. Results for concept *pgr_744*

pgr_2572	ct	cf
t	633	14
f	16	6426

pgr_744	ct	cf
t	123	371
f	75	6520

pgr_1391	ct	cf
t	487	52
f	24	6526

pgr_16	ct	cf
t	5	399
f	32	6653

Fig. 4. Contingency table for the top 4 concepts

As it can be seen, concepts *pgr_744* and *pgr_16* show a high level of false negatives and, as a consequence, the IR measures are quite low. Further work needs to be done in order to explain why some concepts are modeled so well by the linear SVM and others perform so poorly.

As a consequence of these experiments, we decided to focus our work in the $R55$ documents (documents represented by the words that appear in at least 55 documents) because they showed no loss of performance and they have a smaller complexity (5388 attributes versus 38703 attributes for $R1$).

4.2 SVM Evaluation

As explained in the previous section we focused our experiments in the $R55$ set of documents and, in this section, we will evaluate the obtained results against two other standard learning methods: Naïve Bayes and the decision-tree C4.5 classifier.

Naïve Bayes classifiers uses a probabilistic model of text to estimate the probability of a document d to be in class $y - P(y|d)$. However, in order to make the estimation of parameters possible, some assumptions are made. For instance, words are assumed to occur independently of the other words in documents, given its class. Moreover, all documents associated with a particular class are assumed to be modeled accordingly with a unique model for that category. Naïve Bayes classifiers try to maximize $P(y|d)$ using these assumptions and the well-known

Bayes rule for conditional probabilities (see, for instance, [5] for a description of experiments using Naïve Bayes classifiers).

C4.5 [7] is one of the most well-known decision tree classifiers and it has shown good results in a quite diversity of classification problems. We have used the WEKA Java latest version – J48 – with its default parameters.

Figure 5 shows the results obtained for the top concepts (accurate rate and computation time in a P4 at 2.8GHz with 1GB RAM).

pgr_2572

test set			time consumed		
SMO	NaiveBayes	J48	SMO	NaiveBayes	J48
99,577	25,081	99,619	11m	41m	4h10m

pgr_1391

test set			time consumed		
SMO	NaiveBayes	J48	SMO	NaiveBayes	J48
98,928	26,661	99,267	7m	38m	8h11m

Fig. 5. Classification comparison

From these results it is quite clear that Naïve Bayes classifier performs quite worse than the other two classifiers: 25-26% vs 98-99%! The computation time showed also quite different values: from a minimum of 7 minutes (SVM) to a maximum of 8 hours (J48).

For this reason we have excluded Naïve Bayes classifier from the other experiments.

Our next experiment was to evaluate and to compare the results for the $R55$ document classification using SVM and C4.5/J48. Figure 6 shows the results obtained for the top-5 concepts.

	SMO				J48			
	acc %	K	t Fmeasure	f Fmeasure	acc %	K	t Fmeasure	f Fmeasure
pgr_2572	99,577	0,975	0,977	0,998	99,619	0,977	0,979	0,998
pgr_1391	98,928	0,922	0,928	0,994	99,267	0,948	0,951	0,996
pgr_744	93,709	0,329	0,461	0,973	94,738	0,592	0,620	0,972
pgr_16	93,920	0,013	0,023	0,969	93,144	0,267	0,302	0,964
pgr_1877	94,555	0,138	0,157	0,972	93,441	0,218	0,251	0,966

Fig. 6. SVM vs. J48

After analyzing the results it is possible to conclude that the overall correction rate is similar (although a little bit better for J48) but J48 statistics for K and F_{true} are better for the worst classified concepts. This values can be explained by the capability of J48 to build quite complex models with decision trees with many levels. However, it is important to point out that the temporal complexity of C4.5/J48 is much higher than SVM algorithms (10min vs. 8 hours) and the worst SVM classification models remain bad classification models in C4.5/J48.

As a conclusion of this evaluation section, we may point out that SVM linear learning algorithms for documents written in the Portuguese language showed to be, a least, as good as the two other learning algorithms (Naïve Bayes and C4.5) and they produced quite good results.

Similar results were already obtained for other sets of documents, such as the Reuters [4]. Nevertheless, our results showed to be better than the results obtained by Joachims in his experiments. Further work needs to be done in order to explain these differences.

5 Conclusions and Future Work

A methodology for the automatic classification of the Portuguese documents from the Attorney General's Office was proposed. The methodology tries to integrate machine learning algorithms (SVM) with natural language processing tools (part-of-speech tagging and lemmatization) and information retrieval techniques (stop words, documents as bag-of-words, evaluation measures).

The obtained results showed to be, at least, equivalent with similar approaches and they proved to be adequated for the Portuguese language and for the law domain.

As future work, we intend to evaluate our approach against standard document sets, such as the Reuters set. In this way, we will be able to fully compare our results with others researchers' results.

Nevertheless, for some concepts, the obtained results were not quite good and further work needs to be done in order to explain them and to improve the classifiers. Our hypothesis is that these classifiers need more powerful document representations. As a consequence, we intend to use more linguistic knowledge in the document representation, namely, moving from a vector-based representation into a structured syntactical and/or semantical representation. This document representation change will have, as a consequence, the need for new and more adapted kernels.

References

1. N. Cancedda, E. Gaussier, C. Goutte, and J. Renders. Word sequence kernels. *Journal of Machine Learning Research*, 3:1059–1082, 2003.
2. C. Cortes and V. Vapnik. Support-vector networks. *Machine Learning*, 20(3):273–297, 1995.
3. N. Cristianini and J. Shawe-Taylor. *Support Vector Machines*. Cambridge University Press, 2000.
4. Thorsten Joachims. *Learning to Classify Text Using Support Vector Machines*. Kluwer academic Publishers, 2002.
5. A. McCallum and K. Nigam. A comparison of event models for naive bayes text classification. In *Learning for text categorization Workshop of the ICML/AAAI-98 conference*. AAAI Press, 1998.

6. Paulo Quaresma and Irene Pimenta Rodrigues. PGR: Portuguese attorney general's office decisions on the web. In Bartenstein, Geske, Hannebauer, and Yoshie, editors, *Web-Knowledge Management and Decision Support*, Lecture Notes in Artificial Intelligence LNCS/LNAI 2543, pages 51–61. Springer-Verlag, 2003.
7. R. Quinlan. *C4.5: Programs for Machine Learning*. Morgan Kaufmann, 1993.
8. G. Salton and M. McGill. *Introduction to Modern Informatin Retrieval*. McGraw-Hill, 1983.
9. B. Schölkopf and A. Smola. *Learning with Kernels*. MIT Press, 2002.
10. V. Vapnik. *Estimation of Dependencies based on Empirical Data*. Springer, 1982.
11. V. Vapnik. *The nature of statistical learning theory*. Springer, 1995.
12. I. Witten and E. Frank. *Data Mining: Practical machine learning tools with Java implementations*. Morgan Kaufmann, 1999.

Synonymy for Query Expansion in Information Search

Rove Chishman, Renata Vieira, Isa Mara Alves, and Sandro Rigo

Universidade do Vale do Rio dos Sinos
{rove, isa}@icaro.unisinos.br, {renata, rigo}@exatas.unisinos.br

Abstract. This paper presents our work towards the use of domain ontology for information search in university web sites. We evaluate the adequacy of semantic relations for query expansion. We discuss, in particular, synonymy and its role in information search on specific domains.

1 Introduction

One of the main challenges for search systems is the matching of user's information need with the most relevant documents in a collection. In our work we are developing a search system that makes use of Portuguese domain ontology. Our ontology is related to university domain, and we are investigating the appropriateness of query expansion for searching the university web site on the basis of this ontology. In this paper we discuss, in particular, problems related with the specification of synonymy relations in an ontology built with such purpose.

2 An Ontology for the University Domain

Our study is focused on the university domain. Often, in this domain, different terms can specify the same entity (such as *teacher* and *lecturer*; *center* and *department*). When considering different university web sites, this problem may be worsened due to local choices of terms. Ontologies provide accurate definitions of terms and allow the automatic use of them. In the context of web information search, the application of our interest, we can consider conceptual similarity in search mechanisms on the basis of an ontology [2].

In our work we are developing both a search system supported by an ontology and the ontology itself, which is in Portuguese. For the terms selection we considered a) the most frequent key-words typed by users when using the university search system; b) knowledge about the organization structure of the university and c) specific documents that describe university courses in terms of their goals, programs, evaluation criteria, teaching methodology and bibliography. These sources lead us to domain terms such as *lecturer, course, subject, university, center, student, units, departments, people* or *services*. Once the initial vocabulary was defined, the explicit description was based on the relational semantics [3], [6] and the Theory of the Generative Lexicon [9]. Wordnet [5] was used for the initial study of meronymy,

Fernando Moura Pires, Salvador Abreu (Eds.): EPIA 2003, LNAI 2902, pp. 445–449, 2003.

holonymy, hyponymy and hypernymy relations for our terms. Following [3], we considered *part-of* relations as a general denomination for relations such as *member*, *section* or *segment*. The telic role, that defines the purpose of a lexical item, was applied to terms such as *lecturer, rector, researcher*, by describing their typical activity. A *lecturer* for instance is associated to teaching events, together with their arguments: course, time, room, etc.

The identification of synonyms enriches the semantic network. These relations are relevant for query expansion in search systems, since usually the term that the user has in mind is not the same one in the web site documents. In other words, the inclusion of synonymous terms in the ontology allows the system to associate new terms to the term informed by the user. The definition of synonymy and its appropriateness for information search, however, is not a simple question. In the next section we discuss it in detail.

3 The Adequacy of Synonymy Relations for Information Search

Our study is intended to enlarge the list of terms in the ontology by providing synonymous relevant terms. Some terms may be equivalent in some contexts but not in others. The fact is that the more traditional of the semantic relations has not a straightforward definition. Comparing the definitions given in the literature, we realize that there is consensus in at least two aspects: (i) synonymy depends on the context in which terms are used and (ii) it is impossible to find absolute synonymy if the significance of a term is the set of linguistic contexts in which it can occur.

In [6] the idea of relative synonymy is proposed: two expressions are synonymous in a context C if the substitution of one for the other in C does not change the truth-value. That is the definition that better applies to the semantic relation holding between *cadeira* and *disciplina* considering the context of our application. It also allows us to exclude terms like *lente* (archaic form of academic teacher) found in the dictionary [7].

With the intention of introducing the idea of continuity, and avoiding the dichotomy between synonyms and non-synonyms, other expressions started to be used: sense similarity, semantic distance or semantic similarity. The advantage is to be able to consider the notion of typicality, including intermediary values of semantic similarity. A conception for synonymy based on degrees is proposed in [1]. Identification of synonymy is conditioned to the identification of necessary similarities and permissible differences. Alsation and spaniel, for example, have a high degree of semantic overlap, but they are not synonymous. Synonyms should have a low degree of implicit contrast. In other words, the semantic similarities should be more salient than the differences, what does not occur in the pair alsation-spaniel, which, actually, represent a relation of co-hyponymy in relation to the hypernym dog.

Based on these propositions, we elaborated two tests in order to determine what set of synonymous terms should be included in the ontology. One of them considers the consensual idea about the synonymy reliance on the context in which words are used. It considers a substitution test, but which also has the objective of identifying synonymy degrees. The basic strategy consists in testing synonymous sets of terms extracted from the university web site in appropriate contexts.

As an initial experiment of application of our test, we check in the dictionary [4], [8] the synonyms for some representative classes of the ontology. We also look for the synonyms used as key words in the log of the search, because we intend to make the ontology sensitive to the vocabulary used in the domain.

As an illustration of our approach consider the following sets: a) *Professor: educador, instrutor, mestre, mentor, lente, docente*; b) *Aluno: estudante, acadêmico, colegial, discípulo, educando*. Sentences from the university web site are used for the context test: we replace the original term by its synonyms and present it to native speakers to judge the appropriateness of the resulting sentence according to a scale (0,1,2,3). We consider that non-linguistic information that the participants of the research have about the university domain also influences the analysis. Therefore, we are considering context here in a wide sense. The procedure was applied to 6 native speakers. Table 1 shows the individual ratings and the average ratings of native speakers judgments of substitution adequacy. We present first the sentence used as context, then the table with the results.

Context: *Após o primeiro contato do cliente com a Unicon, busca-se um professor orientador que se enquadre no perfil da consultoria e os alunos, na que tenham os pré-requisitos exigidos para a realização das atividades.*

Context: *O aluno é responsável por todas as etapas dos projetos, do primeiro contato com o cliente até sua conclusão.*

Table 1. Context test

Professor	Ratings	Avarage	Aluno	Ratings	Avarage
Docente	2-3-3-1-3-2	2,3	Acadêmico	2-3-3-2-3-3	2,6
Educador	1-1-2-3-3-1	1,8	Estudante	2-3-3-3-2-3	2,6
Mestre	1-1-3-3-1-0	1,5	Discente	2-3-3-2-2-1	2,1
Mentor	2-1-0-3-0-0	1	Educando	1-2-3-1-2-2	1,8
Instrutor	1-0-1-2-1-0	0,8	Colegial	1-1-3-3-1-0	1,5
Lente	2-0-0-1-0-0	0,5	Discípulo	1-0-3-1-0-0	0,8

As the context test is not completely efficient, because it does not exclude hyponyms, co-hyponymy or hiperonyms, like *docente* and *instrutor* (staff and lecturer), for example, we apply a second test to those pairs rated above 1,5, the symmetry test, taking the pairs of terms and verifying de adequacy of the statements *X is a Y and Y is a X,* for each pair *X,Y* (see Table 2).

The accomplishment of that two tests lead us to determine in a more discerning way which synonym terms are relevant to our semantic domain. We start by a set of synonymous terms considered in wide sense, extracted from thesaurus, and concluded with the synonyms identification in strict domain relevant sense.

For the cases above, we have the following sets of terms with average rating greater or equal to 1,5 which also pass the symmetry test with true values equal to or greater than false): a) *Professor: docente* (2,3), *educador* (1,8); b) *Aluno: acadêmico* (2,6), *estudante* (2,6), *educando* (1,8).

Table 2. Simetry test

Professor	(T/F)	Aluno	(T/F)	Aluno	(T/F)
Docente	6/0	Acadêmico	4/2	Educando	5/1
Educador	4/2	Estudante	5/1	Colegial	2/4
Mestre	2/4	Discente	2/4		

4 Expanded Search

In order to validate the use of our ontology in the search system, a prototype was developed. The prototype provides query expansion by consulting an ontology codified in OWL (Ontology Web Language). Synonymous terms can be described by *equivalentClass* definition in OWL. In order to discover similar terms that can be of interest to the user, an access to the OWL description of the synonymous terms is performed. The expanded search is submitted to the search engine and the documents containing the synonymous terms are obtained. The access to the ontology is implemented with the use of Jena[1]. Since we use a Java API, the Apache Tomcat[2] servlet container was chosen in order to support the prototype. We ran a few tests on the university web site, as illustrated in the tables below. We show the number of returned documents for each term (RD), an analysis of the adequacy of the first 10 returned documents (10F) and their relation with the results of the context (CT) and symmetry tests (ST).

Table 3. Expanded query

Terms	RD	10F	CT	ST T/F	Terms	RD	10F	CT	ST T/F
Professor	1550	10	-	-	Aluno	1670	10	-	-
Docente	309	10	2,3	6/0	Estudante	163	10	2,6	5/1
Mestre	231	2	1,5	2/4	Educando	74	10	1,8	5/1
Educador	153	10	1,8	4/2	Acadêmico	5	5	2,6	4/2
Lente	20	0	0,5	-	Discente	64	10	2,1	2/4
Instrutor	18	6	0,8	-	Colegial	3	0	1,5	2/4
Mentor	8	2	1	-	Discípulo	0	0	0,8	2/4

In Table 3 we can see for the term *professor* that the three higher rated terms in the context set (*docente, mestre, educador*) result in a greater impact on recall. There is a precision loss for the tem *mestre,* which corresponds to a lower rating in the symmetry test. For *aluno,* again, we can see a relation between higher recall and higher rating in both tests. In one case, however, the impact in recall was not very representative: for the term *acadêmico* only other 5 documents were returned, the precision however was 100%. As a result of this test if we consider the terms passing the two tests, we have: a) *Professor, docente* (2,3), *educador* (1,8): greater recall with 100% precision; b) *Aluno, acadêmico* (2,6), *estudante* (2,6), *educando* (1,8): greater

[1] available at http://www.hpl.hp.com/semweb/index.html
[2] available at http://jakarta.apache.org/tomcat/

recall with 100% precision. In general the terms passing the test show an improvement in the search results.

5 Concluding Remarks

In this paper we have discussed the use of an ontology as an aid to information search, in special we investigate the adequacy of synonymy as a valuable semantic relation to expand search queries. Other works have shown problems when using pure thesaurus based query expansion for information retrieval, an example is [8]. In this paper we bring an explanation for these problems and we propose a method for tailoring such information for search in specific domains. To make the synonymy specification in the ontology useful for query expansion we propose the application of context and symmetry tests to identify synonymous groups. This proposal is feasible since we are limiting the scope of our search engine to specific domain web sites (as is the case of our university web site). Our tests show that the better valued terms in the context and symmetry tests had a higher impact in recall and precision. In order to improve search results, the applicability of the synonymous terms may be indicated, as a result an analysis as presented in this paper, and this can be used in the ranking of the returned documents. An additional feature to be developed and tested is the treatment of the inheritance between the synonymous terms.

Acknowledgments. The group is financed by CAPES/GRICES, FAPERGS and CNPq. We would like to thank Lilian T. Figueiró for the help with the tests.

References

1. Cruse, A.: *Lexical semantics*. Cambridge: Cambridge Univ. Press (1986)
2. Erdmann, M. et al.: From manual to semi-automatic semantic annotation: About ontology-based text annotation tools. In Buitelaar, P. Hasida, K. (eds), *Proceedings of the COLING2000* (2000)
3. Evens, M. (ed.): *Relational Models of the Lexicon*, Cambridge University Press, Cambridge (1998)
4. Houaiss, A.: *Dicionário da Língua Portuguesa*. Objetiva, Rio de Janeiro (2001)
5. Miller, G.: Dictionaries in the mind. *Language and Cognitive Processes*, **1.3** (1986) 171–185
6. Miller, G., Fellbaum, C. Semantic network of English. *Cognition* **41** (1991) 197–229
7. Nascentes, A.: *Dicionário de Sinônimos*. Nova Fronteira, São Paulo (1981)
8. Pizzato, L., Strube, V.: Query Expansion based on Thesaurus Relations: Evaluation over Internet In: CICLing-2003, Computational Linguistics and Intelligent Text Processing, Cidade do México, México. *Lecture Notes in Computer Science N 2588* (2003)
9. Pustejovsky, J.: *The Generative Lexicon*. Cambridge University Press, Cambridge (1995)

Web Information Retrieval with Result Set Clustering*

Mário J. Silva and Bruno Martins

Departamento de Informática
Faculdade de Ciências da Universidade de Lisboa
1749-016 Lisboa, Portugal
mjs@di.fc.ul.pt, bmartins@xldb.di.fc.ul.pt

Abstract. Existing web IR systems where users have to describe information needs using terms and operators are not without problems. Particularly, they fail in helping users with information needs that are broad, vague, or hard to express through a set of keywords. This paper reports our work on enhancing a web search engine with a clustering interface. Our algorithm builds an index with the textual descriptions from search results and uses term subsumption to derive a cluster hierarchy.

1 Introduction

Web search engines and general information retrieval (IR) systems aim to find the documents that best satisfy user queries. In a typical system, users start by specifying an information need through a set of keywords and operators. The system then retrieves and ranks documents according to their similarity to the query, obtained through techniques that range from keyword matching to advanced graph connectivity analysis [8]. Finally, the resulting ranked list is presented. While experienced users can make effective use of typical search services, those systems are still not suited for a wide range of important tasks. Particularly, they fail in helping users with information needs that are broad, vague, or hard to express through a set of keywords.

With existing tools and given the dimension of the web, a typical query of one to three terms [9], often ambiguous, returns a list with thousands documents. Daunted with so much information, users take a glimpse at the first page of results and quickly give up the search process.

This paper reports our work on extending tumba! [15], a search engine specialized on the Portuguese web, with a clustering interface. By grouping retrieved documents together, basing on their similarities, we intend to improve results visualization through the separation of different thematic categories. This can help users both in locating interesting documents more easily and in getting an overview of the retrieved document set.

* Study partially supported by FCCN and FCT, under grants POSI/SRI/40193/2001 and SFRH/BD/10757/2002.

Fernando Moura Pires, Salvador Abreu (Eds.): EPIA 2003, LNAI 2902, pp. 450–454, 2003.

2 Concepts and Related Work

In IR, clustering is seen as the grouping together of similar documents to expedite information retrieval [11,19]. The cluster hypothesis of van Rijsbergen states that closely associated documents tend to be relevant to the same request, i.e. documents relevant to a given topic are more similar to each other than to non relevant documents [16].

Many document clustering algorithms rely on off-line clustering of the entire collection [13,2], but on the web the collection is too large and fluid to allow an off-line approach. Clustering should be applied to the much smaller set of documents returned in response to a query, a process known as on-line ephemeral clustering [7] or search results clustering. With clustering performed dynamically for each query, the discovered groups can depict the real structure of results and not predefined categories, this way clearly differentiating this from off-line clustering or classification.

Results clustering is not common on commercial search engines, with the notorious exception of Vivísimo[1] and its hierarchically sorted category folders. Sadly, the technology behind it is not public, but from our observations the system is very accurate and can be considered state-of-the-art in current research.

The first published query result clustering algorithm was presented in the Scatter-Gather system [3], using a hybrid approach involving both k-means [14] and hierarchical agglomerative clustering (HAC) [6]. HAC methods have been used for document clustering in IR with mixed success, but several reports indicate they are too slow and sensitive for use on the web.

With the Suffix Tree Clustering (STC) technique [20], the field of search results clustering gained popularity. STC works on the textual snippets returned by search engines as descriptions for the results to a query and builds a suffix tree within linear time on the number of snippets. Each internal node in this suffix tree captures a phrase, associating it with the respective snippets. After obtaining base clusters in this way, final clusters are generated by merging two base clusters if they share majority (more than 50%) members.

In [18], the authors questioned the applicability of STC to other languages. Results suggest that the properties of a language strongly affect performance and the authors argue high quality stemming [10] is a necessity. The use of n-grams [1] instead of phrases may be advantageous, as word order in some languages may be tricky and this way eliminates the need for stemming.

Other promising methods have been reported [17,4], but further experiments are needed in order to confirm their usefulness.

3 The Result Set Clustering Algorithm

The clustering algorithm that we implemented in tumba! [15] can be seen has six steps:

[1] http://vivisimo.com/

1. **Document retrieval** – Results for a given query are retrieved. From each document we take the title, the URL and a snippet from its textual content.
2. **Document cleaning** – The text strings representing each document (concatenation of title, URL and snippet) are processed. Sentence boundaries are identified via punctuation and HTML tags, redundant spaces are compressed and non-word tokens (numbers, HTML tags and punctuation) are stripped.
3. **Index building** – Strings are tokenized. Words separated with hyphens are considered as a single entity (a common characteristic of the Portuguese language.) We associate each "term" with the documents containing it through a structure resembling an inverted index. "Terms" are not just individual word tokens but also groups of two words which occur together and groups of 3 words with the middle one belonging to a list of typical "connectors" (for instance "cidade de lisboa" or "peças em cena" could be index terms). A stop-list is also used, containing not only the most frequent words in both English and Portuguese, but also Internet-specific words (e.g., "java" or "frames"). Terms appearing in too few or too many documents are also discarded, according to frequency thresholds.
4. **Building the subsumption hierarchy** – Clusters are formed hierarchically using a term co-occurrence measure called "subsumption" [12]. Each node is considered a cluster defined by a term. For two terms, x and y, x is said to subsume y if $P(x|y) = 1, P(y|x) < 1$. In other words, x subsumes y if the documents containing y are a subset of the documents containing x. Because x subsumes y and because it is has a higher document frequency, x becomes the ancestor of y in the resulting hierarchy. In practice, as the number of terms that adhere to this strict notion of subsumption is relatively small, the condition is relaxed as $P(x|y) >= 0.8, P(y|x) < 1$.
5. **Assigning documents to clusters** – A document is on a cluster if the representing textual string has the term that defines the cluster. For each node in the hierarchy, we lookup the index for the documents that contain its defining term and mark the association.
6. **Pruning results** – Pruning the resulting hierarchy is essential, as subsumption produces many meaningless clusters. This is done with simple heuristics like:
   - Only keep the association of a document to a node if the document cannot be assigned to one of the node's descendants.
   - Eliminate each node that only has one document and associate the document to the parent node.
   - If two nodes with the same parent have exactly the same documents as children, we only keep the node with the largest defining term.

Once clusters are formed, the user interface displays the resulting structure as an hierarchical organization of the documents in the result set, allowing users to expand and navigate items. Figure 1 shows a screen-shot of the system for a search on "fernando pessoa".

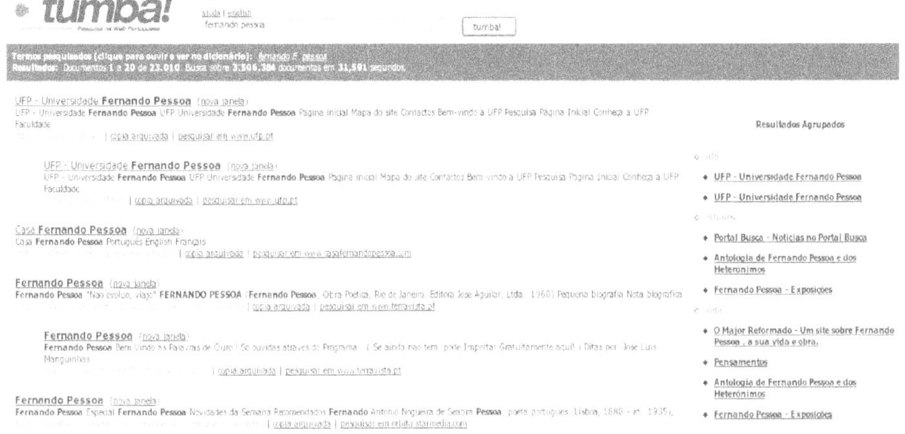

Fig. 1. Results for a search on "fernando pessoa".

4 Evaluation

Our evaluation studies are still at an early stage, but we have a good general road-map. There will be two main stages:

Tunning and evaluation of the algorithm – Search results (the first 50 hits) to 5 queries will serve as test data. Multi-topic queries (i.e. "java", "artificial", etc) will be chosen, so that a structure of clusters definitely exists. This data will then be clustered manually by 2 individuals and the final ground truth set of clusters for each query will result from discussion and unification of both results. For each query we will then apply the algorithm and compare the generated clusters to the ground truth, using a measure of quality based on information-theoretic *Entropy* [5], as used in [7].

Final evaluation – The system obtained by extending a typical search engine with clustering will be evaluated through a user survey. A few "personal" questions will be used to set apart different levels of expertise in web search. The actual evaluation will consist of a small set of questions with mixed difficulty levels, each reflecting an information need. The user is asked to find the answer to each question, mark the start and end-time spent on it, assess the confidence level in the answer and the usefulness of the new clustering interface versus the traditional one.

5 Conclusions

This paper presented the clustering functionality under development for tumba!.

Detailed analysis and interpretation of results is our next step, as well as further experimenting with different settings in the presentation interface. Comparisons with other known algorithms is also an objective for the near future.

Experiments so far have already given precious indications. The quality of the textual snippets is very important and special care should be taken in the selection, as it strongly influences results. A more advanced reduction of meaningless terms, during the index building stage, should also improve quality. In the future, this reduction could even go as far as discarding all non-nouns and non-verbs. Finally, we are also considering additional pruning heuristics for the last stage of the algorithm, in order to discard more meaningless clusters.

References

1. W. Cavnar and J. Trenkle. N-gram-based text categorization, 1994.
2. D. R. Cutting, D. R. Karger, and J. O. Pedersen. Constant interaction-time scatter/gather browsing of very large document collections, 1993.
3. D. R. Cutting, J. O. Pedersen, D. Karger, and J. W. Tukey. Scatter/gather: A cluster-based approach to browsing large document collections. In *Proceedings of the Fifteenth Annual International ACM SIGIR Conference on Research and Development in Information Retrieval*, pages 318–329, 1992.
4. Z. D. and D. Y. Hierarchical, online clustering of web search results. In *3rd International Workshop on Web information and data management*, 2001.
5. B. E. Dom. An information-theoretic external cluster-validity measure, 2001.
6. B. Everitt. *Cluster analysis.* Edward Arnold and Halsted Press, London, 1993.
7. Y. S. Maarek, R. Fagin, I. Z. Ben-Shaul, and D. Pelleg. Ephemeral document clustering for web applications, 2000.
8. L. Page, S. Brin, R. Motwani, and T. Winograd. The pagerank citation ranking: Bringing order to the web, 1998.
9. B. Pinkerton. Finding what people want: Experiences with the webcrawler, 1994.
10. M. F. Porter. An algorithm for suffix stripping. *Program*, 14(3):130–137, 1980.
11. E. Rasmussen. Clustering algorithms in information retrieval: Data structures and algorithms, 1992.
12. M. Sanderson and W. B. Croft. Deriving concept hierarchies from text. In *Research and Development in Information Retrieval*, pages 206–213, 1999.
13. H. Schutze and H. Silverstein. Projections for efficient document clustering, 1997.
14. M. I. Selim, S.Z. K-means-type algorithms: a generalized convergence theorem and characterization of local optimality, 1984.
15. M. J. Silva. The case for a portuguese web search engine. DI/FCUL TR 03–03, Department of Informatics, University of Lisbon, March 2003.
16. C. J. Van Rijsbergen. *Information Retrieval, 2nd edition.* Dept. of Computer Science, University of Glasgow, 1979.
17. Y. Wang and M. Kitsuregawa. Link based clustering of Web search results. *Lecture Notes in Computer Science*, 2118:225ff, 2001.
18. D. Weiss. A clustering interface for web search results in polish and english, 2001.
19. P. Willet. Recent trends in hierarchical document clustering: a critical review, 1988.
20. O. Zamir and O. Etzioni. Web document clustering: A feasibility demonstration. In *Research and Development in Information Retrieval*, pages 46–54, 1998.

ASdeCopas: A Syntactic-Semantic Interface*

Luísa Coheur[1,2], Nuno Mamede[1], and Gabriel G. Bès[2]

[1] L^2F INESC-ID/IST – Spoken Languages Systems Laboratory
{luisa.coheur,numo.mamede}@l2f.inesc-id.pt
[2] GRIL/Université Blaise-Pascal
Gabriel.Bes@univ-bpclermont.fr

Abstract. ASdeCopas is a syntactic-semantic parser, implemented in Prolog, which uses hierarchically organized order-independent rules. This paper focuses on the formalization of semantic rules, presenting the concepts of well-formed semantic rule, rules hierarchy, and the conditions for rules application. If two rules can apply, only the most specific one does so. Examples are given and some properties of the system are pointed out.

Keywords: Syntactic-semantic interface, semantic rules, rules hierarchy, 5P, Minimal Recursion Semantics

1 Introduction

ASdeCopas[1] is a syntactic-semantic parser that takes a graph representing the input sentence and returns a formula, according with a set of semantic rules. The paper focuses on the formalization of semantic rules. Section 2 describes ASdeCopas's input, semantic rules are formalized in section 3, section 4 presents simplified examples and section 5 lists some of the system properties and discusses perspectives on future work.

2 ASdeCopas's Input

Ideas, formalisms and data from the 5P paradigm [1,3,6,2] are followed/used to obtain ASdeCopas' input: a text with an associated graph. A graph is defined as follows (let C be a set of category labels, W a set of words and _ the empty field):

Definition 1. *Graph*
A graph is a pair $G = (\Delta, \Psi)$, *where:*
• Δ *is a set of nodes, each one noted* $node(w, c, p)$, *where* $w \in W$, $c \in C$ *and* $p \in \mathbb{N}$ *(p represents the node's position).*

* Paper supported by FCT (Fundação para a Ciência e Tecnologia).
[1] ASdeCopas stands for "Análise Semântica depois de Completada a análise sintáctica".

Fernando Moura Pires, Salvador Abreu (Eds.): EPIA 2003, LNAI 2902, pp. 455–459, 2003.

• *Ψ is a set of arrows, each arrow noted* $arrow(p_1, p_2)$, *where* $p_1, p_2 \in \mathbb{N}$ *(*p_1, p_2 *being the position of the source and the target, respectively).*
A well formed graph (wfg) verifies:
• $(\forall\ arrow(p_1, p_2) \in \Psi)(\exists\ node(w_1, c_2, ps_1), node(w_2, c_2, ps_2) \in \Delta)(p_1 = ps_1 \wedge p_2 = ps_2)$*(that is, each arrow connects existing nodes)*
• $(\forall\ arrow(p_1, p_2), arrow(p_3, p_4) \in \Psi)(p_1 = p_3 \Rightarrow p_2 = p_4)$*(that is, each node is the source of at most one arrow)*
• $(\forall\ node(w_1, c_1, p_1), node(w_2, c_2, p_2), node(w_3, c_3, p_3), node(w_4, c_4, p_4) \in \Delta)[(p_1 < p_2 < p_3 < p_4 \wedge (\exists\ arrow(p_1, p_3) \vee \exists\ arrow(p_3, p_1) \in \Psi)) \Rightarrow \neg(\exists\ arrow(p_2, p_4) \vee \exists\ arrow(p_4, p_2) \in \Psi)]$*(that is, no crossing of arrows is allowed)*

Each category is a set of attribute/value pairs[2], *i.e.*, feature structures hierarchically organized (see [1] for details). Notice that no constraint is set on the nature of those pairs: they can have a syntactic or a semantic motivation. Arrows are somehow related to dependencies, but, contrary to mainstream dependency theories, arrows go from dependents to the head [6]. Their motivation is simply to connect two elements, because the established relations are needed to reach the desired semantic representation (see [1,3] for extra details about this concept). An example of a graph is shown in the next figure, where *A pequena Maria* means *Little Mary*:

Fig. 1. Graph example.

3 Semantic Rules

Definitions 2 to 8 define the syntax of a well-formed semantic rule, while Definitions 9 to 11 define rules hierarchy and Definitions 12 and 13 rules applicability conditions.

Definition 2. *Element (to transform)*
An element has the form $e = elem(w, c)$, *where* $w \in \{\_\} \cup W$ *and* $c \in \{\_\} \cup C$.

Definition 3. *Arc*
An arc has the form $a = arc(c_1, c_2, d)$, *where:*
• $c_1, c_2 \in C$ *(*c_1 *and* c_2 *are, respectively, the source and the target of the arc);*
• $d \in \{\_\} \cup \{L, R\}$ *(L when the arc goes from right to left, R from left to right).*

[2] For expository reasons we use a unique label to identify those sets.

Definition 4. *Semantic Rule*
A semantic rule is a triple $R_i = (\Sigma, \Theta, \Gamma)$ *(also notated* $[R_i]\ \Sigma : \Theta \looparrowright \Gamma$*), where:*
- Σ *is a (non empty) set of elements;*
- Θ *is a (possibly empty) set of arcs;*
- Γ *is a set of translating functions.*[3]

For the following definitions, let $R_i = (\Sigma, \Theta, \Gamma)$ be a semantic rule.

Definition 5. *Connections between elements*
Let $e_1 = elem(w_1, c_1)$, $e_2 = elem(w_2, c_2) \in \Sigma$.
e_1 *and* e_2 *are said to be directly connected* ($e_1 \bowtie_e e_2$) *if and only if (iff) there is an arc* $a = arc(c_3, c_4, d) \in \Theta$, *such that*
- $(c_1 = c_3 \land c_2 = c_4) \lor (c_1 = c_4 \land c_2 = c_3)$

e_1 *and* e_2 *are said to be connected* ($e_1 \bowtie_e^* e_2$) *iff*
- $(e_1 \bowtie_e e_2) \lor (\exists\ e_3 \in \Sigma)(e_1 \bowtie_e e_3 \land e_3 \bowtie_e^* e_2)$

Definition 6. *Connections between arcs*
Let $a_1 = arc(c_1, c_2, d_1)$, $a_2 = arc(c_3, c_4, d_2) \in \Theta$ *and* $a_1 \neq a_2$.
a_1 *and* a_2 *are said to be directly connected* ($a_1 \bowtie_a a_2$) *iff*
- $c_1 = c_4 \lor c_2 = c_3 \lor c_2 = c_4$

a_1 *and* a_2 *are said to be connected* ($a_1 \bowtie_a^* a_2$) *iff*
- $(a_1 \bowtie_s a_2) \lor (\exists\ a_3 \in \Theta)(a_1 \bowtie_a a_3 \land a_3 \bowtie_a^* a_2)$

Definition 7. *Relation arc/element*
Let $a_1 = arc(c_1, c_2, d_1) \in \Theta$ *and* $e = elem(w, c) \in \Sigma$.
a_1 *and* e *are said to be directly connected* ($a_1 \twoheadrightarrow e$) *iff*
- $c = c_1 \lor c = c_2$

a_1 *and* e *are said to be connected* ($a_1 \twoheadrightarrow^* e$) *iff*
- $(a_1 \twoheadrightarrow e) \lor (\exists\ a_2 \in \Theta)(a_1 \bowtie_a^* a_2 \land a_2 \twoheadrightarrow e)$

Definition 8. *Well formed semantic rule*
$R_i = (\Sigma, \Theta, \Gamma)$ *is a well formed semantic rule (wfsr) iff:*
- $(\forall\ e_1, e_2 \in \Sigma)(e_1 \bowtie_e^* e_2)$*(all the elements are connected)*
- $(\forall\ a_1 \in \Theta)(\exists\ e \in \Sigma)(a_1 \twoheadrightarrow^* e)$*(all the arcs are related with an element)*

Example 1. Well formed semantic rule
The following rule, whose target is Minimal Recursion Semantics (MRS) [5], is a wfsr (`n` is the label of the category associated with nouns):

$[R_1]$ `{elem(_,n,_)}` $: \emptyset \looparrowright$ `{handle(n) : sem(n)(var(n))}`

For the following definitions let $\sqsubseteq$ be the subsumption relation between two sets.

---

[3] For expository reasons we will not detail translating functions. However, consider defined sem(c), var(c) and handle(c), returning, respectively, the semantics, a variable and an handle [5] associated with the element identified by category c.

Definition 9. *Element subsumption*
$e_1 = elem(w_1, c_1)$ *subsumes* $e_2 = elem(w_2, c_2) (e_1 \sqsubseteq_e e_2)$ *iff*
$(c_1 \sqsubseteq c_2) \wedge (w_1 \neq \_ \Rightarrow w_2 = w_1)$

Definition 10. *Arc subsumption*
$a_1 = arc(c_1, c_2, d_1)$ *subsumes* $a_2 = arc(c_3, c_4, d_2)$ $(a_1 \sqsubseteq_a a_2)$ *iff*
$(c_1 \sqsubseteq c_3 \wedge c_2 \sqsubseteq c_4) \wedge (d_1 \neq \_ \Rightarrow d_1 = d_2)$

Definition 11. *Rule subsumption*
Let $R_1 = (\Sigma_1, \Theta_1, \Gamma_1)$, $R_2 = (\Sigma_2, \Theta_2, \Gamma_2)$ *be wfsr.*
R_1 *subsumes* R_2 $(R_1 \sqsubseteq_r R_2)$ *iff*
$(\forall\ e_1 \in \Sigma_1)(\exists\ e_2 \in \Sigma_2)\ (e_1 \sqsubseteq_e e_2) \wedge (\forall\ a_1 \in \Theta_1)(\exists\ a_2 \in \Theta_2)(a_1 \sqsubseteq_a a_2)$

Example 2. Rule subsumption
As n $\sqsubseteq$ np, rule R_1 subsumes the following rule:

$[R_2]$ {elem(_,np,_)} : $\emptyset \looparrowright$ {handle(np) : NAME(var(np), sem(np))}

Definition 12. *Conditions for the application of a semantic rule*
Let $R_j = (\Sigma, \Theta, \Gamma)$ *be a wfsr and* $G = (\Delta, \Psi)$ *a wfg.* R_j *can apply to G iff:*
- $(\forall\ elem(w_i, c_i) \in \Sigma)(\exists\ node(w_j, c_j, p_j) \in \Delta)[(w_i \neq \_ \Rightarrow w_i = w_j) \wedge c_i \sqsubseteq c_j]$
- $(\forall\ arc(c_n, c_m, d) \in \Theta)(\exists\ arrow(p_k, p_l) \in \Psi, \exists\ node(w_k, c_k, p_k), node(w_l, c_l, p_l) \in \Delta)(c_n \sqsubseteq c_k \wedge c_m \sqsubseteq c_l \wedge (d = R \Rightarrow p_k < p_l) \wedge (d = L \Rightarrow p_k > p_l))$

Definition 13. *Application of a semantic rule*
Being given a wfg, let R_1 *and* R_2 *be wfsr, verifying the conditions to be applied to it. If* $R_1 \sqsubseteq_r R_2$, *then* R_1 *is not applied.*

Example 3. Semantic rules applicability
Both rules R_1 and R_2 are in conditions to be applied to the graph from Fig. 1. As $R_1 \sqsubseteq_r R_2$ only R_2 is triggered.

4 Example

If rule R_1 is applied to the graph from Fig. 1, the following formula is obtained: h_{393} : Maria(x_{393}) (notice that variable generation is not carried out randomly: variable indexes are given by the position of the associated element or of the element it arrows). However, as only R_2 is triggered, we obtain: h_{393} : NAME(x_{393}, Maria).

Next we present a rule for intersective and subsective adjectives [4] (we will use the notation from [7]).[4]

$[R_3]$ {elem(_,adj,_)} : {arc(adj, n)} $\looparrowright$ {handle(n) : AM(var(n), sem(adj))}

After adding this rule to the system, the following formula is generated is addition to the previous: h_{393}: AM(x_{393}, pequena).

[4] We should point out that reification of variables [8] over adjectives will be needed to allow modification. However, we will ignore this problem for expository reasons.

5 Brief Discussion and Future Work

Briefly, ASdeCopas has the following properties:

- propagation of ambiguous values can be precluded through the use of (syntactic) information presented in the rules;
- rules can be applied in any order, as they are intrinsically independent (that is, their output does not depend on the output of other rule);
- information can be modularly added by profiting from the hierarchical organization of both categories and semantic rules;
- partial results can be produced;
- different semantic processes (such as role extraction, anaphora resolution, ...) can run at different times and their final results merged, due to the controlled generation of variables.[5]

The main problem with this system is that the immediate production of a structured formula is not easy, even though equivalent "flatter" structures can be easily produced. Moreover, the production of partial results should be taken carefully, as inconsistent representations can be produced.
ASdeCopas is implemented in Prolog and is being tested in question interpretation and in a more formal framework where the output is Minimal Recursion Semantics.

References

1. Gabriel G. Bès. La phrase verbal noyau en français. In *Recherches sur le français parlé, 15*, pages 273–358. Université de Provence, France, 1999.
2. Gabriel G. Bès. Empiricité en linguistique et grammaire de montague: la sémantique en 5P et la compositionnalité (avec en annexe grammaire de montague et ambiguïté). Technical report, GRIL, Université Blaise-Pascal, Clermont-Ferrand, France, Avril, 2001.
3. Gabriel G. Bès and Caroline Hagège. Properties in 5P (soon in the GRIL web page). Technical report, GRIL, Clermont-Ferrand, France, November, 2001.
4. Gennaro Chierchia and Sally McConnell-Ginet. *Meaning and Grammar – an Introduction to Semantics (second edition)*. The MIT Press, 2000.
5. Ann Copestake, Dan Flickinger, and Ivan A. Sag. *Minimal Recursion Semantics. An introduction. CSLI, Stanford University*. 1997.
6. Caroline Hagège. *Analyse Syntatic Automatique du Portugais*. PhD thesis, Université Blaise Pascal, Clermont-Ferrand, France, 2000.
7. Daniel Jurafsky and James Martin. *Speech and Language Processing*. Prentice Hall, 2000.
8. Diego Mollá. Ontologically promiscuous flat logical forms for NLP. In *IWCS-4, Tilburg, The Netherlands*, 2000.

[5] We are not assuming DRT to solve anaphora.

Automatic Selection of Table Areas in Documents for Information Extraction

Ana Costa e Silva[1], Alípio Jorge[2], and Luís Torgo[2]

[1] Banco de Portugal*, Portugal, acsilva@bportugal.pt
[2] Faculdade de Economia do Porto, LIACC, Universidade do Porto, Portugal,
{amjorget, ltorgo}@liacc.up.pt

Abstract. The information contained in companies' financial statements is valuable to several users. Much of the relevant information in such documents is contained in tables and is currently mainly extracted by hand. We propose a method that accomplishes a prior step of the task of automatically extracting information from tables in documents: selecting the lines that are likely to belong to tables. Our method has been developed by empirically analyzing a set of Portuguese companies' financial statements using statistical and data mining techniques. Empirical evaluation indicates that more than 99% of table lines are selected after discarding at least 50% of all lines. The method can cope with the complexity of styles used in assembling information on paper and adapt its performance accordingly, thus maximizing its results.

1 Introduction

Companies have the legal obligation of publishing reports accounting for their activities. These are called financial statements and contain tables with information that supports the decisions of a variety of economic agents, for whom, it is often necessary to combine information from several documents. However, such aggregate analysis requires the time consuming activity of capturing the data manually. Although it is expected that, in the future, financial statements will be published in predefined structured formats such as XBRL (eXtensible Business Reporting Language, [9]), in many countries it will take time before they are fully adopted.

To automatically extract information from tables five tasks must be fulfilled,[2]: 1. *Location*: "differentiating tables from other elements", [7]; 2. *Segmentation*: delimiting the table's physical units, its columns and lines, its simple and spanning cells (those spreading over more than one column or line); 3. *Functional analysis*: identifying the function each physical unit plays; there are two basic functions: containing data and describing data; 4. *Structural analysis*: detecting relationships between cells; 5. *Interpretation*: knowing what the relationships mean, e.g. if the cells "assets", "5" and "PTE" have to be read conjointly, interpreting is saying "assets equal 5 PTE". The task we approach in this paper is a preliminary step to this

* The opinions in this article do not necessarily coincide with the Banco de Portugal's.

Fernando Moura Pires, Salvador Abreu (Eds.): EPIA 2003, LNAI 2902, pp. 460–465, 2003.

process: given a text document, automatically select groups of lines that are likely to belong to relevant tables, thus reducing the search effort in the subsequent tasks.

2 Selecting Target Areas

Current software to locate tables in documents is generally based on detecting the alignment of certain characters, either words, e.g. [3], non-space characters, e.g. [7], or white spaces, e.g. [5]. Other methods, such as [4], examine the contents of each line in the document to gather information that is presented to a decision tree. In these methods, all parts of the document are given equal attention.

To serve as training examples, we downloaded 19 financial reports published by 13 Portuguese companies on the Web from a period ranging from 1997 to 2000. On the whole there were 87,843 lines, of which 70,584 were not table lines and 9,685 were part of tables containing the information we wish to extract. We then proceeded to convert the original files to plain text files using the 'pdftotxt' linux utility, and imported them to a database table. Each line in the report became a distinct record.

2.1 The Main Criterion for Table Line Location

To classify each line as being likely to belong to a table or not, our method basically relies on one feature – the total number of contiguous inner spaces in the line. To determine this, the leading and trailing spaces are removed; all substrings with more than one consecutive space characters are isolated; and the sum of the lengths of these substrings is the total number of contiguous inner spaces in the line. The effectiveness of this feature relies on the idea that a line having more inner spaces than what is "normal" will hold a distinctive graphical element (such as a table or a chart), which is worth inspecting more closely. A Chi-square test was able to confirm the validity of this empirical observation: with significance 10^{-6} and on the basis of our sample, a statistical dependence was found between the number of inner spaces in a line and whether the lines belong to a table. Thus, our main criterion will be

$$E_\ell > \lambda \rightarrow \ell \text{ is a } \textit{candidate table line} \quad (1)$$

where E_ℓ is the number of contiguous inner spaces in line ℓ, and λ is a threshold.

2.2 Robustness of the Criterion to Different Layouts

Intuitively, one can foresee that the threshold could be much smaller in a text written in one single column than in a text entirely written in two or more columns. To verify this observation, we applied the Kruskal Wallis test, [1], which proved, with 10^{-6} significance and on the basis of this sample, that the distribution of inner spaces is statistically different within the reports in the sample. To determine whether a given pair of reports had contributed to this result, we compared each pair at a time and found that only 22,8% of possible pairs were similar. A Chi square test also revealed statistical evidence of independence between whether or not a line is in a table and the document it originates from. As such, the threshold to distinguish the two types of lines should be established differently according to its source document. In other words, we want the criterion to generalize to (where D is a document)

$$E_\ell > \lambda(D) \rightarrow \ell \text{ is a } \textit{candidate table line} \tag{2}$$

To determine the optimal threshold in each document we labelled each line as being in a table or not and counted its number of inner spaces. We then used the J48 algorithm from the data mining suite Weka, [8] to build a one-node decision tree which classifies unlabelled lines according to the logical value of the test "Number of contiguous inner spaces<Threshold", setting it at the most informative possible value.

We would now like to be able to determine how this optimal threshold can be estimated given a document's global features, without prior knowledge of which of its lines belong to tables. We have made two empirical observations: 1. documents with more lines tend to have higher thresholds (because their authors tend to invest more resources to make them graphically appealing and used a more diversified style for accommodating elements on page); 2. in documents where the *most frequent number of positive inner spaces* (or *Mode*) is high enough (but not too high), the optimal division tends to be increasingly higher (because the mode occurs farther from zero when the text is organized in two or more columns).

As such, it should be possible to use measurable features of document, which reflect the style used by the authors in organizing graphical elements on the page, to estimate the best threshold. Options for defining $\lambda(D)$ are given in Section 3.1.

However, one extra characteristic has to be taken into account when deciding whether a line belongs to a table: its neighbourhood. No matter how many inner spaces a line has, it is not in a table if the lines around it are plain text; and a line with no inner spaces is not plain text, if table lines surround it. [4] found an interesting way of incorporating this: when deciding about each line, characteristics of those lines that fall within a fixed 1-line band around it were considered.

Our method, rather than considering a band of invariable size, defines its size according to the characteristics of the page in question. This is done because the information we want to extract is more likely to be in pages with a high concentration of table lines, with either one big table or several small tables. In our sample, a significant positive correlation was found between the *proportion of table lines* in a page and a variable taking value 1 when the page contains a relevant table. Since we do not know in advance which lines belong to tables, we estimate that proportion by counting the number of *candidate table lines* identified by criterion (2).

3 The Algorithm

For each page p with more than a given minimum of m candidate table lines, we identify areas within which to look for tables. If the proportion of candidates on the page, $Weight_p$, is high enough, all lines between the first and the last candidates, c_a and c_z, are included in the area. Otherwise, we may have more than one area per page, each corresponding to a sequence of at least m candidate lines no more than k lines apart. The distance between any two lines is measured in terms of the total number of non-empty lines that separate them; this makes the method robust to the existence of long sequences of empty lines within tables, which is common in this context. Areas always include i lines above the first candidate line, c_a, and f lines below the last, c_z. The values of k, i and f are determined according to the proportion of candidate lines per page. Each line in the area thus defined will be classified as *target* if it has any contiguous inner spaces or if its total string length is smaller than x% of the maximum length of the candidate lines on the page. The procedure is iterated until there are no more close candidate lines on the page and no more pages with enough candidates.

Instead of simply labelling each line as belonging to a target area or not, an absolute index is assigned as a first approach to the delimitation of different tables. Consecutive non-empty lines classified by the algorithm as *target areas* are assigned the same table identifier, which facilitates the subsequent table processing steps.

3.1 Parameters

We considered three manners of estimating the optimal threshold, λ [6]:
- γ standard deviations, $S_X(D)$, from the mean of inner spaces in report D, $\bar{X}(D)$, being γ the value that minimizes the average square error when estimating the ideal threshold for the sample of 19 reports;

$$\lambda_1(D) = \bar{X}(D) + 0{,}46 * S_X(D) \quad (3)$$

- an equation based on the most common number of positive inner spaces found in the 19 reports ($Mode_X$), using the ordinary least square method (which minimizes the average square error of the estimates of λ given $Mode_X$) to determine the coefficients;

$$\lambda_2(D) = 17{,}9 + 1{,}4 * Mode_X(D) \quad (4)$$

- and the minimum of equations (3) and (4). This achieved better experimental results The parameters of the algorithm were set at default values, which we empirically tested: m=3 or m=2 (m=3 was found to be better), x=75% and y=50%. We have determined k, i, and f as a function of the weight of candidate lines per page, as described in Table 1. The user can manipulate the values of m, k, i and f, as well as their relationship with the concentration of candidate lines in the page, to best seize the types of tables that hold the information he wants to extract.

Table 1. Default rule for the definition of k, i and f

	k	i	f
Weight < 30%	1	1	1
30% ≤ *Weight* < 50%	2	2	2
Weight ≥ 50%	3	4	2

4 Evaluation

We first evaluated the methods ability to recognize tables with relevant information, *context-specific evaluation*. For the group of reports used as training examples, with 87,843 lines (9,685 relevant for extraction; 70,584 non-table) using default values, in

17 of the 19 reports, the algorithm was able to discard in average 74,4% of the lines (*economy*) while keeping 99,6% of the interesting lines (*recall*). In the other two reports, by manipulating default values, the algorithm detected the only problematic table to identify 100% of the desired information while discarding in average 62,3% of the examples. In an unseen test group of three reports, with a total 9,470 lines (1,386 relevant for extraction; 7,388 non-table), average recall was 99,4% and economy 73,6%. All interesting tables were at least partially detected in both groups.

For a *generic purpose evaluation*, in which we aim at recognizing all tables, we set parameter values $k = f = 31$, $i = 5$, $m = 3$, independently of the weight of candidate lines on the page. Average results were 98,5% recall and 62,6% economy over the 19 examples; and 99,7% recall and 63,6% economy in the unseen group. The only types of tables this method could not detect were very narrow tables standing horizontally isolated in otherwise text pages, when in source documents mostly written in two or more columns. This happens because not enough candidate lines exist on the page. With $m = 1$, we could detect 99,9% of table lines, with 47,7% economy.

5 Conclusion

We have developed a method to locate portions of ASCII documents with high likelihood of holding tables displaying the information we wish to extract. This is a necessary step in a longer process of information extraction from tables in text. The method, which works on ASCII inputs, has been developed by applying data analysis techniques, from statistics to data mining, on a set of 19 financial statements published on the Web by Portuguese companies. It identifies sequences of potential table lines based on the characteristics of their neighbouring lines, their page and their source document as a whole. The method is able to adapt to the different styles used in organizing graphical components on page, which can be very diverse in this marketing influenced context. Furthermore, it allows User parameterisation to adapt it to the specificities of different contexts. Another main advantage of this method is that virtually any type of document can be converted to ASCII. Performance was measured on the given set of reports and on a separate test set. Results show that a lot of work can be saved right away, without losing relevant information.

Awareness to certain keywords and future recognition of titles has the potential of bringing recall even closer to 100% with very low economy costs, and will be sought in future work. The remaining tasks for extracting information from tables will also be addressed in the future and will include different features related with the structure of the document and linguistic information, among others.

References

1. Conover, W. J, Practical nonparametric statistics. John Wiley, USA, 1999.
2. Hurst, Mathew, "The interpretation of tables in text", PhD. Thesis, School of Cognitive Science, Informatics, The University of Edinburgh, UK, 2000.
3. Kieninger, Thomas, "Table structure recognition based on robust block segmentation", IS&T/SPIE's 10th Annual Symposium Electronic Imaging, USA, 1998.

4. Ng, Hwee Tou, Chung Lim and Jessica Koo, "Learning to recognize tables in free text", Association for Computational Linguistics, USA, 1999, pp. 443–450.
5. Pyreddy, Pallavi, Bruce Croft, "A system for retrieval in text tables", Technical report 105, Dep. Computer Science, University of Massachussets, USA, 1997.
6. Silva, Ana Costa e, "Extracção da informação de tabelas em texto", MSc Thesis, Faculdade de Economia, Universidade do Porto, Portugal, 2003.
7. Tupaj, Scott, Zhongwen Shi, C. Hwa Chang and Hassan Alan, "Extracting tabular information from text files". EECS, Tufts University, Medford, USA, 1996.
8. Witten, I, Frank, E., Data mining: practical machine learning tools and techniques with java implementations, Morgan Kaufmann, 2000.
9. XBRL, http://xbrl.org

Mandarin Question Sentence Detection: A Preliminary Study

Ping-Jer Yeh and Shyan-Ming Yuan

Department of Computer and Information Science
National Chiao Tung University
1001 Ta Hsueh Road, Hsinchu 300, Taiwan
{pjyeh, smyuan}@cis.nctu.edu.tw

Abstract. Detecting Mandarin question sentences is both interesting and difficult. To tackle this new topic, our strategy is first to try to increase recall and then precision. To achieve higher recall, we not only review relevant linguistic literature but also re-examine relevant issues from a new statistical and corpus point of view, and discover more comprehensive and precise question-related words than before. Next we present our statistical approaches and procedure, and discuss our findings. We achieve good recall and modest precision in the preliminary study, and pioneer the computational study of indefinitives.

1 Introduction

This paper presents a new topic in the field of natural language processing (NLP): Mandarin question sentence detection.[1] Its importance is twofold. The first is human-computer dialogue system, and the second is punctuation processing. First, a non-toy human-computer dialogue or question answering system needs to distinguish between background information and foreground queries, in order to interact more like human-to-human conversation. Imagine that you are asking a digital assistant for help:[2]

(1) I have installed and configured Wine, but Wine cannot find MS Windows on my drive. Where did I go wrong?

If the assistant program fails to pinpoint the foreground query and surrounding context, how can it work out a search plan to answer your "where" question?

Second, punctuation has been neglected in the NLP. For example, speech recognition software maps acoustic signals to text, but it seldom places appropriate punctuation marks in the output text. Word processors have built-in or plug-in spelling and grammar checkers, but they seldom try to check punctuation.

[1] To our knowledge, no such prior art exists.

[2] This phrase is excerpted from *The Wine FAQ*.
URL: http://www.winehq.com/site/docs/wine-faq/index

Fernando Moura Pires, Salvador Abreu (Eds.): EPIA 2003, LNAI 2902, pp. 466–478, 2003.

The reason why it has been neglected is that, punctuation is such a complex coding device that challenges computers. It is, as defined in *The American Heritage Dictionary* (Pickett et al. 16), "the use of standard marks and signs in writing and printing to separate words into sentences, clauses, and phrases in order to clarify meaning." Therefore, it involves not only syntactic but also semantic and pragmatic levels of processing. For example,

(2) a. Is this yours? *syntactic level*
b. I beg your pardon? *semantic level*
c. This is yours? I don't think so. *pragmatic level*

Sentence (2a) is obviously a question because of its verb BE-initial syntactic pattern. Sentence (2b), which begins without a verb BE, an auxiliary verb, or a WH word, is regarded as a question only if the meaning of the word "pardon" is taken into account. Furthermore, Sentence (2c) is regarded as a question only if the pragmatic context is taken into account.

It is even more challenging for the Mandarin language because there is no syntactically decisive and reliable marker and word order in Mandarin question sentences (Cheng 2), let along semantic and pragmatic clues.

The goal of this paper is to detect Mandarin question sentences. To put it more concretely, our task, in respect of training and validation, is to label unpunctuated input text with appropriate question marks. This paper is organized as follows. Section 2 reviews linguistic literature on Mandarin question sentences. Section 3 describes our feature-selection stages and findings, and in the meantime re-examines literature from a different angle: statistical point of view. Section 4 presents our training procedures and discusses our findings. Section 5 concludes our main contributions.

2 Linguistic Background

2.1 Use of Mandarin Question Marks

Modern Mandarin punctuation system, inspired by the western culture, was stabilized and formalized in the 20th century (Wu 17). Since then, prescriptive guidelines have been announced by authorities in major Mandarin-speaking regions, including Taiwan and mainland China (MPC 15; GB/T 15834-8). In general, question marks are used at the end of three kinds of question sentences: interrogative, dubitative, and rhetorical questions. For example,

(3) a. 這是什麼？ *interrogative*
What is this?
b. 那麼用功的學生，會考不上學校？ *dubitative*
Can such a diligent student fail the school entrance exams?
c. 難道你還不了解我？ *rhetorical*
Don't you understand me?

However, these vague statements touch only superficial mood issues. For NLP purpose, we need more information on their linguistic structures.

2.2 Ways to Express Questions

There are, in general, two ways to express questions in Mandarin: prosodic and grammatical devices. It is not necessary for the scope and purpose of this paper to enter into a detailed discussion of the former issue. Therefore we only summarize intonation patterns from relevant literature. In an interrogative sentence, the focal words are usually stressed and the whole sentence usually ends with a rising intonation. In a dubitative sentence, the focal words are often lengthened, possibly with a high pitch. In a rhetorical question, it is usually spoken with a sustained or falling intonation. Interested readers may consult more literature on this topic, such as (Zhang 20; Fan 6).

As for grammatical devices, various classification schemes have been proposed in literature. Some are compiled for educational purpose (Zhang 20; Liu et al. 10; Chu 3), and others are for linguistic research purpose (Li and Thompson 9; Lyu 12; Fan 6; Zhang 19; Chu and Chi 4). Some are classified mainly on the basis of morpho-syntactic forms (Li and Thompson 9; Fan 6; Chu 3), some semantic types (Lyu 12; Liu et al. 10; Zhang 19; Chu and Chi 4), and others pragmatic functions (Zhang 20).[3] While the big picture is now widely accepted, there is still considerable disagreement about details.

2.3 Exceptions: Question Words and Referentiality

Since no syntactically reliable marker exists in Mandarin question sentences, as mentioned near the end of Sect. 1, exceptions are inevitable. In most of the exceptional cases, the WH words are used as indefinitives or compound relatives (Chu 3; Chu and Chi 4). There are roughly 5 cases as pointed out by (Chu 3; Chu and Chi 4). The case for indefinitives, as shown in Sentence (4), can be (and possibly can only be) identified from the context since there seems no obvious syntactic pattern. On the other hand, the case for compound relatives can be identified from syntactic patterns, as shown in Sentences (5)–(6).

(4) a. 我 要 幾個 人 幫忙。
Wǒ yào jǐ-ge rén bāngmáng
I need how many people help
I need some people to help me.

b. 我 來 買 點 什麼 吧。
Wǒ lái mǎi diǎn shénme ba
I come buy some what
Let me buy something.

(5) a. 什麼 事 要 做？
Shénme shì yào zuò
What things need do

[3] The literature review is not meant to be definite. Some of them use hybrid criteria for classifying question sentences since there is no strict dividing line between morpho-syntactic, semantic, and pragmatic issues. Most of them also discuss more than one level of linguistic issues. Here we only point out the most prominent point of view.

What things do we need to do?

b. 沒有 什麼 事 要 做。
Méiyǒu shénme shì yào zuò
Not exist what things need do
Nothing needs to be done.

c. 什麼 事 都 要 做。
Shénme shì dōu yào zuò
What things all need do
Everything needs to be done.

d. 什麼 事 也 要 做。
Shénme shì yě yào zuò
What things also/even need do
Everything needs to be done.

(6) a. 誰 先 到？
Shéi xiān dào
Who first arrive
Who arrived first?

b. 誰 先 到， 誰 先 做。
Shéi xiān dào shéi xiān zuò
Who first arrive who first do
Let those who arrive first do it first.

c. 誰 先 到， 就 (誰) 先 做。
Shéi xiān dào jìu (shéi) xiān zuò
Who first arrive then who first do
Let those who arrive first do it first.

2.4 Exceptions: The Influence of Higher Verbs

In his articles (Cheng 1; Cheng 2) Cheng investigated an interesting issue: higher verbs in a complex sentence may influence the decision whether the proceeding question form is interrogative or not. He concluded in (Cheng 1) that inquisitive and cognitive verbs will make the embedded question forms non-interrogative because the focus is shifted to the higher verbs, while other types of verbs may or may not. However, in his subsequent article (Cheng 2) cognitive verbs were classified into the "may or may not" case without further explanation.

There are still open issues regarding the influence of higher verbs. To name a few: Is the classification scheme of verb types exhaustive, complete, and accurate? How to explain the exceptions to these higher-verb rules? Is there another theory to explain the phenomena better?

3 Feature Selection

Our overall machine learning strategy is first to try to increase recall and then precision. In many applications recall and precision are two competitive goals.

One target at one time makes the learning process more focused and easier for performance tuning.

To maximize recall, we need to discover all features that may constitute a question. In Sect. 2 we have reviewed linguistic literature on Mandarin question forms, but the literature does not stand on a corpus and statistical basis. To be useful in statistical NLP methodology, however, a quantitative investigation is necessary. Another reason to conduct a quantitative survey is that the features listed in literature are neither comprehensive nor precise enough for NLP purpose. In this section, therefore, we re-examine several issues in statistical point of view. The main purpose is to pave the way for devising programmable rules and heuristics. The fuller linguistic and qualitative study of them is beyond the scope of this paper.

3.1 The Corpus

The corpus used in this study is Academia Sinica balanced corpus of modern Chinese (or the Sinica corpus for short).[4] It comprises about 5 million words, tagged with part-of-speech information and segmented according to the draft standard in Taiwan. Detailed information of the corpus can be found in (CKIP 5).

Clauses are the basic analysis unit used in this study. The corpus divides every complex sentence into clauses that end with commas, periods, colons, semicolons, ellipses, exclamation, or question marks. There are 20,228 question clauses (2.70%) out of total 749,984 clauses. The register distribution of question clauses is listed in Table 1. If we look at the 4th column (q_i/t_i), we may find that questions are more frequent in the oral forms than written, which is consistent with our intuition. If we look at the 5th column ($q_i/\sum q_i$), however, the corpus is biased severely toward the written forms. Therefore, our results may have the same bias, too.

The choice of Sinica corpus, however, restricts us from fuller investigation. The most serious problem is that it is not a treebank. Since there is no hierarchical information available, we cannot handle properly question clauses embedded in complex or compound sentences.

For convenience, we use the format "(*file name* : *serial number of the clause*)" to indicate where the quotation comes from. For example, "(ebach1 : 80)" indicates that we quote the clause numbered 80 from the file "`ebach1`".

3.2 Finding Question-Related Words

As a beginning, we will examine what set of words constitutes a question sentence. These "question-related words" (hereafter, QRWs) may be content words

[4] The latest public version of the Sinica corpus is 3.0, released on October 1997. Since then, there has been minor fixes on inconsistent formats, tagging, and data cleaning (e.g., about half of the file "`t820902`" was duplicated in the first release of version 3.0). The revision used in this study is dated April 19th, 2001.

Table 1. Register distribution of question clauses in the Sinica corpus 3.0

Register	# of question clauses (q_i)	# of clauses (t_i)	q_i/t_i	$q_i/\sum q_i$
Written	13,821	645,767	2.14%	68.33%
Written to be read	257	10,315	2.49%	1.27%
Written to be spoken	1,168	12,736	9.17%	5.77%
Spoken	4,915	76,470	6.43%	24.30%
Spoken to be written	55	2,944	1.87%	0.27%
Unknown	12	1,752	0.68%	0.06%
Total:	20,228	749,984	2.70%	100.00%

or particles. We coin the term "QRW" in order to avoid confusion with another term used frequently in linguistic literature: "question words" (Li and Thompson 9; Chu 3), which should mean the interrogative words or WH-words (e.g., what, which, who). The set of Mandarin interrogative words is therefore a subset of QRWs.

To find QRWs, we need to calculate four counters a, b, c, and d (as listed in Table 2) for every candidate word w_i in the corpus. The algorithm for finding QRWs, as shown in Fig. 1, undertakes a chi-square (χ^2) test for independence of two variables: words and question clauses. Lines 1–2 initialize the sets $\mathcal{S}_{\mathrm{Q}}$ and $\mathcal{S}_{\mathrm{NQ}}$ to hold all question and non-question clauses, respectively. Line 3 initializes the set $\mathcal{W}$ to hold all QRW candidates. The main loop of the algorithm is contained in lines 4–12. The loop iterates through each word $w_i \in \mathcal{W}$ to compute its χ^2 statistic. Partial results are listed in Table 3.

Table 2. Contingency table for finding question-related words (QRWs)

Clauses	Is w_i in the clause? Yes	No
Ends with '?'	a	b
Ends without '?'	c	d

$$\chi^2 \text{ statistic of } w_i = \frac{(a+b+c+d)(ad-bc)^2}{(a+b)(a+c)(b+d)(c+d)}$$

$$\text{Frequency of } w_i = a + c$$

$$\text{Precision of } w_i = a/(a+c)$$

$$\text{Recall of } w_i = a/(a+b)$$

The χ^2 statistic in Table 3 seems too large because the "No" column may contain something that acts similar to the "Yes" column. Such lurking variables have side effects that falsely increase the χ^2 statistics. Therefore, a higher χ^2

Algorithm input: corpus
Output: associative array $C[w_1 \dots w_n]$ mapping from w_i to χ^2 statistic, where $n = |\mathcal{W}|$
Begin:

```
1     S_Q ← all question clauses in the corpus
2     S_NQ ← all non-question clauses in the corpus
3     W ← all words in S_Q
4     for each w_i ∈ W do
5         a, b, c, d ← 0
6         for each s_j ∈ S_Q do
7             if w_i in s_j then ++a
8             else               ++b
9         for each s_k ∈ S_NQ do
10            if w_i in s_k then ++c
11            else               ++d
12        C[w_i] ← compute χ² statistic for w_i via a, b, c, d
13    sort C in descending order
```

Fig. 1. Algorithm for finding question-related words

Table 3. Top ranks of question-related words

Rank	QRW	χ^2 statistic	Rank	QRW	χ^2 statistic	Rank	QRW	χ^2 statistic
1	嗎 (T)	88941.79	11	難道 (D)	5861.16	21	如何 (VH)	2857.26
2	呢 (T)	72731.19	12	怎麼樣 (VH)	5464.69	22	會不會 (D)	2774.36
3	什麼 (Nep)	37515.11	13	不 (D)	4982.97	23	你們 (Nh)	2173.73
4	為什麼 (D)	26622.68	14	是否 (D)	4540.90	24	還是 (Caa)	2169.88
5	怎麼 (D)	18747.55	15	哪 (Nep)	4376.40	25	怎麼 (VH)	2169.03
6	你 (Nh)	11060.08	16	何 (Nes)	4307.55	26	麼 (T)	2128.01
7	誰 (Nh)	9161.25	17	哪裡 (Ncd)	4086.19	27	何必 (D)	2076.27
8	到底 (D)	8221.60	18	有沒有 (D)	3959.01	28	吧 (T)	1919.64
9	怎麼辦 (VH)	7372.23	19	究竟 (D)	3554.16	29	多少 (Neqa)	1844.61
10	如何 (D)	7369.35	20	為何 (D)	3003.16	30	好不好 (VH)	1809.61

critical value (i.e., a lower Type I error probability α) is required to claim that the result is significant.[5]

In theory, if we accept all top N QRWs as our features, say $N = 300$, we may reach a high recall up to 95%. Though the goal in this stage is to maximize the recall, but pursuing this goal blindly may fall into the trap of overfitting.

[5] Note that in many NLP applications, as Manning and Schütze (14) pointed out, "the level of significance itself is less useful... All that is used is the scores and the resulting ranking."

Roughly speaking, the amount of noise increases steeply when the rank is greater than about 130. Another reason that forbids us to maximize the recall is that precision drops steeply as the recall increases, as shown in Fig. 2.

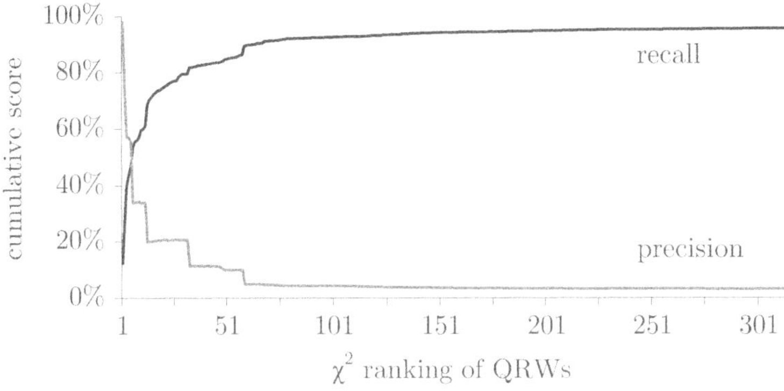

Fig. 2. Cumulative recall and precision of question-related words

3.3 Discussion of the Finding

On closer inspection, the result reveals something not addressed explicitly in linguistic literature. We shall now look more carefully into the following issues: inconsistent segmentation, person, lexical semantics, modality (evaluative adverbs), and rhetorical questions.

Inconsistent Segmentation in the Sinica Corpus. The Sinica corpus does not segment words in a purely consistent manner. Take the Mandarin alternative or disjunctive question form "A-not-A" for example. In some places the rank 22 entry "會不會" (*hùibúhùi*; capable or not) is treated as one word, while in other places it is segmented into 3 individual words. Similar cases are "好不好" (*hǎobùhǎo*; good/agree or not), "要不要" (*yàobúyào*; want or not), "可不可以" (*kěbùkěyǐ*; can or cannot).

The inconsistent segmentation in the Sinica corpus raises some problems in automatic analysis. What is worse, these inconsistently segmented forms cannot be blindly merged into one word since some are not alternative questions, as shown in the following example:

(7)	雨(Na)	該(Nes)	下(VC)	不(D)	下(VC)	(a472a:2160)
	Yǔ	*gāi*	*xià*	*bú*	*xià*	
	rain	should	to rain	not	to rain	
	It should rain, but it doesn't.					

Person. One may wonder why the word "你" (*nǐ*; you; second person singular pronoun) is ranked 6th since intuitively it is irrelevant to questions. Let us look at this issue from another angle: recall. Recall is the ratio of the number of relevant items correctly identified to the total number of relevant items in the population, i.e., recall $= a/(a + b)$. From this point of view, Table 4 shows an interesting finding. The word "你" has such a high recall (12.93%) that for every 7.7 question clauses, there is about one clause containing the word "你". In other words, people tend to express questions with the word "你".

Table 4. Top 10 recalls of question-related words

QRW	Recall		Precision		QRW	Recall		Precision	
	Rank	%	Rank	%		Rank	%	Rank	%
的 (DE)	1	24.71	862	1.97	你 (Nh)	6	12.93	95	15.79
是 (SHI)	2	19.48	329	4.85	嗎 (T)	7	12.39	1	98.12
呢 (T)	3	16.80	25	61.04	有 (V'2)	8	9.64	375	4.38
不 (D)	4	15.78	172	8.42	我 (Nh)	9	6.92	497	3.66
什麼 (Nep)	5	13.39	59	41.26	這 (Nep)	10	6.32	455	3.86

One may argue that the recall of "你" is high simply because it is a high-frequency word and that it is irrevelant to questions. The argument is partially true in that "你" is the 19th most frequent word in the corpus, and the correlation coefficient of recall and frequency is +0.73, indicating a modest positive association. However, it should be notice that not only would recall and frequency but still other factors as well would affect the degree of relevance to question. Some high-recall words (such as "的" and "是") are merely high-frequency words since they have much lower precision measures, implying a smell of stop words.

We also find that the second person pronouns (singular, plural, feminine, and honorific forms) have higher χ^2 statistics than the first person pronouns (singular and plural), and much higher than the third person pronouns (singular, plural, and feminine). It seems that case roles and discourse functions also determine whether the person has remarkable influence, but the lack of a large set of treebank prevents us from automatically mining definite information on the person issue.

Lexical Semantics of Honorifics. We find that lexical semantics play a certain role in determining or predicting a question clause. Take the rank 81 entry "貴姓" (*gùixìng*; your last name) for example. Intuitively, it is typically used in interrogative sentences for asking other person's last name. Statistically, although it is a low frequency word (occurrence = 12, recall = 0.05%), its high precision (91.67%) suggests high validity in predicting a question sentence. The only one false positive found in the corpus is a chapter title of a textbook on conversation:

(8)	請 問(VE)	您(Nh)	貴 姓(VH)	。	(ebach1:80)
	Qǐngwèn	*nín*	*gùixìng*		
	ask	you	last name	period	
	May I ask your last name, please.				

In fact, either a period or a question mark is acceptable here. Different people have different opinions.

The lexeme "貴" in this sense is labeled as an honorific, similar to another lexeme "尊" (*zūn*). But not all such honorific words are used for asking questions. Consulting an authoritive dictionary such as (Xu 18), we may find that "貴庚" (*gùigēng*; your age), "貴幹" (*gùigàn*; your intention), and "貴處" (*gùichù*; your native place) are labeled explicitly as interrogatives, but "貴戚", "貴賓", "貴子", "貴手", "貴恙", and "貴地" are not. To discover more exhaustive and precise knowledge about such interrogative use of honorific or still other lexemes, we need machine-readable dictionaries (MRDs) with quality linguistic information.

Modality and Rhetorical Questions. Another interesting examples showing the importance of quality MRDs are evaluative adverbs and words for rhetorical questions. The former are the rank 8 entry "到底" (*dàodǐ*), rank 11 entry "難道" (*nándào*), and rank 19 entry "究竟" (*jīujìng*). As for the latter, we discover more cases in (Lyu 12): the rank 27 "何必" (*hébì*), rank 71 "何不" (*hébù*), rank 80 "何嘗" (*hécháng*), rank 72 "何苦" (*hékǔ*). Again, the lack of precise morphological markers and quality MRDs designed for computational linguistic research prevents us from further study.

4 Rule Construction

In Sect. 3 we have focused on recall and identified a rich set of QRWs. In this section we focus on devising rules to increase precision without hurting recall too much. We first define a rule specification, and then describe the question detection process, and finally discuss the results.

4.1 Syntax and Semantics of Rules

The syntax of detection rules is listed in Fig. 3. To handle irregular morphological patterns, positions, and exceptional context, we devise our rules around regular expressions, especially the Perl 5.8 favor (Friedl 7). The pros of regular expressions are that they make rules more concise and flexible. The cons are that they may over-generalize the patterns and then decrease recall or precision, and also slow down the training process.

```
RuleList          → Rule+                                # disjunction of rules
Rule              → PositiveAtom+  NegativeAtom*         # conjunction of atoms
PositiveAtom      → 'P'  PositivePosition  Regex
NegativeAtom      → 'N'  NegativePosition  Regex
PositivePosition  → '['                                  # head
                  | ']'                                  # tail
                  | 'x'                                  # don't care
                  | '%'                                  # middle
NegativePosition  → '<'                                  # before
                  | '>'                                  # after
                  | 'x'                                  # don't care
Regex             → any legal Perl 5.8 regular expressions
```

Fig. 3. Grammar of question-detection rules. The quantifier symbol '∗' attached to nonterminals means "zero or more," and the symbol '+' means "one or more"

4.2 The Training Process

The whole training process is iterative, as shown in Fig. 4. Steps 5 and 7 are not entirely automatic since for now there remains many sophisticated facets to analyze further. For example, we discover in step 5 many subtle patterns not stated explicitly before, such as the flexibility in the negation-type words and the lexeme "何" (*hé*; what). Due to the lack of quality machine-readable dictionaries, these patterns are hardly recognized correctly by machines.

```
1   Construct plain rules using QRWs found in Sect. 3
2   while the result does not converge do
3       Train the rules using the training set
4       if the number of false negatives is not acceptable then
5           Investigate if there is any missing feature
6       if the number of false positives is not acceptable then
7           Investigate if the rules are too general
8       Merge similar rule patterns
```

Fig. 4. Overall training process of question detection

4.3 Discussion

For now our system has recall 76.17% and precision 45.79%. Let us devote a little more space to examining the result and possible ways to improve the performance.

False Negatives. Our experience shows that the most fatal obstacle to improve recall is pragmatic issue. Some false negatives are truly our faults, but others (especially those with sentence-end particles) can also be considered euphemism, irony, exclamation, or any other illocutionary act.

To reduce the number of false negatives, the most challenge is that programs should be able to recognize some kinds of speech acts.

False Positives. Our experience shows that the most fatal obstacle to improve precision is referentiality. As stated in Sect. 2.3, there seems no obvious syntactic pattern to identify indefinitives. Another difficulty is complex and compound sentences. The inclusion of higher verbs, as suggested in Sect. 2.4, improves the precision only by 0.32%. It is doubtful whether higher verbs worth further study.

To reduce the number of false positives, we may need some black-box statistical models like HMMs to try to identify indefinitives more accurately, and a little tree parsing may also help.

Clause or Sentence Boundary. The syntax of Mandarin is very flexible compared to Indo-European languages. Such flexibility, however, increases the search space for parsing. As stated in Sect. 1, there is no syntactically decisive and reliable marker and word order in Mandarin question sentences. In real setting, therefore, given a series of clauses, a question-detection program must be able to identify where is the beginning and where is the end of every sentence. Otherwise it may be confused about complex sentences or serial clauses, and has trouble dealing with alternative questions spanning over several clauses.

5 Conclusion

In this paper we have pointed out the problem of detecting Mandarin question sentences and reviewed relevant linguistic literature. Then we have outlined our strategy to this problem: first we try to increase recall and then precision. We have presented our statistical approaches and procedure, and discussed our findings. The lack of quality machine-readable dictionaries limits our pursuit of several subtle issues.

This is a new topic in NLP community as far as we know. Our contributions are twofold. In the linguistic field, we re-examine relevant topics from a new statistical and corpus point of view, and discover more comprehensive and precise QRWs. In the NLP field, we achieve good recall and modest precision in the preliminary study, and pioneer the computational study of indefinitives.

References

Cheng, R. L.: Chinese question forms and their meanings. Journal of Chinese Linguistics **12** (1984) 86–147. Also in Temporal and Spatial Relations, Questions and Negatives in Taiwanese and Mandarin. Yuan-Liou Publishing Co., Taipei (1997) 273–312

Cheng, R. L.: Mandarin and Taiwanese question sentences. Temporal and Spatial Relations, Questions and Negatives in Taiwanese and Mandarin. Yuan-Liou Publishing Co., Taipei (1997) 357–402

Chu, C. C.: A Concise Grammar of Mandarin Chinese. Wu-Nan Book Inc, Taipei (1999)

Chu, C. C., Chi, T. J.: A Cognitive-Functional Grammar of Mandarin Chinese. Crane Publishing Company, Inc, Taipei (1999)

CKIP: A Guide to the Academia Sinica Balanced Corpus of Modern Chinese. Technical Report no.95-02/98-04. Institute of Information Science, Academia Sinica, Taipei (1998)

Fan, X. et al. (eds.): Studies on Mandarin Sentence Types. Shuhai Publishing House, Taiyuan, Shanxi, China (1998)

Friedl, J.: Mastering Regular Expressions. 2nd edition. O'Reilly & Associates, CA (2002)

GB/T 15834-1995: Use of Punctuation Marks. National Standard of the People's Republic of China (1995)

Li, C. N., Thompson, S. A.: Mandarin Chinese: A Functional Reference Grammar. University of California Press, New York (1981)

Liu, Y., Pan, W., Gu, W.: Modern Chinese Grammar. Foreign Language Teaching and Research Press, Beijing (1983). Reprinted by Shih Ta Book Ltd, Taipei (1996)

Luo, Z. et al. (eds.): Unabridged Chinese Dictionary. The Publishing House of the Unabridged Chinese Dictionary, Shanghai (1993). Reprinted by Taiwan Doughua Bookstore, Taipei (1997)

Lyu, S.: An Outline of Chinese Grammar. The Commercial Press, Beijing (1982)

Lyu, S. et al. (eds.): Eight Hundred Words of Modern Mandarin. Revised edition. The Commercial Press, Beijing (1999)

Manning, C. D., Schütze, H.: Foundations of Statistical Natural Language Processing. MIT Press, Cambridge, MA (1999)

MPC: A Manual of Punctuation Marks Revised. Mandarin Promotion Council, Ministry of Education, Taipei (1987)

Pickett, J. P. et al. (eds.): The American Heritage® Dictionary of the English Language. 4th edition. Houghton Mifflin Company, Boston, MA (2000)

Wu, B. J.: Prescriptive Usage of Punctuation Marks. Joint Publishing (H.K.) Co., Hong Kong (1998)

Xu, Z. et al. (eds.) Dictionary of Mandarin. Sichuan Dictionary Publishing House and Hubei Dictionary Publishing House, China (1995)

Zhang, B.: Functional interpretation of Mandarin question sentences. In: Xing, F. (eds.): Various Characteristics of Mandarin Grammar. Beijing Language and Culture University Publishing House, Beijing (1999) 291–303

Zhang, Z.: Common Sense of Mandarin Grammar. Shanghai Education Publishing House, Shanghai (1959). Reprinted by Joint Publishing (H.K.) Co., Hong Kong (1999)

Acquiring Semantic Classes to Elaborate Attachment Heuristics

Pablo Gamallo*, Alexandre Agustini**, and Gabriel P. Lopes

CITI, Faculdade de Ciências e Tecnologia, Universidade Nova de Lisboa, Portgual
{gamallo,aagustini,gpl}@di.fct.unl.pt

Abstract. We use an unsupervised method for learning word classes from partially parsed text corpora. A word class consists of those words that can appear in similar contexts of subcategorization. The main objective of this paper will be to describe an evaluation procedure based on attachment resolution. We will evaluate whether the classes that have been previously learnt are useful in that syntactic task.

1 Introduction

We use an unsupervised method for learning word classes from partially parsed text corpora. The words that occur with similar contexts of subcategorization are aggregated in semantic classes. The main objective of this paper will be to describe an evaluation procedure based on attachment resolution. Attachment resolution consists in providing a parser with information to disambiguate arcs. We will evaluate whether the classes that have been learnt previously are useful in that syntactic task. The degree of efficiency in such a task may serve as a reliable evaluation for measuring the soundness of our learning strategy.

The learning method has been accurately described in [4]. For the purpose of this paper, we will only outline the basic assumptions the acquisition strategy is based on, as well as different steps and modules that are involved in it (section 2). In section 3, two tasks are focused: first, we will describe how the learnt information is used to characterize attachment heuristics, and finally, we will evaluate the performance of these heuristics.

2 Learning Word Classes from Subcategorization Contexts

2.1 Basic Assumptions

Two theoretical assumptions underlie our method: one is based on word co-specification and the other on context similarity.

* Research supported by Program POSI, FCT/MCT, Portugal; ref: SFRH/BPD/11189/2002

** Research sponsored by CAPES and PUCRS – Brazil

Fernando Moura Pires, Salvador Abreu (Eds.): EPIA 2003, LNAI 2902, pp. 479–487, 2003.

First, we assume a very general notion of linguistic subcategorization. More precisely, we consider that in a Head-Modifier syntactic dependency, not only the Head imposes constraints on the Modifier, but the Modifier also imposes linguistic requirements on the Head in return. This idea stems from the Pustejovsky's "co-specification" hypothesis [10]. So, for a particular word, we attempt to learn what type of both modifiers and heads it subcategorizes. For instance, consider the compositional behavior of the noun `republic` in a domain-specific corpus. On the one hand, this word appears in the Head position within dependencies such as `republic of Ireland`, `republic of Portugal`, and so on. On the other hand, it plays the role of Modifier in dependencies like `president of the republic`, `government of the republic`, etc. So, given `republic`, we attempt to learn both what kind of complements and what kind of heads it subcategorizes. As there are interesting semantic regularities among the words co-occurring with `republic` in the above expressions, the aim of our learning method is to extract two different subcategorization contexts:

- $< of; republic, [M] >$, where position M must be filled by words referring to particular nations or states. Indeed, in semantic-pragmatic terms, only nations or states can be republics;
- $< of; [H], republic >$, where position H must be filled by head words denoting specific parts of the republic: e.g., institutions, organizations, functions, and so on.

The second assumption concerns the procedure for identifying and clustering *similar* subcategorization contexts. We assume, in particular, that different contexts are considered to be semantically similar if they have similar word distribution [3]. Let's take, for instance, the following set of contexts:

$$\begin{gathered}\{< of; [H], republic > \\ < of; [H], state > \\ < of; delegate, [M] > \\ < iobj\_by; sign, [M] > \\ < iobj\_on; be\_incumbent, [M] >\}\end{gathered} \tag{1}$$

All contexts in (1) share the same semantic preferences provided they require words denoting the same semantic class. Contexts with the same semantic preferences are likely to possess similar word distribution. Moreover, we also assume that the set of words required by similar subcategorization contexts represents the extensional description of their semantic preferences.

2.2 Method Overview

Our learning method consists in the following steps. Raw Portuguese text is automatically tagged and partially analyzed in sequences of basic chunks. Then, binary syntactic dependencies are identified on the basis of some symbolic attachment heuristics. Then, we extract subcategorization contexts from the binary dependencies, by following the first assumption outlined above (co-specification).

Finally, subcategorization contexts with similar word distributions are clustered into more general classes (second assumption). Similarity between contexts is calculated by using a particular version of the Lin coefficient [7]. For instance, the class illustrated above in (1) is constituted by contexts considered as similar. These contexts have as features those words co-occurring at least once with them, e.g.:

`president, assembly, minister, ministry, government, administration`

This is the way we build classes of words representing the semantic preferences of similar contexts. Such word classes represent contextual senses of words.

Note that this acquisition method permits to associate a polysemic word to different clusters, where each cluster represents one of its senses. For instance, word `administration` not only may appear in the cluster sketched above in (1), but also in:

$$\begin{aligned} &\{< of; [H], drugs > \\ &< of; process, [M] > \\ &< in; [H], course >\} \end{aligned} \tag{2}$$

This word does not mean here a kind of institution any more, but a type of action: `administration of drugs, process of administration`, etc.

2.3 Experiments and Results

We tested our learning strategy over a Portuguese corpus with 6,643,579 word occurrences, selected from the *P.G.R.* (*Portuguese General Attorney Opinions*) text corpora. The data concerning the information extracted from this corpus is presented in Table 1.

Table 1. Corpus data

Word Occurrences	6,643,579
Binary Dependencies	1,543,659
Syntactic Contexts	178,522
Final Clusters	16,274

In order to evaluate the linguistic relevance of these clusters, we will check in the next section if they are useful in a parsing task. The degree of efficiency in such a task (parsing) may serve as a reliable evaluation for measuring the soundness of the learning strategy.

3 One Application: Attachment Resolution

The acquired classes are used to provide the lexicon with subcategorization information. Then, this information is used to improve the parsing task.

Table 2. Dictionary entry of `secretário`

secretário *(secretary)*

· *< de, [H], secretário >* *([H] of secretary)* =
`cargo, carreira, categoria, competência, escalão, estatuto, função, remuneracaão, trabalho, vencimento`
(post, career, category, qualification, rank, status, function, remuneration, job, salary)

· *< de, secretário, [M] >* *(secretary of [M])* =
`administração, assembleia, autoridade, conselho, direcção, empresa, entidade, estado, governo, instituto, juiz, ministro, ministério, presidente, serviço, tribunal órgão`
(administration, assembly, authority, council direction, company, entity, state, government , institute, judge, minister, ministery, president, service, tribunal organ)

· *< iobj_a, [H], secretário >* *([H] to the secretary)* =
`aludir, aplicar:refl, atender, atribuir, concernir, corresponder, determinar, presidir, recorrer, referir:refl, respeitar`
(allude, apply, attend, assign, concern, correspond, determine, resort, refer, relate)

· *< iobj_a, [H], secretário >* *([H] to the secretary)* =
`caber, competir, conceder, conferir, confiar, dirigir, incumbir, pertencer`
(concern, be-incombent, concede, confer, trust, send, be-incombent, belong)

· *< iobj_por, [H], secretário >* *([H] by the secretary)* =
`assinar, conceder, conferir, homologar, louvar, subscrito`
(sign, concede, confer, homologate, compliment, subscribe)

· *< subj, [H], secretário >* *(the secretary [H]))* =
`definir, estabelecer, fazer, fixar, indicar, prever, referir`
define, establish, make, fix, indicate, forsee, refer

3.1 Lexicon Update

Table 2 shows how the acquired classes are used to provide lexical entries with information on the word classes which we have learnt previously. These classes represent subcategorization information that will be useful in the parsing procedure. The entry `secretário` (*secretary*), for instance, is associated with six subcategorization contexts: two nominal and four verbal ones. Concerning the nominal contexts, we learn that *secretary* selects for nouns such as *post*, *rank*, etc. in position H of preposition *de* (*of*), whereas it requires a class of nouns denoting institutions and functions in position M of this same preposition. Concerning the verbal contexts, we also learn that *secretary* subcategorizes various verb classes in different verbal positions: two classes in the H position of the *iobj_a* prepositional dependency, one class as H of *iobj_por*, and one more class as H of the subject relation: *subj*.

Notice that it is the notion of co-specification that allows us to acquire a great number of subcategorization contexts , which are not usual in the standard approaches to subcategorization. Five contexts of *secretary* do not subcategorize standard dependent complements, but different types of heads. This is a significant novelty of our approach.

3.2 Parsing with Co-specification

The syntactic and semantic subcategorization information provided by the lexical entries is used to improve the parsing task. Details of a symbolic DCG grammar with information on linguistic co-specification can be found in [1,4]. In this paper, we briefly outline how the parser uses this information to solve syntactic attachments. Co-specification is at the center of attachment resolution. It is used to characterize the main attachment heuristic. This heuristic states that two chunks are syntactically attached only if one of these two conditions is verified: either the *Modifier* is semantically required by the *Head*, or the *Head* is semantically required by the *Modifier*. Take the expression:

{1} `...compete ao secretário ...`
(*is incumbent on the secretary*)

This expression will be analyzed as a VP-PP construction if and only if, at least, one of the two following requirements is satisfied:

requirement M: context $< iobj\_a\ competir, [M] >$ (*be-incumbent on [M]*) subcategorizes a class of nouns to which `secretário` (*secretary*) belongs;
requirement H: context $< iobj\_a; [H], secretário >$ (*[H] on the secretary*) subcategorizes a class of verbs to which `competir` (*be-incumbent*) belongs.

According to the lexical information illustrated in Table 2, the expression {1} can be analyzed as a VP-PP construction because, at least, requirement H is satisfied. Note that, even if we have no information on the verb subcategorization, the attachment is allowed because of the noun requirements in the H position. Co-specification is also used to solve long-distance attachments [4].

3.3 Evaluating Performance of Attachment Resolution

We evaluated the performance of the parsing strategy based on co-specification. The general aim of this evaluation is to check whether the subcategorization information we have learnt is adequate to be used in a parsing task. The degree of efficiency in such a task may serve as a reliable evaluation for measuring the soundness of our learning strategy.

Test Data. Most work on attachment resolution [5,11,2,6,8,9] uses as test data expressions with three basic phrases (or chunks): $vp - np - pp$. These approaches consider that each expression selected for evaluation can be syntactically ambiguous in two ways. For instance, the partial parse:

{2} [$_{vp}$ cut] [$_{np}$ the potato] [$_{pp}$ with a knife]

can be disambiguated either by the parse:

{3} [$_{vp}$ cut [$_{np}$ the potato [$_{pp}$ with a knife]]]

which represents a syntactic configuration based on proximity (*phrase1* is attached to *phrase2* and *phrase2* is attached to *phrase3*), or by:

{4} [$_{vp}$ cut [$_{np}$ the potato] [$_{pp}$ with a knife]]

which is the correct configuration. It contains both a contiguous and a long distance attachment: *phrase1* is attached to *phrase2* and *phrase1* is attached to *phrase3*.

We consider, however, that the process of attachment resolution should be generalized to other syntactic sequences and ambiguity configurations. Our test data consists of 633 manually disambiguated expressions, which have been selected randomly from a test corpus. These expressions are not only $vp - np - pp$ sequences of phrases. They were divided into three groups according to three different syntactic sequences (see table 3). Moreover, they cannot be reduced to only two syntactic configurations (two parses). They can be syntactically ambiguous in several ways, including adjective and adverb associations. In table 3, the two first expressions contain adjective attachments, while the third one introduces the first part of an adverbial sentence: `na medida [em que]` (*in the sense [that]*).

Table 3. The three syntactic sequences evaluated

$np - pp - pp$	`[`$_{np}$ `o artigo relativo] [`$_{pp}$ `ao decreto] [`$_{pp}$ `da lei]` (*the article referring to the decree of the law*)
$vp - pp - pp$	`[`$_{vp}$ `publicou] [`$_{pp}$ `nos estatutos anexos] [`$_{pp}$ `ao citado diploma]` (*published in the statutes joined to the cited diploma*)
$vp - np - pp$	`[`$_{vp}$ `tem] [`$_{np}$ `acesso] [`$_{pp}$ `na medida]` (*has acess in the sense*)

Baseline. Concerning the ability to propose correct syntactic attachments, we made a comparison between our method and a baseline strategy. As a baseline, we used the attachments proposed by Right Association. That is, for each expression of the test data, this strategy always proposes the attachment by proximity, that is: *phrase1* is attached to *phrase2*, *phrase2* is attached to *phrase3*, and *phrase1* is not attached to *phrase3*.

Precision and Recall. Each expression selected from the test corpus contains three phrases and three candidate attachments. So, given a test expression, three different attachment decisions will be evaluated. The evaluation of each attachment decision taken by the system can be:

- true positive (*tp*): the system proposes a correct attachment
- true negative (*tn*): the system proposes correctly that there is no attachment.
- false positive (*fp*): the system proposes an incorrect attachment
- false negative (*fn*): the system proposes incorrectly that there is no attachment.

The evaluation test measures the ability of the system to make true decisions. We call both *tp* and *tn* "true decisions" (*td*). As far our strategy is concerned, a false negative (*fn*) is interpreted as the situation in which the system has not enough subcategorization information to make a decision. Concerning the baseline, the *fn* decisions correspond to those situations where there is a true long distance attachment: *phrase1* is attached to *phrase3*.

Taking into account these variables, *precision* is defined as the number of true decisions suggested by the system divided by the number of total suggestions. That is:

$$precision = \frac{td}{td + fp} \tag{3}$$

Recall is computed as the number of true decisions suggested by the system divided by the decisions that are actually correct:

$$recall = \frac{td}{td + fn} \tag{4}$$

Note that we do not define precision and recall in a standard way. Unlike most related work, precision and recall are defined here with respect to the decisions made by the system given a candidate attachment, and not given the whole configuration of the expression. This more accurate evaluation gives us more significant information on the system capabilities concerning attachment resolution.

Results. Table 4 reports the test scores concerning the precision and recall of the two comparative experiments performed. The total precision of our method reaches more than 90%, whereas the total recall is about 75%. These results can be hardly compared to related approaches given that: i) there is no related work on Portuguese; ii) our test corpus is not restricted to the two standard ambiguity configurations defined above; we also take into account expressions containing adjective attachments and adverbial phrases; iii) we use three types of phrase sequences, and not only the $vp - np - pp$ sequence used by most related work; iv) the precision and recall definitions are not the standard ones.

This makes it difficult to compare the performance of our method to other unsupervised strategies. We consider, however, that the recall we have obtained should be higher. In order to improve it, we need to provide the dictionary with more items of subcategorization information. One of the main challenges of our current work is to tune the clustering constraints so as to reach high recall by keeping a reasonable precision. This should make the parser more efficient concerning the attachment resolution task.

Table 4. Evaluation of Attachment Resolution

BASELINE			
Syntactic sequences	**Precision (%)**	**Recall (%)**	**F-Score (%)**
$np - pp - pp$	70.81	78.93	74.65
$vp - pp - pp$	71.90	77.83	74.75
$vp - np - pp$	75.49	79.22	77.31
Total	72.74	78.66	75.58
CO-SPECIFICATION			
Syntactic sequences	**Precision (%)**	**Recall (%)**	**F-Score (%)**
$np - pp - pp$	87.15	74.13	80.11
$vp - pp - pp$	92.23	70.36	79.82
$vp - np - pp$	94.23	76.36	84.36
Total	91.20	73.62	81.47

4 Conclusion and Future Work

This paper has presented a particular unsupervised strategy to automatically acquire syntactic and semantic subcategorization requirements. Our strategy is mainly based on two linguistic assumptions: First, it was assumed that not only the syntactic Head imposes restrictions on its Dependent word, but also the latter selects for a specific type of Head. This phenomenon was called "co-specification". Second, we claimed that similar syntactic contexts share the same selection requirements. So, we measured, not similarity between words on the basis of their syntactic distribution, but similarity between syntactic contexts on the basis of their word distribution. It was assumed that the latter kind of similarity conveys more pertinent information on linguistic subcategorization than the former one. The learning process allowed us to provide the lexicon with both syntactic and semantic subcategorization information. This information was used to constrain attachment heuristics.

In future work, our aim is to extend the subcategorized lexicon in order to increase the coverage of the parser. For this purpose, we will use the partial results of the parser to discover new subcategorization information. That is, the new long distance attachments identified by the parser will serve to learn more syntactic and semantic restrictions. The lexicon will be provided with these new restrictions and thereby the coverage of the parser will be increased. The successive "learning + parsing" cycles will stop as no more new information is acquired and no more new dependencies are proposed.

References

1. Alexandre Agustini, Pablo Gamallo, and Gabriel P. Lopes. Selection restrictions acquisition for parsing improvement. In Oskar Bartenstein et alii, editor, *Web Knowledge Management and Decision Support*. Berlin:Springer Verlag, 2003.
2. Michael Collins and James Brooks. Prepositional phrase attachment through a backed-off model. In *Proceedings of the Third Workshop on Very Large Corpora*, pages 27–38, Cambridge, 1995.
3. David Faure and Claire Nédellec. Asium: Learning subcategorization frames and restrictions of selection. In *ECML98, Workshop on Text Mining*, 1998.
4. Pablo Gamallo, A. Agustini, and Gabriel P. Lopes. Learning subcategorisation information to model a grammar with co-restrictions. *Traitement Automatic de la Langue*, 44(1):93–117, 2003.
5. Donald Hindle and Mats Rooth. Structural ambiguity and lexical relations. *Computational Linguistics*, 19(1):103–120, 1993.
6. Hang Li and Naoki Abe. Word clustering and disambiguation based on co-occurrence data. In *Coling-ACL'98*, pages 749–755, 1998.
7. Dekang Lin. Automatic retrieval and clustering of similar words. In *COLING-ACL'98*, Montreal, 1998.
8. Michael Niemann. Determining pp attachment through semantic associations and preferences. In *ANLP Post Graduate Workshop*, pages 25–32, 1998.
9. Patrick Pantel and Dekan Lin. An unsupervised approach to prepositional phrase attachment using contextually similar words. In *ACL'00*, pages 101–108, Hong Kong, 2000.
10. James Pustejovsky. *The Generative Lexicon*. MIT Press, Cambridge, 1995.
11. Adwait Ratnaparkhi, Jeff Reymar, and Salim Roukos. A maximum entropy model for prepositional phrase attachment. In *Proceedings of the ARPA Human Language Technology Workshop)*, pages 250–225, 1994.

Managing Dialog in a Natural Language Querying System

Luis Quintano[1] and Irene Rodrigues[2]

[1] Serviço de Computação
ljcq@sc.uevora.pt
[2] Departamento de Informática
Universidade de Évora, Portugal
ipr@di.uevora.pt

Abstract. A Natural Language Querying System is presented (NL-SIIUE). It enables the access to the Universidade de Évora Information System (SIIUE) heterogeneous databases.
Dialog management is essential for the correct interpretation of the user's intentions and to answer accordingly. Following the ISCO language guidelines, in which NL-SIIUE development is based on, some basic principles of dialog management are described and discussed.

Keywords: Natural Language, Logic Programming, Dialog Systems

1 Introduction

The need for information is growing in our days. The management and day-to-day tasks in an institution as Universidade de Évora demands high information availability.

Universidade de Évora Integrated Information System (SIIUE) [3] was built to gather, organize and structure all the institution's information, aiming to build a solid base for the University development, increasing efficiency in information treatment and analysis.

Along with this knowledge repository, a large group of applications are supported by SIIUE (Academic Services System, Universidade de Évora's web site, etc.).[1]

SIIUE has become the main source of information for Universidade de Évora faculty, students and staff. Its availability and accessibility has become one of the major concerns of SIIUE developers and administrators. The Natural Language system here referred (NL-SIIUE) [11] is one solution for the accessibility and "ease of use" concerns, making it possible for non technically-savvy users to question SIIUE in their own, directly in written Portuguese.

[1] As a support for SIIUE's development a new logic-based development tool was built: ISCO [1]. Initially, ISCO was developed to face the needs of SIIUE in the context of Universidade de Évora but has outgrown its initial purpose: at present, ISCO can be described as a new logic-based programming framework which is being extended in many directions (relational database integration, web-based development, etc.).

Fernando Moura Pires, Salvador Abreu (Eds.): EPIA 2003, LNAI 2902, pp. 488–501, 2003.

Different users will have different needs for information. What better way for users to acquire the information they want than to let them question SIIUE in it's own language? This is what NL-SIIUE tries to accomplish.[2]

For example, if a teacher wants to know how many students have enrolled in his degree he will just have to ask:

```
Quantos estudantes se inscreveram no curso de Inform\'{a}tica?
(How many students have enrolled in the Informatics degree?)
```

instead of accessing some Academic application (which needs extra knowledge to extract information) or of asking it directly to the Central Services whose answer could take some days.

With NL-SIIUE, instead of going to the Central Services, students could make questions like:

```
Qual \'{e} a minha m\'{e}dia?
(What is my average?)

O curso de Economia est\'{a} dispon\'{\i}vel este ano?
(Is the Economics degree available this year?)
```

getting the desired information with no need for extra knowledge and almost instantly.

More than an alternative way of getting information, NL-SIIUE grants access to information that could not be reached in any other way with such a small amount of effort. Users need no extra knowledge to use the system, because they can interact with it in they're own natural language, the Portuguese.

NL-SIIUE's answer quality must be assured. To achieve this the system must interpret correctly the user's intentions and clarify any ambiguity it may get. This clarification is needed when NL-SIIUE gets distinct answers for the user's question. The clarification process is based on a dialog between NL-SIIUE and the user, which purpose is to restrict the possible answers base on the user's answers and intentions.

The remainder of this article is structured as follows: in section 2, NL-SIIUE architecture is briefly analyzed. In section 3 dialog management is described and it will be presented a detailed example pointing out the need of dialog in such applications. Finally some conclusions and future work is described in section 4.

2 Natural Language System

The main goal for this system is to give an easy way in on the SIIUE relational information repository [11] [12]. Its architecture is built of 5 modules (fig. 1):

- Syntactic Analyzer

[2] Although the system only works with Portuguese sentences, the examples given in this article will also be written in English.

- Semantic Interpreter
- Pragmatic Interpreter
- Evaluator
- Dialog Manager

If someone wants to know if the teacher `Cristina Silva` teaches the Economics degree, he will just have to question the system in it's own written language:

```
A Cristina Silva lecciona o curso de Economia?
(Does Cristina Silva teaches the Economics degree?)
```

NL-SIIUE receives the user sentence as input sending it to the first of its four modules:

2.1 Syntactic Analyzer

This module receives the user sentence in Portuguese written language and builds a list of possible syntactic representations according to the Portuguese grammar.

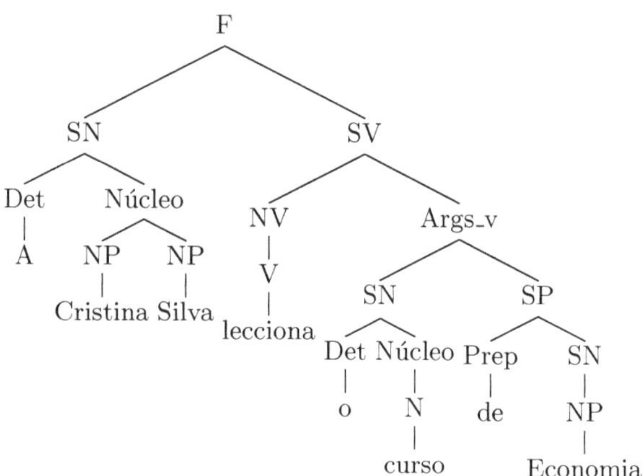

2.2 Semantic Interpreter

Receives the syntactic representations rewriting them on a set of semantic interpretations using a first-order logic form. The example in analysis has two semantic interpretations due to the prepositional predicate (PP) movement ("de Economia"):

```
Sem1:

nome(C,economia), curso(D), nome(E,silva), nome(E,cristina),
leccionar(E,D), rel(E,C)
```

```
Sem2:

nome(C,economia), curso(D), nome(E,silva), nome(E,cristina),
leccionar(E,D), rel(D,C)
```

While Sem1 associates individuals of name "cristina silva" with "economia, Sem2 associates the degree with "economia". Sem1 identifies all "cristina silva" related to an economics entity that teaches any degree, while Sem2 refers to all "cristina silva" that teaches an economics degree.

This interpreters implementation is based on DRS's [9].

2.3 Pragmatic Interpreter

Applies a set of knowledge rules to the semantic interpretations building a set of ISCO expressions [1] that will directly query the Information System.

These knowledge rules are previously (and automatically) built based on SIIUE. For that the system only needs to know the SIIUE databases schema which is available through ISCO's ability to describe external relational repositories. These rules are generated according to the existent relations (classes) and its attributes [11].

The pragmatic interpretations generated for the current example are:

```
Prag1:

si_funcion\'{a}rio(id=E,unidade=C), si_lecciona(docente=E,curso=D),
si_indiv\'{\i}duo(id=A,classe=indiv\'{\i}duo), si_curso(c\'{o}digo=D),
si_departamento(id=C,classe=departamento)
```

with the referent restrictions:

```
E = _#3055(4549:4980:4982:5092:5278)  %% all ''cristina silva''
D = _#1028(1274..1397)                 %% all degrees
C = 1096                               %% economics department
```

```
Prag2:

si_lecciona(docente=E,curso=D), si_indiv\'{\i}duo(id=E,classe=
                                                indiv\'{\i}duo),
si_curso(c\'{o}digo=C)
```

with the referent restrictions:

```
E = _#4068(4549:4980:4982:5092:5278)  %% all ''cristina silva''
D = _#2029(1319:1395)                  %% economics degrees
C = D
```

Prag1 is generated from semantic interpretation Sem1 while Prag2 is generated from Sem2.

The construction of the pragmatic interpretations is based on abductive inference [7]. With this abduction process, NL-SIIUE tries to find the best explanations to the rewritten (LPO) sentence accessing the relational data through ISCO and the generated knowledge rules [11].

As an example, one of the knowledge rules that would be activated by the current example would be,

```
curso(A,Lin,Lout) <-
   check(si_curso,A),
   abduct(si_curso(c\'{o}digo=A),Lin, Lout).
```

which would abduct the ISCO predicate:

```
si_curso(c\'{o}digo=A)
```

The use of finite domain (FD) variables [6] to represent the referents possible values reduces the representation complexity and avoids the treatment of logic expressions on the Dialogue Manager (section 3). FD constraint solver is implemented in GnuProlog [5] based on the clp(FD) solver [4].

2.4 Evaluation Module

This module receives the pragmatic interpretations (ISCO expressions) and processes them, querying the SIIUE for solutions. Not only the interpretations with solutions (`S`) are kept but also those which have no solution `S'`. Both of them are essential for the next step: the dialog.

E.g.: for pragmatic representation `Prag2` which identifies the teachers with names "cristina" and "silva" that teach an Economics degree, the sets are:

```
S =
 [
  [ E = 4980, %% teacher ''Ana Cristina Lopes Silva''
    D = 1319, %% Economics degree
    C = D
  ]
 ]

S' =
 [
  [ E = _#4068(4549:4982:5092:5278),  %% all others ''cristina silva''
    D = _#2029(1319:1395),            %% all degrees with ''economia''
    C = D
  ],
  [ E = 4980,   %% teacher ''Ana Cristina Lopes Silva''
    D = 1395,   %% other degree with ''economia''
    C = D
  ]
 ]
```

2.5 Dialog Manager

The Dialogue Manager (DM) is responsible for analyzing the evaluation results (solution and non-solution sets) and answer the user accordingly.

The results of the ISCO expressions evaluation are parsed by the DM and (in the end) an answer is built. NL-SIIUE may need to clarify some information before getting the answer requested by the user. This clarification is done through a dialogue with the user [12].

In the previous example, clarification is needed because neither S or S' are empty. One possible question for clarification could be:

```
''Refere-se ao docente Ana Cristina Lopes Silva?''
(Do you refer to the teacher Ana Cristina Lopes Silva)
```

If the user answers "no", then DM could answer negatively to the user once S remains empty (the unique possible solution is removed) and S' does not:

```
S = [ ]
S' =
 [
  [ E = _#4068(4549:4982:5092:5278),  %% all others ''cristina silva''
    D = _#2029(1319:1395),            %% all degrees with ''economia''
    C = D
  ],
 ]
```

If the user answers "yes", then no conclusion could be taken. The resulting sets would be:

```
S =
 [
  [ E = 4980, %% teacher ''Ana Cristina Lopes Silva''
    D = 1319, %% Economics degree
    C = D
  ]
 ]


S' =
 [
  [ E = 4980,   %% teacher ''Ana Cristina Lopes Silva''
    D = 1395,   %% other degree with ''economia''
    C = D
  ]
 ]
```

Further clarification would be needed, for example questioning:

```
Refere-se ao curso de Economia?
(Do you refer to the Economics degree?)
```

If the user's answer is "yes", DM would answer affirmatively. If the user's answer is "no", DM would answer negatively.

The Dialog Manager and the clarification process will be explained with more detail in the section 3.

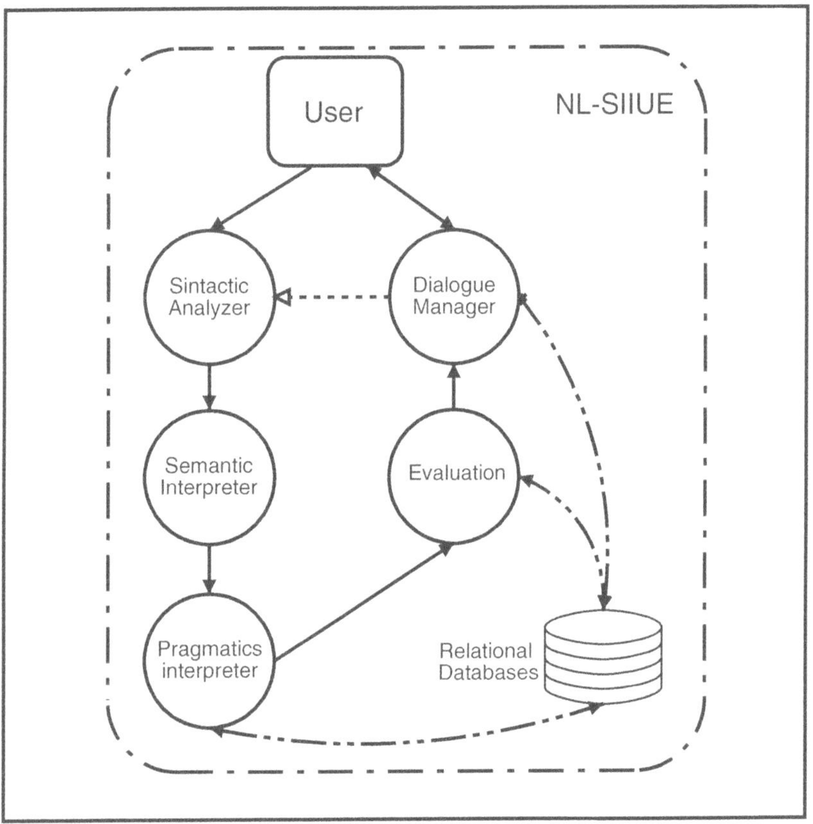

Fig. 1. SIIUE-NL Architecture

3 Dialog Management

3.1 Description

In order to answer correctly, NL-SIIUE must interpret the users intentions. This interpretation may lead to ambiguity problems in which several solutions are found according to different possible interpretations.

The clarification process is based on the knowledge achieved by the solutions found and on a dialog between NL-SIIUE and the user. The dialog's purpose is to understand if the user's question has a solution or not. This process may lead (or not) to the knowledge of the correct user's intention[3].

Assuming the existence of sets `S` and `S'` (section 2):

- If `S` is empty, then no solution is found. NL-SIIUE will answer negatively to the user.
- If `S'` is empty, then all interpretations are possible solutions (belonging to `S`). NL-SIIUE will answer affirmatively.
- If both `S` and `S'` are not empty, it means there are some interpretations with solution and others without. In this case NL-SIIUE will try to find if the user interpretation has a solution or not through a process of clarification.

Based on the knowledge from the pragmatic evaluation (`K`), NL-SIIUE must "decide" what question to place to the user. This questions must minimize the number of elements in `S` or `S'`[4] , until one of them is empty, so that an answer can be sent to the user. This is the *terminal condition* of the clarification process.

To achieve this, the following algorithm was considered:

1. Based on the actual knowledge, checks for the need of the clarification (if the *terminal condition* does not succeed). If it succeeds the process stop and a final answer is sent to the user, else it continues.
2. Select a question (`Q`)
3. Send `Q` to the user
4. Receive the answer (`A`) from the user
5. Interpret and evaluate `A`, achieving an extra knowledge (`k(A)`).
6. Adds `k(A)` to `K`.
7. Return to the beginning.

The process of selection of the question is of most importance. It's efficiency will get the system to a quicker solution. The selection algorithm is described as follows:

1. Identify the referent `X` (more relevant referent) which:
   a) has the smallest set of **instantiation values**;
   b) **type** differs in different interpretations;
   c) **property** differs in different interpretations or referent instantiations.
2. Identify the more relevant referent characteristic (`c(X)`), i.e. the one, within those presented (instantiation values, types or properties), that may eliminate a larger set of referent instantiations or interpretations. If more than one is found, the preference order presented is advisable.
3. Build a yes/no question with `c(X)`.

The user's answers must be "yes" or "no" helping, in this way, to reduce the set of solutions in the clarification process. The user may also say he doesn't know the answer in which case the DM must ignore it and choose another question.

[3] In this process description, there will only be considered *yes/no* questions

[4] The decision of which set to minimize may be taken according to several criteria: the set's cardinality, the set's number of distinct referents, the set's number of distinct pragmatic interpretation, etc.

3.2 Example

```
O Paulo lecciona inform\'{a}tica?
(Does Paul teaches Informatics?)
```

This question has only one semantic interpretation

```
S1: nome(C,inform\'{a}tica), nome(D,paulo), leccionar(D,C)
```

with two distinct referents:

```
C: (_+_+_)
D: (sin+masc+_)
```

and two pragmatic interpretations which, in these case, will both lead to possible solutions. `P1` identifies all teachers with the name "paulo" `D` which teach a degree with the name "informatics" `C`.

```
P1:

si_lecciona(docente=D,curso=C),
si_indiv\'{\i}duo(id=D,classe=indiv\'{\i}duo),
si_curso(c\'{o}digo=C)
```

with

```
C = _#2(1319:1395)
D = _#4068(3845:3851:3945:3951..3956:3958..3962:4005:4130:4203:
          4226:4240:4274:4483..4485:4510:4512:4589:4648:4663:4686:
          4717:4796:4833..4834:4861:4930:4949:4952:4979:5040:5063:
          5071:5073:5088:5090:5115:5142:5233:5246:5248:5282:5289)
```

`P2` identifies all teachers with the name "paulo" `D` which teach a course with the name "informática" `C`.

```
P2:

si_lecciona(docente=D,disciplina=C),
si_indiv\'{\i}duo(id=D,classe=indiv\'{\i}duo),
si_disciplina(c\'{o}digo=C)
```

with

```
C = _#2(5644:5811:6063:6224:6457:6726:6814:6845:6931:7306:7348:7487:
       7494:7506:7508:7510:7751:7755)
D = _#2029(3845:3851:3945:3951..3956:3958..3962:4005:4130:4203:4226:
          4240:4274:4483..4485:4510:4512:4589:4648:4663:4686:4717:
          4796:4833..4834:4861:4930:4949:4952:4979:5040:5063:5071:
          5073:5088:5090:5115:5142:5233:5246:5248:5282:5289)
```

NL-SIIUE will then search for all possible solutions and non-solutions of the pragmatic representations, achieving two sets of referent instantiations, `S` with the solutions and `S'` with the non-solutions.

```
S:
 [
  [ C = 1319,                        %% informatics degree
    D = _#23(3959:4226:5073:5233)    %% teachers with the name ``paulo''
  ],
  [ C = _#1(6224,7494),              %% informatics courses
    D = 5233                         %% teacher ``Paulo Torres''
  ],
  [ C = 6814,                        %% course ``inform\'{a}tica de
                                                          gest\~{a}o''
    D = 5289                         %% teacher ``Paulo Silva''
  ]
 ]

S':
 [
  [ C = _#2(1319:1395),
    D = _#2029(3845:3851:3945:3951..3956:3958:3960..3962:
       4005:4130:4203:4240:4274:4483..4485:4510:4512:4589:4648:
       4663:4686:4717:4796:4833..4834:4861:4930:4949:4952:4979:5040:
       5063:5071:5088:5090:5115:5142:5246:5248:5282:5289)
  ],
  [ C = 1395,
    D = _#23(3959:4226:5073:5233)
  ],
  [ C = _#2(5644:5811:6063:6224:6457:6726:6814:6845:6931:7306:7348:
        7487:7494:7506:7508:7510:7751:7755),
    D = _#2029(3845:3851:3945:3951..3956:3958..3962:
       4005:4130:4203:4226:4240:4274:4483..4485:4510:4512:4589:4648:
       4663:4686:4717:4796:4833..4834:4861:4930:4949:4952:4979:5040:
       5063:5071:5073:5088:5090:5115:5142:5246:5248:5282)
  ],
  [ C = _#2(5644:5811:6063:6457:6726:6845:6931:7306:7348:
        7487:7506:7508:7510:7751:7755),
    D = 5233
  ],
  [ C = _#2(5644:5811:6063:6224:6457:6726:6845:6931:7306:7348:
        7487:7494:7506:7508:7510:7751:7755),
    D = 5289
  ]
 ]
```

At this point NL-SIIUE needs to do some clarification once several possible solutions (and non-solutions) were found.

As seen in section 3.1, the process of clarification starts by choosing a question to place to the user. To select this question the referents and their instantiations must be analyzed.

Looking at set `S` we can see that the referent `C` has two possible classes `degree` and `course`. One possible (class) clarification question could be:

```
Inform\'{a}tica refere-se a uma disciplina?
(Does informatics refers to a course?)
```

The answer to this question will reduce the possible set of solutions. Assuming the user's answer is "no", the new S and S' will be:

```
S:
 [
  [ C = 1319,
    %% informatics degree

    D = _#23(3959:4226:5073:5233)
    %% teachers with the name paulo
    %% (that teach the informatics degree
  ],
 ]

S':
 [
  [ C = _#2(1319:1395),
    %% all degrees with the name ''inform\'{a}tica''

    D = _#2029(3845:3851:3945:3951..3956:3958:3960..3962:
        4005:4130:4203:4240:4274:4483..4485:4510:4512:4589:4648:
        4663:4686:4717:4796:4833..4834:4861:4930:4949:4952:4979:5040:
        5063:5071:5088:5090:5115:5142:5246:5248:5282:5289)
    %% all teachers with the name ''paulo''
  ],
  [ C = 1395,
    %% other degree with the name ''inform\'{a}tica''

    D = _#23(3959:4226:5073:5233)
    %% teachers with the name ''paulo''
    %% (that teach the informatics degree)
  ]
 ]
```

Once there are no more class ambiguities (it's now clear that the user is talking about someone who's name is "paulo" and that teaches an informatics degree), the referent properties must be analyzed so that further clarification may be done.

In S referent D identifies (four) teachers with several "direct" properties:

- Name
- Birth Date
- Sex
- etc.

Other "indirect" properties may be considered. These properties are not directly associated with the individual/teacher but can be extracted of its relations with other entities, for example:

- The department where the teacher belongs to
- The courses he teaches in the degree 1319
- etc.

In this case the property `Sex` is not relevant because all of these teachers are males. `Name` seems to be a good clarification property, but (normally) every person has a different name so we had to ask one by one until we found the user's intended teacher. If a careful analysis is made we can see that two of these teachers belong to the Informatics department while other two don't. This seems to be a good question, because it restrains in half the set of possible teachers and these are the **only** teachers with the name "Paulo" from the Informatics department.

```
O docente \'{e} do departamento de Inform\'{a}tica?
(The teacher belongs to the Informatics department?)
```

Assuming the answer is "yes", the new sets are:

```
S:
 [
  [ C = 1319,
    %% informatics degree
    D = _#23(5073:5233)
    %% teachers with the name ''paulo''
    %% that teach the informatics degree
    %% and belong to the informatics department
  ]
 ]

S':
 [
  [ C = 1395,
    %% other degree with the name ''inform\'{a}tica''

    D = _#23(5073:5233)
    %% teachers with the name ''paulo''
    %% that teach the informatics degree
    %% and belong to the informatics department
  ]
 ]
```

A question that seems concluded would refer the degree we're talking about:

```
O curso \'{e} a Licenciatura em Engenharia Inform\'{a}tica?
(Is the degree Informatics Engineering?)
```

Supposing this is degree the user wanted (1319), he would answer affirmatively and NL-SIIUE would recognize the solution:

```
Sim!
(Yes!)
```

4 Conclusions and Future Work

The growing complexity of an institution as Universidade de Évora demands available and easy-to-handle information. This information must be accessed by all kinds of users (teachers, students, staff, etc.) disregarding their technical knowledge. The natural language system presented in this article is designed to give all users a simple interface for the SIIUE information.

In this paper we have discussed how we can handle the yes/no questions in an natural language interface to databases. We claim that the clarification process is critical in order grant that the system will not answer wrongly to an user. We also claim that in large databases with users that are not fully aware of the databases structure and information, ambiguity is something that will arise frequently.

Current research in this area such as the Precise system [13], focus their work in the correct translation of natural language sentences into sql queries, leaving out the problem of solving ambiguities in the user sentence. This strategy will lead to answers (the sql query result) that an non expert user will have problems to interpret.

Our system architecture has some characteristics of traditional natural language dialogue systems such as [14] [10] [8]. Namely, we infer the users dialog plan and represent and infer the user intentions. The knowledge base used for this inference process is automatically generated from the ISCO databases description.

An important issue that we have not addressed in this paper is the evaluation of our system that we plan to start in a near future.

The evaluation process will have to infer some characteristics of the system, namely:

- If its answers are correct. (the retrieved information is correct)
  This is a very important issue, since only a 100% correct system will be useful. A system that will give a wrong answer will have no purpose.
- If it is possible to retrieve the intended information
  This will be difficult to evaluate and we do not expect a full precision system with respect to this parameter.
- If the system is useful.
  This parameter is important in order to infer the utility of the natural language interface.
  In order to evaluate this parameter we shall compare the answers obtained by two sets of users. One set will try to obtain the answers to a previous defined set of questions using the natural language interface, and the other one will use the other interfaces to the databases, such as the university web pages.

One of the main topics to be handled in the future is the access control of the SIIUE information. Some information may be restricted to a set of users and the system must guarantee that no one else accesses it. To achieve this NL-SIIUE uses ISCO's Rule-based Access Control [2].

Afterwards, in an experimental stage, the purpose of the work described herein is to become available to all users using the University's internal web interface, through Universidade de Évora's web page (*http:// www.uevora.pt/*).

References

1. Salvador Abreu. Isco: A practical language for heterogeneous information system construction. In *Proceedings of INAP'01*, Tokyo, Japan, October 2001. Prolog Association of Japan.
2. Salvador Abreu. Modeling Role-Based Access Control in ISCO. In Lígia Maria Ribeiro and José Marques dos Santos, editors, *The 8th International Conference of European University Information Systems*. FEUP Edições, June 2002. ISBN 972-752-051-0.
3. Salvador Pinto Abreu. A Logic-based Information System. In Enrico Pontelli and Vitor Santos-Costa, editors, *2nd International Workshop on Practical Aspects of Declarative Languages (PADL'2000)*, volume 1753 of *Lecture Notes in Computer Science*, pages 141–153, Boston, MA, USA, January 2000. Springer-Verlag.
4. P. Codognet and D. Diaz. Compiling constraint in clp(fd). In *Journal of Logic Programming, Vol. 27, No. 3, June*, 1996.
5. D. Diaz. http://www.gnu.org/software/prolog, 1999.
6. P. Van Hentenryck. *Constraint Satisfaction in Logic Programming.* Logic Programming Series. The MIT Press, 1989.
7. Jerry Hobbs, Mark Stickel, Douglas Appelt, and Paul Martin. Interpretation as abduction. Technical Report SRI Technical Note 499, 333 Ravenswood Ave., Menlo Park, CA 94025, 1990.
8. M. Dzikovska G. Ferguson L. Galescu J. Allen, D. Byron and A. Stent. An architecture for a generic dialogue shell. In *Journal of Natural Language Engineering, special issue on Best Practices in Spoken Language Dialogue Systems Engineering, December*, 2000.
9. H. Kamp and U. Reyle. *From Discourse to Logic.* Kluwer, Dordrecht, 1993.
10. Diane J. Litman and James F. Allen. Discourse processing and commonsense plans. In MIT Press, editor, *Intentions in Communication, chapter 17, pages 365 388*, 1990.
11. Irene Rodrigues Luis Quintano and Salvador Abreu. Relational Information Retrieval through natural language analysis. In *INAP'01, Tokyo, Japan*, 2001.
12. Irene Rodrigues Luis Quintano, Paulo Quaresma and Salvador Abreu. A Natural Language dialogue manager for accessing databases. In Mamede N. and Ranchhod E., editors, *Proceedings of PorTAL'02, Faro Portugal*, 2002.
13. H. Kautz O. Etzioni and A. Popescu. Towards a theory of natural language interfaces to databases. In *Intelligent User Interfaces (IUI)*, 2003.
14. Martha E. Pollack. Plans as complex mental attitudes. In MIT Press, editor, *Intentions in Communication*, 1990.

Author Index

Lecture Notes in Artificial Intelligence (LNAI)

Vol. 2699: M.G. Hinchey, J.L. Rash, W.F. Truszkowski, C. Rouff, D. Gordon-Spears (Eds.), Formal Approaches to Agent-Based Systems. Proceedings, 2002. IX, 297 pages. 2003.

Vol. 2700: M.T. Pazienza (Ed.), Information Extraction in the Web Era. XIII, 163 pages. 2003.

Vol. 2702: P. Brusilovsky, A. Corbett, F. de Rosis (Eds.), User Modeling 2003. Proceedings, 2003. XIV, 436 pages. 2003.

Vol. 2703: O.R. Zaïane, J. Srivastava, M. Spiliopoulou, B. Masand (Eds.), WEBKDD 2002 – Mining Web Data for Discovering Usage Patterns and Profiles. Proceedings, 2003. IX, 181 pages. 2003.

Vol. 2705: S. Renals, G. Grefenstette (Eds.), Text- and Speech-Triggered Information Access. Proceedings, 2000. VII, 197 pages. 2003.

Vol. 2711: T.D. Nielsen, N.L. Zhang (Eds.), Symbolic and Quantitative Approaches to Reasoning with Uncertainty. Proceedings, 2003. XII, 608 pages. 2003.

Vol. 2715: T. Bilgiç, B. De Baets, O. Kaynak (Eds.), Fuzzy Sets and Systems – IFSA 2003. Proceedings, 2003. XV, 735 pages. 2003.

Vol. 2718: P. W. H. Chung, C. Hinde, M. Ali (Eds.), Developments in Applied Artificial Intelligence. Proceedings, 2003. XIV, 817 pages. 2003.

Vol. 2721: N.J. Mamede, J. Baptista, I. Trancoso, M. das Graças Volpe Nunes (Eds.), Computational Processing of the Portuguese Language. Proceedings, 2003. XIV, 268 pages. 2003.

Vol. 2734: P. Perner, A. Rosenfeld (Eds.), Machine Learning and Data Mining in Pattern Recognition. Proceedings, 2003. XII, 440 pages. 2003.

Vol. 2741: F. Baader (Ed.), Automated Deduction – CADE-19. Proceedings, 2003. XII, 503 pages. 2003.

Vol. 2744: V. Mařík, D. McFarlane, P. Valckenaers (Eds.), Holonic and Multi-Agent Systems for Manufacturing. Proceedings, 2003. XI, 322 pages. 2003.

Vol. 2746: A. de Moor, W. Lex, B. Ganter (Eds.), Conceptual Structures for Knowledge Creation and Communication. Proceedings, 2003. XI, 405 pages. 2003.

Vol. 2752: G.A. Kaminka, P.U. Lima, R. Rojas (Eds.), RoboCup 2002: Robot Soccer World Cup VI. XVI, 498 pages. 2003.

Vol. 2773: V. Palade, R.J. Howlett, L. Jain (Eds.), Knowledge-Based Intelligent Information and Engineering Systems. Proceedings, Part I, 2003. LI, 1473 pages. 2003.

Vol. 2774: V. Palade, R.J. Howlett, L. Jain (Eds.), Knowledge-Based Intelligent Information and Engineering Systems. Proceedings, Part II, 2003. LI, 1443 pages. 2003.

Vol. 2777: B. Schölkopf, M.K. Warmuth (Eds.), Learning Theory and Kernel Machines. Proceedings, 2003. XIV, 746 pages. 2003.

Vol. 2780: M. Dojat, E. Keravnou, P. Barahona (Eds.), Artificial Intelligence in Medicine. Proceedings, 2003. XIII, 388 pages. 2003.

Vol. 2782: M. Klusch, A. Omicini, S. Ossowski, H. Laamanen (Eds.), Cooperative Information Agents VII. Proceedings, 2003. XI, 345 pages. 2003.

Vol. 2792: T. Rist, R. Aylett, D. Ballin, J. Rickel (Eds.), Intelligent Virtual Agents. Proceedings, 2003. XV, 364 pages. 2003.

Vol. 2796: M. Cialdea Mayer, F. Pirri (Eds.), Automated Reasoning with Analytic Tableaux and Related Methods. Proceedings, 2003. X, 271 pages. 2003.

Vol. 2797: O.R. Zaïane, S.J. Simoff, C. Djeraba (Eds.), Mining Multimedia and Complex Data. Proceedings, 2002. XII, 281 pages. 2003.

Vol. 2801: W. Banzhaf, T. Christaller, P. Dittrich, J.T. Kim, J. Ziegler (Eds.), Advances in Artificial Life. Proceedings, 2003. XVI, 905 pages. 2003.

Vol. 2807: V. Matoušek, P. Mautner (Eds.), Text, Speech and Dialogue. Proceedings, 2003. XIII, 426 pages. 2003.

Vol. 2821: A. Günter, R. Kruse, B. Neumann (Eds.), KI 2003: Advances in Artificial Intelligence. Proceedings, 2003. XII, 662 pages. 2003.

Vol. 2829: A. Cappelli, F. Turini (Eds.), AI*IA 2003: Advances in Artificial Intelligence. Proceedings, 2003. XIV, 552 pages. 2003.

Vol. 2831: M. Schillo, M. Klusch, J. Müller, H. Tianfield (Eds.), Multiagent System Technologies. Proceedings, 2003. X, 229 pages. 2003.

Vol. 2835: T. Horváth, A. Yamamoto (Eds.), Inductive Logic Programming. Proceedings, 2003. X, 401 pages. 2003.

Vol. 2837: N. Lavrač, D. Gamberger, H. Blockeel, L. Todorovski (Eds.), Machine Learning: ECML 2003. Proceedings, 2003. XVI. 504 pages. 2003.

Vol. 2838: N. Lavrač, D. Gamberger, L. Todorovski, H. Blockeel (Eds.), Knowledge Discovery in Databases: PKDD 2003. Proceedings, 2003. XVI. 508 pages. 2003.

Vol. 2842: R. Gavaldà, K.P. Jantke, E. Takimoto (Eds.), Algorithmic Learning Theory. Proceedings, 2003. XI, 313 pages. 2003.

Vol. 2843: G. Grieser, Y. Tanaka, A. Yamamoto (Eds.), Discovery Science. Proceedings, 2003. XII, 504 pages. 2003.

Vol. 2850: M.Y. Vardi, A. Voronkov (Eds.), Logic for Programming, Artificial Intelligence, and Reasoning. Proceedings, 2003. XIII, 437 pages. 2003.

Vol. 2854: J. Hoffmann, Utilizing Problem Structure in Planning. XIII, 251 pages. 2003.

Vol. 2871: N. Zhong, Z.W. Raś, S. Tsumoto, E. Suzuki (Eds.), Foundations of Intelligent Systems. Proceedings, 2003. XV, 697 pages. 2003.

Vol. 2873: J. Lawry, J. Shanahan, A. Ralescu (Eds.), Modelling with Words. XIII, 229 pages. 2003.

Vol. 2891: J. Lee, M. Barley (Eds.), Intelligent Agents and Multi-Agent Systems. Proceedings, 2003. X, 215 pages. 2003.

Vol. 2902: F. Moura Pires, S. Abreu (Eds.), Progress in Artificial Intelligence. Proceedings, 2003. XV, 504 pages. 2003.

Lecture Notes in Computer Science

Vol. 2856: M. Smirnov, E. Biersack, C. Blondia, O. Bonaventure, O. Casals, G. Karlsson, George Pavlou, B. Quoitin, J. Roberts, I. Stavrakakis, B. Stiller, P. Trimintzios, P. Van Mieghem (Eds.), Quality of Future Internet Services. IX, 293 pages. 2003.

Vol. 2857: M.A. Nascimento, E.S. de Moura, A.L. Oliveira (Eds.), String Processing and Information Retrieval. Proceedings, 2003. XI, 379 pages. 2003.

Vol. 2858: A. Veidenbaum, K. Joe, H. Amano, H. Aiso (Eds.), High Performance Computing. Proceedings, 2003. XV, 566 pages. 2003.

Vol. 2859: B. Apolloni, M. Marinaro, R. Tagliaferri (Eds.), Neural Nets. Proceedings, 2003. X, 376 pages. 2003.

Vol. 2860: D. Geist, E. Tronci (Eds.), Correct Hardware Design and Verification Methods. Proceedings, 2003. XII, 426 pages. 2003.

Vol. 2861: C. Bliek, C. Jermann, A. Neumaier (Eds.), Global Optimization and Constraint Satisfaction. Proceedings, 2002. XII, 239 pages. 2003.

Vol. 2862: D. Feitelson, L. Rudolph, U. Schwiegelshohn (Eds.), Job Scheduling Strategies for Parallel Processing. Proceedings, 2003. VII, 269 pages. 2003.

Vol. 2863: P. Stevens, J. Whittle, G. Booch (Eds.), «UML» 2003 – The Unified Modeling Language. Proceedings, 2003. XIV, 415 pages. 2003.

Vol. 2864: A.K. Dey, A. Schmidt, J.F. McCarthy (Eds.), UbiComp 2003: Ubiquitous Computing. Proceedings, 2003. XVII, 368 pages. 2003.

Vol. 2865: S. Pierre, M. Barbeau, E. Kranakis (Eds.), Ad-Hoc, Mobile, and Wireless Networks. Proceedings, 2003. X, 293 pages. 2003.

Vol. 2867: M. Brunner, A. Keller (Eds.), Self-Managing Distributed Systems. Proceedings, 2003. XIII, 274 pages. 2003.

Vol. 2868: P. Perner, R. Brause, H.-G. Holzhütter (Eds.), Medical Data Analysis. Proceedings, 2003. VIII, 127 pages. 2003.

Vol. 2869: A. Yazici, C. Şener (Eds.), Computer and Information Sciences – ISCIS 2003. Proceedings, 2003. XIX, 1110 pages. 2003.

Vol. 2870: D. Fensel, K. Sycara, J. Mylopoulos (Eds.), The Semantic Web - ISWC 2003. Proceedings, 2003. XV, 931 pages. 2003.

Vol. 2871: N. Zhong, Z.W. Raś, S. Tsumoto, E. Suzuki (Eds.), Foundations of Intelligent Systems. Proceedings, 2003. XV, 697 pages. 2003. (Subseries LNAI)

Vol. 2873: J. Lawry, J. Shanahan, A. Ralescu (Eds.), Modelling with Words. XIII, 229 pages. 2003. (Subseries LNAI)

Vol. 2875: E. Aarts, R. Collier, E. van Loenen, B. de Ruyter (Eds.), Ambient Intelligence. Proceedings, 2003. XI, 432 pages. 2003.

Vol. 2876: M. Schroeder, G. Wagner (Eds.), Rules and Rule Markup Languages for the Semantic Web. Proceedings, 2003. VII, 173 pages. 2003.

Vol. 2877: T. Böhme, G. Heyer, H. Unger (Eds.), Innovative Internet Community Systems. Proceedings, 2003. VIII, 263 pages. 2003.

Vol. 2878: R.E. Ellis, T.M. Peters (Eds.), Medical Image Computing and Computer-Assisted Intervention - MICCAI 2003. Part I. Proceedings, 2003. XXXIII, 819 pages. 2003.

Vol. 2879: R.E. Ellis, T.M. Peters (Eds.), Medical Image Computing and Computer-Assisted Intervention - MICCAI 2003. Part II. Proceedings, 2003. XXXIV, 1003 pages. 2003.

Vol. 2880: H.L. Bodlaender (Ed.), Graph-Theoretic Concepts in Computer Science. Proceedings, 2003. XI, 386 pages. 2003.

Vol. 2881: E. Horlait, T. Magedanz, R.H. Glitho (Eds.), Mobile Agents for Telecommunication Applications. Proceedings, 2003. IX, 297 pages. 2003.

Vol. 2883: J. Schaeffer, M. Müller, Y. Björnsson (Eds.), Computers and Games. Proceedings, 2002. XI, 431 pages. 2003.

Vol. 2884: E. Najm, U. Nestmann, P. Stevens (Eds.), Formal Methods for Open Object-Based Distributed Systems. Proceedings, 2003. X, 293 pages. 2003.

Vol. 2885: J.S. Dong, J. Woodcock (Eds.), Formal Methods and Software Engineering. Proceedings, 2003. XI, 683 pages. 2003.

Vol. 2886: I. Nyström, G. Sanniti di Baja, S. Svensson (Eds.), Discrete Geometry for Computer Imagery. Proceedings, 2003. XII, 556 pages. 2003.

Vol. 2887: T. Johansson (Ed.), Fast Software Encryption. Proceedings, 2003. IX, 397 pages. 2003.

Vol. 2888: R. Meersman, Zahir Tari, D.C. Schmidt et al. (Eds.), On The Move to Meaningful Internet Systems 2003: CoopIS, DOA, and ODBASE. Proceedings, 2003. XXI, 1546 pages. 2003.

Vol. 2889: Robert Meersman, Zahir Tari et al. (Eds.), On The Move to Meaningful Internet Systems 2003: OTM 2003 Workshops. Proceedings, 2003. XXI, 1096 pages. 2003.

Vol. 2891. J. Lee, M. Barley (Eds.), Intelligent Agents and Multi-Agent Systems. Proceedings, 2003. X, 215 pages. 2003. (Subseries LNAI)

Vol. 2893: J.-B. Stefani, I. Demeure, D. Hagimont (Eds.), Distributed Applications and Interoperable Systems. Proceedings, 2003. XIII, 311 pages. 2003.

Vol. 2895: A. Ohori (Ed.), Programming Languages and Systems. Proceedings, 2003. XIII, 427 pages. 2003.

Vol. 2897: O. Balet, G. Subsol, P. Torguet (Eds.), Virtual Storytelling. Proceedings, 2003. XI, 240 pages. 2003.

Vol. 2899: G. Ventre, R. Canonico (Eds.), Interactive Multimedia on Next Generation Networks. Proceedings, 2003. XIV, 420 pages. 2003.

Vol. 2901: F. Bry, N. Henze, J. Maluszyński (Eds.), Principles and Practice of Semantic Web Reasoning. Proceedings, 2003. X, 209 pages. 2003.

Vol. 2902: F. Moura Pires, S. Abreu (Eds.), Progress in Artificial Intelligence. Proceedings, 2003. XV, 504 pages. 2003. (Subseries LNAI).

Vol. 2905: A. Sanfeliu, J. Ruiz-Shulcloper (Eds.), Progress in Pattern Recognition, Speech and Image Analysis. Proceedings, 2003. XVII, 693 pages. 2003.

www.ingramcontent.com/pod-product-compliance
Ingram Content Group UK Ltd.
Pitfield, Milton Keynes, MK11 3LW, UK
UKHW021901190726

13853UKWH00003B/1364

* 9 7 8 3 6 6 2 2 0 3 1 4 9 *